Cultural Studies

Cultural Studies

The Basics

Jeff Lewis

2nd edition

Los Angeles • London • New Delhi • Singapore

First Published 2008

SAGE Publications Ltd
1 Oliver's Yard
55 City Road
London EC1Y 1SP

SAGE Publications Inc.
2455 Teller Road
Thousand Oaks, California 91320

SAGE Publications India Pvt Ltd
B 1/I 1 Mohan Cooperative Industrial Area
Mathura Road
New Delhi 110 044

SAGE Publications Asia-Pacific Pte Ltd
33 Pekin Street #02-01
Far East Square
Singapore 048763

Library of Congress Control Number: 2007935998

British Library Cataloguing in Publication data

A catalogue record for this book is available from
the British Library

ISBN 978-1-4129-2229-6
ISBN 978-1-4129-2230-2 (pbk)

Typeset by CEPHA Imaging Pvt. Ltd., Bangalore, India
Printed in Great Britain by TJ International Ltd, Padstow, Cornwall
Printed on paper from sustainable resources

To Jay and Sian

Contents

List of Tables, Figures and Plates

TABLES

FIGURES

PLATES

Preface

Together, we weave what we can from the warp and woof of one another's experience. For the scholar, I suspect that he had unburdened himself . . . He left here knowing that he had contributed important information to the map I had in mind. (James Cowan, *A Mapmaker's Dream*)

I introduced the first edition of this book through a reference to James Cowan's novel, *A Mapmaker's Dream*. The mapmaker is attempting to conceptualize his vastly expanding horizons; his cartography, however, is perpetually frustrated by the exquisite, even miraculous, vitality and detail of the world. Even so, the frustration of the cartographer, as with his servant scholars, is ennobled by the splendour of the journey – that expedition of knowing which is both transient and endless, and which is ultimately the expression of our singular and collective dreaming.

My aim in writing the first edition of *Cultural Studies* was to make a similar contribution to this journey of knowing. I attempted to create a textual cartography which drew together the rich and complex intellectual genealogy that marks the formation of the cultural studies discipline and our understandings of contemporary culture. Since completing the first edition, however, I have found my own horizons expanding, eliciting new insights into the nature of meaning-making in a globalizing cultural setting. Internationally significant events like 9/11, along with the seemingly intractable momentum of globalization, have contributed to a distinct shift in the consciousness and formative modes of cultural meaning-making. This second edition of *Cultural Studies*, therefore, is once again attempting to map the dynamic state of the world, bringing forward my own dynamic understandings and apprehensions of this miraculous cultural sphere.

As in the first edition, I have sought in this new edition to present and critique the major modes of cultural analysis; I have used this critique to develop a specific theory of culture which is then applied to the study of specific cultural sites and spaces. However, I have attempted in this new edition to account for changes in the discipline itself, as well as in the significance of the sites being analyzed. I have added an entirely new chapter on the culture of terrorism. This has proved an essential addition, not only because of the preoccupations of contemporary global cultures, but because these changes have stimulated some compelling revisions within the discipline itself. In particular, events like 9/11, the 'war on terror', the oil wars and conditions of global warming, are all stimulating a revival of cultural studies' deep roots in cultural politics.

To some extent, the interest in political violence and global terrorism is part of a broader cultural and disciplinary development, most particularly associated with globalization. As I outline in Chapter 1 of this new edition, globalization has numerous effects, and cultural studies is extremely well-placed among the social sciences and humanities to account for these 'expanding horizons'. To this end, this new edition of *Cultural Studies* is projecting a more globally focused interrogation of culture(s). This broader focus on globalism and the conditions of global insecurity is a critical part of my own scholarly journey.

This new edition of *Cultural Studies* represents another dimension of this expedition and of our shared project of contemporary cultural mapping.

Acknowledgements

My particular thanks are due to the School of Applied Communication, the Globalism Institute and the office of the Pro-Vice Chancellor Research at RMIT University. All these bodies have provided resources for the completion of this text.

I would also like to thank the following people – Belinda Lewis, Jay Lewis, Sian Lewis, Sonya DeMasi, Kirsty Best, Alice Sherlock, Diana Bossio, Jessica Raschke, Kristen Sharp and Louise Refalo. These people have made an absolutely invaluable contribution to the *Cultural Studies* genealogy and to my own personal and intellectual life.

Thanks to a range of colleagues who have supported my work – John Handmer, Paul James, Damian Grenfell, Jack Clancy, Sheldon Harsel, Christine Hudson, Alan Cumming, Tony Dalton and Brian Henderson.

My thanks to Terry Batt for allowing me to use *Forthcoming Attractions* (Cover and Plate 7.1). Thanks to Thea Linke (Plate 1.2), Pia Interlandi and Devika Bilmoria (Plate 4.1), Pia Interlandi and Optic Photography (Plate 8.1), and Michael Cresswell (Plate 1.1).

I'd also like to acknowledge the support and guidance provided by the Sage team, most particularly Chris Rojek, Jai Seaman and Mila Steele.

Part One

Forming Culture/Informing Cultural Theory

1

Contemporary Culture, Cultural Studies and the Global Mediasphere

INTRODUCTION: THE CONTEMPORARY SETTING

In 1997 Diana Spencer, Princess of Wales, was killed in a car accident in Paris. The driver was well over the legal alcohol limit and was travelling at speeds in excess of 200 kilometres an hour. While we might condemn the recklessness of the group, a global audience of around 2.5 billion people watched the laying to rest of the 'People's Princess', making it the most watched event in all human history. Also in 1997 the highest grossing movie of all time, *Titanic*, was released; over the following decade the film earned around $US600m and reached audiences in 120 countries. Around the same year the annual earnings of the North American pop singer Celine Dion were $US55.5 million, although this figure is well short of the Rolling Stones' tour earnings in 2005 which reached $US135m. In 2006 the annual earnings of movie director Steven Spielberg had topped $US360 million, which was about the same as the annual profit of global news broadcaster CNN. All of these figures, however, seem modest when measured against the annual earnings of the Fox Entertainment Group, which generates annual revenues of $US10 billion and holds around $US24 billion in media assets worldwide.

Such immense sums have been generated through the expansion of major media corporations and the absorption of media audiences into global networked communication systems. Satellite, cable and wireless digital technologies have allowed media organizations to distribute their products across most areas of the world, from affluent urban centres to provincial villages in Suluwesi, Nigeria and the Amazon Delta. But these technologies are not, of themselves, a reason for the extraordinary growth in global media that has occurred over the past two to three decades. Media texts – music, TV, film, print, Internet – meet their audiences in a complex intersection of systems and personal imaginings. To this end, the transformation of the world into a *global media sphere* is the result of a dynamic interaction between macro processes (history, economy, technology, politics and modes of social organization) and the profoundly intimate and intricate microcosms of a person's life – the realm of the individual subject. Culture, in a very profound sense, is formed through these processes: an assemblage of dynamic engagements that reverberate through and within individual subjects and the systems of meaning-making of which they are an integral part.

In this way, the collective 'audience' and each individual viewing subject contribute significantly to the formation and representation of events like the Diana funeral. Viewers of the funeral, like the audiences of the Twin Towers attack in 2001 or the World Cup Football of 2006, were participants in the dynamic of culture and the transformation of global spaces into the new media sphere. Significantly, many people continue to speculate that Diana's death was caused by the media, both literally and metaphorically. At the time of the accident, Diana and her companions were attempting to escape the intrusions of the rogue celebrity press, the paparazzi. Of course, Diana was also part of a broader public interest and imagining. She had appeared often in the major, mainstream media, and her life and personal struggles had become a significant part of the everyday lives and experiences of 'ordinary' people. To this extent, Diana was a media and cultural product like any other 'text' or celebrity. However partially or impermanently, the characters, events, celebrities and texts that are constituted through the media are a fundamental part of our culture.

Warfare, tragedy, love, desire, struggle, relationships – all are mediated for us and implicated in our everyday experiences. The Rolling Stones, Tom Cruise, the attack on the Twin Towers in New York and the Columbine High School killings become real for us – emotionally and cognitively present in our daily contemplations, conversations, pleasures, imaginings and pains. They provide a resource for the management of our own problems, relationships, actions, politics, judgements and processes of persuasion. They become part of who we are and how we understand the world around us. They become our reality.

Thus, the media is not just a conduit for the transfer of meanings from the central corporation to audiences; the media are part of a generalized context and interplay of meaning-making. The media do not exist 'out there', but are immersed in the everyday practices and meaning-making of individuals and communities across the globe: they are a significant resource in the formation and construction of contemporary culture(s).

Yet culture is shaped through two quite contrary impulses: one toward the greater congregation of shared meanings (values, practices, texts, beliefs); the other toward change and greater dispersal. While we will speak a little more about dispersal below, we can establish here that the media is profoundly implicated in the process of meaning aggregation, a process that is essential through all gradients of cultural formation. All societies, that is, must communicate and commune through the formation of overlapping or contiguous social imaginings – the sense of participating in 'the group' through the mutual and interdependent construction of meaning. Thus, culture is that

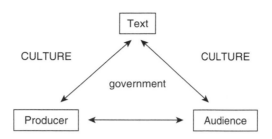

Figure 1.1 *Culture, the media and meaning-making.*

Source: Lewis 2005, p. 6.

shared (imagined-meaning) space where the media and audiences interact. Figure 1.1 gives us some sense of how this interaction takes place.

Each apex in Figure 1.1 is interacting with all other elements. This is a dynamic and ceaseless inter-flow of parts, moving through various social gradients in order to generate meaning –

- *Media producers* include all those people, institutions, regulations and processes who/which contribute to the formation of texts. Text producers may be professional and corporate, or non-professional individuals and communities who create texts online, photographs, home videos, art, poems and so on. Producers draw on the vast 'library' of meanings that already exist in culture, including their own professional judgement, to create their texts.
- *Texts* include every form of mediation in language, sound, smell and image. Media texts may include handycam home videos, garage music, blockbuster movies, websites, books, Internet downloads, TV news, and so on. These texts may be broadcast distribution (including global), or narrowcast (including person to person).
- *Audiences* include any form of text consumer at any level of production or reception. Audiences are not passive receivers of messages, as early media theory imagined (see Chapter 8). Rather, they are active creators of meaning, drawing on their own personal store of pre-existing experiences and meanings, as well as specific texts and the vast 'library' of imaginings and meanings that are held within culture itself. To this end, an audience body may be formed across broad social gradients from huge, global constituencies, to highly localized and specialist consuming communities.

As will be outlined below, this pre-existing library of meanings that are held within culture might equally be understood as the invisible 'knowledge' which shapes, and is shaped by, the individual and collective consciousness of a given social group. This consciousness is itself shaped in terms of this exterior 'semiotic' (meaning-based) architecture, as well as more ineffable states of the human mind – those that operate at the liminal and subliminal levels. Thus, while consciousness refers to knowledge and meanings which can be explicated and articulated in some form of language and text, the liminal and subliminal levels of human cognition generally cannot. There are many words used to describe this 'pre-lingual' dimension of the human mind – intuition, the sub-conscious, the 'unconscious', sensations, emotions, spirit, imagination, 'gut feeling' and so on. While this dimension of culture, meaning-making and knowing will be discussed in later chapters, the concept of 'imagining' is offered here as a way of describing the *confluence* of consciousness, the liminal and subliminal levels of human cognition and meaning-making.

At this point of the discussion, it is also worth noting that these meanings, and indeed audiences themselves, are engaged in complex processes of social and political organization, which in the contemporary capitalist-economic context are generally hierarchical. Thus, different groups have greater and lesser access to the resources of text construction and distribution. To this end, a particular group's preferred meanings may be privileged over others. Quite obviously, major media corporations like the Fox Network have the power to create and distribute their version of the world (e.g., the Iraq War) more than smaller companies, community broadcasters or individuals. Particular meanings, therefore, may carry the interests and ideologies of dominant social and economic groups.

Thus, the death of one woman, Princess Diana, has carried an extraordinary density of meanings because it appears consonant with the interests and ideologies of dominant social elites *and* the broader cultural values of vast numbers of 'ordinary' people. Similarly, the reporting of 9/11 was largely shaped by the perspective of the US administration and meanings that are deeply embedded in American culture; these meanings were privileged over alternative meanings, such as the criticisms of American foreign policy and economic exploitation of the Middle East.

- *Culture*, therefore, is constructed out of consonant and aggregating meanings that are shaped in relation to a given social group's values, ethics, interests and ideologies. Culture may become evident in the material text (speech, image, sound, words) and in practices (human actions, audience behaviours, and so on). However, as we have also said, culture is also dynamic and replete with disputes over meaning and various claims for meaning primacy. New meanings are shaped in terms of the ceaseless interaction of humans and their diverse communicational forms. As we will discuss below, this dynamic contributes to the transfer, implosion, creation and re-creation of meaning.
- *Governments* and government regulations are a significant sub-category of culture, since they are able to exert considerable influence over the regulatory environment in which the media operate. For example, the expansion in global corporate media during the 1980s and 1990s was facilitated by the deregulation of the US media industry, allowing corporations to grow exponentially and absorb larger markets.

The contemporary cultural setting, which blends mediated with politically inscribed meanings, needs to be understood as a new public sphere. Historically, the modern European nation-state was constructed around an ideal of free expression and the participation of citizens in government. This free expression took place in the public sphere – initially the public square and other public forums, and eventually through the medium of print. Mass societies have now come to rely on the electronic broadcast media as the centrifugal force of democracy. This new public sphere can be regarded as the *mediasphere* – a critical 'culturescape' in which meanings flow through various channels of human and technologically enhanced modes of communication (Lewis, 2005; Lewis and Lewis, 2006). The mediasphere is the compound of the media and the public sphere, the conflux of macro and micro processes of communication and social engagement.

Global Capital, Cultural Value and the New Televisual Reality

The 'media', therefore, is best understood as a set of dynamic communicative and culturally constituted relationships, rather than simply as a particular industry or conglomerate of corporate organizations. While they are not the same thing, mediation is embedded in culture and culture is embedded in mediation. This more inclusive conception of the media is clearly critical for our understanding of contemporary, televisual culture and its various permutations across modernizing and globalizing human societies. Most recent social theorists, in fact, recognize that communication and culture are central contingencies in the current phase of globalization, noting that the new transnational economy has been largely constructed around the instantaneous transfer of information (see Castells, 1997; Sklair, 2002; Roseman, 2003; Urry, 2003; Nairn and James, 2005). Most commentators also agree that this compression of time and space constitutes a new historical epoch of 'contiguous distance' by which the immediate transfer of finance, news or entertainment can draw people from their distant cultural and physical spaces into the virtual world of mediation – and its distinctive culture of televisualization. Thus, while capitalism has always carried its products across spatial and cultural borders, the new economy concentrates *value* into forms that can be instantaneously transacted across vast distances in an instant.

Pierre Bourdieu (1977, 1984, 1990; see also Baudrillard, 1981) argues that the foundation for this new form of symbolic exchange was established around the beginning of the twentieth century. According to Bourdieu, the meanings and social values attached to capitalist products transmogrified, as the basic needs of modern societies were largely satisfied. As Karl Marx had noted, capitalism depended for its survival on constant and unconstrained growth: that is, the capacity to invent new products to meet new markets and new demand. With the need for basic food, clothing and housing satisfied by the early twentieth century, capitalism became reincarnated as 'consumer capitalism', whereby individuals and families became concentrated into the consuming 'household'. But this was not simply an economic or social reorganization. Media, culture and communications were at the centre of these transformations; from the 1920s until the emergence of television, the wireless radio was the 'magical voice' of electricity and all the wonderful new products that a modern home could possess. Marketing, branding and advertising strategies contributed to the shaping of a new cultural and social consciousness which enabled communities, families and individuals to re-imagine themselves in terms of a new collective order, that is, as a 'society' that had a shared ideology and national trajectory. Thus, the communities that had been so severely strained and fragmented during the period of urbanization and industrialization were being re-welded through a sense of national belonging and the communal practice of capitalist consumerism. Pleasure, therefore, became the solder which bound political ideology to a new sense of community and shared culture.

To this end, capitalist products not only supported the economic sustainability of the developed societies; they also provided for society a new fabric of values and meanings, a *raison d'être* (reason for being) which gave direction and focus for the new consuming household. In a highly competitive and hierarchical society, where the distribution of wealth is often unjustly meted, it is largely this ideal and aspiration of pleasure that enables the overall system to sustain itself. According to Bourdieu, elite social groups have become particularly adept at 'reading' the values and meanings that are inscribed over particular capitalist products and practices. Thus, the products themselves are not politically neutral since their consumption reinforces the distinctions that are implied in the capitalist production process.

The concept of 'taste' becomes a rubric for social distinctions that are constituted around income, education, social refinement and class. In this way, a consumer or group of consumers will shape their own consciousness and identity around the ascribed value of particular products and services. At its simplest level, an individual distinguishes him/herself by driving a BMW to work, while another rides a Vespa. More subtly, an individual purchases department store clothing in the hope that it will pass as expensive designer wear. The social background of another individual is exposed when the etiquette of dining and utensil use is transgressed.

Of course, there has always been a level of symbolic value attached to products, but these were constrained by the limited incomes and purchasing power of the majority of the population. The continued expansion of the middle class and the proliferation of consumable products in developed societies stimulated an exponential growth in symbolic exchange value. From the early part of the twentieth century the household became increasingly populated by furniture, fashion, decor, trinkets, cutlery, washing products and a vast array of comfort products that enhanced the lifestyle of the new bourgeoisie. Different social groups actually came to recognize one another through the exercise of product preference and the presentation of their 'style'. A number of cultural commentators have suggested that the expression of style is not simply about power differentials, but about differentiation or fragmentation more generally: thus, different social groups or 'sub-cultures' adopt a particular style of dress or consumption practice in order to identify themselves within the great morass of contemporary society (Stuart, 1984; Muggleton, 2002).

Jean Baudrillard (esp. 1981, 1984a) is somewhat critical of Bourdieu's reading of symbols and social distinction, arguing that contemporary sign systems cannot be so simply correlated with forms of social power. For Baudrillard, the symbolic force of a BMW is created less through the discrimination of consumption and class, and more through its ability to 'arouse' consumers. Beginning from a very different theoretical base from Bourdieu, Baudrillard argues that contemporary culture is a deluge of signs, symbols and images. These 'signs' are proliferating through the volumes of media and informational processes that now distinguish and create contemporary culture. Yet, while other theorists believe that these signs are conduits of meaning, Baudrillard regards the meanings themselves as vacuous because there is no social agreement about their value and durability. In this sense, they are merely simulacra or imitations of imitations which dissolve before they are even comprehended by media audiences. The Princess Di phenomenon, the killings at Columbine High School, the sexual adventures of Paris Hilton are all constituted through a new, televisual culture – a new reality or hyperreality. This hyperreality creates new forms of stimulation, new forms of arousal and demand, new forms of erratic consumption. The product becomes intensely exalted and sexualized, often through the deployment of a young female body – but this arousal is a stimulation and can never be satisfied. The consumer is prompted to act and consume; however, the deluge of images and signs is unending and the urge to consume is never consummated, never quite complete.

In Baudrillard's terms, therefore, the sign overtakes the product as the primary source of arousal, action and economy. Because it is nothing more than a sign, a powerfully sexualized sign, the consumer can never escape its abstraction. The proliferation of signs continues to stimulate. The BMW is sexually imaged and motivates some form of consumption – if not the car, then something else. The arousal prompts the desire to buy, but ultimately there is nothing there. The sign is empty, leading merely to another sign, another amorphous arousal, another vacuous avatar.

For Baudrillard, contemporary culture is marked by this absence of material reality. Everything is mediated, and in Baudrillard's extreme view this means that everything is an imitation of an imitation – a simulacrum. In these terms, it is possible for Baudrillard (1995) to contend very seriously that 'the Gulf War did not take place' because the whole event was pre-prepared for televisual consumption, pre-digested and presupposed in its outcomes.

Fredric Jameson (1990, 1991) suggests, however, that this new culture is evinced through a deeper logic by which the news media are constantly reconstituting themselves in the condition of 'the perpetually new'. The electronic media and the proliferation of signs and symbols actually reduce human value and human culture by compressing time and space. According to Jameson, contemporary culture has 'finally transcended the capacities of the individual human body to locate itself, to organize its immediate surroundings perceptually, and cognitively to map its position in a mappable external world' (1990: 85). The news media, that is, function to concentrate time and information in particular ways that separate us from the past, constituting all knowledge as an historical amnesia. Mediated culture, in this sense, is both a phantasm and a condition of severe loss. Our sense of presence in the culture and in meaning-making has been seriously compromised by the proliferating omnipresence of the media and information systems.

While many analysts of contemporary culture share Jameson's critical concerns, others treat the proliferation of signs and images more optimistically. Richard Dyer (1985), John Fiske (1987, 1989b), David Muggleton (2002) and Henry Jenkins (1992; Jenkins et al., 2002), for example, have seen significant connections between the production of popular media texts and the cognitive and sensual satisfactions of audiences. 'Celebrity', in particular, is identified as the communal link that reconciles consumption capitalism with the everyday practices and pleasures of individuals within mass, contemporary society. For these authors, and many others impressed by the social and personal potential of popular media, the rendering of human experience in images and information is not to be feared, but to be explored, enjoyed and used by the people who integrate these texts into their own lifeworlds and imaginations. This perspective has become particularly prevalent in studies of the Internet and virtual cultures.

Globalization and a Politics of Contemporary Culture

We have established that contemporary culture is shaped in relation to pre-eminent forms of televisual and globally networked media. We have also recognized that the meanings and meaning-making processes which determine, and are determined by, culture are always formed in relation to audiences and their everyday lifeworlds and social practices. Of course, meanings are also shaped in relation to other significant communicational nodes, including other media (print, aural), social institutions (government, law, education, family), friendship and community groups, and the imaginary of an individual's personal history. All of these interactions take place within a more generalized and collective history, in which particular memories are privileged and preserved in text, and are thus available for the meaning-making of the present (de Certeau, 1988).

Many recent studies in the social sciences have been particularly interested in the cultural and economic transformations associated with globalization processes and the new communications technologies. The primacy of the image as a communicative mode has been central to these transformations, most particularly through the global networking of media systems. The German philosopher Martin Heidegger (1952, 1977) referred to the arrival of the moving picture and the grand proportions of the cinema image as historically transformational: in the 'world as picture', the image becomes 'gigantic', overwhelming humans by its deceptive scale and presentation of the appearance of something which is actually absent.

While Heidegger did not live to see the full force of media globalization, it is clear that he recognized that the image spectacle would contribute significantly to the transformation of human consciousness – and that this change would filter back through all levels of human social experience. Heidegger feared that this new consciousness would veer human thinking away from deeper contemplation and the written word, thus depriving humans of their rational capacity to determine right from wrong. This mesmeric fascination with the image and (American) individualism would ultimately distract humans from the pursuit of freedom of thought, replacing it with a specious pursuit of freedom of (consumer) choice. The Marxist cultural theorist Theodor Adorno (1994) fortified these views, claiming that consumerism and popular culture transformed the individual into a pseudo or false individual who would slavishly follow fashion and the dictates of the powerful culture industries. Adorno was especially concerned about popular music and the power of melodrama to control and constrain human creativity.

Robert McChesney (2004), among many other recent writers, has claimed that media globalization has generally reduced the capacity of individuals to access the media, thus limiting diversity of views and consolidating elite ideologies across the globe. This is a particularly acute problem for English-speaking communities, since American media corporations dominate the global markets. In the context of the 9/11 attacks on New York and the global 'war on terror', Noam Chomsky (2001, 2003a, 2003b) argues that the corporate media and US government have simply asserted their interests and elite ideology over the citizens of the US and indeed the whole of the world. Similarly, Douglas Kellner (2005) claims that the combination of global power and the predominance of the media spectacle have debased democracy and the capacity of citizens to exercise clear political choices.

While there is some truth in these claims, they only partly explain the role of the global networked media in shaping global culture and the new media spaces (Lewis, 2005). The media is not simply motivated by the desire to dominate political spaces; it is driven by its own internal deficiencies and deficits –

Each media pronouncement or text is shaped through a deferral narrative in which the meaning of the story is linked in perpetuity to its supplement – the next news bulletin, episode, CD release, film, PR campaign or advertisement. Each new discourse or text is gestant, that is, with its own arrival and departure, and with the gestational connection to past and future texts. This system of connectedness creates a fiscal and semiotic debt which can only be redeemed through the exigency of the next instalment, the next great event, the next epiphanal spectacle. In order to support this semiotic exigency, media organizations within the industrial complex must invest in new technologies, strategies, productions and personnel. Everything must be the newest and the latest: ratings, market data, advertising contracts, licences, boards of directors, shareholders, parliamentary hearings, audiences, and creditors – all contribute to a sense of informational volition for media professionals. This 'imperative for information' drives journalists and editors, with an accelerating momentum, toward an ever greater level of production and productivity in an increasingly vigorous and contested semiotic and financial environment. (Lewis, 2005: 35)

In the context of increasing global insecurity, this situation has led many cultural analysts to conclude that the global networked media is the political affiliate of other dominant (hegemonic) organizations. In particular, authors like McChesney, Kellner and Chomsky equate the volume and prevalence of global media with a form of cultural imperialism. These views accord with globalization theories which identify western-US economic and military domination with a new kind of world order within which culture is becoming increasingly homogenized (see Chapter 10). The global corporate media works with the US-based political hegemony to ensure the spread of western interests through the ideology and practices of 'free-market', capitalist economics. Thus, the meanings and products that are generated through the new form of capitalism outlined above are supported by a dominant ideology – which itself is distributed through western-based signs and symbols.

While the ubiquity of US-based cultural products is clearly evident, this standardization argument has nevertheless been widely challenged. As we have already noted, the tendency toward the greater agglomeration of people and culture into a single economic and social/political order has created a range of effects. And indeed, globalization theorists such as Arjun Appadurai (1990, 1996, 2006), David Held (Held et al., 1999) and John Urry (2003) have maintained that the move to greater economic and cultural consolidation has necessarily involved countermoves toward local transformations and forms of social fragmentation. Roland Robertson refers to these counterflows in global and local effects as 'glocalization': the process by which local communities and cultures absorb and transform the globalizing elements of culture and economy. Manuel Castells (1997) has investigated these changes in terms of a reverse process of identity reformation, a process by which local communities adapt their sense of self in terms of global trends and local history.

Within this framework, globalization and the global culture are returned to the level of 'ordinary' people and their everyday lives. Some theorists refer to this process of re-absorption and adaptation of cultural products and their inscribed meanings as a form of 'hybridization'. That is, the corporate media and other powerful groups generate their products, ideologies and texts across the globe; these materials and meanings are 'consumed' by different local communities but their inscribed values and meanings are changed *in relation to* the interests, history, values, institutions, beliefs, identities and practices of the local people. These groups then produce their own meanings and texts out of the hybrid of cultural elements. Perhaps the most spectacular example of this is the Bollywood phenomenon, which has adapted Hollywood movie styles, production systems, technologies and financial models into Indian expressive forms. Thus, the Indian movie industry has been constructed through the hybridization of western cinema and local

Plate 1.1   *Six Months after the Tsunami in Arugambay, Sri Lanka*

The global disaster as global (dis)unity

On December 24, 2004, a massive earthquake on the northern tip of Sumatra, Indonesia, generated a tsunami event which wreaked incredible death and devastation across the region. While over 200,000 people were killed in Indonesia itself, many tens of thousands more fatalities were recorded in Thailand, southern India and Sri Lanka. Like other natural disasters – disease, hurricanes, floods – the impact of a tsunami is critically linked to the human conditions in which it occurs. Unlike the Pacific, which is rimmed by developed world economies and technology, the Indian Ocean had no tsunami warning system or effective protection devices for coastal communities. The photograph above was taken six months after the tsunami struck a small fishing village, Arugambay, on the eastern coast of Sri Lanka. The concrete wells are filled with sand, appearing like gravestones for the once-thriving communities that occupied the shoreline.

(Cont'd)

> While international aid organizations swept into the areas to support the recovery, their presence created as much harm as good. Complex ethnic, cultural and political conditions were destabilized, as the three main community groups – Tamil, Muslim, Sinhalese – competed for aid and recovery resources. The Muslim community, in particular, felt alienated by the majority Sinhalese government and aid agencies from the US, which was regarded as anti-Muslim in its war on terror. Tamils felt equally aggrieved, viewing themselves as victims of the government's ongoing civil war against the separatist Tamil Tigers. When the government constructed a Buddhist temple in the middle of the township to give hope to the victims of the tsunami, a community war erupted with each of the ethnic groups accusing the other of corruption and banditry.
>
> Thus, when the terrible devastation of the tsunami was reported across the globe, the news generated unparalleled sympathy and donations from the developed world. However, in a tragic reverberation of globalization, the combination of natural disaster and transnational interventions seems to have deepened the horror. Globalization might be bringing peoples and cultures closer together, but this new contiguity is exacerbating complex tensions and instabilities: the world remains critically divided, even in the midst of increasing communication and information distribution.

customs, narrative styles and preferred modes of entertainment. Now the biggest movie industry in the world, the Bollywood system is being mimicked and adapted by various smaller countries and cultures, which are re-hybridizing the form to suit their own, local conditions and forms of cultural practice.

CASE STUDY 1: Defining Di

It must already be clear that this assemblage of cultural discourses and imaginings can never be reduced to a single and all-embracing 'grand narrative' (Lyotard, 1984a). Indeed, one of the significant points of agreement amongst recent cultural theorists is that contemporary culture is multi-forming, divergent and constantly in dispute. 'Language wars' are formed, that is, not only in actual military or physical conflicts, but through all conditions of meaning-making and culture. The celebrity status of Princess Diana serves to illustrate this point, even though, on the surface, the Diana funeral appears to be one of the most unifying experiences in human history. The life and death of Diana Spencer need to be understood as a series of calamitous and struggling discourses which engage with an enormous number of people's pleasures and pains. Diana's funeral established a new horizon of global media consumption and cultural participation across the globe: around 2–3 billion people watched the memorial service, and the Elton John tribute song remains the highest selling music single ever produced. Even in the decade or so since her death, the imaginary of the 'people's princess' continues to stimulate the production of books, videos, websites, news stories and charity activities across the world. *The Queen* (Stephen Fraser, 2006) is the most recent example of the continued force of the Diana mythology for the popular imaginary.

The person of Diana – whoever that might have been – is represented or constructed through the mass media and through general public discourses that interact with media texts (Davies, 1999). Her clothes, her hair, her palace, her title, her 'image', her sex, her relationships – all are representations or texts in as much as we attach meaning to them in our everyday practices and communicative encounters. And while this is true for each of us and has always been the defining feature of culture, the Princess Diana phenomenon illustrates the particular capacity of contemporary culture to construct and radiate meanings, even through the vacuum of personal knowing. That is to say, our society and culture can function as a mass of accumulated parts because mediated knowing has been able to replace immediate or personal knowing of the other members of that huge communal formation (modern society). Though we know relatively few members of that mass group personally, we are nevertheless able to imagine and identify with a culture or community of other humans because of the mass media, their images, narratives and information. We didn't know Diana personally, but we developed a personal knowing and an emotional engagement through the operations of the media.

The position of the celebrity is therefore fundamentally paradoxical (see Marshall, 1997; Turner, 2004; Jaffe, 2005). Diana is 'of the people' and yet prominent among us. She is constructed by our own capacity for meaning-making and yet delivered to us through the dissemination power of the mass media. Whoever-she-is must respond to what we think and feel she is, and yet we contribute significantly to the discourses that surround, attach themselves to, and produce her. The Diana we know and respond to becomes implicated in our own life experiences; she is not 'out there' as a distinctive, singular and objective fact. Rather, Diana is known only as she is 'mediated' through the texts and discourses that produce her. Thus, she becomes one of us, a living being in the fold of our own relationships, loves, fears, and homes.

Let us consider this in more detail. At the simplest level, of course, Diana Spencer came to represent charm, spontaneity and glamour for the popular imagination (Drew, 1998). This regal beauty hearkens to a range of already existing texts, images and imaginings that have been drawn through the fairytale and popular texts of childhood and beyond. Jacques Derrida (see 1979, 1981) calls this linking of texts and the accumulating of interdependent meanings 'intertextuality'. Thus, our sense of Diana is built around other texts and textual experiences, some of which we might regard as adapted mythologies: narratives that are so frequently repeated that they become embedded in our belief systems or taken-for-granted truths and ideologies. The mass media also rely on, and textually appropriate (borrow from), these textual experiences to enrich, enliven and emotionally inscribe their own particular stories of Diana and her life (see Richards et al., 1999).

The 'celebration' and celebrity-making of Diana can only be understood in terms of these other texts and the propensity of a consumer capitalist culture to *commodify* people as media products. As John Taylor (2000) argues, Diana's appeal is certainly driven by the imaging of regal grace, beauty and charity, though inevitably this commodification implicates certain political and ideological considerations. Specifically, the image is self-legitimating: it confirms its own value and right to give pleasure to its audiences as indeed it confirms the validity of capitalism, capitalist institutions and its media, and the status and substance of the royal heritage itself. John Hartley (1996) has argued that the very idea of a constitutional monarchy continues to be legitimated through the popular media's continual re-presentation of the royal family: 'The "tabloid" and "gossip" media's obsession with the royal gonads is at the cutting edge, as it were, of political journalism in this context' (Hartley, 1996: 12). The image and the institutions that support it are entirely self-interested, driven by an ideology that is predicated on production, consumption, power and profit. Politics and ideology, that is, are necessarily implicated in the construction of the Diana character in the same way as they are implicated in the celebrity creation of movie and popular music stars.

However, and as Hartley himself goes on to ponder, the ideological context of the culture is itself formidably ambiguous. The Diana image is delivered to us by a plutocratic institution which might well have vested interests in the maintenance of elite power formations – celebrity sells, creating wealth, legitimacy and status for the media owners who create 'fame'. Even so, we need to recognize that it is the interests and consumption practices of ordinary people that actually determine the 'success' of those constructed images. The people ultimately select the image for their own everyday purposes and pleasures. Diana's privilege and power within the culture are sanctioned and permitted, that is, by the interests of her audience – her media subjects (Turnock, 2000).

But even this does not explain the incredible popularity and durability of the image in life and in death. As we examine it more closely, the Diana character was constructed through a remarkable range of competing signs and symbols. Yes, she was charming, gracious and beautiful, and ultimately these qualities were able to evolve into more mature narratives of maternity, abandonment and profound feminine integrity. But equally, Diana's political presence seemed strangely reconciling. The iniquities of inherited privilege and despotic rule are neutralized through the popular imaginings and presentation of Diana's more charitable and democratic demeanour. Those tiaras and dresses that might have radically distanced Diana from her consuming public became relativized – symbols of her charity, her work for the poor and impoverished of the world. As befitting the mythologies of benevolent authority, Diana's charity was both a demonstration of popular and community participation and a validation of her right to prominence and privilege. This 'charitable' demeanour was able to camouflage, it would seem, the social privilege which facilitated the sale in 1997 of one of Diana's dresses for over $200,000 (a silk gown Diana wore when dancing with John Travolta at the White House).

Diana's celebrity, therefore, was intensely political, although the direction and exercise of that 'power' remain invisible or at least evasive. In the clamouring of grief that followed her death, there seemed no space at all for criticism or negative review. The opulent lifestyle and the inebriant circumstances of the accident were largely ignored by the serious and popular press, though had the same fate befallen socially ascribed villains – criminals, blacks, poor single mothers – the treatment of the issue would have been entirely different. In Diana's case the paparazzi, those voracious and marauding media hyenas, provided an effective focus for public blame – the paparazzi refused to comply with Diana's highly managed image manufacture. The public seemed strangely to forget that the paparazzi and the official press were merely the conduits for its own rabid consumption of the Diana narratives.

Indeed, one of the most telling features of Diana's celebrity was the ongoing battle for control of her image and representation. While the Diana celebrity had an immense capacity to increase audience ratings and circulation figures, control of the image was more extensively waged between different commercial, ethical and institutional interests. This 'struggle to signify', as Stuart Hall calls it, was most intensely manifest in the aftermath of Diana's death when the official Diana media machine was railing against the tabloid press, which was in turn railing against the paparazzi. For their part, the paparazzi, or unofficial celebrity press, represented themselves as the defenders of 'free speech' and editorial independence; they told the true stories because they were not constrained by Diana's public relations machinery. It was the paparazzi who released 'unofficial' photographs of Diana's life for the intrigue and pleasures of the general public. The paparazzi fed the rabid and salacious interests of Diana's public, contributing to her fame and her celebrity mystique.

These internal media ructions seemed peculiarly subdued during the period immediately following Diana's death. As Mick Hume (1998) has pointed out, the petty ethical squabbling turned to a general mood of embarrassment, if not shame. The Diana consumers articulated their grief through blame of others. The media culture that pursued all in order to make it available for the sensate pleasures of the consumer was suddenly under scrutiny. The media were blamed for Diana's death and an ethical truce was called as the assembly of televisual global citizens watched the regal coffin as it was charioted through the streets to Westminster. The media had gone too far and brought about her death, but at least they were available for our own personal grieving.

What is clear, then, is that our ability to make sense of the world we live in is now absolutely dependent on our relationship with the media. It is not that we are 'conditioned' by the various information and entertainment media, but rather that we are a part of them since our knowledge of ourselves and our world is filtered through their images and language. It may well be that the increasing abstractness of the world actually elicits an equally strong, though contradictory and unconscious, desire for moral and ideological substance – a 'grounded' reality that is not so evanescent, ephemeral and contingent. The mythology of Diana, her regality and substantive links with the deep past, represent a way of imagining the world as a 'community' of subjects or citizens. The Diana narrative, that is, may well provide for people that sense of community and social consensus which contemporary culture, for all its pleasures, plenitude and possibilities, has rendered more abstract, if not elusive.

CULTURE AND CULTURAL STUDIES

A Definition of Culture

As noted, much recent commentary distinguishes contemporary culture in terms of the global communications systems and the compression of time and space. The formation of celebrity is one dimension of these new historical conditions; in rendering the familiar exceptional and the exceptional familiar, celebrity and televisual culture more generally contribute to the creation of an impression of global community. However, as we have also indicated, these impressions are accompanied by an equally forceful politics of hierarchy and differentiation – a sense in which the *notion* of global community and global culture are merely propagated by powerful elites who have most to benefit from the illusion of an integrated and homogenous social order. In either case, culture exists within the meaning-making of individuals and groups through the relationships formed in communication. The mediasphere brings text-producer-audience into a dynamic relationship that forms and is informed by culture (including political culture). We can thus define culture in the following terms –

Culture is an assemblage of imaginings and meanings that are generated by a given social group. These meanings may be consonant, disjunctive, overlapping, contentious, continuous or discontinuous. The given social group may be formed around a broad gradient of human communities, activities and purposes. Communication is the central force which binds social groups to culture; in contemporary culture these communicational processes are dominated by various modes of global networked media.

We can look at each of these definitional attributes in greater detail:

1 *Culture is an assemblage of imaginings and meanings.* I have already suggested that culture is constructed around collective and individual human consciousness. The term 'consciousness' generally refers to that mode of human thinking which is self-aware and shaped in relation to social experiences and social knowledge. Clearly, an individual's consciousness is shaped around the dominant values, beliefs and significant 'knowledge' of the social group. But also the individual's own 'mind' and personal history filters these experiences to form a distinctive, individual consciousness. The inventor of psychoanalysis, Sigmund Freud, claimed that this latter process is further complicated

by the human 'sub-conscious', which operates at a subliminal level beyond the direct awareness of individuals.

Meaning-making is thus a very complicated set of processes. As noted earlier in the chapter, the concept of 'imagining' is applied in order to capture the conscious, liminal and subliminal mental operations which are mobilized by individuals and groups as they create meaning. The term does not refer exclusively to those zones of human creativity (imagination) which may be opposed to the faculty of 'reason'. Rather, 'imagining' refers to the forming power of mind, sensibilities, emotions and experience as they become the embryo of knowledge and its articulation in language. This 'experience' may be delivered by the mass media, as we have suggested, or other significant institutions such as the government, law, education or the family. Experience may also be that broad raft of interactions and activities which constitute an individual's everyday experience. The 'knowledge' which is the kernel of meaning, therefore, may be articulated as attitudes, beliefs, values, opinions, ideas, identity, art and even actions – all of which constitute 'expressivity' (Deleuze and Guatarri, 1987) and a 'readable' cultural text.

And just as the meanings of a text may change over time, so too can an individual's imagining of him/herself and the external world. Because imagining may be rational, irrational, creative and emotional – it is the ferment and site of change and the re-ordering of self. The 'imaginary' is the locale of an individual's complex engagement with the culture, with one's own aesthetic and creative re-processing of change, confusion and illumination. Thus, we can entirely re-configure or re-imagine our relationship with another human being: for example, a former lover toward whom we have become indifferent or even hostile. The concept of imagining might also help to explain the reconstruction of our individual identities through different social and temporal contexts: for example, through the experiences of migration or education. It explains how an industrial, working-class slum can be re-configured and re-imagined as a trendy, inner-city lifestyle. The physical space may be only moderately changed, but the cultural imagining is radically altered.

We are thus extending the definition of culture well beyond the notion of 'way of life', which has evolved in anthropological studies (see Chapter 2). Even so, social practices, beliefs, rituals and artefacts are all meaningful and hence part of the general definition.

2   *These imaginings and meanings may be consonant, disjunctive, overlapping, contentious, continuous or discontinuous.* As we shall see, language and meaning systems have often been treated as solid and fixed formations. However, meaning systems like language are capable of producing misunderstandings and non-meaning, as well as meanings. At any one time, a culture can be subject to an infinite array of meaning disputes and gaps. There may be 'dominant' meanings, values and ideologies that seek to determine a particular social order; however, a culture can never be entirely closed since it is made up of competing interests and many different individuals (subjects) and groups. Even relatively isolated tribal communities were comprised of different age groups and gender, and engaged in various forms of external interaction. Modern societies are extraordinarily complex, mixed and heterogeneous, rendering them vulnerable to an infinite array of external and internal disputes of meaning.

3   *The given social group may be formed around a broad gradient of human communities, activities and purposes.* As we have already noted, culture and society are not the same thing, though they are clearly contingencies of one another. Individuals belong to various forms of social groupings, each with their own 'cultures'. This means that we can speak of a family culture, a national culture, an ethnic culture, a global culture, a work culture, a religious culture, a university culture, a football culture, a technological culture, a gay culture, and so on. A number of these cultures are attached to major social institutions which can assert considerable influence over its constituency. Nation and national culture, for example, have proved both durable and powerful, creating conditions in which individuals will surrender their lives in their defence.

All cultures, macro and micro, operate through particular discourses, rules, belief systems, values, rituals and practices that are imbued with meaning. Part of this meaning-making involves the construction of an individual's personal identity (or 'subjectivitiy') through the internalization and re-projection of attributes that are specific to that particular culture. In a complex, modern society, where an individual may participate in a range of different social groupings and hence cultures, identity formation may produce contradictory effects. Thus, an individual may encounter more and less contention between various cultural affiliations and sources of identity construction. Ravers, for example, may love their nation but transgress nationally constituted drugs laws. The young Muslim men who perpetrated the attacks on the London underground (2005) were second generation immigrants and were clearly torn between an affiliation with the laws and values of nation and democracy, and the *jihadist* values which condone murder as retribution for Britain's invasion and occupation of Iraq.

Reading the veil: A contemporary cultural analysis

In 2004 the French parliament passed legislation banning the wearing of all religious icons in all public schools. The law was greeted with considerable consternation by many of France's six million Muslims, as well as numerous civil rights groups. While the ban was placed on all religious iconography, it was generally recognized that the Muslim headscarf or *hijab* was the primary target of the new law. In the midst of global agitation around Islamist militantism, the war on terror and the calamitous US-based occupation of Iraq, the new French law created distinctly polemical responses. On the one side, many people saw it as a reassertion of modernist, democratic principles, most particularly the separation of 'church and state'. On the other hand, it was seen as the over-assertion of western secularism, and the transgression of the religious and civil rights of France's Muslim community.

Other pluralist western nations seemed somewhat dismayed by the French government's anxieties about domestic Islamism, preferring to manage Muslim communities through the general ambit of religious freedom and anti-discrimination processes, rather than a generalized process of control or prohibition. French sensitivity to the 'excessive' expression of religion, it was assumed, derived from the deep history of religious politicism which led to the exclusion of the Catholic Church from state affairs. The rupture of the French Revolution (1789–99), in particular, continues to affect contemporary French cultural and political life.

Protests about the laws in France were truncated, however, by the kidnap of two French journalists, who had been covering the Iraq War and occupation. While France was not part of the occupying forces, the Iraqi kidnappers used the two journalists as hostages, demanding that France repeal its religious icon laws. While the journalists were eventually released unharmed and the laws remain in place, similar controversies have arisen in the UK following the Islamic militant attacks on the London underground in 2005. As in the US after 9/11 and Australia after the Bali bombings, the 7/7 underground attacks in the UK stimulated some profound hostilities toward Muslim communities and Islam more generally. Since the underground attacks, the Muslim veil has been frequently identified as antagonistic to the values of democracy and public 'transparency'. The former British Home Secretary, Jack Straw, refused to meet with any person who 'covered her face', and novelist Salman Rushdie reportedly described the veil as 'shit'.

These sorts of views have been fortified by a number of 'modern' Islamic women who regard the veil and the burqa as an abomination which oppresses women. Other members of the Islamic community, including those who describe themselves as Muslim feminists, regard the burqa as a legitimate expression of femininity which liberates women from the male gaze and social judgements based on sexual attractiveness. Thus, while many in the west regard the burqa and veil as oppressive, many Islamic women see their traditional mode of dress as an expression of freedom and personal agency.

4   *Communication is the central force which binds social groups to culture; in contemporary culture these communicational processes are dominated by various modes of global networked media.* As we have discussed earlier, the electronic media intensified particular cultural trends and processes during the twentieth century. The particular characteristics of electronic communication have rendered the conditions of cultural dispute, dissonance, instability and transition even more acute. Previously distant human cultural formations have been brought into greater propinquity, creating the circumstances for a proliferation of cultural discourses. These proliferating discourses stimulate ever-increasing possibilities for new meanings and new non-meanings or communication gaps.

For example, as the media products of the United States penetrate non-Anglo/European cultures, there is a remarkable proliferation of new discourses and disputes. In the period since World War II (1939–45), American films have introduced the discourse of romantic love and mouth kissing to cultures which had only deployed it as a marginal or fetishistic practice. The meaning of mouth kissing and the sexual mores associated with its deployment have been widely contested in countries like Japan, Korea and Indonesia. In Indonesia, especially, the cultural transitions that are accompanying globalization and the prevalence of western cultural styles and products are causing considerable consternation among more conservative community leaders. These leaders are sponsoring a new 'anti-pornography' law which is designed to ban publications like *Indonesia Playboy,* as well as gay and transvestite sexual practices and public kissing. Ironically, the invocation of traditional moral values against gay and transvestite practices seems to ignore or override Indonesia's long history of tolerance and social recognition of these practices. Thus, it is not the practices themselves which appear to be the problem, but the new globalizing cultural context in which they are represented as 'modern' or 'western'.

Postmodern Culture_www.the.postmodern.turn.com

The concepts of 'the postmodern', 'postmodernity' and 'postmodernism' have become widely used in various forms of social and cultural analysis over recent decades. While an entire chapter of this book has been devoted to this topic, it is worth noting immediately that these terms are not used consistently and many commentators, in fact, reject them altogether (see Habermas, 1984b; Kellner, 1995; McGuigan, 1997). Even so, it is critical for all students of cultural studies to understand these terms and their application for the analysis of contemporary culture. Thus, since the 1980s, numerous commentators across a range of disciplines have characterized the cultural changes we have been describing above as 'the postmodern turn': that is, as a new historical epoch which can be distinguished from the previous, 'modern' period. The differences between the two can be summarized as in Table 1.1.

There are several things to be said about this typology –

1   A number of cultural commentators reject the claim that we have moved into an entirely new historical phase, arguing that the current epoch is just another permutation of modernism. For these commentators, contemporary culture has become increasingly global, free-market, 'mediated', 'networked' and complex. But these characteristics are essentially 'modern', extensions of the cultural, political and socio-economic institutions that have been forged over the past several centuries. These commentators are usually most interested in the structures of power that have been constructed around various forms of western, capitalist societies. While they might accept that culture is changing, these commentators view the various cultural elements outlined in Table 1.1 as continuous, rather than oppositional.

2   A number of politically conservative scholars reject the whole notion of an epochal change, regarding the elements in Table 1.1 as a dangerous bi-product of social and aesthetic radicalism. Many of these scholars argue that postmodernist ideas (relativism in particular) are socially threatening and should be rejected. Unlike their left-liberal

Table 1.1   *The Modern/The Postmodern*

The modern	The postmodern
Enlightenment	Post-Enlightenment
Logic-centred	Image/media
Scientific method	Chaos/Quantum
Absolute truth	Relativism
Humanism/liberalism	Cultural specificity
Homogeneous	Heterogeneous
Europe-centred	Global/multicultural
Universal laws	Deconstruction
Social structure	Individual pleasure
Industrialism	Post-industrialism
Materialism	Symbolism
Atoms	Information
Patriarchy	Sexual fluidity
High art	Popular media
Chronology	Time/space compression
Broadcast	Multiple creators
Reality	Simulation
Conclusion	Inconclusive/language play

counterparts, however, they do not accept the need for a new social, economic or political system.

3   Some commentators accept the notion of a 'global postmodern' (see Hall, 1991a, 1991b), but seek to apply a critique of culture that is essentially modern. That is, they critique the elements on the right-hand side of the table (the global postmodern) using the elements on the left-hand side (modern logic and political strategies). Fredric Jameson (1991, 1998), most notably, established a critique of postmodern consciousness which clearly derives from a commitment to a neo-Marxist tradition.

4   Some commentators welcome the new historical epoch and its potential for emancipation from modernist social structures and the limitations of its critique (see Jencks, 1987b, 1995; Hutcheon, 1988; Giddens, 1994; Duvall and Dworking, 2001). Thus, rather than replace the oppressive institutions of modernism with a different set of potentially oppressive institutions, the postmodernists advocate a new form of individualism and free expressivity (Deleuze and Guatarri, 1987). The right-hand side of the table replaces the left-hand side, creating new conditions for the exploration of personal autonomy and alternative values.

5   For many scholars, this new critique is the province of new disciplines such as 'cultural studies'. Even if it is no longer specified, many scholars and students working in cultural studies are adopting a postmodern perspective, one which celebrates cross-disciplinary models, creative thinking, diversity, and relativism. Many scholars now simply accept that these attributes are a genuine and well-recognized dimension of the cultural landscape, whether it is tagged 'postmodern' or not.

Each of these positions has a place in the study of contemporary culture, as each has its particular insights and value. As we have already noted, the disputes between these various perspectives centre largely on definitions of power, the strategy of critique and respective conceptions of 'value', 'structure', 'aesthetics' and 'ideology'. Disputes around the analytical efficacy of the term 'postmodernism' in many ways cloak broader disciplinary contentions over the meaning of 'culture' itself, and its significance relative to other analytical foci such as society and social institutions, politics, policy and materialism. The general strategy of this book is to give voice to these relative claims in order to illuminate the various ways in which culture and meaning-making have been examined and formed through the broad lineage of cultural analysis, theory and cultural studies. Through these broadly evolved insights into the *concept* of culture, the processing and operations of contemporary 'culture' will be revealed. That is, the concepts become a lens through which students and scholars may view the world within which they are so entirely and intimately immersed.

Of course, the analysis offered in this book is neither politically nor heuristically neutral. One of the lessons of cultural studies is that language is always formed in terms of a specific political space: that is, it is *positioned* in accordance with the analyst's own views, modes of reading and expressivity. This book, in other words, is simply one other cultural utterance, one other cultural text. My voice, like yours, is subject to the same complexion of power, meaning-making and dispute, as any other text. To this end, I have already privileged particular perspectives and models, and as we proceed, my preference for the complexities of meaning-making and resistant agonisms will become increasingly revealed.

Even so, the general aim of this book is to present cultural studies in its broadest terms, acknowledging the significant contribution of alternative modes of cultural analysis. To this end, this book rejects the dichotomous approach to cultural studies that has evolved since the 1980s (see Chapters 3 and 12). To some extent, this dichotomy is related to the concept of postmodernism, with particular schools of thought embracing the concept with others rejecting it. But, more broadly, the dichotomy can be summarized in the following terms –

1   A number of scholars believe that the material conditions of life determine the semiotic (meaning-making) and cultural dimensions. Culture is to be studied as an outcome of social structures, institutions and government policies. These scholars have usually been trained in Marxist and liberal politics, and sociology.
2   A second group focuses on the aesthetics of text, meaning construction and text reading. Within this group is another division between those who focus more specifically on aesthetics, and those who focus on the political (cultural politics) of textual construction and consumption. The policy and materialism cultural scholars tend to see the focus on aesthetics as solipsistic, overly theoretical and impracticable. They are usually regarded as 'postmodernists' by the materialists.

Plate 1.2 *The 2006 World Cup Football, Germany*

Plate 1.3 *Cremation Ritual on Nusa Lembongan*

Global and local interflows

Culture is formed around specific social groups – their customs, beliefs, practices, values and predominant modes of meaning-making. The 2006 World Cup Football (soccer) event based in Germany brought around 3.5 billion people into a single, televisual community. While this community was ephemeral and shaped by an extraordinarily tenuous media imagining, it was nevertheless a clear manifestation of a constituent, global culture. For all their immense internal diversity, this televisual community shared significant values, practices, rules, norms and meanings through their experience of the World Cup text. Plate 1.3 presents a far more localized ritual event. This cremation was witnessed by most of the 150 community members on the small Indonesian island of Nusa Lembongan. Cremation ceremonies of this kind are linked to older Vedic-Hindu practices, which were once dominant across South and South East Asia, pre-dating the arrival of Islam around the tenth century.

   Thus, while the World Cup is clearly a global event constituted around an evolving global culture, the highly localized cremation on Nusa Lembongan has also been shaped by historically resonant 'global' rituals. In the contemporary context, such ceremonies contribute to the maintenance of local 'traditions' and culture, even as they are being absorbed into the televisual practices (like photography) of international visitors. Thus, like the World Cup, these customary practices are now the subject of a new form of globalization – international tourism.

The approach of this book is more inclusive and less divisive. To this end, the dichotomy itself appears largely unproductive since, as it is argued in Chapter 12, both sides of the polemic emphasize different dimensions of the cultural process, using variations of the same methodological framework. Thus, the book explores the various genealogies of cultural analysis, applying its own conceptual hybrid for the elucidation of contemporary culture in the latter chapters.

CASE STUDY 2: Terrorism: A Postmodern Attack on America

The al-Qa'ida attacks on Washington and New York represent a pivotal moment in American and world history. I have argued at length (Lewis, 2005) that these attacks not only created a void in the New York skyline, they also constituted a rupture in the meaning of 'America' – and in particular the American people's faith in their nation's global primacy and inviolability. In particular, the attacks challenged many of the assumptions that had been inscribed over American culture, identity and sense of historical destiny. Not surprisingly, the social status quo with most to lose from this new vulnerability rushed forward in order to fill the void, to restore meaning to the condition and status of 'America'.

Journalists and politicians, in particular, invoked the discourses of 'nationalism', tradition and the 'deep past' – a common strategy in times of national crisis and instability. As we have outlined above, the aim of such strategies is to ground the modern state in a sense of 'origin' and purpose, thus providing a greater sense of durability and destiny. Thus, in order to truncate the possibility of fragmentation and the emergence of alternative (perhaps revolutionary) meanings, the US President, George W. Bush, sought to fill the semiotic void with a highly integrated and homogenizing ideology of nation, action, vengeance and destiny. In the speeches which followed the calamity, this ideology was concentrated in an Absolute Truth, a polemic which could in no way be challenged or repudiated, was formed around a mission of retribution. Operation Infinite Justice was the original title of this mission, and an 'infinite' justice, of course, is one that marshals the divine powers against evil. Bush called on such retribution in his hastily coined, but extraordinarily effective, 'war against terror'. The ritual of prayer and the interlacing of blessings on the nation, its people and its ideology constituted a new crusade, one which would restore the meaning of America and its divine destiny as 'the chosen' (Nairn and James, 2005). These views were fortified by the archetypal American journalist and novelist, Norman Mailer, who spoke for much of the media as he declared –

> [T]he best explanation for 9/11 is that the Devil won a great battle that day. Yes, Satan as the pilot who guided those planes into that ungodly denouement ... Yes, as if part of the Devil's aesthetic acumen was to bring it off, exactly as if we were watching the same action movie we had been looking at for years. That may be at the core of the immense impact 9/11 had on America. Our movies came off the screen and chased us down the canyons of the city. (Mailer, 2003: 110–11)

Thus, the meaning of America, which had been articulated in its popular culture, comes 'off the screen' in a radical disjunction of what was, and what is. The glory and heroism of the movie screen would now be invoked as the solution to this rupture.

Within the context of such centralized and bedazzlingly potent political discourse, the voices of moderation, let alone dissent, were heavily muted. Susan Sontag (2001) queried the broad aesthetic by which American cultural politics constructs itself. The description of the perpetrators of the 9/11 attacks as 'cowardly' confounded Sontag. In essence, she argued, 9/11 was not an assault on 'liberty', 'civilization' or 'the free world', but was rather a response to America's own policies and actions in foreign territories. This perspective was also echoed in the *London Review of Books* special edition on September 11, where Mary Beard boldly suggested that 'however tactfully you dress it up, the United States had it coming'. These comments precipitated a deluge of responses, most of which attacked Beard's perspective. One American academic from Stanford University , for example, was incensed by the lack of sensitivity expressed by the British journal, claiming that she rejected the idea that America was 'to blame' for the attacks and that she would cancel her longstanding subscription to the *LRB* as a matter of protest. An equally forceful response to criticisms of US foreign policy was directed against Bill Maher, the host of US TV show *Politically Incorrect*. Explicating a point made by guest Dimesh D'Souza, Maher suggested that 'Lobbing cruise missiles from two thousand miles away, that's cowardly'. Like Sontag, Maher was savaged by the media, the public and the White House. A major sponsor cancelled their contract and Maher was abandoned by his network; the programme was cancelled several months later.

Thus, for many American journalists and social commentators the 9/11 attacks crystallized the nation's cultural status – its values, heritage and politics. Those who dared to criticize US foreign policy or ideological integrity in the midst of such an egregious assault, and such profound grief, were not simply insensitive: they were 'traitors'. To this end, many public commentators vilified those intellectuals who, like Sontag, had been captured by postmodernism and its facile moral relativism. Where the world was so clearly divided between good and evil, a postmodernist relativism seemed as impotent and impure as the terrorists themselves. Writing in the *New York Times*, Leonard Piekoff claimed that the greatest obstacle to US victory in the 'war against terror' was 'our own intellectuals, … multiculturalists rejecting the concept of objectivity'. And in a similar vein, John Leo denounced the 'dangerous ideas' of 'radical cultural relativism … and a postmodern conviction that there are no moral truths worth defending' (cited in Fish, 2002: 28).

In many respects, all of the comments cited above, along with the grand pronounce-ments of the US President himself (see Chapter 12), are based on some form of cultural analysis – and they are all formed around critical assumptions about the nature of American culture. Thus, they are all inscribed with a particular conceptual framework which defines the interests, perspectives and cultural politics of the speaker. Those that seek to impose an homogenised and absolute set of values and ideologies are, undoubtedly, inspired by a particular vision and meaning of 'America', one which privileges the US and the west in a more generalized 'clash of civilizations' (Huntington, 2002). As we discuss in Chapter 12, these privileged discourses form the basis of a new global cultural divide that now undermines the very basis of that privilege – a democratic social order. A significant role of cultural analysis, therefore, is to interrogate these assumptions and the basis of dominant discourse. The language wars that irradiate through global media networks expose themselves in the agonistic conditions of imposed and privileged order. The war on terror is, above all other things, a cultural trope which seeks to inscribe itself on the imaginings of all audience meaning-makers and their respective reading of this dynamic globalizing culture.

METHODOLOGIES AND METHODS

Our task in this book is to interrogate the various ways in which culture is formed, theorized and studied. An important part of this project is to present the most significant models of cultural studies analysis and methodologies. By 'methodologies' we mean the theoretical, epistemological (knowledge) and heuristic (discovery) context in which specific investigative techniques (methods) are applied. While some cultural studies practitioners use various combinations of these models, others tend to privilege specific techniques and methods of investigation (see McGuigan, 1997; Giles and Middleton, 1999; White and Schwoch, 2006). Cultural studies, in fact, is noteworthy among the humanities and social sciences for its deployment of diverse methodological designs. This 'interdisciplinary' approach to the study of culture brings together many of the intellectual and methodological traditions of the humanities (literature, media studies, history, aesthetics, philosophy) and the social sciences (sociology, anthropology, political science). While these different traditions have produced some quite passionate debates and disagreements about the 'true mission' of cultural studies, their confluence has also produced an extraordinarily productive and incisive body of work. These methodological models can be summarized in terms of theoretical analysis, critical investigation, deconstruction, textual studies, empirical studies and policy-based research.

Theoretical Analysis

Most cultural analysts use theory and conceptual frameworks in order to identify, clarify and speculate over specific cultural sites and issues. Some cultural theorists seek to establish the conceptual parameters within which cultural analysis should take place. They raise questions such as: What is culture? What is the appropriate focus of cultural studies? What is the relationship between power and culture? What role do the media play in constructing culture? How does representation – including the aesthetics of representation – contribute to the formation of cultural knowledge and the cultural episteme? Are social practices more or less important than textual analysis? These sorts of questions have already been raised in this chapter. In this sense, we can define theory as a form of conceptualization in language (see Milner, 2002; Lewis, 2002a).

Thus, a critical part of cultural studies is the formulation of 'concepts'. A concept provides a lens through which to view cultural sites, practices and other theorizations. For example, Antonio Gramsci adapted the concept of 'hegemony' (lit. 'leadership') to describe the ways in which institutional elites in a society 'negotiate' their power with those whom they lead. This concept has become popular in cultural studies as it provides a useful mechanism for explaining the ways in which powerful groups interact with less powerful groups. For cultural studies scholars the concept of hegemony enables a description of various forms of organizational and social hierarchy without erasing the potential for liberation across the broader community. The Gramscian concept, therefore, has been adapted and redeployed for a description of the relationship between media and their audiences.

Other cultural analysts (e.g., Hall, 1991a, 1991b) argue that theory is only a means to an end: it frames the questions which should then be directed toward specific research of specific texts, policies, social practices, institutions and relationships. In either case, theory is no more and no less than our way of knowing the world through its transformation into language. It takes us out of the quotidian immediacy of experience and allows us to see how various elements relate and intersect with one another. In other words, theory operates like a cognitive map. Our immersion in the world of action is relieved by theorization: by our capacity to step back and frame our contemplations in an orderly, established and systematic way.

Critical Investigation/Cultural Politics

As outlined earlier, cultural studies is embedded in questions of power and ideology. While 'ideology' has a number of definitions (see Chapter 3), we are speaking here about a systematic formulation of politically derived beliefs, values and discourses. These questions of power and ideology are articulated through symbolic forms of social practice, institutions and texts. As we noted above, different schools of cultural analysts privilege the material or 'corporeal' dimensions of politics over the symbolic – and vice versa. And some schools focus specifically on the ways in which discourses are engaged in policy formulation which impacts directly on the corporeal and material conditions of citizens. In all cases, these analyses incorporate an investigation of the meanings associated with political conditions.

In order to conduct these studies, cultural analysis has developed and deployed varied and extremely potent techniques, most particularly in terms of identifiable differentiations in economic, social and cultural power. In many areas, such as postcolonial/decolonization studies, queer studies and feminism, cultural studies has quite deliberately challenged particular regimes of power, particularly as they are expressed in discourse and texts. At their most polemical and overt, these critical studies begin from a specific oppositional position and 'criticize' the orthodoxies of dominant and oppressive ideologies. The early work of Raymond Williams and the Birmingham Centre for Contemporary Cultural Studies (see Chapter 4) focused very directly on an agenda of social and political reform.

More recently, critical cultural studies has focused on questions of liberation and identity. As we have noted, identity is formed around cultural experiences and facilitates some level of subjective choice in determining 'who I am'. This identity politics often examines the 'representation' of particular social groups in terms of a dominant ideology. This dominant ideology attempts to prescribe identity for the individual, which the analyst in turn seeks to overthrow. A feminist reading of the Diana story may, for example, emphasize the political construction of female identity and the limits that are placed on Diana's (and other women's) subjectivity. Similarly, a postcolonial analysis of the current 'war on terror' would critique the US-dominated cultural construction of 'Islam';

according to the postcolonial critique, the 'west' constructs Muslim people as monolithic, belligerent and necessarily antithetical to freedom, democracy and western values.

As we have suggested, culture cannot be disengaged from its symbolization and imagining, nor can these imaginings be disengaged from the power relationships that form and inform them. To this extent, then, our interrogations of culture will regularly encounter questions of power, liberation and resistance. Power is ubiquitous, as Michel Foucault claims, and all power involves the struggle to signify, construct meanings and control language and mediation generally. Politics and power, therefore, are not simply contingencies of democratic processes or governance. Rather, power is fluid, pervasive and inevitably bound to all processes of meaning-making, dispute and dissolution. As we shall see throughout this book, questions of power and ideology arise at the moment of utterance, the moment of forming the imagination in discourse. Whether they concede it or not, all cultural theorists and analysts are engaged in the operations of language struggles and language war.

Deconstruction

The technique of deconstruction has become an important and distinctive part of the critical lexicon. Jacques Derrida (1974, 1979) pioneered the technique, applying it to the study of European philosophy. Basically, Derrida seeks to illuminate the historical and linguistic assumptions that underpin the formation and cultural status of certain dominant ideas. Derrida examines the 'construction' of these ideas by questioning their underlying legitimacy; once the social legitimacy is cast into doubt, then the idea begins to unravel or become 'deconstructed'. Derrida's strategy of deconstruction points specifically to the language structures and rhetorical techniques used in European philosophy. This rhetoric, Derrida argues, is based on forms of 'binary opposition', where two elements are juxtaposed in order to demonstrate the superiority of one over the other: for example, reason over unreason, civilization over nature, man over woman, West over East, speech over writing, and so on. Deconstruction seeks to dissolve these binary formations by showing that, since everything is a mere construction of language, neither of the binary opponents can exist without reference to the other. Both sides of the opposition are relative to one another so neither can be absolutely and everlastingly true: their 'truth' is only a claim against the other pole. As language unravels, so does truth.

Cultural studies practitioners have adapted Derrida's methods for a more general analysis of cultural phenomena. In particular, analysts have sought to expose and deconstruct the discourses (power and language) which inform particular texts, institutions and social practices. Edward Said (1993), for example, has demonstrated how the liberalist and bourgeois morality that underpins nineteenth-century English literature was informed by imperialist, xenophobic and racist ideology. Similarly, the representation of Princess Diana confirms particular political and social attitudes, most particularly the legitimacy of capitalist hierarchy and the mediated artifice of feminine glamour. Deconstruction techniques can also be applied to less obviously polemical conditions such as the representation of specific racial groups in various forms of contemporary advertising. The deployment of a Japanese person in English-speaking advertisements, for example, is not necessarily Orientalist or overtly racist, but may configure a new kind of ethnic typology: it may represent innovation, digital expertise and organizational efficiency. Deconstruction seeks out the assumptions which lead to the formation of typologies in this kind of textualization.

Textual Studies

The study of texts (books, news, magazines, films, TV programmes, webpages and musical recordings) has emerged as a significant part of the humanities. Some traditional forms of textual analysis seek to illuminate the aesthetic qualities, moral values and immanent meanings held within a quality art or literary text (high art). By and large, contemporary cultural studies has dispensed with this methodology and the distinction between high and popular art which grounds it. Indeed, cultural studies has developed a particular technique of textual analysis, one which seeks to locate the text within its historical, material and cultural context. Thus, rather than consider meaning to be something inherent in the text or as something which elevates art over all other aspects of life, cultural studies has treated texts as cultural documents. These documents cannot be separated from the circumstances and conditions of their production and consumption. Thus, cultural texts are fundamentally and inescapably embedded in social practices, institutional processes, politics and economy. The meanings of texts cannot be treated as independent of the broader flows and operations of the culture in which the text exists.

As we have already noted, of course, this interconnectedness of text and context may be studied in many ways, and indeed the definition of what constitutes 'a text' is also quite variable. Some analysts seek to separate media texts from everyday practices and experiences. Others, like Roland Barthes (1975, 1977), claim that since everything is symbolic or meaningful, everything can be treated as text. For Michel Foucault (1974, 1977a, 1980), everything is mediated in terms of power relationships and so everything can be regarded as 'discourse' (language and power). In any case, the symbolic conditions of textuality remain a central and critical focus for cultural studies. For some analysts the text is a primary indicator of the context; for others the context presents insights into the text and its representations.

In cultural studies, popular media texts are as significant as the more complex and abstruse art forms. TV soap operas and commercials reflect important aspects of everyday culture. Some forms of cultural inquiry concern themselves with the structure of textual narratives (story-telling), most particularly as these narratives reflect broader cultural patterns and processes of conflict resolution. This 'structuralist' or 'semiological' approach suggests that textual narratives are the aesthetic manifestation of deeply rooted cultural patterns: 'myths', for example, which are part of the essential patterning of a given culture (see Barthes, 1973; Fiske et al., 1987). More recent analysis has tended to move away from this approach, adopting a more open and fluid analysis of representation and culture. This approach may be critical or deconstructive, or it may be designed to elucidate the complex interrelationships that operate through culture. Our analysis of the Diana story constitutes a textual analysis which seeks to illuminate the complex nature of identity construction, textual representation and textual reception. It also reflects on the institutional processes that are engaged in the promotion of a celebrity.

Empirical Methods

Some cultural studies practitioners like to distinguish between 'empiricism' as a methodology, and the empirical methods it deploys. In this sense, empiricism is an epistemological (knowledge) framework by which the world can be described and measured in an objective form (facts-data). Empirical methods, however, may be viewed as strategies that can be used for the illumination of facts, *or* the illumination of the perspectives (multiple truths) generated in human interactions with each other and the world of phenomena (natural and human made objects). It is this latter approach which has become increasingly popular in cultural and media studies. The findings generated by these techniques are not treated as a universal truth, as in the natural sciences, but rather as part of a multi-forming picture. In this general sense, 'empirical' might be simply defined as 'experience'.

As early forms of social science became more interested in the symbolic dimensions of social experience, a range of empirical methods were developed and applied. In particular, anthropology and sociology became interested in recording the social and symbolic practices – that is, the 'way of life' – of specific social groups. This 'way of life' included all symbolic activities (including rituals and economic activities) and artefacts (e.g., implements, art objects, paintings), both of which carry significant meaning. The methods of 'ethnography' were devised in order to record and map the ways in which human groups participated in and constructed culture.

Sociological analysis applied various forms of ethnography to the study of so-called 'deviant sub-cultures' (e.g., biker gangs, drug users, naturists). While some of these studies involved direct immersion in the sub-culture (participant observation), they could also apply various forms of interview strategies and discussions called 'focus groups'. In work more directly articulated through cultural theory, Dick Hebdige (1979, 1988) adapted these methods for the study of youth culture and 'style' in the United Kingdom. Similarly, some areas of audience studies have sought to elucidate the ways in which audiences 'consume' and use media texts in their everyday lives. This form of ethnography records ordinary people's practices and application of texts. Morley and Silverstone (1990), for example, have used empirical methods to show how audience/consumers use the technology of the TV in their normal, domestic lives. Video recordings, questionnaires and focus groups are all commonly used to study people and their relationship to texts within a given cultural context.

Ethnography of this kind tends to produce very descriptive or 'qualitative' data. This approach is achieving considerable popularity within cultural studies as it remains embedded in a notion of 'way of life'. Ien Ang's study of the audiences of *Dallas* (Ang, 1985) was not ethnographic, but nevertheless sought information about the experience of ordinary viewers. Some research, however, applies more rigorous quantitative or statistical methods to gather data. These sorts of studies use, for example, extensive survey techniques and statistical data gathered from TV ratings or from government bureaus. These sorts of research models have difficulty justifying their theoretical connection to cultural studies since they present such data in terms of objective truth. Cultural studies tends to treat reality and truth as forms of cultural construction: that is, the truth is only ever partial as it is shaped in the unstable and uncertain materials of language and culture.

Policy-based Studies

Policy-based studies have always been a part of cultural studies. Since the 1990s, however, particular schools of cultural studies have fixed their identity around a more focused style of cultural policy analysis, especially in terms of major technologies such as TV and digital communications (see Lewis and Miller, 2002). There may be many reasons for this more exclusive focus on policy, not the least of which is the propensity of governments to fund empirical and policy-directed social science. Policy research applies a range of strategies in order to elucidate the economic, social and cultural implications of some more or less specific cultural/media issue. For example, the public anguish over the death of Princess Diana prompted various governments to consider the question of individual privacy and the media. Cultural studies presented various perspectives on the issue of privacy and the popular media; cultural policy research asked whether some greater level of regulatory protection was required. Cultural policy studies have also examined issues such as the public funding of national film and television programmes, funding of public and community broadcasters, ownership of media corporations, and public ownership of telephone services. Issues of access, surveillance and censorship have also been regularly canvassed in policy-based cultural research.

Empirical and statistical methods, case studies and direct interviews are all common strategies in policy research. Close reading, textual analysis and deconstruction are less common in research, which is often directed toward 'reports' and audiences outside the academy.

ADVANTAGES OF THE CULTURAL STUDIES APPROACH

As we have noted throughout this chapter, contemporary developed societies are characterized by the following:

1   *Increasing differentiation and diversity.* There are increasing levels of social, economic and cultural interaction between humans across the globe. Migration, workplace structures and practices, tourism, business travel, education exchange and global communications are creating more varied and less unitary social and cultural conditions. Individual human subjects live in increasingly complex circumstances where they are constantly exposed to alternative ways of living, acting and making meaning.
2   *Increasing consumerism.* Capitalism continues to mutate as it seeks out new and different products for new and different markets. The practices of consumption lead onward to problematics of newness, taste and fashion, sexualization, and environmental calamity.
3   *Increasing density of televisual product and modes of knowing.* The proliferation of the visual image has led to new problematics in thinking and experiencing the world. The culture is saturated with aural and visual images. Digitization and computer networking are contributing to the transformation of work and of information and entertainment-based practices. Subjects are exposed daily to multiplying modes of televisual stimulus.

As we have outlined in this chapter, the concept of culture provides an invaluable tool for the exposition and analysis of these characteristics and of the contemporary world more generally. Of course, our task of explaining and analysing culture is a formidable one: culture is a work in progress which is thoroughly implicated in all matters of human activity and thinking. Yet the magnitude of the task is commensurate with the rewards. Culture, as a diverse assemblage of meanings and meaning-making processes and practices, is an enthralling and extremely rewarding field of inquiry. This chapter has established the scope of our challenge; the remaining chapters in Part 1 will examine in more detail how culture came to be formed in various modes of analysis and theory.

2

Social Theory and the Foundations of Cultural Studies

INTRODUCTION: FOUNDATIONS OF 'CULTURE'

In Chapter 1 we distinguished between 'society' as an organized congregation of people, and 'culture' as a social group's aggregated meanings and meaning-making processes. Many earlier definitions regarded culture as the relatively homogenous and integrated symbolic 'web' which provided stability and coherence to a given society. These definitions regard society itself as highly integrated, since it is formed around durable and powerful social 'structures'. In attempting to define and explain this relatively new form of social organization, mass society, social theorists in the seventeenth and eighteenth centuries adapted the notion of structure from the natural sciences and engineering. In these terms, social structure is the invisible framework over which the material, institutional and organizational fabric of a society is woven; as in 'primitive' societies, culture provides the symbolic weave that gives coherence and meaning to this new form of large-scale society.

The development of a distinctive cultural studies discipline, therefore, is clearly implicated in the emergence of social theory and the social sciences, especially anthropology and sociology (see Lewis, 2002b: 40–56). Enlightenment philosophy was particularly interested in questions of epistemology or knowing, and the ways in which humans interacted with one another and with nature. Dissatisfied with the explanations offered by traditional theology, many of these philosophers claimed that the human mind, most particularly the faculty of reason, was the fundamental source of knowing in the universe and the cradle of the human spirit. Thomas Hobbes (1588–1679), for example, believed that humans have the capacity to construct their societies in a reasoned and rational manner, deriving the greatest social satisfaction for the majority of the populace. Immanuel Kant (1724–1804), most notably, argued that the faculty of human reason mirrors the intrinsic creativity and orderliness by which the universe itself is governed. G.W.F. Hegel (1770–1831) claimed that the universe – including the human spirit and socially constructed morality – is shaped by a fundamental balance of opposing parts (thesis and antithesis). The objective of human advancement is to bring these opposing forces into resolution (synthesis) through an ascending scale of ontological perfection (the actual).

The writings of Kant and Hegel represented an attempt to understand the new human-nature relationships which modern society and the economic system of capitalism were forging. This important concept, 'society', had once been restricted to the social elite, as in 'high society'. Ultimately, however, the need to understand and conceptualize the increasing scale of human congregation in cities and regional territories led to a more inclusive deployment of the term. The peace treaty signed at Westphalia in 1648, which brought to an end a thirty year war between various European powers, became the template for the modern, sovereign *state* – the entity which established the political boundary for 'rationally' constituted societies and the complex administrative and cultural processes that gave them legitimacy. Urbanization, improved communication and transportation networks, electoral suffrage, and the expansion of ideologies such as nationalism and imperialism, all contributed to a widening of the conception of 'the society of man'.

Karl Marx (1818–1883; see Chapter 3) conceived of this great human mass as the outcome of distinct social and historical forces. In Marx's view, 'mass society' was characterized by struggle and conflict. Large groupings (class) within the social formation struggled against one another until social change was achieved; this change, however, brought new groups into conflict. Marx's model of social and historical conflict contrasted with other theorists who believed that stability and durability were the most notable and determining characteristics of society. Auguste Comte (1798–1857) was among the earliest theorists to consider 'the society of man' in terms of scientific or 'empirical' enquiry. Comte's aim was to produce a naturalistic method of analysis which would account for the stability of society at any given moment, but which would also explain its change over time. Comte applied the principles and methods of the natural sciences – observation, experimentation and comparison – for the study of the *laws* which govern human community.

CULTURE AND SOCIETY

Émile Durkheim and Social Structure

Perhaps more than any other scholar of the time, Émile Durkheim (1858–1917) is responsible for establishing the theoretical parameters of the science of society, directing both the focus and methodology of enquiry. Thus, while 'culture' remains a somewhat amorphous concept for Durkheim, 'society' is defined in terms of a cohesive and integrated organization of people into a locatable, hermetic form. Durkheim's approach to the study of society, however, contributes directly to the evolution of a cultural sociology in two significant ways: first, in his account of social structure; and secondly, through the analysis of symbolism and religion which takes place in his later works. It is certainly true that Durkheim's early analysis of social structure is characterized by a significant devotion to the externality of social structure, quantification and data collection. His work at this level appears to be invested in mathematical methodologies, maintaining an adherence to the Enlightenment principles of rationality and objectivity. Even so, the concept of social structure – the invisible pillars that hold society together – is one of the most important in sociology, providing the focus and raw materials for much of the discipline's development during the twentieth century.

Structure is a rather elusive concept, since it refers to phenomena which are not in themselves visible, but which are known through their effects on human action. Social structures are the building blocks (framework) of social bonds and interrelationships. In his explanations of the functioning of integrated social systems, Talcott Parsons (1961: 36–7) adapted Durkheim's notion of structure in his own explanation of social action and how integrated social systems function for the satisfaction of individual and collective needs. According to Parsons, structure is able to influence the thinking, attitudes and behaviours of social actors (individuals engaged in action in society). Structures are large, slow-moving and constant when compared with the rapid and ever-fluctuating 'empirical' experience of everyday life. Moreover, these structures are external and objective, impervious therefore to the caprice and control of small groups and individuals. Even so, structures and social systems are stable because they correspond to the interests and the shared, normative expectations (what is expected and normal) and values of individuals within the society.

What constituted society for Durkheim was not so much the attributes of individuals, but rather the social and historical forces that bring a group and its structure into being. This is something more than the assemblage of individual consciousnesses; the group comes to take a life of its own.

> The determining cause of a social fact should be sought amongst the social facts preceding it and not among the states of the individual consciousness. (Durkheim, 1960: 110)

If we were considering a political party as a structure, then the social facts of that party would be constituted from those forces which brought the party into being and which sustain it through the present. Social facts could not be determined by the individual party member's consciousness, personal attributes or moral perspectives. While the collective of these elements may contribute to the sustainability of the party, they cannot, of themselves, explain its existence.

Durkheim and Symbolism
Durkheim's second major contribution to the development of cultural studies and cultural theory came in his later works on primitive religion and symbolism. While there are various

ways of defining symbolism, Durkheim applies the concept as a set of complex associations where religious rituals, icons and artefacts are interpreted by members of the social groups (tribe, community, congregation). Meaning, therefore, is a matter of interaction between the symbol, the group and individuals within the group. This hermeneutic or interpretive definition of symbolism suggests an open, relative and flexible relationship between the cultural artefact and its meaning. It may be contrasted to Talcott Parsons' later and more deterministic definition of symbol which suggests an absolute relationship between the two. In this latter application the symbol is treated as a sign which has a fixed relationship with the thing it represents: that is, there is a direct line between the sign and its referent. Durkheim's notion of the symbolic tends to be more open and flexible. Parsons was interested in the ways a particular sign – the value placed on a new automobile, for example – fits into a generalized system of social order and how the sign motivates and directs individuals' goal attainment. Durkheim was interested in the way a ritual may be interpreted and used to explain the complex matrices and interrelationships of life.

Durkheim's theory of symbolic or cultural sociology appeared most earnestly from the 1890s and dominated his work until his death in 1917. While distinguishing between the profane and the sacred, Durkheim nevertheless insisted that an analysis of religion would necessarily illuminate a culture's general symbolic environment: 'A great number of problems change their aspects as soon as their connections with the sociology of religion are recognized' (Durkheim, 1960: 351). Thus, while Durkheim's interest in primitive religions may appear to invest itself in the more comparative or anthropological dimensions of sociology, his intention was to use the particular instances of his investigations to illuminate the symbolic and cultural character of modern society as well. Certainly, the posthumous publication of many of Durkheim's lectures demonstrates quite directly that symbolic systems, subjectivity and solidarity were central issues for the analysis of contemporary as well as primitive human groups. Issues of education, politics, professional organizations, morality and the law were all appropriate for analysis within the general sphere of symbolic classification (see, e.g., Durkheim, 1977).

It is this classificatory system which problematizes the relationship between symbolic culture and social structure. In particular, Durkheim suggests that there is an emotional hierarchy which symbolizes human relationships within social groups. While this is most obvious in primitive societies, symbolic relationships are also discernible within complex societies: we may feel closest to our immediate family, less so to cousins and less so to neighbours and associates. This emotional or 'affective' hierarchy parallels broader social and cosmological hierarchies which are ordered and articulated according to principles of thought or 'cognition'. In other words, the cosmos can be divided between the most intimate and least intimate intensities – from the sacred to the profane. The sacred, through its symbology, is condensed, solid, pure and unifying; the profane is diffuse, potentially threatening, disruptive and precarious. Durkheim goes on to explain that many primitive religions also employ forms of naturalistic totems which symbolize particular familial groups or clans, and which locate that group within a geographical and social/symbolic system. Totems provide temporal, spiritual and socioeconomic identity for the group, setting them in a fixed relationship with other groups and within the broader natural and cosmological order.

While it is important not to conclude that Durkheim's symbolism constitutes a radical break from the epistemological heritage of German Idealism, it is certainly true that Durkheim raises important questions about the relationship between symbolism and social structure. Therefore, while he readily concedes that not all societies share the same classificatory symbolic system, Durkheim does privilege the notion of a social unity built around a common symbolic system. Thus, even though there are patterns of classification common to all (sacred–profane most obviously), Durkheim attempts to maintain the specificity of different social groups by admitting a certain flexibility into the interpretation process. Certainly, as he considers the more open and complex conditions of modern society, he readily concedes that the classificatory system is necessarily subject to more challenging and disruptive hermeneutic processes. This dualism in Durkheim's work has been recognized by his followers, including Talcott Parsons. Thus, while praising the attention Durkheim pays to symbolic and cultural systems, Parsons (1967) is critical of the later works' emphasis on autonomous symbolic processes rather than values and their institutionalization. The work of Durkheim's more immediate associates and students demonstrates the same shifting emphasis from systemic social order to autonomous and free-functioning hermeneutics: Halbwach (working-class consumption), Mauss (exchange) and Bougle (caste) have all demonstrated that symbolic culture is not merely the servant of social structure and social system, as Parsons claims.

It should be remembered, of course, that these are the seminal years of sociological research and it was not until the rise of Parsons' empirical positivism during the 1940s through to the 1950s that the discipline was really able to declare itself as a cohesive and formidable body of knowledge. Until that time, the research fields were sporadic and somewhat inchoate. Alexander (1988) points out that sociology's interest in Durkheim diminished somewhat during this period, though his influence continued to develop in other theoretical and heuristic fields interested in culture and symbolism. The work of French structural anthropology and linguistics (see Chapter 5) and American anthropology, for example, absorbed significant aspects of Durkheim's later work in the development of their own definitions and deployments of the notion of culture. Thus, while it is fair to say that Durkheim's dual interest in social structure and symbolic processes is never fully realized as an integrated theory of modern culture, the work provided a framework for elaboration by later cultural theorists.

Max Weber

As mentioned in Chapter 1, one of the great problems for modernism has been the persistent tension between collective and individual interests – between the macro and micro levels of society and culture. In many respects democracy and the modern state have been forged precisely around the need to reconcile these contending human impulses. This tension has underpinned, yet continued to trouble, a whole range of philosophical and empirical investigations into the human condition. It lies behind the universal–particular tension that Kant and Hegel attempted to reconcile; it persists in the structure–symbolism dualities of Durkheim; and it is again central to the methodological precepts outlined by Max Weber (1864–1920). Along with Durkheim, Weber is generally cited as one of the founders of modern sociology, and is a major contributor to the development of cultural theory based around the concept of social action. Weber's major contributions to the development of cultural sociology are as follows:

1   The development of sociological methods which are not grounded in the assumptions of natural science but which are directed specifically toward the study of human society. These methods, while constituted around reason and objectivity, are specifically designed to account for the investigation of social actors in action.
2   The development of a social theory which centres on the subjective meanings social actors attach to social action. These actions (and their meanings) are directed toward mutual interests, and they always occur within a particular social and historical context. Behaviour that falls outside these parameters is not available to sociology.

According to Weber, there are four types of social action:

(a)   purposeful or goal-oriented rational action, such as the construction of a steam engine to carry goods and people over vast distances;
(b)   value-oriented rational action, such as the pursuit of an ascetic lifestyle for the sake of (irrational) salvation;
(c)   emotional or affective social action, such as committing murder in a fit of rage; and
(d)   traditional action, such as the reproduction of traditional artefacts or enactment of traditional rituals.

While there may be some level of overlap in these categories, Weber was most intrigued by the rising predominance of purposive action in modern society. In many respects, Weber's analysis of law, economics, politics and personal relationships returned to the question of how modern society had come to be dominated by goal-oriented rationalization. As is frequently the case, the answer centred on the ways in which human action and social and historical contexts shifted in relation to one another. Weber could not settle on a (Hobbesian) materialist version of social reality, or on a (Kantian) idealist version. Instead, he fixed his analysis on the concrete experience of the common subject as the fundamental unit of sociological enquiry:

Interpretive sociology considers the individual and his action as the basic unit, as its 'atom'. … The individual is … the upper limit and the sole carrier of meaningful conduct. … Such concepts as 'state', 'association', 'feudalism' and the like, designate certain categories of human interaction. Hence it is the task of sociology to reduce these concepts to 'understandable' action, that is, without exception to the actions of participating individual men (Weber, 1946: 55).

For Weber a method of social enquiry must account for the problem of 'facts'. Social and cultural enquiry cannot be directly paralleled with the laws and methodologies of 'natural' science since nature is largely static, material and presumes a certain determinancy or directly observable causality. While the laws of nature cannot entirely exhaust all there is to know about nature, they function sufficiently as 'representations' of nature – as 'reality'. Humans, however, are more complicated. Their behaviour, knowledge and symbolization cannot be treated or 'revealed' as a mere mirror of reality. Indeed, following Kant, Weber believed that the essences of culture and nature could not be revealed; only the phenomenal or surface forms of that reality were available to enquiry and observation. It was not appropriate, therefore, for cultural or social science to seek laws or empirical generalizations that would elucidate phenomenal essence. Rather, it was the task of the researcher to reveal phenomena as *social action* within the realm of reason and reasoned investigative frameworks.

Reason is absolutely critical to Weber's schema, not because he wanted to mimic the natural sciences and their positivist empirical frameworks, but because he recognized the theoretical and heuristic dangers of his own departure from generalized facticity. That is, if facts are not to be regarded as universal and absolute representations of reality, then it becomes immediately possible that social and cultural enquiry could be no more than a series of dissociated and limitless accounts of a purely individual or idiosyncratic version of the world. Weber's deviation from the standards of empirical science and the assumption of its reality opened his work to a twofold problem:

1 Is the social and cultural merely a dissociated collection of individual perceptions of the real constituted by wholly separate and individualized particles of knowledge? Is the social world a loose assemblage of subjective experiences that have no greater bond than the assumption of a shared reality?
2 Is the social researcher reduced to a mere recording function for these particularized bits of knowledge, with his or her own work constituting merely one more version of the idiosyncratic?

In response Weber argues that cultural and social knowledge is formed through a kind of intersubjective consensus, a consciousness that is constituted in the interests of collective gratification. 'Knowing' is thus a form of cultural action which is constrained, as it is constituted, by morality, heritage, tradition, conventions and reason. Members of a social group 'create' a reality for a given purpose at a given time. This intersubjective reality is not haphazard or speculative, but operates through the collective consciousness of individuals in action.

Equally, cultural analysis is shaped and informed by its own historical conditions; it too is subject to the collective values that are ascendant and which operate through institutional conventions. That is, cultural and social research are very much 'of their times', part of the context they themselves are investigating. For Weber, this 'empathy' between cultural analysis and its focus does not reduce the need for researchers to be 'value'-sensitive in their work. Rather, it inclines social science away from relativism and toward a paradigm of 'consensual' truth where 'values' are acknowledged and interpretation is a delicate process of judgement and discrimination. Weber's empirical social and cultural science is, therefore, a finely positioned methodology which distinguishes between relativism, on the one hand, and numerical positivism, on the other. It is science because it is constituted through rigourous, repeatable and agreed standards of 'data' collection and analysis. It is 'objective' yet subject to the particular conditions prevalent in a particular place at a particular moment in history. Weber attempts, that is, to mediate polarities of knowledge: one which is universal and applicable in all circumstances, and the other which has particular paradigmatic value for a particular social group at a particular moment.

While Weber's essays on methodology (Weber, 1949) have contributed significantly to the evolution of social science and its research strategies, considerable debate surrounds the theoretical and ideological efficacy of the overall body of his writing. In particular, Marxist critics are suspicious of Weber's neo-Kantianism, which consistently integrates social values, and which places the concept of culture before the structural discriminations of class and production. Weber, like Kant, seeks an almost Romantic solution to the problem of collective and individual interests. His emphasis on social action tends to privilege individual subjectivity over and above the sorts of structured discriminations and politics that surround capitalism. Indeed, the belief that society and culture are constituted forms of consensus tends to camouflage the conflicts and antagonisms that persist in all social formations, especially mass society.

In fact, Weber employs a particular concept, the 'ideal type', which is designed to reconcile the tension between universal typologies and the actuality of individual actors. Numerous critics have suggested that this utopianism actually distracts social enquiry from the specific disorders and oppressions that are suffered by particular social groups. To this extent, the ideal type acts as a metaphor for Weber's notion of a culture built around discrete values: culture is not the mirror or 'superstructure' of economy or politics, but is rather an autonomous producer and reproducer of social order and social relationships as they are structured through social action. Culture is, therefore, a cognitive rather than a material category. It is a way of thinking which consistently returns from a potentially threatening diversity into a more comforting mode of consensuality and collective consciousness.

Not surprisingly, a number of modern Marxists have been highly critical of texts like *The Protestant Ethic and the Spirit of Capitalism* (1930), in which Weber attempts to explain the 'culture' of capitalism in distinctly Kantian terms. Thus, the 'spirit' of capitalism refers to a way of being in the world which is predicated on values, morality and rationality. This complex of rationalized and rationalizing values is reciprocally experienced by entrepreneurs seeking profit and workers seeking to articulate themselves in labour. Culture is present in every act and cannot be treated as divisible, a separate modality, or mirror of economic imperatives. For the Marxist commentators, however, Weber's account is not merely a description of capitalist cultural processes, but is informed by intense ideological presuppositions. In accordance with his own methodological precepts, Weber's description of capitalism and Protestantism is value-neutral, or at least embedded in the values of his times. Marxism, as we shall see in the following chapter, regards this 'value-neutrality' as a surrender to the *dominant* values and ideology which it supposedly analyzes.

PHENOMENOLOGY AND CULTURAL STUDIES

Sociological Roots

The work of Weber and Durkheim provided a significant platform for the development of social enquiry during the twentieth century. As we have seen, Talcott Parsons adapted the empirical model established by Weber and Durkheim, developing his own distinctively 'objective' and statistically oriented model of sociology (American positivism). The work of Karl Marx (see Chapter 3) provided a second strand for the emergence of a systematic approach to the study of society and culture, one which is shaped by a concern for ideology and social reform. Issues of social inequity and 'social problems' are also central to the sociological research conducted at the University of Chicago early in the twentieth century. The work of Robert Park (1864–1964), in particular, integrated an interest in the everyday experiences of cultural sub-groups, such as immigrants, with a broader vision of American society. This interest in everyday experiences and the perspective of sub-groups forms the basis of a 'phenomenology' of society which focuses on the way individuals and communities make meaning out of their experience of the world of things (phenomena).

  The Chicago School scholars were significant to the development of this branch of sociology in that they established an unashamedly popular culturalist paradigm for the study of society. Notions of power, hierarchy and ideology were present in their work, though they generally resisted an elaborate Marxist analysis of social problems and social injustice. Park's interest in Marxism was more intellectual than political, and in most cases the Chicago School maintained a powerful liberalist and pluralist perspective on the phenomena they studied. Park's own journalistic ethics clearly influenced the formulations of his projects and analyses. In particular, he believed that the objective rendering of the complex details of everyday life would contribute more to the alleviation of social problems and social injustice than to the overthrow of governments. The task was to illuminate, and the techniques of observation and recording were not dissimilar to those employed by the journalist. Park's own interest in radio and the popular media, and the wider patterns of investigations within the School, reflected a substantial confluence with the ethics and heritage of modern journalism – a ground-level, real-life humanism that protected the interests of the everyday citizen, as well as the institutions of democratic liberalism.

In many respects, the Chicago School provided an heuristic paradigm for other forms of research based around popular culture. The rise of journalism and communication studies in the US, for example, helped to focus the social sciences on the effects of the popular media on individuals and particular sub-classes of the mass society. Beginning in 1933, the Payne Fund studies, for instance, were designed to analyze the impact of film on children and other social sub-groups. While the results were largely inconclusive, this new form of social research demonstrated that audiences interacted with their culture and political contexts in complex and often contradictory ways. Blumer (1933), for example, found that criminals and criminal behaviours might be affected by a film, depending on the themes, attitudes and characters being depicted, and the social environment of the viewers.

These sorts of studies, which focused on the everyday experiences of ordinary people, also paved the way for a more theoretically grounded sociology. Phenomenology – the investigation of phenomena in the world – was adopted into sociology through the writings of Peter Berger in the 1960s. However, the work of the Chicago School and their descendants might well be identified as confluents of a phenomenological tradition. In particular, the face-to-face, ground-level research of sociologists like the Lynds (*Middletown*, 1929) and William Whyte (*Street Corner Society*, 1943) maintained, and indeed enhanced, the interests of community-based social enquiry. While it is true that the Lynds excluded marginal groups (African Americans, divorcees) from their snapshot of community life, Whyte was much more adventurous in his explorations of the street-life textures of Boston's North End, and his examination of everyday Bostonian life drew on the anthropological precepts of inclusiveness and ritualized power. The social mapping of later sociologists such as Elliot Liebow (*Tally's Corner*, 1967), Kai Erikson (*Everything in its Path*, 1976) and Berger himself, owes much to the evolution of urban anthropological methods.

Martin Heidegger

As a theory of 'society' and 'culture', phenomenology remains both marginal in sociology and somewhat elusive. This is partly because the two great progenitors of phenomenology, Edmund Husserl (1859–1938) and his student Martin Heidegger (1889–1976), held quite divergent positions on the definition and application of the concept. What is common to both positions, however, is the restoration of the subjective ('I', 'me') over the objective (all that is external and real). Husserl, in fact, rejects G.W.F. Hegel's transcendental rationalism, which privileges the objective as the central sphere of ontology (being in the world). Instead, he revives René Descartes' epistemology (account of knowledge), which sought to confirm the substantiveness of knowledge by the method of doubt: to doubt is to render knowledge ultimately immune from skepticism. To achieve this level of scientific knowledge, Husserl argues, the knowing subject or 'knower' must be centralized in the process of knowing. That is, the knowing subject must precede the externality of the world of objects.

Martin Heidegger rejects Husserl's transcendental Idealism and with it the transcendental ego. For Heidegger, it is not the irreducible and ultimate fact that 'man' exists in a world that transcends him; rather he exists in a state of 'givenness': *Dassein* or 'there-being'. For Heidegger, the question of what it is *to be* must continually be raised because Idealism fails to present it. We find ourselves 'flung down' into the world and into a time and place we did not choose. We cannot adopt the perspective of disinterested observer because we are always and forever part of the fabric of objects that exist in and of our own consciousness. It is this being-in-the-world which Heidegger claims to be constrained by the Idealist ego and its essentialism. The only significant standpoint, the only one open to investigation, is the one Husserl describes as 'natural' where the subject remains fixed in ordinary judgements with other ordinary people. Phenomenology, in this sense, becomes a way of being and a methodology rather than a transcendent experience:

> The expression 'phenomenology' … signifies primarily a methodological concept. This expression does not characterize the *what* of the objects of philosophical research as subject-matter, but rather the *how* of the research. (Heidegger, 1952: 50)

Heidegger's version of phenomenology differs markedly from Husserl's in as much as the ordinary experience of phenomena is its primary focus of study. Our experience of a tree is determined not by its transcendent presence in our consciousness, but by the mere fact of its existence in relation to ourselves. Heidegger's view that we are 'flung down' into the world of phenomena heralds the sort of existence-in-the-world thesis presented by existential philosophy. Søren Kierkegaard, Jean-Paul Sartre, Friedrich Nietzsche and Heidegger himself all share a view that the mere fact that we are here in the world is the fundamental fact. The Viennese philosopher Alfred Schütz brought these notions of phenomenology into the realm of social enquiry, adding a further level of sophistication to the Chicago School approach to everyday life.

Alfred Schütz

After his arrival in the United States from Vienna in 1939, Alfred Schütz made a significant contribution to the development of a phenomenological perspective in American sociology. He combined aspects of phenomenology with Weber's theory of intersubjectivity. Schütz was interested in developing a social theory which, focusing on social action, could account for the capacity of subjects to be conscious of themselves in relation to others. That is, subjectivity, since it had to be conscious of something, would necessarily be involved in 'constructing' meaning *of something*. Subjects would construct meaning through their everyday practices and in relation to other constructing, conscious subjects. Again following Weber, Schütz was interested in the notion of intersubjectivity: that is, subjects interact and communicate in order to produce some sharable meaning or meaning consensus. Schütz provides for later sociologists a theoretical grounding for the analysis of a social reality that is shaped by subjects' interaction in everyday contexts.

Peter Berger

Much of Schütz's work resembles earlier phenomenology, most especially in its ontological, almost theological, interest in 'ultimate' questions of being, existence and the meanings that constitute human consciousness. While Schütz's work draws these questions more fully toward matters of society and social interaction, the more complete translation of phenomenology as a sociology of subjectivity is provided by Maurice Merleau-Ponty and Peter Berger. Like Schütz, Berger was born in Vienna and was heavily influenced by notions of 'intersubjectivity' as the basis of social construction of meaning. That is, our awareness of the world of objects (our consciousness) is largely facilitated through our mutual interests with other conscious subjects; we work together to create our version of the world. Also like Schütz, Berger emigrated to the United States, and in his prolific writings dating from the 1960s, he urged a mode of empirically grounded sociological research which described the 'phenomena' of everyday actors in everyday life. Berger's greatest contribution to contemporary sociology and cultural analysis resides in a theoretical competence which facilitated the study of microtic (personal) experiences such as the internalization of values, as well as macrotic (major) phenomena such as the social construction of institutions (see Berger, 1967; Berger and Luckman, 1966).

Berger does not offer us a distinct and detailed theory of culture, though his philosophical assumptions and the character of his work certainly express a fundamental interest in the processes of meaning-making and the 'consciousness' that underpins everyday social experiences. Essentially, culture for Berger may be summarized as 'the totality of man's problems' (1967: 6). Such a totalizing definition is typical of phenomenological thinking; society is merely a portion of culture, and culture appears as the reflection of the ontological dimensions of all human consciousness. What it is to be human continues to preoccupy the phenomenologist, framing the content and conceptual analyses the empirical researcher presents. For the phenomenologist, culture exists only in as much as people are conscious of it (Berger and Luckmann, 1966: 78). Sign systems and language, in particular, are seen as the primary conduits of intersubjectivity and meaning (Berger and Luckmann, 1966).

Central to this conception of language is the notion of dialectic, which Berger uses (unlike Hegel and Marx) to denominate a form of subjective interplay. These interplays exist in many forms, though the interplay of self and body and self and the sociocultural world are fundamental to Berger's understanding of culture. Berger's discussions of the body and organicism, for example, lay the foundations for more recent cultural studies interest in the body and bodily inscriptions of meaning (see Chapter 9). Most importantly, Berger explains how a person's individual biology can limit his or her experiences in life, noting that the world one has created also acts in return upon the body (Berger and Luckmann, 1966: 181). Sexuality and intake of food are necessities of biological existence; the body lives, seeks sexual release and nourishment, but particular circumstances of life impact upon the behaviours that determine how these phenomena are experienced. Humans are socially conditioned into certain values, belief systems and behaviours, and these sociocultural forms will necessarily determine the means by which individuals experience nourishment and sexual release.

The interplay of body and self parallels the broader interplay of self and general sociocultural forms. By and large, Berger is arguing here that society and culture are the collective manifestations of the inherent interests of individuals. Society and culture and the individual necessitate each other. Individuals do not create reality in their own terms but must always and inevitably refer to the collective conditions of their world. Socialization conveys to the individual all the knowledge that is required for social functioning. Individuals create culture out of what is passed on to them; they are motivated to do this, Berger argues, as a substitute for what is denied them by their instinctually deprived organicism. In other words, society and the individual are both manifestations and constructions of each other. This fundamentally dialectical relationship, Berger claims, draws together the two opposing pillars of social theory: the Weberian notion of individual meaning and the Durkheimian interest in facts and social structures. In fact, they are two sides of the same coin, and each must be understood in terms of the other.

There is no doubting the significant contribution that Berger's work has made to the development of sociology and a sociological form of cultural studies. Berger's work needs to be understood, however, as a fundamentally humanist and ontological pursuit. There is little in the work that demonstrates a significant commitment to radical social reform, nor indeed to the political dimensions of social and cultural experience. Indeed, while Berger's writings during the early 1970s betray a level of political awareness (*The Homeless Mind*, and *Pyramids of Sacrifice*, 1973), his discussions of language and social reality fail to acknowledge the significant relationship between culture and power that was being pursued by his contemporaries in Britain and continental Europe. The controversies surrounding Berger's work, like that of his symbolic interactionist colleagues, related more to validity of method. Berger's phenomenological methods presented a significant challenge to those forms of quantitative and objectivist social science that had been popularized by Talcott Parsons and his followers. Berger's interest in ethnographic mapping and speculative phenomenology are characterized by positivism as a form of intuitive and descriptive narrative which lacks empirical or scientific precision.

As sociology has begun to incorporate more fully a cultural perspective, various theorists and empirical researchers have integrated theories of language with the phenomenological lineage. Phenomenology, in fact, provides a quite particular account of culture, one which identifies the *essential* features of a context and the invisible *consciousness* of everyday social actors. The collective of these individual consciousnesses comprises the 'lifeworld' of a culture. In textual studies critics have often concentrated on the 'lifeworld' of characters within the text (e.g., The Geneva School of literary critics), though more recent work has attempted to account for the interplay between text and reader/audience (see Wilson, 1993, 1995, 2004). In a sense, this shift from a text-centred criticism to an investigation of the subjectivities of audiences reflects a similar move in phenomenology from Husserl's more scientific or objectivist interests to Heidegger's more free-flowing adventures into the lifeworld of everyday people.

Phenomenology and *Thin Red Line*

Phenomenology has been adapted into various forms of literary and film studies. From its Greek derivation, phenomena refers to 'that which appears'. In early adaptations of phenomenology for the study of texts, critics sought to reveal the essential character or underlying consciousness which patterns the aestheticized world. Phenomenology at this level is really attempting to reveal some fundamental qualities which are shared by human minds and their consciousness (awareness or knowledge) of the world. J. Hillis Miller, for example, examines Thomas Hardy's novels to reveal certain repeated patterns of the author's consciousness; these patterns are formed through metaphors of distance and desire.

While critics may use a phenomenological framework to analyze fictional texts, authors and film-makers have also been influenced by the ideas of Husserl and Heidegger. Terence Mallick's films clearly reflect an interest in 'flung downness' and the web of consciousness. In *Thin Red Line* (1998), for example, the camera provides a rich aesthetic perspective of internal and external conditions of warfare and its horror. The film opens with a low angle view of a forest canopy and audiences are immediately engaged by the point of view of the film's protagonist, Witt, a World War Two US soldier. The poetic reverie of his internal monologue is cinematographically juxtaposed with a vision of chaotic and often bloody combat. This apparent disjunction between subjective and objective 'spaces' is disrupted by Witt's own shifting vision. In the midst of the horror, Witt's camera eye penetrates the chaos, fixing itself momentarily on the emergent beauty of nature and his own besieged humanity: the wings of a butterfly, breezes on the grass, the desperate love of a comrade, the transcendence and affirmation of death. This flow

(Cont'd)

of conjunction and disjunction provides the aesthetic momentum of the film, creating for Witt and the audience a mood of bewilderment and elevation, even through the worst excesses of human action, brutality and violence.

Mallick invites us to share in this journey of consciousness and in Witt's sense of being 'flung down' into a world that makes no clear sense in and of itself. As viewers, of course, we are required to take the details of the text and relate them back to our own experience and interpretive order. We are left with a sense of profound tragedy and waste, but the vision is not finally nihilistic. Rather, we are encouraged to uncover the deep beauty of the loss – the sacred moment in which Witt himself is sacrificed. His vision, his memories and ultimately his life are surrendered to the conditions of an ineffable but significant cosmological occlusion. The mystery of the human aesthetic, that is, must ultimately triumph over the misery of its reality.

Symbolic Interaction

Symbolic Interaction(ism) is another branch of sociology which derives from Chicago-style subjectivism, psychology and a general reaction against the ascendancy of structural functionalism. Norman Denzin (1992: 3) explains that symbolic interaction combines aspects of behaviourist language theory with interpretive phenomenology; the major distinction between phenomenological approaches and interactionism rests primarily in the latter's greater interest in the microcosm of individual social actors' participation in specific situations where meaning is negotiated and exchanged. While Denzin (1992), and Becker and McCall (1990) have traced the emergence and development of symbolic interactionism through social psychology (esp. George Herbert Mead), anthropology and philosophical pragmatism (esp. John Dewey), it was not until the 1950s and 1960s that a fully theorized interactionist approach became available to sociological enquiry. Most notably, the new symbolic interactionists brought a more systematic empirical methodology to the study of meaning exchange, as well as a more sustained substantive cohesion to the notion of symbolism and meaning construction.

In *The Presentation of Self in Everyday Life*, Erving Goffman (1959) suggested in a vaguely ironical way that the modern self was, in fact, a series of responses to given symbolic contexts. That is, notions of an essential self needed to be measured against the tendency for individuals to 'dress themselves up' in order to satisfy the requirements of a particular situation. Goffman constructed a framework, for example, for reading the 'man in the grey flannel suit', observing that social status could be dressed up according to norms and expectations of a particular situation. While Goffman's analysis may seem rather tame when measured against the radical subjectivities discussed in current cultural analysis, his work did lay the foundations for new ways of understanding social contexts.

During the 1960s, Howard Becker's work on deviance brought symbolic interactionism into the mainstream of a more inclusive and expanding field of sociological enquiry. This invigoration of sociology, in fact, accompanied wider social trends of the 1960s and early 1970s, whereby particular areas of public discourses were engaging with ideas of socialization, alternative lifestyles, youth culture and the questioning of value-systems that had led to the Vietnam War and the threat of a nuclear Armageddon. Popular films such as *The Wild One* and *Rebel without a Cause* and the rise of youth music had alerted sociologists and the general public to the paradoxes and potential efficacies of social deviance. Reaction against McCarthyist conservatism and Parsons' positivism drew sociologists out of obscurity, stimulating a more widespread engagement with phenomenological and symbolic interactionist theories and methods.

There can be little doubt that the work of phenomenology and symbolic interaction on deviance and sub-culture influenced the work of British cultural theorists like Raymond Williams, Dick Hebdige and Stuart Hall (see Chapter 4). Even so, these methods and theories may, in a sense, have reached their pinnacle in Becker's work, and while interactionism continues today, recent developments in language or discourse theories have highlighted the limitations of a social psychological approach that emphasizes the microcosm of interaction as the central unit in cultural enquiry. Becker's own work on deviance in a sense legitimates the whole notion of normalcy and deviance; a cultural studies perspective would certainly reject that sort of dualism as it would reject the very idea of 'difference' being articulated as negative or aberrant. Clearly Becker's point is that society constructs notions of deviance, but for the current generation of cultural criticism, such an approach would be the 'bottom-line' or 'given' of any form of cultural enquiry. More generally, the belief that 'society' is a constitution of individual meaning exchanges is never fully realized in the interactionist analysis. The body of qualitative research which comprises the interactionist tradition never actually conceives of, nor adequately accounts for, 'culture' as such. Discussions and analyses satisfy themselves with the minimalist position; the psychological condition of the individual actor seems never to escape into the broadening processes of the 'lifeworld'. The interactionist analysis of deviance, for example, seems satisfied in its reports of the psychological state of interacting subjects and the ways in which their meanings are coded within a highly localized context of interaction – the sharing of drugs, the purchase of a new motorbike.

While some interactionists claim that their approach does indeed facilitate an investigation of social structure (see Denzin, 1992: 61–2), there is no doubt that any attention paid to broader social formations is incidental to the primary and microscopic view of specific social exchanges. Some critics have also suggested that interactionism tends to reproduce, in fact, microtic versions of larger social structures, forming as a consequence a reification of structure as 'context', 'meaning' or 'activity' (Prendergast and

Knottnerus, 1990). This reduction of larger systems produces a rationalistic, cognitive and emotionless rendering of the meaning exchange process.

Above all, however, the interactionists remain fundamentally liberal and indeed politically neutral (see Reynolds, 1990). While this criticism was common in neo-Marxist writings of the 1950s and 1960s, most especially in the work of C. Wright Mills, the complaint persists in the writings of more culturally oriented commentators like James Carey in the United States and Stuart Hall in Britain. Moreover, recent language theory (poststructuralism and postmodernism) has argued that all texts are problematical renderings or constructions of reality, rather than mirrors of reality itself. While phenomenology grounds itself in fundamental ontologies (essential truths), symbolic interactionism satisfies itself with an empiricism which it claims will produce its own conceptual or theoretical groundings. The methodologies (ethnography or participant observation) of symbolic interactionism are offered as the epistemological substance of the world as experienced. The theory or way of framing and understanding an event will necessarily arise through the data collection process – all will be revealed. Contemporary language theory, however, argues that such renderings are themselves supplements to the original experience: that is, they mediate rather than mirror reality, forming a secondary text which is itself subject to construction and interpretation. What is revealed in symbolic interaction research is an interpretation of an interpretation, and barely constitutes an empirical fact. This problem of methodology continues to haunt sociology, even as it has embraced many of the principles and precepts of cultural analysis.

CULTURAL ANTHROPOLOGY

Anthropology can be understood as a form of comparative sociology. Generally speaking, the discipline emerged out of an interest by European and American scholars in the cultures of colonized peoples. During the eighteenth and nineteenth centuries, the various fields of naturalism, philology (study of languages), archaeology and anthropology were not distinctly bordered; the invading nations sanctioned and encouraged the examination of the conquered people not merely to substantiate military, commercial and administrative efficiency, but also to fortify the conquering civilization's intellectual superiority. Artefacts, biological samples, primitive peoples themselves, were all treated as specimens or curiosities, and were appropriated for the universities, museums and private collections of the conquering country. The moral legitimacy of this barbarism was provided by intellectuals like Adam Smith (1723–90) Herbert Spencer (1820–1903) and Robert Malthus (1766–1834), whose ideas on self interest became vulcanized to Charles Darwin's evolutionism to produce the first major globalization theories: the survival of the fittest nation or civilization. We have already seen that nineteenth-century German philosophy was very much entranced with the idea of *Kultur* or the advance of individuals and civilizations. Nineteenth-century British philosophy articulated a more pragmatic though equally forceful interest in the necessities of usefulness, prosperity and the advance of superior nations.

Edward Said (1978, 1993) has mapped the discourses of colonizing nations, arguing that the entire culture of the conquering nations was predicated on differentials of power that incorporated the territories and cultures of invaded peoples. For Said, the production of nineteenth-century art and scholarship was bound by an identity which distinguished the civility of the home culture from the primitivism of alien 'others'; the discipline of anthropology emerges out of that dualism, that sense of curiosity, Romanticism and even guilt. Whether motivated by compassion, dispassion or celebration, the very presence of the Westerner in the alien culture, Said argues, served merely to reinforce the privilege and status of the investigator over the investigated. The ethic of liberal humanism – democracy and freedom – seemed never to extend to the interests and dignity of the conquered people, except in terms of philanthropy or charity, which were themselves markers of a superior condition.

From these beginnings, however, anthropology has developed sophisticated techniques of analysis and societal comparison. Into the twentieth century, anthropology generally evolved into two broad fields of analysis:

1   Structural or cultural anthropology, as practised by Claude Lévi-Strauss, Ferdinand de Saussure and Mary Douglas, examines the cognitive structures that distinguish cultures. These structures arise through language systems and may be manifest as mythology, kinship or, in the case of contemporary culture, consumer goods (see Douglas, 1978). We will examine this field of structural anthropology in detail in Chapter 5.
2   Interpretive anthropologists are more keenly interested in cultural textures and forms of cultural relativism; the methods, which are far less scientifically precise, seek to elucidate the personal and subjective sensibilities which constitute meaning-making. This field of anthropology, examined in detail below, is closest to the humanist subjectivism and phenomenology which rises through Chicago sociology and blooms during the 1960s and 1970s.

Clifford Geertz

The work of American anthropologist Clifford Geertz has been most frequently presented as seminal in the development of interpretive anthropology. Underpinning Geertz's work is a reading of Weber's famous description of society in which 'man is an animal suspended in webs of significance he himself has spun'. Geertz takes 'culture to be those webs, and the analysis of it to be, therefore, not an experimental science in search of law, but an interpretive one in search of meaning' (1973: 5). Geertz's work demonstrates, in fact, a blurring of cultural boundaries whereby the researcher as interpreter invokes his/her own experiential knowledge in order to elucidate the text of his/her investigations.

Thus, in his famous essay on Balinese cockfighting (see insert) Geertz invokes the non-Balinese texts of psychology and aesthetics (*King Lear*) in order to explain significant social relationships and 'personalities' in Balinese culture. Anthropology, according to Geertz, is a multi-disciplinary activity which must confront the wide range of human activities – including 'power, change, faith, oppression, work, passion, authority, beauty, violence, love, prestige' –within the context of their doing (Geertz, 1973: 21; see also 1988).

The Balinese cockfight

Clifford Geertz's anthropological studies of non-modern societies have provided a useful methodological and theoretical paradigm for contemporary cultural studies. In particular, Geertz seeks to illuminate the 'web of meaning' by which members of a given social group are bonded. These meanings, however, are not unitary or homogeneous, but are formed through struggle and conflict as well as consensus. Geertz's studies constitute a form of 'ethnography': a mapping of people, practices, artefacts and meaning-making processes. The following excerpt is taken from Geertz's study of the Balinese cockfight. The meaning of the fight is not immediately obvious; the task of the analyst is to draw these meanings into the light and interpret them for the non-Balinese.

Of cocks and men

To anyone who has been in Bali any length of time, the deep psychological identification of men with their cocks is unmistakable. It works in exactly the same way in Balinese as it does in English, even to producing the same tired jokes, strained puns, and uninventive obscenities. Bateson and Mead have even suggested that, in line with the Balinese conception of the body as a set of separately animated parts, cocks are viewed as detachable, self-operating penises, ambulant genitals with a life of their own…

In the cockfight, man and beast, good and evil, ego and id, the creative power of masculinity and the destructive power of loosened animality fuse in a bloody drama of hatred, cruelty, violence, and death. It is little wonder that when, as is the inevitable rule, the owner of the winning cock takes the carcass of the loser – often torn limb from limb by its enraged owner – home to eat, he does so with a mixture of social embarrassment, moral satisfaction, aesthetic disgust, and cannibal joy. Or that a man who has lost an important fight is sometimes driven to wreck the family shrines and curse the gods, an act of metaphysical (and social) suicide. Or that in seeking earthly analogues for heaven and hell the Balinese compare the former to the mood of a man whose cock has just won, the latter to that of a man whose cock has just lost. (Geertz, 1991: 243–4, 245)

Geertz's work, while distinguishing between society (social relationships) and culture (symbols), confirms the significance of their interaction. Indeed, as we consider the deployment of the concept of culture as 'way of life', Geertz's studies on Bali raise the important question: is culture no more than an expression, mirror or confirmation of existing social order? In reply Geertz suggests that culture actually and actively constructs meaning by providing social actors with the space for considering, reviewing and feeling what it is to be Balinese. That is, culture is not merely a confirmation of social and personality processes, but a field of creativity and production: symbolic production. Thus, art and all other expressive modes become forms of collective thought-experiment where members of the group can explore and wonder about the many things that perplex and intrigue them: works of art 'materialize a way of experiencing, bring a particular cast of mind into the world of objects, where men can look at it' (Geertz, 1976: 1478).

Geertz's own methodology of interpretation and elucidation is characterized as 'thick description' (1973), a form of ethnography adapted from literature studies as much as from the sociological analyses of Durkheim, Weber or his more immediate mentor, Gilbert Ryle. For Geertz, this ethnography may in fact apply the broadest range of data-collecting techniques in order to grasp and then render the complex of cultural meaning-making comprehensible to outsiders:

> [I]nterviewing informants, observing rituals, eliciting kin terms, tracing property lines, censusing households. ... Tracing his journal. Doing ethnography is like trying to read (in the sense of construct a reading of) a manuscript – foreign, faded, full of ellipses, incoherences, suspicious emendations, and tendentious commentaries, but written not in conventionalized graphs of sound but in transient examples of shaped behaviour. (Geertz, 1973: 10)

Geertz's work is mobilized through this form of investigative and interpretive practice, allowing the theoretical dimensions of his analysis to emerge in context. Just as culture is relativistic, so theory is multilayered and expressive of the texture of the investigative focus – that is, of culture itself. Theory is bound by culture. The best thing about interpretation techniques, according to Geertz, is that they eschew the necessities of conceptualization and therefore they are able to resist 'systematic modes of assessment' (Geertz, 1973: 24). Geertz insists that the whole point of a semiotic investigation is that it elucidates the signs and *concepts* as they are used by the subjects of the study, thus enabling access and 'conversation'. In other words, Geertz is recommending a theory or conceptual framework that is 'grounded' in the field, that arises from the data rather than being imposed upon them by the theoretician, abstractionist or scientist. While invoking the theories of key sociologists, Geertz's approach resembles the sort of thinking that informed Robert Park and others of the Chicago School. Geertz prefers to map his cultural subjects, allowing the descriptions to run as closely as possible to the texture of their lives.

3

Marxism and the Formation of Cultural Ideology

INTRODUCTION

The concept of 'power' is central to many areas of contemporary cultural studies. While particular zones of cultural aesthetics and postmodernism have parenthesized issues of power, for most scholars working in the discipline it remains a key concept and focus of study. As Stuart Hall has argued, many of the most important studies of culture involve questions of social injustice and inequity – and in this context, Hall claims, Marx and Marxism 'are never far away'. Karl Marx (1818–83) thus remains a towering figure in modern social, cultural and political theory. His revolutionary views on power and social relationships have influenced many generations of radicals and critical thinkers. His work continues as a point of reference in academic and public discourse, even as his followers adjust to dramatically altered historical circumstances. The collapse of the USSR and communist states in Eastern Europe, the liberalization of the Chinese and Vietnamese economies, the contraction of communist revolutionism in the developing world, the rise of radical Islam, and the fragmentation of the reformist agenda in developed democracies, are all cited as evidence of the demise of Marxist ideals. Marx's theories on the mode of production, division of labour and class warfare seem no longer relevant in a culture so far removed from the conditions of nineteenth-century Europe. Even so, the philosophical underpinnings of Marx's critique continue to attract interest, most particularly as theorists attempt to understand the evolution of privilege, oppression and social hierarchy in contemporary culture.

Of course, it would be entirely unfair to expect that any social commentary could survive in its literal form much beyond its own immediate historical context. The power of Marx's analysis rests in its compassion and its recognition that the new economic system of capitalism created great comfort and pleasure for some but great injustice and hardship for the majority. Thus, while moving beyond the literalism of Marx's political prescience, contemporary cultural theorists have found Marxist notions of power and ideology particularly valuable for the development of their own critical perspectives. The substance of this influence is quite variable. American pluralist/liberalist cultural theory has tended to resist issues of power, at least until relatively recently. British cultural studies (see Chapter 4) has been strongly influenced by the neo-Marxist analyses of Louis Althusser and Antonio Gramsci. More recent forms of postmodern cultural theory have tended to extend the French poststructuralist critique of Marxist analysis, rejecting in particular the austerity and class basis of Marxist analysis.

MARX AND HEGEL

Marx was born in Germany, but after suffering the indignities of social exclusion and anti-Semitism moved to France and on to London, where he spent most of his adult life. While Marx himself was not a member of the working class (proletariat), he identified this social group as the victim of oppressive social conditions. Throughout his writing career, Marx worked toward the emancipation of society through the formulation of a self-consciously radical programme which would liberate all society from the ills of industrial capitalism. In reading Marx, however, we must remember that his ideas changed, as indeed did his social and intellectual circumstances; we should not expect too absolute a consistency in the overall body of his work. Some of the most interesting and important aspects of Marx's thought are to be found in the earlier writings, where he struggles to liberate his own theorizing from that of his major mentor, G.W.F. Hegel. In order to understand some of the complexity in Marx's approach to culture, we need to appreciate Marx's intellectual relationship to Hegel's dialectics and the transcendental rationalism which underpins his work.

Hegel's Dialectics

Hegel's transcendental rationality views the real world as merely an appearance of underlying epistemological structures (the 'actual'). Hegel believed that the real and actual worlds could only be resolved through a spiritual ascent, a form of self-consciousness which would allow a complete reconciliation of human thinking (concepts) with the actual conditions of nature. This synthesis would finally reconnect the human mind (subjectivity) with the world of objects (objectivity). Reason and reasoned thinking lay at the centre of this progress.

Marx rejects the idea that the essential character of reality is spiritual, and that freedom and conflict in the world might be resolved through reference to the synthesizing power of essential nature. He does not accept Hegel's reduction of things and human activities

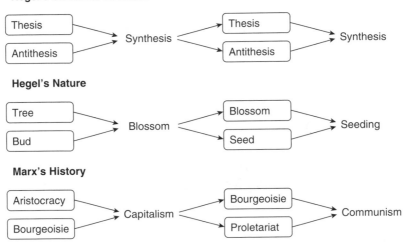

Figure 3.1 *The dialectics of Hegel and Marx.*

to modes of consciousness, nor does he accept the distraction of human suffering from the real conditions of politics and economy. Hegel's dialectical theory, in fact, describes nature as a series of perpetually evolving conflicts and resolutions: all phenomena present themselves as thesis for which there is a natural and inevitable antithesis; the eventual crisis of opposition leads inevitably to synthesis. This synthesis ultimately expresses itself as a further thesis with consequent antithesis. Moral wisdom and freedom, according to Hegel, are achieved via an evolutionary progress through oppositional claims or conflicts to wisdom as consciousness and knowledge. Put simply, Hegel's dialectics in nature function as shown in Figure 3.1. Hegel claims that this fundamental structure of nature compares with the spiritual ascent of human subjects. The principal difference, however, is that human morality can aspire to the bosom of God and ultimate spiritual/moral knowing.

Marx's Materialism

Marx's materialism is material in as much as it questions the value of such theories for the real-life attainment of human values and liberation. In the context of social and environmental degradation, Marx sought to break with the metaphysics of Hegel and his philosophical tradition. In fact, while acknowledging the brilliance with which Hegel pursued the logical conclusions of this tradition, Marx wanted to install a form of philosophical naturalism. In the *Critique of Hegel's Philosophy of Right* (1970), Marx claims, against Hegel's notion that 'man' is essentially spirit, that he is rather 'real, corporeal man with his feet firmly planted on the solid ground, inhaling and exhaling all the powers of nature' (orig. 1843, 1970: 206). Marx takes this metaphor of nature to express the suffering of 'man' as much as his capacity for self-assertion and pleasure beyond the mere abstractness of Hegel's conception:

> As a … natural, sentient, objective being, he is a suffering, conditioned and limited being, like animals and plants. … The fact that man is an embodied, living being with natural powers means that he has real, sensuous objects as the objects of his being. (Marx, 1970: 206–7)

Hegel's idealism, therefore, is brilliant but overly abstracted (or in Marx's terms 'alienated') thought. And while Marx himself adapts the dialectical model (thesis–antithesis) for a reading of the major movements and conflicts of history, his ultimate aim is to ensure a perspective of the human experience which is grounded in the real conditions of human life.

Marx's Naturalism

Marx's naturalism, however, indicates a certain ambivalence (or internal dilemma) which persists through much of his work and which continues to plague critical writing today. This is the question of determinism and free will. Marx offers for us an image of history and of the human experience which is coloured by suffering and structurally determined oppression. The lasting impression of Marx's work is of an alienated individual and social class whose only possibilities for freedom are revolutionary uprising. Free will, most particularly as it is envisaged in *The Communist Manifesto* (1848), is an act of collective determination, though even here the collectivity is conditioned by 'class struggle' and the inevitability of dialectic determinism. Yet pencilled through the writings is a naturalism which, like the naturalism and idealism of particular Romantic writings, opens a space for individualized pleasures, including the pleasures of aestheticism. In opposing the alienating effects of industrialization by which the product of labour belongs to the capitalist, Marx refers to the possibilities of creative and natural being. In *The Economic and Philosophical Manuscripts* (1844) he refers specifically to the 'species being' by which humans confirm their uniqueness as animals by aestheticizing the products of their labour 'according to the laws of beauty'.

Thus, while Marx generally rejects Hegel's notions of spiritual nature, he clearly articulates in some of his writings the belief that humans must satisfy bodily and social needs. That is, while history is shaped by struggle, the end of these conflicts is the completion of their natural as well as human needs. Nature is ontological and independent of consciousness. Its value for human life is twofold: it provides resources for the satisfaction of needs, and it provides an aesthetic resource for the gratification of sense and individual pleasure. At this point, however, Marx again resists the Idealism and Romanticism of Hegel and philosophers like Jean-Jacques Rousseau, both of whom implicate human consciousness and freedom in the spiritual exigencies of nature.

For Marx, nature does not hold the promise of pure reason nor spiritual ascent, but it does offer the individual the opportunity to shape and experience his or her humanity in the fullness of aestheticized sense.

Above all things, Marx's ideal brings history to account. While Hegel posits a utopia of pure reason, Marx's own logics lead him to the actualization of an egalitarian condition, where humanism and nature are fully resolved and mutually supportive. This new communalism is achieved through the real struggles of real human beings; there can be no recourse to the imagining of the spirit.

> Communism is the positive supersession of private property, of human self-alienation, and thus the real appropriation of human nature through and for man. It is, therefore, the return of man himself as a social, i.e., really human, being. … Communism as a fully developed naturalism is humanism and as a fully developed humanism is naturalism. It is the definitive resolution of the antagonism between man and nature, and between man and man. It is the true solution of the conflict between existence and essence, between objectification and self-affirmation … between individual and species. It is the solution of the riddle of history, and knows itself to be the solution. (Marx, 1963: 155)

Marx's answers to the problem of history and conflict, therefore, are political. Communism promises the 'complete emancipation of human qualities and senses', including 'not only the five senses, but also the so-called spiritual senses, the practical senses [of] desiring, loving' (Marx, 1963: 160). While these largely incidental comments about the liberation of the senses appear at various points in Marx's writings, his most significant contribution to the theory of symbolization and meaning-making appears in his discussions of the relationship between economy and culture, most notably through the theory of ideology and the base–superstructure model.

SYMBOLIC CONTROL

Marx's somewhat sporadic discussions on naturalism and individual fulfilment present a rather limited perspective of free will. As with numerous other social commentators of the nineteenth-century, Marx's structuralism tends to limit opportunities for the exertion of individual will, presenting a view of humans as victims of history, large social movements and institutionalized structures such as class. As we shall see, this problem of how individuals and groups might construct their freedom remains a problem for many other critics influenced by Marxist reformism. But for Marx himself it is particularly problematic, given that his liberationism is vested in a class of people of which he is not even a member. If the working classes are to act upon and achieve their freedom, then presumably they must be able to conceive of it in some way. Marx claims to resolve this question by producing his dialectical version of human history: it appears that the working classes must necessarily rise up against their oppression because history compels them. In other words, the proletariat's history appears to be predestined, a template that determines their actions.

The German Ideology

There is a logical problem here, for if the working classes are able to conceive of their freedom, it may be that they have already reduced their oppression. That is, the very act of thinking may constitute an overcoming of the limits of oppression. Freedom is difficult to conceive when we don't have it; it's a lack, an absence, an abstraction. If we can conceive of what we don't have, then perhaps it is the oppression that is the abstraction, an imagination of our present condition. In *The German Ideology* (1932) Marx attempts to articulate this conundrum by suggesting that our capacity to 'think' our freedom is itself determined by the ruling classes. These classes, who have a vested interest in extinguishing challenges to the validity or actuality of their 'right to rule', actively construct modes of compliance through the promotion of ideology (ideas, beliefs, values). To achieve this, the rulers attempt to transform the conditions of their self-interest into 'universal' social values. That is, social values that encourage obedience, loyalty to authority, legitimacies of blood, religion, social pragmatism, commercialism, and so on, are disseminated as the general conditions of goodness.

Ideology, therefore, is false consciousness because it derives from the interests of the present ruling class. In aristocratic times regal imagery and rituals confirmed the status and superiority of the aristocrats. The notion of 'blue blood' was conceived as a restrictive analogue, a means of distinguishing ruler from ruled. Shakespeare's plays are riddled with evidence of royal patronage, praise for kings and kingly deeds, and persistent reminders of the sacred lineage of royal blood. In Marx's time, the bourgeoisie constituted their power through public and popular discourses. Street signs, coins, education institutions, public hangings, all legitimated the rule of plutocrats. The obedience of the proletariat was constituted through this false consciousness, a belief that things were as they should be and that the proletariat's social, political and economic privations were justly ordered, if not ordained. Only in times of significant social stress can these ideologies be stripped bare and recognized as class-based rather than universal. Thus, in Marx's dialectics of history, the transformation from aristocratic pre-eminence to bourgeois pre-eminence would have been accompanied by a significant re-alignment of social values and ideology.

The imposition of ideologies, therefore, cannot extinguish entirely the possibilities of change and reform. Even so, Marx's description gives us a particular insight into the operations of culture as directing and determining human 'nature'. But his position is incomplete. His naturalism suggests that humans will inevitably suffer and experience pleasure and that culture will both provide the expression of that suffering and the source of its overcoming. In the midst of this uncertainty Marx continually returns to generalized explanations of determining social structures. These structures, as we have noted, are built around economy and labour, rather than its expressive or aesthetic modes. In conceding that ideology is the construct of class interests, Marx opens the way for a full account of symbolization and meaning construction. However, he lacks the conceptual armoury needed to attack this problem as fully as have later analysts. That is, he travels to the edge of some extremely incisive analysis of the political operations of language, symbolization and ideology. However, there are simply not enough intellectual resources, not enough concepts and theories available to him in order to take the next step. Rather, he confines himself to a more concentrated rendering of the economic structures which determine human suffering and oppression.

The Base and the Superstructure

The base–superstructure model outlined in *A Contribution to the Critique of Political Economy* (orig. 1859, 1976) was designed to elucidate the relationship between the distinctly economic structures of a society and the institutional and behavioural articulations of those structures. The 'base' refers to 'forces' of economy and production (tools, technology, workers' skills) and the relationships of class that are mobilized in the application of those forces. The superstructure refers to institutions (political, educational, legal, etc.) and the forms of 'consciousness' that are the expression or outcome of these institutions (see Figure 3.2). These 'expressions' might be understood as ethics, values and ideology, though Marx and Engels never adequately explain the relationship between these categories. This elision has given rise to a multitude of subsequent interpretations, debates and applications.

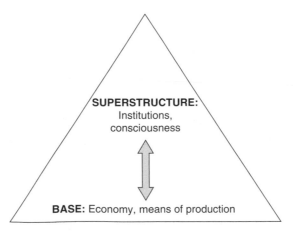

Figure 3.2 *Marx's base–superstructure model.*

Importantly, however, Marx and Engels' perspective in the *Critique* most certainly presents culture as the expression and servant of economy. Engels himself attempted to clarify the idea after Marx's death, suggesting that the relationship between the base and superstructure (economy and meaning-making) was not entirely deterministic because there is a degree of reciprocity: 'The economic situation is the basis, but the various components of the superstructure … also exercise their influence upon the course of the historical struggles and in many cases determine their form' (1994: 194). Engels suggests here that the superstructure does more than just reflect the underlying determinations of economy. Rather, the superstructure – institutions, symbolizations, culture – actively participates in the form and shape of society and political relationships. That is, the base produces the actual character of a particular superstructure (feudal, agrarian, industrial), but the relationships between institutions and individuals inside the superstructure will clearly produce their own effects. Engels, that is, permits a level of 'free will' within the superstructure which, presumably, provides the opportunity for resistance, class warfare and revolution. Ultimately, however, this free will is limited by the underlying character of history and political economy. Only certain things are possible within the superstructure, and these are the limits set by the economic base.

The primacy of economy in Marx's theoretics limits his view of culture and symbolization. His unyielding resistance to Romanticism and the ideals of transcendent consciousness perhaps impairs his ability to think outside the limits of that particular epistemology. It's not consciousness that determines life, but life that determines consciousness, Marx argues. But in many ways his view of consciousness, as a way of knowing that is thoroughly implicated in economy and relationships of production, restricts his conception of how that knowing might proceed. In particular, Marx fails to see how knowing and symbolization might create the circumstances of the liberation he seeks. Even so, while other nineteenth-century social theorists were formulating a disinterested, 'scientific' account of human experience, Marx was cognizant of the influences of power and politics in all realms of human activity. He believed that power was fundamentally embedded in culture, and it was this point that was to be elaborated by later theorists.

CRITICISMS OF MARX AND MARXIST ASSUMPTIONS

The cultural critique of Marx's theories can be summarized in the following terms:

1 Marx conceived of human relationships primarily in terms of political economy and materialism. For cultural theory this emphasis limits the possibilities of analysis to investigate abstract forms of symbolization.
2 This materialism is essentialized in Marx's theory of labour and the mode of production. Class is the major social determinant, and constitutes foundational social structures.

Poststructuralist and postmodernist criticisms of Marx see this emphasis as overly simplistic and excessively all-encompassing or 'universalizing' (see Poster, 1989)

3 This tendency to view the world in terms of class or collective groups has restricted Marx's analytical breadth. In particular, Marx constructs a limited perspective of the individual, and of individual pleasures, expressivities and gratifications.

4 Marx's theory of alienation suggests that the mode of production and the conditions of labour reduce individuals (and their subjectivity) to the condition of 'commodity' (a thing to be bought and sold).

5 Marx's account of history tends to *totalize* or *universalize* all human experience in a single, grand theory that explains everything.

6 Marx relies on the Cartesian/Kantian view of the split between the subjective and objective worlds. He sees humans in terms of external or objective forces which determine subjective experiences and actions. He devotes the majority of his interest and work to these external conditions and to the possibilities of class action.

7 Marx is suspicious of belief systems that are built on non-rational or excessively emotional, spiritual or artificial grounds. Marx's view that religion is the 'opiate of the masses' indicates a general suspicion of abstractionism and irrationality. His work is very much embedded in the traditions of scientific rationalism; his followers have consistently struggled with his limited perspective of symbolization, spiritualism and metaphor.

8 Marx directs his hopes for emancipation in the actions of the proletariat or working class. Emancipation is a contingency of the conditions of oppression.

Karl Marx and Homer Simpson

Karl Marx's *Communist Manifesto* provided the basis for a good deal of reformist thinking during the nineteenth and early twentieth centuries. The *Manifesto* explains how the revolutionary overthrow of the ruling classes by the proletariat or working classes will lead to a ruler-less utopia (anarchic communalism). The communist state, temporarily governed by the proletariat, will ultimately dissolve into a global community in which individual autonomy and collective responsibility will be reconciled and meld harmoniously into one another.

Of course, Marx's ideals have never been realized. The communist state was to evolve out of the ruins of bourgeois, industrial capitalism. In fact, social experiments with communism have emerged in largely pre-industrial states during times of severe social crisis, usually precipitated by some form of imperial war (e.g., Russia, China, Vietnam). In modern, industrialized capitalist states the concept of 'class' has become increasingly problematic and difficult to define. In the United States, for example, a country which has never developed a strong labour politics, the idea of class consciousness appears particularly dubious. Pre-eminent ideologies constituted around capitalist consumerism, individual prosperity and success, and social pluralism seem to have muted any significant formulations of class. If ever there was a strong identification with social class, it is seriously threatened by new forms of social fluidity and cultural imagining. The contraction of manufacturing and heavy industry has been accompanied by new informational and entertainment economies and lifestyles.

Homer Simpson, the hapless nuclear power plant worker from the animated TV series *The Simpsons*, personifies the condition of the working class in contemporary culture. Homer is the source of much of the programme's comic despair. He appears almost entirely unaware of the iniquitous social forces that oppress him, preferring a televisual bliss to the cold realities of his condition. Homer is a perpetual loser, unable to organize industrially, unable to deal with the grotesque perversities of his boss at the nuclear power plant. Instead, he barely acknowledges the truth of his oppression, escaping into sport, TV and the quotidian trials of family life. The popularity of *The Simpsons* over a very long period derives largely from its subtle interplay of pathos and ridicule. We sympathize with Homer, but we examine him from the safe distance of a middle-class, consumerist lifestyle. Homer inevitably belongs to some other social group, some other epoch; he is not a member of a social class with which the audience can identify. He is merely Homer Simpson – comic, pathetic, ignorant, and a true representative of Marx's proletariat 'false consciousness'.

The complaints against Marx by cultural theorists are generally threaded through a more substantive interest in symbolization, a more complex view of power, and a greater sense that capitalism is more perplexing and complex than Marx had appreciated. While some theorists claim to have rejected Marxian views outright, others have attempted to manipulate and adjust the theories in order to embrace more contemporary intellectual and social conditions. In the remainder of this chapter we shall examine how Marx's theories have been adapted, most especially for a broad understanding of power, symbolization and culture.

THE FRANKFURT SCHOOL

The Frankfurt School is the name given to a group of Marxist scholars who were exiled from Nazi Germany in 1933. The group worked in New York before returning to Frankfurt in 1950. The Institute for Social Research at Frankfurt practised a 'Critical Theory' which rejected notions of realism in favour of a blend of Marxist social criticism, aesthetics and Freudian psychoanalysis. Among the major members of the group were Max Horkheimer (1895–1973), Theodor Adorno (1903–69) and Herbert

Marcuse (1898–1979). Walter Benjamin (1892–1940), who committed suicide after failing to escape to Spain and freedom from the Nazis, is also associated with the Frankfurt School, though his work and experiences remain distinct. With the exception of Benjamin, whom we will deal with separately, the Frankfurt School members were particularly interested in the relationship between the mass media as a 'culture industry' and the working classes.

Distinctively, the group focused attention on popular culture and popular media texts. However, unlike earlier work done through the Payne Fund and the Chicago School of Sociology, the Frankfurt group brought a far more radical approach to the critique of the (American) mass media. The cognitive effects model, which investigated the media's impact on individuals, and the anthropological inquiries of Chicago-style sociology were suddenly overwhelmed by the systematic and substantially theorized critique of the modern media and the culture in which they operated. As Lukács and Brecht had argued, culture could work against oppression; the Frankfurt School focused on mass culture and its propensity for social control. Culture was therefore foregrounded in the revolutionary struggle. Undoubtedly, the work of the Frankfurt School provided a basis for a new and more radical approach to the sociology of culture and the media.

Adorno and Mass Culture

Having escaped the horrors of the German Third Reich and the Jewish Holocaust, the Frankfurt School intellectuals became quickly disillusioned with American materialism and the 'pseudo-individualism' it propagated. Thus, the apprehension of the mass-mindedness and social acquiescence that had led so easily to the disintegration of German culture was rendered even more disturbing by the School's engagement with American mass consumerism. In particular, the 'culture industry', with its capacity for the delivery of messages to mass audiences, was considered the principal agent of control and social conditioning. The masses' immersion in highly schematized popular culture texts paralleled for Adorno the 'opiate of the masses' thesis outlined by Marx. That is, entertainment texts such as film, radio and later television stifle the political imagination. Herbert Marcuse made a similar point in *One Dimensional Man* (1964), suggesting that popular culture texts indoctrinate and manipulate people into glib gratifications that ultimately create a 'false consciousness', an ideological positioning which accords with the interests of the ruling classes. In fact, a common theme in Frankfurt School writing on popular American culture is that social classes and individuals will necessarily be distracted from serious social and political issues as they are constantly seduced by superficial entertainments and consumer hedonism. The culture industry, like all other capitalist institutions, has a vested interest in hierarchies of power and the control of messages and ideologies supporting capitalist economics and the rights of privileged elites.

In *Dialectic of Enlightenment* (1972, orig. 1944) and a range of other writings, Adorno claims that the actual narratives of popular texts distort reality in order to obscure the real conditions of human life. Social conflict is resolved through the production of popular narratives and melodramas. The privileging of narratives of authority, control, heroics, the moral primacy of the bourgeois family and the myth of success tend inevitably to neutralize opposition by constituting a false ideology. These distorted ideologies are supported by what Adorno calls an 'instrumental rationality', which is the rationalization of human behaviours through schedules and technology. The peculiar power of the leisure and entertainment industry is that it is able to reproduce the same schedules and controls that are prevalent in workplaces. Individuals are obedient to the work schedule and to the TV and radio programme guides, sitting passively and attentively in front of the medium when the programme and time slot commands. That is, the radio, cinema and television construct a rationalized environment in which time and behaviours are controlled by the owners of capital, who are also the owners of time. Freedom, therefore, is surrendered through the momentum of technology and rationalized social authority. Thus, mass society itself replaces the ego-ideal of the father; people come to obey and are controlled by the 'massification' of society and the capitalist forces that lie behind it.

Clearly Adorno, Horkheimer and Marcuse do not equate the modern consumerist culture with the folk culture and folk art of the past. Indeed, the Frankfurt School regard popular culture generally as an illusion created by the owners of capital in order to maintain their own privileges. Folk art comes from the people; modern popular art comes from the large capitalist institutions. A number of more recent cultural theorists have argued that the Frankfurt School's distinction between folk and commercial, popular culture is excessively simplistic and elitist. In particular, the Frankfurt School's disavowal of popular music misunderstands critically the complex relationship between text, audiences and ideology (see Chapter 8). Critics like Frith and Horn (1987; see also Bennett et al., 1993), for example, regard Adorno's essay 'On popular music' as a privileging of elite and intellectual tastes over the interests and aesthetic preferences of ordinary people: the classical music Adorno admires has little to do with the lives of the 'working people' whom Adorno claims to defend.

Adorno argues in this essay that the mass production of musical texts tends to produce a constraining effect on imagination. Texts are thus standardized in a cyclical process whereby successful lyrical and melodic patterns are copied and repeated in order to satisfy the 'conditioned' tastes of audience consumers. These audience consumers are thus conditioned by the repeated patterns and seek nothing more than the replication of these familiar and comfortable, if unimaginative, gratifications. These gratifications, Adorno argues, derive from certain psychosociological needs within audiences, most particularly those relating to affiliations with dominant social structures. As with his other writings on popular culture, Adorno claims that popular music inclines audiences toward a form of obedience or capitulation that may be either a distraction from more serious or troubling aspects of life (rhythmic obedience), or a more complete immersion in the sentimentalism of the text (emotional obedience).

There is a certain and often cited pessimism about the Frankfurt School's account of the social world and its cultural conditions. Adorno and Horkheimer do, however, offer some possibilities of escape but this tends to parallel both the Romanticism of nineteenth-century literary theory and Hegelian Idealism. Specifically, Adorno locates freedom in the fissures of dialectical conflict which will be most evident in complex forms of art. The prevailing ideologies (or false consciousness) can be challenged by an art form that does not have to collude with dominant economic structures. Unlike popular cultural products, therefore, art and literature are distanced from reality and are capable of exposing the serious deficiencies of economy and dominant social forms. Thus, while Lukács criticizes modernist texts for reflecting the alienating conditions of modern existence, Adorno praises the avant-garde for challenging orthodoxies and creating 'negative knowledge'. The experimentation of modernist texts is seen as a virtue precisely because it is distanced from reality and because it attempts to re-form and restructure that reality. It is crucial, Adorno claims, for art to make the downtrodden aware of the real conditions of their existence and to make them angry about it. Both in content and in form, the modernism of Proust, Beckett and Schoenberg demonstrates for Adorno the power of alienation in modern times. The subjective experience of an individual's alienation is thus rendered objective by the work of art, creating new possibilities for resistance and change.

WALTER BENJAMIN AND MECHANICAL REPRODUCTION

As in much of Adorno's work, Walter Benjamin's famous essay 'The work of art in the age of mechanical reproduction' (1977, orig. 1935) acknowledges the importance of art in social criticism and culture. However, Benjamin does not share Adorno's outright rejection of the new technologies and their particular modes of communication: radio, cinema, telephone and gramophone. Benjamin, in fact, inverts the focus of Adorno's work, arguing that the new technologies release art from the possession and control of the bourgeoisie. The notion of an authentic and unique work of art must be rethought because art now can be mechanically reproduced and multiply distributed. Audiences can experience a film or photograph simultaneously across the globe and across social borders.

Benjamin's theories have been highly influential in cinema and more latterly cultural studies, most particularly as they resonate with an egalitarianism rooted in the everyday practices of ordinary people. Benjamin argues that the 'aura' of a work of art – that unique, perhaps mystical, power that separates the art work from the everyday fleshliness of its audience – is irretrievably compromised by the work's reproducibility. The authority (the author) of the text and its ritualized aesthetic integrity can no longer be sustained in the face of mass distribution and mass consumption. The deconstruction of rituals and the dimming of aura, Benjamin argues, release the text to politics at the level of consumption. Thus, while Adorno maintains that the content and form of the art object hold the promise of politics, Benjamin sees this promise in the action of consumption. While Adorno fears the power of the culture industry to create standardized texts for obedient audiences, Benjamin identifies in capitalism itself the potentialities for its own demise.

Meaning, therefore, is less a contingency of mode of production than a participatory process, engaging producers, texts and audiences. Once meaning is released from the localized control of bourgeois ritual, the revolutionary potential of the text is released to audiences. In ways that parallel the interests of Weberianism, symbolic interaction and phenomenology, Benjamin's contemplations on meaning provide a more optimistic vision of everyday practices and the potential for humans to create their own freedom. In a more practical sense, Benjamin also locates this potential in text-writers and film-makers, who, within the confines and constraints of their own historical contexts, have the capacity to liberate ideas from the prevailing economic structures. Like Brecht, Benjamin suggests that socialist artists and writers should, in fact, become 'producers', and where possible take responsibility for the whole process of text-making. An artist, therefore, would actively revolutionize text production using the correct 'techniques'; these techniques, however, will always be subject to the complex set of associations, influences and constraints of the times.

LOUIS ALTHUSSER AND STRUCTURALIST MARXISM

From Russian literary formalism through the Frankfurt School, and including the Second and Third Communist and Socialist Internationals, Marxism was continually reviewing its origins in economics and scientific rationalism. Thus, the interest in the base–superstructure model was supplemented by increasing fascination with the ways in which the superstructure operated as ideology and within the general frame of culture. Unlike many other Western Marxists, Louis Althusser (1918–90) determined to rethink significant issues of structure and ideology from within the French Communist Party. Althusser's significant contribution to the development of a critical cultural studies, therefore, emerges through his commitment to a 'scientific' re-rendering of Marxist historical materialism, most particularly through the perspective of a 1960s French philosophy that was turning against existentialism and phenomenology. Paradoxically, and as Gregory Elliott (1994) has argued, Althusser's efforts to renovate Marxist structuralism contributed to the ferment of post-Marxist thinking that seized Parisian intellectual life after the débâcles of the 1968 revolutionary skirmishes. Althusser's revision of Marxist precepts is characterized by its remarkable eclecticism:

> [E]xpelling ... the Hegelian heritage, renouncing autarky, and restoring dialogue with non (or even anti) Marxist traditions, assimilating Nietzschean–Heideggerian, as well as Spinozist–Bachelardian, motifs, the Althusserian renovation of historical materialism intersected with broader currents in Celtic philosophical culture, associated with the names of Claude

Lévi-Strauss, or Jacques Lacan, Michel Foucault, or Jacques Derrida … assembled under
the flag of … theoretical anti-humanism. (Elliott, 1994: viii)

Overdetermination

In his review of Marx and Engels' base–superstructure model, Althusser borrows from
Freud's concept of overdetermination. Thus, while Marx and Engels saw economy as the
fundamental determinant of the superstructure (social and cultural features of a people),
Althusser imagined that the superstructure could function independently from, though
in concert with, the economic base. In *For Marx*, Althusser refers to Lenin's question
on why the socialist revolution occurred in Russia, which was not the most advanced
industrial state (where Marx had predicted revolution would occur). Althusser answers
that the revolution was not determined by economy alone, but was acting in concert
with other significant cultural features not necessarily determined by economy at all –
national character, traditions, history, international events and 'accidents' of history.
Economy works with 'various levels and instances of the social formation' (Althusser,
1969: 101).

Overdetermination, then, refers to the complex set of elements and associations that
comprise the social formation. Economy may ultimately be a determinant of these complex
forms of life, but it does not and cannot stand alone; it must interact with and diffuse
itself through all other elements in social life, and as such forms part of the matrix of
overdetermination. For Althusser, these social formations may be broadly categorized
into three levels: the economic, the political and the ideological. In any given historical
epoch, one level may have greater influence and determinacy than others. Althusser's
thesis significantly modifies Marx's original conception of base and superstructure,
opening the way for a more considered approach to the influence of language and
symbolization.

Significantly, Althusser distinguishes his own version of Marxist scientific analysis from
Hegel's dialecticism, which he sees as overly totalistic and unitary. Althusser's reading
of Hegel is significant because it provides the foundation for his own identification
of contradictions and complexities in the relationship between the base and the
superstructure. According to Althusser, Hegel sees history in terms of substantive phases
that are dominated by a single idea. This single idea is informed by an overriding spiritual
principle, which is the most abstract form of consciousness of itself. That is, an historical
phase will know itself by being aware of itself in terms of an abstract philosophical or
religious consciousness. This internal and mystical knowing will necessarily constitute the
'ideology' of that epoch (Althusser, 1969: 103). Althusser contrasts Hegel's understanding
of history with his own Marxist conception of the base–superstructure relationship.
The Hegelian conception of an historical epoch, Althusser claims, will be necessarily
unitary and governed by one significant causality with one overriding idea. Althusser,

echoing Antonio Gramsci (see below), rejects this unitary and totalistic notion of history, as he also rejects the mechanistic or deterministic views of particular Marxists who imagine history and social change to be a linear and uncomplicated function of will.

Althusser, therefore, seeks an explanation of the complex associations in a society, avoiding a conception of the social formation which is excessively homogenizing, unitary or simplistic. In fact, he is careful to avoid concepts like 'social system' which suggest a uniformity and level of integration, functionalism and co-operation which is both false and overly compliant. He recognizes that a social formation is an aggregate of people, elements and structures, and that an explanation of the processes which constitute hierarchical relationships within the formation cannot be reduced to single causes. Althusser offers various perspectives on oppression and emancipation; his notion of 'ideology', however, has provided one of the most important analytical concepts for the development of a critical cultural studies.

Althusser's Ideology

Althusser's concept of ideology was developed to articulate more fully these complex and contradictory associations which function through the various structures of a social formation. While the term has been adapted from Althusser by more recent British cultural studies, its use by Althusser is relatively consistent, emphasizing the capacity of a set of ideas to predominate within a social formation. In particular, he identifies ideology as a 'system' of practices and representations by which people 'imagine' the conditions of their life: 'By practice in general I shall mean any process of transformation of a determining given raw material into a determinate product, a transformation effected by a determinate human labour, using determinate means' (Althusser, 1969: 166). Practice, however, does not refer solely to labour and the means of production; practice may transform aspects of political life, and ideological practice may transform a person's relationship to the general conditions of the social formation.

Ideology might best be understood, then, as 'a representation of the imaginary relationship of individuals to their real conditions of existence' (Althusser, 1971: 152). To put this another way, ideology refers to the way we live out the real conditions of our life at the level of its representation in discourses and texts. Our imaginations are mobilized through the 'superstructure' which convinces us that our lives are better than they really are. It is important to consider this idea carefully because the relationship between the real and imaginary remains significant for cultural studies, most especially as it has integrated important areas of language theory. Althusser asks the question: why is there a need to represent the real conditions of life at all? Why not deal directly with the source? His answer takes the notion of ideology beyond mechanistic interpretations which might say simply that the powerful install these ideologies in order to control the less powerful. In fact, Althusser suggests that ideology functions across all levels of the social formation, influencing the practices, imaginations and belief systems of both ruling and subordinate classes.

Ideology, therefore, constitutes a 'closed' system: there can be no 'distance' from its influence, no identification of the 'real' except by virtue of a scientific, analytical, Marxist discourse. The notion of 'imagined relations' is critical because it limits the escape and the possibility of a critical distance and knowing. We cannot interpret the relation of people's imagination to their real conditions because the conduit between the two is also imagined or represented. Althusser (1971: 155) suggests, then, that the question of interpretation must be replaced by questions: why is representation necessary at all, and what is the nature of these imaginings? In terms of text analysis, Althusser applies the concept of the 'problematic' by which a text will frame and organize its ideas according to ideology; the problematic of a text must, in fact, function according to the information it includes (answers to questions it poses), as well as the information it does not include. The task of the Marxist analyst is to elucidate these inclusions and exclusions, illuminating the ideology by which the text is constructed.

Subject Positions

Althusser's use of the concept of ideology, therefore, differs from Marx's in at least one very important way. For Althusser, ideology is not so much 'false' consciousness, as Marx claims; rather, ideology constitutes a sort of 'misrecognition' of the real condition of one's existence. To this extent, ideology returns important information or knowledge about the world to the reader/viewer of a representational text. The reader/viewer is to an important extent 'created' or at least 'positioned' by this information. In his essay 'Ideology and the Ideological State Apparatuses' (1971) Althusser argues that ideology interpellates concrete individuals as concrete subjects. In other words, individuals are effectively transformed into ideological subjects through their engagement with the imaginary world created through representation. The world is rendered intelligible for the subject as s/he takes up a position provided by the text. In very important ways, texts provide subjects with the discursive resources necessary for comprehension of themselves and the world – but both the subjectivity and the world can only exist in terms of representation and the 'imaginary'.

Again, unlike the German Idealists and Romantic philosophers, Althusser presents an image of individuals and their subjectivity as multi-forming and 'fragmentary'. That is, human subjects are not unitary and integrated through the function of reason or spiritual essence. Different modes of representation create different subject positions; subjects encounter various ideologies and subject positions through class, gender, race and social position. For example, class is not a singular and fixed condition that may be objectively recounted; rather, it is constituted through a range of representational processes by which the subject comes to identify a certain reality. This class awareness or consciousness is shaped by ideology which necessarily produces gaps between the imagined and real conditions of life. A subject and his/her consciousness, therefore, will be only partial or incomplete since these gaps, along with the ever-unfolding of new or alternative representations, will frustrate any attempts at complete integration.

Ideological State Apparatuses

The principal problems with Althusser's approach to ideology have been well canvassed (see esp. Hall, 1982). We can, however, summarize these difficulties by highlighting the two somewhat irreconcilable aims of Althusser's deployment of the concept:

1   Ideology is understood as the representation of the imaginary relationship of individuals to their real conditions of existence. The world, therefore, is a vortex of representation in which the subject is positioned and repositioned by an ineluctable symbolic order. At this level, ideology constitutes an essential process by which individuals live their lives and make sense of the world.
2   Ideology is produced by the superstructure in relation to the conditions of overdetermination. Althusser's political position, therefore, seeks to identify the operations of representation, not merely to identify the reality beyond representation, but to clarify the question: why represent the world at all? His scientific, Marxist analysis becomes the only valid tool for irrupting the ideological nexus of imagination and reality. At this level, ideology becomes far more than a matter of imagination, fragmentation or misrecognition. Ideology is a systematic mode of oppression which operates through significant and powerful social and economic 'apparatuses'.

Althusser's work has been most influential in cultural studies largely through this latter deployment of the concept of ideology. Althusser writes quite specifically about Ideological State Apparatuses (ISAs) which promote and distribute various forms of ideology through the dominant context of economic capitalism. As we noted above, the processes of overdetermination are formed through these apparatuses: family, education system, church and mass media. These apparatuses have become ubiquitous and effective in promoting and maintaining dominant order and the interests of powerful oligarchies. According to Althusser and other Marxists interested in the symbolic patterning of ideology, ISAs operate to supplement and often lead the social controls of threat and physical coercion.

The analysis and exposure of ISAs and ideological processes more generally have continued to be an important part of the work of cultural studies. There have been various attempts to integrate Althusserian theory into a more consistent and flexible analytical paradigm (see Hall, 1982; Laclau and Mouffe, 1985). In particular, and as we shall see below, the coupling of ideology with Gramsci's notion of hegemony has enabled cultural analysis to elucidate some significant and complex representations of power and power relationships. In a film like *Toy Story 2*, for example, we might identify ideologies which support patriarchal and capitalist interests. Even toys, it seems, are distinguished by gender (the cultural construction of sex typologies). The male heroes save the victim/female from the evils of exploitation. Family and middle-class values are restored through a symbolic order which confirms for children that women and men are necessarily constituted in this way. The subject/viewer is thus positioned by the film's narratized ideology; both the positioning and the ideology clearly serve the interests of the media-based, corporate ISA that produced the film in the first place. In this way, the legitimacy of capitalism, consumption, industrial cartels, social hierarchy and fixed labour are confirmed. Viewers anticipate a life in which they are placed as gendered and class-directed labour within a confined and highly managed social order. The fantasy of the film operates as a solution to the complex relationships and ideological forces that surround and challenge the subject/viewer.

Plate 3.1 *Slum Tourism in India*

Marxism, Mumbai and the end of history

Many commentators believe that the collapse of the Berlin Wall in 1991 marked the end of the Cold War – and Marxism! Advocates of free market (neoliberal) global economics, in particular, argue that the Marxist social and economic experiment imploded with the capitalist conversion of former communist states – the USSR, Yugoslavia, Poland and East Germany. The supremacy of global capitalism has been further confirmed by the integration of existing communist states, China and Vietnam, into the global capitalist economy. For Francis Fukayama the end of communist economics can be celebrated as an end to ideological combat and ideological 'history'.

It may be, however, that the celebrations are premature. Marx predicted that capital and wealth would flow, like water, to the lowest point of a social terrain. Because capitalism seeks principally to eradicate costs in order to maximize profit, it will always flow toward the cheapest costs in labour and infrastructure. In this sense the base for the current consumer economy is situated in the areas of cheapest costs and labour. Since World War Two, capital has moved to Japan to Korea, Taiwan and other parts of South East Asia. It is currently nestling in China and India. Both these mega-nations with populations of around a billion people are seen as the superpowers of the twenty-first century. Their economies are growing at around ten per cent per annum and virtually all the world's cheap labour products (textiles in particular) are being manufactured in these two regions.

And yet the vast majority of the people in these countries remain destitute, undernourished and unemployed. The pleasures and largesse of the west are being constituted around a deep poverty that remains obscured by the chrome hanging racks and pleasant disposition of first world clothing stores. The vast slums of Mumbai are rarely depicted in western advertising. And even when western visitors come to Mumbai to explore the wonders of the exotic east, the penury and horror of the slums are transformed as tourist curiosities, another product for the delight of the west.

Liberation and Literature

Part of the problem for an Althusserian analysis is that ideology appears to be too successful, providing little space for escape from its control. To a degree, however, art and literature are capable of creating a critical distance by which the subject may at least partially escape the controlling power of the ideological imaginary. The great work of art is, of course, subject to the predominance of epochal ideology; but the relationship between the imagined and real conditions of life, though it is itself 'imagined', can somehow fracture the substance of the ideology by making us 'see'. Althusser's essay 'Letter on art' (1971) has provided the analytical paradigm for Pierre Macherey's (1978) outline of literary theory. Rather than treat a text as an autonomous and integrated (unique) artefact, Macherey sees the work as a 'product', the outcome of a wide range of criss-crossing processes and elements. These processes constitute a form of social 'unconscious'. As Althusser explains, ideology normally functions to subsume social contradictions in an apparent harmony, a commonsense and naturalistic view of reality. As Macherey argues, however, once the ideology is aestheticized, its inconsistencies, fissures and contradictions become obvious once again. Most particularly, the 'absences' or excluded information which correspond to the ideological interests and failings of the text become available for elucidation by the critic. The task of analysis, therefore, is not to harmonize the fissures and absences of a text, but to illuminate them and their ideological sources.

ANTONIO GRAMSCI

One of the major questions posed by the social theorists who followed Marx concerned the apparent willingness of subordinate classes to co-operate with the means of their oppression. In his discussions on bureaucracy and capitalism, the liberal sociologist Max Weber (see Chapter 2) surmised that much of the symbolic activity of modern society was devoted to the legitimation of economy and politics; Adorno argued that popular culture and its institutions consciously sought to control the 'thinking' of audiences; and Althusser demonstrated that dominant ideologies were capable of diverting individuals' imaginations and practices away from the real conditions of their existence. While it is true that Marxism concerned itself with matters of violence, threat and social coercion, it is equally true that the left-wing lineage continued to puzzle over the apparent consensus which enabled capitalism to advance, despite the obvious and often brutal discrepancies in the distribution of its prosperity.

Hegemony

The work of Antonio Gramsci (1891–1937) was adapted into cultural studies in an attempt to overcome the limitations of Althusser's ideology. Stuart Hall (1982) and others in the Birmingham Centre for Contemporary Cultural Studies (see Chapter 4) identified particular value in Gramsci's somewhat more flexible approach to the operations of ideology and power. Gramsci saw the relationship between state coercion and legitimation as central to an understanding of constituted consensus and co-operation. Gramsci, a revolutionary and founding member of the Italian Communist Party, saw leadership or 'hegemony' as the pivotal issue. Gramsci, who had himself been imprisoned by the Fascists in 1926, argued that the state and other hegemonic institutions could not rely on force or coercion to control opposition and challenge authority. The maintenance of social order or consensus is achieved by 'strategic management'. In a point later taken up by Althusser, Gramsci claims that social elites constitute their leadership through the universalizing of their own class-based self-interests. These self-interests are adopted by the greater majority of people, who apprehend them as natural or universal standards of value (common sense). This 'hegemony' neutralizes dissent, instilling the values, beliefs and cultural meanings into the generalized social structures. Althusser's notion of Ideological State Apparatuses of family, education, media, legal institutions, and so on, echoes Gramsci's belief that consensus is achieved through the general distribution of values, beliefs and cultural practices. The stability and normality of capitalism in Western democratic states has been achieved, according to the Gramscian theory, by this consolidation of the conditions of hegemony.

The Organic Intellectual

This universalizing is not, however, a simple act of coercion or imposition. To this extent, Gramsci transforms Marx's base–superstructure model into something that Marx himself (following Hegel also) considered: the state = political society + civil society. In this famous formulation political society refers to the coercive elements within the social totality, and civil society refers to the non-coercive elements which produce the conditions for the absorption and generalized dissemination of values, behaviours and beliefs. Part of this dissemination is achieved through the function of what Gramsci calls the 'organic intellectual'. While everyone has the potential for intellect, Gramsci insists, only particular people perform the function of intellectual leadership. All social groups produce their own organic leaders whose role it is to organize, negotiate, reform and distribute values and behaviours within their group or class. That is, the organic intellectual will construct the group's identity by giving 'it homogeneity and awareness of its own function' (Gramsci, 1971: 5).

Importantly, organic intellectuals are responsible for 'negotiating' consensus and the distribution of values throughout their constituency. This negotiation implies processes of cajolement, persuasion and threat, on the one hand, and resistance, engagement and incorporation, on the other. It may of course involve some levels of compromise and reform, and will always carry with it the possibility of violence, coercion and subjugation. The economic interests of the controlling group will always be the central, if subliminal, issue, but this interest may be achieved through a range of strategies, including the promise of some forms of personal or collective gratification in the present and future. This 'compromise equilibrium', as Gramsci calls it, though it may give the impression of completion, allows for the possibility of challenge and resistance.

In fact, hegemony can never entirely erase the discrepancies created by an unequal system of power and reward. In the flow of capital and imperial power into the non-European world, this hegemony might stimulate the paradox of an armed resistance movement which mimics the political character and institutions of its oppressors. Ho Chi Minh's nationalist uprisings which led to the Vietnam War were formed around a constellation of militarism, nationalism and administrative processes, all adapted from the French and US occupiers. On the other hand, the consensus might be more clearly negotiated, and armed resistance avoided, through the compromise equilibrium. In British colonies like Australia, New Zealand and Canada, for example, this equilibrium was facilitated through a torpid but constant release of imperial power. The economic interests of the oppressing group remained intact though the direct control of the territories was surrendered. In other words, a 'negotiated leadership' maintained the interests of the oppressors while presenting an impression of self-determination for the oppressed.

Gramsci and Cultural Studies

Resistance, however, was not guaranteed, and Gramsci himself identified a 'traditional intellectual' who might have sustained some level of historical continuity or critical distance beyond the class interests of the organic intellectual (Gramsci, 1971: 7). This distinction, however, proved ultimately unsatisfactory and Gramsci's hope for reform rested finally with the formation of a working-class organic intellectual. Raymond Williams (see 1981: 214–17), one of the founders of British cultural studies (see Chapter 4), adopted the theory of hegemony for a more broadly encompassing analysis of culture and the media. Williams attempts to expand Gramsci's notion of an intellectual and the potential for resistance across culture. For Williams and other cultural commentators interested in popular media texts, Gramsci's notion of hegemony provides a Marxist framework for elucidating power relationships, but without the pre-eminence of economy and the mode of production thesis. The intellectual might constitute himself or herself through a productive relationship with consumers of media culture. Unlike Adorno's analysis, which is so scornful of the popular text's imposition of meaning, and the instrumental rationality and institutionalized structures it represents, Williams' Gramscian approach to text allows more room for the 'negotiation of meaning'. The popular text is not a simple coercion or exertion of cultural control; text consumers have a good deal more say in the way the text and its meanings operate.

Stuart Hall (1982), also from the British cultural studies lineage, argues that Gramsci's hegemony is ultimately a far more productive concept than Althusser's ideology. Hall claims that Althusser's ideology leaves far less room for resistance and agency than does Gramsci's negotiated hegemony. In either case, Gramsci's notion of hegemony provides a useful insight into the complex exchanges that take place within the broad dominion of the 'superstructure'. It provides that important space, missing in Marx's original thesis, in which control by powerful groups and institutions remains incomplete. Culture thus provides the means of oppression but also the means of liberation.

The organic intellectual might therefore emerge from within the ranks of any social interest group or movement since the 'common sense' by which people organize their everyday lives is fundamentally embedded within popular culture. While Gramsci invested his resistance in the organic working-class intellectual, cultural studies has widened the scope of this liberationism, most especially through the construction of identity and other forms of popular cultural politics. Acknowledging the importance of subject positioning, the formation of identity through representation, and the centrality of popular media for the organization and intelligibility of everyday life, cultural studies has focused its attention on the ways in which meanings are negotiated through complex relationships of power and resistance. In many respects, and as Stuart Hall (1996) himself concedes, cultural studies intellectuals sought the common ground of the everyday people and practices they studied; they sought to arise from the ranks of the oppressed in order to liberate their voices. In other words, in the great contest of meaning-making they hoped to be organic intellectuals who would lead the charge of resistance. Some examples of this sort of work include studies by Judith Williamson on advertising (1978), David Morley on news and current affairs (1980a), and Tony Bennett et al. (1986) on popular film.

SCIENCE, LANGUAGE AND CRITICAL THEORY

The influence of the Marxist intellectual heritage remains evident in cultural studies, most particularly as it has been filtered through radical sociology, feminism, the Birmingham Centre for Contemporary Cultural Studies and the various permutations of postcolonial theory. This filtering process, most particularly as it has been influenced by the work of Gramsci and Althusser, has shifted the Marxist project away from economic politics toward a more generalized cultural politics. Even so, this greater interest in language and symbolization has led to an even more sustained interrogation of the new or neo-Marxist project. Coming through the broad sweep of cultural theory, the source of these challenges can be summarized as follows:

1 *Fragmentation of the political field.* Marxist concentration on class has overemphasized a dialectical or dualistic conception of the social formation. Liberation has been defined in unacceptably narrow terms, neglecting the emancipatory claims of women, colonized peoples, ethnic minorities, gays, the disabled and other social sub-groups.

2 *The extension of interest in popular culture and consumption as pleasure.* Marxist denunciation of capitalism, and especially the austerity of theorists like Adorno, tends to overstate the vulnerability of ordinary people and their everyday practices. Mikhail Bakhtin (1984) provided some insights into the possibilities of the 'carnivalesque' or folk culture as a site of people's pleasure and hence resistance to dominant rationalities of

order and control. In contemporary culture, these pleasures and consumption practices have led many social reformers to seek liberation in theory which embraces rather than entirely denounces the 'practices of capital'.

3 *The challenge of poststructuralism.* Poststructuralism and other recent developments in language theory (areas of postmodernism, discourse theory, reading theory, etc.) challenge the material and rational basis of Marxism and liberal humanism by shearing away the notion of a grounded or substantial and absolute truth.

Jürgen Habermas: Critical Theory and Communicative Action

While we will pursue all of these challenges in their own terms in later chapters, the attempts by Marxist-derived analysis to resist or accommodate the challenges are worth investigating as they herald a new phase of critical study. Jürgen Habermas is generally regarded as part of a second wave of 'critical theory' which derives directly from Marxist modes of analysis. While not a contemporary of the first wave Frankfurt School, Habermas nevertheless has sought to extend and elaborate on the Marxist project, identifying the principal deficiency of modern society with 'a lack of freedom'. In 'Towards a reconstruction of historical materialism' (1975) Habermas explains that his principal difficulty with Marxism is that it fails adequately to address the problem of lack of freedom in modernizing societies. In particular, Habermas finds fault with Marx's assumptions that historical and economic evolution is linear and deterministic: for Habermas, in fact, progress and the rise of modern society have been far more unpredictable. To this end, Habermas, like most other critical theorists, erases the idea of class struggle as the source of revolution, replacing it with a broader panegyric which espouses the importance of individual and collective freedom and the formation of a new public sphere.

Habermas (1983) argues, nevertheless, that a retreat from the purity of the Marxist project constitutes a retreat from modernity and its unfinished project. In a significant debate with the French poststructuralist philosopher Jean-François Lyotard, Habermas argues that the filtering out of modernity's rational project of reform leaves the contemporary condition vulnerable to ongoing modes of oppression and social disorder. The Habermas–Lyotard debate centres on the two theorists' respective approach to language, truth and social criticism. Poststructuralists believe that all reality is formed through the mediation of language and therefore there can be no absolute or universal reality. The question of social criticism is opened up because no critical position is grounded in truth – critique only exists in the ungrounded perspective of the critic. Habermas argues, on the contrary, that a rationally derived truth, and hence critique, is both possible and desirable. A rationally derived truth remains the ultimate object of knowledge, Habermas maintains, but the fascination with poststructural and postmodern theoretics exposes philosophy and social science to substantial accusations of political and intellectual capitulation (if not conservatism).

While Habermas's conclusions remain problematic, his identification of the challenges of poststructuralism to the solidity of the Marxist project are significant, and have been central to many of the debates surrounding the respective theoretical claims during the past two decades. Habermas's utopianism attempts to integrate aspects of language theory with more conventional modes of historical materialism. While he begins with Max Weber's theory of modernity, he rejects the notion of consciousness as the central feature of modernist reality, the transcendent unity by which reality is ultimately experienced and known. For Habermas, the limitations of critical theory, most especially as it was articulated in the work of Adorno and Horkheimer, rests on their reliance on Hegelian/Marxist modes of dialectics and transcendent epistemology (modes of knowing). Habermas, therefore, wants to restore the power of a grounded, absolute, rational truth for a critical theory which could provide the directions for a better society.

As we recall, the principal focus of Frankfurt-style theories of consciousness rests on the separation of the subject (the individual who will know) from the object (the external phenomena that is to be known). The relationship between the subject and object is resolved, first, through *cognition,* where the object is represented to the subject as it really is; and, secondly, through *action,* whereby the object is transformed by the things the subject will do. These functions will always take place within the context of self-preservation. Cognition and action, then, implicate the mentality of 'survival of the fittest' – competition for control. From Weber through to the Frankfurt School this pessimistic vision seems to underpin theories of society. Habermas, however, attempts to construct a more optimistic and pragmatic social vision which is not dependent on notions of transcendent consciousness, or on relationships of power (control and manipulation). Like the intersubjectivity of Schütz's phenomenology, though without the unifying consciousness, Habermas creates a notion of consensus that is constituted around communication between subjects. This 'intersubjectivity' is formed through a mediated reality that operates necessarily through human communicative action. The key is the collective constitution of shared reality, including the meaning that is attached to processes of cognition and action. Communicative action becomes the central theme of human truth-value:

> If we assume that the human species maintains itself through the socially co-ordinated activities of its members and that this co-ordination has to be established through communication – and in certain central spheres through communication aimed at reaching agreement – then the reproduction of the species also requires satisfying the conditions of a rationality that is inherent in communicative action. (Habermas, 1984a: 397)

Rationality remains central to Habermas's theory of modernity and to the utopianism which, he claims, would take modernity beyond the threshold of despair. Thus, Habermas conceives of modernity in Weberian terms as the differentiation of science, morality and art into relatively autonomous zones. The advance, 'perfection' and integration of these various spheres into the everyday experiences or *lifeworld* of ordinary people would mark the completion of the modernist project. The means by which these spheres could achieve perfection was never provided by Weber. Habermas, however, explains that rationality and the liberation of communicative action within the public sphere would certainly provide the appropriate conditions for a true human emancipation.

This rationality, however, was not the 'instrumental' or technical rationality to which Weber refers. Such a rationality, deriving from institutions, economy and bureaucracy, always risks the imposition of the will of the state over the potentialities of liberation. Habermas, therefore, follows Weber in distinguishing between instrumental rationality and communicative rationality, which functions most directly in the lifeworld of everyday practices and representations. That is, Habermas's communicative rationality is the site of culture and cultural exchange. This public sphere facilitates the free presentation of truth or validity claims which are challenged and modified in order to produce the effect of consensual, rationalized truth. In the utopian circumstances, this free exchange produces the best possible conditions – the 'ideal speech situation' – for the perfection of art, science and morality, and hence liberation. This ideal speech situation lies effectively outside history and is therefore universal in its intent. Habermas assures us that humans will naturally and inexorably seek to represent themselves and their culture in language, and that these representations are the fundamental constituencies of society. Of course, the lifeworld is bound by specific historical contexts, but in the 'dynamics of development', circumstances will necessarily be impelled toward the ultimate rationality of language and the formation of a situation in which this rationality can be expressed. So, beyond the specifics of the particular language interaction, the ideal speech situation becomes a universal ideal.

Habermas's views on various aspects of social and critical theory appear to have shifted during the course of his writing career. Some commentators would even challenge the suitability of the appellation 'Marxist' as applied to Habermas's theories, most especially as he has moved away from the base–superstructure model in favour of a more language-oriented theory of action. Indeed, Habermas has claimed quite explicitly that notions of a working-class politics must yield to a more complex assemblage of political and scientific discourses, most particularly as they are built around the notion of 'the public sphere' and universalized notions of communication, 'symbolic interaction' and language. On the surface, it may appear that Habermas is subscribing to those theories of language like poststrucutralism which place language at the centre of culture and which accept the fracturing of social agency and ideology. However, Habermas remains fixed in his view that communication is a rationality that is historically patterned, if not inevitable. He would take history beyond the causal structures of Marxist dialectics, but his vision remains centred in the logics of scientific discourse. 'Modern science … [is] governed by ideals of an objectivity and impartiality secured through unrestricted discussion' (Habermas, 1987b: 291). Lyotard (1984a) disputes this point, arguing that modern science is a positioned and self-legitimating narrative, comparable in many respects to the narratives of literature or politics.

4

From British Cultural Studies to International Cultural Studies

INTRODUCTION

The development in the 1960s and 1970s of a distinctively British style of cultural studies can be traced through two significant and related tensions. First, British cultural studies, especially as it became articulated and practised at the Birmingham Centre for Contemporary Cultural Studies (BCCCS), sought to distinguish 'popular' culture as a mode of textual and everyday practice from 'mass' or 'consumerist' culture. The need for a distinction of this kind arose out of the British and European intellectual traditions which privileged high art over popular or low art. British and German Romanticism had exerted enormous influence over the development of educational and academic practices. In forging the humanities and liberal humanism, for example, the Romantic aesthetic had argued that civility and the elevation of consciousness were only possible through the experience of sophisticated forms of music, art and literature.

As we have also seen, the Hegelian lineage in Marxist aesthetics also looked to high art to provide liberation from oppression, ideology and intellectual confinement. British cultural studies, however, drawing on the broader lexicon of social history, anthropology and Chicago-style sociology, felt deeply disturbed by the elitism of the Romantic heritage. A study of culture needs to incorporate the widest possible field of symbolic activities; expunging the idea that social 'value' and political emancipation are the exclusive province of complex intellectual and aesthetic forms. As Jim McGuigan (1992, 1996) suggests, the formation of British cultural studies is necessarily an engagement with, if not a celebration of, popular or everyday culture. This notion of the popular directly challenges those critiques that identified popular art with 'low', 'mass', 'commercial' or 'consumerist' art. The replacement of these pejorative epithets with the notion of 'popular' was designed to remove the assumption underlying the high art–low art distinction.

The second tension which underpins the development of British cultural studies emerges directly out of this challenge to the literary and critical heritage. The distinction between the Frankfurt School's pessimistic appraisal of mass-produced culture and other, more anthropological, notions of the 'people's art' created significant theoretical challenges for the practitioners of British cultural studies, most particularly in their desire to create a critical framework for the reading of texts and culture more generally. Indeed, and as Graeme Turner (1996) has noted, the principal question for cultural studies theory and practice relates directly to the problem of freedom and agency. To what extent is an individual subjectivity free and capable of independent thought and action, and to what extent is s/he a predetermination of institutional and structural power? The various answers British cultural studies offers to this question are rooted in a diverse and often antagonistic history.

It is important to note at this stage that our emphasis on a national typology in this chapter – that is, *British* cultural studies – is only justifiable in terms of the very distinctive attitudes and attributes that developed around the work of Raymond Williams and the various Birmingham Centre scholars. Chris Rojek (2003) has suggested that the formation of a distinctly British (or more precisely *English*) cultural studies is the result of quite clearly identifiable historical conditions, the intersection of the country's own history, intellectual tradition and culture within a very specific political and policy environment. In either case, the Williams and BCCCS heritage has provided a significant basis for the internationalization of British cultural studies and its adoption into broader fields of enquiry across the globe.

LITERARY FOUNDATIONS OF CULTURAL STUDIES

F.R. Leavis

During the nineteenth century, England became the predominant world industrial and economic power. As we have noted in previous chapters, however, the immense wealth generated by industrialization was not evenly distributed and many people in England lived through appalling conditions of squalor, environmental degradation and community dislocation. Romantic literature, among many things, was a response to these conditions. Authors as diverse in their interests as Samuel Coleridge, Matthew Arnold and Thomas Carlyle contributed to a new form of idealism which was based on humanist principles, aesthetics and various kinds of reformist cultural politics. Along with other social reformers of the time, including Charles Dickens, these writers believed that human redemption was only possible through the exercise of reason and the artistic imagination – both of which contributed to the formation of an ascendant 'culture' or 'civilization'.

These ideals might seem to have been realized at the beginning of the twentieth century with the consolidation of universal suffrage, public education and mass literacy. In this context, the admission of Frank Leavis (1895–1978) and Queenie Leavis (1900–82) at Cambridge University after World War I (1914–18) is notable on two counts: first, it announces the entrance of a new social class, the lower middle classes (petite bourgeoisie), into the highest levels of British educational and intellectual life; and, second, it forecasts a significant change to the focus and curriculum of university study. The discipline of English literature was brought out of the margins and placed at the centre of the liberal arts education. The Leavises, along with a number of other young scholars of the time, brought to the humanities, and to British intellectual life generally, a fresh approach to social investigation, one which embedded social knowledge in moral and aesthetic elevation. As the nineteenth century Romantic poet and scholar Matthew Arnold had insisted, humanism, liberalism and moral improvement were all facilities of *culture* and cultural knowledge: for Arnold and other Romantics 'culture' was thus the predicate of refined knowledge and moral purity.

This concept of 'culture' deviates significantly from the one that we outlined and developed in Chapter 1. Following the ideas of the German philosopher Immanuel Kant, the Romantic approach to culture (as the ultimate expression of human refinement and 'civilization') derives from the notion of culture as 'cultivation' (Germ. *kultur*) – the processes of growing or enhancing human capacities through reason, spiritual elevation and aesthetics. It is precisely this idea of culture being expressed through high art which generated the oppositional dichotomy of high art–low art. This dichotomy was situated, of course, within a social hierarchy that distinguished those who did and did not engage in the production and consumption of these high art texts (literature, philosophy, fine art, classical music). The artistic/expressive practices, or meaning-making, of groups outside this elite was simply not acknowledged (see Figure 4.1).

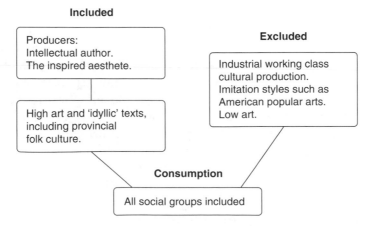

Figure 4.1 *Leavis's culture.*

The arrival of people from the lower middle classes into the university sector might seem to have broken this dichotomy. Critically, however, this broadening of the social constituency of the university sector did not lead to a more inclusive definition of culture; it led merely to a more energetic and expansive distribution of those texts which the Leavises and other scholars regarded as virtuous and worthy. That is, culture was not to include the meaning-making of the lower classes, but the lower classes were to be 'included' in the audiences that these elite, high art texts attracted. Public education, which was advocated by the Romantic reformers of the nineteenth century, was now able to provide a pathway for the lower classes into the bourgeois culture from which they had been excluded. Thus, from the early years of the twentieth century, the lower classes were admitted into what Leavis called 'the great tradition' of English literary culture – and its elevated moral vision.

This moral vision may be understood in several ways:

1   It was a genuinely political tenet, supporting the precepts of liberal humanism. Leavisite Romanticism sought to resolve the ongoing problematic of alienation. Just as institutional democracy was designed to reconcile individual and collective interests, Romanticism and liberal humanism sought to elevate the individual from the immediate conditions of life, reconciling each member of the society with the needs, interests and demands of the whole community. A shared morality, a shared aesthetic, a supreme knowledge – all would bring people together in a community of reasoned and respectful interdependence.

2   The aesthetics were humanist and constituitive of social order. Like the empirical social sciences, the liberal arts were developed as a counterpoint to the genuine terrors of modern life. The Great War (1914–18) demonstrated for all the peoples of 'civilized' Europe that the advanced condition of their technology and lifestyles could turn vicious and bloody. The morality constituted in literature, and the pedagogical and critical processes that would elucidate artistic vision for the masses, would necessarily contribute to social order. The liberal arts would help us avoid the degeneracy and excesses that led to the devastation of war, poverty and social chaos.

3   The moral vision and the liberal arts contributed significantly to the ideology of nation and nationhood. Leavis's humanism and his notions of the 'great tradition' were tinged with a crippling and fearful xenophobia. Presented through the most utopian and heroic images of Britannia, the Leavisite construction of the artistic ideal was deeply vested in communal nationalism.

4   The terrors of modern life and the devastating effects of warfare had led to a deepening mood of nihilism and despair, most especially in continental philosophy, where, of course, the effects of war had been most profound. Leavis's moral vision was seen as an antidote to capitulation and the relinquishment of religious faith.

In fact, Leavis's rendering of the 'great tradition' seeks to reconcile the substantive moral and existential tensions that had been narratized in the English novel and which were representations of the broader cultural dialectics of modernism. In this sense, his work represents a point of scholarly departure, bringing Romanticism into the mainstream of institutional education. However, it is also a hearkening back to the past whereby the consummate threads of moral and spiritual idealism are theorized against the overwhelming pressure of philosophical and everyday negativism. In particular the events of the Great War and the continuing degeneration of industrialization had stimulated enormous fears and doubts amongst everyday people and scholars of the early twentieth century. The Existential philosophers – Kierkegaard, Heidegger, Nietzsche and Sartre – who sought to break with the Romantic idealist tradition, were delivering messages of serious doubt. The absence of God and an ultimate moral referent had inspired thinkers like Søren Kierkegaard, for example, to distinguish between those people who could make some irrational and mystical 'leap of faith', and those, like himself, who could never find it in themselves to believe. Leavis and the other British literary scholars seem to have made that leap, despite the confronting and devastating experience of warfare and mechanical existence, despite the absence of God, and despite the overwhelming knowledge of death and meaninglessness as it was being explored by the artists and philosophers of the early twentieth century – including the novelists whom they studied and admired.

Popular Culture and the Leavisite Legacy

While there can be no doubt that the Leavises and the body of scholars who followed them were politically moderate and that their new discipline of literary studies supported an intellectual utopia, it is inaccurate to characterize them as either quaint or wholly conservative. Very often, such characterizations have been made by recent scholars seeking to demarcate their own liberatory projects against an intellectual corpus which fails to appreciate the significance of popular culture (e.g., Docker, 1994: 20–32). Frank Leavis and others did, in fact, celebrate the sort of folk culture in which a number of later British cultural analysts located their studies and utopian values. Moreover, Leavis's interest in texts and cultural formations, his bland optimism and the tepidity of his political humanism are sometimes repeated in postmodern cultural analysis. As we shall later see, particular zones of postmodernism (the aesthetics of Charles Jencks, for example) constitute a 'leap of faith', a belief in a humanist and bourgeois aesthetic, which would save humanity from the terrors of modernist expressionism, minimalism and existential nihilism.

Mass Culture vs Popular/Folk Culture

We have seen that the Chicago School of sociological and cultural enquiry developed a more inclusive, pluralist and less fearful approach to everyday practices and culture (see Chapter 2). Indeed, the School sought to elucidate the matrices of social relationships, experiences and attitudes which contribute to the formation of culture. It should be remembered, however, that the Chicago School tended to adopt the methodologies and perspectives of journalism and anthropology, and that their work tended to examine and understand particular sub-sets of people: immigrant groups, urbanized neighbourhoods and ethnic sub-cultures. Neither their methodology nor their theoretical frames of reference inclined Chicago sociologists toward an examination of the social whole, the mass of people who might collectively be regarded as the society, nation or culture. When social science did turn its attention toward the conglomerates – as in the Payne Fund studies – it generally did so with some sense of misgiving. The primary questions for the Payne Fund researchers revolved around the impact of mass media messages on the well-being of individual citizens: for example, how were these messages affecting democratic sensibilities, moral perspectives or the mental health of children? Both the Chicago and the Payne studies were conceived from a liberalist and pluralist ideological perspective. Both sought to maintain and protect the individualist ethic, morality and democratic institutions. But both also wanted to contribute to the enhancement of the ideology of prosperity and freedom which was the persistent ideological framework around which pluralism was built. The rise of the mass media and profound suspicions about its messages may have constituted a threat to pluralism, which, in essence, was a finely balanced social compound which adhered a varied constituency to a homogenizing ethos of assimilated Americanism.

The ascendancy of Talcott Parsons, an immigrant intellectual who had seen the worst excesses of human divisiveness and disorder, might be explained partly in terms of this precarious compound, partly by the instabilities being generated by the Cold War. In either case, Parsons' devotion to social order and to the positivist rendering of complex social phenomena represents a broader commitment in American scholarship to the values of assimilated individualism. Parsons contributes to an American approach to popular culture which is both partial and suspicious, vacillating between complete fear and pragmatic recognition. There are, in fact, two significant omissions from American analysis of the popular media:

1   There is an absence of interest in the ideological and political dimensions of the popular media. While the Frankfurt School brought an interest in the mass media and ideology, their analysis, as we have seen in Chapter 3, was based on notions of social control and a pessimistic rendering of resistance. In many ways the Frankfurt School echoed the sorts of suspicions that motivated the Payne Fund studies.

2   The radical potential of popular culture and the popular media doesn't appear in American sociology and cultural studies until at least the 1970s. Sociologists like Herbert Gans (1973) provide a critique of the mass culture–popular culture division. Others, like Alvin Gouldner (1976), explain how ideologies are multiplied through the rise of popular media technologies and texts; these multiple ideologies present opportunities for alternative social ideas and readings.

Herbert Gans was one of the first American sociologists to critique the mass culture perspective. The notions of mass culture and culture industry were developed by the Frankfurt School to distinguish folk or popular art (art of the people) from mass-produced or commercial art (produced by industrialists for consumers). While folk art was positive and generative of positive and creative values, mass culture was formulaic, superficial, commercial, as well as morally, politically and artistically destructive. The Frankfurt School and the Leavisites both condemned mass-produced art, while celebrating folk or popular art. Gans, however, was alert to the fundamental contradictions of this distinction. He was also alert to inconclusive findings of a phalanx of media studies in the United States:

> A ... far more serious theme of the mass culture critique accuses popular culture of producing harmful effects on the people who use it. A number of specific effects have been postulated: that popular culture is emotionally destructive because it provides spurious gratification and is brutalizing in its emphasis on violence and sex; that it is intellectually destructive because it offers meretricious and escapist content which inhibits people's ability to cope with reality; and that it is culturally destructive, impairing people's ability to partake of high culture. (Gans, 1973: 30)

Gans explains that there is no evidence to support the idea that the vast majority of Americans who are exposed to popular culture are 'atomized, narcotized, brutalized, escapist, or unable to cope with reality' (1973: 31). He goes on, in fact, to claim that the criticisms of both high and mass culture are delivered by those who have a vested interest in one dominion of expression over the other. Gans' apologia for popular culture disavows the distinction between mass, popular and high culture, claiming that there is a continuum and that all expressive forms are valid in themselves, and all should be available for sociological analysis.

Gans' relativism introduces a much broader scope for media and cultural analysis in America. However, this relativism also introduces new problems for media criticism, as it problematizes the whole notion of value. Gans' perspective provides for the popular media a new status and centrality in contemporary cultural analysis, as it dissolves the dialectic that has always positioned the popular media as an inferior expressive mode. British cultural studies, as it progressed during the twentieth century, was also forced to confront this problem. Birmingham-based British cultural studies sought, that is, to reconcile the conceptual division that had been established between mass and popular culture: first, by a general re-rendering of the dignity and social value of working-class community and history; secondly, by dissolving the elitism of Leavisite and Frankfurt School analytical paradigms; and, thirdly, by adopting modes of enquiry which had been developed in American sociology and various zones of social history, linguistics and anthropology.

Even so, the British/Birmingham approach could not accept entirely the relativism which Gans and others recommended. In particular, it wanted to maintain its allegiance to critical traditions, forestalling the embrace of American liberal pluralism. In order to maintain this critical distinction, British cultural studies established, or at least reconfirmed, another analytical dialectic: between cultural production and cultural consumption. At the level of consumption, British cultural studies dissolved the distinction between high, popular and folk art. In this sense, notions of 'low', 'mass', 'consumerist', or 'commercial' art were replaced by a non-pejorative, generic and non-hierarchical concept of 'popular' art – that is, art of the people. What mattered to British cultural studies were the processes of meaning-making; these processes implicated media institutions and media consumers in a particular, culturally constituted communicative context. The challenge for British cultural studies, that is, was to build a new premise for critique and analysis without recourse to elitist perspectives, and simple conceptions of text, reader and culture.

CULTURALISM AND THE FORMATION OF A NEW CULTURAL STUDIES

While neither Raymond Williams nor E.P. Thompson was directly associated with the BCCCS, their work, along with various members of the Centre, is regarded as central to the formation of a substantially new form of cultural enquiry. According to Richard Johnson (1979), the second director of the Birmingham Centre, the concept of 'culturalism' most succinctly describes this new mode of cultural analysis. Initially applying the concept to the work of Williams, Thompson and Richard Hoggart, Johnson refers to a particular kind of theoretical coherence and mode of analysis which has since proved enormously influential across the humanities and social sciences. Culturalism, in this sense, suggests that a social group's behavioural and social patterns can be revealed through the analysis of textual production and documented practices. For many analysts today, culturalism also implies a broader interest in questions of ideology and hegemony as they are articulated in popular culture. This mode of analysis is clearly manifest in the writings of the various members of the Birmingham Centre and those, like Williams and Thompson, who are engaged in their respective forms of culturalist exposition.

The Birmingham Centre: Brief Overview

Before looking at some of the most notable, individual contributors to the development of the Birmingham-style cultural research, it is worth examining briefly the genesis and development of the Birmingham Centre itself. The Birmingham Centre for Contemporary Cultural Studies grew out of a significant shift in the mood and direction of British social, aesthetic and cultural enquiry. While the Leavisite paradigm had remained largely ascendant during the early and middle years of the twentieth century, sociology, anthropology and historical studies were seeking new heuristic terrains, new ways of considering the relationships that defined human practices and meaning-making. In particular, scholars influenced by Marxism were seeking alternative perspectives on a post-World War II society that was racked by guilt, Cold War tensions, the nuclear arms race, and a profoundly vociferous conservatism which insisted that prosperity and social order were mutually dependent. Underlying this conservatism, however, were the stirrings of two significant social movements: the beginnings of youth culture in the developed world; and the ascent of the working classes into positions of cultural and social leadership.

Having never developed a strong class system, and being driven by a pluralist and liberalist ethos, American politics resisted the formation of a formidable industrial-based political party. However, in Britain and Europe, with their strong traditions of class polemics, critical theory and radical politics, the post-World War II period offered significant opportunities for social progress. Prosperity, conservatism, an expanding youth population (the baby-boomers), labour shortages, changes from manufacturing to service-based industries – all contributed to a vastly increased demand for education and educators. The influx of young teachers and academics brought new ideas which sought to resolve the social degeneracies that had led to World War II and the Cold War, and which now expressed themselves through a repressive regime of social conformity. These young educators influenced the rising generations, giving legitimacy to the new styles of music and cultural discourses as they questioned the validity of previous generations' social values and ideas. In Britain during the 1950s and 1960s, in particular, many of these new educators were drawn from the working classes. Their specific interrogation of prevailing social norms directed a new approach to the academy, critical thinking, and education generally.

Certainly in Britain there had existed in the earlier part of the century a persistent, though marginal, interest in the culture and heritage of the industrial working classes. While the Leavisite paradigm continued to exclude the cultural productions of those outside the intellectual elite, areas of community studies and community-based arts groups supported an interest in working-class practices and modes of expression as forms of folk culture. Thus, while particular zones of public and academic discourse were arguing that culture was largely an homogenized, centrist and bourgeois phenomenon, a minority of scholars were projecting a distinct social and cultural status for working people and their community. The Centre for Contemporary Cultural Studies was set up at the University of Birmingham in 1964 with Richard Hoggart as its first director. In many respects, the Centre functioned within the general context of interest in a more egalitarian approach to culture, its institutions and social practices. It became the nucleus for the burgeoning and maturing of that interest. From its beginnings, the Centre seemed to occupy a privileged position in researching and articulating contemporary, especially working-class, urban culture, with the majority of its work being dedicated to postgraduate studies and publications.

Significantly, the Birmingham Centre, most particularly under the influence of Raymond Williams and its second director, Stuart Hall, deviated from the American effects model of social enquiry. While the Leicester Centre for Mass Communications Research remained fixed in statistical and empirical methods, Birmingham aimed to explore culture and the media anthropologically and discursively – as lived experiences.

The difference between the Leicester and Birmingham approaches is significant since the Leicester Centre had adopted the communications research model developed in America early in the twentieth century. The aim of this approach was largely scientific: researchers measured the cognitive and attitudinal effects that a media message would have on its recipients. The methods of measurement were scientific, disinterested and quantitative. The Birmingham Centre, however, treated the media as a fundamentally ideological and cultural phenomenon. Their meaning-making processes were essentially and inescapably problematic, rather than assumed, as in the theoretical premise of the Leicester approach. The interaction between audiences, texts, producers and culture was complex, and could only be elucidated through the application of discursive and ethnographic methods: that is, through interpretations, detailed language-based descriptions and detailed qualitative interviews and observations.

Through the work of Williams and Hall, in particular, the media were considered in terms of political processes and language systems. Drawing their influences from French language theory, as well as Marxist theory, the Birminghams regarded culture as a diffuse matrix of linguistic and ideological relationships. Text, textual meanings and culture functioned reciprocally, necessarily implicating social differentials of power and knowledge. Under Hall's directorship, in particular, the work of the Centre and its students explored an ever-widening corpus of cultural phenomena, applying an ever-widening set of methodologies. Dick Hebdige's anthropology on youth culture, David Morley's ethnographic work on television audiences, Angela McRobbie's engagement with feminism and culture – all contributed to the breadth of heuristic activities by which the Centre expanded its influence.

Richard Johnson replaced Stuart Hall in 1979 and took a more restrained approach to the diversifying field of the Centre's work. As an historian, Johnson was a little sceptical of some of the ethnographic work in which the Centre was engaged. Jorge Larrain replaced Johnson and oversaw its transformation into a standard university department, teaching undergraduate programmes and suffering from seriously reduced research funding. Since the resignation of Larrain in 1991, the department has had a succession of heads, including Michael Green, Ann Gray and Frank Webster. Prior to this conversion, the Centre never had more than three full-time staff at any one time yet managed to produce an extraordinary volume of work and publications.

Richard Hoggart: Working-Class Culture

One of the earliest analyses of British industrial working-class culture was carried out by Richard Hoggart. In *The Uses of Literacy* (1958), Hoggart explores the relationship between working-class culture and folk culture, and the 'imposed' and 'external' culture of mass-produced popular texts. Unlike Leavis, Hoggart is interested in the fabric of industrial and urbanized working-class experience; like Leavis, however, Hoggart maintains a deep suspicion of externally contrived cultural production, most especially as it floods into the creative quarters of the working-class community. Laing (1986) and Turner (1996) have suggested that Hoggart's own working-class background and his experiences in teaching literature to adults from his own social background helped maintain his interest in the conditions and culture of his class. While this is probably true, there is an ambivalence in Hoggart's work, a certain abstraction, which clearly demonstrates his uncertainties and subliminal doubts about the treasure of working-class culture. In many respects, this ambivalence is a symptom of the abstraction itself, the need to record the very immediacy and spontaneity of the cultural practices of the working-class community. But it also reflects a sense of alteration, of loss, the very thing which Hoggart regrets but of which he is necessarily a part.

This nostalgia for the pre-World War II working-class culture, the culture of his childhood, tends to skew Hoggart's sensibilities. Indeed, his repudiation of popular culture – American popular music, jukeboxes, popular novels – refers both to the superficiality of the texts themselves and to the threat these texts pose to the maintenance of the class and its culture. That is, American jukebox culture constituted an allure, a distraction, for the youth who were to inherit the deep traditions of the industrial, urban working-class culture. While Hoggart believes the working classes and their codes of practice and morality are sufficient to withstand the invasion, there remains a distinct sense of foreboding in his writing, one which derives as much from his 'bourgeois' intellectual training as from a loyalty to his cultural heritage. Indeed, there exists in Hoggart's work a profound and occasionally puritanical suspicion of America and American popular culture, a fear of its superficial and sensual engagements, a fear of its glitter and surface glamour. Like the Leavises, Hoggart seeks a nobility that could be projected as a universal moral paradigm. His disappointment with contemporary youth and the mutating effects of introduced culture reflects a utopianism that spreads well beyond his repudiation of institutional power and obsessive consumerism.

Hoggart's contribution to the evolution of cultural theory is certainly significant. *The Uses of Literacy* helped to refocus interest in a 'bottom-up' conception of culture: culture that is segmentary, specific and deriving from the symbolic and everyday practices of lower-level community. However, like the Leavises and the Frankfurt School theorists, Hoggart was deeply suspicious of the imposed culture of mass-produced texts. He simply found the invasion of American alien culture overbearing and necessarily attached to dubious relations of power and production. Even so, he was responsible for establishing the Birmingham Centre in 1964, after which (1968) he became Assistant Director-General of UNESCO. He was never able to reconcile his anthropological interests in working-class culture with his distaste for what he regarded as 'phoney' American popular culture. To a degree, this ambivalence reflects not only his personal disjuncture but the absence of a theoretical framework which could allow the analyst to negotiate the very difficult path between understanding and sympathy. That is, Hoggart was not able to comprehend adequately the role of mass-produced culture in the lives of working-class people because he had no way of framing it critically. He saw the changes the invasion was making to the class structure of his youth, but he lacked the theoretical tools necessary to accommodate these changes. The only means of comprehending and analyzing mass-produced culture were provided by Leavis and neo-Marxist works on the one hand, and the sympathetic engagement with the texts by the working-class consumers themselves on the other. In many respects, the history of British cultural studies after Hoggart is characterized by various attempts to negotiate this path. McGuigan (1992, 1996) argues that British cultural studies resolves the problem by wedding popular folk culture to mass-produced culture. While this is true to an extent, McGuigan's conclusion that British cultural studies then attempts to imitate the focus of its analysis – i.e., populism – is far from accurate. As we shall see, the cultural theorists who follow Hoggart constructed extremely sophisticated strategies for elucidating and critiquing the production and consumption of media texts.

The working classes and british punk music

It is widely argued that contemporary first world cultures have become 'post-industrial', and thus the whole notion of an industrial working class is obsolete (Bell, 1973; Giddens, 1994; Poster, 1995). Even so, the resonance of industrial working-class history and culture remains a powerful presence in various zones of contemporary discourse and textualization. British punk music of the 1970s and 1980s, for example, articulated a strident and self-consciously offensive working-class identity. Bands like the Sex Pistols and the Blockheads represented a cultural positioning which, while engaging thoroughly in global media commerce, deliberately assaulted bourgeois taste, 'mainstream' popular musical styles and social hierarchy, particularly as it was represented in the heritage of the British aristocracy. Punk musicians challenged the increasing tendency in popular music toward high levels of production, commercial formulae, and what they regarded as an intellectual or virtuoso pretentiousness amongst certain musicians. The irony is, of course, that punk music itself quickly became part of the commercial music lexicon and is now filtered through various forms of independent styles such as American (Seattle) grunge.

Punk clothing styles, moreover, have been incorporated into various forms of (bourgeois) fashion motifs, expressing an alternative sub-culture that is largely eroticized through gendered motifs and an industry of working-class nostalgia. These sorts of working-class motifs continue in British popular media, with punk music and working-class films experiencing a significant resurgence during the 1990s and 2000s. While Thompson's book on the English working class establishes a typically Marxist tension between the working classes and the bourgeoisie, this tension has largely dissolved in contemporary textualizations. The tension that is more often dramatized

(Cont'd)

and represented in current music and film texts is between the imagined possibility of a working-class culture and its complete dissolution. Indeed, rather than offer a celebratory depiction of the working classes, films like *The Full Monty* offer a somewhat deflating nostalgia in which genuinely good people are seen as the victims of social progress and the dissolution of their class dignity. We are led to ask, therefore, is the resurgent interest in working-class industrial culture an exercise in nostalgia comparable to Leavis's invocation of a nineteenth-century provincial folk culture?

This transformation of city spaces has motivated film-makers and musicians to document an atrophying culture. Mike Leigh's *Secrets and Lies*, for example, addresses these questions through a general exploration of cultural dilution. The transformation of urban spaces is analogous to the cultural transformation of a particular working-class family. Leigh, however, is not nostalgic in his depiction of the family. In fact, *Secrets and Lies* dramatizes the tensions that persist within a transforming working-class culture: the limits of educational, vocational and material ambition are set against the dignity of individual and collective struggle. The miscegenation reveals a new era for the family and for a British working class that must confront itself and the limits of its own condition. The 'illegitimate' black daughter, thereby, transcends her white mother and the old urban working class, bringing a new legitimacy and vision to the post-industrial world of global London.

Raymond Williams: The Problem of Culture

Raymond Williams, the son of a Welsh collier, also taught in adult education in the post-World War II period and also sought to integrate the Leavisite methodology with a left-wing political perspective. Between 1946 and 1960 Williams' involvement with the adult education journal *Politics and Letters* demonstrates an increasingly sophisticated interest in the whole idea of culture. In many respects, *Culture and Society* (1958), one of the most important books in the development of British cultural studies, represents a flowering of this effort to understand the relationship between literature and politics. Williams employs the technique of close textual reading, but he is most concerned to illuminate the context within which the literary text functions. His notion of culture remains largely untheorized, but there is a strong sense in which the social and political processes that surround and inform the text are necessarily integrated into the meanings that the text offers.

Williams' account of the literary history of Britain is fundamentally liberated from the confinements of Romantic immanence and transcendence. Of course Leavis himself would acknowledge that an author works within a context, but for the Leavisite tradition the 'genius' of the author is always a contingency of moral and spiritual elevation. Society is filtered by the author's imagination so that the narrative of the novel or poem becomes ahistorical, a moral and spiritual exigency that denies the immediacies of historical context. Williams, therefore, also defies the direction of the American New Criticism, which attempted to revitalize Leavisite Romanticism by an even more extreme theorizing of the 'poem' as an inviolable and self-contained corpus of meaning – the thing Cleanth Brooks calls a 'well-wrought urn'. While American literary scholars like W.K. Ranson and Cleanth Brooks were seeking to liberate literature from the imperatives of social and political context in order to establish its uniqueness as human articulation, Williams was trying to fix the meaning-making process within the immediate social conditions of the contemporary context. A text, for Williams, was necessarily a contingency of social relationships, including relationships of power.

Of course, Marxist scholars like Georg Lukács had developed an alternative to the Leavisite position, though there is no real evidence that Williams had access to the critical Marxist perspective and only late in his career did he acknowledge directly his indebtedness to that creed. Moreover, Williams did not have available to him the increasingly sophisticated lexicon of French language theory; writings on complex language systems like semiotics and structuralism were not readily available in translation. Terry Eagleton (1978: 35–40) has argued that Williams' work, in fact, lacks a truly socialist perspective as it remains faithful to Leavisite notions of nostalgia and provincial Romanticism. While it is true that Williams fails to confront the issues of industrialism directly, it is also true that he conveys in his writings generally a desire for justice and social equality. Significantly, he remains caught between the notion of culture as an aesthetic category (literature specifically) and culture as a generative and ubiquitous set of everyday practices (the anthropological notion of 'way of life'). To this extent, *Culture and Society* does not quite resolve or abandon the Leavisite perspective, and we find the same ambiguities in his more elaborated attempt to define culture, *Keywords* (1976). Culture is 'one of the two or three most complicated words in the English language' (1976: 76), Williams tells us. But we are never able to escape the intransigence of a definition which is distinctly qualitative and entirely incorporative.

Williams' conclusion to the entry on culture reflects his contrary inclinations toward inclusiveness, on the one hand, and intellectual or social leadership, on the other:

It is significant that virtually all the hostility … [to the notion of culture] has been connected with uses involving claims to superior knowledge (cf. the noun INTELLECTUAL), refinement and distinctions between 'high' art (culture) and popular art and entertainment. It thus records a real social history and a very difficult and confused phase of social and cultural development. It is interesting that the steadily extending social and anthropological use of culture and cultural … has, except in certain areas (notably popular entertainment), either by-passed or effectively diminished the hostility and its associated unease and embarrassment. (1976: 82)

From *The Long Revolution* (1965) to *Culture* (1981), Williams demonstrates his desire to converge these definitions, identifying culture as the organization of complex relationships 'between elements in a whole way of life' (1965: 63). Popular arts remain regrettably poor quality, Williams maintains, but there is no special place for the 'arts' as a privileged and transcendent discourse, as Coleridge, Arnold and Leavis had claimed. Rather, Williams treats the arts as practice or 'elements' within the complex of the whole way of life. In *Culture* (also titled *The Sociology of Culture*), in particular, Williams seeks to elucidate a sociology which engages fully with the popular arts and the media. In the later works, especially, Williams is interested in the social conditions and social relationships that inform and surround the arts through the operation of ideology (Williams, 1981: 26–30) and institutions. He remains untouched, however, by the influences of French structuralism, and even in an important book like *Television, Technology and Cultural Form* (1974) there is a certain failure to appreciate the full implications of his analysis of contemporary popular media. For example, while Williams points to the unique conditions of television programming and institutions, and while he incisively attacks technological determinist and effects analysis of television, he remains distinctly suspicious of TV's intent and popularity.

Once again, we can see that Williams is sensitive to the institutional and ideological processes that contribute to the formation of texts and textual meanings. He is also aware that the meanings constituted in these texts are substantive and contribute themselves to the construction of culture as a way of life. However, the resonances of his Leavisite training and his own preference for more complex artistic forms seem to limit his analyses, drawing him back into a more restrained account of the 'value' of TV texts in aesthetic and cultural terms. That is, Williams recognizes, that television is a major part of contemporary culture, but he retains his right to question its worth.

E.P. Thompson and Historical Cultural Studies

More so than Williams, who retained some residual affiliations with Leavisite textual values, E.P. Thompson's monumental study *The Making of the English Working Class* (1980) represents a substantiation of a critical link between cultural theory and politics. Like the French Annales school of historiography, Thompson sought to articulate the lives, as well as the social and political conditions, of the common people. Thompson's work, however, is not satisfied with a mere wresting of history from the control and interest of elite groups. Rather, he seeks to produce a history of the working class themselves, one which is experiential and vested in everyday practices and everyday culture. That is, Thompson's historiography avoids the sorts of sentimentalism and nostalgia that are evident in Leavis's provincialism, and which can be seen in traces in Hoggart's comparative study of pre- and post-World War II working-class England.

Moreover, Thompson's project is not merely descriptive. Beginning from the per-spective and experiences of the industrial working class in the period leading up to the

1830s, Thompson seeks to explain its condition and cultural formation in terms of the progress of capitalism. While he had resigned from the British Communist Party by the time of the book's publication, he demonstrates a significant allegiance to Marxist conceptions by which class is defined as 'a social and cultural formation arising from processes which can be studied as they work themselves out over a considerable period' (1980: 11). This 'making' of a class, Thompson explains, 'happens when some men, as a result of common experiences (inherited or shared), feel and articulate the identity of their interests as between themselves, and as against other men whose interests are different from (and usually opposed to) theirs' (Thompson, 1980: 8–9). This description engages an anthropological approach to human groups with Marxist precepts. It is comparable to the Chicago School approach to social mapping in that it seeks to explain processes and identity through complex associations and influences. It is unlike Chicago sociology in its focus on class and on the political context in which class is formed.

Thompson, thereby, diverges significantly from Williams' approach to culture, which focuses on the capacity of people to produce an organic, interactive and consensual whole. Thompson begins with notions of class and struggle, but insists that culture can never constitute a single way of life, only conflict between different ways of life. Clearly, his work is based around macro structures of class. However, the conflict model he applies to an analysis of culture informs much of the thinking about culture and cultural difference that has arisen in more recent years. Thompson's Marxism, nevertheless, treats the structure of class as a more or less homogeneous category, though, unlike Marx, he does not see this category as the outcome of the economic 'base'. That is, Thompson, along with Williams, rejects the base–superstructure model, insisting that economy and culture must necessarily interact to produce effects in identity, behaviour and belief. Also like Williams in *The Long Revolution*, Thompson rejects entirely the notion of class domination, postulating rather that power difference contributes to, rather than determines, the formation of class culture. The dignity and freedom of the working classes are as much self-determinations as acts of resistance. Thompson's picture of the working class is not of an oppressed and inert social formation, but of a dynamic and complex mixture of oppression and agency. The working classes are not merely determined, but determining.

Thompson's major contribution to the development of cultural theory may be summarized in terms of his complete rejection of the Leavisite high art–low art dialectic. For Thompson, everything contributes to the formation and legitimation of culture. Notably, he seeks to explain the experience of being immersed in culture without direct reference to external determinations independent of the perceptions and experiences of the cultural group under focus. For Thompson, this means that the 'blind alleys' of history, those elements which Michel Foucault later calls 'discontinuities', are necessarily integrated into the general cultural mosaic. Thompson, therefore, is not merely interested in historical causalities which lead one event or phenomenon into another; he is equally concerned with the details and immediacies that contribute to the mood and appearance of a particular historical moment.

Thompson's approach sets him against other significant cultural theorists at the time. In particular, he became engaged in a significant debate during the 1970s over the relative value of what may be called culturalism and structuralism (see Thompson, 1976; Neale, 1987). Structuralism, as we have noted in our discussions on Durkheim (Chapter 2), Marx and Althusser (Chapter 3), concerns itself with those social structures which bind and determine the major forms of a society and culture. While Durkheim is interested in legal and religious structures, Marx, of course, is primarily interested in the structure of class. Structural anthropologists such as Lévi-Strauss and Saussure (see Chapter 5), and neo-Marxists like Louis Althusser, are interested in the structures of language – those macro formations which function to produce major cultural and social adhesions. Structuralists tend to be more interested in these substantive forms rather than the infinite and constitutive details that make up the structure. Culturalism, as Richard Johnson (1979) defines it, concerns itself precisely with those details: local practices and symbolic microcosms in which everyday life is patterned and experienced. Once again, this divide represents a tension between collective patterns and microtic level details – the collective and the individual. Among numerous others, Thompson, Richard Johnson and Stuart Hall argued out the relative value of structuralist and culturalist propensities, with the most acid and passionate articulations appearing in the journal *History Workshop*. Johnson, who espoused the values of an Althusserian approach to cultural history over excessive humanism and localism, applied the critique of 'culturalism' against Thompson and others. Thompson rejected the nomenclature, criticizing the implied determinism of the structuralist approach. The notion of structure, Thompson claimed, inevitably lessened the power of working people to determine their own life experiences, culture and freedom. It limited descriptions and explanations of the world to structured causes.

Stuart Hall: The Transformation of Cultural Studies

Stuart Hall's personal struggle with Althusserian structuralism, and indeed the whole Marxist project, in many respects parallels the Birmingham-based cultural theory's struggle to produce a productive theoretical framework for the analysis of popular culture. In his own account of this struggle, Hall contends that British cultural studies is necessarily implicated in the politics and postulates of Marxism; indeed that cultural studies exists 'within shouting distance of marxism, working on marxism, working against marxism, working with it, working to try to develop marxism' (1996: 265). For Hall, the theoretical interests of Marxism and cultural studies were never perfectly matched, most particularly because Marxism fails directly to address the key concerns of cultural studies: culture, ideology, language and the symbolic.

Thus, Birmingham cultural studies turned to the ideas of structural anthropology and Althusserianism to explain the problem of language and power: 'The power involved here is an ideological power; the power to signify events in a particular way' (Hall, 1982: 69).

But for Hall, with his particular interest in popular media texts, the Althusser–cultural studies nexus remained problematic. Hall's own experiences as a West Indian immigrant might seem to have complicated his willingness to accept the structuralist explanations of power. That is, ethnicity seemed to add a further dimension to the Althusserian notion of domination, which tends to locate power in the relatively closed categories of social class. Ethnicity, migration, social mobility and the shared product of popular culture seemed to create for Hall a more complex social scenario than could be explained by Althusser's notion of ideology. Unlike Hoggart, Williams and Thompson, Hall was not part of the British working-class heritage, and the inclination of Birmingham theory to aggregate the particulate experiences of so many people, communities, rituals and practices into the one, distinctly British, symbolic system seemed overly reductionist to him. If nothing else, it placed Hall himself on the outer of the theoretical and analytical activities of the Centre; it marginalized him as a social being.

In his account of the move from structuralist to Gramscian cultural analysis, Hall notes that Marxism and its derivatives remain decidedly 'Eurocentric' (1996: 269). In his co-authored book *Policing the Crisis: Mugging, the State and Law and Order* (Hall et al., 1978), his own ethnicity becomes foregrounded as he provides a view of culture which emphasizes localism and subversion, as well as active participation in the mediation of people's lives. While race has not been a central theme in Hall's writings, there can be little doubt that the absorptive interests of nation and national culture represented in the works of Hoggart and Thompson would be of less concern to him than interplays of ideology and power. While this is partly due to Hall's own fascination with theoretical problems, it is also a measure of his interests in the broader constitution of culture which is not vested in class and nation but which is engaged through much more expansive cultural and textual practices. This is not the pluralism of American communications research – Hall explicitly denounces pluralism as artificial and assimilative – but rather it is an exploration of wider fields of oppression, privilege and resistance.

From Althusser to Gramsci The need for a theoretical perspective which could accommodate social diversity, popular media, power and resistance led Hall away from Althusser toward Antonio Gramsci's notion of hegemony. Certainly, the 'turn to Gramsci', as Tony Bennett (1997) calls it, provides for Hall a more engaging and productive approach to the analysis of media texts. Gramsci's concept of the 'organic intellectual' (see Chapter 3) presents a critical space in which both free agency (the ability to act independently) and oppression can be seen to operate. Challenging Althusserianism, Hall notes that it is difficult 'to discern how anything but the dominant ideology could ever be reproduced in discourse' (1982: 78). The Russian linguist Volosinov (sometimes identified with Bakhtin) provided the basis for a more thoroughgoing analysis of the 'struggle to signify':

> For if the social struggle in language could be conducted over the same sign, it followed that signs (and by a further extension, whole chains of signifiers and discourses) could not be assigned, in a determinate way, permanently to any one side in the struggle. (Hall, 1982: 79)

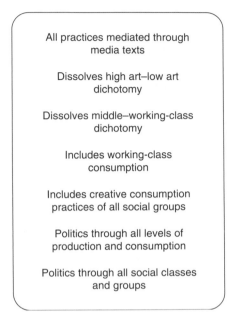

All practices mediated through
media texts

Dissolves high art–low art
dichotomy

Dissolves middle–working-class
dichotomy

Includes working-class
consumption

Includes creative consumption
practices of all social groups

Politics through all levels of
production and consumption

Politics through all social classes
and groups

Figure 4.2   *Stuart Hall's culture.*

Antonio Gramsci's theories of hegemony and the organic intellectual, Hall contends, provide the facility for the construction of, and resistance to, power. When leadership must be negotiated across a whole range of 'organic' fields of interest, space is opened up for the everyday citizen to challenge, query and demand. Ideology, as Althusser imagines it, is a blanket effect; in Gramsci, however, individuals and groups might form pockets of resistance, creating their own symbolic nodes which challenge the imposition of external culture. The problem of social control is mediated, therefore, by the everyday practices and agency of smaller and 'less powerful' groups in the community. Leaders can only lead when they are sanctioned in respect of these smaller symbolic nodes. The 'struggle to signify' is not a uni-dimensional process, but an ongoing act of power, resistance and negotiation. This approach to power and symbolization allows Hall to maintain his adversarial politics without surrendering to the pessimism of Frankfurt-style social control theory. Hegemony and its functioning through the mass media necessarily open the culture to the possibilities of subversion, change and reform. In reviewing his adoption of Gramsci's theoretics, Hall acknowledges the theoretical 'conundrums' with which Gramsci was forced to work:

[T]he things about the modern world which Gramsci discovered remained unresolved within the theoretical framework of grand theory – marxism – in which he continued to work.

> At a certain point, the questions that I still wanted to address in short were still inaccessible
> to me except via a detour through Gramsci. Not because Gramsci resolved them but because
> he at least addressed many of them. (1996: 266–7)

The Gramscian notions of hegemony and the organic intellectual allowed Hall to
examine media texts in terms of challenge and struggle, as much as domination.
Moreover, it allowed him to admit into the nexus of his cultural analysis an approach
to the media that was not restricted by the claims of class and structure. Indeed,
while other zones of cultural analysis were being influenced by the ideas of French
poststructuralism and American postmodernism, Hall's own Gramscian theoretic was
sufficiently positioned to admit a broader political field, including feminist, race-based
and postcolonial analysis. Even so, Hall concedes that the admission of these wider
politics into cultural studies strained the efficacy of the Birmingham Centre's theoretical
conceits:

> [A]ctually getting cultural studies to put on its own agenda the critical question of race,
> the politics of race, the resistance to racism, the critical question of cultural politics, was
> itself a profound theoretical struggle.... Again it was only accomplished as the result of
> a long and sometimes bitter – certainly bitterly contested – struggle against a resounding but
> unconscious silence. (1996: 270)

Hall also concedes, however, that these struggles were a necessary, and, we might add,
paradoxical, process of change.

Encoding/decoding Hall's methods are as varied as his theoretical encounters. His
approach to textual analysis, however, is clearly outlined in his essay 'Encoding/
decoding' (1980). For Hall, a text is thoroughly embedded in its cultural context,
which, in turn, is determined by relationships of power and hegemony. In many
respects, Hall's approach to text and context resolves the dichotomy that developed in
Birmingham studies between culturalism, as elucidation of particulate cultural details,
and structuralism, an investigation of ideology and structures as sources of power
(see Bennett, 1986). The encoding/decoding process is designed to supplant simple
notions of authorship and interpretation. Essentially, various agencies contribute to
the formation of a textual 'code': investors, media institutions, creative staff, and so
on. Each is informed by particular cultural experiences, including various ideological
perspectives and convictions about what would constitute a successful media product.
Textual coding engages these aspects through a dynamic of meaning potentials known
as signifiers. The text is a product, therefore, of individual, hegemonic and cultural
ingredients. Texts carry a series of meaning possibilities whereby signifiers can be
interpreted in a variety of ways. This potential for varied 'interpretation' is known as
polysemy.

Coding and representation

A text represents (re-presents) the world around us. It is not a mirror or identical reproduction of everyday reality, but creates a version or impression of that reality. In other words, texts mediate and in a sense create a new 'reality' out of the cultural resources of life. In a process he calls encoding, Stuart Hall (1980) argues that cultural resources are shaped into sharable textual codes (language systems); these textual codes are then decoded (or interpreted) by audiences. Through this representation of the world, text-makers and text-readers are able to share and create meanings for themselves and for one another. Ideology and hegemony play an important role in this encoding/decoding process, since they enable members of a society and culture to locate specific meanings out of a given text's range of possible meanings. Dominant groups within a social formation are able to exert greater influence in what Hall calls the 'struggle to signify': that is, the battle over cultural resources which enables some individual and groups to have their own specific interests and needs satisfied.

One of the most common motifs in contemporary culture is the body of the thin, young woman. Text-producers deploy this motif or symbolic form for a range of libidinal, narrative and commercial purposes. Feminist cultural theorists like Angela McRobbie (1982) have argued that texts like that in Plate 4.1 'position' readers and therefore reinforce dominant ideologies of sexism and patriarchy. The ad tells teenage girls, for example, who they are and how they should act. Similarly, Laura Mulvey (1975) argues that the perpetual availability of women's bodies in contemporary visual culture satisfies the interests of the dominant gender, men. Naomi Wolf (1991) argues that the depiction of generally unattainable body shapes in advertising serves to discipline and control women. Real women are perpetually dissatisfied with their bodies and hence spend excessive energy and time on the project of thinning.

In all cases, this disproportionate representation of attractive young women distorts the actual conditions of everyday life. Stuart Hall's point is that the media create their own representational 'reality' which is formed through the interests of dominant groups, hegemony and ideology. The abundance of attractive, usually Anglo-Celtic, young women in the media is not an accident, but represents a very specific cultural predilection.

Decoding is a mirror process by which the audience or consumer is confronted with a series of meaning potentials in the text. These meaning potentials struggle for prominence, but audiences tend to aggregate around what is known as the dominant or preferred reading. Dominant readings are derived through hegemonic processes whereby audience members draw on their knowledge of culture, cultural values and cultural norms. Where the audience is more alike or homogeneous, the likelihood of a dominant reading is greater. Hall insists, however, that the decoding process is far from unilateral and variations in reading are always possible. Certain textual meanings – the value of capitalism, nation,

Plate 4.1   *The Beauty Economy.*

The image of young female bodies is the mainstay of modern advertising and patriarchal cultural systems. Advertising sells its products by connecting the desire to buy with sexual desire and desirability. The sexualized images stimulate the viewers, creating the desire to 'become' the image, or be engaged sexually with the image. Thus, the image 'situates' or 'positions' viewers by telling them who they are in relation to the image – and how they should act and think in order to satisfy the new desire.

individualism, for example – are repeated and presented so frequently and unreservedly that they appear as forms of ideology. Others are presented in more varied ways and may be subject to what Hall calls the 'struggle to signify'; these more contested areas of discourse can lead to more varied decodings. In either case, Hall recognizes that the mass media offer opportunities for the presentation of significant cultural values and ideologies which may reinforce the interests of dominant groups (organic intellectuals, as Gramsci calls them). Equally, however, polysemy offers opportunities for challenge and varied decoding practices. Social challenge and social reform are possible through the fissures and imperfections of the encoding/decoding process. The task of the analyst is to illuminate the processes by which preferred or dominant readings are constructed; close textual analysis can illuminate particular assumptions and ideologies that are engaged in cultural representation.

Identity Politics – In a number of important essays on globalism and identity written during the 1990s we can see once again Hall's own personal struggles with the atrophy of Marxism and Marxist solidarity. The well-canvassed fragmentation of the social and cultural landscape, accompanied by an equally fragmenting theoretical landscape, has led to further and more profound abandonments of the Marxist polemic. Indeed, while Hall is prepared to maintain his disavowal of psychoanalytic and poststructural theory that is not informed by political intent (see Hall, 1988, 1991a, 1991b), his more recent writings on identity appear to be seeking a more inclusive and flexible approach to the mutability of subjectivity and personal identity. The paradigm of political resistance is now a matter of diffusion and identity creation:

> The more social life becomes mediated by the social marketing of styles, places and images, by international travel and by globally networked media images and communications systems, the more identities become detached – disembedded – from specific times, places, histories, and traditions, and appear 'free-floating'. We are confronted by a range of different identities, each appealing to us, or rather to different parts of ourselves, from which it seems possible to choose. (Hall et al., 1992: 303)

While the postmodernists appear to welcome this new permutation of individual freedom, Hall's mood is a little more restrained, betraying an ambivalence which hearkens to his Marxist, reformist heritage.

THE INTERNATIONALIZATION OF BRITISH CULTURAL STUDIES

Graeme Turner has argued that cultural studies cannot easily be separated into specific fields of interest; nor is it a discrete constellation of disciplines: 'Cultural studies is an interdisciplinary field where certain concerns and methods have converged; the value of this convergence is that it has enabled us to understand phenomena and relationships that were not accessible through the existing disciplines' (1996: 11). Cultural studies, however, is not just an interdisciplinary 'field', as Turner suggests. It is also a set of concepts and apprehensions which necessarily problematize the focus and methods of the traditional humanities and social sciences. Cultural studies, that is, raises the question of how reality is constituted. Its answer is that all reality is culture, since all reality is mediated by discourse and meaning-making processes. These processes are not simply abstract expressivities; they are restored to the world of action within a context of power relationships and their various motifs of social differentiation – class, gender, race, sexual orientation, ethnicity and so on. The traditional disciplines which have assumed their realities must choose either to ignore this insight or accommodate it through the transformation of their scholarship. If culture is always the starting place of reality, then literature, sociology, politics, history and anthropology must redefine themselves in terms of cultural analysis, or else surrender entirely to the new humanities, the new 'field' of study.

What distinguishes British cultural studies is that it was perhaps the first in the English-speaking world to address the problematic of meaning-making and the need to conceive more fully of the broad field of human experience known as culture. While the Birmingham Centre seems remarkably organic with the hindsight of history, as both Johnson and Hall record, there were many bitterly contested battles over methods, strategies, resources, theories and values. By the time the Centre was folded back into the academic mainstream during the 1980s, these wide-ranging programmes and strategies had been variously adopted by emerging cultural studies schools and traditional disciplines around the world. While it is true that many of the Birminghams' ideas on culture, power and language were being explored in various ways, the Centre (Stuart Hall in particular) provided an extremely systematic and coherent approach which synthesized many of these ideas into a workable programme.

This model of cultural scholarship, which blends various forms of textual studies with a broadly conceived analysis of power, has clearly resonated with many academics across an increasingly globalized university sector. Ackbar Abbas and John Nguyet Erni (2005) argue that the emancipatory mission and theoretical cogency of cultural studies has been particularly appealing for scholars in the postcolonial world. The internationalization of cultural studies is being accomplished, according to Abbas and Erni, through the dissemination and deployment of its key concepts in the study of decolonization, subaltern and diaspora studies. This form of 'transculturalism; (Lewis, 2002a), however, has also proven appealing to various forms of scholarship, particularly in the United States, which had been interested in marginality (deviance, sub-culture, youth culture), but which lacked a strong theoretical core.

Moreover, through its further engagement with forms of ethnography, French poststructuralism and American postmodernism, British cultural studies is now barely distinguishable from cultural studies in Australia, Canada or the United States. In fact, while particular areas of communications and media sociology maintain an adherence to positivist principles, especially in the United States, the hybridizing of various areas of cultural studies through the English-speaking world has significantly transformed the demarcations that once separated the disciplines. For American sociology and communications studies, the Birmingham theoretics articulated in a formidable way many of the ideas that had been explored through Chicago sociology, phenomenology and symbolic interactionism. The elision of hardline Marxism in a generalized cultural critique seemed somehow to bring to American cultural analysis a vigour that was not threatening to the liberalist and pluralist ideals of its scholarship.

James Carey's *Communication as Culture* (1989), for example, represents a significant departure in American communication studies. Carey's analysis of communications technology brings British notions of culture into the foreground. Carey insists, in fact, that the symbolic and political dimensions of culture were as significant in the formation of 'America' as were economic and industrial processes. Similarly, Lawrence Grossberg's essay 'Birmingham in America' (1997: 1–32) explores the problematic of culture through an adoption of British cultural studies strategies. Grossberg's work has been heavily influenced by Birmingham writers like Dick Hebdige, who pioneered analysis of youth culture in the 1970s. Contemplating the various permutations of American youth and popular culture, Grossberg argues that culture cannot be parenthesized or reduced to concepts of social control:

> Cultural studies believes that culture matters and that it cannot simply be treated (dismissed) as the transparent – at least to the critic – public face of dominating and manipulative

capitalists. Cultural studies emphasizes the complexity and contradictions, not only within culture, but in the relations between people, culture and power. (1997: 12)

This transatlantic adaptation of Birmingham-style cultural studies rejects the economic bottom-line as the determinant of cultural forms. Grossberg's cultural studies, while not a mainstream in American cultural sociology and communications studies, nevertheless constitutes a significant heuristic zone, one in which the problematics of power and popular culture are centralized. America's long-standing interest in popular culture is now reframed in terms of power and ideological formations.

Significantly, however, Birmingham-style cultural studies is being forced to accommodate the new theoretical inflexions of poststructuralism and postmodernism. While particular zones of cultural studies have tried to resist the effects of these inflexions, others have been much more absorptive. In the United States, in particular, the mutating aesthetics of postmodernism has found its way into various fields of cultural analysis. Grossberg himself struggles with the contending influences of postmodernism and the residual Gramscian politicism of Birmingham-style cultural studies. While the details of this tension are more clearly outlined in Chapter 8, there is certainly a crisis of emphasis in the minds of many cultural theorists: in crude terms, critics of postmodern cultural studies believe that it has surrendered excessively to the claims of consumer capitalism and has lost its capacity for social and cultural critique.

It may be, in fact, that the liberalist pluralist scholarly tradition in American cultural studies leads it more fully toward a postmodern, as opposed to a Birmingham, style of cultural studies. In this sense, the liberalism of the Chicago School, the localism of symbolic interactionism and the transcendentalism of phenomenology, constitute forms of rehearsal for a more complete and indigenous analysis of American popular culture. In fact, Birmingham-style cultural studies has transmogrified into various forms of cultural politics, opening the way for the appropriation of popular culture by a more expansive and celebratory popular cultural studies. The residues of Gramscian analysis can be located in various universities around the world, but this is less typical than Hall and others would certainly have preferred. A crisis in cultural studies may be prevalent, as Grossberg (1997) laments, but in other respects we are witnessing a ferment of theoretical and methodological expansionism as the humanities and social sciences attempt to redefine themselves and their interests in terms of culture and mediation. Old methods and ideas are being welded to new. Various forms of scholarly hybridization are taking place. Conferences are replete with calls for a return to empiricism or political economy or the purity of Gramscian concepts. What is clear, however, is that the new disciplines can no longer function without recourse to significant debates about language and culture. Whether these debates encompass issues of power, ideology and emancipation is a function of emphasis and definition. Certainly, the British tradition of cultural studies has provided, above all else, a way of thinking about culture which makes such issues ineluctable.

5

Language and Culture: From Structuralism to Poststructuralism

INTRODUCTION

As we noted in the previous chapter, British cultural studies moved away from a Marxist-based analysis of working-class life towards a broader field of cultural enquiry. While politics and everyday practice remained pivotal to cultural studies, scholars like Raymond Williams and Stuart Hall brought a greater focus on media and media texts into the field, arguing that 'representation' was a critical part of the formation of meanings and culture more generally. Hall (1982), in particular, sought to free cultural and media analysis from the linear reductionism of the American effects tradition, on the one hand, and the materialist determinism of Marxism, on the other. Hall recognized that both the effects tradition and the Frankfurt School of neo-Marxism presented a limited vision of the relationship between culture, media institutions, texts and audiences. The effects model treated language as a given and the process of communication as a simple matter of message transmission: a message and its effect on an audience could be simply measured by the application of 'objective', statistical methods. The Frankfurt School also applied a transmission model, though messages were intrinsically ideological; media messages always carried the political interests of the elites who generated them. Adorno, Horkheimer and Marcuse believed, it would seem, that the masses were passive and uni-dimensional victims of the overbearing power of state and media institutions. The material and political privation of the masses was legitimated through the ideology of mass-produced texts.

For Hall and many others working in the field, however, these transmission models failed adequately to explain the complex processes which form meaning, culture and cultural politics. Indeed, the theory of semiotics – or more precisely 'semiology' – provided the most compelling insights into this process. The merging of French language theory with Birmingham-style cultural studies contributed significantly to the widening of the cultural studies project in Britain and elsewhere. Undoubtedly Hall's personal qualities and experiences provided an ideal conduit for the hybridization of Gramsci, Althusser, French semiology and materialist politics.

Even so, the ferment of interest in French language theory in the English-speaking world eventually reached well beyond the interests of Hall and the other Birminghams, most especially through the emergence of a *post*structuralist theoretic which invaded cultural studies from the 1980s onwards. In this chapter we will look at the lineage of French language theory from structuralism through to poststructuralism. Many scholars might object to this juxtaposition, arguing that the rupture between structuralism and poststructuralism constitutes a distinctive and categorical break. My own view is that the challenge presented by poststructuralism to structuralism, while significant and defining, does not erase the substantive issues, interests and themes that connect the two within the genealogy of contemporary cultural theory. Many of the debates within current-day cultural studies centre on the viability of poststructuralism for the analysis and comprehension of postmodern culture.

STRUCTURALIST LANGUAGE THEORY

Ludwig Wittgenstein and C.S. Pierce

As we have noted in previous chapters, modern scientific principles and methods were developed through the philosophical writings of people like René Descartes, John Locke and Immanuel Kant. Descartes, for example, explains that knowledge is only possible through the removal of doubt, and by the application of universal principles expressed through a universal language, specifically the language of mathematics. The social sciences, developed during the nineteenth and early twentieth centuries, also adopted principles of reason and universalism.

The studies of C.S. Peirce (1839–1914) and early Ludwig Wittgenstein (1889–1951) provided a basis for the 'science' of linguistics and, in particular, the emergence of the concept of 'the sign' as the universal unit that underpins all languages and language function. According to Peirce, a sign is something that stands for something else in the mind of an individual. A sign may construct an 'equivalent sign' or a 'developed sign' in an individual's cognition. Peirce recognizes that the sign of an object will necessarily produce a further sign for the individual; he calls this the *interpretant* of the original sign. A sign is not just a public notice like 'Keep off the Grass' or 'Enter'; it is a symbol which signifies for the reader some form of meaning. A sign, therefore, might be smoke indicating fire, a word or a visual image. A red traffic light indicates stop; the word 'cat' refers to a fluffy creature with four legs and an appetite. The reason why signs can present meaning is because they belong to and operate within a system.

Early in his writing career, Ludwig Wittgenstein was also interested in the universal principles which govern the operations of language. In particular, Wittgenstein was interested in the possibilities and limits of language, most especially as the world of phenomena is translated into a universal truth – a philosophical proposition. In the most widely cited of his writings, *Tractatus Logico-Philosophicus* (1922), Wittgenstein 'explores' this process of translation, arguing that the logical forms of language must necessarily operate to reproduce the logical forms of the 'lifeworld':

> In a proposition a situation is, as it were, constructed by way of experiment. ... One name stands for one thing, another for another thing, and they are combined with one another. In this way, the whole group – combined like a tableau vivant – presents like a state of affairs. (Wittgenstein, 1922: 4.031–4.0311)

Wittgenstein's later work on 'ordinary language' deviates significantly from the earlier analysis of logical forms. In many respects the earlier phase supports the structuralist approach to language, while his later writings, focusing on the interplay of meanings he calls 'language games' (see Lewis, 2002b: 149–50), is more closely aligned to a poststructuralist paradigm. Wittgenstein's great contribution to the development of cultural theory and a specifically defined cultural theory of language centres on his understanding of the importance of context and the imprecise nature of it. The system of signs and the language games that render them meaningful are never free of their context; the rules, the games and the communication occur directly through the context of their activation. Freeing himself from an 'algebra' of language, Wittgenstein came to understand that language is never independent of its operational context.

Semiology: Ferdinand de Saussure

The Swiss linguist Ferdinand de Saussure (1859–1913) extends many of the arguments and interests of C.S. Peirce. Saussure's work proceeds from the basic premise that the relationship between symbols (signs) and the things to which they refer (referents) is arbitrary. Saussure's project, therefore, is to elucidate the operations of language, particularly through its relationship with culture. Like Marx, Durkheim and Weber, however, Saussure understands these operations in terms of major, determining forces and formations called structures. Less like the earlier social theorists and more like Wittgenstein and Peirce, however, Saussure sees language as the principal agent in the foundation and formation of these structures. According to Saussure, therefore, society, culture and meaning-making are contingencies of language and language structure. Language is conceived in terms of rational, totalistic and orderly frames which integrate the multitude of complex associations and relationships underscribing human experience. Saussure, again like the early Wittgenstein, offers us a science of language. This science provides universal explanations for the formation and operation of language across all cultures and contexts. Saussure's 'semiology' seeks to elucidate, that is, the principles underlying the formation of any language within its given context. While these contexts vary across culture, the principles which organize human languages do not.

For Saussure, therefore, the operations of language can only be understood in terms of the system of that given language. A system or set of structures will determine the discrete relationships between words and their formation into sentences (syntax). A word has no meaning except through its relationship to other words and hence its deployment within a system of words. In Saussure's terms, 'language has neither ideas nor sounds that exist before the linguistic system, but only conceptual and phonic differences that issue from the system' (1974: 120). A given culture will have a particular need to discriminate between two or more objects or experiences. Consider, for example, the rapid invention of new words in the current computer boom: bytes, webpages, URL, email, digitization, .com. The culture requires new ways of discriminating objects and experiences, so old words may also be reinscribed with new meanings (virus, crash, superhighway). Similarly, the Inuit people of North America (Eskimos) have a vast array of words that describe discrete differences in what the English language categorizes as 'snow' or 'white'. The culture and its needs determine the categories of meaning.

Saussure's interest in discrete differences and the systems within which these differences function informs his scientific account of semiology. Some writers like to distinguish between 'semiology', as the science of signs or language systems, and 'semiotics', as a form of cultural and textual analysis developed at the Birmingham Centre for Contemporary Cultural Studies (see Chapter 4). In either case, the semiotics practised in the English-speaking world has been critically influenced by Saussure and his science of semiology. The difference between the two resides mainly in semiotics' less substantial adhesion to scientific principles, and its greater focus on particular forms of textual representation, most especially in film and television.

Saussure believes that semiology should concern itself with the current-day (synchronic) conditions of language and language use, rather than with its historical development (diachronic approach to structure). Accordingly, analysts may elucidate the structures of language in terms of *langue*, the overall system, and *parole*, the particular operations and selections which determine meaning in a given context. Specifically, Saussure claims that in order to construct meaning (*parole*) a language user will select words, syntactical forms, grammar, and so on, from all the possible operations and categories available within the system of a language (*langue*). Comparing these operations to a game of chess (cf. Wittgenstein's language games) Saussure suggests that the homogeneity of the structure or system is what makes possible the heterogeneity of the individual actions and meaning-makings of the *parole*. The system is what holds the details together.

Recalling Peirce's conception of the sign, Saussure's science attempts to extend a theory of language to all meaning-making or sign systems. Saussure observes that the same principles of operation, discrete differences and similarities, and rules, may be applied to all human communication. To explain this more clearly, he separates the sign into its two constituent parts thus:

SIGN = signifer (material sign)/signified (mental concept of sign)

Saussure argues that the signifier can be sounds, marks on a page, light, colour, images, and so on, but the signifier has no inherent meaning. The mental picture or concept which is produced as a person interacts with the particular signifier is the fount of meaning. However, this interaction between the person and the sign (both the concept and the material signifier) only creates meaning when the sign is understood in relation to its *langue* or system. Like Wittgenstein and Peirce, Saussure insists that the mental concept and the material sign can only produce meaning when the sign is functioning in relation to its system. The red light is the signifier; the concept of stop is the signified; the system of traffic codes is the *langue*.

This means, of course, that a word and its assemblage in syntax must be constantly referred by the user to the *langue* from which the words and rules are drawn. The *langue*, as we have noted, is inevitably bound to the social and cultural context in which the language *parole* (specific utterance) is operating. Similarly, a photograph will have its material dimensions (signifiers), but this assemblage of colour tones, images, shapes and textures is meaningful only in terms of the contexts within which they function. This context will necessarily include the space or place within which the photograph appears: newspaper, art gallery, friend's photo album, the Internet. Both the photograph and the contexts will relate to further contexts in time, space and culture. The *signified* is produced through a complex interaction of these various levels of *parole* and *langue*: specific instance and containing context.

Structural Anthropology: Claude Lévi-Strauss

Beginning with a similar interest in language systems, the French anthropologist Claude Lévi-Strauss adapted Saussure's semiology for the analysis and elucidation of culture. In particular, Lévi-Strauss wanted to describe the unconscious frameworks or formations which bind and define so-called 'primitive' culture. His analysis explores a wide range of cultural practices, including language, rituals, modes of dress, art works, myth and language. As with Saussure, Lévi-Strauss sees these practices as expressive of the essential culture. Perhaps the most resonant and certainly most frequently visited dimension of Lévi-Strauss's work relates to his account of myth. Myth, however, should not be conceived in terms of 'untruth' or an unscientific account of spiritual reality. For Lévi-Strauss, in fact, myth functions like language whereby individual myths must rely on the whole system of myths in order to produce their meaning. The comprehensibility of these myths by members of the culture relies on the distinction and heterogeneity of the individual narrative as it interacts with and draws from the system of myths which govern rules, operations and available interpretations or meaning-making. Like a single word, a single myth has very little meaning. Placed alongside the corpus of a culture's mythologies, the individual myth becomes meaningful.

Lévi-Strauss is particularly interested in the narrative shapings of the human mind and how the world is comprehended through those fundamental structures. Specifically, he believes that all myths share a common structure, one which divides the world into binary oppositions: good/bad, culture/nature, insider/outsider, male/ female, material/spirit. One of the functions of myth, therefore, is to resolve these contradictions in narrative. Thus, while the story establishes fundamental tensions, it also provides the mechanisms for resolution, which, according to Lévi-Strauss, leaves the cultural participant in a kind of satisfied or cathartic condition. The narrative is satisfactorily resolved and the world is rendered comprehensible.

Lévi-Strauss's analysis became particularly popular in contemporary film analysis during the 1970s and into the 1980s. Will Wright's *Sixguns and Society* (1975) applied Lévi-Strauss's analytical methods and principles to reveal the underlying structure of the Hollywood Western. For Wright, the Western is built around oppositional structures such as insider/outsider. Wright argues that, for all the specific variants and institutional forces that inform different Westerns, their fundamental oppositional structures create character and narrative types that are essential to the American consciousness. Thomas Schatz (1981) extends Lévi-Strauss's and Wright's perspectives by arguing that all commercial film-making is fundamentally a process of constructing contemporary myths. Schatz argues that the development of film genres during the twentieth century is a form of 'compulsion repetition' arising from collective responses to mass audience interests and tastes. As with more general semiotic adaptations of Lévi-Strauss's structural anthropology, Schatz's analysis claims that film-making divines the underlying social conditions and mythologies that constitute contemporary culture. Film and other texts are our window to ourselves.

EARLY ROLAND BARTHES AND THE SEMIOLOGICAL MOMENT

Myth and Ideology

Roland Barthes's work is often regarded as the crossover between structuralism and poststructuralism. Certainly, in his discussions of myth and his re-rendering of Saussure and Lévi-Strauss, Barthes seeks to elucidate contemporary French culture in terms of fundamental, mythic structures. His project, however, may be distinguished from those of Saussure and Lévi-Strauss in as much as he is far more concerned with the political dimensions of mythology, and the important problem of its taken-for-grantedness. In particular, Barthes seeks to elucidate the ideological foundations of contemporary myths, arguing that particular narratives are so frequently repeated in culture that they are essentialized or 'naturalized' as absolute and commonsense truth. In *Mythologies* (1973), *The Fashion System* (1990) and *Elements of Semiology* (1967), Barthes maintains an adherence to scientific semiological principles as he describes the complex chain of cultural operations that produce signification.

In a manner that anticipates his later works, Barthes emphasizes the *process* of signification, arguing that meanings continue to accumulate over signs through what he calls 'connotation'. That is, a sign might have its literal, primary or 'denotative' meaning, but through the operations of signification further layers of meaning are attached as connotations of the original. Words are literal, but their operation in context produces meanings that may be psychologically, emotionally or ideologically charged. The word 'black', for example, has a literal meaning, but further meanings are connoted by the word's deployment in specific cultural, social and political contexts. These are what Barthes calls the secondary level of meaning. While these meanings may be unstable over time, at any given moment they will be attached to specific systems of social knowledge and socially constructed truths. When the word 'black' is attached to a person from a particular ethnic, racial and social background, it may be connoted in terms of crime, villification, prejudice or hatred.

For Barthes, these accretions of meaning constitute cultural myths. These myths or 'second-order semiological systems' may also be understood as ideology: those prevailing ideas, narratives and representations which support dominant socio-cultural structures. For Barthes, contemporary cultural myths form a fabric of belief upon which politics are built. A number of critics have pointed out that Barthes doesn't fully distinguish between myth and ideology, claiming that the two concepts seem to be entirely interchangeable. He does, however, point to the polysemic nature of signs: that is, their capacity to carry alternative meanings. Let's consider again the word 'black' and its attachment to a human type. As we have noted, the word may be used in support of a dominant ideology, a set of 'myths' or narratives which identify whiteness as the norm or standard for the developed, advanced world. Whiteness is often attached to the notion of goodness, purity, clarity and enlightenment. Blackness, on the other hand, is often attached to the notion of darkness, salaciousness, poverty, marginalism, and so on. The white culture remains the dominant ideology or paradigm on TV and in contemporary films. Whiteness orders itself in terms of success, legitimacy and beauty.

The mythology of blackness may be understood in terms of the media's frequently repeated stories. News stories very often present blackness in terms of crime, sexuality or physical performance. In many respects, black is associated with a narrative of essential nature. Blackness appears in the sporting pages of the newspapers. In film, blackness is related to street crime, or as the sacrificial partner of a (benevolent) white hero-cop. Blackness is often anti-authority, presented through narratives of bodily excess and a wildness resistant to bourgeois standards of normality. The exceptions to these narrative standards constitute, Barthes would claim, the polysemy of the concept. Popular music has been particularly robust in its challenges to the ideology and mythology surrounding blackness, though in all the media there are opportunities for repositioning the term's cultural connotations. Black people themselves have sought to redeem these connotations, rebuilding their own identity as black. 'Young, gifted and black', 'black power', 'black music', 'black style', 'black liberation' – all phrases designed to challenge the prevailing order.

Barthes claims, and this is a point which Stuart Hall and many others have appropriated in their development of British cultural studies, that this polysemy constitutes a 'struggle' for domination: the struggle to signify, as Hall himself puts it. The 'reading' or 'viewing' of a text by an audience is therefore historical and political. It is the task of the textualist to produce the second-order signification through an effective selection of signs; the reader draws on the same system of cultural and social knowledge in order to construct his or her own meanings from the text. The task of the analyst, however, is to de-naturalize or 'de-doxify', as Barthes puts it, the assumed naturalness of the second-order meanings, most especially as they inscribe dominant ideologies.

THE POSTSTRUCTURALIST CRITIQUE OF STRUCTURALISM

The most commonly noted problem with structuralism is also its strength. That is, structuralism, with its invocation of underlying grammar, structures, ideology and social knowledge, tends toward a social and theoretical universalism. In emphasizing shared social knowledge, structuralism seeks a commonality, a shared objective space which crosses temporal, spatial and even cultural boundaries. Like Marxism and other forms of 'rationally' construed social knowledge, structuralism has sought to explain the world and human actions in terms of major, inclusive and universally applicable conditions. We can summarize structuralism's attempt to resolve this problem in the following terms:

1 Structuralism seeks to explain society and culture in terms of major structures which are common to all societies, cultures and languages. The particular is drawn into, though never extinguished, by the universal.
2 An analysis may thus begin with a particular instance and context: for example, the exclusion of black people from news broadcasting on television in Jackson, Mississippi USA. Structuralism explains this example in relation to overall structures such as:
   (a) dominant cultural myths;
   (b) underlying pattern of ideology: shared values, beliefs, norms, symbols;
   (c) forms of signification which are rooted in power structures in a society; and
   (d) broad linguistic patterns which are common across time, space and culture.

The discrete differences between signs, which Saussure highlights and which constitute the operations of language, are subjugated, therefore, to broader structural categories. These categories are the *langue* or referential language system. According to structuralism, specific socio-cultural instances or contexts (*parole*) are inevitably referred back to the system of social knowledge. The *langue*, the underlying linguistic and social order, will therefore always predominate over the particular instance or *parole*.

It should not surprise us, then, that the scientific methods used to divine this underlying order are themselves constructed around an assumed objectivity and orderliness. Thomas Kuhn (1970) and, later, Jean-François Lyotard (1984a) have argued that the whole of modernist scientific method is implicitly designed to articulate an order that is a predicate of itself: science, scientific methods and scientific principles are formed around orderly processes and are designed to uncover the underlying patterns of natural order. The social sciences conceive of society in a very similar way, applying very similar methods and principles. Structural linguistics, like social and critical structuralism, is built around a social scientific paradigm; the social knowledge it assumes is designed to prove the existence of social and cultural order. While this order may need to be re-formed or reshaped, it nevertheless exists according to fundamental and underlying patterns. The objective of structuralist critique is to expose these patterns and bring to bear a new social order.

Poststructuralism, however, has suggested that this underlying linguistic order, the referential system, is conceived through certain leaps of faith which override the actual functioning of language and discourse. In particular, the stability of the relationship between the *parole* (instance of language use) and the *langue* (system) is achieved only through the parenthesis of history's vast array of details and the local conditions of culture. It is this problem of detail, change and instability which continually challenges the systems that structuralists claim are the foundations of signification and meaning. Poststructuralist theory, in general terms, sees the formations of stable and orderly systems – including the theories and methods of structuralist language analysis – as just another language gesture, just another *parole* or instance of language use. For poststructuralism, language is bound absolutely to its context of use, its moment of utterance, and all efforts to form language into orderly patterns, categories, systems or *langue* merely corrupt the context in which the discourse is operating. Order, that is, is imposed by the structuralist and is not a characteristic of language itself.

This problem has many sides to it. In particular, Saussure and other structuralists like to maintain the stability and unity of the sign, even though they have theoretically divided it into two not entirely connected parts: the signified and the signifier. Saussure suggests that the actual operations of language use incline signifiers toward their particular signifieds or concepts. Language-users need this secure attachment in order to make sense of one another. Poststructuralism, however, has emphasized the gaps and incompleteness in this process, suggesting that the signifier and signified are as arbitrary in their relationship as the sign and the thing to which it refers. The sign is not a unity of two fused parts, two sides of the one coin; rather, poststructuralism suggests that signifiers and signifieds are two operational layers which momentarily touch in an almost accidental intersection of highly unstable and temporary meaning. The emphasis, thus, is on the *problem* of meaning and not its systematic certainty.

While this problem is clearly evident in the translation of one language into another, since there is often no equivalence in grammar and vocabulary, it is also a problem within the one language 'system'. The dictionary, for example, is generally regarded as the ultimate referent, the principal means by which a signified (word) is fixed to its signifier or meaning. However, when we look in the dictionary we will often find a number of definitions for the same word. Each of these definitions is of course a signifier in its own right and impels the reader toward further signifiers and signifieds in order to locate meaning. Thus, the word 'stable' will be defined as: something persistent; unchanging; not unstable; secure; a place to house horses or other livestock; and so on. Each of these words will also be defined in the dictionary and in pursuit of meaning we can look them up only to find more words that need to be looked up – the trail is endless. Meaning is processed through a matrix of complex relationships which clearly challenge the unity of the signifier/signified. The operationalization of the signifier is possible, not in spite of these deferrals, but as a result of them. By placing the signifier into a language context, language-users problematize meaning in their attempts to create it. Meaning is never assured; it is merely sought as it is deferred.

This problematization of meaning is also profoundly related to the issues of ideology. Those areas of structuralism which contend a necessary relationship between language systems and ideology assume a certain stability in the sign and in the struggle to signify. While Hall and others in the Birmingham tradition acknowledge a degree of uncertainty in these struggles, their polemic relies on structural divisions by which power is fixed within particular social groups. Gramsci's negotiated hegemony and Barthes's notion of variant interpretations or polysemy are concepts that Anglophone cultural structuralists developed and deployed as a way of evading Marx's more totalistic explanations of power and ideology. Even so, the British cultural studies lineage, with its particular interest in class, power divisions and language structure, retained an interest in ideology as the political manifestation of language war (Lewis, 2005). And indeed, for those cultural theorists who remain interested in a reformist politics, the structuralist concept of ideology has proved extremely difficult to surrender (see Hall, 1991a, 1991b; Kellner, 1995, 2005). The significant problem for structuralist cultural politics, however, is that polysemy doesn't begin and end with its own frame of interest. Ideology begins to fracture under the stress of multiple audiences and multiple interpretations; the instabilities of meaning run entirely through a reformist politics and its aspiration for a logics of change.

Structuralist and Poststructuralist Approaches to Culture

Structuralist and semiological language theory was adopted into the Birmingham Centre for Contemporary Cultural Studies during the 1960s and 1970s (see Chapter 4). The influence of writers like Saussure, Lévi-Strauss and Althusser has been enormous, most especially as cultural studies has expanded its interests from an analysis of

Table 5.1   *Structuralism and Poststructuralism*

Structuralist cultural studies	Poststructuralist cultural studies
Language systems	Language as diffuse
Signifer/signified	Slippery signifer, language wars
Way of life	Meaning-making
Class structures	Cultural communities
Ideology/hegemony	Everything as representation
Institutional and fixed power	Power as personal relationships
Structural resistance	Power at the level of the body
Democratic socialism	Democratic multiculturalism
Media institutions	Media-making

class-based culture to the broader fields of ideology, popular media and representation. The penetration of poststructuralism, however, has been far more diffuse, though no less significant. Table 5.1 highlights some of the major differences in emphasis between a structuralist and poststructuralist style of cultural analysis. It is important to note that these differences are not entirely chronological, and that specific zones of contemporary cultural studies may prefer one style of analysis over another.

Stuart Hall and numerous others working in contemporary cultural politics continue to struggle with this problem. Hall (1991a) identifies culture as the radiation of media and its discourses within a broad global postmodernism. As he moves away from class and other levels of cultural localism, Hall conceives of a cultural whole in which power and structure arc unevenly experienced and distributed. In order to critique the condition of contemporary culture, then, Hall must match these macro formations with macro challenges. Hegemony or negotiated leadership remains valid because it conceives of meaning-making in structural terms. Poststructuralism and the theoretical wing of postmodernism, however, challenge the Gramscian approach by limiting the scope and relevance of structure. Power and ideology, therefore, are conceived in vastly different terms, terms which for many working in the field constitute a reactionary politics and a capitulation to those powers which exert disproportionate influence within the culture.

THE LATER BARTHES

Barthes' earlier works are characterized by a certain ambivalence toward signification and meaning-making. While subscribing generally to the Saussurian paradigm which analyzes systematically the structures and stability of language, Barthes was also interested in the processes of signification and the possibilities of polysemy or multiple interpretations of words. In *Elements of Semiology* (1967) the same glimpses of a poststructuralist awareness emerge from some otherwise standard structuralist precepts. In particular, while claiming that semiology could explain all the operations of language, Barthes comes to recognize that his own semiological discourse functions as a 'second-order' language which could be seen to substitute for the 'first-order' textual discourses under study. Thus, his analysis of Baudelaire, which produces a new 'version' of the original text, could be seen as a form of metalanguage; this new (secondary) text might now be placed in the position of Baudelaire's text, making it available for further analysis. Barthes recognizes that his own interpretive discourse had become a substitute for the original text and that this 'second-order' text might itself now be interpreted or analyzed, setting forth an ongoing trail of replacement discourses. Thus, there emerges a whole series of metalanguages which inevitably replace the original Baudelaire text. All texts are equally fictional, therefore, and should not be read in terms of absolute truth or origin.

This realization marks a major departure from semiological scientism; it establishes a level of interest which is to blossom in Barthes's later writings. In his collected essays *Image–Music–Text* (1977), for example, Barthes announces quite clearly that the notion of authorial authority can no longer be assumed. In essays such as 'The photographic message', 'Writers and readers' and 'The death of the author', Barthes problematizes the relationship between the author, the text and the reader, noting in particular that a text should be understood as a 'multi-dimensional space in which a variety of writings, none of them original, blend and clash. The text is a tissue of quotations drawn from the innumerable centres of culture' (1977: 146). The semiological assumptions about stability and secure meaning-making are thereby surrendered as Barthes seeks more acute insights into the uncertainties of reader meaning-making and what he subsequently calls the pleasure of the text. The author's role in text construction is parenthesized, not simply in a gesture of isolating the text from intentional design, but as a more complete acknowledgement of the active engagement of audiences with the polysemic multidimensionality of discourse.

In *The Pleasure of the Text* (1975) Barthes seeks some further clarification of the reader's power to pursue his or her own capricious delights. Barthes notes that, in an engagement with the text, a reader is free to abandon the directives of the signifier in favour of his or her own cognitive and sensual responses. In other words, the polysemy or multiple interpretation which is available for a reader's cognitive engagement is also available for sensual or bodily response. Different readers will respond differently to the meanings and sensual pleasures that are generated from the signified. In many respects, Barthes is seeking an explanation for textual engagement and meaning-making that moves beyond his earlier interest in myth and binary resolutions. Even so, the notion of pleasure is founded upon two distinct dimensions of response: 'pleasure' and a more concentrated, more intense experience which he calls 'bliss' (*jouissance*). It is at the level of bliss that Barthes again approximates a poststructural positioning, if only because 'bliss' is characterized by an unstable, contradictory intensity which comes to defy the stable and secure conditions of language (mere pleasure).

Mere pleasure is typical of a 'join' or contact between two surfaces: garment on bare skin, or the reading act and the text. In the reading act, pleasure is likely to be engaged as the reader remains fixed and aware of the action of reading. If the reader skips pages, or reads particular realist discourses, the pleasure arises out of the contact or join that is facilitated in the act of signifier and signified. However, when the reader is engaged beyond awareness, then s/he is approaching the condition of bliss. These moments of complete aesthetic immersion render the reader oblivious to all external conditions and to the reading act itself. There arises now the possibility of an intensity of experiences which may 'transcend' the join – transcend language itself – since the reader is now thoroughly engaged in his or her own bliss. Now the reader risks the collapse of cultural assumptions. Meaning is precarious; politics are precarious; culture and language are precarious. If the reader resists this ecstatic condition, however, the intensity might collapse into boredom.

Barthes's pleasure of the text, therefore, is an account of some more sublime, post- or pre-linguistic condition. His theories have proved particularly well suited to Anglophone analysts who have been interested in the processes of textual reading and more particularly the pleasure-giving dimensions of textual consumption. That is, Barthes's later interest in pleasure has provided a theoretical framework for those cultural theorists, like John Fiske, Henry Jenkins and Richard Dyer, who have sought to celebrate in varying ways the significance of popular culture for the lives, pleasures and cultures of everyday consumers of the popular media. This style of cultural analysis, with its emphasis on multiple meanings and individuated pleasure, provides a significant theoretical bridge not only to poststructuralism, but also to the expanding territory of postmodern cultural studies.

Undoubtedly, Barthes's work moves toward the edges of a poststructuralist theoretic, yet his account of 'bliss' also carries an unmistakably Romantic resonance with it. In particular, there is a certain level of essentialism in his account of textual bliss, a sense in which the pre- or post-linguistic condition of bliss is analogous to the 'finer tone' referred to in John Keats' letters and poetry. This finer tone, Keats explains, is a kind of ecstasy where the sublime aesthetic washes over the poet in an ephemeral but unmistakable fusion of opposite intensities. Moreover, Barthes's turn toward Japanese art and culture in his later writings is reminiscent of the Romantic poets' interest in an Orient which transcends the lineality of decay and the oppositionalism that underpins European culture.

The Difference between poststructuralism and postmodernism

For many cultural commentators there is very little difference between post-structuralism and postmodernism. Both emphasize cultural diversity, the individual emancipation, the impossibility of an absolute truth, the unstable nature of history and a politics which is broad and inclusive and not restricted to issues of class or social order.

(Cont'd)

Both, in fact, are critical of notions of structure. Both tend to be interested in the popular media, globalism and new expressive forms and identities.

However, there are significant differences in the heritage and history of the two terms. Poststructuralism tends to rise through certain areas of French language theory. Its principal exponents are later Roland Barthes, Jacques Derrida, Jacques Lacan, Julia Kristeva, Michel Foucault, and Gilles Deleuze and Félix Guattari. For all their significant differences, these writers represent a radical break from the philosophical tradition which treated reality as a distinct, epistemological fact. Poststructuralism challenges us to think about the world in terms of language and mediation, the problematic of meaning and non-meaning, and the rupture of taken-for-granted and universal Truth. Poststructuralist writing is often difficult because it accepts the improbable nature of any logical order and claims to knowledge – including its own.

Postmodernism has two distinct sources. One of them is philosophical and derives from poststructuralism. The theoretical bridge between poststructuralism and postmodernism has been provided by Jean-François Lyotard, Jean Baudrillard and the American Marxist literary critic Fredric Jameson. The other source of postmodern theoretics comes through American aesthetics, where the term was conceived in order to describe a particular style of art and literature.

Postmodernism can sometimes be used to describe the historical phase that follows modernity (some time in the last thirty or so years). It has also become a popular way of describing the cultural 'condition' or ways of thinking that currently predominate. Theoretically, it is a very loose collection of ideas which has traces of poststructuralism, utopianism and celebratory popular culture.

DECONSTRUCTION: JACQUES DERRIDA

Subject and Language

While Roland Barthes drifts unevenly between a structuralist and poststructuralist perspective, Jacques Derrida is unrelenting in his pursuit of the gaps and irregularities of language and meaning-making. From his earliest investigations of Husserl's phenomenology, Derrida has been suspicious of the project of structuralism and the idea that a fundamental 'grammar' underpins culture, language and the human mind. In particular, he challenges the notion of a sub-stratum or 'essence' which grounds, as it makes possible, a re-rendering of consciousness through highly abstracted theoretical or empirical methodologies. In his early discussions on discourse and structuralism in the human sciences (see 1970), Derrida argues that the human sciences, like the natural sciences, are engaged in an enterprise which would force the fluidity and imprecise nature of language into structures which effectively legitimate themselves as absolute and unassailable truths. These truths or true findings, Derrida maintains, are merely transgressions, denials of the natural operations of language. That is, language, according to Derrida, is not of itself constructed out of truths, essences or ultimate reference points – there is no origin that lies behind language. Rather, language is a restless and ever-moving mass of imprecise details, constantly seeking, but never quite achieving, some approximation of meaning.

Derrida refers to this meaning as a kind of 'presence': that is, he claims, people seek some confirmation of knowledge of themselves and their capacity to make sense of who they are in relation to others. Their *presence* in the world is substantiated, therefore, by the exchange of absolute meanings. We need to note here that Derrida is moving far beyond the epistemological problem of the subject–object split (see Chapter 2), which preoccupied philosophy and social science during the eighteenth and nineteenth centuries. The problem of language and the self (the subject in the lifeworld) overthrows epistemology as the major concern of philosophy and cultural theory during the twentieth century. The notion of a unified subject – that is, the unity of the 'me' or 'I' of the world – is generally assumed in pre-Freudian descriptions of the self. Western culture has produced a substantial vocabulary which describes this condition of fixity: origin, essence, consciousness, structure, centre, being, substance, truth.

Psychoanalytic theory, especially the adaptation of Freud by Jacques Lacan and Julia Kristeva, opens the way for theorizing the subject as 'unfixed'. Psychoanalysis also theorizes a more precarious and indeterminate relationship between subjects and the language that connects them. That is, the subject no longer exists as an absolute condition, a deeply rooted and basically unchangeable entity; the subject is dynamic, mutable, open and formed through various relationships and experiences, all constituted in language. Derrida, therefore, is highly dubious about the possibility that a subject 'originates' in some essential form. Rather, the subject exists as a contingency of language. The question of origin, therefore, is placed under erasure, as Derrida explains it.

This process is rather tricky. The concept of 'origin' continues to be claimed in language, but because language itself has no origin, 'origin' cannot be replaced or substituted. That is, Derrida's methods prevent him from critically obliterating the concept of 'origin' since that would require some substitution in language. Derrida's methods of analysis, therefore, do not seek to replace origins or centres but merely highlight the problems associated with false foundationalism. This is true not only for the concept of 'origin' but for any concept, any word. If he were to substitute the origin of the concept of 'origin' or any other word with another possibility, then he would be risking the re-establishment of a different origin for the one he has dismissed. Therefore, Derrida's analysis merely exposes the principles and processes which inform specific instances of language use without offering alternatives.

Derrida's strategy of critique, therefore, is quite deliberately focused. He wants to remove the notion of essence, centre, presence or origin from all language acts. Language exists as a particulate and incomplete gesture which operates within a particular context and perpetually seeks, though never actually fixes on, meaning. Derrida cannot substitute this dynamism with a fixed meaning alternative. He doesn't claim that we can think outside or beyond a particular concept, for to do so would entrap us in the (false) gesture of origination. It is not what a concept can 'really' tell us, or what it really means, but rather what is missing (or absent) in the concept itself. For example, if we were to critique the concept of 'knowledge' as it was being used in a particular instance – by someone with whom we violently disagree, for example – we may wish to substitute this person's claim about knowledge with an accusation of 'ignorance'. In other words, we would seek to substitute the centre/presence of the concept 'knowledge' with the alternative concept 'ignorance'. Derrida, however, warns us against this sort of critical approach, which, he argues, merely transgresses the basic principles of language. Because language has no centre or origin and because our subjectivity is open and unfixed, our claim to truth is false, our substitution is misguided. All we can do, in fact, is *expose* the binary nature of this claim to meaning and truth (knowledge/ ignorance) without preferring one over the other – without, that is, restoring a centre to the status of fixed and absolute language presence. This method of 'deconstruction' is fundamental to our understanding of what Derrida calls 'writing'.

Deconstruction

Derrida's methods are established in his two early works *Of Grammatology* (1974) and *Writing and Difference* (1979). Essentially, his interest in language emerges through an initial analysis of the phenomenology of Edmund Husserl and the processes by which the Western philosophical tradition constitutes itself as paradigm knowledge. The methodology associated with Derrida's key concept 'deconstruction' has been adapted in a variety of ways by recent cultural analysis. Derrida himself uses the technique to illuminate the processes by which philosophy legitimates itself in language, most especially the language of writing. His method is similar to Barthes's 'de-doxification' in that it seeks to demonstrate how particular writing positions are constructed in meaning, even though those meanings must constantly elude definition. That is, Derrida explains throughout his work that philosophy has legitimated itself by its own constant self-reflexivity, one philosopher referring to his/her precedent. The meanings of the text are thereby constructed around these intertextual references.

Unlike the political intent of de-doxification, however, the primary task of decon-struction is to expose the principles and processes which construct language and history, especially as it is articulated in Western philosophy. To this end, Derrida accepts the general notion that European thought and language have been built around systems of opposition (good/bad, life/death, present/absent). These binary poles insist for their resolution on the domination of one over the other, a 'presence' which is facilitated by its opposite's 'absence'. Conventional 'critical' methods merely engage in shifts within the system, allowing for the predominance of one pole over another. As in the above example of knowledge/ ignorance, this selection of one pole over the other merely shifts the centre and origin of the binary oppositions. We remain trapped within the system. Deconstruction, however, seeks to elucidate and therefore override the binary oppositions through a questioning of their legitimacy and a recognition that they are merely formations in language (writing especially). Deconstruction attacks the centre and the system not by attempting to replace it (for that would be yet another origin), but by elucidating it and its infinite deferrals of meaning – by removing the grounds upon which it is built.

Writing

Derrida, in fact, contrasts this oppositionalism in language with non-Western linguistic possibilities. He uses the notion of 'logocentricism' (*logos* = word) to illustrate how Western philosophy is structured through systems of opposition and logical inference. Thus, proposition A may be contrasted to proposition B but the inference of this *logos* is proposition C. It works like this:

> Men grow beards. Women do not. I have a beard, therefore, I am probably a man.

This form of philosophical processing is built into the very foundations of our language. While this point was well established in the writings of Russell, Wittgenstein and Saussure, Derrida seeks a complete rupture of its value and values, a radical overthrow of the *logos* that is mobilized through a system of meaning-making. *Logos*, as Derrida reminds us, is the full attachment of logics with the origin of 'the word'. It is this word, most especially the spoken word ('phonocentrism'), which presents itself as the 'non-originary origin', that seeming absolute presence which is articulated in the Bible as the first of human presence: 'In the beginning was the Word'. Thus, 'the spoken word' presents itself as the centre and beginning point of our European culture; the word is the foundation upon which our civilization is constructed.

In *Of Grammatology* (1974) Derrida claims that, rather than the spoken word, it is writing which constitutes the articulation of the system of the sign. Writing (*écriture*), which forms itself in and around the presence of an imagined origin, substitutes for the possibilities of language. *Écriture* is able

> to designate not only the physical gestures of literal pictographic or ideographic inscription, but also the totality of what makes it possible and also, beyond the signifying face, the signified face itself. And thus we say 'writing' for all that gives rise to an inscription in general. … The entire field covered by the cybernetic *program* will be the field of writing. (Derrida, 1974: 9)

Language and writing, however, are never fully able to establish this origin and presence, since they are always in a state of deferral: every word and every text can only be understood in terms of other words and other texts. Moreover, the meanings of words can never avert fundamental gaps, fissures and slippages which are always engaged through the processes of communication. To illustrate this point, Derrida invokes the concept of 'difference', which was so important in the structuralist account of language systems. Difference, for Derrida, cannot be simply equated with the discrete discriminations which fix a word to particular categories of meaning. That is, Saussure sought to understand the differences between words in terms of the system of differences which constitute a language: the difference in meaning which is constituted between the signifiers dog and cat, or dachshund and poodle, are provided by the system of signifiers.

Derrida, however, is interested in the differences between and within words which frustrate the formation of meaning and which disable the movement toward systematic categorization of things. He explains that difference can operate to confuse meanings and produce ambiguities; these ambiguities constantly propel language into receding dispersals of meaning. As is common with Derrida, he illustrates this problem through the concept under scrutiny. In French the pronunciation of the word difference could itself be written with an 'e', as it is, or with an 'a' to form '*différance*' – a word that doesn't actually exist in the dictionary. In either case, the word would sound the same when spoken; only in writing would a difference be discernible. Derrida goes on to suggest that this dualism is contained further in the word's meanings, where the verb *différer* means both 'to differ' and 'to defer'. Derrida combines these literal meanings in order to construct the problematic of writing and 'difference'. To differ, Derrida explains, is a spatial concept by which a system places some semantic or categorial distance between one word and the next. To defer, however, is a temporal concept whereby the signifying system is in a state of perpetual delay of its meanings. In writing, these deferrals are constantly exposed, whereas in speaking they are disguised within the general claim of presence. *Différance* is hidden, that is, because the spoken word seems to be constantly present in the presence of the speaker and the speaking. *Écriture* displays the signifiers in their raw, agitated and ever-referential (intertextual, deferred) condition.

Derrida suggests in *Writing and Difference* and *Of Grammatology* that writing has been generally regarded as an impure version of speech language. This 'violent hierarchy' constitutes a coupling of superior and inferior conditions or cases where speech is preferred to writing. Thus, in Derrida's reading of Rousseau, he sees Rousseau's privileging of (natural) speech over (dangerous) writing as a form of supplementarity. Rousseau sees writing as a supplement to speech, something which adds an inessential quality to the primary condition:

> Rousseau considers writing as a dangerous medium, a menacing aid, a critical response to a situation of distress. When Nature, as self-proximity, comes to be forbidden or interrupted, when speech fails to protect presence, writing becomes necessary. It must be *added* to the world urgently. ... Writing becomes dangerous from the moment that representation claims to be presence and the sign of the thing. (Derrida, 1979: 144)

In French the word *suppléer* means both to supplement and to substitute. Derrida seeks to reverse the writing–speech hierarchy by identifying common characteristics and by arguing that privileging of any kind implicates the processes of supplement (and substitution). As with the interdependence of self and other as outlined in psychoanalytic theory, conceptual couplets like speech/writing, presence/absence, nature/civilization, necessarily engage each pole in the supplement and substitution of the alternative. In Derridean terms they are already always present in the other. Speech, therefore, is already always written, nature is already always present in civilization, and so on. Deconstruction takes place as the text dissolves the hierarchical structures which privilege one position or concept over another, when the supplementarity, that is, is lain to rest.

Derrida and Cultural Studies

It must be said, however, that deconstruction is simply the strategy of exposing these processes. Derrida's deconstruction is no longer analogous to Barthes's 'deconstruction' in that it cannot and will not offer an alternative. Since no alternative is possible, Derrida's work has limited political interests, most especially when compared with either Barthes or Michel Foucault. In fact, Derrida's position in cultural studies is politically ambiguous. Many critics have condemned his resistance to direct political and contemporary cultural engagement (see Dews, 1984; Poster, 1989), arguing that the elliptical nature of his analysis produces a witty but redundant form of rhetorical sophistry. This sophistry, because of its resistance to real-world problems, contributes to the formation of a distracting and reactionary political field. Other cultural critics, however, have seen enormous potential in deconstruction for the location and exposure of the ideology which functions through language, most especially through forms of textual representation. In particular, cultural politics has used a 'deconstruction' method to illuminate the normative values that inform representations of gender, race, ethnicity and sexual orientation. This adaptation of the concept is well removed from Derrida's original deployment and in many respects is a hybrid of conventional critique, though with an added assumption about the inadequacies of pure structuralism.

This transformation of Derrida's ideas and methods for the analysis of popular culture is sometimes attached to notions of postmodernism. A good many of the discourses which celebrate postmodernism deploy various versions of Derrida's key concepts: deconstruction, difference and logocentrism. Most particularly, this form of postmodernism uses these concepts to position itself against the prevailing standards of modernism: postmodern analysis deconstructs the high arts, scientism, hierarchical homogeneity and logocentricism of modernism. However, these adaptations are not strictly within the field of Derrida's analysis. Christopher Norris (1987, 1990) has suggested, in fact, that Derrida's work sits comfortably within the heritage of Western philosophy as it employs standard practices of reason, critique and rhetoric. Norris contrasts Derrida's work with the openness and illogicality of postmodernism. Don Thade (1991) goes further, suggesting that Derrida's recent work on the white spaces and margins of a page of writing is largely encompassed within the frame of contemporary hermeneutical (interpretive) phenomenology. Thade places Derrida beside interpretive phenomenologists like Paul Ricoeur, who shares an interest in the problematic of non-meaning and meaning. This positioning of Derrida, once again, returns his radical conceit, his deconstruction, to the more general and conservative realm of the philosophical tradition he seeks to overthrow.

These ambiguities in Derrida's critical reception are puzzling in some respects, but understandable in others. Derrida's reluctance to deal directly with real-world issues and culture – especially prior to 1990 – created an elusiveness about his work which fundamentally confirmed the precepts of his analysis. Language is an imperfect conduit or mediation that both binds and separates human subjects. Not surprisingly, the deconstruction method has been as popular with conservative critics as it has been with more reformatory interests. Derrida's great insight is that language processes and structures can be readily reversed. While Derrida advocates against using this reversal to re-originate or re-privilege particular perspectives, the temptation to do so seems irresistible to many critics. Indeed, even in producing this reversal, many critics have been subtly able to instate the conditions of the binary structure in order to serve the interests of conservatism: again this is understandable for an analytical strategy which insists we should elucidate, but not alter, the course of things.

Thus, the conservative American literary critic Paul de Man has adapted this solipsistic spirit for the deconstruction of the underlying principles of fictional prose and poetry. Equally, however, deconstruction has been adapted for radical postcolonial, queer and feminist cultural analysis. It was, perhaps, Derrida's reluctance to engage directly in cultural politics which contributed to a decline in his popularity in France, even as interest in his work continued to rise in the US and other parts of the Anglophonic world. In either case, Derrida appears to have responded to these exhortations during the 1990s and 2000s when his writing began to focus more directly on political and social issues. In texts like *Politics and Friendship* (1997) and *Specters of Mark* (1994) Derrida engages in a moral and political analysis of contemporary culture, though with his familiar flair and complex irony.

MICHEL FOUCAULT

Foucault's Poststructuralist Writing

Perhaps the most often cited and accessible of the French poststructuralists is Michel Foucault. Foucault's work is far less consistent than the writings of Derrida, and many critics have questioned the efficacy and exact character of his contribution to cultural studies and cultural history. In particular, a number of critics have suggested that his work is riddled with contradictions and ambivalence, suggesting variously that it might be characterized as existentialist, structuralist, poststructuralist, radical, reactionary, anarchic, feminist, anti-feminist and even Islamicist (see Hoy, 1986a, 1988; Arac, 1988; Rabinow, 1991; Hekman, 1996; Afary et al., 2005). In fact, Foucault's work is an exhilarating exploration of the possibilities of language, culture and power. This exploration seems necessarily to impel Foucault into forms of self-conflict and toward the limits of his own conceptualizations. Both within particular texts and across his career, his work is clearly pushing the boundaries of what might be said about human meaning-making within a context of complex associations of power and historical rupture. Indeed, while Derrida's great strength is the playful but unremitting consistency of his argument, Foucault's work is more agitated and dissatisfied, seeking to create the conditions of political, as well as intellectual, liberation.

Yet, as has been discovered by Barthes and numerous others espousing an emancipatory cultural politics, liberation is difficult to realize through an analysis of the abstruse and complicated processes of meaning-making and language formation. Against the primacy of economy, social structure and material conditions, Foucault came to argue that power was formed through 'discourse' (or language) as it operated in human relationships and experienced at the level of the an individual's own body. Liberation, Foucault contends in the poststructuralist phase of his work, is not a revolutionary Marxist enterprise, nor is it a matter of structuralist realignments of language systems. Rather, he insists, liberation is a process of identification – of exposing the social and cultural–historical assumptions which seek to fix and rigidify the relationship between discourse and power. The liberation of the self is conceivable only in terms of the unfixing of those assumptions and the release of the body from the historical inscriptions which construct identity in discourse. In other words, Foucault seeks to free the individual self from totalizing discourses which falsify power and the subject. These totalizing discourses may be instituted through the state and its apparatuses of surveillance and discipline; they may also be produced by the pseudo-liberationism of Marxism, which fixes the self (the individual) in structures of class and revolution.

Foucault wanted to free the individual/subject from the constraints of other people's and institutions' discourses. To this extent, he claims that his books are 'bombs for others to throw', and 'tools for the revolutionary demonstration of the established apparatus' (see Foucault, 1977a: 113–38). In his poststructuralist phase, that is, Foucault wanted to be sure that his liberational enterprise would not slide away into some other form of discursive hegemony where the intellectual would 'speak for others', leading them into the artifice of someone else's freedom. He criticizes Marx and others for falsely investing their own liberation in the conceptions of class warfare. The proletariat would not save the world; this was the duty of individuals, including individuals in the middle classes.

Foucault did not wish to be accused of fixing other people's liberation within the walls of his own discourse:

> What, do you think I would take so much trouble and so much pleasure in writing, do you think that I would keep so persistently to my task, if I were not preparing – with a rather sticky hand – a labyrinth in which I can venture, in which I can move my discourse, opening up underground passages, forcing it to go far from itself, finding overhangs that reduce and deform its itinerary, in which I can lose myself, and appear at last to eyes that I will never have to meet again. I am no doubt not the only one who writes in order to have no face. Do not ask who I am and do not ask me to remain the same. Leave it to our bureaucrats and our police to see that our papers are in order. (Foucault, 1972: 17)

Taken from his mid-career text *The Archaeology of Knowledge*, these comments indicate clearly that Foucault's thinking is diverging decidedly from a view of the author and the intellectual – indeed the self generally – as a fixed and immovable presence in the construction of text and discourse. As with Barthes's rejection of authorial authority, Lacan's unfixing of the self and Derrida's denial of origin, Foucault is requesting that any subject should be allowed to shift ground and become something other than what he or she is at any given moment of the present.

In fact, we can identify three distinct phases in Foucault's writing career, and *The Archaeology of Knowledge* marks a shift away from an earlier historicism which was grounded in existential variations of Marxist teleology (theory of ultimate causes). This, the second phase of Foucault's writing career, incorporates the following texts: *The Archaeology of Knowledge* (1972), *The Order of Things* (1974), *Discipline and Punish* (1977a) and *The History of Sexuality, Volume One* (1981). This poststructuralist phase of his career is characterized by the following:

1. Foucault rejects Marxist materialism. The disturbances that took place on the streets of Paris during the 1968 student agitations left many left-leaning intellectuals disappointed and disillusioned. Foucault, along with other French poststructuralists, was already developing doubts about the structuralist approach to power and ideology, but the disturbances seem to have galvanized these thoughts into a clear rejection of Marxist precepts. In particular, Foucault rejects the Marxist explanation of history and the investment of revolutionary authority in structural revolution.
2. Foucault rejects notions of a unified subject, preferring instead a notion of the subject as an open and mutable site for the construction and exchange of discourse.
3. Foucault rejects biological or social determinist theories. In particular, he argues against the idea that the body is an outcome of biological imperatives. Rather, biology serves the interests of discourse, culture and history.
4. Foucault develops the notion of archaeology, then genealogy, to explain the operations of history. History is replete with imprecise and capricious details: elements, characters and issues which discontinue as often as they continue. This is not to say that Foucault does not uncover patterns and links in history; rather, like E.P. Thompson, he insists

that history is not about the movement of large structures and significant historical events. It's about people and their relationships within a broad context of power and knowledge.

5   Power and knowledge are not embedded in social structure. Power is a process, a matter of exchange. Where there is power there is challenge. Power is unstable, processual and forever switching direction. People and structures do not possess power, they merely transmit it. Power is always experienced at the level of the individual subject's body, the local level, the level of 'microphysics'.

The Problem of Power

In fact, for Foucault's poststructuralism, power, knowledge and discourse are the central contingencies of history. Foucault's basic method is to examine an historical period which for him constitutes the building blocks of cultural modernism. That is, he examines particular phenomena (hospitals, mental institutions, prisons, sexual technologies) of the eighteenth and nineteenth centuries, using his historiography to shed a broader light on modern culture. He follows Nietzsche's strategy of compounding concepts which are so thoroughly embedded in one another as to make them entirely interdependent. Power/knowledge and discourse/power are mutually reflexive; culture is fundamentally constituted around these key compounds. At one point Foucault claims that everything is discourse and power is everywhere. According to Foucault, then, nothing in culture exists that is not mediated in some way by the meaning-making of discourse (language, images, etc.) and its corollary of power. This is not the same as Althusser's claim about the ubiquity of ideology, which is a mechanism of social control and domination (see Chapter 3). Foucault, rather, is suggesting that power exists at the level of everyday practice and everyday exchanges between subjects. Power is personal, immediate and unavoidable.

> [I]t is in discourse that power and knowledge are joined together. And for this very reason we must conceive of discourse as a series of discontinuous segments whose tactical function is neither uniform nor stable. To be more precise, we must not conceive of a world divided between accepted discourse and excluded discourse, or between the dominant discourse and the dominated one; but as a multiplicity of discursive elements that can come into play in various strategies. It is this distribution that we must reconstruct, with the things said and those concealed, the enunciations required and those forbidden, that it comprises; with the variants and different effects – according to who is speaking, his position of power, the institutional context in which he happens to be situated – that it implies; and with the shifts and revitalization of identical formulas for identical objectives that it also uses. (Foucault, 1981: 100)

Thus, in his analyses of sexuality (1981), prisons (1977a) and the social sciences (1974), Foucault demonstrates that power is never separable from the instance of its expression. Power and knowledge are inevitably identifiable with one another since each is productive of the other. It is not simply that knowledge produces power and works its way out from the centre as a universalizing and hegemonic exigency, but rather that power/knowledge exists at all points of the particular.

Foucault and the power of the particular

Foucault refers to the immediate and particular levels of power as its microphysics. He illustrates the operations of the microphysics of power in the historical development of prisons and modern sexuality. However, he is strangely reluctant to apply these precepts for an analysis of contemporary culture. Even so, we can observe the operations of the microphysics through an infinite range of personal interactions and experiences: for example, in the ways in which the medium of TV is consumed. A *macrophysics* would emphasize the power of institutions to produce and distribute messages. A *microphysics* would be interested in the ways audience members interact with one another, with the medium and with TV texts. A range of complex interactions may take place over the selection of a TV programme. These negotiations may mobilize institutional power (justice, income, paternity), emotional power (tantrums, sulking, imploring) or sexual power (favours for favours, seduction). In an analysis of these relationships and discourses, power is treated as unstable and exchangeable. Thus, a victory in the negotiations over the TV programme may be 'hollow' and may result in various forms of loss: the victor may be treated by other members of the family as selfish, unreasonable or conniving. The victor, therefore, may ultimately surrender important dimensions of power in other contexts and conditions (e.g., seeking approval or affection). Power exists only in discourse and can therefore never be fixed in structures; power operates always at the level of the individual body.

The Problem of Truth and Theory

Foucault attempts to go beyond the Enlightenment dialectic (power/powerlessness), leading him, as it leads Derrida and others, away from the very centralizing postulates of rational theory itself. It is on this point that liberational theorists like Edward Said and Stuart Hall have distanced themselves from Foucault's argument, arguing that Foucault never fully realizes the liberational potential of his claims. However, just as Gilles Deleuze insists that theory be 'partial and fragmentary ... functional, disposable and unrenewable' (1977: 205), Foucault insists that authorial reason (logocentricism) should function to undermine its own discursive and self-validating power. Like Derrida, Foucault wants to resist the temptation to re-centre the language of argument or critique: he wants to leave theory to destabilize itself. If it were not to do so, then it would simply reproduce the sort of grand and encompassing claims that so severely impede Marxist writings.

In fact, as Foucault reminds us throughout this phase of his career, power can only be produced as a localized 'microphysics' (Foucault, 1977a), an outcome which produces and is produced by its own impulses away from the centre. Thus, 'truth', like 'power', can only ever be partial and incomplete, existing in the matter of human action and beyond the isolating closures of theory:

> [I]f it exists at all … truth is a thing of the world. It is produced only by virtue of multiple forms of constraint. And it produces regular effects of power. Each society has its own regime of truth, its own 'politics' of truth: that is, the type of discourse it accepts and makes function as true. (Foucault, 1980: 131)

Foucault's 'archaeological' method is designed to uncover historical discontinuities as much as continuities: that is, his history is one which is as interested in the particulates and details of history as much as those things which progress toward subsequent events and subjectivities. While some critics have been confused by this notion, essentially Foucault is trying to distinguish his own exposition of localized truths from the Marxist historiography which constantly seeks grand explanations of structures, causes and outcomes. In particular, his key texts *Discipline and Punish* (1977a) and *The History of Sexuality, Volume One* (1981) demonstrate the effectiveness of this strategy.

Discipline and Punish

Discipline and Punish maps the experiences of prisoners during the modern period, and, in particular, how these experiences are formed through their representation in discourse. Foucault attempts to maintain a liberationary intent in his account of the 'body' as it is inscribed by power relationships. Thus, his description of the change from torture to imprisonment in the eighteenth century interrogates the basic assumptions and 'discourses' of Marxism and liberal humanism. Marxism sees the change as an exercise in the division of labour: the capitalist classes seeking new ways of controlling the proletariat and exploiting their labour. Liberal humanism, especially as it is articulated in the utilitarian philosophies of Jeremy Bentham, conceives of the prison as a more humane and reformatory mechanism for the treatment of miscreants. Foucault, however, sees the prison as a means of constituting the self and the body. In particular, he is interested in describing the apparatuses by which the body is inscribed with power/discourse. The 'panopticon', a prison blueprint drafted by Jeremy Bentham himself, becomes the metaphor for Foucault's understanding of the relationship between the state and the individual. In a panopticon system the individual is always under the observation of the prison wardens; for Foucault, this system of continuous and ubiquitous surveillance is a reflection of the modernist predilection for power/discourse and the 'disciplining' of the citizenry. It is precisely the relationship which his discursive liberationism would seek to unfix.

More broadly, *Discipline and Punish* continues Foucault's interest in the modernist predisposition for drawing the world and individuals out of the immediacy of their experience and into the constructed world of language or discourse. This reconstitution of individuals and their subjectivity is clearly an exercise in the formation and re-formation of power relationships. Thus, at the time when British cultural studies is preoccupied with structural linguistics and 'the struggle to signify', Foucault is exploring how power is experienced at the level of the individual subject. In *The Order of Things* (1974) he had described the emergence of the social sciences in terms of this increasing need for the social organization of language, most particularly the need to fix individuals in social and psychological description. The social sciences, Foucault argued, were a means of placing the human experience into forms of knowledge that were not so much humanistic or liberational, but were rather constituitive and administrative; in a sense, human subjectivity was invented by the social sciences and rendered available for state administration. In *Discipline and Punish* Foucault also argues that the emergence of criminology is a discursive process aimed at administering and 'surveying' individual subjectivities and bodies in a collective and organizational stream. Moreover, the scientific discourses of criminology are inevitably woven into practices and technologies of power which undermine completely science's claim to be disinterested, objective or impartial.

The History of Sexuality

In *The History of Sexuality, Volume One* Foucault extends these arguments into the sexual and reproductive experiences of individual subjectivities and bodies. Again, he examines the discursive dimensions of sexuality in the modernist period. Foucault argues, against the claims of recent liberalists, that the eighteenth and nineteenth centuries were not periods of sexual repression so much as they were periods of sexual transformation. The immediacies and openness of sexual and reproductive experiences, Foucault contends, were transformed into various forms of discourse: religious, educational and social scientific. This transformation allows the experience of sexuality to be both stimulated and surveyed by the state. The contradictions, displeasures and pleasures that are associated with sex and sexuality are thereby engaged through new ways of speaking and writing about sex. On the one hand, sex is facilitated by its articulation in bio-medical and psychological discourses; but, on the other hand, the state, through census and educational processes, is able to observe the sexuality of its citizenry. Foucault suggests that these articulations are sexual experiences in much the same way as actual physical engagement is. There can be no sexuality, Foucault insists, without discourse.

Clearly, Foucault is arguing here that the biological and materialist interpretation of sexuality is misguided and that all reality is mediated through discourse and culture. These arguments are most forcefully articulated in the *History of Sexuality, Volume One*, where he outlines his project as the exposition of these discourses, rather than the examination of actual practices. In the later volumes of the series, however, he retreats significantly from this position, marking a third and final shift in his theoretical positioning. In fact, the latter volumes of *The History* might be conceived as 'straight' histories, outlining practices and events without the problematization of their discourse. In the first volume of the series Foucault is interested in the disturbances and obsessions of middle-class sexuality, and his liberational intent seems to be invested in the potential of the discursive release of sexualized bodies: new ways of articulating and experiencing the individual's sexual subjectivity. However, he never completes this project, preferring, it would seem, to prepare the way for others to take more deliberate or active steps toward their own liberation.

Foucault and Cultural Politics

Edward Said (1986), among many others, has rebuked Foucault for this retreat. In particular, Said expresses his frustration with Foucault for not fully embracing the political corollary of his studies. Mark Poster (1989) has explained the retreat in terms of Foucault's own gay sexuality and the occlusion of his liberational designs. Certainly, Foucault's final major essay, which preceded his death from an AIDS-related condition, demonstrates a significant and somewhat puzzling attempt to reconcile his thinking and writing career with what he imagines to be his philosophical heritage. In 'What is Enlightenment?' (1984), Foucault places his work within the general project of the Enlightenment. Jürgen Habermas, in particular, finds this reconciliation puzzling since Foucault's poststructuralism had been so antagonistic toward the structuralist, rationalist, materialist heritage which is generally associated with Enlightenment philosophy. Foucault's poststructuralist work would seem to question the very grounds upon which the Enlightenment liberational enterprise is founded. His emphasis on discourse and the instability of power/knowledge seems very clearly to repudiate any notion of social structure. Interestingly, however, many of the liberationists who have followed Foucault's work have tended to focus on the formation of power/discourse in particular zones of cultural and institutional interest. To this extent, Foucault's poststructuralism has provided some theoretical substance to a cultural politics which seeks to destabilize power/discourse formations that are centred on gender, ethnicity, imperialism and sexual preference. Foucault's poststructural writings, therefore, have proved enormously influential even though he found himself retreating form the whole project of discourse analysis at the end of his career.

Foucault and Governmentality

There is yet an even more lingering, and to an extent puzzling, adaptation of Foucault's intellectual legacy. A number of authors have attempted to ground their work on culture, policy and democracy in a set of lectures and writings which Foucault himself had decided not to publish. To this extent, cultural theorists like Tony Bennett (1999) have sought to liberate the notion of governance and democracy from the rationalist order defined by Jurgen Habermas. Bennett, in fact, argues that contemporary, postmodern culture is thoroughly infused by the conditions of regulatory processes and practices – these processes and practices can be conscripted into the cause of democratization and liberation. In other words, matters of governance and government policy are inevitable, and so cultural analysis needs to engage thoroughly with regulatory processes in order to enhance democratic potential, as well as the freedom and quality of life of citizens.

In support of these arguments, Bennett invokes the work of Michel Foucault, most particularly his work on state power and 'governmentality'. For some (e.g., see McGuigan, 1996), this use of Foucault's writing is a misappropriation, since Bennett's aim is to provide some normative values and principles for the practical analysis of government cultural policy, and Foucault is regarded by many of his followers as something of an anarchist. Jim McGuigan points out, however, that Foucault's slippery and generally ungrounded historical analyses render his work available for quite contrary theoretical readings:

> Because he refused to ground his subtle and compelling analyses of power in norms of critical judgement, Foucault's work lends itself to radically dissimilar forms of interpretation and application. That the anarchist Foucault should have become, in effect, a theoretical source for a kind of management consultancy in the service of cultural administration is oddly plausible. (1996: 176)

Plausible or not, the application of Foucault's ideas is constituted around a fundamental belief that 'governmentalism' is pervasive throughout culture: that is, throughout the processes by which meanings are formed, distributed and consumed. For Bennett, it is the institutions and material effects of this process that need to be central to the cultural studies project.

If we return to Foucault's essays on 'governmentality', we can certainly identify a preoccupation with the pervasiveness of power. However, the notion of governmentality is only partially developed, unlike Foucault's more substantive theorizations on the state, populations, administrative technologies, power, discourse and knowledge. In fact, Foucault's 'writings' on governmentality are based on a particular series of lectures, most of which have been prohibited from publication by the literary executors of his estate (Burchell et al., 1991). The somewhat disproportionate interest being expressed in the concept indicates the seriousness with which political and cultural theory are attempting to reconcile the precepts of poststructural and postmodern theory with the demands of practical political action. Perhaps the development of the concept in the first instance was motivated by Foucault's own desire to accomplish the reforms his major writings simply intimated. In effect, governmentality is distinguished as a modern political practice which deviates from pre-modern, sovereignty-based theories of legitimation. That is, governmentality dislodges sovereignty as the essential fabric of the state from the rise of the Enlightenment. While sovereignty was concerned with obedience to law (and hence to the sovereign), governmentality is concerned with the tactics of governance: governmentality is about the filtering through of regulatory practices, including the practices of self-regulation and the management of material products or things.

> Government is defined as a right manner of disposing things so as to lead not to the form of the common good, as the jurists' texts would have said, but to an end which is 'convenient' for each of the things that are to be governed. This implies a plurality of specific aims: for instance, government will have to ensure that the greatest possible quantity of wealth is produced, that the people are provided with sufficient means of subsistence, that the population is enabled to multiply. … [W]ith government it is not a matter of imposing laws on men, but of disposing things: that is to say, of employing tactics rather than laws, and even of using laws themselves as tactics – to arrange things in such a way that, through a certain number of means, such and such ends may be achieved. (Foucault, 1991: 95)

PSYCHOANALYTIC THEORY: JACQUES LACAN

Western intellectual thought has explored the notion of subjectivity in various ways. The concepts of 'subjectivity', the 'subject', the 'self' and the 'ego' generally refer to the 'I' (me) of any particular human context. Descartes and Kant established the conception of a divided (split, dual) self, distinguishing between the subject as internal and contained, and the object as all phenomena external to the subject including other people (selves). Descartes' famous 'I think, therefore I am' directs Kant's later epistemological (through knowledge) conception of an intrinsic conceptual framework by which the human subject is able to 'know' the external world of objects. Romantic philosophy and aesthetics project over Kantian epistemology a view of the subject as a profoundly mystical exigency. The 'I' of Romantic poetry, for example, frequently seeks to transcend the cloying and demeaning circumstances of the material world through a form of spiritual ascent, an apotheosis which liberates the self from oppression and degeneration. Phenomenology, most especially as it is represented in the work of Edmund Husserl and Martin Heidegger, also seeks to explain the 'reality' of the world – phenomena – through the direct experiences of the subject. Marxism and its various derivatives reject all notions of the subject that are not fixed in material and economic conditions: for Marxism and other forms of structuralism the subject is necessarily situated in its relationship to material, economy and social organizations.

Psychoanalytic theory, most particularly Jacques Lacan's poststructuralist adaptations of Sigmund Freud, examines in detail the relationship between the various 'I's of the world and their wider experience of language. Following Émile Benveniste's idea of subject positions, Lacan argues that the self exists only in relation to other subjects. This means that when I say, 'I am hungry' and the other person says, 'I will give you food', the two 'I's are functioning in a delicate and highly unstable relationship with one another. Each 'I' exists only at the moment of utterance; the receiver of the utterance is delicately poised to take up the subject position 'I' when it is his/her turn to speak. Psychoanalytic poststructuralism, therefore, seeks to understand the gaps and the instabilities that operate through, and mediate, these shifting subject positions. Language is pivotal to the self's ability to locate an appropriate subject position, and Lacan's adaptation of Freud centres on the relationship between human experience of language (the conscious) and that dimension of human experience which pre-figures language (the unconscious).

This relationship between the conscious and unconscious dimensions of human experience is complex and often unstable. Lacan, again following Freud, distinguishes between various developmental stages in a person's life which place him or her in relation to language and levels of consciousness or adulthood. The unconscious, however, is never obliterated in this process; rather, it is subsumed beneath the surface of language and consciousness, ready to re-emerge through critical moments and experiences. A central motif in psychoanalytic writing, then, is the notion of 'lack', a form of loss which has various manifestations in human experience. In the three critical developmental phases outlined by Freud/Lacan – mirror, *fort–da* and Oedipal – the condition of lack constitutes a central and defining characteristic. As we progress through life, we are driven by the desire to recover this lack; as we look back, we idealize a condition of completeness or plenitude when we were one with the mother. This mythical phase of plenitude engages the self in a complete identification with the mother, and a complete union of subject and object. The recovery of this lack and lesion directs the three stages in the following ways:

1 Birth disrupts the union of the infant in the womb and now the infant must be satisfied with intermittent contact with the breast. This 'fragmentation' of the completeness of the union impels the infant toward a form of self-awareness. This 'mirror phase' occurs (around 6–19 months) as the child develops a sense of self through self-observation in a real or imagined mirror. At this point too, Lacan/Freud introduces the notion of *misrecognition*, whereby the infant (mis)recognizes its self in the mirror which is not the actual self, but a representation of the actual self. In fact, this image gives the impression of a more unified and complete subject than the life-stage actually warrants. The mirror phase is characterized by the experience of the 'imaginary', which Lacan distinguishes from 'the symbolic'. Thus the child imagines its unity through a real or imagined mirror, failing to notice fully that this 'image' of the reflected self may not even be itself but may be another child which the infant confirms as itself. The imaginary continues even through the full formation of the ego (self) since the myth of the unified selfhood depends on the ability to identify with 'objects'.

2 This construction of self or ego also depends on the child's ability to distinguish between itself and objects. The father's prohibition marks the child's entrance into the 'symbolic'

by which s/he learns to distinguish differences (right/wrong, male/female, son/father, present/absent, etc.). Thus, the *fort–da* (gone–here) game phase is really about identifying oppositions. The principal part of this game is the recognition that things are present and then they are absent; the child articulates this entry into language through this simple game of recognition.

Lacan, also following Freud here, makes particular note of the symbol of the penis (the 'phallus'). The penis is not merely a physiological apparatus, but is meaningful in many different ways. The symbolic penis or phallus can be projected in many ways and attached to many different symbolic contexts. For Lacan, the most important dimension of the symbolic penis is its capacity to unite meanings generally: the 'phallus' becomes the privileged signifier in Lacan's system, as it allows all other signifiers (material symbols) to make contact with their signifieds (concepts or meanings). (This relationship remains unstable, however, since the phallus is also constituted around the problem of 'lack' or absence which becomes intensified during the Oedipal stage.)

Thus, this entry into language intensifies the experience of 'lack' since we are able to articulate our needs and recognize the lack of satisfaction. Gesture, therefore, runs on a series of discourses and is necessarily implicated in language. As we have noted, the subject and subjectivity are themselves contingencies of language. There is no essential or 'pre-linguistic' self but merely an imaginary and its productive misrecognition. The subject shifts in relation to other subjects and their subject positions. The 'I' about which I speak in a sentence is never the same 'I' which is doing the talking. Thus, the unity of signifier and signified is constituted on an unstable premise. Language shifts and so do signifiers and subjects.

3   In the Oedipal stage the child subject achieves sexual maturity. Lacan's rewriting of the Oedipus complex treats the unconscious as though it were structured like a language. As we have seen, Saussure attempts to weld together the separate systems of signifiers and signifieds in order to unify the sign. According to poststructuralists, however, this adhesion fails because the two systems are subject to the incessant deferrals of meaning over time. As we have just noted, this problem is exacerbated when the subject is considered, since the 'I' of any utterance is never a complete fusion between the material sign and the conceptual meaning. Sexual maturity intensifies the subject's desire to recover his or her 'lack' through the reunification of self and language. Desire, in fact, represents the process of pursuit, whereby the subject seeks to fix the signifier to the signified: the 'other', the 'real', the moment of plenitude. In order to resolve this 'lack' the subject seeks to fix his or her body to the object of desire but is forever confronted with a further signifier in much the same way as the seeker of meaning is haunted by the forever receding possibilities of definition in a dictionary. One signifier is met with more and yet more signifiers.

Lacan's outline of these three stages is significant for our general understanding of poststructuralist notions of subjectivity. The subject's immersion in the symbolic (language, discourse) is never complete because neither the self nor the sign is unified. Even sexual desire, which might seem to override or escape language, is symbolic because the object of an individual's desire is always produced symbolically in language. When I desire a person I am seeking to reunify myself, to recover that loss which separated me from the completeness of gestation. My desire is therefore generated by a need to reunify signifier with signified, conscious with unconscious, self with other. My hope is that the person whom I desire and the act of sexual engagement will liberate me from language, but inevitably the person whom I desire will exist for me in language. My desire is bound by language.

Lacan's work has been highly influential in cultural studies, both for those working in a direct psychoanalytic line and for others applying a more generalized version of his key concepts. In feminist film studies Lacan's theories have influenced notions of visualization and 'the male gaze' (see Chapter 6). In postcolonial theory his notion of the 'other' (or 'otherness') has been variously interpreted and applied, most frequently to refer to the European construction of identity against the otherness of non-Europeans. In cultural politics more generally Lacan's theories about open subjectivity and the construction of identity have been particularly significant. This poststructuralist perspective of an unfixed self has also been adapted in various domains of postmodernism where individual pleasure and the liberatory potential of the self are broadly canvassed.

POLITICS AND DIFFERENCE: DELEUZE AND GUATTARI

Anti-Oedipus

The relationship between poststructuralism and cultural politics is highly problematic. As we shall see in later chapters, the primary criticisms of poststructuralism are generated through structuralist and related political perspectives. In many respects the perception of poststructuralism's political limitations has prompted a more strident postmodernist critique which seeks to transform poststructuralism's interest in language and authoritative discourse into a more radical and culturally oriented politics of difference. Indeed, while we have investigated the political interests of Michel Foucault, his work remains framed by a certain resistance to contemporary social and cultural critique; his books are 'bombs for others to throw', and his analysis is generally restricted to earlier periods of modern history. Equally, Jacques Derrida confines his interests to the textual and philosophical processes by which meanings are formed, deferred or dissolved. Although his key concepts of deconstruction and difference have been clearly appropriated for popular and political critique, Derrida himself remains politically elusive, even though the last part of his career was centred on a moral and political engagement of sorts.

Gilles Deleuze and Félix Guattari are perhaps more self-consciously political than either Foucault or Derrida, and in many respects their work represents an embryonic postmodern political critique. Deleuze was a radical philosopher, a type of anti-philosopher, who sought to remove social and metaphysical thinking from the hierarchies of elite intellectualism and intellectual discourses. Guattari, on the other hand, was a practising, Lacanian-trained psychoanalyst who sought the overthrow of historical and hierarchical discourses by which the doctor–patient relationship was inscribed by savage divisions of power and knowledge. Both Deleuze and Guattari wanted to produce a form of political criticism which was liberated from the artifice of intellectual hegemony and Marxist structuralism, both of which fixed human groups within immutable and historically persistent divisions of power. To this extent, Deleuze and Guattari's early writings are devoted to a triad of tensions – Marxism, Nietzschean existentialism and Freudian psychoanalysis – which are explored in order to produce a more radical account of human desire and politics.

In *Anti-Oedipus* (1983), for example, Deleuze and Guattari examine human desire in terms of authoritarianism and the codes which construct it. Like Adorno, they are interested in the relationship between human desire and the ascent of authoritarian subjectivities (versions of the self) which lead in the most spectacular instance to the formation of totalitarianism. This condition, extending Nietzsche's extension of Marx's concept of 'alienation', is a manifestation of the pandemic desire for security, the need to be led, the need to be affirmed and fixed in the leadership of others. Thus, Nietzsche's repudiation of the church in *Antichrist* is invoked by Deleuze and Guattari in order to repudiate the codes of conventional, Freudian psychoanalysis. From its inception, Deleuze and Guattari argue, psychoanalysis has constituted a kind of church with stipulated rules of order and behaviour. Its treatments, predicated upon the separation of power and the definition of neurosis, rely on a faithfulness which is unassailable and which divides humanity between the leader who treats and the herd which is to be treated. Subjectivity for the neurotic is self without distress, self without pain (Deleuze and Guattari, 1983: 428), a tranquillized position which faithfully restores the might of the herd.

Like R.D. Laing and other psychiatric practitioners who seek to free the individual from this pathologic definition of neurosis, Deleuze and Guattari pursue the possibilities of 'breakdowns' and 'breakthroughs' (original insights and experiences) as expressions of desire, intensity and what they refer to as the general flows of human experience. They describe their approach as 'schizoanalysis'. This method of engagement with the subject contrasts in every way with the pathological impetus of conventional, Freudian psychoanalysis, which, they argue, measures everything against divisions of Oedipal theory, 'castration' and neurosis. Schizoanalysis begins with the 'schizo', the individual's subjectivity and his/her breakdown and breakthrough – the 'schizophrenic out for a walk' is a better model than a neurotic lying on the analyst's couch.

The Oedipus complex, according to conventional Freudian theory, refers to the Greek story of Oedipus, who mistakenly kills his father, marries his mother and ascends to the throne. Freud adapts the story to explain a neurosis involving sexual disruption. Deleuze and Guattari argue that this breakdown and the schizophrenia which is involved are not an illness at all, but a breakthrough, bringing particular insights, opportunities and pleasures to the problematic of open subjectivity. Deleuze and Guattari contrast the Oedipal discourses and territorialities of individual, family, church and state against the possibilities of deterritorializing experiences of desire and subjectivity that have not been confined by the codes of the Oedipus complex and neurosis – these are the free flows, the lines of escape which lead us elsewhere. Desire is not to be abjured or feared, but released for the greater purposes beyond restrictive and pathological codes:

> Desire then becomes the abject fear of lacking something. But it should be noted that this is not a phrase uttered by the poor or dispossessed. On the contrary, such people know that they are close to the grass, almost akin to it, and that desire needs very few things – not those leftovers that chance to come their way. (Deleuze and Guattari, 1983: 27)

Anti-Oedipus should not simply be read, however, as a retreat into hedonism and sensual pleasure, as escape from the authoritarian discourses of psychoanalysis and capitalism. In fact, Deleuze and Guattari seek a social and cultural critique that moves beyond Marxist structuralism on the one hand, and bourgeois psychoanalysis on the other. *Anti-Oedipus* is explicitly an optimistic text, Deleuze and Guattari explain, but this optimism is built around the dissolution of all authoritarian discourses. In many respects, the Marxist–Freudian opposition is neutralized by the book's discussion of Friedrich Nietzsche's account of alienation and desire. Most particularly in *On the Genealogy of Morals*, Nietzsche illuminates the relationships between desire, will and the processes of capitalism. The history of humanity is identified as an alienating process toward 'becoming reactive'. Nietzsche's escape from reactivity through the assertion of an existential will provides for Deleuze and Guattari the possibility of a revolutionary subjectivity, a freedom which liberates desire rather than confines it in the terminal conditions of class warfare or Oedipal concessions.

A Thousand Plateaus

In *A Thousand Plateaus* (1987) Deleuze and Guattari extend the liberatory impulses of subjectivity into the realm of all language codes, including their own. Like Derrida, Deleuze and Guattari seek to neutralize their own textual predispositions to authority by offering a de-centred, non-originary structure to their book. To this extent, they suggest that the reader need not follow the hierarchies that are generally built into texts – linear processes which privilege particular orders, sequences, chapters or sentences. The book, therefore, might be read from any angle and at any beginning point that the reader desires. The book has no linearity, no beginning, middle or end, but is part of a free flow of discourses, each neutralizing the authority of the other. Like Barthes and Foucault, Deleuze and Guattari introduce *A Thousand Plateaus* through the denial of their own fixed identities and authorship, moving on, however, to renounce the presence of the book itself:

> A book has neither object nor subject; it is made of variously formed matters, and very different dates and speeds. To attribute this book to a subject is to overlook this working of

matters and the exteriority of their relations. … A book is an assemblage of this kind, and as such is unattributable. It is a multiplicity – but we don't know yet what the multiple entails when it is no longer attributed, that is, after it has been elevated to the status of a substantive. (Deleuze and Guattari, 1987: 3–4)

Deleuze and Guattari imagine, then, a discourse that is unbordered and which flows with the associative alacrity of the memory or the unconscious. *A Thousand Plateaus* is an assemblage of thoughts, 'nomad thoughts', which are liberated from the strictures and structures of author and reader.

The notion of 'nomad thought' constitutes a central motif for *A Thousand Plateaus*, though Deleuze and Guattari are careful not to allow any notion to take on the solidity of a 'concept'. Concepts may be useful as 'the founding bricks of a courthouse', but Deleuze and Guattari are seeking a more unstable and ephemeral language form, one in which assemblages replace fixed, organic systems composed of discretely organized and hierarchical components. An assemblage of like matters, therefore, is not a fixed concept or category; it is always a heterogeneous and convenient arrangement. Thus, in analyzing the world, Deleuze and Guattari insist on their own immersion and on the continuing possibilities of rearrangement, disassemblage and the integrity of components. The primary condition of nomad thought is affirmation, even when the focus of the thought is negative. An assemblage of like matters, therefore, is not a fixed concept or category; it is always a heterogeneous and convenient arrangement.

In the hands of Deleuze and Guattari, in particular, poststructuralism becomes a utopia which distinguishes itself from the alienation of Marx and the nihilism of Sartre. The enabling capacity of this affirmation is 'force': the ability to break the walls at any moment and move on to a new thought, a new condition. Force is to be distinguished from power which builds walls. Force facilitates the 'smooth space' by which thinking travels from point to point. Consequently, *A Thousand Plateaus* might be read as a forcefield of pleasures where thinking across the many expressive media – most notably in mathematics and music – carries the potential for creating smooth space and new ways of conceiving of things. The music of the text is specifically noted in terms of its potential for flow and exploration. In particular, the musical refrain, evident in infants' *fort–da*, ethnic music, mothers' ditties and Schubert's songs, facilitates the forever-becoming potentials of human identity:

It's not really known when music begins. The refrain is neither a means of preventing music, warding it off, or forgoing it. But music exists because the refrain exists also, because music takes up the refrain, lays hold of it as a content in a form of expression, because it forms a block with it in order to take it somewhere else. *The child's refrain, which is not music, forms a block with the becoming-child of music.* An assemblage of like matters, therefore, is not a fixed concept or category; it is always a heterogeneous and convenient arrangement. (Deleuze and Guattari, 1987: 300)

Part Two

Cultural Locations

6

Feminism: From Femininity to Fragmentation

INTRODUCTION

Modern feminism is often dated to the French Revolution; it is suggested that the social revolutionary Charles Fourier coined the term at the beginning of the nineteenth century. However, while once it may have been possible to define feminism quite precisely and unproblematically, recent developments have brought significant changes and fragmentation to feminist and gender studies. The basic aspiration of feminism may still be the liberation of women from gender-based oppression: however, the meaning of 'oppression', 'liberation' and even 'femininity' have become highly contested, most particularly as they relate to the cultures, lifestyles and choices of different women and female communities across the globe. The influence of poststructuralism, postmodernism, postcolonialism, psychoanalytic theory and new modes of political and cultural analysis has undermined several core assumptions of earlier models of feminism. In this context, a number of key theorists claim that feminism is itself ruptured and that the older interests should now be replaced by a more contemporary perspective – something which some commentators might refer to as cultural politics, new feminism or even postfeminism. In any case, these new debates in feminist theory are now critically embedded in contemporary cultural theory.

Recent histories of the feminist movement have located women's liberational activities in terms of three distinct waves:

1   The first wave refers to the suffragette movement, which was seeking primarily to have women's political rights inscribed into the democratic process. The suffragette movement was part of a general middle-class agitation that began during the nineteenth century.

2   The second wave occurs from the 1960s, where specific legislative and social processes excluded women from full and equal participation in public life, work and culture. This phase of agitation begins as the 'women's liberation movement' and evolves into the common nomenclature of feminism.

3   The third wave refers to the current period. Women's rights are now enshrined in legislation in western developed nations; within this legislative framework, however, the 'culture' and its ideologies remain fundamentally 'patriarchal', sexist and prejudiced against women. Men and male interests still dominate the culture, and women have to confront implied limits on their social and economic progress. Issues such as work/family balance, sexual assault, career impediments, political participation and income disparity continue to motivate feminist politicism.

While these broad temporal categories provide some useful insights into the feminist critique, they tend to reduce the history of gender relations to a simple progression. In fact, the story of gender relations is complicated and there are many cultural elements and tributaries which the 'three wave' theory ultimately subsumes within its teleological (cause and effect) framework. The lives, struggles and experiences of the many women who have lived through this three-phase period cannot necessarily be explained in terms of the liberational momentum described by this form of feminist historicism. In the current phase, in particular, the whole ideal of 'being liberated' means many different things to many different women: as Michel Foucault has noted, emancipation is itself a matter for the individual's discretion, rather than the judgement of an 'intellectual' or 'historian'.

While we will address key aspects of the historical development of feminist theory, the primary aim of this chapter is to elucidate the key assumptions that inform cultural and theoretical perspectives of gender. The chapter examines feminism as a cultural positioning as well as a cultural politics. The objective is to move away from treating feminism teleologically, as an outline of ultimate causes; rather, the chapter wants to explore the disputes as much as the continuities which form feminism. For the purposes of this chapter, feminism is understood as the collection of ideas and practices which are centred on the liberation of women.

FEMINISM AND MODERNISM

Modernism and the Suffragettes

As we have noted throughout this book, modernism's principal economic system, capitalism, is constructed around a fundamental contradiction between constraining supply and expanding demand. Supply is privileged and seeks to limit itself in order to create value, while demand is designed to be limitless in order to ensure the scarcity and value of supply. Supply is privileged and elite; demand is democratic and inclusive. The owners of supply (capital), therefore, seek to maintain their privilege without alienating those people (lower classes) who provide the demand for their products and services. For those who demand the products (the market) capitalism appears to be advancing their interests, as it provides the materials and services necessary for a comfortable life. In this context, capitalism survives upon a finely mediated tension between privileged and general interests.

Of course, capitalism has not operated independently of culture; quite the contrary. The three great pillars of cultural modernism – capitalist economics, humanism and democratic political institutions – have worked through various forms of co-operation and dispute in order to maintain the opposite trajectories of privilege and freedom. The complex codes that underwrite the modern era are best understood, therefore, as ideological battlegrounds where notions of equality of opportunity and equal rights clash persistently with new forms of privilege, cultural manipulation and oppression.

Gender, like class, has been a central category in the unfolding of these ideological and language wars. Marxist feminists argue that women's labour is exploited by capitalism, most particularly as women have been excluded from the ownership of capital and property. Whether or not this is the case, there is no doubt that the confinement of women to nurturing, domestic and sexual services is associated with a general exclusion from other, more prominent, cultural zones. In particular, women were far less prominent in public debate and political processes than were men during the reform period of the nineteenth century. The Suffragettes, a group of largely educated, middle-class women, sought to redress this situation, arguing specifically that political representation and the right to vote should be extended to their own class of women, if not to all citizens. While their aims were in one sense quite specific, there is no doubt that the Suffragettes were motivated by broader ideological concerns about the role and rights of women in a patriarchal culture. In particular, concerns over the legal rights of women in marriage and property were inscribed with a cultural politics that had emerged through the significant fictional writings of Jane Austen, the Brontë sisters and George Eliot.

While these texts represented many of the injustices and indignities that were being suffered by middle-class women during the nineteenth century, a more specific women's liberation was being articulated in British utilitarianism. Utilitarianism was largely committed to the prevailing economic and social systems, though it sought a general improvement to the conditions of life through a strategic implementation of social and political reforms. In particular, the utilitarians believed that the general good of a society would be served by the enhancement of individuals' own 'usefulness' or utility. Public education, public works and eventually universal suffrage would enhance the pride and moral condition of individuals and the citizenry. If individuals could enhance their own usefulness and the conditions of their own personal morality, then there would be a general improvement to society at large. According to John Stuart Mill and Harriet Taylor Mill

(1970), this principle of utility extended to women as well as men. Properly educated and informed in the ways of economics and business, women could contribute equally to the public good – including the political well-being of the nation. In achieving their own personal sense of utility, women could mobilize their own special faculties for the betterment of the nation as a whole. Moreover, according to Mill and Taylor Mill, if women are to be most responsible for the education of the young, then it would be far preferable that women themselves were well educated and capable of sharing their knowledge and abilities.

Women and High Modernism

Kate Millett (1971: Ch. 4) claims that the period from 1930 through to the 1960s constitutes a general reversal of the sexual liberation of the previous century, which had culminated in the granting of universal suffrage. For Millett and other feminists of the 1960s and 1970s, this 'decline' of feminism represents a certain slackening of focus, a sense in which the war had probably already been won. The emergence of consumer capitalism during the early part of the twentieth century had shifted the force of exploitation from production to consumption. Women's labour had continued to be exploited, but with the emergence of the household as a primary cultural unit, women were also being conditioned into the role of domestic consumer. Advertising and the new electrical communications media were creating new cultural spaces for the exploitation and oppression of women – not only were women targeted and positioned by product marketers as the source and stimulant of new forms of household consumption, the sexualized image of a woman's body became a central motif in the new televisual culture. Continuing into the present, this form of bodily representation of women contributed to the construction of an ideal femininity which was sexual, maternal, 'natural', emotional and obedient to the desires and rational power of men. Thus, the hard-won victories of the Suffragettes were being eroded by a new form of exploitation constituted around mass consumption, mass communication and normative representations of the female body.

According to Kate Millett, however, the writings of Virginia Woolf and Simone de Beauvoir constituted an important alternative to this form of political degradation in the first half of the twentieth century. Woolf's *A Room of One's Own* (1978, orig. 1929) and de Beauvoir's *The Second Sex* (1972, orig. 1949) attempt to place women very directly within the matrices of cultural representation in language. Woolf, a member of the Bloomsbury group of literary critics, sought to reorder Matthew Arnold's aesthetic and social criticism through the development of a distinctively female literary voice.

Woolf's aesthetic and literary criticism has provided recent feminism with a framework for reading and writing, as well as a cultural perspective of what numerous commentators refer to as 'modernism' or 'high modernism'. We should note that this use of the concept of modernism is quite restrictive, referring to a narrow cluster of ideas and texts, mostly appearing between 1890 and 1930; this is a common categorization used in areas of literary and aesthetic history (see Wolff, 1990: 79). (Our own, much broader and more culturally oriented use of the concept refers to ideas and texts from the Enlightenment through to the present.) Woolf is highly regarded in terms of aesthetic modernism, most particularly because she polemicizes the social and material conditions within which art and literature are produced. The inventiveness of avant-garde literature and art, Woolf insists, necessarily implicates the issue of gender. Women, she urges, need to liberate themselves and their aesthetic from the constraints of the male 'sentence', both literally and metaphorically. Woolf uses Dorothy Richardson as an example of the expressive potential of all women writers:

> She has invented, or, if she has not invented, developed and applied to her own use, a sentence which we might call the psychological sentence of the feminine gender. It is of a more elastic fibre than the old, capable of stretching to the extreme, of suspending the frailest particles, or enveloping the vaguest shapes. (Woolf, 1979: 191)

Woolf claims, therefore, that women need to move beyond the sentences provided by men, adapt and extend the existing discourses in order freely and openly to articulate their own sense of the world. 'A room of one's own' becomes the cry for space, both intellectual and material – the minimum resource for the full participation of women in culture.

Simone de Beauvoir: French Marxist Feminism

Woolf's arguments maintain the logics of British liberalism and a humanism which now specifically includes women. While anglophone feminists of the 1960s and 1970s would return to this theme, Simone de Beauvoir's assault on patriarchal capitalism and the confinement of women's expression and cultural participation has a more radical edge to it. Unlike Woolf's extension of Matthew Arnold's literary humanism, de Beauvoir is influenced by Marxist and existential raillery against the standards and norms of bourgeois society. Indeed, while Woolf's discourses never threaten the formidable elitism of British 'high culture', de Beauvoir takes a more expansive view of social discourse and power. In particular, she establishes the important relationship between identity and gender, noting that the fundamental issue for a woman in defining herself is: 'I am a woman'. A man, de Beauvoir maintains, would never feel the need to begin with this fundamental, genderized statement of identity. Women's dispersal in history is always measured against the primary definer of masculinity; this dispersal has prevented women from developing a collective identity, as is the case with other oppressed groups. Women, therefore, are fixed in an asymmetrical relationship with men; he is the norm(al), the One, while she is the abnormal, the Other. Her identity is measured necessarily against what a man is. Her exclusion from public participation constantly and permanently confines her identity.

Clearly influenced by Marxist existentialism, de Beauvoir rails against the artifice of 'equality' which never fully extends to women, because the ideology of equality assumes the inferiority of women, creating belief in both men and women that this is the normal state of affairs. Women themselves, rather than sympathetic men, are best placed to comprehend the actual conditions of their own existence, and thereby create the conditions for genuine equality and liberation. De Beauvoir lays the blame for this co-operative oppression at the feet of patriarchal capitalism. Women become the construct of men and surrender their potential for freedom, through insidious processes of discourse and history. Femininity construes women as the pleasure and labour objects of men, as 'men compel her to assume the status of Other' (de Beauvoir, 1972: 29). The solution, de Beauvoir considers, is a form of socialism which radically alters the hierarchical predispositions of capitalism, preferring a human nexus which liberates women and men from the limitations and unfreedoms of patriarchy.

De Beauvoir's existential socialism bears the marks of her long-term friend and periodic lover Jean-Paul Sartre, who identified freedom as the major project of human existence. This more radical assault on the standards of bourgeois life, aesthetics and sexuality also challenges the fundamental links between liberal humanism and women's liberation. In a society where women were becoming increasingly embedded in capitalist consumerism, de Beauvoir's socialist feminism sought to unravel the capitalist commodification process and the restrictions capitalism imposed on women's lives. Her desire to liberate femininity from the constraints of male proprietorialism and romantic idealism was to prove a major inspiration for the sexual liberationists of the 1960s and 1970s.

SEXUAL AND POLITICAL EMANCIPATION

The 1960s was a period of major political and cultural reawakening. During the post-war years and into the 1950s, the world was gripped by the deep freeze of Soviet and capitalist polemics. America had reasserted itself as the major world military, economic and cultural power. Its solipsistic and jingoistic views became expressed in terrible forms of conservatism and internal repression. The so-called 'McCarthyism' of the 1950s led to deep internal rifts as the right of politics became increasingly paranoid, accusing America's own citizens of Soviet sympathy, sedition and treason. Communist sympathizers were spotted at all levels of American society. Bohemians, artists, intellectuals, actors, writers – indeed anyone who dared challenge the rigidities of authority and the overriding ideology of societal unity – were immediately suspected of anti-Americanism. Undoubtedly, the ferment of artistic, cultural and intellectual activities of the 1960s was a response to the suffocating conditions of the previous decade. The emergence of the teenager as a new, autonomous consumer, the arrival of the contraceptive pill, and the widening distribution of media technologies like TV – all contributed to a political mood that incorporated the revival and popularization of the women's liberation movement.

Sexual Politics

Kate Millett's *Sexual Politics* (1971) seeks to define contemporary politics in terms of two distinct social classes – not the proletariat and bourgeoisie, but men and women. While this definition might most obviously accord with a structuralist perspective of human society, Millett makes it clear that her politics functions very much through the levels of personal relationships. Sexual politics, even in the era of supposed political equality and equality of opportunity, works beyond the level of traditional Marxist definitions; patriarchy, Millett declares in a sustained and vitriolic critique, is an insidious undercurrent which barely admits the humanity, let alone the status and dignity, of women:

> The rationale which accompanies the imposition of male authority euphemistically referred to as 'the battle of the sexes' bears a certain resemblance to the formulas of nations at war where any heinousness is justified on the grounds that the enemy is either an inferior species or really not human at all. The patriarchal mentality has concocted a whole series of rationales about women which accomplish this purpose tolerably well. And these traditional beliefs still invade our consciousness. (Millett, 1971: 46)

While Millett's book lacks the theoretical density of Althusser's 'ideology', she is speaking here about a similar exigency: patriarchy is an economic and cultural system which forms around the subordination of a whole class of people, women. The major focus of *Sexual Politics* is the exposition of these negative stereotypes and images of women, the mechanisms which justify the control and oppression of the sexual Other. Millett makes clear that she is distinguishing between the biological condition of the female and the culturally constructed conditions of gender and femininity. Accordingly, Millett's analysis of Henry Miller, D.H. Lawrence, Jean Genet and Norman Mailer elucidates a patriarchal intensity which constantly validates the perspective of the male as sexual activist and female as sexual focus. Like de Beauvoir and Germaine Greer, Millett sees the female experience of sex and sexuality as fundamentally constrained by the need to satisfy male's material and ideological interests. Thus, Norman Mailer's *The American Dream* is impugned as a murderous and sodomite attack upon women. Henry Miller's *Sexus* – 'she kneeled at my feet gobbling it' etc. – is regaled for its tone of 'one male relating an exploit to another'.

Defenders of the works of writers like Henry Miller and Jean Genet have suggested that Millett's reading is both too narrow and too literal. Miller's work was significant in as much as it brought the whole experience of sex and the problematic of idealized love into a new critical and aesthetic focus. Millett sees the surrealism and homosexuality of Jean Genet's *The Thief's Journal* only in terms of female subjugation and degradation. Millett, it is argued, tends to homogenize the complex associations and meanings offered in these works, reducing them to a monochrome of her own polemic. Indeed, just as critics had seen Georg Lukács's Marxist interpretations of particular novels as reductionist, Millett's reading of Mailer, Miller and Genet might seem to bracket out a broader potential for liberation and subversion. Certainly, this is the defence mounted by Mailer himself in *The Prisoners of Sex*, where he accuses Millett of deliberately altering the meanings of the texts she analyzes to suit her political project. Mailer repudiates Millett's critique, arguing that she fails to acknowledge that a text may not simply mirror the sexist attitudes of its cultural context. Artists and writers, Mailer argues, create the conditions of experience which might challenge the assumptions of the exterior world – a male author does not necessarily reproduce nor confirm the ideology of the world from which he draws his discourse.

The Mailer–Millett debate, in fact, raises a significant issue for feminist strategies, one which is taken up more fully in poststructuralist and postmodernist accounts of feminist politics. That is, the text and its interpretations are fundamentally problematic. Millett's framework of reading provides particular insights into the culture, and cultural politics generally. Mailer argues that this framework is only one possible approach to the text, and a highly polemicized and inadequate one. According to Mailer, Millett and others, including Germaine Greer (*The Female Eunuch*), have *mis*interpreted the text, imposing meanings that are not necessarily the intention of the author nor the mirror of the culture. These sorts of debates persist, even through the application of more sophisticated semiotic techniques of reading.

The Male Gaze: Laura Mulvey

In her essay 'Visual pleasure and narrative cinema' (1975), Laura Mulvey attempts to integrate feminist precepts with Freud/Lacan's language-based psychoanalysis (see Chapter 5). In many respects, Mulvey's reading of popular cinema texts parallels the feminist textual studies of Angela McRobbie at the Birmingham Centre for Contemporary Cultural Studies. Mulvey seeks to understand the processes and power relationships in culture which consistently represent women (and men) in socially idealized roles, using sexually idealized imagery. In particular, Mulvey is interested in the relationship between the sexualized and stereotyped image of women as they are subjected to, and produced out of, the focus of the male gaze and male desire. While Mulvey's gender distinction remains typically structuralist, the innovative application of psychoanalysis to explain the relationship between men and women in textual processes has proven enormously influential for feminist media studies, especially during the 1970s and 1980s. It is central, for example, in the formation of what Stuart Hall (1988) calls '*Screen* Theory', cinematic analysis formed in and through the journal *Screen*; it has also been prevalent in feminist analysis of television (Moores, 1993).

Mulvey's objective is consciously political, seeking to deconstruct the fundamental patriarchal conditions of 'phallocentricism': 'the paradox of phallocentricism in all its manifestations is that it depends on the image of the castrated woman to give order and meaning to its world' (Mulvey, 1975: 746). Phallocentricism is not merely the pre-eminence of the male sexual organ, but the symbolic and cultural pre-eminence of the gender male. Mulvey's analysis attempts to demonstrate how the ubiquity and centralization of the male gaze upon the female form is an outcome of significant psychological and therefore cultural processes. Cinema, for Mulvey, constitutes an 'advanced representation system' through which a range of pleasures may be derived. 'Scopophilia', for example, is a fundamental sexual drive, a form of voyeurism, which the conditions and text of cinema-viewing facilitate. Scopophilia, in fact, is a conscious and concentrated way of 'looking' which engenders feelings of lust and satisfaction that are not necessarily directed toward concupiscence; at its more extreme, scopophilia manifests itself as a kind of Peeping Tom syndrome. The cinema, Mulvey argues, has consciously evolved a viewing context which promotes scopophilic pleasures, presenting 'a hermetically sealed world which unwinds magically, indifferent to the presence of the audience, producing for them a sense of separation, and playing on their voyeuristic phantasy' (Mulvey, 1975: 749). The darkness, beamed light and the dream-like qualities of the cinema create a mood of privacy and the illusion that the spectator is looking alone and from a distance.

The second major pleasure associated with cinema spectatorship derives from the complicated processes of narcissism (self-love) and identification. The identification of spectator with spectacle is a necessary part of self-definition. Mulvey parallels this process with Jacques Lacan's description of a child's mirror phase, where the child misrecognizes his/her 'reflected' image as more complete, powerful and perfect than is actually the case (see Chapter 5). Mulvey argues that this misrecognition occurs in cinematic identification. This matrix of recognition/misrecognition constitutes the significant articulation of the 'I' of the world, the viewer's fundamental experience of self:

> This is a moment when an older fascination with looking (at the mother's face for an obvious example) collides with the initial inklings of self-awareness. Hence it is the birth of the long love affair/despair between image and self-image which has found such intensity of expression in film and such joyous recognition in the cinema audience. (Mulvey, 1975: 749)

The dual move in cinema spectatorship leads the viewer to identify with the perfection of the screened image, creating a false sense of completeness, while at the same time drawing the viewer into the pre-recognition phase of the unconscious, that condition in which viewers forget time, place and their own self. As we have noted in various discussions, this condition is a form of unconscious textual immersion, comparable to Barthes's concept of textual bliss, and what Lacan describes as the phase of immersion in the identity of the mother prior to the recognition of 'lack' and entrance into the symbolic world of language.

Mulvey points out that these two pleasures are necessarily in tension: scopophilia is based on the separation of the spectator from the spectacle; narcissism is a function of the engagement of the spectator with the 'ego-ideal' (the image of a perfected self) represented in the spectacle. These contradictions, however, are resolved somewhat through the social functioning of cinema, a functioning which ascribes the role of spectator to men and spectacle to women. Hollywood cinema, in particular, actually systematizes these roles through highly efficient practices. Camera techniques reinforce modes of looking by drawing the eyes of the audience into the eyes of the male protagonist; the female star is eroticized by the male protagonist and hence by the male audience, reinforcing the disciplinary and controlling processes on the female body. Such pleasures, however, constitute a dominant patriarchal order which needs to be challenged in order to 'conceive a new language of desire' (Mulvey, 1975: 748).

While Mulvey's essay has been enormously influential in the development of a feminist media and cinema studies, more recent appraisals of audiences and visual pleasure have asked disarmingly simple questions about the essay's validity. In particular, the issue of the female gaze and eroticization of the male body has caused remarkable perturbations for Mulveyan analysis. That is, Mulvey's essay ideologically connects the repetition of female images types in cinema with broader social control mechanisms; is it then not possible that the repetition of male body images might provide symbolic material for sexual and ideological reversal? Just as the female body is repeated and centralized for spectatorship, the male body is clearly rendered for the fantasy and freedom of female spectatorship (see Williams, 1992; van Zoonen, 1994). Moreover, Mulvey's essay assumes a heterosexual engagement; it's becoming increasingly clear that gay, lesbian and bisexual spectatorship will appropriate 'straight' imagery for an adaptive homosexual pleasure (see, e.g., Cowie, 1984; Matthews, 1997).

Of course, these variations in spectatorship processes may reflect the realization of Mulvey's objective, which was to dismantle the patriarchal continuities of Hollywood cinema. Certainly, during the 1970s, the articulation of women's visual pleasure was considerably more constrained than is presently the case. Mulvey's own psychoanalytic schema, nevertheless, clearly restricts the acknowledgement of a varied visual erotica, maintaining, as it does, that the underlying structures of patriarchy determine male as normative and female as other. Mulvey's own experimental films (with Peter Wollen) represent a strident assault on patriarchal looking and the Hollywood template. But even these efforts have encountered criticism, as commentaries have accused Mulvey of elitism and inaccessibility. In the context of an increasing academic interest in the 'value' of popular arts and popular cinema, Mulvey's critique of Hollywood and TV imagery has been seen as limiting and limited, denying women's sexuality and capacity for erotic looking, rather than liberating it.

POSTSTRUCTURALISM AND FEMINISM

The theorists discussed above share a common belief that the two human genders, women and men, represent more or less distinctive social classes. Patriarchy is an historically constituted political, economic and cultural system which necessarily facilitates the domination of one group over the other. These two classes may not be the only significant structural divisions functioning within a society, but for many feminists they are the principal determinants of a person's life experiences – more so than social class, which may be abrogated or transcended by individual effort and the greater facilitation mechanisms of patriarchal social mobility. A woman may learn to speak, dress and act in ways that belie her social class, but she can never escape the inscriptions of her gender.

Clearly, this form of structuralist feminism tends to homogenize the experience and cultural constituency of the respective conditions of male and female. Both Millett's repudiation of patriarchal objectifications of women and Mulvey's psychoanalytic model of eroticization 'reduce' much of the complex interplay of identity, gender and culture to a simple ideological polemic. Poststructuralism, as we have noted in the previous chapter, questions the stability of signification processes, thereby casting doubt over the oppositions and fundamentalism of structuralist polemics. For feminism, this is particularly pertinent since the reformist agenda of first and second wave feminism relies so critically on the homogenized poles of male–female and on the historically perpetuating *system* of patriarchy. Not surprisingly, many feminists reject poststructuralism's emphasis on language and the limits of structure, most particularly those feminists who have sought the democratic or revolutionary overthrow of structured male privilege.

Even so, particular zones of poststructuralism have presented themselves in terms of political objectives. Michel Foucault, for example, seeks to expose personal or microphysical dimensions of power, most particularly as it is experienced at the level of the individual body. Deleuze and Guattari seek to undermine normative discourses which treat human desire and psychology as pathology. In both cases, power is conceived as a formation in language and knowledge, as a matter of process and unstable exchange, rather than as a fixed and inherent facility of structure. For a feminist analysis, this means that the social and cultural construction of gender can no longer be conceived as a necessary outcome of social structures. The symbolic constitution of male and female is problematized as the categories themselves become contingencies of uneven and unstable language processes. Poststructuralist feminism, therefore, could no longer accept the feminist project which sought to overthrow the old structures of male–female and replace them with new ones. Rather, a poststructuralist feminism had to dissolve the fixed position of structure altogether and open the question of gender to a general deconstruction.

A poststructuralist feminism, that is, needs to focus on the personal and unstable dimensions of power without reducing the complexities of sexuality to essentialist or generic statements. This means that poststructuralist feminism could not make broad claims about the way 'men' look or the way particular representations gratify a patriarchal system. Poststructuralism attempts to dispense with the notion of 'system', as it dissolves generic and structuralist statements like 'women are nurturers'. Poststructuralism can then go on to explore the possibilities of new language formations, but without certainty or stability. This emphasis on language games and the immediate and personal experiences of language disinclines poststructuralism from a direct assault on the structures of power. That is, power is analyzed at the level of the personal, the individual body and individual subjectivity. While structuralism seeks to replace iniquitous social structures with more just and compassionate structures, poststructuralism is more interested in elucidating power as it functions in personal relationships. Therefore, poststructuralism rejects Mulvey's approach to the gaze, arguing that the assumption of a structural difference in the way men and women 'look' is dubious. Nor, indeed, can poststructuralism accept the basic feminist precepts which might claim 'all men are sexist', or 'all men are rapists'. For poststructuralism, these statements are as unsustainable as 'all women are nurturers'.

Desire and Freedom: Julia Kristeva

Julia Kristeva, a French theorist, has attempted to produce a poststructuralist feminist theory based on Jacques Lacan's psychoanalytic model. Lacan's theories, of course, were adapted by Laura Mulvey's more structuralist analysis of cinema in order to explain the system of Hollywood movies in terms of distinct gendered differences. Kristeva (see 1980), however, sought to extend her analysis of texts and representation beyond the limits of 'system'. In particular, she wanted to develop Gail Rubin's theory of a sex–gender system, exploring the possibilities of subjectivity and desire without recourse to prescriptive differences between men and women. Kristeva uses Lacan's description of subject-splitting to emphasize the instability of knowledge and identity. Like Derrida, Kristeva challenges the 'logocentricism' of Western philosophy, arguing that the whole notion of a unified, knowing subject is fundamentally designed to exclude the possibilities of the 'subversive noise of pleasure'.

Desire, according to Kristeva, unfixes the subject, creating new possibilities for experiencing self and identity. In particular, poetic language demonstrates how 'new' discourses might penetrate the authority and standardization of familiar and constrained discourses and subject positions. Thus, unlike Mulvey's subject, who appears, in the end, to be a victim of the subject-making of systematic, male, authority discourses, Kristeva's subject is always in process and capable of choosing alternative subject positions. Kristeva's psychoanalytic model for a revolutionary feminism emphasizes continually the potential for the liberation of desire. The rhythm and sound of poetic language mimic the sense experiences of sexual engagement. Poetry liberates the individual from the unconscious. Only when these raw materials of sense – the semiotic – become regulated do they return to the conditions of logics, order, authority and fixity.

Other French Poststructuralist Feminists

Thus, while Mulvey appears to offer little escape from the socially contrived unconscious (other than perhaps her own unapproachable filmic texts), Kristeva seeks constantly an anarchical discourse for the liberation of women and men from the limitations of logocentricism and the authority of phallocentric 'symbolic' order. This revolution of language is closely linked to avant-garde artistic and literary expression and to the actual overthrow of political and legal processes that limit women's full participation in culture. Other French feminists (Chantal Chawaf, Xafière Gauthier, Luce Irigaray, Hélène Cixous) argue similarly that female sexuality is an immense and mysterious force for revolutionary reconstruction. Irigaray and Cixous, for example, have each argued that women need to present the fundamental differences inscribed in their bodies and sexuality as formidable revolutionary tools.

In this sense, French poststructuralist feminism marks its distinction from earlier anglophone feminist writings which seek primarily to expose the material and symbolic deprivation of women's lives. For Kate Millett, the differences between males and females have been exaggerated as they have been inscribed by the systematic conditionings of patriarchal society; biology has been used in the rhetoric of control and subordination: 'weaker sex', 'irrational', 'emotional', 'nurturing', 'passive'. For French feminists like Irigaray and Cixous, however, these biological differences can be harnessed in the celebration and articulation of feminine power. Women, therefore, cannot be conceived as merely one thing, but are infinite and expanding. Rather than emphasizing the negative conditions of patriarchy, French poststructuralist feminists have tended to seek an articulation of new possibilities, new differences, new horizons.

In her co-authored essay 'The laugh of the Medusa', Cixous (with Clément) outlines a formidable and almost joyous account of female bodies and their articulation in text. While acknowledging the potentialities of female masculinity and male femininity, Cixous nevertheless insists that female writing is inevitably an expression of women's own distinctive corporeality: 'The difference becomes most clearly perceived on the level of *jouissance*, in as much as a woman's instinctual economy cannot be identified by a man or the masculine economy' (Cixous and Clément, 1986: 81). Thus, echoing Roland Barthes' notion of textual bliss, *jouissance*, Cixous is referring to some finer and more complete state of writing and reading. The nexus of text and body is a condition of cultural advance – that new and irretrievable expansion of the female experience.

The Problem of Representation

Clearly, the approach of Cixous, Irigaray and Kristeva to sexuality and text provokes further complexities for feminism and feminist thought. In particular, the desire to articulate the uniqueness of the female aesthetic and unconscious – the heightened and celebrated state of difference – risks a return to essentialism ('women are *essentially* like this'). That is, while opposing the possibilities of a biological essentialism which can be articulated as a reason for subjugation, the French poststructuralists seek another brand of essentialism which broadens rather than diminishes the horizons of female sexuality and subjectivity. In many respects, this theoretical complexity parallels broader difficulties within poststructuralism itself, most especially as it attempts to translate its notions of discourse and power into political strategy. Notions of language instability – the unfixing of signifiers from their signifieds – open the way for the removal of all forms of essentialism, fixed systems and categories, and structure. A feminism that seeks to restore the unique conditions of the 'female' tends to risk the subversion of its own theoretical premise.

As it merges with cultural studies, feminism has confronted the issue of how women are represented in texts, and how those texts function at a political level. A good deal of feminist cultural analysis has tried to reconcile the structuralist and poststructuralist approaches to the question of representation. In its efforts to present a genuinely political account of representation, feminist cultural studies has offered a range of arguments about the absence, presence and nature of these representational discourses. These arguments continue to inform and frustrate contemporary feminist textual analysis. They can be summarized as follows:

1a   Women are historically absent/ excluded from public discourse because men have controlled the facilities of representation. This means that women (or 'non-idealized' images of women) are absent because men like to tell their own stories about their own interests and objects of desire. This classical feminist argument suggests that structural forces operate to exclude women from full participation. While recent textualizations are attempting to redress this historical exclusion, it is still obvious in the arts, politics, business and commerce.

1b   Alternatively, women are actually present in public discourse but this presence is not acknowledged because women's discourses have been seen as 'inferior' to men's; men, in fact, control the mechanisms of acknowledgement. Women actually tell their own stories, but the texts are more locally distributed, more personal or not appealing to mass market and popular cultural consumption. The significance and value of these texts (novels, poems, conversations, short films, family photos, etc.) are not seen as important by hegemonic cultural discourses controlled by men. Women will not participate, for example, in the aggressive, adversarial political institutions that have been established by men; women's politics are more personal and quotidian, involving creative and community participation.

2   Men are not able to represent women accurately because they are not corporeally or experientially capable of knowing what it is to be a 'woman'. This is the French poststructuralist feminist approach discussed above. Women and their experience of their lives and bodies are unique and can be only adequately represented by women themselves. The completion of women's liberation is only possible with the release and exploration of desire through the woman's own body and through artistic representation. Women are *essentially* different and must be given the means of expressing that difference.

3   As a corollary of (2), it must follow that men and women experience their lives differently. As only women can genuinely represent the female experience, women should be absent from representations by men and men should be absent from representations by women. This extreme poststructuralist perspective suggests, further, that each subject and subjective experience is unique, casting doubt on the whole enterprise of representation.

Foucault and Feminism

Attempts to overcome these difficulties have produced some interesting and diverse arguments both within and outside feminism. In particular, a number of feminists have applied Michel Foucault's conceptions of discourse/power for the broader analysis of representation and sexuality. Foucault's *History of Sexuality, Volume One* has provided feminists with a view of power which acknowledges the imperatives of representation (discourse) and the processes of control and liberation. Thus, while Marxist and liberal materialist visions of sexuality tend to seek liberation in the specific conditions of social revolution or legislation, Foucauldian liberation is premised on discursive and ideological transformation. As we noted in the previous chapter, however, Foucault presents his books as 'bombs for others to throw', a challenge which poststructuralist feminism applies to the analysis of the textual representation of women in a multitude of contemporary discourses. Foucault has pointed out that sexuality as a set of texts and practices (all discursive or carrying meaning) is fundamentally in dispute. Bodies as sets of discourse are never finalized, never complete, but always in a state of flux, always under siege, always a site of power and discursive contestation. Thus, the bourgeois sexuality of the nineteenth century was not repressed, as is so often reported. Rather, the discourse of sexuality was transformed into something new and different: medical, population, educational, social scientific and even confessional discourses all provided a conduit for sexual language and sexual expression. Thus, while the European *scientica sexualis* contrasts with the *ars erotica* of the East, there was nonetheless a discourse available for the constant pleasures, anxieties and disputes in power of modern, bourgeois sexuality.

Foucault's poststructuralist phase, thereby, provides a conception of subjectivity and identity which acknowledges the multiple levels of discourse and power. The subject, like discourse itself, is never complete but is always in a state of flux. In following Foucault, recent feminists (e.g., Sawicki; Moi, 1991; Meyerowitz, 2002) have left the question of biological difference entirely open, acknowledging further that gender is only one discursive inscription among others (such as class, ethnicity, identity and sexual orientation). That is, feminism has tried to move away from conceptions of the feminine which re-essentialize the experience of women and which seek liberation through the elite or avant-garde arts. The eschewal of sexism, therefore, is not to be found in the unique (and generic) female experience nor in the aesthetics of an avant-garde poem or film. Rather, the liberation of women must be viewed as a more inclusive but personal and particular project, one which may engage with other aspects of an individual's identity and experience of the world. The liberation of women, to put it simply, is about the liberation of each woman as opposed to the collective class.

This quite radical move provides a certain freedom for Foucauldian feminism; Theresa de Lauretis, a poststructuralist feminist film theorist, conceives of identity, for example, in terms of a subjectivity which is

> constituted in language, to be sure, though not by sexual difference alone, but rather across language and cultural representations; a subject engendered in the experience of race and class, as well as sexual relations; a subject therefore not unified but rather multiple, and not so much divided but contradicted. (1987: 2)

Gender, in this sense, is conceived in terms of process and exchange rather than as a fixed condition. Foucauldian poststructuralism, therefore, declares that the subject is ultimately open. Foucauldian feminism slips away from the semiotic–symbolic dichotomy outlined by Julia Kristeva. Kristeva criticizes the symbolic as it relies on realistic or direct representations of the world in accordance with prevailing (patriarchal, post-Oedipal) ideological order. The eschewal of these authoritative discourses exists only in the pre-symbolic (pre-Oedipal, semiotic) dimensions of the unconscious/poetic. It should be remembered that the terms 'symbolic' and 'representation' are being used here to locate a particular set of popular texts (filmic, photographic, literary). These popular texts are distinguished from more complex and poetic, avant-garde textualizations which defy the symbolic because they produce a sort of 'new' or 'original' discourse that parallels the pre-linguistic demeanour of the unconscious (pre-linguistic, before the discovery of 'lack').

A Foucauldian approach tends to reject such distinctions, parcelling all forms of meaning-making (practices and texts) into the one category of 'discourse'. This is more than a semantic difference, however, since the Foucauldian approach would see all meaning-making as cultural contingencies and subject to the analytical strategies of deconstruction and discourse/power. Foucauldian feminism would claim, therefore, to present a broader strategy of sedition; this strategy seeks to undermine both the authoritative, realistic texts impugned by Kristeva and any other discourse (poetic, avant-garde or otherwise) which would fix the subject in a particular subject position, including positions based on the prescription of gender. Foucauldian subjectivity is always in process, always seeking that new and untraversed possibility. Both audience-based and postmodern feminisms have adapted this approach in order to explore a broader notion of gender and gendered identity. Unlike Kristeva's approach, therefore, a Foucauldian feminism would avoid the restoration of the 'unique' or 'essential' experience of being a woman; gender is opened to an infinite array of possibilities.

MAGAZINES AND CULTURAL FEMINISM

Foucauldian feminism provides a significant facility for those feminists interested in liberation and individual freedom. The move, which takes gender issues away from notions of a fixed or essential identity and the determining conditions of gendered structure or class, clearly releases the potential for individual agency and self-determination. The limits of this approach, however, relate to a broader problematic in the relationship between poststructuralism and cultural politics: that is, can we have a politics which opposes oppression or injustice but which is not rooted in structure or structured ideology? Critics of the Foucauldian approach argue that the de-centered subject must ultimately be conceived in terms of language, and language must ultimately re-centre (re-originate, re-fix) its content as a claim to knowledge or truth. Foucault's particular deconstruction of gendered knowledge, it is argued, must inevitably constitute an alternative discourse, a new way of conceiving the subject, and thus of re-centring the subject. This alternative, revolutionary discourse will be centred or positioned somewhere: it can't exist in a vacuum.

These critics of Foucauldian feminism argue, further, that the emphasis on discourse inevitably limits the very real conditions of female poverty, disadvantage and underprivilege. The material world is necessarily parenthesized in Foucauldian analysis (Mitchell, 1984). Marxist and liberal humanist feminists retain their interest in what they see as the conditions of cultural and economic privations, pointing out, for example, that women on a global scale have incomes of less than half that of males. Postcolonial feminists point to the high mortality rates, debilitating poverty and excessive labour-loads of women in the non-developed world; they also point to the continuing political and public exclusion of women, and to the oppressive legal conditions in nations that execute women for sexual infidelity or for being the victim of sexual assault. This material and physical oppression is measured through vigorous ideological processes which continue to represent women as socially and culturally abnormal.

Angela McRobbie and British Cultural Feminism

We have discussed in detail the development of a particular form of cultural studies at the Birmingham Centre for Contemporary Cultural Studies during the 1960s and 1970s (see Chapter 4). The Centre's emphasis on the material and ideological privileging of particular groups within a culture over the interests of others contributed significantly to the evolution of contemporary cultural analysis. As Stuart Hall (1996) has noted, the question of politics was never too far away in any of the work carried out at the Centre. Angela McRobbie, who was one of Hall's associates at Birmingham, brought a vigorous and determinedly feminist perspective to those politics, challenging the Centre's own dominant approaches of class, ideology and culturalism.

McRobbie's early work on gender and youth culture is framed around Althusserian ideology. In particular, McRobbie illustrates how text, audience and industry interact to produce specific significations and ideological effects. In her essay on the teen magazine *Jackie*, McRobbie (1982) defines the publisher, D.C. Thompson, in terms of a capitalist logics and anti-unionist politics. She argues that the producers of the magazine consciously seek to produce a social and cultural order 'in terms of femininity, leisure and consumption' (1982: 87). McRobbie follows Althusser's notion of Ideological State Apparatuses in pointing to the manufacture of images, discourses and ideas which lead young women to consent to the conditions of their oppression and control. That is, young women are 'disciplined' into a patriarchal way of thinking about themselves and their femininity through a repetitive exposure to idealized feminine forms.

Publishing houses, which have a particularly invisible but significant status within a culture, are able to exert excessive power within the 'struggle to signify', despite the uncanny capacity of youth to subvert imposed culture. McRobbie acknowledges the potential for internal disruption to the conditions of cultural hegemony (social and cultural leadership), though for young women this capacity is limited by their gender. That is, in the normal conditions of hegemony the followers are able to manoeuvre and 'negotiate' certain aspects of the leaders' control. Youth culture, as Dick Hebdige (1979) demonstrates, is particularly well versed in taking the artefacts of an imposed culture (the transistor radio, clothing and hairstyles, street corners, etc.), adding to them and making them part of their own cultural experience. However, the restricted access of girls to the public sphere limits their ability to reappropriate cultural products and hence disturb the predominant processes of control and consent. McRobbie argues, in fact, that girls' use of teenage magazines tends to take place within private spheres, and that cultural practices, which Gramsci believed would produce the conditions for negotiated domination, are never really available for them.

McRobbie uses standard semiotic analysis to demonstrate how particular images and motifs are repeated in order to produce gender-based stereotypes. Sex and love become the defining qualities of life. Boys are classed in terms of action and access; girls are blonde and sexy, brunette and unreliable, or plain and uninteresting. The major objective is to attract the interest, love and fidelity of a boy, and hence female relationships are defined in terms of competition and threat: 'The girl's life is defined in terms of emotions – jealously, possessiveness and devotion. Pervading the stories is a fundamental fear, fear of losing your boyfriend or never getting one' (McRobbie, 1982: 107). Overall, McRobbie's analysis treats *Jackie*, in her own words, as 'a massive ideological block in which readers were imprisoned' (1991: 141). Her later work on teen magazines, influenced by some revisionary analysis of audiences and texts, tends to admit a greater possibility for feminine subversion. In particular, McRobbie appears to have moved beyond dismissive accounts of women's magazines (cf. Jackson, 1996) which condemn them universally for their imposed and controlling images of female femininity.

Cultural Feminism and Postmodernism

McRobbie (1997) notes that poststructuralism and poststructuralist psychoanalysis have extended the boundaries of feminist analysis beyond the sort of 'austere' Althusserianism which had directed her own work on *Jackie*. According to McRobbie (see also Winship, 1987; Driscoll, 1995), poststructuralism opens up the question of meaning and identity for women, illustrating a more complex relationship between what is known and what might function at the level of the unconscious. Battles for meaning, power and identity rage across the broad gamut of discourses, including the discourses of commercial women's magazines, feminism and the private imaginings of the mind. In the progress of her work, McRobbie comes to question her earlier assumptions about girls' capacity to interpret and reject cultural texts and artefacts. She adopts a more Gramscian approach to feminism and to the ways in which discourses are evolved; she argues, in fact, that adolescent girls' identities are negotiated through these various discourses. Ultimately it is these battles and exchanges which lead McRobbie to acknowledge the possibility that there may be

> no truth of womanhood, just as there can be no single or true feminism. Power resides in the currents of meaning which condense at key cultural sites in society, including magazines. Hence one important task for feminism is to show how magazines compete to construct the subjectivities of millions of female readers by producing these great bundles of meanings on a weekly basis. So familiar are these that they enter our unconsciousnesses producing desires and pleasures even when consciously we might not want them to. (1997: 193)

This question of pleasure has become central to postmodern and audience-oriented cultural theory. McRobbie herself concedes that it is women's pleasures, filtered through the feminist critique, which ultimately disrupt the monochrome of ideological analysis. Feminists themselves experience a love–hate relationship with the popular texts they study, seduced perhaps by the feminine imagery and the romantic narrative of popular women's magazines.

This new or diversified brand of feminism facilitates a critical efficacy which brings feminism back into a more empathic relationship with women's (as opposed to 'feminist') culture. Feminists are now able to admit their own pleasures and anxieties into the broad lexicon of everyday women's experience, deconstructing the loftiness or superiority of their academic knowledge and facilitating a significant engagement with the broadly based political potentialities of popular culture. In this sense, McRobbie's recent studies have sought to explain the transformation of women's, especially young women's, magazines and the reformulation of the notion of femininity. In particular, she notes in her analysis of the British magazine *More* that there has been a movement away from sexual restraint and the obsessive interest in *the* boyfriend toward images of sexuality and identity 'which break decisively with the conventions of feminine behaviour by representing girls as crudely lustful, desiring young women' (1997: 196). For McRobbie, this new identity marks a significant moment in which the relationship between feminism and femininity is loosened; the new teenage girl is free to seek her fun and pleasures, though ultimately, even in this liberated territory, the question of power and capitalist consumption remains problematic.

FEMINISM IN CONTEMPORARY POLITICS

McRobbie's account of current-day feminism demonstrates clearly that the field of gender critique is far from monodic and singularly motivated. From the 1980s through to the 2000s this greater interest in pleasure and identity, and the shifting nature of gender analysis continued to challenge the conventions of structuralist feminist analysis. Contemporaneously, women's liberation penetrated broad areas of popular, personal and governmental discourses, bringing significant changes to the way the culture conceived of and experienced gender. Even so, the liberation imagined by feminists like Simone de Beauvoir and Kate Millett has evolved and fragmented in ways which have produced often contradictory and unanticipated consequences. Perhaps the most notable manifestation of these unexpected consequences has been the appropriation of feminist ideologies and aspirations by conservative politics. In particular, the rise and dominance of Margaret Thatcher in British politics has illustrated the double-edge of contemporary feminism. The economic and social policy success of Thatcherism has been mimicked, not only by subsequent British and Australian governments, it has powerfully influenced a generation of feminists on the political right across the globe. Thatcher's austere contraction of public welfare, the arts, health, education and public transport, along with her vicious assault on labour organizations and the public services, marshalled a policy position which shattered the optimistic visions of 1970s political feminism. Thatcher's free-market philosophy exposed an unsettling dimension of feminism which demeaned weakness and vulnerability – especially in men – in favour of a performative competitiveness which hearkened to the deep values of British conservativism. The consequences for feminist philosophy can be summarized as follows:

1   Thatcherism shattered the traditional image of the 'female' as nurturer and carer, the keeper of community and personal welfare.
2   Thatcherism demonstrated that women could be just as vicious, imperious, chauvinistic and brutal as any man, shattering the stereotype of masculinity which had informed earlier feminist critique.
3   The unleashing of Thatcherist power illustrated that power was more than just a fixity of gender, but could easily be moved to the female. The essentialization of gender needed to be modified against other conditions of class, education, race, sexuality, nation.

4 Thatcherism raised the question of the purpose of liberation. If a woman were to accede to power and act so terribly against other women (and men), then what had feminism achieved?

5 A number of feminists explained Thatcherism as another manifestation of patriarchy, that Thatcher merely took on the characteristics of males in a male political context. If this were so, then how could a feminine power be conceived as an alternative? And is feminine power to be conceived as some mysterious, ineffable and essential force?

6 The rise of a conservative feminism obliterated the putative disadvantages of gender, arguing that if an individual were good enough, he or she would necessarily succeed.

This conservative feminism has been particularly prominent in English-speaking nations with a Westminster system of government: Britain, Canada and New Zealand have all had conservative female prime ministers or opposition leaders. It may be that the absence, until the 2008 Presidential round, of such significant female political leaders in the United States has contributed to a more assertive affirmative action legislation. It may also be that feminist politics in the United Kingdom has been mollified by the potency and austerity of Thatcherist feminism. In either case, feminism has been forced to confront a potential for deep, economic and social conservatism (see Heywood and Drake, 1997). Certainly some feminists dismiss Thatcherist feminism as either no feminism at all, or an inevitable part of female participation in public life. In the latter sense, feminists continue to impugn a social and political system which still limits female representation, arguing that parliament, congress and the presidential office will never be truly democratic until all forms of female experience are represented there. Only when women have an equal presence in government will the Suffragette project and democracy itself be fully realized.

As we have noted, a significant strand of feminist politics has been grounded in capitalist and bourgeois ideology. Even Jane Austen's *Mansfield Park* celebrates a kind of bourgeois prosperity and the advancement of middle-class women over the servitude and poverty of West Indian black workers upon whom the wealth is clearly founded (Said, 1993). Utilitarian feminism embraces the opportunities of market-based economy, and certainly this brand of feminism is present in Thatcherist politics. It should not surprise us, therefore, that one of the most prominent demonstrations of feminist political success has been associated with classical, free-market economics and the rights of the individual to succeed. The conservative political position which promotes individual progress as the root of social progress lies at the heart of Thatcherist feminism. It may be that the final lesson of Thatcherism is that the liberation of women is more likely to be accomplished through an aggressive individualism, rather than through an intricate rendering of collective, leftist agitation. That is, conservative individualism may well produce the reforms and successes sought by feminism.

Certainly, the successes of an individualist or right-wing feminism, along with a general diversifying and modulating of the politics of the Left since the 1980s, has contributed to a significant fracturing of the feminist project. The increasing gap between rich and poor inside and between nations is facilitated by a brand of capitalism which is necessarily associated with free-market ideology. Conservative feminism has certainly played its part in this extension of hierarchical principles, urging a liberation of the (female) self which is bound by an ideology that celebrates personal gratification and the accumulation of personal wealth.

The success of conservative politicians such as US Secretary of State Condoleeza Rice is a more recent example of the accomplishments of feminism, although there is no doubt that many left-leaning feminists feel aggrieved at the choices some women are making. Rice, for example, who supported the US-led invasion and occupation of Iraq, seems more interested in the ideology of American global domination and personal prosperity than in the fate of the multitude of her Iraqi sisters. As a feminist, Rice represents the acme of personal self-realization – but she appears less interested in any form of collective female consciousness or responsibility.

Other feminists, however, remain less enthusiastic about this ideology, attaching their liberational feminism to the other reformist issues: social equity, social welfare, poverty alleviation, education, ethnicity, sexual orientation, environmentalism. In either case, it is clear that the older style of feminism, which was largely monophonic and which tended to locate the female experience as the 'victim' of history, has been transformed into a new and radically more diverse political movement.

CONTEMPORARY FEMINIST CULTURAL POLITICS

Affirmative Action/Sexual Harassment

Equal opportunity, sexual harassment and affirmative action legislation has been enacted in most developed nations. The aim of this legislation is to reduce discrimination and promote greater access to public life by women and other disadvantaged groups. These types of legislation have been designed to draw women into the protection of the state and redress historical modes of gender-based discrimination. Such legislation has produced uneven results, prompting continuing debates over their efficacy and necessity. With the notable exception of Scandinavia and several other developed nation contexts, women remain significantly underrepresented in government legislatures, executive management and the higher income categories. And this is despite education and early career participation levels which are comparable to men.

To this end, career interruptions associated with family duties and child-rearing remain a primary obstacle to occupational fulfillment for many women. Scandinavian countries appear to have adopted more elaborate and 'family-friendly' childcare and workplace systems, allowing women an earlier and more conducive return-to-work than in other, more free-market models. Yet, even for those women who are not impeded by fertility

Women, girls and global power

While women in the first world debate different perspectives on career and 'femininity', many women in the developing world continue to live in the most abject conditions of poverty, disease, and political violence. According to a report by aid agency Plan International (2007) females make up the poorest class of people living on the planet, with over a billion women and girls living on less than a dollar a day. In many parts of the world, most notably the Middle East and Africa, females are entirely excluded from formal education; nearly 80 million girls worldwide are forced into marriage before the age of 18; and over 100 million girls each year are the victims of infanticide in countries where males are the preferred offspring.

These figures are corroborated by UNICEF (2007: 5), which points out that in 2002 there were around 150 million girls who had been the victims of forced sexual intercourse. Of the nearly 2 million girls under 18 who are working in the commercial sex trade, many have been abducted through the global sexual slave trade. In this context, it is not surprising that there are now around 3 million more women than men infected with HIV AIDS – a crisis which UNICEF attributes to women's general state of poverty, a lack of literacy amongst girls and the relative powerlessness of sex workers and wives. UNICEF also points out that the misery experienced by fertility-age women continues into later life, when elderly widows are often deprived of inheritance rights by patriarchal traditions and social customs.

While many commentators would point out that global poverty affects men as well as women, there can be little doubt that as a general class, women in the developing world are doing worse than a comparable category of males. While women and children are very rarely the perpetrators of political violence and oppression, they are most prolifically their victims. For many western feminists the poverty and misery of developing world women are a direct outcome of global systems of patriarchy and economic capitalism – western feminist issues such as sexual harassment, the cosmetics industry and the problematics of 'femininity' are qualitatively linked to women's poverty and oppression in the developing world. That is, both developing world poverty and modern conditions of social limitation are the result of culturally constituted patriarchy.

and family issues, the continuation of patriarchal codes and practices in business and public life is also often cited as a major obstacle to women's progress and full social participation (Moe, 2003). That is, through the economics of capitalist and professional competition, women as a class of workers are subject to the prejudice and self-interests of males. In this sense, sexual harassment is more than just a form of libidinal violation, it is an occupational strategy designed to humiliate and disadvantage women within a competitive work environment.

Of course, there are a number of more individualistic and free-market feminists who exhort women to conquer these disadvantages through personal effort, rather than

Plate 6.1   *The Slums of Mumbai in India where Women and Children are the Poorest of the Poor*

legislative process. As we noted in our discussion on utilitarianism and Thatcherism, there are certainly a number of feminists who argue against the proliferation of welfare style legislation, which imposes recruitment and promotion quotas for women and other disadvantaged groups. The major complaint against these affirmative action strategies is that they risk rewarding deficient performance in order to meet quotas; such situations could prove demoralising for other workers, reduce efficiency and contribute to corrupt workplace practices (Bacchi, 1996).

Separational and Cyborg Feminism

While the policy model of women's liberation is designed to serve the interests of the majority of women living and working in relatively 'mainstream' social circumstances, a more radical resonance of structural feminism proposes more forceful measures for the overthrow of patriarchy and the re-alignment of social history. This type of feminism, most particularly as it has attached itself to other liberational ambitions such as lesbian separationism, remains determinedly adversarial. The notion of 'difference' becomes the rallying point for the social and sexual fulfillment of women. 'Woman', in this sense, is a radical concept which ultimately seeks the erasure of *man* – not just patriarchy or 'phallocentricism'. This form of separationism is advocated by radical structuralists like Sheila Jeffreys who contends that male sexual penetration of women is generally tantamount to rape. In this broader context, woman to woman sexual engagement would replace heterosexuality, applying technological solutions to the 'problem' of reproduction. Believing that male sex hormones condemn men to dispositions of violence and control, radical separationists argue that lesbian sexuality is necessarily founded on social and sexual equality (Jeffreys, 2004, 2007).

Such views remain hostile to the notion of postmodern pleasures and the ultra heterosexuality of many contemporary women. Heterosexual female liberation, which manifests itself in sexual display, 'style', make-up, clothing, dance and even (heterosexual) 'promiscuity', is largely a delusion perpetrated by contemporary capitalism, men and patriarchy (Jeffreys, 2007). Within this context, it is not only patriarchy and history which is to blame for the oppression of women, but men. Jeffrey's own decision to adopt lesbian sexuality was largely political – a direct rejection of the social class of men who are the perpetrators of cultural oppression.

Sexuality, therefore, is a political weapon which needs to be used 'strategically'; difference is an essential and fundamental condition which necessarily assaults the idealized imagery, deceptive pleasures, sentimentalism and political relativism of particular versions of postmodern theory. Donna Haraway (1991), for example, anticipates the collapse of gender through the ascent of a cyborgian woman. Men, masculinity, patriarchy and capitalism will all implode through the evolutionary reign of the cyborg.

Postcolonial Feminism

Postcolonial feminism (see Spivak, 1987, 1992; Gunew, 1993; McClintock et al., 1997; Gauch, 2006) has generally been influenced by Foucauldian and psychoanalytic theory. However, rather than filtering these theories into a new mode of pleasure and personal creativity, postcolonial feminism has seen the issue of representation in terms of a transnational patriarchy or patriarchal imperialism. Here, the notion of 'self' and 'other' becomes highly politicized; the white, colonizing male is seen as the dominant or normative self and the Oriental or colonized female is seen as alien and the object of sexual and material 'colonization'. Thus, the women of colonized territories are 'doubly colonized' as imperialism is fortified by patriarchy.

Thus, while postcolonial theorists like Edward Said (1978, 1993) seek to liberate conquered peoples from the historical resonance of imperialism, feminist postcolonialists focus specifically on the condition of women in developing states and within migrant communities of developed (formerly colonizing) nations. The postcolonial or decolonization analysts frequently apply poststructuralist notions of subjectivity and language to their emancipatory project. The 'construction' of meaning through text is treated as entirely ideological: male conquerors justified their conquest, administration and exploitation of foreign peoples through the formation of a range of politically constituted texts. These texts included literary, philological and various forms of 'scientific' studies, as well as a raft of administrative and governmental documents. In essence, the texts sought to re-shape the law, culture and social knowledge of the conquered peoples, constituting their 'otherness' (difference to the colonial masters) as normal and a predicate of the more powerful colonizer. Such texts, of course, legitimated the rule of the conqueror as well as the superiority of the developed world culture and system of knowledge. The position of women in the colonized territories, which was generally subordinate to the men, became subject to the social and sexual interests of the conquering, white males. The Oriental woman – primitive, natural, sexually available – became thus iconicized in imperial texts, a condition of the aesthetic and libidinal imaginings of European culture.

More broadly, this eroticization of the Orient necessarily creates a control relationship between the male colonizer and the feminized Orient. This eroticization is expressed through notions of the Orient as 'exotic', feminine, mysterious and unruly. The art and poetry of the colonizing nations of Europe are replete with images of bare-breasted women, sleek and feminine-looking males. This sexualization matches femininity with subordination. Postcolonial feminism seeks to 'deconstruct' the images of the non-West by interrogating the colonial and patriarchal systems which give them legitimacy. The concept of 'difference' (diversity, multiculturalism, etc.) becomes the political alternative to a deconstructed cultural imperialism.

Transculturalism and Non-western Women

These arguments and modes of analysis have been particularly compelling, as they have been applied to particular problems in the developing, previously colonized world. Studies by UNESCO and other bodies have demonstrated that women and children in the non-developed world are the poorest and most malnourished humans on the planet. It is also clear that the education of women in these territories provides the most powerful opportunity for development, disease management and social improvement. In Africa, in particular, aid organizations and Non-government Organizations are now seeking to alleviate horrendous levels of poverty and suffering through a programme which 'emancipates' women from patriarchy and servitude. An educated and liberated mother provides the greatest hope for the education of children and a more broadly-based social mobility.

Even so, contemporary postcolonial feminism has been forced to confront a key paradox within its own theoretical grounding, most particularly as it seeks to impose its political perspective over Islamic women in the previously colonized territories of the Middle East. Indeed, the liberal humanist tradition from which feminism evolved in western culture has at times appeared disjunctive and even imperialist in its encounters with various forms of Middle Eastern and Islamic 'feminism'. As western feminists have sought the liberation of their Islamic sisters from patriarchal practices, including religiously derived cultural practices, Islamic feminists have often accused their liberators of cultural hubris. Such practices as polygamy and head-face coverage have been regarded by many western feminists as a form of male-imposed confinement of women's rights and sexual freedom; Islamic women, on the contrary, believe that they are expressing a choice within the boundaries of their faith and cultural traditions.

In discussing the war on Iraq, Wendy McElroy (2003) argues that the contiguity of military engagement is forcing western feminists to review their own solipsistic understandings of culture and the role of women. The feminism of the Middle East, according to McElroy, insists that women's liberation is absolutely integrated with religion, the family and men. Unlike the ideology of familiar second wave feminism which identifies religion and the family with the hegemony of patriarchy, Middle Eastern feminism seeks continually to reconcile gender roles within an Islamic culture that is constituted around the identity of the devout, family matriarch. This leaves the liberal feminist in the west with a serious and confronting problem –

> Western feminists cannot resolve their ideology with that of Islam. War and its aftermath will bring the two movements into intimate contact and conflict. The result is likely to be a recasting of the definition of feminism. (McElroy, 2003)

This form of feminist cultural hubris is resonant of precisely the cultural imperialism which postcolonial feminists have sought to overthrow. More generally, it recalls the central problem of a feminism which is largely constituted around an elite, educated, wealthy and western-centric social class. Western feminism, especially its universalistic structuralist incarnation, seeks to speak on behalf of *all* women across all cultures, contexts and territories. This approach not only subsumes the considerable aspirational variations between women, it also neglects the emancipatory needs of men – including those indigent, oppressed, violated and damaged men of the postcolonized world.

Postfeminism?

A number of commentators claim that we are now entering a 'postfeminist' cultural phase. There are three major reasons for this transformation: first, so-called

(Cont'd)

'second wave' feminism has produced the desired effects of focusing attention on the oppression of women during the modern period; second, legislation protecting the economic and social rights of women has been established in the major developed nations of the world; and, thirdly, the fragmentation of the feminist project has led to serious questions about the validity of treating women as a single social category, supported by a single political vision.

In a sense, the move to a postfeminist perspective has been motivated by the success of feminism. However, the very serious divisions and disputes within the field of feminism have led a number of cultural commentators to query the validity of the whole notion of 'feminism'; a number of women interested in the female experience have questioned whether their particular reformist project and their own identity can be productively associated with the nomenclature of 'feminist'. Whether we use the notion of 'postfeminism' or not, the problematic of contemporary feminism may be summarized as follows:

1 The strict categories of 'male' and 'female' are based on biological differences and cultural ascriptions. The liberating of these social and cultural ascriptions has led to a far more mixed social scenario where the historically ascribed characteristics of femininity and masculinity may be attached to either gender. Contemporary men and women may be more or less nurturing, athletic, aggressive, sexually assertive, and so on. Feminism which essentializes femaleness but excludes qualities of traditional 'femininity' risks being authoritarian and prescriptive. That is, feminism may commit women to social ascriptions which they may not wish to employ in their subjectivities.

2 Men's own subjectivity may be prescribed by a feminism which is supposedly dedicated to liberation.

3 This greater mixing of gendered subjectivity has led to a range of revisions within feminism. One of the most important questions is: can 'men' be directly linked to 'patriarchy', and are men responsible for patriarchy? Many women interested in the liberation of women have come to dissociate 'particular' men from the sins of sexism and patriarchy. (In many respects, this question parallels the problematic of racism: can all whites be held responsible for racism?)

4 Can women still be treated as a distinct, homogeneous and unitary social category independent of race, ethnicity, sexual orientation, education levels, income, community and age? Can we assume in contemporary society that being female is necessarily a subjugant social position? Is this really plausible or valuable for a politics of reform?

5 Patriarchy and capitalist specialization had allocated the roles of carer, educator, nurturer and community-builder to women; these roles had been regarded

as generally inferior to the tasks allocated to men. Rather than seeking to elevate the value and social status of caring work, feminist advocacy has been largely devoted to increasing women's access to areas of economic and public activity. Women's successful penetration into these areas has further diminished the status and value of caring activities, leaving a good deal of 'community' work vacant or devolved to low-paid and low-skilled workers. A good deal of public discussion on family, nurture and community care centres on the general absence of appropriate resources and personnel to ensure the emotional and mental health of the community. Postfeminism is asking difficult questions about the efficacy of this general exodus by women and men from the responsibilities of care.

THE IMAGING OF THE FEMALE BODY

Beauty and the Body

While much of the institutional and legal discrimination against women has been overcome in modern, western societies, many feminists argue that contemporary culture remains replete with discriminatory practices and various forms of symbolic oppression. In particular, women's bodies continue to be 'positioned' in terms of men's sexual desire and patriarchal imaginings of power and control. In a culture which is now dominated by visual imagery, the commodification of female sexuality has caused considerable consternation for many feminists. Naomi Wolf's widely read text *The Beauty Myth* argues, for example, that women's subjectivity has been crippled by a pervasive and pernicious patriarchal strategy of control and discipline. According to Wolf, legal and social liberation has not protected women against the 'beauty economy', which manacles women to impossible images, cosmetic products and modes of patriarchally imposed starvation diets and diseases:

> Beauty is a currency system like the gold standard. Like any economy, it is determined by politics, and in the modern age in the West it is the last, best belief system that keeps male dominance intact. In assigning value to women in a vertical hierarchy according to a culturally imposed physical standard, it is an expression of power relations in which women must unnaturally compete for resources that men have appropriated for themselves. (1991: 10)

Wolf's book, which has proven one of the highest grossing feminist texts of all times, simplifies and popularizes the work of earlier feminists such as Sandra Bartky and Andrea Dworkin.

Over the past two decades, in fact, many feminists have identified the beauty industry and body-modelling practices as the new incarnation of cultural patriarchy. This new submission to male sexual desire and imagining is not only insidious and oppressive, it creates serious harm to women's bodies, psyches and social dignity. Eating disorders, facial scarring, breast and genital damage, ingestion of toxins, infections, and even death – are all outward manifestations of a resurgent patriarchy. Sarah Shaw (2002) invokes a strong structuralist feminist critique against patriarchy and men who inflict various forms of 'mutilation' on women whose life mission becomes the visual gratification of men. According to Shaw, women have historically mutilated their bodies in order to satisfy the standards of normality and beauty set by men. The availability of new forms of cosmetic technology – face lifts, liposuction, breast augmentation, genital modification – have imposed new performative standards and expectations on women. Sheila Jeffreys (2005) argues that these new forms of mutilation accord with the United Nation's Fact Sheet on 'Harmful Traditional Practices', which seek to prohibit the inimical modifications of women's bodies. Stiletto shoes, push-up bras and even lipstick constitute a form of harmful social practice designed to stimulate male libido and assertions of control.

The feminist critique of sexual desire and beauty assumes that women are merely the passive subjects of male control and desire. As with the Marxist critique of class-based ideology, structuralist feminism provides few pathways to emancipation other than a revolutionary overhaul of the structures that govern patriarchal ideology. However, because patriarchy is so pervasive and entirely dominates women's minds and bodies, there appears no way of thinking outside the controlling structures: women simply can't see the reality of their situation. In this sense, the notion of 'choice' or personal agency is entirely misplaced, as women are deluded by a culture industry that is dominated by the interests, economic power and sexual desires of men.

As in other areas of the culture, this notion of choice has become a central battleground of social meaning-making. Alternatives to the structuralist perspective of desire, beauty and femininity have been generated through new forms of feminism. Liberal-utilitarian and postmodern feminism, in particular, regard the sexual pleasure of women to be the principal source of female liberation, beyond equality of opportunity and legislative protection against discrimination. This sexual pleasure is not merely the gratifications associated with carnal engagement; rather, 'pleasure' is connected to a broad range of feminine expressivities, including clothing, display, cosmetics and even surgery if a woman chooses. Natasha Walter, for example, argues that the problem with feminism is that it seeks perpetually to impose its social and political agonisms over every aspect of a woman's personal life. Learning from the sexual power represented in the imagery of Madonna,

Walter seeks a liberation that is infused with pleasure and a capacity for self-determination. In the contemporary context –

> Most women feel free, freer than their mothers. Most women can choose what to wear, whom they will spend their lives with, where to work, what to read, when to have children. (1999: 10)

A new feminism will feel 'easier' about the female experience, as women are able to 'spend time waxing their legs or painting their nails', indulging their 'often wickedly enjoyable relationship they have with their clothes and their bodies' without being made to feel guilty by an old, puritanical feminism (Walter, 1999: 86).

In *Fresh Lipstick* (2005) Linda Scott also invokes the Madonna motif, arguing that the anti-beauty feminists are merely self-serving as they seek to homogenize the immense diversity of women and women's experience in the cause of their own dull and monochromatic revolution. To this end, Scott's arguments invoke the postmodern perspective which treats power as a matter of personal exchange and expressivity, and which seeks to emancipate all subjects from the congregational impetus of mass 'society' and ideology. Thus, while feminists like Sheila Jeffreys might equate the Muslim veil and western cosmetics as comparable forms of patriarchal oppression (2005: 37–40), postmodern feminists argue that such cultural manifestations are merely surface tensions gathered around the broad problematics and celebratory value of human diversity. Women, that is, are not a single class of being, but a widely distributed and amorphous assemblage of characteristics, biology, cultural traits, manifestations, desires and imaginings, The condition of 'being female', in this sense, is formed around a diverse range of cultural options based on religion, ethnicity, skin colour, language, class, sexual orientation, style, age, and even the choice of eye-shadow. It is therefore an act of extraordinary hubris for middle-class, white, western intellectuals to prescribe the fits-all-sizes liberation for all women.

Grrrl Power and Transgendered Bodies

The celebration and exploration of new sexual imagery is most clearly evident in the analysis of rock and popular music, where Madonna, perhaps more than any other single female figure, has self-consciously 'explored' and displayed women's sexuality through the aesthetic of her music and visual imagery (see Fiske, 1989a; Walter, 2002; Scott, 2005). The Madonna image has been presented and used as a source of arousal, sexual pleasure and identity exploration. This mainstreamed and heavily corporatized Madonna imagery, however, contrasts with the more aggressively marginalized sexual imagery of other female rock musicians. As with broader debates surrounding the popular and the artistic in contemporary entertainment, many rock musicians find themselves contemplating the dilemma of personal, artistic control on the one hand, and commercial imperatives on the other. Popularity and the sale of CDs and concert tickets are the means by which most artists measure their success. However, there are a number of rock musicians who regard their creative activities as far more important than the aspiration of commercial success. The 'grrrl power' movement of the 1990s reflects the desires of a number of young women's bands to maintain the integrity of their creative and political activities and the presentation of themselves and their art through the media. In many respects, grrrl power sought to liberate the message and the messenger from the commercial control of record companies and media meaning-makers.

As female musicians and performers became increasingly popular during the 1990s, a number of younger female musicians sought to pursue a more didactic and assertively feminist polemic in their music. Supported by the Feminist Majority Foundation, the US based riot grrrls set out to encourage audience members 'to educate themselves, speak out, register to vote, and learn what they can do to protect their right to abortion and birth control' (Cause sleeve notes). As the movement spread to the underground rock scene in the United Kingdom, the messages of power and independence were intensified, forming a consciousness which sought collectively to subvert the masculinities which dominated rock culture.

Clearly, the aim of grrrl power and the riot grrrls was to wrest the power of representation away from male or patriarchal control and place it in the hands of the performers. This collective consciousness and the ideal of female emancipation which informs it, however, have not been sacrosanct. As Marion Leonard (1997) has pointed out in her discussion of grrrl power, the movement was simply incapable of sealing itself from the imperatives of ideological and commercial challenge. Grrrl power becomes girl power in the hands of the marketing machinery, and the aspirations of self-representation become modulated through capitalism and the commercial ideology. Highly commercialized and marketable product groups like the Spice Girls and Pussycat Dolls have been able to appropriate the idea of 'grrrl power' for the promotion and consumption of their own musical and image products. Feminism, like any other cultural formation, that is, may be transformed into commodity and dispersed as something predictable, mainstream and comfortable. For the celebrants of popular cultural texts, this form of feminism may represent, in fact, the cultural reality. Spice Girls and Pussycat Dolls feminism – ephemeral, attractively packaged and evasively defined – might prove to be the high point of social transformation. In any case, feminism has been enormously influential in achieving this transformation. Whether it is the pinnacle of its successes is yet to be determined.

But the Madonna imagery has also contributed to other forms of sexualized liberation, including the imagery of submissive males, transgenderism and bi-sexuality. In many respects, Madonna's imagery quite consciously invokes the sexual power and fluidity of earlier *cors celebres* such as Marlene Dietrich. In either case, the motif of women desiring women and cross-bordered bodies inevitably creates difficulties for the anti-beauty feminists whose liberational enterprise is forged largely around a rigid conception of men and women. Thus, while lesbian separational feminists imagine a utopia that has erased men and cosmetics, 'lipstick lesbians' imagine a personal expressivity and relationships that celebrate ultra femininity and its conjugal pleasures. As categories of lesbian sexuality, 'lipstick', 'femme' and particular kinds of female bi-sexuality generate much of their erotica around the same sexualized motifs of femininity which stimulate male heterosexual libido. The politics of lesbianism which inspire 'dyke culture' are thus substituted with a postmodern, style-based mode of female display and pleasure.

The same problems of identity and politics are also manifest in transvestite, transgender and inter-sex modes of expression. Transvestites are biological males or females who dress and express as the 'opposite' gender; transgender subjects change their physiology through medical interventions (hormones, surgery); and inter-sex subjects are born with indeterminate sexual biology, often having both forms of genitalia. In all cases, of course, the deterministic model of structuralist feminist critique barely applies. Male transvestites, in particular, adopt a form of femininity which seeks to parenthesize their male biology, thus defying the simple categorizations upon which sexism is putatively constructed. To this end, transvestites may be attracted to their own biological gender, or to the cultural gender they have adopted: in other words, transvestites may be homosexual, heterosexual or bi-sexual. In all cases, these transgendered bodies are living modes of a postmodern sexuality which challenges the monadic model and assumptions presented by anti-beauty structuralists.

7

Postmodernism and Beyond

INTRODUCTION

Over the past two decades the concept of postmodernism has achieved remarkable currency in cultural and public discourse. It is now virtually impossible to speak of contemporary culture without recourse to this resilient and encompassing concept. Like 'culture' itself, in fact, postmodernism appears to have penetrated every level of academic discourse from the humanities and arts through to the social and natural sciences. The concept, however, remains highly disputed, its mixed history directing scholars and other commentators through a phalanx of cognitive, critical and aesthetic possibilities. In this chapter we will examine the concept of postmodernism in relation to these key cultural debates. However, before proceeding, it is worth clarifying a few significant definitional issues.

Postmodernity and Postmodernism

A number of commentators distinguish between postmodernity and postmodernism. Postmodernity represents an historical phase or period which is characterized by the presence of particular cultural elements. Postmodernity supersedes the previous historical period of modernity. Of course there are many elements of the previous period which continue, but as Fredric Jameson (1991) argues, the new elements are sufficiently prevalent to suggest that we have entered a new historical phase. Postmodernism refers more specifically to a way of thinking, articulating and symbolizing. In other words, postmodernism might refer more specifically to a cultural mode of thought which ultimately expresses itself in discourse (see Hutcheon, 1988; Connor, 1989).

The periodizing of cultural history allows us to conceive of social elements which constitute a distinctive chronological order; however, there is little agreement about the nature, definition or date of postmodernity. The concept of the 'modern', for example, is sometimes restricted to a period of art production between 1880 and 1940 (see Bradbury and McFarlane, 1978; Gilbert and Gubar, 1988). Jean-François Lyotard, in his famous work *The Postmodern Condition* (1984a), allows both cognitive (ways of thinking) analysis and historical description to merge somewhat, creating the distinct sense that the 'knowing' in postmodernism is fundamentally inscribed in the condition itself: being part of the historical times, we necessarily 'think' in accordance with conditions of the culture. Meaghan Morris (1993, also 1998) goes as far as to suggest that our capacity to elucidate contemporary (postmodern) culture is linked fundamentally to our adoption of contemporary cognitive modes: analysts retaining older theoretical and analytical frameworks simply cannot understand the contemporary condition.

This interconnectedness of the two concepts, postmodernism and postmodernity, has discouraged many commentators from bothering with a distinction. Even so, the problem of how to define the postmodern and what should be included under its heading remains highly contested in aesthetics, sociology and cultural studies. In this chapter we will look at the ways in which the concept of 'postmodernism' has evolved and contributed to our broader understanding of contemporary culture. Specifically, we will explore the ways in which the concept has evolved through the development and integration of American aesthetics, social analysis, French poststructuralism and British cultural studies. Of particular interest are the ways in which the concept has been broadened and now applies across a wide field of disciplinary categories: aesthetic, social–historical, cognitive (way of thinking) and cultural (way of representing).

It is possible that the great surge in scholarly interest in the concept of postmodernism has been somewhat eclipsed by the emergence of new concepts and paradigms within the broad field of cultural analysis, particularly since the events of September 11, 2001 and a resurgent engagement in the cultural conditions of globalization. However, it is equally important to acknowledge that 'postmodernism' has become an integral, if not standard, component of the analytical lexicon – a rubric for the complex and often contradictory trends and elements which comprise contemporary culture.

LITERARY AND AESTHETIC DERIVATIONS OF POSTMODERNISM

The New York Experimental Art and Literature Scene

There is general agreement that the term 'postmodernism' was introduced by Frederico de Onis in the 1930s to describe some marginal reaction against the ascendant aesthetics of modernism (see Hassan, 1985). During the 1960s a loose collective of writers, musicians and artists adapted the term as a means of distinguishing their own avant-garde and rejectionist style of art from what has been referred to as the high modernism of the mid-century and post-World War II period. In particular, New York aesthetes and commentators like Susan Sontag, Ihab Hassan, John Cage, William Burroughs and Leslie Fiedler rejected the codes and status of institutionalized artistic forms.

William Burroughs, for example, sought to reinvigorate language and everyday experience through the exterior of human experience, rather than through the profound and intellectual mimesis of James Joyce or William Faulkner. Like Jack Kerouac and the Beat poets, Burroughs' language is experiential, liberated from the constraints of grammar and form. This paragraph from *Exterminator* represents the sort of muted and everyday epiphany that underscores the postmodern style proclaimed in Burroughs' writing:

> You couldn't say exactly when it hit familiar and dreary as a cigarette butt ground out in cold scrambled eggs the toothpaste smears on a washstand glass why you were on the cops day like another just feeling a little worse than usual which is not unusual at all well an ugly thing broke out that day in the precinct this rookie cop had worked a drunk over and the young cop had a mad look in his eyes and he kept screaming. (1966: 162)

This sort of everyday apocalypse has often been associated with forms of popular pleasure and hedonism. Burroughs' engagement with street life and with the language of street talk brings high literature into contiguity with popular cinema. This is the surface texture of language rather than the profound inner expressionisms of the individual as it had been explored by William Faulkner and other modernists. Burroughs' postmodernism is an excursion which directly challenges the borders between language and image, vision and collapse, high art and popular discourse.

Susan Sontag (1966) seems to parallel the rising interest in popular culture in Britain in her repudiation of academic textual studies which emphasize elite artistic forms and the activity of 'interpretation'. She rails against the exclusion of popular art forms such as photography and film from the academic canon. The reinvigoration of culture and cultural activities, she argues, is only possible through the radical reformulation of what it is that constitutes art and legitimate artistic expression. Interpretation serves merely to gratify the interests of academic institutions and the interests of a bourgeois cognoscenti. In particular, Sontag rejects the processes of canonization by which the avant-gardism of modernist texts – the literature of Joyce, T.S. Eliot and William Faulkner – becomes stabilized by bourgeois academic discourses and institutions. What might have been a radical transgression of artistic and cultural standards becomes stifled by institutional acceptance. 'Interpretation' is the act of normalizing texts; the radical elements of a text are transformed by forming them as palatable and recognizable tropes for consumption in schools and universities.

In *The Dismemberment of Orpheus: Towards a Postmodern Literature* (1982), Ihab Hassan attempts to explain the emergence of a literature which explicates, as it questions, its own literary and narrative techniques. This meta-fiction (see also Hutcheon, 1995) reworks a number of self-reflexive strategies that had been present in earlier literary forms, including Shakespearean and Jacobean dramas, and the eccentric tale-telling of Laurence Sterne (*Tristram Shandy*) and Henry Fielding (*Joseph Andrews* and *Tom Jones*). For Hassan, the most significant literature of the twentieth century reaches beyond the nihilism of high modernism; postmodernism is formed around a 'literature of silence' which succumbs to an Orphean dismemberment, but which nevertheless 'sings on a lyre without strings' (Hassan, 1982: xvii). Orpheus is the Greek poet/musician who is slain and dismembered by the Maenads because they were jealous of his attention to young men. Orpheus and the dismembered head are cast into the river Hebrus, where the dead poet continues to sing and defy his death. For Hassan, the poetics of postmodernism defies the logical conclusions of modernism (i.e., that all is death, that God is absent, that the universe makes no sense). The voices go on, despite the implications of despair which a nihilistic modernism brings to cultural knowledge.

Hassan, however, is not speaking so much about a rupture or jettison of modernist sensibilities as about an intensification of modernism's absurdist heroics. Postmodernism, that is, is somehow coiled into the imperatives of modernism, whereby the absurdism and alienation explored in the literature of William Burroughs represents another resonant tune, another silence, in the sexualized heroics of alienation. Madness, sexual ecstasy, the unstitching of form, the uneasy slippages of tragedy and comedy – all represent the extremes of modernism through the incarnation of postmodernism. In the 1982 edition of the book Hassan adds a 'Postface' which attempts to delineate the differences between the modern and the postmodern. Table 7.1 presents a summary of his distinctions.

Table 7.1   *Modern and Postmodern Literature*

Modernism	Postmodernism
Romanticism/symbolism	Pataphysics/Dadaism
Form	Antiform
Purpose	Play
Design	Chance
Hierarchy	Anarchy
Mastery/*logos*	Exhaustion/silence
Art object	Creative process
Synthesis	Antithesis
Preference	Absence
Centring	Dispersed
Root/depth	Rhyzome/surface
Origin/cause	Difference
Metaphysics	Irony
Determinacy	Indeterminacy

Source: Hassan, 1987: 267–8.

Literary Postmodernism and Popular Culture

Significantly, Hassan's account of literary postmodernism relies on a rather separatist view of the expressive power of literature. Indeed, despite their attempts to integrate various literary genres, including the popular genre of mystery and detective novels, into the lexicon of the postmodern, the aesthetic commentaries of the 1960s and early 1970s fixed their vision on avant-garde arts rather than on the mass-produced texts of popular culture. Popular culture was treated as a resource which the avant-garde could use for the construction of its own texts. Andy Warhol's texts, for example, mimicked popular iconography in the same way Burroughs' language imitated the openness of everyday street talk. This artistic 'egalitarianism' became a favoured trope for avant-garde postmodernism. Literary analysts like Ihab Hassan and Brian McHale, in fact, maintain an adherence to the Romantic idea that literature possesses a unique capacity for the articulation of culture beyond the confines of space and time. Brian McHale (1987), for example, sees the modernist literature of James Joyce, William Faulkner or even Franz Kafka as being fundamentally epistemological: the way human consciousness knows, understands or interprets the world. Postmodernism is more interested in what McHale calls an ontological (essential) rendering or construction of the world. That is, while McHale accepts that modernism is interested in the structures and processes involved in literary form, this interest is driven by a continuing desire to know the world from which the individual has become alienated. Postmodernism releases the world to the 'possibilities of impossibilities'; the individual capitulates to his or her alienation and explores the processes of construction and the multiplicity of form, rather than his or her own alienated state of mind. Postmodernism, therefore, is a building and working of textual styles – a 'carnivalesque' of styles, registers and possibilities which may be marked by joy as much as by terror. These cacophonies and heterologies nevertheless remain fixed in the stable progress of an organic literary history, a history which remains accessible to genealogy and comprehension. Thus, novels like Joseph Heller's *Catch-22*, Ralph Ellison's *Invisible Man* or Thomas Pynchon's *Gravity's Rainbow* should not be read as a protest against alienation so much as a recognition of absurd social and human conditions, and an attempt to endure them.

More recent commentators, such as Umberto Eco (1984), Linda Hutcheon (1988), Jim Collins (1989) and Daniel Fischilin (1994), have extended McHale's definitions, insisting that postmodernism, in fact, deconstructs the boundaries that contain literary interaction. In particular, the boundaries between literature and other forms of discourse, including 'popular culture', are dissolved in favour of a more embracing and inclusive reading of media and mediation processes. While these analysts begin with an interest in literature and derive their analytical reference from the traditions of literary analysis, their work reflects a broader interest in the theories of structuralism and poststructuralism.

Postmodern media texts

There are many different ideas about what constitutes a postmodern media text. Some observers argue that films like Francis Ford Coppola's *Apocalypse Now* mark a significant move from a modern to a postmodern aesthetic style. The nihilism of modernism is replaced by uncertainty, a 'singing silence' as Ihab Hassan calls it. In Coppola's film there is a dualism or tension between, first, the possibilities of the complete vision ('the horror') as it was articulated in Joseph Conrad's novel *Heart of Darkness,* around which the film is based; and, second, an apocalyptic hedonism which is never complete but which becomes part of a spurious and absurd game of images and incompatible ideals. The 'smell of napalm in the morning', the pointless journey, the battleground surfing – all are part of the uneasy pleasure/terror of warfare and imperialism, and their atavistic aspirations.

Other commentators have seen the combination of textual elements in David Lynch's films *Blue Velvet* (1986) and *Mulholland Drive*(2001) and TV series *Twin Peaks* (1990–1) as fundamentally postmodern. The emphasis here is less on the thematic content of the text and more on its formal organization of elements. These texts, and many others of the 1980s and 1990s, combine allusions to, and elements of, other texts and textual styles. This bricolage or pastiche formation seeks to create a sense of textual and cultural inclusiveness. Generally, the texts dissolve the distinction between high and popular art, creating new ways of 'being popular' and speaking through the everyday discourses of everyday audiences.

The appellation 'postmodern' has also been applied to 'cult' films like *Clerks,* which has been sometimes called a popular grunge movie: a transgressive text designed to destabilize institutional filmic and cultural norms. *Clerks* tells of the relationship and vocational problems of a young college dropout who now works in a convenience store and is caught between the loves of two women. The multiple ironies, crudity and basic carnality of the film betray a deep sense of loss and hopelessness. The dissolution of institutions and prescriptive relational forms creates new freedoms, subjectivities and terrains of pleasure. However, these pleasures are tinged with the persistent threat of loss and meaninglessness. This film is postmodern because it reflects faithfully the everyday experiences of everyday members of the postmodern tribe.

Postmodernist expressive forms – in Collins' terms, everything from literature, architecture and film to pornography – construct 'a vision of cultural production that is decentered without being anarchic, heterogeneous without being "democratic"'(1989: 26). Collins' version of postmodernism sifts various aspects of poststructuralist theory to produce a political postmodernism which rejects the centring and homogenizing impulses of modernist democracy. Postmodern cultural production is always 'political' in that texts, Lacan (1977) explains, actively 'position' individuals in relation to one another. That is, the text and the reader/viewer interact in order to form meanings; these meanings are only possible because the reader/viewer shifts (positions) his or her perspective, identity and subjectivity in relation to the text.

Jim Collins' work emerges out of that line of postmodernist aesthetics which challenges elite, bourgeois distinctions between high and popular art. As we noted, such precepts underscore the aesthetics and critical commentary of the 1960s American avant-garde. Andreas Huyssen has suggested, in fact, that the 'great divide' that separates high and popular art is mediated, if not dissolved, by the emergence of 'postmodernism'. For Huyssen, the postmodernism of the 1970s replaces an exhausted avant-garde aesthetics:

> By the 1970s that avantgardist postmodernism of the 1960s had in turn exhausted its potential, even though some of its manifestations continued well into the new decade. What was new in the 1970s was, on the one hand, the emergence of a culture of eclecticism, a largely affirmative postmodernism which had abandoned any claim to critique, transgression or negation; and, on the other hand, an alternative postmodernism in which resistance, critique and negation of the status quo were redefined in non-modernist and non-avantgardist terms, terms which match the political developments in contemporary culture more effectively than the older theories of modernism. (1986: 188)

This split which emerges in American postmodernism mirrors a similar division in British cultural studies between those who sought to extend poststructuralist analysis into forms of audience and youth culture studies, and those who wanted to pursue a more politically oriented neo-Gramscian approach to cultural politics. For Huyssen, the political or critical postmodernism is most evident in the writings of women and minority groups, those who have done most to recover 'buried and mutilated traditions' (1986: 198).

Huyssen, nevertheless, rejects the idea that poststructuralism constitutes the critical or theoretical parallel of aesthetic postmodernism, most especially as the French theories have been adapted in the United States. His questioning of the poststructuralist contribution to critical thinking in the US, however, neglects seriously the catalyzing effects of writers such as Lyotard, Deleuze and Guattari, and Foucault. Indeed, since the early 1980s there has been a continuing integration, hybridization and multiplication of the various discourses of British cultural studies, French poststructuralism and American postmodernism such that the three fields of enquiry have at times become almost indistinguishable. In attempting to account for contemporary culture and what Lyotard (1984a) calls the 'postmodern condition', recent analysis has virtually dispensed with substantive lineages or disciplinary borders. The common interest in heterologies, sexualization, multiple discourses, multiculturalism, new political modalities and liberated subjectivities has drawn postmodernism into the widest possible arraign of applications. Huyssen's attempt to quarantine American postmodernism from French poststructuralism has proven to be quite unsustainable. Indeed, one of the earliest proponents of British cultural studies, Dick Hebdige, notes that it is becoming more difficult 'to specify exactly what it is that "postmodernism" is supposed to refer to as the term gets stretched in all directions across different debates, different disciplinary and discursive boundaries, as different factions seek to make it their own' (1988: 181). The American avant-gardist and aesthetic postmodernism with elements of French poststructuralism informs many of these disputes, most particularly as postmodernism extends to social and cultural theory.

JEAN-FRANÇOIS LYOTARD: FROM FRENCH POSTSTRUCTURALISM TO FRENCH POSTMODERNISM

The Modern and the Postmodern in Lyotard's Writing

Jean-François Lyotard combines social critique with an interest in new forms of thinking, art and aesthetics. In particular, Lyotard is suspicious of contemporary divisions between 'the technical intelligentsia who are committed to functional rationality … [and the] literary intellectuals who have become increasingly apocalyptic, hedonistic and nihilistic' (Lyotard, 1984a: 46). Like Daniel Bell (1973, 1976), who predicted the rise of a post-industrial society, Lyotard is seeking an explanation for the current 'state of knowledge'; this explanation should engage with the tensions, continuities and discontinuities of an evolving historical epoch. Lyotard, unlike Bell, defines these historical and social transformations in terms of what he calls the 'cultural condition'. For him, this general assemblage of elements – economic, political, intellectual, cognitive, artistic, industrial – marks a change from a modern to a postmodern condition. By comparison, Bell's historicism concentrates primarily on the mode of economy and the move from an industrial, technocratic society to a post-industrial society in which abstract scientific thinking is ascendant.

In fact, Lyotard never entirely resolves the relationship between modernism and postmodernism, as either an historical or a cognitive dialogue. As noted at the beginning of this chapter, Lyotard does not distinguish between postmodernism (cognitive system or way of thinking) and postmodernity (historical and cultural elements which define an epoch). For him the way of thinking about a culture and the various economic, social, political and discursive elements that comprise it are integrally, if not absolutely, linked. The modern and the postmodern, therefore, represent an interplay ('language games') of elements and discourses, with each cognitive system informing, as much as challenging, the other. For Lyotard, the modern and the postmodern are a mixture of historical and cognitive (knowledge-based) modes of reference; postmodernism is a 'gestant' form of modernism, a mutually dependent permutation. Much of the confusion surrounding Lyotard's work assumes that he is advocating the replacement of the modern by the postmodern, and that the two 'conditions' can be clearly marked in terms of rupture and separation. As we shall see, this is not generally the case, and in fact his engagement with the postmodern is rather ambivalent, reflecting a genuine desire for liberation without the complete surrender of modern modes of social or aesthetic critique.

Ihab Hassan (1987) argues that Lyotard was influenced by American avant-garde postmodernism, and that his extension of the term for social and historical criticism confuses the term by restoring it to a modernist framework. According to Hassan, Lyotard's use of the concept of postmodernism to describe the state of contemporary 'knowledge' is not a radical challenge to bourgeois aesthetic (and social) values. Rather, Lyotard's criticism of modernism and modernity is framed in terms of modernism itself, its own principles and ways of thinking. Lyotard is not able to escape the modernist mode of thinking, Hassan argues, and merely corrupts the concept of 'postmodernism' by applying it as a general description of history and culture. Hassan, as we have noted above, prefers to restrict the concept to an aesthetic or cognitive category, rather than one which embraces all culture.

Gillian Rose (1988) claims something similar in her discussion of Lyotard's adaptation of the term from a style of art and architecture to a tool for social enquiry. According to Rose, the transmission of the term from literary and aesthetic criticism to social and philosophical analysis removes a good deal of its potency and precision. Lyotard himself, in fact, has elaborated his position on the relationship between aesthetics, philosophy and postmodernism, noting that postmodernism is 'undoubtedly part of the modern' (Lyotard, 1984b: 79). Equally, '[m]odernity is constitutionally and ceaselessly pregnant with its postmodernity' (Lyotard, 1991: 25). Thus, while most commentators read Lyotard's *The Postmodern Condition* (1984a) as a celebration of the arrival of the postmodern, across the breadth of his work there is a much clearer recognition of the interdependence of the modern and the postmodern. To a degree, Lyotard's own elaborations might seem to support Andreas Huyssen's claim that 'deconstructionist' or 'poststructuralist' postmodernism remains somewhat fixed in the parameters of modernist critiques of itself (Huyssen, 1986: 208–16); Huyssen, and others, however, fail to appreciate the efficacy of Lyotard's perspective for cultural and political analysis, most especially as it attempts to reach beyond the flagging limits of Huyssen's own literary postmodernism.

The Postmodern Condition

Lyotard's *The Postmodern Condition*, along with his contiguous essay, 'Answering the question: what is postmodernism?' (1984b), seeks to illuminate the present 'condition of knowledge in the most highly developed societies' (Lyotard, 1984a: xxiii). This condition of knowledge, culture and history is characterized in terms of transformation and 'crisis'. The source of this transformation is the fracturing of discourses and systems of knowledge that had informed the progress and ideology of what Lyotard defines as 'the modern'. While directing attention toward this dismantling of systems of knowing in literature, religion, Marxist politics and the arts, Lyotard is most concerned to demonstrate the dislocating effects of postmodernism on the truth claims of science. Modernist science, Lyotard explains, is constructed around a form of self-legitimizing narrative (metanarrative) which confirms its own validity through the imposition of its own self-justifying and self-reflecting standards of knowledge. Modern science, that is, proclaims its own value in its own terms; its truth is therefore a grand truth, a universal truth, which underscores the methods and belief system of the whole modernist culture. Thus, as with other commentaries on postmodernism, the definition of the postmodern is fundamentally embedded in the definition of the modern.

Lyotard's interrogation of modernist metanarratives clearly draws on his own disappointment with the imaginary potential of modernist discourses, especially in reformist politics and avant-garde aesthetics. Indeed, his discourse wavers between a description of social and cultural processes, and a form of cultural advocacy. In *The Postmodern Condition* he describes his methodology in terms of Wittgenstein's 'language games' (see Chapter 5): a remodelled analysis of discourse and the processes of meaning-making. Lyotard claims that his analysis of these language games provides a means of elucidating and deconstructing modernist metanarratives. This poststructuralist technique is designed to expose and ultimately dissolve the assumptions which support the 'truth' claims of modernism's grand explanations and theories: for example, Marxism, capitalism, and Enlightenment science. For Lyotard, however, these language games are like Stuart Hall's notion of 'the struggle to signify' (see Chapter 4): the games are formed around adversarial conditions by which one discourse will impose itself over another. In particular, Lyotard emphasizes the agonistic dimensions of language games; rules are produced by players in order that they may 'play' or 'fight', and thus engage in speech acts: 'Great joy is had in the endless invention of turns of phrase ... [b]ut undoubtedly even this feeling depends on a feeling of success won at the expense of an adversary, and a formidable one: the accepted language, or connotation' (1984a: 10). Lyotard's method, in fact, establishes a tension between, first, the language', their productive pleasures and inclination to heterogeneous meaning-making (culture and imagination); and, second, those broader language 'moves' which produce conformity, homogeneity and metanarratives.

Lyotard clearly sees the new, postindustrial societies as facilitating new modes of heterogeneous language games. However, the persistence of modern predispositions in science and technology threatens to refurbish 'systems' of knowledge and discourse which are fundamentally oppressive and self-legitimating. Lyotard's description turns again to advocacy as he seeks the invigoration of human imagination and the deconstruction of these knowledge systems:

[F]unctions of regulation, and therefore reproduction, have been and will be further withdrawn from administrators and entrusted to machines. Increasingly, the central question is becoming who has access to the information these machines must have in storage to guarantee that the right decisions are made. Access to data is, and will continue to be, the prerogative of experts of all shapes. The ruling class is and will continue to be the class of decision makers. (1984a: 14)

Lyotard's political or ideological intent, therefore, is inscribed with this deep suspicion of systems of control – the discourses that constitute a privileged social status. However, while his advocacy creates a political space for deconstruction, this politics is construed in terms of thought and aesthetics, rather than direct action. Lyotard's alternative political discourse provides later postmodernists with a facility for further political exploration, although Lyotard himself rarely ventures beyond the realm of modernist political engagement: that is, he applies a modernist mode of deconstruction to expose the deficiencies of modernism.

Quantum mechanics and postmodern science

A number of commentators, including Jean-François Lyotard and Charles Jencks, have argued that the new physical sciences are exposing the deeper dimensions and true character of 'nature'. Enlightenment science, borrowing from classical Greek mathematics, had believed that the universe functioned according to relatively straightforward laws of causality in three-dimensional space: the universe operated like a machine. The scientist's task was to uncover, define and prove these laws by the processes of objective observation. Albert Einstein's general theory of relativity, which identified time as the fourth dimension of space, required science to re-conceptualize the universe; however, scientific method remained largely unchanged.

The study of sub-atomic particles or 'quanta', however, has created significant problems for traditional scientific methods of observation. Quanta are the smallest particles of matter and hence constitute the fundamental building blocks of the universe. These particles, however, do not behave in ways that are familiar to naked-eye observation. Specifically, quanta may behave like a 'wave' sometimes, and like particles of matter at other times. That is, they may behave with quite incompatible properties and propensities. This incompatibility, however, is never simultaneous. Contradicting standard scientific procedure, these contradictory aspects of quanta will be observed in exactly the same experiment, but never at the same time. In fact, the act of observation appears to change the behaviour of quanta, raising critical questions about the value and validity of 'objective' observation itself.

For Lyotard and others, quantum physics can be understood as a postmodern science which fundamentally dissolves traditionally formed systems of knowledge. Postmodern physics, that is, opens the way to the imagination and the creative dimensions of knowledge. The metanarratives of Enlightenment (modern) science are shown to be based on false assumptions. Science is just another discourse, just another language game. Quantum mechanics provides material evidence of those games since, like language, it draws together the practical and technological facilities necessary for human survival with the ultimate mysteries of nature and the universe. As Paul Davies has explained, quantum theory integrates the broadest dimensions of human knowledge from Zen Buddhism to technologies such as the laser, the electron microscope, the transistor and the semiconductor (Davies, 1983: 100). For postmodernism, his integration and reconfiguration of various levels of reality confirms the underlying diversity of the universe and its delicate mediation of complexity and chaos (Jencks, 1995).

Lyotard's reading of contemporary physics – quantum, atomic and fractal theory – functions as both metaphor and panegyric for the dismantling of controlled systems. The new physics, Lyotard explains, disengages nature from modern scientific explanations. According to him, the relation between the scientist's statement and what nature says seems to be organized as a game without perfect information. But science itself needs to be foregrounded as a body of knowledge which legitimates itself as a primary discourse.

When we examine the current status of scientific knowledge – at a time when science seems more completely subordinated to the prevailing powers than ever before and, along with the new technologies, is in danger of becoming a major stake in their conflicts – the question of double legitimation, far from receding into the background, necessarily comes to the fore. For it appears in its most complete form, that of reversion, revealing that knowledge and power are simply two sides of the same question: Who decides what knowledge is? Who knows what needs to be decided? In the computer age the question is now more than ever a question of government (Lyotard, 1984a: 8–9).

The control of knowledge, indeed the very definition of what constitutes knowledge, is central to Lyotard's account. In particular, Lyotard appears to rejoice in the social and cultural potential of the new science, which can no longer 'measure' accurately. Lyotard demonstrates this point by referring to Jorge Luis Borges' story of the emperor who seeks to map exactly the dimensions of his entire empire. The only truly and absolutely accurate map of the empire turns out to be an exact replica in full dimension; the construction of the simulacra ultimately bankrupts the empire. Modern science is caught in precisely the same dilemma; modern science seeks to produce absolute knowledge, even though such knowledge is impossible. A fundamental contradiction necessarily subverts the entire enterprise of modernism and its discourses:

This inconsistency explains the weakness in state and socioeconomic bureaucracies: they stifle the systems or subsystems they control and asphyxiate themselves in the process (negative feedback). ... Even if we accept that society is a system, complete control over it, which would necessitate an exact definition of its initial state, is impossible because no such definition could ever be effected. (Lyotard, 1984a: 55–6)

For Lyotard, the contradictions that beset the modern reveal themselves as opportunities within postmodern discourse. There can be no simple disengagement. The postmodern condition reflects the dialogue taking place through these transitions.

'What is Postmodernism?'

Thus, Lyotard's suspicion of systems might seem to place his discourse clearly in the realm of postmodernism, though his suspicion of computers and the inevitable agglomeration of information 'bits' (see also Lyotard, 1991: esp. Ch. 2) distances him from other areas of postmodern utopianism (see Lewis, 1997a, 1998). Moreover, his interest in 'undecidables' in postmodern science propels him toward broader discussions of agonism in language games, those 'differends' or differences in perspective that defy mediation or resolution. Lyotard himself appears to be engaged with the *differend* of modernism and postmodernism, seeking a mediation which gives voice to the new modes of heterogeneity and the subversion of systems without the complete surrender of the modernist capacity for experimentation, reform and what he calls the sublime. In 'Answering the question: what is postmodernism?' (1984b) he explicates these problems through his criticism both of a consensual language system, proposed by Jürgen Habermas, and a postmodernism which fails fully to embrace the potentials of imagination, including experimentation. The postmodern aesthetic, Lyotard fears, threatens to do away with avant-garde experimentalism, which constituted the 'alternative' discourse within modernism: that is, which provided an escape from the more oppressive, authoritarian and systematizing inclinations of the modern.

Lyotard had already dismissed the philosophy of 'anything goes' (1984a: 76), but in the later essay he is quite specific in his repudiation of postmodern architecture which fails, in his view, to pursue the potentialities of an architectural avant-garde. At its most exhilarating, therefore, postmodernism is that part of modernism which is perpetually 'nascent'; not the conclusion of modernism, but its re-generator, its precipitant. This somewhat contradictory view of the relationship between the postmodern and the modern is expressed in Lyotard's account of the sublime:

If it is true that modernity takes place in the withdrawal of the real and according to the sublime relation between the presentable and the conceivable, it is possible, within this relation, to distinguish two modes. ... The emphasis can be placed on the powerlessness of the faculty presentation, on the nostalgia for presence felt by the human subject, on the obscure and futile will which inhabits him in spite of everything. The emphasis can be placed, rather, on the power of the faculty to conceive, on its 'inhumanity' so to speak ... since it is not the business of our understanding whether or not human sensibility or imagination can match what it conceives. (1984b: 79–80)

Lyotard is suggesting that the modern evolves as a gap between what an individual can conceive or think about, and what can actually be presented as discourse. The art and literature of modernism represent this problem as a withdrawal from what might be regarded as 'realistic'. Picasso's paintings, T.S. Eliot's poetry and James Joyce's novels all are examples of how 'the real' is replaced by this gap. The despair or 'nihilism' (sense that there is no meaning in life) that is evident in much modernist aesthetics expresses this feeling of loss, the feeling that the real is no longer present. Lyotard claims, however, that there is another side to this withdrawal of the real. This 'second emphasis' is more optimistic since it allows us to reflect on this withdrawal, this inhumanity. This is the point of the avant-garde.

When considered in terms of aesthetics, this definition allows modernism to be nostalgic for the thing it no longer can present, but only conceive. The art and literature of modernism are fundamentally fixed in the 'solace and pleasure' of form: that is, of the shape and structure of an artwork. Paradoxically, however, this solace and pleasure are also evident in the pain modernists experience as they realize that the form of an artwork has been depleted of content and meaning. A postmodern aesthetics, according to Lyotard, confronts the same modernist problematic though without the solace of good form and 'the consensus of a taste which would make it possible to share collectively the nostalgia for the unattainable' (1984b: 81). Postmodernism, according to Lyotard, finds itself with a stronger sense of the unpresentable since there can be no pre-established rules which might govern form or the artistic act itself. Rather, the rules are to be reinvented, or at least invented after the fact of the artwork existing. In other words, the work of art or literature comes into being as if it were an event, and as if there were no possibility for content or form. The rules are invented after the work appears and must be conceived *post facto*; the work of art's 'realization' (*mise en oeuvre*) always begins too soon. Postmodern has to be understood according to the paradox of the future (*post*) anterior (*modo*).

FREDRIC JAMESON

Lyotard's deconstructionist postmodernism has influenced many recent commentators, most especially those who have sought to expound a theory of general cultural evolution. The deconstructionist method, however, has been appended to quite varying appraisals of postmodern culture, some of which are highly pessimistic and critical, others of which are more welcoming and celebratory. Of this former group, Fredric Jameson and Jean Baudrillard, in particular, have treated the emergence of a televisual, postmodern culture with deep suspicion. Both Jameson and Baudrillard form their critique of consumerism and televisual culture through a substantive and complex interweaving of structuralist and poststructuralist theoretics. In the end, however, the critique is pessimistic, offering very little relief or alternative to the ubiquity of the postmodern move.

Postmodernism and the Logics of Late Capitalism

Like the British cultural theorists, Fredric Jameson adapted Louis Althusser's notion of dominant ideology in order to elucidate the underlying political and ideological patterns of cultural texts. In *The Political Unconscious* (1981), Jameson articulates for American readers many of the theoretical and critical arguments that had been well established in French semiology and British cultural studies. As with the British literary critic Terry Eagleton, however, Jameson's efforts to reconcile the problematic of fragmentation and unity have drawn him to broader considerations of contemporary culture. In his essay 'Postmodernism and consumer culture' (1983), subsequently revised as 'Postmodernism, or the cultural logic of late capitalism' (1984), Jameson theorizes postmodernism in terms of an Althusserian model.

Postmodernism is thus conceived as social fragmentation, a new historical phase in which the dominant ideology or 'cultural logic' is characterized by what Ernest Mandel calls late or multinational capitalism. This third-phase capitalism, following market and then monopoly capitalism, 'constitutes … the purest form of capital into hitherto uncommodified areas' (Jameson, 1984: 78). As with Pierre Bourdieu's analysis of contemporary French culture, Jameson recognizes that this new capitalism is built upon 'symbolic exchange-value'. That is, once capitalism has satisfied basic needs (food, clothing, shelter), it must necessarily seek new phenomena to sell. Products and services, therefore, have a new value attached to them, a 'symbolic' value whereby the culture discriminates value according to status, fashion, prestige, and so on. For example, a pair of sunglasses bought from the Two Dollar Shop will perform the same function, but attract less value, than the 'name-brand' equivalent (Oakley, Arnette, Polaroid). In postmodern culture this symbolic value is produced through the 'ephemera' of televisual imagery and 'information' processes. In a sense, the symbol (name-brand, image-endorsing celebrity, etc.) becomes the commodity. These highly valued 'ephemera' underscore the fragmentation of a culture, which is being produced through increasingly large and globally oriented corporations.

Culture, therefore, is inescapably embedded in the processes of capital. For Jameson, the cultural dominant is fundamentally expressed through this proliferation of symbolic products and images. Not surprisingly, contemporary artists and writers have sought to articulate this new expressive verbiage, the popular symbols and texts which proliferate in postmodern culture:

> The postmodernisms have been fascinated precisely by this whole 'degraded' landscape of schlock and kitsch, of TV series and Readers' Digest culture, of advertising and motels, of the late show and the grade-B Hollywood film, of so-called paraliterature with its airport

paperback categories of the gothic and the romance, the popular biography, the murder mystery, and science fiction or fantasy: materials they no longer 'quote' as a Joyce or a Mahler might have done, but incorporate into their very substance. (Jameson, 1984: 55)

Jameson thus acknowledges the power and ubiquity of new cultural forms and modes of expression. However, unlike postmodernists such as Charles Jencks, he maintains a level of distance and critique, arguing, for example, that postmodern architecture is merely an outward expression of modernist capitalism. Jameson's critique, therefore, is constructed, a little like Lyotard's, around a sense that certain elements in the new (postmodern) culture are politically, socially or even aesthetically bereft. Thus, the postmodern culture, as the embedded expression and logic of third-phase capitalism, is more than a mere style and more than the individual elements that constitute modes of popular expression. For Jameson, postmodernism is a 'periodizing concept':

whose ultimate function is to correlate the emergence of new formal features in culture with the emergence of a new type of social life and a new economic order – what is often euphemistically called modernization, postindustrial or consumer society, the society of the media or the spectacle, or multinational capitalism. (Jameson, 1983: 113)

This cultural dominant is of course both implicitly and explicitly political. Even so, this new social order cannot exclude alternative elements, oppositions and the cultural legacy of previous social constituencies; in keeping with Althusser and Raymond Williams, Jameson's theory of postmodernism provides space for contradictions and countervailing movements:

The 1960s are in many ways the key transitional period, the period in which the new international order (neocolonialism, the Green Revolution, computerization and electronic information) is at one and the same time set in place and is swept and shaken by its own internal contradictions and by external resistance. (Jameson, 1983: 113)

While he is careful to avoid a determinist perspective, Jameson seeks to illuminate these contradictions in terms of the new social order's compression of time and space. To this extent, pastiche and 'schizophrenia' become the principal markers of the new modes of cultural expression. Pastiche articulates in texts the sort of de-centred globalist capitalism which dominates the new economic and political order. Pastiche, being the combination of elements and styles into an assemblage of form, is distinguished from modernist parody: the deployment of specific tropes or styles in a text in order to mock them. Parody is used in modernist literature and film as a comic technique which substantiates the central aesthetic and moral perspective of the text; pastiche mimics styles and tropes in order to give the sense of dispersal and multiple dialogues or perspectives.

In broader cultural and political terms, pastiche becomes the articulation of the unleashing of the individual and individual subjectivity. According to Jameson and many others, modernism is marked by a substantial cultural investment in the individual subject. The highly stylized and unique author is the cultural articulation of these earlier periods of capitalism. The dissolution of the unique and unifying authorial voice and its replacement by assemblages of ephemeral elements and voices indicates a broader shift in cultural conceptions of subjectivity itself. Postmodern pastiche, therefore, represents a dissolving of bourgeois subjectivity, as much as the end of individualized imagination and aesthetic invention. The models of Proust, Picasso and T.S. Eliot 'do not work anymore … since nobody has that kind of unique private world and style to express' (Jameson, 1983: 115). Jameson struggles to disguise his ambivalence about these changes, noting again that pastiche, as a series of de-centred imitations of style, produces the fundamental effects of dislocation:

> [I]n a world in which stylistic innovation is no longer possible, all that is left is to imitate dead styles, to speak through the masks and with the voices of the styles in the imaginary museum. But this means that contemporary or postmodernist art is going to be about art itself in a new kind of way; even more, it means that one of its essential messages will involve the necessary failure of art and the aesthetic, the failure of the new, the imprisonment of the past. (1983: 115–16)

Enthusiasts of contemporary popular culture (cf. Chambers, 1988; Grossberg et al., 1988; McRobbie, 1994) often identify Jameson's collapse of high art into the amorphousness of 'mass' cultural production as a revivification of the Frankfurt School critique (see Chapter 4). Yet Jameson's position is somewhat more subtle, even ambivalent, as it seeks to illuminate a new social order in terms of fragmentations rather than simple social control. Jameson's unease with the new social order and with capitalist consumption and production practices arises not so much out of a desire to reinstate homogenizing modes of centred culture, but out of a disappointment with its alternative. That is, for Jameson the postmodern solution to modernist social and political oppression is fundamentally deficient.

To this extent, the 'nostalgia film' (e.g., *Back to the Future, Blue Velvet, Angel Heart*) is a spectral imitation of a lost time. Postmodernism regresses, in Jameson's view, not by producing historical drama, but by creating as new and with an overload of sentimentality a time when desire was pure and privileged. This commercial reproduction compares with postmodern architecture, which Jameson views with equal suspicion, an architecture that parades its pastiche of elements in a thorough and unremitting bonding of commerce and capitalist hegemony. This perpetuation of the past in the present dislocates time, producing the effect of unreality or schizophrenia. The history of aesthetic style replaces real history and temporal continuities break down. Historical amnesia thus intensifies time as an internal experience, rendering it more vivid and more dislocating, creating moods that glow 'with hallucinatory energy'. This new culture, then, is both morally and imaginatively bereft. The deep seriousness and utopian imagery of modernist thought are dislodged by a radiating triviality, a superficiality which constantly eludes critical analysis and political hope.

Certainly, Jameson's disappointment with postmodernism is more acutely expressed in the later essay, 'Postmodernism, or the cultural logic of late capitalism', where he seems to despair of the possibility of ever fully grasping the political and epistemological implications of this new (dis)order. For Jameson, the spatial and temporal co-ordinates that provide for us a sense of our world have been swept over by the new cultural conditions. Jameson's great contribution to discussions on cultural postmodernism (see also Jameson, 1998) rests in his transferal of various aspects of structuralist and poststructuralist theoretics. Like Lyotard, Jameson draws poststructuralism away from its somewhat solipsistic interrogation of modernist texts to focus on the problematic of contemporary culture. The gloom that occasionally descends over his analysis, and which is especially evident in the cultural logics essay, is not just a residue of Marxist structuralist pessimism. He seeks genuinely to understand the new culture and appreciate its potential for liberation. Unfortunately, he is forced to concede that the postmodern presents a set of problems that are at least as intimidating as the modernist ideologies it seeks to replace.

JEAN BAUDRILLARD

Criticisms of Jameson's perspective have tended to be situated within the broad corpus of postmodern and popular consumerism theories. In particular, critics have argued that his critique is written from the position of a high modern neo-Marxist. According to these criticisms, his residual Althusserian structuralism confounds his attempts to embrace fully the political and aesthetic projects of postmodernism. Jean Baudrillard's writings on postmodern culture have also been attacked for being excessively pessimistic and for their barely acknowledged undercurrent of modernist (especially Marxist) nostalgia. His analysis of postmodernism, however, is less easy to situate than the analysis of either Lyotard or Jameson. The main reason for this is that Baudrillard assumes the position of the postmodern poet; his own writings are characterized by a discursive tenor which seems to mimic the phenomena he is exploring. Some critics, such as Christopher Norris (1990), have found his style of analysis frustrating, illogical and deliberately obscurist; others have rejected it as gloomy or even nihilistic. In either case, Baudrillard's recent writings centralize the media and media images as the defining force in cultural analysis. In fact, media imagery, Baudrillard claims, creates the discourses upon which the culture – or the phantom of the culture – is formed. Baudrillard's own apocalyptic and hedonistic discourse betrays a particularly elusive ambivalence, an ambivalence which, in its own way, has proven remarkably penetrative, alluring and controversial.

Baudrillard's analysis of postmodern culture combines elements of technological determinism, pessimism, Gnostic dualism and wonder in a discourse that often evades substantive critical analysis. In fact, one of the most distinctive features of his cultural theory is its self-reflexive engagement with the postmodern funhouse of meaning, meaning gaps and multiple ironies (see Kellner, 1989; Norris, 1990; Smith, 2004).

Early Writings

Baudrillard's earliest writings, *The System of Objects* (1996, orig. 1968) and *The Consumer Society* (1998, orig. 1970), adapt Marxist analysis of economic production for the study of the processes and effects of capitalist consumption. Baudrillard's application of semiology (the study of signs, see Chapter 5) for an understanding of how consumer culture functions stimulated his broader interest in communication processes. Signs themselves, Baudrillard explains, attach themselves to consumer products; these products become identified with the signs which carry them, and consumer behaviour becomes largely classifiable according to its relationship with coded products. Meanings are transferred to the consumer through the act of consumption.

In *For a Critique of the Political Economy of the Sign* (1981, orig. 1972) Baudrillard begins to question the structuralist strategy both in his own analysis and in the semiology of Saussure (see Chapter 5). Retaining an interest in Marxist critique, Baudrillard applies a vaguely poststructuralist or deconstructivist analysis of the two halves of the sign: the signifier (physical symbol) and the signified (the mental concept). Saussure had pointed out that the relationship between sign and its referent (the thing to which it refers) was arbitrary, and that meaning only occurs when the sign is functioning in relation to other signs. Meaning, that is, is created through the interaction of various signs, not because there is a 'meaningful' relationship between the sign and its referent: the word 'dog' has meaning because we know that 'dog' is defined as 'a hairy, canine creature with four legs and a tail', not because the word has an intrinsic relationship to the creature itself. The sign is therefore a contingency of particular categories of signs within a context of their use. Baudrillard argues that political economy (Marx's description of capitalism) functions in a similar way: a commodity may be divided into its two operational parts: exchange-value (price) and use-value (the actual use and 'meaning' of the commodity). In fact, Baudrillard tells us, the price or exchange-value obscures the utility of the product, just as the symbol obscures the meaning of a sign. Baudrillard uses this critique to examine the historical functioning of capitalism, deconstructing its obscure operations to reveal its underlying mode of signification.

The End of Marxism

In *The Mirror of Production* (1975) and *Symbolic Exchange and Death* (1993, orig. 1976) Baudrillard breaks entirely with political economy and structuralism, marking a broader interest in the territories of proliferating communication, images and information.

These books also announce the beginnings of Baudrillard's epiphanic and hyperbolic style, where the thought of a new social epoch becomes an opportunity for prophetic vision. In a later text, *The Ecstasy of Communication,* Baudrillard expresses his bleak vision in terms of an end to all meaning:

> The end of labour. The end of production. The end of political economy. The end of the dialectic signifier/signified which permitted the accumulation of knowledge and of managing the linear syntagm of cumulative discourse. The end simultaneously of the dialectic of exchange value/use value, the only one to make possible capital accumulation and social production. The end of the linear dimension of discourse. The end of the linear dimensions of merchandise. The end of the classic era of the sign. (Baudrillard, 1988: 127–8)

These conclusions are fundamentally social, brought about by the unfixing of symbols and signs from familiar, historically determined references. For Baudrillard, this new epoch is dramatically symbolized by the arrival of new temporal and spatial conditions, a highly mediated reality or 'hyperreality' which renders all former social theories and accounts obsolete.

In arriving at this conclusion, however, Baudrillard seeks to understand its implications. The new mediated reality is double-edged, bringing together the ecstatic possibilities of unrestrained communication and the inevitability of loss and alienation. Thus, while other postmodernists rejoice in the ascendancy of mediated and prolific popular culture, Baudrillard's apocalypse is both hedonistic and anxious. The proliferation of signs and information in the media challenges the possibility of meaning, imploding the media themselves into a fluid and indistinct series of simulations: 'Information devours its own contents; it devours communication and the social' (Baudrillard, 1983a: 100). In essence, Baudrillard is erasing the message and its content from primacy in the communications process, emphasizing instead the importance of the conduit or carriage of these messages. However, the medium which carries the message is also less significant than the sheer volume of communication itself. McLuhan's centralization of the medium ('the medium is the message'), which Baudrillard had earlier rejected as technological determinism, is rejected a second time because the medium can no longer mediate messages at all; it can no longer carry the information about 'the real':

> Strictly speaking this is what implosion signifies: the absorption of one pole into another, the short-circuit between poles of every differential system of meaning, the effacement of terms and distinct oppositions and thus that of the medium and the real…. This critical – but original – situation must be thought through to the very end; it is the only one we are left with. It is useless to dream of a revolution through content or through form, since the medium and the real are now in a single nebulous state whose truth is undecipherable. (Baudrillard, 1983a: 102–3)

Simulacra, Seduction and Hyperreality

Thus, while structuralist and poststructuralist theories might concede a place for 'reality', even though it may be highly mediated and barely relevant, Baudrillard extends Umberto Eco's notion of hyperreality, arguing that all is simulation – the imitation of an imitation. This proliferation of 'simulacra' renders the real inert, dispenses with the representational imaginary, and entirely obliterates the need for empirical theories of knowledge:

> No more mirror of being and appearances of the real and its concept. No more imaginary co-extensivity; rather, generic miniaturization is the dimension of the real. The real is produced from miniaturized units, from matrices, memory banks, and command models – and from these it can be reproduced an infinite number of times. It no longer has to be rational, since it no longer has to be measured against some ideal or negative instance. It is nothing more than operational. In fact, since it is no longer enveloped by an imaginary, it is no longer real at all. It is a hyperreal, the product of an irradiating synthesis of combinatory models in a hyperspace without atmosphere. (Baudrillard, 1984b: 254)

The other side of this bleak vision, of course, is the recognition that the conditions of hyperreality are perpetually stimulating. A person can no longer be conceived in terms of a rational relationship with the external, objective world. A subject is a communicating process, constantly aroused through the unceasing flow of images, source-less and destination-less simulations. In *Seduction* (1990, orig. 1979) Baudrillard prefigures later readings of the free-flow of arousal and simulacra, arguing that 'seduction' is the most appropriate mode of human interaction, replacing intersubjective or objective modes of 'truth' which would penetrate beyond the surface play of sense and stimulation. But this seduction, which is a perpetual play at the surface of all communication, including sexuality, can no longer facilitate the types of 'carnality' which once functioned to inform and challenge the rationality of modern social practices. The modern subject maintained a private space where the tensions between rationality, sexual ecstasy and sexual repression could be played out. In hyperreality there is no private space, no depth; sexuality and communication must constantly and relentlessly be experienced at the surface: 'Unlike this organic, visceral, carnal promiscuity, the promiscuity that reigns over the communication networks is one of superficial saturation, of an incessant solicitation, of an extermination of intestinal and protective spaces' (Baudrillard, 1983b: 131). This 'ecstasy of communication' defines for Baudrillard the fundamental conditions of culture. The obsessive sexual imagery deployed in all communicative modes explicates sexuality and constantly stimulates a desire that cannot possibly be satisfied, nor indeed is it meant to be satisfied. While Baudrillard's earlier writings on commodity and symbolic exchange emphasized the (capitalist) functionality of these proliferations, the later writings have emphasized the boundless waste that now accompanies sexual desire.

In *Forget Foucault* (1987) Baudrillard contrasts his own theories on communication and sexuality with those of Michel Foucault. Baudrillard's wish to think through the implications of poststructuralism 'to the very end' lead him to a condemnation of Foucault's account of sexuality and power. Baudrillard argues, in fact, that Foucault's centralization of desire largely extinguishes it in much the same way as 'Marxism put an end to the class struggle, because it hypostatizes them and buries them in their theoretical project' (1987: 13). Significantly, Baudrillard dismisses Foucault's political interests, suggesting that 'power' ultimately unravels itself in direct proportion to its self-assertion. Baudrillard's politics therefore are fundamentally dismissive of activism since activism itself depends upon content. If there is no content, only stimulation and simulation, then power itself is a baseless imitation: neither a fixity of structure, as in the Marxist imagining, nor a process of exchange, as in the Foucauldian schema.

> What Foucault does not see is that power is never there and that its institution ... is only a simulation of perspective – it is no more reality than economic accumulation – and what a tremendous trap that is. ... There is something in power that resists as well, and we see no difference between those who enforce it and those who submit to it; this distinction has become meaningless, not because the roles are interchangeable, but because power is in its form reversible; because on one side and the other something holds out against the unilateral exercise and the infinite expansion of power. ... This resistance is not a 'desire'; it is what causes power to come undone. (Baudrillard, 1987: 42)

For Baudrillard there can be no hierarchy of ordered positions, nor battles between differently situated and empowered groups. Power is always and forever played out in the simulations of hyperreality. For this reason, he can claim in all seriousness that the Gulf War did not take place (Baudrillard, 1995), not only because the images were a manipulation of coded interests, but because there were no actual adversaries, no real challenges, no essential disputes in power: 'This war is an asexual surgical war, a matter of war processing in which the enemy only appears as a computerized target, just as sexual partners only appear as code-names on the screen of Minitel Rose' (Baudrillard, 1995: 62). In other words, the passion and bodily sensations that might accompany a real war, in Baudrillard's view, were entirely missing from the screen-and information-based war that was simulated as the Gulf War. Just like a TV soap opera or the Olympic Games, the Gulf War was a production event, something lacking the sex and carnality of previous times, a dissolving event that had already finished before it had begun, an exercise in global entertainment.

Baudrillard's current writing continues this theme of proliferation and waste. We have become so implicated in this production of information and imagery, so completely embedded in the imagery itself, that we can no longer expect anything productive or useful to be achieved. In fact, the images are already waste before they appear. Humans themselves are waste before they have done anything useful:

> The worst of it is that, in the course of this universal recycling of waste, which has become our historic task, the human race is beginning to produce itself as waste-product, to carry out this work of waste disposal on itself. What is worse is not that we are submerged by the waste-products of industrial and urban concentration, but that we ourselves are transformed into residues. (Baudrillard, 1994: 78)

Baudrillard's postmodernity offers little political or cultural relief from this pessimistic vision. Indeed, while we may find ourselves wallowing in the delights of Baudrillard's own linguistic and theoretic excesses, being 'seduced' by the imagery and decadent sexual allusions, we are never allowed to release ourselves from the sense that the present and culture itself have already disappeared into the waste of history. For Baudrillard, the generation of waste by humans has ultimately constructed us as imagery and residue, prior to the operations of any productive value.

As noted earlier, Baudrillard's work has been severely criticized by other postmodern theorists for its pessimism and deterministic political vision. Of course, Baudrillard would himself explain his work in terms of the shattering of conventional social theory and social critique. Very simply, he is not interested in maintaining a critical trajectory which, for all intents and purposes, was designed for a previous historical epoch and which failed to deliver fundamental social reform anyway. Even so, his complete erasure of familiar discursive strategies and the common discipline of logical analysis or measured argument may be regarded, on the one hand, as original and exhilarating, but, on the other as confusing and pointless. His method, that is, might seem to be faithful to the thing it claims to analyze: meaningless hyperreality, lack of content, lack of sequential order. The question that is often asked of Baudrillard, however, is not merely one of usefulness or comprehensibility so much as: does his writing genuinely lack content, as he might claim, or is he pretending that his own text has meaning when nothing much else does? In fact, Baudrillard never escapes these contradictions, and at times defends them as a virtue in his work (see Baudrillard, 2002).

POSTMODERN ARCHITECTURE

Up to this point, we have discussed three more or less distinct categories of postmodernism:

1 *Avant-garde postmodernism.* This attaches the concept to a particular style of aesthetics.
2 *Deconstructionist postmodernism* (Lyotard). This combines a more general discussion of aesthetics and representation with a discussion of 'knowledge' and history. These poststructuralist-inspired theories have influenced other forms of postmodernism, most especially those that see 'postmodernism' as a general cultural and social description.

3   *Pessimistic critical postmodernism* (Jameson and Baudrillard). This views postmodern culture with deep suspicion.

To this list we need to add a fourth category:

4   *Celebratory postmodernism.* This group theorizes postmodernism in a far more welcoming and celebratory manner than the deconstructionists and critical pessimists. In fact, it combines elements of deconstruction theory with an interest in the stylistics of avant-garde postmodernism. In many respects, Andreas Huyssen's book *After the Great Divide* (1986) represents an attempt to reach beyond the early avant-gardist postmodernism by relinquishing its residues of modernist negativism or nihilism in favour of an aesthetics that could incorporate popular creativity and a more egalitarian spirit. For Huyssen, the postmodern sensibility is different from avant-gardism and from that modernism that is constantly in revolt against itself: postmodernism 'raises the question of cultural tradition and conservation in the most fundamental way as an aesthetic and political issue' (Huyssen, 1986: 216). This fourth group, therefore, is interested in themes of pleasure, multiple discourses, individualism and the emancipation of subjectivity. (Particular fields of celebrationism are also interested in consumerism; this issue will be taken up more fully in the next chapter.)

Art, Architecture and History

The art historian Charles Jencks has transformed the concept of postmodernism from its avant-garde roots and applied it in a more general taxonomy of architectural and aesthetic style. Jencks' major contribution to the development of the concept rests largely in his notion of 'double-coding'. By this, Jencks suggests that postmodern artistic and intellectual modes are dialogic, drawing together various 'voices' or components into the one text and allowing them to speak without resolution. In other words, a postmodern form of expression does not try to obliterate or replace one voice with another (as modernism would do), but facilitates an ongoing dialogue between various parts. In his earliest writings on postmodernism, Jencks applies the notion of double-coding to refer specifically to the interrelationship between modernism and postmodernism, an idea he maintains throughout his work. In architecture he claims that double-coding could be understood as

the combination of modern techniques with something else (usually traditional building) in order for architecture to communicate with the public and a concerned minority, usually other architects. The point of this double-coding was itself double. Modern architecture had failed to remain credible partly because it did not communicate effectively with its ultimate users … and partly because it did not maintain effective links with the city and history … To simplify, double-coding means elite/popular, accommodating/subversive and new/old. (1986: 29–30)

Jencks' categorization of architecture applies across a whole range of expressive and social processes, even though 'postmodern movements vary in each cultural form' (1986: 29). His further subdivision of postmodern art and architecture (see also Jencks, 1987a) emphasizes the capacity of postmodernism to restore aesthetics to a human scale for human pleasures. In particular, the postmodern style of new or neo-classicism celebrates the human form, liberating it from nihilism, expressionism and the abstract or geometric rationality of modernist art styles. This revivification of the recognizable, sensual and pleasurable dimensions of the human form re-places art into the context of everyday practices – even as these representations of the human form are 'double-coded' and pluralized in the expanding embrace of postmodern aesthetics. Postmodernism, therefore, includes all expressive modes, allowing the interaction of popular culture with the intensity and complexity of profound thought. In Jencks' terms, postmodernism is everything that can be articulated, imagined and enjoyed in human terms.

To this extent, Jencks also sees postmodernism as a periodizing concept. Art and especially architecture, which is the most highly corporatized, physically extant and expressive form in contemporary culture, are indicators of broader social and historical trends. Jencks (1987) outlines thirty-two characteristics or 'variables' which constitute the defining assemblage of postmodern aesthetics – these include ideological, stylistic and design qualities. While these variables are common to many definitions of postmodernism and embrace such things as humour, pastiche and language play, Jencks' later definitions tend to celebrate postmodernity against the limits of modernity.

Considered in these terms, Jencks defines the world as a distinct advance on previous epochs. This new world is a multinational constituency which is ordered through its major cities: New York, London, Paris, Tokyo, Hong Kong, Singapore and Frankfurt. The 'radical eclecticism' and humanly scaled architecture of these cities draws together the broad span of human cultures and human history, allowing them to exist in a heterogeneous harmony of parts. Nothing is subsumed by the homogenizing force of cultural imperialism; the multiplication of ideologies and bourgeois pleasures facilitates the capitalist desire for difference and change. These new cities and the postmodern context through which they function are predicates of pleasure and function. Beauty and joy are reintroduced to the increasingly human spaces. The old, grey and falsely egalitarian monoliths of the 'modern' city are being replaced by consumerized funhouses, open and eclectic settings where people of all types might congregate, converse, do business and enjoy the allusions and interplay of cultures, spaces and time. Postmodern architecture, according to Jencks, 'calls up the memories of a culture to which we were connected, and by respecting these associations, by giving them the honour of transformation, it manages to have a dimensionality greater than the present' (1987a: 8). This new world is inclusive and de-centred, offering immense possibilities, in Jencks' mind, for a post-cultural eclecticism which would liberate all humanity from the intensity, limits and dangers of modernist national allegiance. These new transnational experiences are being accompanied by a move to economic and industrial reformation: post-heavy industry, post-Fordist mass production, and an information age that offers small-scale economies, flexible work and business operations, new pleasures and new expressive modes.

Like many other postmodern utopians, Jencks tends continually to parenthesize the more negative implications of his vision, while simultaneously caricaturing modernism and its failings. This optimism underscores virtually all of his writing, and we are left with a sense that anything that is good must be postmodern, and anything that is bad must be modern.

While Jencks himself leaves a space in postmodernism for modernist perspectives, he constantly presents the two in polemical terms. According to Jencks, the contradictions which had plagued and critically limited the modern vision have been overcome through postmodernism's greater emphasis on the individual and personal pleasure. Jencks' radical eclecticism, which functions at a human scale of experience and perspective, provides new opportunities for enhanced, complex lifestyles. Capitalism can now be harnessed and re-shaped through these lifestyles, creating more choice and an even greater potential for aesthetic experimentation, social diversity, inclusiveness and sensate gratifications. Capitalism is no longer a master, but a servant of choice and of a pluralized society. Public and private interests are no longer in conflict since the ascendant self will always find a place, a niche, in the ever broadening eclecticism of the global postmodern.

Postmodern Nature

Jencks' theory of postmodern satisfaction reaches its zenith in *The Architecture of the Jumping Universe* (1995), where postmodernism and its aesthetic forms are validated in terms of a theory of nature. As with Andrew Ross's *Strange Weather* (1991) and Jean-François Lyotard's *The Postmodern Condition* (1984a), Jencks develops a social and cultural theory which derives in part from a reading of contemporary science, most particularly the so-called 'new physics'. Postmodernism generally, and postmodern architecture in particular, is explained in terms of theories of 'complexity' and a 'purposeful' universe. Thus, the universe is not interested in the petty human squabbles which characterize modernity; it

> is always seeking out the tenuous position of maximum choice, maximum computability, where almost any outcome might occur. Creativity is balanced at this knife-edge between predictability and randomness. A completely ordered or completely chaotic system is not very valuable because it cannot evolve very far; it cannot improve or progress. By contrast, a system pushed far-from-equilibrium to the boundary between order and chaos – to that crucial phase transition – is rich in possibilities. (Jencks, 1995: 85)

These progressive or transitional phases represent evolutionary 'leaps' or 'jumps' where a plateau of increasing complexity in the universe and nature is replaced by a rapid advance. The history of the universe can be chronicled in terms of these varying phases: stable or

Plate 7.1   *Terry Batt, Forthcoming Attractions (Oil and wax on canvas, 6' x 7')*

Postmodern art is characterized by pastiche, wit, multiple ironies and images from popular culture. The paintings of Terry Batt, like those of many other postmodern artists, are rich with warm and vibrant colours and scales of human responsiveness. The works engage the viewer in the experiences of everyday life, including the life of mass media and popular characters. Terry's work hearkens back to the New York *avant garde*, reflecting a clear homage to painters like Andy Warhol.

plateau periods; periods of modestly increasing complexity; and leaps in which stability is replaced by this knife-edge of chaos and order. For Jencks, the progress of natural evolution and ultimately human history can be chronicled in much the same way. The present postmodern phase is a transition; its complex associations integrate potential chaos (drastic decline in biological diversity, human population explosion, greenhouse effect, the depletion of the ozone layer, etc.) with new forms of order (radical eclecticism, fractal theory, global village, etc.). The outcome is a more complex and more beautiful (human) condition, a postmodern culture. These complexities can be represented architecturally, which for Jencks is their ultimate truth. The system, which is the architectural design, might thus incorporate references to chaos and order, ecological conditions and natural processes. That is to say, a truly postmodern architecture will appear more like the self-repairing system of a living organism than a nineteenth-century machine. The new architecture may in fact replicate the complex processing of computer systems, or a cybernetic which, 'with its changing software as the driving force, is losing its mechanical nature. In ten years' time the word and concept of "machine" will be self-contradictory because it will have become creative, anticipatory, non-routine – that is non-mechanical' (Jencks, 1995: 160).

So for Jencks, postmodernism promises all. Organic architecture will be integrated with 'smart' machinery (computers) which are no longer constrained by their mechanistic ancestry. This self-organizing cultural system is both a part of, and a representation of, a self-organizing universe. Following theorists like Paul Davies (1987), who also argues that the universe is evolving in accordance with a particular organizational 'blueprint', Jencks' vision is decidedly progressivist, if not precipitative and teleological:

> We are driven from behind by destructive universal forces, and pulled from in front by positive ones. It is to these second, optimistic cosmogenic forces that we, and the many living things and characters who resist entropy, owe our existence. To them, this friendly polemic is dedicated. (Jencks, 1995: 16)

Jencks' 'friendly polemic' argues that the ecological and social traumas being experienced in contemporary culture are to be expected during a time of rupture and transition. What is more important is that nature must run the fine edge between chaos and higher levels of order so as to advance the condition of complexity. Architectural and social forms, therefore, must mimic this natural complexity – fractals, quanta, wave theory – in order to realize fully the promise of postmodernism.

POSTMODERN POLITICS, NEW DEMOCRACY AND THE INVISIBLE ETHIC

The notion of a postmodern politics is highly debated within social and cultural theory. As we have indicated, there are three distinct groups of theorists of the postmodern: avant-gardists, deconstructionists and celebrationists. At this point in our discussion, we might add a fourth group, which would peripherally include Daniel Bell, but which is grounded more fully in a form of materialist and structuralist critique of both the theoretical and cultural dimensions of postmodernism. This group would include Marxists, liberal humanists and liberal phenomenologists. In many respects, the principal question informing this group's critique of postmodernism refers quite directly to the possibility of a postmodern politics. In fact, these theorists argue that postmodernism is both theoretically and culturally conservative. Their reasons for arguing this are threefold:

1   Celebrational and deconstructionist postmodernisms tend to limit their theory in order to reject universal principles of reform. A sense of principled social justice, liberation and reform can never reach to all people in all situations. Universal principles like human

rights, social equity, freedom of speech, freedom of assembly, freedom from poverty, are all too broad and too sweeping for celebrational and deconstructionist postmodernists. Postmodern emphasis on 'difference' risks a complete surrender of universal principles of liberation.

2   The emphasis on discourse or language tends to neglect questions of 'real power' and real material deprivation. Questions of poverty and privilege which are determined by formidable social power can never be tackled by postmodernism. As Charles Jencks has argued, these are the questions of another time. The interests of the bourgeoisie of the developed world are more focused on aesthetic and personal pleasure.

3   The emphasis of celebrational postmodernists on popular culture and consumerist practices tends to legitimate capitalist processes, consumerism and forms of social and cultural hierarchy.

Among this group are theorists like Peter Dews (1984), David Harvey (1989) and Jürgen Habermas (1981, 1983, 1984b). For these commentators, the celebration of a new epoch called 'postmodernity' or 'postmodernism' is premature. Habermas (1983), in particular, has impugned the whole notion of a postmodern condition, arguing that modernism is a political and theoretical project which remains fundamentally 'incomplete'.

Habermas is himself a complex and interesting theorist who sits somewhat outside the canon of postmodern theory (see Chapter 3), even though his work from the 1980s shares a significant interest in the social and cultural dimensions of language. His earliest work engages with major debates on sociological theory and the methods of people like Talcott Parsons and Max Weber. However, when he turns his attention toward the rising influence of French poststructuralism, Lyotard and Foucault in particular, his response is strangely hostile. In many ways, Habermas's debates with Lyotard and Foucault reflect a professional competitiveness, since both sides were seeking to extend cultural and reformist thinking beyond the boundaries of Enlightenment reason and Marxist ideology. Habermas wanted to complete the project of the Enlightenment (or 'modernity') by focusing on the problematic of language and inter-subject communication (intersubjectivity); this interest in intersubjectivity contrasts with the interests of other phenomenologists who are more preoccupied with the 'consciousness' of individual subjects. To develop this reformist analysis of intersubjective communication, Habermas deliberately avoids the sort of pessimism which, in his view, prevented groups like the Frankfurt School from offering a genuine escape from social control and oppression:

> The project of modernity formulated in the eighteenth century by the philosophers of the Enlightenment consisted in their efforts to develop objective science, universal morality and law, and autonomous art according to their inner logic. At the same time, this project intended to release the cognitive potentials of each of these domains from their esoteric forms. The Enlightenment philosophers wanted to utilize this accumulation of specialized culture for the enrichment of everyday life – that is to say, for the rational organization of everyday social life. (Habermas, 1983: 9)

The Ideal Speech Situation

In his most detailed and extended work on the political and social dimensions of language, *The Theory of Communicative Action* (1984a, 1987a), Habermas explains his dissatisfaction with Enlightenment reason in terms of its concentration on epistemology or knowledge. To this extent, he seeks to expound a theory of social reform based on communication and action, rather than on the overthrow and replacement of the structure or the 'system'. Habermas is influenced by the work of Max Weber (see Chapter 2), who distinguishes between instrumental rationality and communicative rationality. Instrumental rationality refers to those practices which are formed through institutions and bureaucracies of state and economy, and which constitute the foundations of social stability. Communicative rationality refers to those everyday practices of everyday people (the lifeworld) which function to socialize people, facilitating a sense of order, social knowledge and cultural reproduction. In communicative action individual 'actors' are able to assert themselves and their knowledge, bringing their private 'truth claims' into a public space.

Communicative rationality, thereby, allows individual actors to present their own personal truths and measure them against the truths of other individuals; this process contributes to the formation of a general, social and consensual truth. This mutual construction of truth becomes culture, and in what Habermas refers to as 'the ideal speech situation' the various truth claims are rationally engaged with and resolved. While this public forum constitutes an idealized or utopianized version of human communicative action, it provides Habermas with a focus for the completion of the modernist project – a space in which politics may be respectfully played out and differences acknowledged and resolved. In this ideal speech situation, communicative rationality overrides the centralizing and excessively bureaucratic controls of instrumental rationality.

Habermas's theory functions as a general elevation of democratic ideals and the significance of public participation and public policy-making. Habermas argues, in fact, that a fully functioning modern, democratic society would draw together its various spheres of activity through the genuine activism of its citizenry. Again, Habermas follows Weber's description of modernization as the separation of art, science and morality into distinct spheres. Modernization can only be completed when each of the spheres is optimized through communicative action and through the confluence of their ideals. That is, the ideals promised in each of the spheres of art, science and morality will only be fulfilled when they are transferred back to the realm of individuals, their communicative actions and their lifeworlds. Emancipation becomes the perfection of these public speech conditions; rationality and society are reintegrated through the experience of publicly fostered consensus.

When the system intrudes on the lifeworld of actors – and this is the deficiency of modernity which must be overcome – pathologies are produced. In an increasingly technical society, where the state continually imposes itself on the ideal speech situation, the instrumental rationality produces hierarchical effects on communicative exchange.

The imperative toward consensus is replaced by communicative rupture as one party tries to overthrow the interests of the other through an instrument of force. Habermas argues, in fact, that the poststructuralist and postmodernist critique of reason is therefore appropriate only in terms of this instrumental rationality, and cannot be used against communicative action. Communicative action, in Habermas's view, facilitates the free flow of individuals and groups through rational and rationalized discourse. A postmodern precept which demands the deconstruction of state apparatuses and the abandonment of hierarchical discourses is provided for in the conception of the ideal speech situation and the intersubjectivity of individual lifeworlds. French poststructuralism and postmodern theoretics, Habermas argues, serve only to mystify modernism's fundamental critique of itself, complicating the project with a fundamental surrender of its positive political aspirations or modernism (see Habermas, 1981, 1983). In other words, Habermas finds some value in the postmodern/poststructuralist critique of state apparatuses and ideologies, but postmodernism/poststructuralism's refusal to offer an alternative politics simply denies the force of modernism's reformist project, its efforts to complete itself.

Much of the debate about the differences and respective value of Habermas and deconstructionist postmodernism centres on the question of truth and science. While Habermas argues that the ideal speech situation of communicative rationality is free of hierarchical distinctions and dominative structural ideologies, Jean-François Lyotard thinks the opposite. According to Lyotard (1984b), Habermas reconstructs the conditions of universal and systematic domination, both in his privileging of scientific discourse and truth validity claims, and in the obliteration of difference through the imagining of 'consensus' resolution. Lyotard's thesis welcomes that part of postmodern culture which allows differences (*les differends*) to assert themselves beyond the homogenizing impulses of scientism, universal values and consensual law. Any rationality which finds itself restoring truth claims and the methodological impositions of science is not to be trusted.

Postmodernism as New Democracy

The most significant problem for advocates of a postmodern politics is the variability in the concept's meaning. In this chapter we have identified four distinct types of postmodernism, each of which bearing its own specific political tenor. And indeed, while postmodernism has become thoroughly absorbed into the lexicon of social and cultural studies, this variability appears to have subdued its efficacy and deployment in the analysis of contemporary culture, most especially within the context of the September 11 attacks and the subsequent 'war on terror'.

In many respects, the radical violence of war and the resurgent cultural divide between the 'east' and the 'west' (Lewis, 2005) has critically problematized the postmodern conceptualization of 'difference' which has become the mantra of its political legacy. Indeed, it has been precisely this mantra of 'difference' which appears to have out-shone the more contentious and theoretically complex concept of 'postmodernism', appending itself to western notions of internationalism, multiculturalism and social pluralism. Difference and diversity, that is, have become central discursive platforms for social and migration programmes in many western nations since the 1980s; they have also formed the basis for more radical theories of democracy and experimental individualism, especially through the new communications technologies (see Chapter 11) and expressive sexualities (see Chapter 9).

As Stuart Hall (1991a) noted some time ago, however, even the mantra of difference is a limited reformist ideal, since it transforms significant cultural 'Difference' into a form of western, capitalist entertainment – a dilute and palatable international cuisine of 'difference'. Moreover, its advocacy for a democratic or radical individualism merely confirms the capitalist ethos of anti-collectivism and a total abdication of social responsibility, including responsibility for the billions of global citizens who live in a state of war, at or below the poverty line. Equally, the political mantra of difference and radical subjectivity seems not to be able to distinguish between, for example, liberated sexuality and diversity of cultural practice on the one hand, and criminal violence on the other. Both constitute a deviation from homogenized and normative social prescriptions, and both form a radical mode of difference and social plurality.

As noted in Chapter 1, the 9/11 attacks on the US and the subsequent 'war on terror' have stimulated a significant review of western social policies on diversity, as well as fuelled conservative scholars' criticisms of postmodernism and the broader project of identity-based emancipation. According to these 'revisions', postmodernism and the diversity mantra are found wanting when they are forced to confront the hard facts of a 'violent and inevitable' civilizational divide. Samuel Huntington (1993), Bernard Lewis (2003) and numerous other conservative commentators argue that war between the west and non-west is inevitable because Islam is fundamentally anti-modern and anti-democratic. Diversity, in this sense, should be a mere constituent of the grand monolith of modern, western, liberal-democracy.

In response to these criticisms, various cultural theorists have attempted to reinvigorate the foundational work of postmodern/poststructural deconstructionists like Ernesto Laclau (Laclau and Mouffe, 1985; Laclau, 1991) and Deleuze and Guattari (1983, 1987). According to Michael Hardt and Antonio Negri (2004), a radical democracy, even within the context of war, can only be shaped through the evanescence of 'the multitudes' – a concept that seeks to extend the notion of diversity through the dissolution of privilege and community. Hardt and Negri speak for many enthusiasts for a new democracy when they postulate a new, radical subjectivity which is shaped through the multitudinous conditions of cultural mixing. Through the mobilization of cultural alterity (Otherness), this new subject will *act* in a way that necessarily extends the freedom of the cultural whole. In this sense, the collapse in support for the UK Prime Minister and US President who led the invasion of Iraq (2003–) and the 'war on terror' is a simple manifestation of the inevitability of democratic radicalism, and the emergent, but irresistible ascent of alterity in contemporary cultural politics. Within a new symbolic order, the radical democratic subject is constituted around a desire for pleasure which is necessarily suspicious of war and war leaders: the failure of the Iraq occupation and the broader Middle East policies merely confirms these deeper (multitudinous) cultural politics.

Other poststructuralist-influenced commentators on the war on terror and contemporary culture are less optimistic, particularly about the postmodern enthusiasm for pleasure and 'enjoyment'. Slajov Zizek (2004), for example, questions the whole notion of the subject determining the act; for Zizek, rather, the act determines the subject. In this sense, the twin tower attacks and the reactive war on terror were not an interruption to the general momentum of democratizing culture – the symbolic order. They were a part of a symbolic order in which the invisible weave of history simply exposed itself in a triumph of violence, a war that had been undeclared and in which the various enmities had merely crystallized as definitive act. Zizek questions the whole notion of 'enjoyment' as a form of political desirability, a sensibility and passion which necessarily confronts the conservative impulse to hierarchy, ideology and authority. The election or non-election of war leaders, to this end, is largely irrelevant to the general order by which the culture impels its actors and actions.

Unlike liberal and Marxist critics of war and political violence, however, Zizek is not frustrated by postmodernist idealism; he doesn't advocate the erasure of poststructuralist ideas on discourse and language. Rather, he suggests an alternative scenario in which actors decline to act, expressing their deviation to the ascendant order by simply 'doing nothing'. Such inertia would not constitute a submission to ideology but its complete rejection – a rejection in radical silence. He asks:

> What if it is only the full acceptance of the desperate closure of the present global situation that can push us towards actual change? (Zizek, 2004: 80)

This is a question to which we will return in Chapter 12.

8

Popular Consumption and Youth Culture

INTRODUCTION

In Chapter 1 it was argued that contemporary culture is characterized by the density and proliferation of mediated communication – radio, television, IPod, movies, internet. While much of the earlier analysis of society and the media focused on the *production* of texts, we argued in Chapter 1 that a more complete understanding of culture also required an analysis of processes of textual *consumption*. Our distinctively televisual culture has been constructed around a form of consumer capitalism which attaches significant symbolic value to products, services and information units. That is, capitalism and its system of exchange imbues its material and non-material products ('artefacts') with certain kinds of meaning. Pierre Bourdieu (1984, 1990), as we have also discussed, claims that these meanings are largely constituted around forms of social discrimination. As an hierarchical and highly competitive economic system, that is, capitalism situates individuals and groups according to their demonstrable economic assets and attributes: the consumption, ownership and display of capitalist products helps to locate individuals within a class–style hierarchy which contributes to the formation of their social identity.

However, while all capitalist products convey meanings, only particular dimensions of those meanings are *directly* linked to power and ideology as Bourdieu claims. Moreover, and as poststructuralist and postmodernist theorists have demonstrated, these meanings are themselves contested and challenged by different individuals and groups within and between social formations. Thus, for some drivers their sports utility vehicle (SUV/4WD) may represent freedom, adventure and strength; to other drivers, however, such vehicles may represent environmental delinquency, danger and a traffic hazard.

Such disputes in meaning (or 'polysemy') are particularly common in media and other cultural artefacts that are designed primarily to convey information via narrative, image or 'style'. Again, as we noted in Chapter 1, producers of such 'texts' may seek to impose a particular meaning over their audiences/consumers, and often these meanings are linked to particular ideological perspectives. The Fox Network in the United States, for example, was strident in its support of the White House administration and the invasion/occupation of Iraq (2003–). In many respects, these 'dominant' political perspectives are formed through a complex aesthetic of information reporting, story-telling and meaning-making that is shaped through various modes of televisualization and a new form of cultural consciousness.

Even so, these dominant perspectives, generated through organizations like the Fox Network, are neither absolute nor impervious to challenge and the assault of counter meanings, counter interpretations and reinterpretation. Both the dominant and counter meanings form the fabric and texture of the contemporary 'public sphere' or 'mediasphere' – a transformed and transformative space of political debate and meaning-making. Audiences, as 'text consumers' are as critical to the operations of the mediasphere as are the texts and text producers. This chapter examines the theoretical conceptualizations of audiences, the politics of text consumption, questions of consumption 'style', and a particular audience sub-set – youth culture.

EARLY AUDIENCE THEORIES

Transmission and Uses/Gratifications Models

Communications and journalism schools in the United States were the first to develop sophisticated audience research models and theories. American academics and community leaders in the early part of the twentieth century were particularly concerned about the negative effects the new electrical media (radio and cinema) may be having on children and the free thought of individuals. The Payne Fund studies (1929–32), in particular, investigated the causal link between the mass media and negative behaviours and attitudes in children. Such studies were pivotal in the development of the communications 'transmission model' and the 'magic bullet' theory – both of which claimed that a 'message' could reach a target audience through the deployment of effective media and professional strategies.

However, while liberal academics and community leaders in the US feared the power of the media to compromise individualism and free thought, European Marxists were afraid that a powerful media would indoctrinate the people with capitalist ideology. In either case, audiences were viewed as passive receivers of messages and highly vulnerable to the meaning-making power of the mass media. Such perspectives continue into the present, although a more sophisticated understanding of audiences has evolved around the notion of media 'uses and gratifications'. In this perspective audiences are not passive receivers or dupes of the mass media; they are active meaning creators who use media texts for their own pleasure, intellectual and emotional stimulation.

Fundamentally, the model switches interest from media institutions and messages to the ways in which audiences use and derive gratification from media messages. This switch in interest begins with the work of Elihu Katz (1959) and is developed in a more complete way by James Lull. Lull introduced important methodologies which drew uses and gratifications research away from a strictly psychological model toward a more ethnographic model. Lull's essay 'The social uses of television' (1980) published the findings of a three-year project in which his team observed the TV viewing practices of over two hundred households in California and Wisconsin. The observation team became 'participant observers' in the household, eating dinner with the families, doing chores, participating in group entertainment and watching TV. Lull argues that the presence of the observer eventually became less exceptional and barely disrupted the families' normal domestic activities. Lull's work is clearly linked with the phenomenological school of sociology, which had achieved some significance in the United States from the 1970s. While the method had been used in a wide range of sociological enquiries (mostly to do with 'deviant' and sub-culture activities), this was the first time a genuinely ethnographic technique had been applied in American media analysis. As we shall see below, this application of an anthropological 'ethnography' brought Lull's sociology of the media quite close to the incipient ethnographies that were being conducted at the Birmingham Centre for Contemporary Cultural Studies, most particularly through the work of David Morley.

Screen Theory

The move toward a postmodern audience theory, however, has been filtered through the heritage of European structuralism and poststructuralism. The translation into English of a largely French structuralist approach to language theory can be traced to a number of British media and cinema analysts working in the 1970s. In particular, the journal *Screen* provided a forum for the exploration of new approaches to the audience and the audience experience of cinema texts. Two of the journal's significant contributors, Colin MacCabe and Stephen Heath, took a particular interest in French structuralist and psychoanalytic theory. Heath and MacCabe constructed a theory of film analysis which integrated Jacques Lacan's notion of 'the gaze' as a cinematic experience with Louis Althusser's concept of dominant ideology. While the relationship between reader and text had been problematized in literary studies through phenomenology and poststructuralism (see Bleitch, 1978; Iser, 1978; Tompkins, 1980), cinema studies was drawn more fully into the cultural studies perspective through a particular interest in the act of watching images and connecting those images with the audience's whole sense of self.

According to the *Screen* theorists, the questions for the study of cinema are: what is the subject, where is the subject and how does the subject exist in relation to the text? Recalling Bertolt Brecht's condemnation of realist literature, MacCabe (1974), for example, criticizes Hollywood realist cinema for 'positioning' the spectator/subject as though s/he were experiencing 'real life' in the text. The classic Hollywood film feigns transparency, creating an illusion for the spectator that what is being displayed can be believed because it is a natural and realistic representation of life. The spectator thus misrecognizes the image as real while at the same time experiencing the perspective or gaze of the camera as actually his or her own. When the image is displayed it is as though the spectator were looking directly from within the fictional construction, projecting him- or herself into the action as the camera eye becomes the spectator's own eye. In contrast, the work of Brecht and the film director Sergei Eisenstein foregrounds the artifice and machinery of art production and constantly turns the camera or textual gaze back on the audience, thus potentially eliding realism and its ideological imperatives.

DAVID MORLEY'S AUDIENCE ETHNOGRAPHY

While still a student at the Birmingham Centre, David Morley (1980b) had critiqued *Screen* theory for its treatment of audiences as being merely 'positioned' by text. Morley's quite seminal work on audiences integrated the Birmingham Centre's increasing interest in empiricism with the encoding/decoding model developed by Stuart Hall (1980, see Chapter 4). According to Hall, text makers draw on prevalent cultural perspectives to 'encode' their narratives, ideas and ideology: audiences draw upon a similar, though not identical, corpus of cultural elements and experiences to 'decode' the text. The consonance of the encoding/decoding process creates the conditions for a negotiated, shared and dominant meaning, as well as the durability of social power or 'hegemony'.

Morley sought to test these ideas empirically: that is, through an accurate recording of experience in the context of the action (see Chapter 1). For a number of researchers coming out of the Birmingham Centre in the 1970s, this form of 'ethnography' provided a mechanism for analyzing the 'decoding' part of the encoding/decoding process. Dissatisfied with the quantitative and effects traditions prevailing in American communications schools, researchers like David Morley and Roger Silverstone embraced the idea of a discursive, anthropological study of audiences which acknowledges the significance of the cultural context of text reading and text consumption. Unlike the uses and gratifications research being conducted in the US by James Lull and others, however, the Birmingham audience research was very much embedded in questions of power and ideology. While qualitative research uses a range of methods, ethnographic audience research tends to examine audience activities within the normal context of their viewing. An ethnographic study, therefore, would tend to record people's activities within the home, where people normally watch TV. The domestic context of TV watching is an essential feature of the process of audiences' meaning-making.

The Nationwide Audience

David Morley's (1980a) early study of the British TV, magazine-style, current affairs programme *Nationwide* marks a significant moment in the development of cultural studies. While American cultural analysis had been influenced by anthropologists like Clifford Geertz and the various permutations of phenomenological sociology, British cultural studies had tended to merge its literary and sociological lineages through the development of a more speculative, textual method. That is, because of their strong interest in questions of ideology and a general belief that all discourse is politically positioned, the British cultural theorists had tended to defer significant questions about science and scientific methods. Even the 'scientism' of Saussure's semiology and Lévi-Strauss's structural anthropology becomes mollified in the translation to British cultural studies. The British practitioners of semiotics were less interested in presenting a scientific edifice and more interested in presenting the processes of textual coding in terms of hegemonic and ideological forces.

As we have noted, the Birmingham methodology tended to concentrate on the text, elucidating its meanings through speculations about how an audience might engage with its discourses, and the dominant ideologies and hegemonic conditions of a culture. Stuart Hall's notion of 'preferred reading' suggests that audiences will select a particular meaning from a text, depending on their social position and the ways in which they relate to the culture. All texts are 'polysemic' (having multiple meaning potentials), so audience members are able to select a 'dominant reading' position in accordance with prevailing cultural norms, standards and ideologies. Polysemy, however, also facilitates forms of 'negotiated' reading, whereby audience members can *actively* engage with the text's meaning potentials to create a more individualized or divergent reading space. As we shall see later in the chapter, these divergent spaces may actually challenge or transgress the authority of the dominant reading.

The first stage of the *Nationwide* project examined the news text and offered speculations or hypotheses about the ideological conditions in which the text would be read. According to the research, *Nationwide* was a common-sense, regionally based interpretation of the main news events of the day. It was designed to speak to, and from, the common person. It also aimed to acknowledge the diversity of Britain, giving a voice to the interests of various social sub-groups. Morley's qualitative analysis sought to uncover the degree to which actual social subjects accepted or rejected *Nationwide*'s reading of the news. Video recordings of the programme were shown to twenty-nine socially located groups comprising either managers, students, trade unionists or apprentices. Morley's research team found significant variations in groups' attitudes toward the programme's style and its readings of particular events. Bank managers, for example, rejected the programme's style as merely entertainment but endorsed its ideological readings, even when they opposed their own. Trade unionists endorsed the style, but rejected the ideology. One group of black students didn't reject the programme's preferred reading of events, but chose not to 'read' the programme at all. Indeed, the strongest conclusion that was drawn from this seminal work was that there is no clear or direct relationship between socioeconomic group and a preferred reading of a text. Morley argued that the various social groups draw on much more complex resources when reading a text than had been assumed. Indeed, the reading patterns that were identifiable linked together various cultural traditions, political allegiances and institutional/professional discourses – black youth culture, Labour Party politics, Marxism, professionalism, bourgeois educational perspectives, and so on, could all be invoked in the course of reading a text.

Family Television Consumption

From its emergence as a distinct discipline Birmingham-style cultural studies was deeply committed to the possibilities of difference and the social margins. Nevertheless, the significant relationship between culture and the contemporary media necessarily admitted debates about the validity of particular types of audience analysis. Morley's experience with the *Nationwide* project demonstrated that the patterns of audience reading were even more diverse and complicated than he had originally anticipated. This discovery encouraged Morley, no doubt, to investigate an even more highly localized cultural zone, the family. At the same time, he came to reject the encoding/decoding model, which concentrates on issues of power, ideology and preferred reading. In a postscript to the *Nationwide* project, in fact, he admits a level of uncertainty about the whole notion of 'preferred reading', suggesting that it is probably no more than 'the reading the analyst is predicting that most members of the audience will produce' (1980b: 6). In centralizing the audience, Morley had come to believe that a more generalized investigative model would be required if the full implications and details of audience practices and readings were to be elucidated. In this sense, his work brings him closer to the sort of anthropological models that had been developing through subjectivist and phenomenological sociology practised in the United States.

In fact, this problematization of the text and the preferred or dominant reading concept was taking place in wider fields of cultural analysis, most especially as poststructuralism was being integrated into theories of consumption and postmodern theory. Barthes, Derrida and Foucault had all deconstructed the notion of the original work of art and the 'authority' of the author; poststructuralism had claimed, in fact, that all discourse was formed in relation to all other discourses and no text could claim to be unique and meaningful in its own right. Morley's *Nationwide* research had convinced him of the validity of these claims, most particularly as the polysemy of texts seemed not to surrender to the structuralist imperatives of homogenizing and dominant ideology. That is, his research seemed to validate the poststructuralist belief that there are as many gaps in meaning-making processes as there are confluences. In *Family Television* (1986) Morley ceases to interrogate the ways texts and readers interact to produce meaning in relation to dominant ideologies. Rather, his research focuses on the way individual family members interact, struggle and create meaning for themselves in relation to other family members. While *Family Television* retains some interest in issues of power, this approach to power is more consistent with Foucault's notion of microphysics or personal power: between men and women, parents and offspring, and siblings. To this extent, the 'content' or texts of the TV medium become less important than the technology or medium itself, since what matters most in the relationships within the family is the symbolic value of the medium in terms of its consumption, rather than the specific readings of specific texts. The important questions for Morley include the following:

1 How do individual family members use the television?
2 Who controls the television and in what circumstances?
3 What do people do when the television is switched on?
4 In what ways does the television confirm the various relationships, including the power relationships, within the family?

Morley and others who have followed the empirical cultural studies model have attempted to graph the culture of television viewing. As the most prominent domestic communications technology, one which constitutes the central entertainment and informational mode, TV occupies an extremely significant cultural space. As with early radio and the rising use of the Internet, television conflates the public and private spheres. Morley's recent work continues to graph the ways in which domestic technologies are constituted through this highly localized culture of the family:

> Broadcasting (along with other domestic technologies of communication) has, therefore, to be understood as enmeshed within the internal dynamics of the organization of domestic space, primarily with reference to gender relations. However, our interest lies in formulating an analytical framework which goes beyond the question of the internal relations of the domestic sphere to include the shifting relations between this domestic or private sphere and the public sphere by which it is framed. From this perspective we see that not only has the development of communications technology been affected by the pre-existing organization of domestic space but that broadcasting, for example, can be seen to have played a significant part in rewriting the relations between the domestic and public spheres – for instance, by increasing the attractiveness of the home as a site of leisure. (Morley and Silverstone, 1990: 38)

Morley's interest in the symbolic dimensions of communications technology parallels the work of James Carey (1989) in the United States. While Carey's methodology is distinctly historical and discursive, there is no doubt that both researchers acknowledge Marshall McLuhan's claim that the 'medium is the message', and that the interaction between a technology and the context of its consumption necessarily and significantly contributes to the shaping of culture. Moreover, Morley's empirical methods have proven highly influential for those researchers who have actively engaged with issues of communications and cultural policy. Governments across the developed world have been more inclined to heed the advice of (and fund) cultural research that is framed in empirical or scientific terms. Morley's insistence that cultural studies research should be empirically based has provided a valuable paradigm for researchers since the 1990s who have sought to examine broadcasting and broadcasting policy.

PIERRE BOURDIEU AND SYMBOLIC CONSUMPTION

David Morley's shift from an investigation of the text–reader relationship to a focus on media consumption reflects wider moves within the field of cultural analysis. In particular, the problematization of the text and textual meanings produced through phenomenology on the one hand, and poststructuralism on the other, has led to some significant rethinking of the status of the text and how it functions in relation to the everyday practices of everyday people. Certainly, the general principle that different people interpret texts differently has led particular theorists to ask questions about how texts and their medium can be related to the broader culture. Significantly, attention has been focused on the value of text as part of the culture of consumer capitalism. The French sociologist Pierre Bourdieu was one of the earliest theorists to examine the question of symbolic consumption, outlining in particular the ways in which consumption, as an everyday practice, is implicated in ideology and capitalist hierarchies. That is, Bourdieu sought to explain how capitalism and its forms of discrimination and social hierarchy sustain themselves through the everyday practice of consumption, rather than through the processes of production and labour.

In *Distinction: A Social Critique of the Judgement of Taste* (1984) Bourdieu articulates, in a distinctly sociological framework, many of the ideas that had been infiltrating British cultural theory. In particular, he demonstrates that the idea of 'taste' – the 'innate' power of consumers to discriminate qualitatively between products – is fallacious. According to Bourdieu, the 'tasteful' selection and consumption of products is used as a social insignia for the privileging of particular individuals and groups. The selection of a product and the display of its value necessarily implicate consumption in the symbolic positioning of people and their everyday lifestyle and practices. Bourdieu argues, however, that symbolic consumption doesn't merely reflect a person's social position, but actively and actually generates it. That is, everyday players are not socially positioned through their variant levels of education, income and occupation; their position in the mode of production and labour. Nor are they merely the victims of ideology and the limiting effects of symbolic information. They are also, Bourdieu argues, constructions of particular consumption practices, practices which produce and reproduce their position in the social hierarchy. Accordingly, the less privileged groups in the community are ideologically infected by 'lack of taste'; however, the choices they make as consumers serve to construct their social roles and reproduce their lack of privilege.

For example, the consumption (and style of consumption) of different types of alcohol reinforces the social position of the consumer. A man in a suit may sip wine at an expensive restaurant or may choose boutique beers at a comfortable bar. By contrast, an unskilled labourer might drink considerable amounts of mass-produced beer in a public bar or pool room. The respective consumption practices reinforce the social position of the consumers, functioning as symbolic indicators of occupation, education and income levels.

In many respects, Bourdieu's empirical work illuminates similar cultural territory to that which Roland Barthes was investigating in *Mythologies* (1973). However, while Barthes was examining the ideological and mythological dimensions of French suburban life, Bourdieu wanted to know how suburban life reproduced itself in terms of actual consumption practices. To a degree, that is, Bourdieu's empiricism begins where Barthes concludes, seeking explanations for the taken-for-grantedness (doxa) of everyday suburban life. Bourdieu's empirical work in *Distinction* consisted of a questionnaire survey of around 1200 respondents, covering a broad sample of occupations and social 'classes'. His analysis linked consumption with social class, noting, for example, that there were strong correlations between social status and such things as housing styles, musical tastes and food preferences (1984: 1). However, 'taste' in Bourdieu's terms refers as much to 'distaste' or disgust as it does to positive preference (1984: 56). In either case, Bourdieu's principal interest is in the systematic accumulation of symbolic power through the act of consumption. This structuralist conception of everyday practice had been discussed in earlier works such as *Outline of a Theory of Practice* (1977), where Bourdieu explains the significant notion of 'symbolic capital' (see esp. 1977: 70). Symbolic capital, however, is more than just a differentiation of incomes or the power of discretionary spending. It is more than just an outline of dominant and subordinate social players. In fact, symbolic value, as we have suggested, attaches to notions of cultural distinction and necessarily produces a cultural economy in which 'taste' becomes the fundamental currency. In this sense, two groups may have the same income, but one has superior knowledge and intellectual or aesthetic discretion. Within the middle classes this discretion might distinguish the vulgar, tasteless *nouveau riche* from the well-educated and highly informed professional.

Again, a simple example might explain this difference in symbolic hierarchies. Bourdieu points to the differences between people of taste and the more vulgar groups who have achieved some level of wealth through a trade or manual labour. Quality or fashionable furnishings in the home, the engagement with classical rather than popular music, speech intonations, and clothes – all may be deployed as symbols of superior taste. Even within youth culture, where income and occupation should barely be relevant, there are the same sorts of discriminatory dynamics. Brand-name clothing, for example, might distinguish the cool or fashionable from the uncool. Schools, which institutionally position young people according to age or academic performance, are replete with sub-cultural hierarchies, all of which are distinguished by symbolic value. Preferences for particular musical or clothing styles distinguish insiders from outsiders; the power elites within the student community are identified as much by symbolic taste as by academic, athletic or sexual performance.

MICHEL DE CERTEAU

Bourdieu's work has proven highly influential for those areas of cultural studies preferring a sociological framework for their analysis (see Featherstone, 1991). However, Bourdieu, like Louis Althusser, has been accused of a kind of intellectual conservatism, despite his desire to present a case for radical social realignment (see Jenkins, 1992; Moores, 1993). Specifically, his empirical structuralist approach tends to reinforce the structures he would subvert by limiting the opportunities for agency and transcendence. Social actors seem to be so completely embedded in their symbolic and cultural conditioning ('habitus') that there appears to be little possibility of subverting the social standards of taste; as with Althusser, Bourdieu offers little space for emancipation.

Michel de Certeau is one of the most significant French cultural theorists to critique and expose these limits. His two major texts, *The Writing of History* (1988) and *The Practice of Everyday Life* (1984), use a psychoanalytic model to develop a liberational space for ordinary people and their everyday practices. Significantly, de Certeau (1984: 45–60) expresses some dissatisfaction with Bourdieu's structuralist polemic. Yet, his dissatisfaction also extends to Michel Foucault's poststructuralism; de Certeau feels exasperated by Foucault's reluctance to provide political solutions for those people whose liberation he claims to encourage. According to de Certeau, Foucault's description of the apparatuses of power neglects those operations which are not 'privileged' by the writings of history, but which are active in innumerable ways in the technological machineries about which Foucault writes: 'These techniques which are also operational, but initially deprived of what gives the others their force, are the "tactics" which I have suggested might furnish a formal index of the ordinary practices of consumption' (de Certeau, 1984: 49). People act within the corporate or state apparatuses and their technologies; Foucault fails to give adequate recognition to these actions. Just as Said (1986) has expressed his disappointment with Foucault's ultimate political inertia, de Certeau rejects Foucault's disinclination to examine thoroughly that 'power' Foucault himself detects in the operations of everyday procedures.

As Frow (1991) has pointed out, de Certeau's writing has focused on popular culture as a set of practices, rather than a set of texts. The sustaining argument of *The Writing of History* centres on the parallel projects of historiography and rhetorical (literary) analysis. According to de Certeau, historiography and literary rhetoric treat 'understanding' as the effects of representation; in other words, a culture may be analyzed and explained through the elucidation of textual representations, through the symbolic force of language and writing. In contrast to this approach, the Lacanian derived notion of the *real* – that unbordered realm of space and time that cannot be mediated or marked by language – provides for de Certeau a compelling alternative to the 'reality' composed through systems of knowledge such as historical or literary writing. The real, that is, exists at the margins of these systems, a matter of sensory apprehension and the unconscious 'other' in the dominion of objects (see de Certeau, 1988, esp. Chs 2, 5, 6, 8). Lacan, we recall, identifies a prelinguistic experience in childhood. At its most perfect, this unconscious, prelinguistic experience exists when the child is part of the mother; when the child is introduced to the world of language and knowledge, he or she becomes aware of his or her separation from that perfect state. The unconscious, therefore, is the ultimate, the 'real' and must be distinguished from the 'reality' of symbolization, representation and language. In other words, the 'real' is the realm of pre-language, of sensory responses to objects, nature, action and practices that are not invaded by knowledge; 'reality' is the realm of knowledge, thought and language.

The writing of history, therefore, invades the spaces of the real by forcing it out of the unconscious and into the rationalized world of knowledge. While culture imposes itself on the real (nature), it is only through the rifts and gaps in this writing system – zones which knowledge can't rationalize – that the true unconscious and otherness of history is revealed. Historiography will assert itself and its rationalist discourse as a will to truth; but the discourse itself betrays its otherness through a paradoxical veracity, a set of details and meanings that defy the imposed order of writing. Thus, history will write about the French Revolution and inevitably the narrative of the event will force the infinite details of people's lives at the time into a systematic discourse. This discourse will transform or 'reduce' the infinity of details to documents of causes, politics, leaders and results. However, the 'other' dimension to this period of the past will defy rationalization. It is the way people will go about their lives amidst the turmoil of the event; will wash, talk, eat and sleep; will seek to protect themselves from disease or pain; will reproduce and care for their children. The writing of history misses these minutiae, since they slip through the ambit of language and writing to exist merely as practices and actions in everyday life. These everyday sensate experiences which motivate and delight us become the unwritten 'other' of history.

In *The Practice of Everyday Life* we can see that de Certeau's interest in the otherness of power (which Foucault neglects) derives from these same precepts. However, here his desire to foreground the lived experiences of ordinary people is more intensely politicized in a contemporary context. The historical 'otherness' of everyday practice is centred, revealed and valorized as a form of 'continuous present'. The alternative 'structures' of power are thus to be apprehended in the *practices* of the everyday raiders of culture within the dominion of the 'real'. 'Writing', with its textualized 'reality', is once again revealed as an ordered and bordered system of knowledge; de Certeau unravels the presence of writing in order to expose its unconscious subjectivity. The everyday practitioners, with their propensity for 'tactical' raidings of objects and meanings, become the heroic 'anti-heroes' of de Certeau's popular culture – the culture of the people and their everyday practices.

Yet these heroes are not the oppressed proletariat of the Marxist mode of production, nor the *extra*-men (or superman) of Nietzschean philosophy, nor the liberated utilitarian entrepreneurs of market-based capitalist economics – all of whom are fixed in structuralist conceptions of culture and 'reality'. De Certeau's heroes are ordinary people, liberated by their capacity to act, to feel, to 'practise' at the level of the pre-symbolic, prelinguistic real of the everyday. The official culture becomes pre-eminent through the evolution of writing:

> But all through this evolution, the idea of producing a society by a 'scriptural' system has continued to have as its corollary the conviction that although the public is more or less resistant, it is molded by (verbal or iconic) writing, that it becomes similar to what it receives, and that it is *imprinted* by and like the text which is imposed on it.
>
> This text was formerly found at school. Today, the text is society itself. It takes urbanistic, industrial, commercial, or televised form. But the mutation that caused the transition from educational archaeology to the technocracy of the media did not touch the assumption that consumption is essentially passive. (de Certeau, 1984: 167)

Text, then, can be identified as a set of machineries, technologies or apparatuses – including televised media – which may be equated with society itself. Text is therefore to be distinguished from the operations or practices that defy their internal logics. The non-text, we might assume, slips out of its discursive boundaries *as operation*, resisting the solidifying impulse of textuality, and eluding the compromising order of society.

Resistance to this official, textual culture, thus becomes the territory of the real, the unconscious, the prelinguistic practices of everyday life. De Certeau argues that in work and leisure everyday practitioners are engaged in the operations of 'making do' – they must take what the society and culture offer and create 'transverse' spaces which become the 'play in the machine', the source of an individual's power and freedom. De Certeau distinguishes between 'strategies' and 'tactics', both of which produce this effect of disrupting or altering the processes of contemporary capitalist culture (de Certeau, 1984: 29–30). Strategies constitute a level of apparent conformity to the conditions offered by social circumstances; tactics are the 'invisible' activities or operations which everyday practitioners employ within the framework of these circumstances. In this sense a North African emigrant may choose (strategically) to live in Paris and take a job in a factory which enables him and his family to survive with a reasonable degree of comfort and security. However, within this general strategy, the immigrant may 'find ways of using (tactically) the constraining order of the place' (de Certeau, 1984: 30) in order to further advantage his life circumstances. De Certeau refers to the notion of *la perruque* or 'wearing the wig'. These are the disguises that are used by everyday practitioners in order to create the illusion of conformity; behind or within this apparent conformity they are creating a space for their freedom. The worker, therefore, may use his or her time to pilfer, send personal emails, run a football betting competition, speak about television programmes, arrange social engagements – all on the company's time and money. But these creative spaces are not simply defined by the workplace; they are created in the home and in the general activities of consumption and 'making do':

> Without leaving the place where he has no choice but to live and where it lays down its law for him, he establishes within it a degree of *plurality* and creativity. By an act of being in between, he draws unexpected results from his situation. (de Certeau, 1984: 30)

For de Certeau there are three significant characteristics of this resistance:

1 It exists at the level of the unconscious (what Lacan calls the real) and is therefore outside the realm of consciousness, language and inherited culture. Resistance or subversion is not achieved through the instructional content of a text, nor by its special aesthetic qualities, as theorists like Julia Kristeva, Bertolt Brecht or the American postmodernists might claim. Resistance exists outside the text altogether, except in as much as the tactical raiders of everyday life make the text, or any other cultural activity, object or artefact, 'their own'.
2 It functions as operations (or actions) at the level of everyday life and is not predetermined by structure or ideology, which are societal and therefore textual. Where an everyday person becomes subversive of rationalized order is where he or she functions against the flow of discourse. Practitioners do not think their liberation; they merely experience it through their everyday activities.
3 It operates necessarily through consumption and consumption practices. These are 'tactical' since they are used by everyday people to maximize their own pleasures and life satisfactions. The everyday raiders act in their own interests without recourse to grand narratives, reformist ideology or direct challenge to authority. Their self-interest is sufficient motivation to disturb the rationalizing effects of social conformity.

The 'Weak' and the 'Strong'

De Certeau's notion of popular consumption practices has proven extremely attractive to those celebrational postmodernists who have sought to raise consumption to a higher theoretical and political plane (see Fiske, 1989a, 1989b; Featherstone, 1991; Featherstone et al., 1991; Jenkins, 1992; Marshall, 1997). Applying his theoretical density for a reading of popular culture, John Fiske, in particular, rejoices in those practices of consumption, which provide for all social groups the opportunity to create meanings and community outside the structures established by the 'official' culture. Fiske and others tend to parenthesize some of the more difficult aspects of de Certeau's theory, including his psychoanalytical ideas on 'writing' and 'the real'. Popular cultural analysis tends, for example, to collapse the distinction between 'writing' and 'practice' into a general theory of transgression which incorporates all forms of textualization and everyday practice. What matters for popular cultural theorists like John Fiske is that all texts (all culture) are available for consumption (using, reading, viewing, listening). The texts provided by capitalist culture are strategically adopted and tactically raided for the personal, transgressive pleasures of the consumer/everyday practitioner.

In this sense, de Certeau and Fiske break significantly with Bourdieu's conception of symbolic value. They reject the idea that taste merely reflects and determines social hierarchy, arguing that Bourdieu seriously misunderstands the power of social groups to form meanings and constitute themselves culturally. De Certeau specifically rejects the idea that the lower classes are 'weak' and vulnerable to the structuralized and controlling powers of the 'strong' and their socially determined privileges and tastes. According to de Certeau, 'the weak' use their consumption tactically to overthrow the putative power of 'the strong', who are fixed and restrained by the rationalized order of language and history. In fact, the 'strong' are weak because they have no idea that they are being duped. The 'weak' wear disguises or 'wigs' (*les perruques*) by which they hide their tactical raidings. As Fiske takes up this idea, he argues that the strong (corporate powers) are vulnerable to these selective practices of the 'weak' (everyday consumers) since it is the consumers who decide what will and won't succeed commercially. The 'weak' select products from the vast array of overly structured and overly invested materials and services on offer. The weak are nimble, deft and creative, while the strong are torpid, culturally and intellectually obese, and fixed in overly rationalized systems of structure. By far the greater majority of all products remain unsold and it is the 'strong' who are left to puzzle over their failure, second-guessing the shifting interests, tastes and sensibilities of the 'weak'.

Fiske argues, in fact, that the 'strong' must anxiously and despairingly wait upon the choices of the 'weak'. The 'weak' form fashion and taste. Their popular consumption liberates them from expectation and the hierarchy of overbloated and competitive superiority. The 'weak' transform products, practices and places and make them their own. Old people use shopping malls to save money on heating and cooling; young people transform street corners into social totems. They raid the second-hand stores, remove labels from expensive items and sew them on to cheaper imitations. They wait for the post-Christmas sales. They tear at the knees of blue jeans and transform them into symbols of a new community. They remove the wheels from roller skates and drill them onto plywood boards. The 'weak', that is, overthrow the reality bondage of the 'strong' through their own (unconsciously) 'tactical' consumption and meaning-making at the level of the *real*.

TRANSGRESSIVE PLEASURES: POPULAR MEDIA CONSUMPTION

John Fiske

John Fiske's celebration of popular culture began during the 1980s when he appended many of the precepts of the Birmingham Centre for Contemporary Cultural Studies to the theories of Bakhtin, de Saussure and Barthes; in the later 1980s and 1990s he further elaborated his analysis of popular culture through the work of de Certeau and celebrational postmodernism. Throughout his work, Fiske has been intrigued with the idea of (bodily) pleasure as the source of popular resistance. Like other English-speaking theorists working in the field (see Hebdige, 1979; Dyer, 1985; Frow, 1991; Jenkins, 1992; Hartley, 1996; Marshall, 1997) his work combines an interest in text with an analysis of audience or reception practices. However, it has continually sought to reconcile the text–audience divide through speculative readings about how a particular audience might respond to a given text. While these speculations were built around notions of preferred reading (encoding/decoding) in his earlier writing, Fiske has later adapted Barthes's notions of pleasure and bliss to develop a politics of audience pleasure.

It is through the reworking of textual polysemy or multiple meanings that audiences are able to experience a pleasure that frees them from the instrumental rationalities and order of patriarchal capitalism. In this way, Fiske clearly moves from investigation to celebration of popular culture, where the 'popular' is conceived as necessarily political and transgressive, and necessarily implicates the bodily pleasures of readers, viewers and users. Texts which are 'popular' or 'of the people' carry far greater potential for bodily liberation than do the putative high arts, which are always constrained by abstruse, overly rationalized and inaccessible discourses. However, Fiske's work, for all its inconsistencies, is not merely populist or opportunistic, as Jim McGuigan (1992, 1996) and others have claimed. A text, which may be anything from a beach to a football match to a television soap opera, becomes liberatory when it engages the viewer/consumer in particular subject 'positions' and practices. Fiske feels genuinely that these engagements constitute the best hope contemporary culture can offer for the liberation of individuals and communities.

Adapting Bakhtin through the Carnivalesque

Clearly, Fiske attaches meanings to the activity of consumption which are distinct from classical Marxist or radical environmentalism, both of which identify consumption with social control, and social and environmental damage. Fiske's work, in fact, follows the lead of Mikhail Bakhtin (Valentin Volosinov), who reversed various aspects of classical Marxism to produce his theory of the carnivalesque. The carnival of the Middle Ages, Bakhtin explains, removes hierarchy and law in what appears to be a sensate, almost Dionysiac, disordering of social norms.

> The laws, prohibitions, and restrictions that determine the structure of ordinary, that is noncarnival, life are suspended during carnival: what is suspended first of all is hierarchical structure and all the forms of terror, reverence, piety, and etiquette connected with it – that is, everything resulting from socio-hierarchical inequality or any other form of inequality among

people (including age). All *distance* between people is suspended, and a special carnival category goes into effect: *free and familiar contact between people.* (Bakhtin, 1984: 122–3)

Clearly, Bakhtin is idealizing a social reversal which dissolves identity, rules and bodily and social distance. As with the early English festival 'Twelfth Night' or the contemporary Mardi Gras of Sydney and Rio de Janeiro, Bakhtin's carnivalesque is a time when sensual experience overtakes logical order; the carnival culture, which privileges laughter, parody, disorder, sexuality, abundance and transparency, overrides official culture, which prefers intellect, order, governance, opacity, stasis and control. Politically, however, the carnival was not merely a temporary negation of the official order, but carried the promise of a better world, a utopia, which could release the common person from the drudgery of his or her obedient and fixed conditions.

Fiske identifies the carnivalesque with the liberationism of popular TV (1987, 1989a). According to Fiske, TV's engagement with excesses of bodily display, grotesqueness, degradation and spectacle identifies the medium as a carnival of carnality and sentimentalism. TV watching thus becomes a source of freedom and reversal, a site in which everyday viewers can relieve themselves of order, obedience and capitalist-directed tedium. We must remember, however, that this television viewing and indeed all the popular practices identified by Fiske and others operate at the level of the unconscious. Consumption is not a deliberately seductive act, but is rather an outcome of self-interest and the maximization of personal pleasure.

Girls, Women, Romance and Soapies

While not directly referencing to Bakhtin or de Certeau, a number of feminist analysts have used the notion of text reading and consumption to inform their research on women as a specific audience sub-set. The most notable of these include Angela McRobbie, a member of the Birmingham group, Ien Ang and Janice Radway. Angela McRobbie's career study of teenage women's magazines shifts from a structuralist repudiation of stereotyped representations (1982) toward a more audience-based analysis of the ways in which these magazines and their discourses are consumed and deployed for pleasure and the formation of female identity (1991). McRobbie and Garber expressed their broad dissatisfaction with resistance and youth culture studies which excluded the interests and textual consumption of girls:

[Girls] are absent from the classic ethnographic studies, the pop histories, the personal accounts and the journalistic surveys of the field. When girls do appear, it is in ways that critically reinforce the stereotypical image of women ... or they are fleeting or marginally presented. (1991: 1)

According to McRobbie, in this latter phase of her work, girls contribute to the formation of their own culture through style, dress and shopping, as well as creative consumption of female-based media texts (McRobbie, 1989).

Similarly, Ien Ang's (1985, orig. 1982 in Dutch) analysis of the American soap opera *Dallas* represents a significant shift in the way feminism considers the text–audience relationship. While earlier feminists and social control theorists condemned soap operas for their restrictive and stereotypical presentation of women and women's lives, Ang's *Watching Dallas* emphasizes the creative, liberatory and meaning-making potential of text consumption. One of the most interesting features of Ang's book is its attempt not merely to elucidate a conception of the audience as active meaning-makers, but also to elucidate that meaning-making in terms of diversity and personal agency. That is, Ang wanted to understand how Dutch audiences responded to, interacted with, and constructed, meanings from this very popular American soap opera. Ang's point of departure was her own contradictory experiences with a TV programme which she found intriguing, stimulating and appealing on the one hand, yet ideologically offensive on the other. Ang confesses that she enjoys soaps for their romantic intrigue, opulence and glamour, but recognizes that they clearly contravene her rationalized ideological sensibilities. That is, her own ambivalence becomes a tacit acknowledgement of the capacity of television programmes to position readings both between various audience members as well as within the one subject reader:

> [M]y own ambivalent relation to *Dallas* will also have its repercussions. This ambivalence is on the one hand connected with my identity as an intellectual and a feminist, and on the other hand with the fact that I have always particularly liked watching soap operas like *Dallas*. At one time I really belonged to the category of devoted *Dallas* fans. (1985: 12)

Other cultural investigators confronted the same problem during the 1980s and 1990s, most especially in their studies of the audience–text relationship. Some, such as Janice Radway, Richard Dyer and Jackie Stacey, have been particularly interested in the construction of women's pleasures and identity through fantasy and romantic imagery. Radway's (1987) famous study of romance readers in the American township of Smithton represents a significant movement in American sociology toward a cultural studies perspective. Radway herself claims never to have heard of cultural studies when she completed her research, though the analysis parallels much of the interest and work being conducted in Europe and Britain under the cultural studies banner. Radway's research involved a community of women who patronized Dorothy Evans' bookshop, famous for its romance listings and Dot's own romantic eruditions. The research consisted of face-to-face interviews, small group discussions and questionnaires – a far more meticulous and carefully managed piece of qualitative research than was conducted by Ien Ang.

Kitsch and the mobilization of popular taste

Andy Warhol was one of the first major artists to recognize the creative and commercial potential of popular culture. Just as works of 'art' have been appropriated into mass consumer culture through industries like poster publishing, tourism and memorabilia, 1960s *avant garde* artists like Warhol began to exploit the creative potential of mass consumer images and forms. Many more recent artists have deployed similar motifs. Terry Batt's painting (Plate 7.1) *Forthcoming Attractions* features a range of motifs drawn from popular film and television.

The Japanese artist Takashi Murakami has taken this blending of art and popular iconography to an even higher level of self-consciousness. While Japanese art has never clearly distinguished between the expressive modes of 'art' and folk craft, Murakami consciously draws this fabled 'Japaneseness' into his own creative work, generating a particular mode of artistic design for an international art market. Using motifs common to contemporary Japanese popular culture, *Anime* and *Menga,* Murakami creates works that have originality and commercial viability. Extending traditional Japanese interest in surfaces, Murakami creates some works for the international exhibition market, and some mass produced products for broader consumption. In this way, Murakami doesn't just exploit mass consumer iconography; he actually produces it in mass production factories.

In many respects, the art of artists like Warhol and Murakami represents the obfuscation of boundaries of social value. This is very similar to the re-ascription of value (moral, financial, aesthetic) and meaning which social groups place on any given 'social artefact'. The immense appetite for new social products in contemporary culture has contributed to the transformation of things into valuable 'collectables' – artworks, trinkets, dolls, rocks, memorabilia. The re-formation and revaluation of everyday things known as 'kitsch' is typical of this re-ascription process. Thus, junk is repackaged and sold on as collectable products. Murakami's mass produced dolls, which present as cute kitsch, are presented as high value and collectable for an unspecified future market.

YOUTH CULTURE

The Idea of Youth 'Sub-culture'

In many respects, the work of McRobbie, Ang and Radway is part of a more general scholarly interest in the behaviours and attitudes of social sub-groups, who use texts to build identity, community and various forms of social 'resistance'. Much of this work has its roots in anthropology and the sociology of sub-cultures, which had emerged in the US in the 1960s (see Chapter 2) and which was adopted by a number of researchers in the

Birmingham Centre for Contemporary Cultural Studies in the later 1970s. In accord with the Centre's broader interest in working class culture and ideology, writers like Paul Willis and Dick Hebdige applied the notion of 'sub-culture' to their analysis of youth. Willis (1978), in particular, developed the concept of 'homology' to describe a social sub-group's distinct cultural attributes: a 'sub-culture' exhibited a level of integration, structure, shared rituals, values, style, and meanings. The combination of homology and 'bricolage' (the combination and reassigning of cultural elements) provided a number of Birmingham Centre scholars with a basis for studying working class youth resistance to dominant cultural values and bourgeois hegemony.

Thus, while 'youth' may be a category of age, 'youth culture', in BCCCS terms, is framed significantly around clothing style, practices, rituals and musical texts. For Dick Hebdige (1979), most notably, youth sub-culture constitutes a significant challenge to inherited social values and lifestyles. Like Michel de Certeau, Hebdige applies Lévi-Strauss's concept of 'bricolage' to describe the ways in which sub-cultures borrow from existing or conventional culture to form new cultural elements. For Hebdige, youth culture constitutes a bricolage of elements which ultimately combine to form a distinctive, expressive and transgressive 'sub-culture'.

Hebdige sees the formation of 'style' as a critical component in sub-cultural identity formation and its potential for resistance. Adding the important element of race to the mix of working-class youth culture, Hebdige argues that 'style' is a cluster of meanings (codes, signifiers) which necessarily disrupts the symbolic order imposed by commercial, bourgeois capitalism:

> We should, therefore, not underestimate the signifying power of the spectacular sub-culture not only as a metaphor for potential anarchy 'out there' but as an actual mechanism for semantic disorder, a kind of temporary blockage within the system of representation. (Hebdige, 1979: 90)

The metaphor, arising through the music of punk band The Sex Pistols (*I am an Anarchist*), is realized in the aggressive and deviant styles which various modes of expressive youth sub-culture represent. Punk music, according to Hebdige and other cultural scholars at the time, represented a rejection of bourgeois history and values: punk styles of music and dress inevitably challenged social decency and an uncritical obedience to capitalist commerce and the orderliness of labour.

From Class to Multivalent Pleasure

Numerous commentators have argued that the Hebdige-BCCCS model –

1   Overstates the political significance of working class youth sub-culture. In particular, critics suggest that the musical and clothing styles of youth sub-cultural groups – including

punk – do not clearly represent the political vision of the group members and their level of social and political awareness (consciousness).

2   In a related criticism, many commentators note that even the most hostile expressive mode (again including punk) is subject to the appropriating power of commercial capitalism. To this end, the Sex Pistols were a commercial fabrication which netted their inventor, Malcolm McLaren, a considerable fortune in international record sales. Far from being a working-class hero, McLaren was a designer and entrepreneur who identified the commercial potential of the Sex Pistols and punk more generally.

3   Widdicombe and Wooffitt (1995) argue, further, that the BCCCS researchers themselves failed adequately to engage in the lives of their working-class subjects, tending to rarefy the experiences in order to inflate the subversive potential.

4   In this sense, there is a general misreading of popular texts and everyday practices. If resistance exists at all, it is rather through the 'pre-lingual' aesthetic of pleasure and 'fun', which is the essential quality of youth and their sub-cultural expressivities.

5   The focus on the 'working class' tends to override other important cultural attributes which are also part of various forms of social hegemony – gender, race, sexual orientation and so on.

Despite these criticisms, the work of Hebdige and Willis, in particular, remains seminal in youth culture studies. Within this context, we can see that 1960s youth culture in Britain was formed through the cultural propinquities and bricolage of urban black migrant culture, the popularization of American black culture and the incorporative commodifications of middle-class white culture. The sub-cultures constituted themselves through a 'style' which might have had little to do with the cultural source but which was 'enabled' through appropriation. In this sense, the mod movements of the 1960s, which formed around the music and style of bands like The Beatles, came to disguise many of their original cultural influences. The Beatles' music and appearance were influenced by black American rhythm and blues, though these roots become obscured somewhat in the development of the new sounds and presentational styles. The Beatles made palatable for white middle-class audiences the sub-culture of former slaves, ultimately creating a new liberatory space for further cultural experimentation and hybridization. For The Beatles and the youth culture which came to surround them, this hybridization later incorporated the musical sounds, religion and cultural narcoses of India.

Hebdige explains the creative and liberatory formation of such sub-cultures in terms of broader historical and social phenomena. The formation of youth culture, therefore, needs to be understood in terms of structural changes as well as community-level experiences. In particular, the experimentations and adaptability of British youth culture during the 1960s can be explained in part by accelerated migration into Britain from Jamaica and elsewhere, and the associated 'decline of empire'.

In many respects, Hebdige's work lays the foundation for wider cultural analysis of youth culture (see Redhead et al., 1997; Skelton and Valentine, 1998; MacDonald, 2001). The work of Lawrence Grossberg in the United States and Simon Frith in Britain centralizes rock music as a cultural and political formation. Frith, in particular, argues that earlier (modernist) paradigms of musical analysis fail dismally to account for the 'popularity' and importance of rock music in contemporary culture. The commodification of music and musical forms has facilitated the ongoing and restless shifts in identity formation which surround the highly particularized pleasures of listening to rock music. Taste not only determines the construction of an individual and group's identity, but it actually calibrates that identity against broader cultural formations, expectations and norms. The way someone 'is' seems closely associated with the type of music he or she chooses. In this sense, the 'meaning' of a musical text is thoroughly bound to the listener and the context of listening:

> To grasp the meaning of a piece of music is to hear something not simply present to the ear. It is to understand a musical culture, to have a 'scheme of interpretation'. For sounds to be music we need to know how to hear them: we need 'knowledge' not just of musical forms but also of rules of behaviour in musical settings. (Frith, 1996: 249–50)

Fandom

Henry Jenkins (1992; see also Jenkins et al., 2003) applies the same understanding of the community of meaning to his analysis of the fans of the long-running TV and film series *Star Trek*. Like John Fiske, Jenkins adapts Michel de Certeau's notion of strategic raiding to explain the way fans 'poach' the meanings of a corporatist, mass-distributed text like *Star Trek*. For Jenkins, 'the fan' constitutes a particular social and cultural category; a fan doesn't merely watch a text but uses it as a central symbol, a way of bringing order, meaning and community to his or her everyday experiences. The text is 'poached' because fans do much more than treat the text as a distraction or escape from everyday experiences. The text helps the fan actually construct those experiences. Jenkins (1992: 277–81) outlines the complexity and diversity of fandom as a sub-cultural community, according to five general levels of activity:

1 Fans are distinguished by their capacity for cultural proximity and critical distance. Fans scrutinize texts multiple times and with considerable expertise; fans discuss, debate and create meaning from texts through enunciative as well as experiential practices.
2 Fans' expertise engages particular kinds of interpretive and critical practices. Fans insist on consistency of detail across a programme and between programmes. Part of 'becoming

a fan' involves the learning of the fan community's particular mode of reading, and the dominant meanings that generally issue through community expectation. Fan criticism often involves filling in the gaps, overcoming inconsistency and rendering the text amenable to the community's preferred reading. That is, the fans 'supplement' the text in order to make it fit with the fan group's preferred way of understanding and relating to the text.

3   Fan expertise also involves consumer activism. Fans lobby TV networks and their advertisers when they feel a series is in jeopardy or when they disagree with a programming decision. They also express their dissatisfaction with any changes to the text, its characters, plot or orientation.

4   Fandom engages with particular forms of cultural production, and aesthetic traditions and practices. 'Fan artists, writers, videomakers and musicians create works that speak to the special interest of the fan community' (Jenkins, 1992: 279). This appropriation and bricolage process draws from commercially available materials in order to produce a highly specific, sub-cultural style which identifies the community members with their group. Again echoing de Certeau, Jenkins claims that this sort of appropriation challenges the corporatist power of institutions which claim to have copyright control over popular media narratives. The art is made for a general sharing, and not for profit – it becomes the basis for a genuine folk culture.

5   Fandom functions as an alternative cultural community, one that is not predisposed to mainstream social and commercial practices. The utopianism of the *Star Trek* text is transferred into a community discourse that challenges mainstream culture. Fandom, that is, offers an alternative reality 'whose values may be more humane and democratic than those held by mundane society' (Jenkins, 1992: 280). For Jenkins, this alternative offers fans options for dealing with the real-world issues of conflict, alienation and despair.

Jenkins, like Dyer, Stacey and Fiske on occasions, tends to utopianize his cultural consumers, projecting for them an identity which evades the homogenizing order of official culture. The carnivalesque celebrated by Mikhail Bakhtin is absorbed into a theory of bodily conviction, a delight in the capacity of ordinary people to make their lives less ordinary (Jenkins et al., 2003). In a sense, this is the fundamental contradiction of Jenkins' analysis: in celebrating the everyday practices of ordinary people, he treats these textual poachers as postmodern heroes, lower-level groups who are able to liberate themselves from the status of their ordinariness to become part of a pre-eminent cultural form – the popular text. The difficulty remains, of course, that the problematic of ordinariness is a statement of desire that would overcome banality, that would invest itself in fame, glamour, social prominence and adventure which their own lives so clearly lack. While Jenkins insists that this desire to overcome lack is both justifiable and positive, it might as easily be conceived as a form of personal and cultural pathology. The idealizing of this desire never quite escapes Baudrillard's dread that the simulacra that drive contemporary media culture, including media consumption, are entirely vacuous, pointless, an endless stream of stimulation, a desire that has no end.

Hip Hop, Drugs Culture and New Forms of Youth Resistance?

As we have already noted, one of the most obvious problems for Hebdige and others in the BCCCS centres on the capacity of capitalism and the culture industries to appropriate style – including resistance style – for their own ends. Numerous commentators on popular music, for example, have asked whether or not it is actually possible for bands to generate genuinely 'alternative' cultural or political perspectives. And while some exceptional musicians like Ani DiFranco have been able to maintain artistic and financial control of their music and political integrity through the maintenance of independent labels (for DiFranco her own Righteous Babe label), in most cases this strategy is simply untenable. The history of independent music artists demonstrates very clearly that it is extremely difficult to resist the power of transnational record companies and the lure of the commercial 'sell out'. When alternative or independent musicians demonstrate any level of commercial potential, they will often exchange their poverty, low-budget record production values and limited success for wealth and fame: the price is often the control of their music and its aesthetic and creative integrity.

These basic financial imperatives are set against the background of significant social changes that have taken place in the west in the several decades since Hebdige first theorized working-class youth culture as a mode of political resistance. Indeed, as numerous commentators have noted, post-industrial societies in the globalizing west have broadly dissolved the distinct social categories based on simple notions of class (Giddens, 1990, 1994; Urry, 2003). These quite distinct socio-cultural changes since the 1990s can be summarized in the following terms –

1 Work patterns have moved many people away from industrial to service based industries.
2 Many workplaces are highly corporatized and global in focus.
3 There have been significant changes in global migration, bringing many people from a wide variety of backgrounds into the west.
4 This has led to various forms of cultural hybridization and the rise of multiculturalism as a primary policy mantra.
5 The increasing globalization of media – including the emergence of the Internet, (Google, Blogs, My Space, YouTube) and convergent telecommunications – has contributed significantly to the formation of new transcultural expressive spaces.
6 Women have entered the workforce in vast numbers, contributing to the very significant changes to women's economic and consumer power, sexual relationships and family.

In the context of this significant re-shaping of the cultural landscape, a politics based on any form of class consciousness or style seems largely obsolete.

It is not surprising, therefore, that new forms of youth cultural practices have also been postulated as forms of 'resistance'. In particular, the musical genres of rap (rhythm and poetry) and techno (computer generated music and sounds) emerged during the mid-1970s and 1980s as new forms of hybrid culture, inspiring 'alternative' forms of youth cultural practice. Rap, with its various forms of hip hop sub-genre, arose out of the confluence of West African, Jamaican and American talking-blues music in the black street culture of New York (Gilroy, 1998; Forman, 2000). As it has spread to various diasporic groups across the globe, rap music has become celebrated as a liberatory mode of expression and critical component for the formation of community identity. Murray Forman argues that the particular qualities of the street form have enabled its adoption within specific city communities:

> As the main form of musical expression within the hip hop culture, the early DJ sound systems featured a series of practices that linked the music to other mobile practices, such as graffiti art and 'tagging'. Together, these overlapping practices and methods of constructing place-based identities, and of inscribing and enunciating individual and collective presence, created the bonds upon which affiliations were forged within specific social geographies. Hip hop's distinct practices introduced new forms of expression that were contextually linked to conditions in a city comprised of an amalgamation of neighbourhoods and boroughs with their own highly particularized social norms and cultural nuances. (Forman, 2000: 67)

This idea of creating community out of dissonance or diaspora represents a form of contemporary utopia, linking disparate individuals and neighbourhoods across the world. In a typically postmodern idealization, hip hop becomes a textual panoply against the continual threat of social collapse and disharmony.

Much of this utopianism subsumes the distinct social problems that are associated with street cultures generally, and hip hop in particular. Sub-genres like gangster rap romanticize drug culture and a form of criminal dissent which presents itself as both glamorous and socially legitimate (see Queeley, 2003). As in gangster films which have heroized criminals and criminal lifestyles, gangster and other forms of hip hop music have personified the negative experience of social sub-classes – especially African-Americans and Hispanics – and created an 'aura' of social resistance. Thus, while early rappers like Public Enemy transformed their negative experiences into explicit social and political commentary, gangster rap imagines Tarantino-like violent heroics in which social oppression is challenged by advocacies of criminal practice and social violence.

Paradoxically, however, these forms of romanticized violence have proven as popular with educated, 'middle-class' youth global markets – especially (though not exclusively) those with migrant or non-Caucasian backgrounds. The gangster idol who dares to swear and thumb his nose at authority creates an appealing, transgressive motif for those audiences who may imagine resistance but who are essentially obedient to the imperatives of capitalist labour and the bourgeois lifestyle. In this context, rap music has become appropriated, packaged and marketed to mass and nuance markets through the global industry networks. Not only have white performers like Eminem mimicked and appropriated the style, rendering the genre even more broadly acceptable to the non-Black marketplace, but rapping styles have been incorporated into mainstream musical genres. This hybridizing of commercial musical forms has tended to neutralize the intensity of 'resistance' as it creates a fantasy of 'difference' for the mainstream, international markets. Commercial hip hop, that is, tends to exploit a middle class yearning for adventure and risk through a musical narrative which celebrates alternative identity and free-wheeling lifestyles that are not constrained by institutional schedules and rationality. As they are woven into the highly produced and corporatized texts of mainstream music charts, the rap beats and spoken 'poems' expose themselves as a flaccid, fraudulent and exhausted musical genre, a parody of the political rage which once inscribed the street life of Black New York.

Ecstasy and Club Culture

Mind-altering narcotics have been associated with youth culture since the 1960s. The adoption of 'psychotropic substances' by sub-sets of western youth can be linked to various sources, including black jazz musicians and immigrant groups, particularly from the Indian sub-continent. While marijuana was the most widely used narcotic in the youth sub-culture of the 1960s and 1970s, more recently a whole class of methamphetamines and pleasure drugs like 'ecstasy' have become extremely popular among youth. Ecstasy, in particular, has been associated with a particular form of youth practice constituted around techno-music, rhythmic and repetitive dance styles and social assemblages like rave parties and youth-based 'nightclubs'.

Ben Malbon (2002) has likened the experience of ecstasy-based (night)clubbing to the sense of 'oceania' described by Sigmund Freud (see Chapter 5). Freud, who developed the theory and methods of psychoanalysis, believed that individuals could experience a heightened sense of bond or belonging through particular states of consciousness. Malbon argues that the confluence of ecstasy and dance assemblages creates a sense of 'being liminal', the cognitive zone between the conscious /unconscious states, experience/language, and in/outside oneself:

> [T]he experience of in-betweenness or liminality – the experience of being taken outside or beyond oneself, especially while dancing – is a characteristic of many crowds and particularly the closely packed, sensorially bombarded dancing crowds of clubbing. At its most intense this sensation of in-betweenness can partly induce or trigger the altered state of consciousness that I am calling, after Freud … the 'oceanic' experience. I use this term in evoking a feeling of an indissoluble bond, as being one with the external world as a whole. (Malbon, 2002: 492)

In fact, many of the personal accounts and analyses of the ecstasy and clubbing cultures frequently invoke a social utopia that is resonant of the hippie movement of the 1960s. Ecstasy is a form of psychotropic drug which triggers the brain's capacity for communion and repetition. The rave and club scenes, along with the favoured techno-music, are constructed around close bodily contact, rhythmic dancing and the pulsing experiences of sexual intimacy. This bodily utopianism is offered as an antithesis to the morality, institutionalism and political violence which governs the social world and perverts its potential for freedom and pleasure. The obsessive sensuality that generally accompanies the consumption of ecstasy is also represented as an alternative to the sexual intensity and singular trajectory of (especially male) climax and deflation.

Ecstasy and amphetamine utopianism is largely a middle class phenomenon, constructed by users and commentators who are seeking some sort of personal transcendence. The social, physiological and psychological problems associated with drug use appear to be strategically parenthesized in much of the literature of popular and youth cultural studies. In this sense, clubbing drug culture eschews a critical analysis which would situate ecstasy and amphetamine use within a criminal code, or as a significant social health issue. Rather, the broadly espoused 'postmodern' celebration of choice and bodily pleasure are invoked as a form of social resistance, a celebratory cultural politics which challenges normative or conservative social values.

POPULAR POLITICS

From the 1980s and 1990s cultural theory and cultural studies have engaged more fully with questions of popular cultural consumption, most particularly through the auspices of postmodernism. This evolving field of enquiry has led to some significant theoretical problems, most particularly as cultural analysis attempts to reconstitute its political and reformist projects. The centralization of 'pleasure' and 'everyday practices' opens the way for a politics of individual agency. Popular culture, therefore, becomes a site for liberation through desire. As Lawrence Grossberg has put it, 'Opposition may be constituted by living, even momentarily, within alternative practices, structures, and spaces' (1988: 169). These alternative spaces are provided through choice and the continuing diversifications that postmodern consumer culture provides. De Certeau's arguments, which have their roots in Bakhtin and others, seek a space in which the overwhelming ubiquity of capitalist structures is neutralized and sent into retreat, a space where capitalism becomes the servant of the strategic raiders, and where the promise of postmodernism can be fully realized. This promise – choice, diversity, multiculturalism, individualism, sexual liberationism, self-constituting identity – becomes the basis for contemporary culture and contemporary cultural politics.

Recent political theory has moved quite markedly from a strictly structuralist analysis of politics toward a politics which acknowledges the significance of culture, identity and the personal or 'visceral' dimensions of democracy and political expression. Writers like David Held (1987, 1992), Ernesto Laclau (Laclau and Mouffe, 1985; Laclau, 1996) and Anthony Giddens (1994) have attempted to construct a democratic cultural politics which liberates reformism from a Marxist 'grand narrative' and universalism on the one hand, and from institutionalized liberal–democratic relativism on the other. Giddens, in particular, expounds a reform theory which would extend the possibilities of democracy and culture beyond what he regards as the stasis and interdependency of Left and Right politics; however, he would also want to conceive of a politics which is not reduced to the kind of convergent, centralist and economic-rationalist relativism which now predominates in Western liberal democracies. Giddens' alternative is a personal politics which restores power to the microphysics of everyday human experience.

Jürgen Habermas (1984a, 1987b, 1989) has also attempted to reconcile the various dimensions of popular culture and political reformism. Habermas's point of departure, however, is markedly different from the poststructuralists, psychoanalytical theorists and postmodernists. For him, the public sphere exists as a transformative space where democracy is removed from the control of the state and restored to the level of public participation. Communication becomes the central focus of democracy, as the 'populace' take control of political discourse in order to create the ideal speech situation – that utopian 'space' where all views are discussed in public and disagreements are resolved through informed and rational debate. Habermas describes the development of modernity in terms of the separation of the state (and its discourses) from the private individual. The state reproduces itself in terms of ideology (false consciousness), public intervention and control of the individual. The separation of the individual from state-sponsored ideology leads inevitably to the diminution of private and public freedom:

> If ideologies are not only manifestations of the socially necessary consciousness in its essential falsity, if there is an aspect to them that can lay claim to truth inasmuch as it transcends the status quo in utopian fashion, even if only for the purposes of justification, then ideology only exists from this moment on. (Habermas, 1989: 88)

Modernity, thus, becomes the unfinished project (Habermas, 1983), the project that will return politics to the public sphere and where governmentality and democracy are refurbished as participative domains of communicative action. This communicative action centralizes individual agency and the capacity of citizens to express and construct their own truths within the bounds of a regulated and secure lifestyle.

Notions of pleasure are not excluded from Habermas's theory, though he would reject its centralization in the organization of social and cultural life; reason and social order are the preconditions of individual pleasure at whatever level it is experienced. Jim McGuigan (1992, 1996) makes a similar point in his critique of popular cultural studies. McGuigan argues that the whole project of cultural studies and cultural theory has fallen into crisis because writers like John Fiske and Henry Jenkins have seriously overstated the political and subversive potential of popular culture. This excessive celebration of popular culture and the transgressive potential of pleasure and textual (symbolic) consumption, McGuigan claims, come about because the finely balanced tensions that exist in Gramsci's theory of hegemony have been tipped in favour of individual choice and agency. Gramsci, we recall from Chapter 3, argues that hegemony (social 'leadership' by organic intellectuals) is actually 'negotiated' by the dominant and subordinated groups in a culture. Leaders in all fields maintain their privilege by adjusting their power to the needs and interests of subjugant groups and individuals. Subordinates feel some measure of engagement with and commitment to the social arrangements to which they themselves have contributed.

According to McGuigan (see also Kellner, 1996, 2005), recent cultural studies, most especially through the analysis of youth culture and popular television, have tended to override important aspects of the political economy of cultural production:

> The uncritical endorsement of popular taste, from an entirely hermeneutic perspective, is curiously consistent with economic liberalism's concept of 'consumer sovereignty', the weaknesses of which are particularly manifest in the debate concerning broadcast policy conducted in Britain since the 1980s. ... An adequate account of contemporary popular culture demands analysis of public communication, institutional power and, in a materialist perspective, socio-economic relations. (1992: 6)

Questions of policy, institutional power, ethics and production, in fact, have been marginalized in theoretical debates and textual studies since the 1980s and 1990s. However, these questions persist and particular areas of cultural analysis, including audience, ethnology and 'materialist' sociological studies, have returned in various ways to questions of government and institutional processes. McGuigan's reference to broadcast policy and the movement in the English-speaking world toward more general laissez-faire social and economic policy (economic rationalism, market sovereignty, neoliberalism) has proven significant.

As we noted above, this movement represents a reorientation of left–right political divisions toward the centre. Globalism, corporatism, competition policy, savage reductions in public services and public employment, and the deregulation of labour, industry, the media and markets – all are symptoms of an ascendant ideology. The problems with balance of trade and enormous debt that had crippled the economies of Britain, Australia, New Zealand and Canada during the 1980s served to fuel the rhetoric of classical economics or 'economic rationalism'. As media industries became over-priced and relatively underperforming, they liquidated and dramatically cut costs; deregulation was a way of both subduing costs and increasing tradability. Government broadcasters were savaged while cable, satellite, video and interactive digital media expanded exponentially.

The classical economic theory of consumer sovereignty placed individual choice at the centre of consumer capitalism. Cultural studies, whatever its motivations, became implicated in the ever-expanding embrace of privatization and commercialization. For McGuigan, the popularity of the media, especially youth media, was seen to infect the academy with its own market sovereignty and populist discourse. To be popular, that is, became an economic imperative for an academy besieged by the demands of economic rationalization.

Beyond McGuigan's general condemnation, however, significant theoretical problems continue to beset popular cultural studies. While the vocabulary of the debate has shifted from 'hegemony' to 'postmodernism', the question of structural controls against individual agency remains. That is, the 'powerful text–active audience' tension remains largely unresolved. Numerous theorists, including Ien Ang (1996), have despaired of ever clearly identifying 'the audience'; Ang, in particular, has presaged a move toward a more direct analysis of the specific industrial, commercial and regulatory context in which the text–audience relationship operates. Feminists like Angela McRobbie suggest even further that the irresolvability of this tension threatens the very basis of her political project. Women are socialized and 'controlled' by a textualized structural patriarchy; however, it is possible that the pleasures that are creatively extracted from these texts by women may constitute a resource for personal liberation. In order to mediate this conundrum, McRobbie (1994) recommends the restoration of a neo-Gramscian approach to media and culture, reformulating the analysis of consumption in terms of the context of production. By treating texts as 'reproductions', McRobbie claims, we will be able to understand the institutional practices which give them form. McRobbie seeks a return to ethnography which would illuminate institutional and audience practices.

Tony Wilson (1993, 1995, 2004) attempts to mediate deconstructionist theory with a fully theorized empirical analysis of audiences. Postmodernism, Wilson considers, is a theory of difference and diversity, a political paradigm which treats audiences and textual reading as necessarily subversive of homogenizing structural intent. In poststructuralist terms, the audience cannot be 'known' as a group of living breathing human beings, but must be regarded as another discourse and as ultimately 'unknowable' (Hartley, 1992: 110). Wilson (also Jacka, 1994), however, argues that these discourses are built around the experiences and interactions of real people with 'phenomena' which are available to knowledge. The link between audience as discourse and the empirical rendering of those discourses can be found in the philosophy of phenomenology and hermeneutics. Put simply, audiences and their interpretation of texts take place within a certain cultural context, a certain system of knowledge or 'consciousness'. Of course audiences are written and spoken about and are therefore discourses; but they are also people who engage with and reproduce their own forms of discourse. The methods of social science – observation, discussion and interview – give the researcher access to these audience discourses. An audience can be therefore 'known' empirically.

Wilson deploys the theoretical frame of phenomenology in order to access the 'everyday' or 'ordinary' lifeworld of television viewers. Following in the traditions developed through Husserl, Weber and Habermas, he seeks to resolve the problematic of subject and object, whereby the individual's 'cognitive horizon' unifies familiar and unfamiliar objects into an organic and comprehensible reality:

> Horizons are frameworks of cognitive knowledge underlying perceptual experience, allowing aspects of that experience to be recognized and identified as types already encountered. Our concept of circularity, this cognitive horizon, both from and with which we interpret the world, allows us to anticipate that half-experienced circles will turn out to be round and to recognize them as familiar when they do. Our horizons of understanding the people around us permit differences to be perceived between human beings and animals, to anticipate and recognize their distinct activities. These frameworks operate as the fundamental basis of expectations about how things will be in the future. (Wilson, 1993: 17)

The phenomenological approach to audiences, then, follows a Kantian precept of pre-existing or essential reality, the source of which unifies subjects and objects. Wilson wants to understand the convergence and divergence of audience perceptions; the concept of horizon neatly represents a perceptual space which nonetheless can be confirmed as a reality. The cognitive horizon of the audience allows for variance in perception while inclining toward a dominant or common reading reality; for Wilson, 'reading' is always and everywhere a 'fusion of horizons' drawing upon, and producing, differences (Wilson, 1993, 1995).

Not surprisingly, Wilson invokes the authority of the phenomenological hermeneutics (interpretive theory) of Paul Ricoeur (see Chapter 3). For Wilson, as for Ricoeur, the convergence/divergence of subject perception challenges structuralist precepts about language and subjectivity. In particular, Ricoeur rejects the substitution of the subject by the dominance of social (or linguistic) structure. In this sense, Riceour's 'new hermeneutics' appears to parallel poststructuralist arguments about the relativity of language and the primacy of the subject in forming reality through interactions with language. Don Thade (1991) argues, in fact, that the deconstructionist method of poststructuralism, Jacques Derrida in particular, clearly parallels the hermeneutical method of Paul Ricoeur. Thade refers specifically to Derrida's shift in reading emphasis from the immediacy of its content centre to the 'edges'. Derrida's focus on margins, borders, signatures, titles, borders, divisions – that is, everything which constitutes background to the text content – is similar to Ricoeur's focus on the linguistic consciousness. Thade argues that Derrida's strategy is fundamentally phenomenological, since reader perception and interpretation necessarily implicates the background in the 'field of perceptivability' (1991: 132). This phenomenological strategy de-centres focal perceptions in order to address the taken-for-grantedness of fringe elements.

Ricoeur himself has opposed poststructuralism for its 'internalism', rejecting the incapacity of Derrida, in particular, to bring the reading act into the lifeworld of narrative and meaning-making subjects. Even so, there is a sense in which the 'cognitive horizon' of phenomenology parallels the interminable play of language where meaning becomes a kind of shadow presence for Derrida and his followers. Vincent Descombes (1980: 136–45) reminds us, in fact, that Derrida's initial writing on Husserl resolves itself into a deconstructive method which nevertheless constitutes an extension and radicalization of the phenomenology he critiques. For Descombes, the whole poststructuralist enterprise is born out of an attempt to extend and radicalize phenomenology, an attempt to understand more thoroughly the act of communication, its facilitations and failings.

Of course the major difference between phenomenology and poststructuralist theory centres on the former's attachment to a transcendental or pre-existing reality. Phenomenology, at least in the hands of Husserl and the new hermeneutics, seeks to identify the possibilities of meaning over the difficulties of variant perspectives. Poststructuralism is more concerned with the impossibilities of meaning, the gaps and limits of language. For phenomenology, the subject seeks to confirm the lifeworld reality of the cognitive horizon; the deconstructionist seeks to explode its illusion. The challenge for postmodern theoretics is to overcome the illusion and the limits of meaning without recourse to a transcendent or pre-existing 'reality' or 'consciousness'. In this sense, postmodernism's emphasis on otherness, difference, identity and consumerist pleasure seeks to hold the subject within the borders of everyday life, while maintaining the possibility of liberation. This liberation is not transcendent, however, nor does it rely on the possibilities of some extra-dimensional consciousness or reality. In a simple materialist sense, what we can experience directly and immediately, the release of bodily experience, has become the centre of much postmodern liberationism.

Postmodern Audiences and the End of Politics?

These various approaches to the audience have tried in their respective ways to explain the complex processes of meaning formation. The Gramscian approach, critical theory and various permutations of interpretive hermeneutics have all sought to resolve the tension between notions of the text as powerful ideology and the creative meaning-making of audiences. They have also tried to integrate some of the important insights of poststructuralism into a theory that maintains some level of materialist interest: that is, they have attempted to combine an interest in discourse with a sense in which the audience is comprised of real people with real sufferings, interests and vulnerabilities. These critical approaches attempt to mediate the text–audience tension within a distinctly political framework. The greater problem for critical analysis is associated with the

Plate 8.1 *Girl Power for Sale*

Popular music and performance have become central components of youth culture. The transgressive potential of music culture, in particular, is constantly challenged by the demands of marketing systems, and corporatized commodity formula.

problematics of audience/consumer pleasure. For critical theory, 'pleasure' can only be conceived in terms of the relief of suffering and oppression. For postmodernism, however, pleasure is not merely the end of political enterprise, but the means and very centre of political engagement. To this extent, the question of whether the audience is comprised of real people or not is entirely irrelevant; the audience is merely an 'engagement', an immersion of imaginations and discourses, which are ultimately constituted through pleasure. 'Meaning' is not something that can be located in an heuristic examination of either text, audience, or both: it is a sensibility which facilitates ongoing discursive imaginings and gratifications.

Andy Warhol wanted to articulate the pleasures of life as they are experienced at the surface and through the proliferation of consumerist images and products. As this theme is taken up by postmodernism and its centralization of the audience/consumer, particular theoretical problems emerge. The theoretical danger for postmodernism is twofold:

1   It threatens to collapse into an irreversible relativism which perpetually separates individuals from one another. If postmodernism is true to its heterogeneity, then it can be little more than a form of indulgent and relativist hedonism. In supporting a consumer sovereignty ethos, postmodernism claims that everything is acceptable if it brings pleasure to the individual. In this sense, postmodernism and popular consumerist theoretics can have little to say about the suffering of others.
2   It threatens to present its politics as a grounded and privileged theory of utility: that is, one in which pleasure, difference, creative consumerism, individualism and audience creativity become the 'essence' of a generalized politics of liberation. Postmodern discourse might actually transgress the imperatives of deconstruction by claiming to be true, absolute, centred and 'essentially' significant. It may return to the conditions of knowledge; it may claim a special insight, a ground which might deny its fundamental constituitivity. That is, rather than the world being mediated by language or discourse, the danger is that the discourse may present itself as the reality.

In this sense, de Certeau's own consumer raiders are suspect since their political reversal is entirely without content or consciousness, being constituted by a popular consumerism and self-interest that pre-exists language. De Certeau's raiders, that is, are the product of psychoanalysis – the pre-conscious, prelinguistic other of history. However, the subconscious and the everyday become essentialized themselves when they are presented in political terms: this special realm of the subconscious defies language and the reality it creates. This prelinguistic realm, the unconscious, therefore, appears a little like phenomenology's special realm of consciousness. Of course the two are deliberately opposed by Lacan and de Certeau, but they are similar in as much as they both provide for the unique possibilities of human liberation. De Certeau's unconscious – mysterious and devoid of content – is nevertheless a resource for freedom which is fundamental to the human condition – something which is greater, it seems, than language itself and which appears to parallel the special transcendence of Romantic aesthetics and philosophy.

While de Certeau and his followers would clearly reject any suggestion that they are returning to a kind of phenomenological or Romantic essentialism, there are clear parallels between the everyday and the lifeworld. The writings of Fiske, Jenkins and others have tended to position everyday reality and popular culture above critique. This optimism is infectious but limiting. Indeed, while the notion of pleasure is significant for an understanding of culture and meaning-making, it has been seriously undertheorized. What is needed in cultural analysis is a more complete rendering of the concept, one which is less reliant on the merely superficial expositions of 'bodily pleasure', and which re-examines these sensibilities through a broader lexicon: happiness, satisfaction, neutralization of displeasure, release, joy, bliss, gratification, and so on.

Not surprisingly, cultural studies and cultural theory have moved somewhat beyond simple celebrationism and are concerning themselves more fully with issues of the human presence in contemporary culture, most especially through the formation of 'identity' or personal subjectivity. In the following chapters we will examine the problematics of contemporary cultural politics, most specifically in reference to key themes: the body, globalism and new communications technologies.

9

The Body

INTRODUCTION

The body has always been a significant presence in anthropological and aesthetic studies. Classical sociology, however, has tended to view the body as a functioning unit which contributes to specific social outcomes. From the 1960s various forms of cultural politics have sought to understand the effects of social processes and power on the individual and individual body. Feminism, in particular, focused attention on the negative effects of social inscriptions on the body: the ways in which a society constructs meanings around the biological conditions of gender in order to discipline and control the body. Poststructuralism and postmodernism have provided a more theoretically substantive framework for analyzing the relationship between subjectivity, language (discourse, symbolization) and the body. According to poststructuralists like Michel Foucault, and Deleuze and Guattari, bodily sensations like pleasure and anxiety are inextricably linked to the formation of subjects in language. In other words, the body and its sensations are 'inscribed' with meanings that are formed through culture; culture stimulates these sensations and gives meaning to their experience. The liberation of individual subjects, therefore, is a contingency of the body as much as it is an articulation of identity formed in language. If an individual subject is to be free, then the body must be mobilized through the cultural expression of difference and pleasure.

The emergence of a cultural theory of the body has been associated with broader historical trends, such as the following:

1 *The intensification of individualism.* As noted in Chapter 7, postmodern culture has extended the modernist ideology of individualism, seeking its solutions to the complex of social claims through a rejection of collective action in favour of individual pleasures and liberation.

2 *The increasing sexualization of culture, including the ever-proliferating discourses of sex and sexuality.* Contemporary culture has become increasingly saturated with discourses on sex and the possibilities of new forms of sexual identity, sexual relationships and modes of pleasure.

3 *The increasing deployment of the body as spectacle and commodity.* During the twentieth century the rise of advertising was coupled with a rise in the deployment of the body as visual spectacle and commodity. This 'symbolic exchange of the body' has often compressed the bodily spectacle with products (like cars, clothing, toothpaste, etc.) or entertainment services (sport, fictional narratives, news etc.).

4 *The paradoxical imaging of idealized youthful bodies against the problematic of bodily flaws, disease, obesity, ageing and death.* Sensate bodies are imperfect, they decay and suffer damage. Contemporary culture has obscured or deflected the negative effects of biology through its proliferation of bodily perfections and projections of pleasure. However, these bodily failings continue at the level of the non-televisual, beneath the surface of culture – an absent presence, as Derrida puts it.

5 *Acceleration in the technologizing of bodies.* Humans have always applied technology to enhance their economic, military and communicational power. Modernity has accelerated these propensities, particularly through the engineering of media networks and various forms of prosthetics. Digital-based technologies, especially, have advanced the integration of bodies *as* communication – as images, cyborgs and sexual play spaces.

Thus, in a culture where images are persistently foregrounded and where desire, consumption and bodily beauty are primary indicators of human value, the body assumes a cultural significance far beyond its biological foundations. The body, that is, becomes a cultural site in which its many competing discourses subsume, though never entirely escape from, its biological, quotidian or mortal limits.

This chapter examines the body as a cultural site. This is not to deny the existence of a biological or sensate condition for the body; rather, it is to place that biology alongside the discourses which produce sensations. Very simply, bodies are biology, they emit and receive sensations; these biological actions, however, are elicited through culture – stimulated, experienced, understood, and made meaningful through culture. Hair grows, but immediately it is subject to the actions of culture – shaved, coloured, combed according to cultural interests. The food we eat and how we eat it, the way we experience sex and sexuality, our shelters, our relationships, our definition and responses to beauty, our desires and needs – all are subject to culture. Equally, however, culture is a contingency of the presence of the body; subjectivity, identity, politics and discourse are formed through the presence of human bodies. Our aim in this chapter, therefore, is to examine the body as a confluence of sensate and cultural processes, recognizing that the mediated and biological bodies are necessarily and interdependently linked, the two sides of the one coin.

MODERNISM AND THE BODY

Most commentators agree that the period of the Enlightenment (esp. seventeenth and eighteenth centuries) lays the foundation for the rise of modernity and modernist ways of thinking. A central feature of Enlightenment epistemology (philosophy of knowledge) is the separation of the mind (reason, the higher spirit) over the sensory and emotional state of the body. This hierarchy of human biology, however, has its roots in classical Greek and Roman philosophy. The ancient Greek philosopher Plato (427–347 BC), for example, identified this duality as a principal challenge for the construction of human civilization, most particularly in the formation of a rational and orderly republic. Plato argues that the body and the sensate need to be disciplined by the higher values of the mind, the soul and the highest form of knowledge, Wisdom. Plato sees the physical world as a denigrated form of what he calls the Idea. This metaphysical explanation of the universe is reproduced in his understanding of the human experience. For Plato, the mind (soul, reason), while it is the prisoner of the body, must necessarily rule sensory or appetitive desire. Personal harmony, like the harmony of the state, is only possible if physical and potentially chaotic urges of the body are governed by reason.

It is for this reason that Plato thought it sensible (though not entirely desirable) to exclude the poet from his ideal republic, since poets are the agents of a miraculous and mutinous aesthetic which defies rational order. René Descartes (1596–1650) adopted the Platonic model for his analysis of 'nature' and the human condition. His famous aphorism *cogito ergo sum* (I think therefore I am) in many ways established the framework for a thoroughly modern strategy of understanding (epistemology). 'I think' constitutes all doubt; and what follows is a confirmation of all objects in nature once proven (therefore I am = I have a body). The Cartesian method, which has influenced the formation and methodology of all modern science and rational thought, insists that all proof requires complete doubt. That is, the truth can only be revealed when it is not assumed or 'given'. Doubt must precede truth. Existence is only possible when it can be proven, and 'proof' necessarily requires the exertion of rational thought. Descartes, therefore, establishes the superiority of the mind over the body by insisting that only knowledge can produce the proof of matter, reality and the sensory experience of the body. Descartes, along with many other Enlightenment scientific philosophers, separates the material world of objects, including the object of the body, from the mind, which has its own metaphysical connections to the spirit, the soul and God. The body is 'nature', while the mind and God are the controllers and creators of nature.

In *The Birth of Tragedy* (1956, orig. 1872) Friedrich Nietzsche identifies this mind–body duality as an historical pattern, arguing that the two opposite human propensities toward order–reason and sensation–chaos are symbolized in the Greek gods Apollo (light, wisdom, civility) and Dionysius (dance, music, desire, wine). This irresolvable duality is recognizable, according to Nietzsche, in the formation of modern societies and the essential condition of being human. Modernism, that is, has tended to construct the human condition in terms of the ontological separation of the mind (consciousness, reason, refinement, spirit) over the body (desire, emotion, 'appetite' sensation). The project of civilization, politics and social order is to reconcile these parts through the primacy of mind. The separation remains, of course, because the reconciliation is constructed in discourses which are themselves formed in terms of the same hierarchy of knowledge. These discourses can be located in several key areas –

1   *The economic body.* Marx complains that the capitalist system conceives of working-class bodies as mechanical units in the mode of production. Capitalism treats both the labour and the body as property, like other material objects. While slavery is the most extreme manifestation of this condition, the various Masters and Servants Acts which defined labour and industrial relations during the eighteenth and nineteenth centuries legally bound workers' bodies to their employers. A worker's body, that is, was a form of property, an economic unit in the production process. Workers were forced to pay fees if ever they wished to leave their place of employment: they had to purchase their freedom. The owners of capital treated the bodies and labour of workers as they would treat any other productive machinery.

2   *The humanist body.* Utilitarianism and liberal democracy sought to ameliorate the excesses of capitalist rationality through a social programme based on individual pleasure, Romantic transcendence and modes of personal improvement. The utilitarianism of Jeremy Bentham and James and John Stuart Mill seeks to reconcile bodily pleasures with reasoned social improvement. Individuals will be motivated by self-interest and personal happiness; they will recognize that personal and social improvement is the most reasonable and logical way of achieving this happiness. Utilitarianism expected that being useful to a society would necessarily implicate personal pleasure. Personal self-interest and personal pleasure, therefore, become the motivation for general social improvement. A democratic state must necessarily issue from self-interest. It is always better to live in a rational state governed by principles of orderly conduct than it is to live in chaos. Public education, manhood suffrage and liberty were the necessary outcomes of personal pleasure and utility. The body and the mind would seem to operate harmoniously, as the mind came to accomplish the self-interests of the body.

3   *The biological body.* Philosophers and scientists like Rene Descartes and Isaac Newton established the fundamental principles for studying the laws of the physical universe (physics). The work of Émile Remarque and Charles Darwin extended these principles to the fields of biology and evolution. Darwin's *On the Origin of Species* (1859) provides a foundation for understanding biological systems. Bodies, in this sense, are treated as orderly and self-determining organisms which are comprised of functioning parts. The development and increasing complexity of the system are constituted out of a fundamental, rational principle: evolution.

    When translated into human terms, Darwin's concept of 'survival of the fittest' became an equally forceful principle for the organization of human civilizations. Humans could be treated as competing organisms; human societies could be treated as competing civilizations. These competitive systems underpin the advance of human civilizations whereby superior biological and social groups would necessarily rule over and perhaps eradicate inferior groups. In this sense, Thomas Malthus's theory of population argues that survival imperatives place pressure on groups to spread and conquer new territories and peoples. This biological imperative provides a moral authority for imperialism and the competitive hierarchies of capitalism generally. That is, biology presents itself as the objective and scientific validation of bodily imperatives. In fact, the discourse of biology and evolution functions as part of the ideology and self-legitimation of capitalism and capitalist economics. In its most recent manifestations in the global 'war on terror', theories like Samuel Huntington's *Clash of Civilizations* (1993) provide a justification for the domination of the United States and its ideologies over the rest of the world (see Chapter 12).

4   *The sociological body.* From its beginnings in the work of Durkheim and Weber, sociology has tended to accept the Cartesian dichotomy of mind–body, focusing interest on the mind as the primary definer of humans as social beings. To this extent, classical sociology has tended to treat the body as an outcome of the mind; the body's actions are therefore measured as units in a mathematical system of descriptions. That is, bodily actions indicate the more important operations of the mind. This objectification of the body and its positioning within a system tends to replicate the reification of modernist science. Marx's interest in the deployment of bodies in capitalism, Weber's interest in the rationalization of the body and in styles of life and status, and Durkheim's interest in symbolism lay the foundations for more substantive analyses of the body which sociology develops during the twentieth century.

THE BODY AS DISCOURSE

The proliferation of signs, images and simulacra accompanying the rise of the mass media has forced theory to re-conceptualize the body and its relationship to culture. The body, in fact, has been at the centre of cultural theory's interrogation of mechanical, humanist and other systems-based theories which are grounded in the primacy of biology and material reality. In moving away from the universal explanations and 'grand narratives' of culture, contemporary cultural analysis has become more concerned with discourse and the processes of meaning-making. The body, therefore, is being conceived in terms of being inscribed, constituted or rendered meaningful in representation and culture. According to poststructuralist and postmodern theories, the body needs to be 'read' in terms of symbolic processes; this reading gives us insight not into what is real, but rather into what is cultural: that is, in terms of what is meaningful for the culture in which the body is deployed. A body, in this sense, may be read in what is conventionally understood to be a 'text' (film, magazine, advertisement, TV programme). But the body may also be read *as* a text in and of itself. It is inscribed with meaning through all aspects of everyday life; through modes of dress and undress, through relationships, through work, through engagement with other discourses. In other words, the body *is* the text.

Sociologists like Bryan Turner (1992) and Chris Shilling (1993, 2005) have sought to develop a generalist mode of analysis, which treats the body as material, functional, sensory and symbolic. In attempting to reconcile social and cultural theories of the body, Shilling in particular has explored the meaning of the body in terms of social power and the parameters of social policy. Poststructuralist, postmodernist and social constructionists, however, have tended to emphasize the discursive and cultural dimensions of the body. Following earlier studies by Georges Bataille, Michel Foucault's studies on prisons (1977a) and sexuality (1981) have presented a direct challenge to modern biological notions of the body, most particularly as they are transformed into forms of social theory. In *The History of Sexuality, Volume One*, for example, Foucault makes clear that discourse always precedes biology. The biology of the body, that is, provides the raw material for sexuality, but it is only in culture and the mediation of discourse that sexuality can actually exist. Sex is not a natural urge so much as a carefully coded discourse, or series of discourses, which social groups deploy in order to have sexuality. Foucault's theories directly challenge the notion that sex is the great taboo of modernism. According to Foucault, religion, the social and medical sciences, families and educational institutions talk about sex in order to control it; sexual discourse, however, will also incite and facilitate modes of sexual experience:

> From the singular imperialism that compels everyone to transform their sexuality into a perpetual discourse, to the manifold mechanisms which, in the areas of economy, pedagogy, medicine, and justice, incite, extract, distribute, and institutionalize the sexual discourses, an immense verbosity is what our civilization has required and organized. Surely no other type of society has ever accumulated – and in such a relatively short span of time – a similar quantity of discourses concerned with sex. (1981: 33)

Foucault's history of these discourses analyzes the body in terms of relationships and processes of power. As with his studies on the medicalized, imprisoned and social scientific body, Foucault's study of sexuality is concerned with the body as a site of power. It is at the level of the body, Foucault insists, that power is experienced, exchanged and reformed. This power/discourse, and the knowledge that it carries, is necessarily imprecise and personal, a matter of exchange and doubt, rather than structure and historical subjugation:

> [I]t is in discourse that power and knowledge are joined together. And for this very reason we must conceive of discourse as a series of discontinuous segments whose tactical function is neither uniform nor stable. To be more precise, we must not conceive of a world divided between accepted discourse and excluded discourse, or between the dominant discourse and the dominated one; but as a multiplicity of discursive elements that can come into play in various strategies. It is this distribution that we must reconstruct, with the things

said and those concealed, the enunciations required and those forbidden, that it comprises; with the variants and different effects – according to who is speaking, his position of power, the institutional context in which he happens to be situated – that it implies; and with the shifts and revitalization of identical formulas for identical objectives that it also uses. (1981: 100)

Power as it is experienced in this sexual 'microphysics' may be usefully engaged for the enhancement of individuals' pleasures.

The Biological Imperative Argument

While *The History of Sexuality* is concerned primarily with the ways in which culture constitutes sexuality and inscribes the body with meaning, this phase of Foucault's work directly challenges biological approaches to the body generally. In fact, Foucault's work on the discursive constitution of the body parallels other approaches to the body which some sociologists refer to as constructionist: the notion that human experience is fundamentally constructed in language or discourse, and that subjects are constructed by culture. Most sociology, and indeed most social science and cultural theory, is more or less constructionist. At its most extreme, however, a constructionist approach would deny any role at all for biology, suggesting that all reality is mediated and therefore constructed by culture. All human problems are to be found in culture and society, as indeed are all solutions to those problems.

The constructionist perspective is most hostile to the 'biological imperative' arguments which suggest that human behaviours are fundamentally rooted in our biology, including our evolutionary or genetic history. Liberal reformism, Marxism and feminism have all had to confront these arguments, whereby biology is invoked as an explanation for, especially hierarchical, patterns of human behaviour: humans are 'naturally' aggressive, discriminatory, self-interested, competitive, and so on; males and male sexuality are naturally predatory, visual, promiscuous, assertive. According to the biological imperative argument, these survival instincts are so completely patterned into our genes or hormones or psychology that we can only modify them at the margins rather than alter them in any essential way. The biological imperative argument suggests that attempts to alter these essential patterns generally lead to some form of mental, emotional or psychological illness, a pathology which fundamentally disrupts not just the minds of individuals but ultimately the social order and the social condition.

At its most extreme and dangerous, the idea that nature precedes and determines culture (social conditioning or 'nurture') continues to be promoted through pseudo-sciences like eugenics. A derivative of Social Darwinism, eugenics theorizes a range of human differences and competencies that are supposedly coded into genes. In this sense, the 'superiority' of specific racial groups is explained and ultimately justified in terms of a genetic history which necessarily manifests itself in terms of civilizational order and power.

While the experience of Hitler's Third Reich might have sensitized human societies to the dangers and stupidity of such arguments, warrior groups continue to invoke such ideas in order to justify the most extreme and brutal forms of violence and genocide. The arbitrary administrative division by which Belgian colonialists defined the people of Rawanda, for example, provided the basis for a eugenic civil war during the 1990s. This kind of essentialization of race and ethnicity remains a powerful source of human insecurity and social slaughter within an increasingly globalized cultural context.

SEX AND SEXUALITY

Feminism and New Sexuality

As may already be clear, a good deal of the recent analysis of the body in contemporary culture is centred on sex and sexuality. Feminism, in particular, has helped to reshape our thinking about the body, personal relationships and the conditions of power. However, as we discussed in Chapter 6, feminism itself has been substantially critiqued in contemporary cultural theory, most especially feminism which invests its politics in a structuralist classification of gender. This critique suggests that the older styles of structuralist feminism (Marxist and liberalist) tend to reduce all males to a particular political, cultural and sexual taxonomy; it also claims that liberation for all women can be reduced to a simple set of prescriptions. More recent feminist theory, influenced by Foucault and postmodern theoretics, has abandoned many of these assumptions, accepting the notion that emancipation is associated with a more fluid and unspecified subjectivity, one which resists the reduction of 'men' and 'women' to any form of assumed sexuality, subjectivity or political preconditions.

There is no doubt, however, that the political and sexual iconoclasm of feminism has contributed in significant ways to contemporary culture. Women's sexuality, which the feminists of the sixties sought desperately to liberate from patriarchal constraints, is now deeply woven into the fabric of contemporary culture. This release of the female body and female sexuality has not necessarily satisfied the higher ideals of structuralist feminism. Women have been released to higher levels of educational, professional business and public participation; however, women's sexuality has also been rendered available for appropriation by capitalist commodification, including the commodification of media imagery. The spectacle of (especially young) female bodies and sexuality has become so prolific as to appear normative, the standard by which all sexuality is to be known, stimulated and mobilized. If, as Foucault suggests, sexuality is primarily an operation of discourse, then the discourse of young women's bodies has become contemporary culture's primary sexuality. The great anxiety of contemporary feminism centres on the question of whether or not this primacy is liberational or another permutation of patriarchal control.

Of course, particular dimensions of feminist analysis would derive significant satisfaction from the emancipation of women's sexuality from the oppressions of sexual conservatism which limits women to domestic or maternal roles and which treats them as the sexual objects of male desire. Certainly, many feminists from the sixties sought a sexuality for women which would be assertive, uninhibited, freely expressed and lustful: that is, a sexuality which allowed females the same sexual privileges as culture accords to men. However, something of a divide has developed between these liberational forms and the sensibilities of younger feminists who feel entirely comfortable with a sexuality that is embedded in commodification and consumerist imagery. Certainly feminists like Germaine Greer and Naomi Wolf have expressed misgivings about a liberation which leaves women sexually complete but emotionally vacant. Greer, in particular, has asked quite directly whether her own project of sexual liberation has not been appropriated by a new kind of cultural superficiality, one which celebrates sex for its own sake but which leaves the questions of relationships and emotional satisfaction largely incomplete.

In 2007 the American Psychological Association Task Force on the Sexualization of Girls reported that the proliferation of sexualized images of young women and girls was having a detrimental effect on a 'whole generation of girls'. Confirming the theoretical reading of many structuralist feminists, the report argued that the explicit and sexual imaging of young female bodies created a permissiveness which distracted young females from emotional, educational and relational fulfillment. Such views corroborate broader concerns about body image diseases like anorexia, and the condition of 'social infertility', by which women reach the end of their biological reproduction phase without a satisfying relationship and children. During the 2000s, anxieties about permissiveness and social infertility have contributed to an increasing sexual conservatism among some women's groups, leading to a 'chastity backlash' in which younger western women are invoking 'traditional' values of celibacy before marriage (Eden, 2006).

This new debate of liberationism stimulates particular hostility among many younger feminists, who accuse older feminists of retreating from the project of women's sexual and libidinal liberation. Thus, the primacy of sexual and consumer-decorative pleasure has clearly become a fundamental factional impasse for contemporary feminism. The presence of the female body and female sexuality in popular culture has left a number of, especially older, feminists worried that liberation has become appropriated by the capitalist machinery, and that women are becoming more incarcerated by the modelling and force of idealized and unattainable pleasures (Jeffreys, 2005).

The Spectacle of the Body

Linda Williams (1989, 2004) in her study of film pornography expresses this feminist anxiety as a debate between feminists who fear the objectification of women's bodies in text, and those who are opposed to censorship. This latter group, Williams contends, remains concerned about certain depictions of women, but sees the control of imagery and expression as fundamentally pernicious: 'These women are interested in ... defending the expression of sexual differences and in opposing the hierarchicalization of some sexualities as better, or more normal, than others' (1989: 23). This liberationism, however, is tested when Williams considers hard-core pornography: on the one hand, hard-core might be conceived as a matter of the free expression of a variant female sexuality; on the other hand, it might represent a form of sexual exploitation. Thus, Williams' ambivalent acknowledgement of these varied sexualities and modes of stimulating pleasure betrays a deep fear that hard-core pornography constitutes political and social harm for women.

Williams recognizes that pornography may be used and interpreted differently by different audiences, and that the issue of 'power' has become problematized in readings of the relationship between a text and an audience. However, neither of these revelations is sufficient in themselves to convince her that the genre is worthwhile, either aesthetically or politically. In film, unlike literature, the complete exposure of the female body implicates not just the imagining of an author and an audience, but the actual presentation of actual women in imaginary forms. The question of liberation and the visualization of the female body remain problematic in Williams' studies:

> But seeing everything – especially seeing the truth of sex – proves a more difficult project than one might think, especially in the case of women's bodies, whose truths are most at stake ... [T]he visual terms of the cinema do not allow the female protagonists of hard-core films to authenticate their pleasure. This may be one reason why the confessing jewels in the filmic case are male, rather than female, genitals. (1989: 32)

In male-oriented pornography the film is climaxed by the 'money-shot', or male ejaculation, rather than in the presentation of female ecstasy, which remains a mere stepping stone. Williams' repudiation of hard-core pornography remains problematic since it is based on the uncertainty of presentational forms. That is, Williams believes that hard-core pornography can be identified as a distinct textual and sexual category. Ultimately, she rejects the idea that 'pleasure' constitutes a moral virtue in itself and that just because something is pleasurable it is necessarily worthwhile or good. Rather, Williams seeks to understand the problematic of a liberational sexuality which is based on the ultimate resolution of male climax. For Williams' feminism, it is this final gesture that reduces the hard-core to a politically unacceptable genre (2004; also see Cornell, 2000).

In his account of the development of anti-pornography politics, Laurence O'Toole argues that an uncomfortable alliance has developed between conservative moralists and particular zones of feminism:

> Although the feminist anti-pornographers may lack the social and political power of the moralitarians, over time their arguments have achieved a considerable cultural sway, with

a profound influence upon the language of censorship, which finds anti-porn feminist terms such as 'objectifying', 'dehumanizing' and 'degrading' tripping off the tongue of patriarchs and old-style moral guardians. Feminist anti-porners have contributed not only a new semantic vigour to the culture of censorship in Britain and the U.S., but also a fresh impetus for a level of policing of visual material that would be considered extreme if ventured by the moralitarians. (O'Toole, 1998: 28)

O'Toole contends that pornography is fundamentally indefinable, except in terms of the discourse of censorship. In other words, only the condition of control and exclusion – the things that others don't want displayed – can consistently define what is pornographic and what is not. For anti-porn feminists, including Linda Williams, this control should be levelled against the visualization of the female form for the satisfaction of the male gaze and male sexuality.

The problem with this approach has been outlined in more general terms in our discussion on feminism (Chapter 6). However, for contemporary feminism, which has the female form at the centre of its interests, there are significant difficulties in sustaining this position:

1 Subjectivity and sexuality become prescriptions of an all-knowing, structuralist authority. Only certain content, subjectivities and viewing positions are permitted. This 'authority' has been challenged from both inside and outside feminism.
2 Anti-porn feminism has trouble defining the exact nature of this permissible sexuality. The same explicit sexual content may be permissible in certain textual contexts, but not in others. When women produce explicit sexual depictions it may be considered 'erotica'; when men produce the same content it risks being damned as 'pornography'.
3 Perhaps the most difficult issue to deal with is the issue of reception. Heterosexual women, gay women and various permutations of loving couples may use the 'pornographic' text to intensify their sexual experiences. The text which is pornographic for heterosexual male onanism may be legitimate for the exploration of female sexuality. The text will be the same, but the audience response will define the status and politics of the text.

Some commentators (including D.H. Lawrence, Susan Sontag and Michel Foucault) have attempted to distinguish between pornography and erotica in more general ways. Such arguments, however, often invoke broader cultural prejudices which locate erotica in complex high art and pornography in the pedestrian world of mass consumerism or unenlightened voyeurism (see Williams, 2004). Erotica may be intellectually or aesthetically elevated, located in the female perspective or in bourgeois culture; pornography has often been located in male sexuality, working-class culture and mass consumerism.

Ara Osterweil (2004) argues that films like Andy Warhol's *Blow Job* mark the intersection of art, popular culture and pornography, where the 'avant garde' denies the boundaries of decency or normative morality to create its particular aesthetic. Similarly, we might compare the French film *Romance* (1999), written and directed by Catherine Breillat, with the 1980s American porn film *Deep Throat*, starring Linda Lovelace. Both films present the sexual odyssey of a female protagonist, and both depict sexually explicit content, including intercourse, oral sex, male and female genitalia and actual male ejaculation. *Romance* is generally conceived and consumed as an art-house movie; *Deep Throat* was produced purely for the pornography market, though in many ways it entered a more general cultural vernacular as a playful and absurd reflection on contemporary sexuality. Fierce battles were fought to protect *Romance* from being banned or censored in various parts of the world. In most cases the defence of the film was built around its artistic merit. *Deep Throat*, on the other hand, became a rallying point for anti-porn feminists, who believed that the depictions in the film debased women and were fundamentally dehumanizing. For a brief time, Linda Lovelace herself became the heroine of the anti-pornography movement in the United States. The bourgeois liberationism and intellectual elevations which protected *Romance* were not available for *Deep Throat*.

Dancing Bodies: Bodies in Motion

Some recent writings have attempted to reach beyond these elitist conceptions as much as they have sought to dissolve the sort of feminist anxieties expressed by Williams and others. In particular, theories based on new subjectivities and the power associated with bodily pleasure have extended into ever-broadening areas of cultural activity and textualization. Arguments which locate emancipation in the consumption of popular music or popular television texts are being applied to the texts and consumers of sexually explicit erotica. John Fiske (1989a) describes the self-presentation of managed nudity by women on the beach as a form of auto-eroticism. Fiske's arguments, drawn from de Certeau's notion of corporate raiding and Bakthin's theories on the transgressive nature of everyday folk culture, liberate individuals from the control of powerful institutions. Bodily pleasure becomes the central and unconscious ambit of emancipation and opposition. This focus on the auto-erotica of personal sexual display underpins similar cultural studies analyses of dance.

Anthropological studies have identified dance as a significant ritualist practice for storytelling and for kinship and fertility activities. In particular, traditional cultures have used dance as a conduit of social and cosmological knowledge, as well as more sensate practices of sexual display and courtship. Dance, in fact, constitutes a language or discourse which is transferred ritually through generations and which constitutes a significant thread for the ongoing identity and self-definition of community and culture. Through emigration, globalization and diaspora – the postmodernization of culture – specific ethnic groups have attempted to sustain elements of this traditional identity through the re-constitution of dance and dance practices. For example, in the city of Freetown in Sierra Leone, Temne peoples have formed voluntary associations called 'dancing compins'. The ostensible function of these associations is to perform music and dance for significant cultural events: weddings, visits of important people, and fund-raising. Most members of the dancing compins have migrated to the city from rural areas and each of the compins is formed around particular regional derivations. While the dancing compins were clearly formed to re-constitute traditional cultural identity, they were also used for community lobbying and for the ascension of political leaders. Dance, that is, became implicated in the maintenance of social and cultural rituals and the formation of modern politics in Sierra Leone.

Dance has also been associated with various forms of courtship, gender display and sexual ritual (McRobbie, 1989; Desmond, 1997). In particular, the interplay of genders have been mobilized in dance practice, as femininity and masculinity (as well as transgenderism and homoerotica) are accentuated through specific modes of dress, rituals and styles of performance. Indeed, while McRobbie et al. (1989) have argued that femininity is the central focus of contemporary dance, it is very clear that cultural fashion also prescribes quite stylized performativities and modes of display for men and masculinity. Thus, we might acknowledge that specific dance forms and display practices are more popular with women; however, as well as 'gazing' at women, men are also participants in the courtship and ritual practices of dance.

Clubs and Ecstasy

While certain images of western hyper-masculinity may have viewed dance as fundamentally 'effeminate' (think of John Wayne movies) or counter-masculine, males have nevertheless continually contributed to the dynamic of dance practice. In the recently established popular forms of dance in both live and club venues young men frequently dance alone or in groups, mimicking the ritual practices evolved by young women over the past several decades. Indeed, the 'mosh pit' – a crowded front-of-stage dance area – has become a place of masculine competitiveness and at times aggression.

This sort of aggressive masculinity, however, is far less typical in 'club culture', a site in which femininity and narcissistic sensuality are intimately coded into the music, dance forms, displays and practices of the rave and nightclub scene. According to Helen Thomas (2003) club culture has been formed around the intersection of historical trends in dance community, display clothing, psychotropic drugs like 'ecstasy', and intensive forms of repetitive dancing (185–87). In fact, the drug-taking associated with rave and club culture is an essential dimension of the experience of auto-erotica and sensate expressivity. Many clubbers report heightened sensation and tactile responses in the crowded conditions of the dance floor and in sexual experiences that might follow. However, while women frequently report a heightened experience of sex, males often consume 'viagra' (Sildenafil citrate) to restore sexual function that ecstasy compromises.

Erotica

Despite these changes, however, the spectacle of a dancing female body remains a central trope in contemporary culture. Historically, bourgeois culture has developed highly skilled and specialized forms of dance, such as classical ballet, which continue to tell stories and explore ideas. Undoubtedly, the presentation of women on stage implicates the possibility of sexual display for the visual and vicarious satisfactions of the viewers. However, while bourgeois culture invoked the notion of 'high art' in order to ameliorate its moral anxieties over the presentation of female bodies and female sexuality, the working classes seemed far less abashed (McNair, 2002). Burlesque and carnival culture in Europe and America frequently flouted obscenity laws, as performers experimented with various forms of nudity and erotic dance. Lucinda Jarrett argues that the emergence of striptease in twentieth-century Europe is replete with the same anxieties and debates that are evident in discussions on text-based pornography:

> The separation of the formal from the informal arts has led to the 20th-century opposition of art and pornography. Erotica sits ambiguously between these two poles on a slide rule where the marker is the censor, positioned by the moral values of a social context. (1997: 3)

Jarrett's primary interest, however, is not the problematic of censorship or the ambivalences of social values. Rather, she explores the activity of stripping in terms of the performers themselves, and how the dancers conceive of their art: 'Female strippers are strong women proud of an expressive sexuality which is not easily contained by the formalism of classical dance' (1997: 4). Jarrett repudiates the pornographer's camera, which reifies the performer and the performance, criminalizing and exhausting its power. Jarrett argues forcefully that striptease is the erotic art of the people and that the history of erotic dancing is very much embedded in connections between 'sexually powerful women' and a culture's desire or libido. Jarrett's thesis moves well beyond the timidity of feminist anti-pornography arguments, claiming that strippers are sexual artists, heroines acting on behalf of all people's liberation.

Jean Baudrillard argues similarly that striptease constitutes a fundamental sexual reality whereby the dancer removes her clothes and puts on her meanings. This carnality contrasts, in Baudrillard's view, with the simulacra of contemporary sexual imaging where the naked female form has become a mimicry or echo of genuine sexuality. The nude female body is, of course, present in advertising, television, cinema and video production, but striptease engages live bodies in ways that are designed to challenge as they interact with the live bodies and living sexuality of the audience. Of course both the live and the televisual bodies are constituitive of fantasy and sexual imagining, but the live body engages much more fully with the cultivation of these imaginings. For Baudrillard, the visceral body, in fact, disappears with the televisualization; the fantasy loses its force and presence.

To this extent, striptease is a more direct and fleshly discourse than other forms of sexualized nudity. In fact, the most recent permutation of striptease, table-top and lap dancing, deliberately exploits the interactive potential of live performance, reducing the psychological and spatial distance between performer and audience in order to produce a more intimate and complete imaginative union. An intimacy is created by a performance which is often one-to-one and which, in many cases, involves conversation, proximity and eye-to-eye contact. In some venues there are also opportunities for the dancer to touch the client/audience, but this is highly specified and discretionary. In peep-shows, however, venues are organized so that audience members can self-stimulate. Touch becomes implicated in striptease through the direct engagement of the viewer on the performing body. As Jarrett argues, the fundamental element of this sexual congress is always the sexual power of the stripper. Erika Langley (1997) confirms this view in her autobiographical account of the peep-show dancers of the Lusty Lady in Seattle. Longley records her first encounter with the eyes of a patron, and her own transformation from vulnerability to sexual power. According to Longley, her work as a stripper liberated her sexuality as it challenged the underlying limits that ideology and morality place on cultural expression.

For Brian McNair (2002) this new sexuality represents the 'democratization of desire', a more broadly dispersed libido which liberates individuals from the moral constraint of elite social groups. The proliferation of table-top and peep-show venues across the major cities of the world reflects a broadening of sexual discourses. Table-top, in particular, constitutes a form of gentrification of striptease as it locates erotic dance in more middle-class consumption contexts; women and couples are also more commonly attracted to these venues than previously. The proliferation of the naked female form has become so significant that it may provide a facility and stimulus for all sexuality – not just the sexuality of heterosexual (patriarchal) males. Table-top dancing blurs the boundaries between performance and prostitution (though venues and dancers would reject this claim). The intimacy that the performance engages is more analogous to intimate contact than the more vicarious representations of the electronic media. The popularity of the live performance might partly be explained by the general trend in contemporary culture toward a more open and prolific sexuality, and a more transient sexual experience. This sexuality is one which:

(a) permits an intimacy that is not bound by commitment, permanence or ongoing responsibility;
(b) acknowledges the unparalleled ascendancy of consumerism in human relationships;
(c) avoids the problematic of love but which acknowledges the extravagant beauty of youthful femininity;
(d) permits a sexual polygamy, a desire, that is never quite consummated and never quite fulfilled; and
(e) avoids the problematic of sexually transmitted diseases such as AIDS through the vicarious experience of multiple sexual partners.

Within this context, however, the transgressive potential of table-top dancing becomes muted within the broader commodity conventions of bourgeois culture. Pole dancing classes now attract a wide variety of participants, including many who have no intention of working professionally but who use the classes for fitness, auto-erotica and personal development. Clustering around the 'pole' as a playful but mildly parodic phallic symbol, many of these women are simply engaging in a gendered community activity from which they derive some innate pleasures. Sex industry advocates, while tolerating this form of pornographic impersonation, are nevertheless deeply concerned about a more general dilution of their trade. In particular, advocates bemoan the invasion of soft porn into everyday television, most particularly through 'reality' TV programmes like *Big Brother*. While in its twilight, the *Big Brother* series brought a high level of explicit sexual discourse, various forms of sexual engagement and nudity into domestic living rooms across the developed world. For the sex industry the everyday nature of this new form of pornography seriously threatens the taboo and prurient context through which their products and services attract value. The everyday nature of explicit sexual display, that is, constitutes a danger to the libido and desire that underpins sexual commerce.

ALTERNATIVE SEXUALITIES

Gendered Sex

While bodies are clearly designed to experience sex and sexual pleasure, the meaning, management and expression of these sensate experiences are clearly formed in culture. In this sense, the social management of sexuality is fundamentally political. In feudal and agricultural societies, social power and the ownership of economic resources like land were often exercised through the control of fertility, kinship and 'blood-lines' – as well as military force. Powerful groups created complex laws and religious dictums around sex, ensuring their own privileges, pleasures and inheritance rights while maintaining a constant supply of agricultural and military labour through the management of social fertility and prohibitions on the sexual excesses of the commoner. This fine balance of social libido and sexual prohibition underscored the cultural formation of class and gender hierarchies. Patriarchy, which seeks to fix gender through distinct dispositions of masculinity and femininity, was largely shaped by elite interests and the scrupulous management of desire, controlled breeding and the requirements of labour.

The prohibition on homosexuality was formed largely out of this same historical and political imperative. However, while same-gender sexual expression has been ignored, tolerated and even sanctioned across many cultures, the evolution of modern societies appears to have been accompanied by a particular contempt for this form of sexual expression, especially when practised by men. The legislative prohibition of homosexuality in England during the nineteenth century was embedded in a discourse of moral, religious and scientific outrage against these 'unnatural' and Sodomistic practices. For many of the legislators and enforcement agencies, homosexuality was clearly the articulation of a profound personal depravity and psychological pathology. Indeed, much of the modernist discussion of homosexuality, until quite recently, has been constituted around the question of whether homosexuality is a physical or social pathology. In either case, Queen Victoria's scrutiny of the original homosexual prohibition bill prompted her to exclude women from the law, since she believed that the fairer sex had neither the biological apparatus nor base disposition to indulge in such bestial activities.

And while gay political advocacy and a more enlightened and progressive conception of homosexuality have largely erased these conceptions of same-sex desire as 'disease', debates about the derivation and source of homosexuality persist. The alternative theories on these sources can be summarized in the following terms –

1. *Homosexuality is a basic biological or genetic orientation.* It is estimated that around 10 per cent of adults have had sex with a person of the same gender. Of this group some people believe that they are essentially gay or lesbian and that they are biologically programmed to be attracted to the same gender. This group of sexual exclusivists often build their identity and community around the sense of being distinctly different. Some recent, though not unquestioned, science has suggested that there is, in fact, a 'gay gene' which predisposes particular individuals toward same-gender attraction. This science also claims that the gay gene has always been present in human populations; the high proportion of gay individuals within specific family groups is cited as proof of the existence of the gene.

2. *Gay orientation is formed through particular cultural groups and modes of expression.* While there are clearly a proportion of people who regard themselves as exclusively gay, there are many more who have a mixed orientation. This suggests that culture and cultural expressivity are implicated in same-gender orientation. Thus, some specifically patterned cultural practices and behaviours are more likely than others to produce homosexual modes of expression. Historically, we can see that particular societies and cultures were supportive of same-gender sexual practices (e.g., Classical Greece), while others were more hostile. In modern, western societies there are certain social practices which appear to generate a higher proportion of same-gender sexual practice. Single sex Catholic schooling, prisons, cultural contexts which encourage sexual experimentation (Bohemian communities, gay parents, specific popular cultural texts and environments etc.) – have all been cited as social stimulants to gay sexual expression.

3. *Hyper-masculinity and patriarchy* are also often cited as a cultural source of the rejection of heterosexual relations. Some male homosexuals report that the intense expectations of masculinity disinclined them toward a heterosexual identity. Excessively austere or prohibitive fathers have long been cited as a source of homosexual orientation

for sons. Similarly, lesbian women have cited 'bad experiences' with aggressive and patriarchal men as a reason for engaging with women. These bad experiences may include physical or sexual abuse, or the severe restrictions imposed by patriarchal male partners.

4. *Everyone has the potential to experience same-sex attraction*, but only particular individuals are prepared to experiment with this form of sexual expression. In this sense, there is no patterned social conditioning but a random intersection of individual conditions, life-history, influences and personal psychology.

Being Queer: Queer Theory

In many respects, these theories on the sources of gay and lesbian sexual practices are also implicated in the ways in which same-gender attractions are expressed in culture. The modern state, as we noted above, had employed various mechanisms to suppress these practices, including the application of criminal and pathological labels and sanctions. Thus, an individual subject became a 'homosexual' ('fag', 'poofter', 'dyke') as the culture fixed the practice against the human typology. Paradoxically, the gay liberation movement which emerged in the 1960s exploited the cultural typology and its intrinsic dualism (gay/straight) in order to overthrow the legislative prohibitions on homosexuality. As in the broader civil rights movement, the liberation of same-gender sexual practices was shaped by an identity politics which was largely conditioned by the values of the oppressive state apparatuses and the language–knowledge that it had imposed. The gay movement sought to reverse their exclusion from the freedoms and human rights upon which the modern state had been founded (Jagos, 1996; Patton and Eppler, 2000). The cry of 'pride' encoded a belief that individuals were born homosexuals and they simply wanted to be able to express their orientation without legislative or social injunction.

This fixing of the straight/gay dichotomy, however, has been seen more recently as itself a restrictive typology which limits expression and choice. While the essentialization of gayness might suit the identity and political interests of particular same-gender oriented individuals and communities, it also limits the scope for mixed attractions and mixed identity, including transgenderism. 'Queer theory' has evolved as a way of wresting the expressive power of same-gender sexuality from the rigidities and essentialization of the modernist project. Derived through poststructuralist theories on language, power and knowledge, queer theory seeks to deconstruct the straight/gay binary and its notions of a fixed and integrated identity. To this end, queer theory usurps the labels of 'queer' as it was applied by the official, 'straight' culture (see Seidman, 1996; Huffer, 2001; Halle, 2004). Queer theory, therefore, sees identity as open and expansive, a projection of complex discursive effects which may be marshalled for specific social settings and then released into the dynamic of further incarnations of cultural expressivity.

Challenging gender liberation stereotypes: The Indonesian *Waria*

Second wave feminism is being seen increasingly as a peculiar blend of political critique and political conservatism. In order to liberate women from patriarchal gender prescriptions, second wave feminism has often created its own version of the liberated woman – a well educated and androgynous looking person who is not the victim of male-based consumer fashion. This stereotype has been rejected by many women, including a new wave of feminists who seek to express their own version of liberated femininity and sexual interaction with men (and women). Significantly, the notion of 'femininity' has also been adopted by another radical social category – transvestites – who use femininity to usurp broader social prescriptions of gender, including their own masculinity.

Paradoxically, a feminist critique that seeks to deconstruct femininity must necessarily abjure the gender-blend of these 'in-between' cultural categories. To this end, second wave feminism becomes an oppressive political framework, which aligns itself with conservative and censorial political forces.

The Indonesian transvestite group known as *waria* have a long history in traditional and modernizing Malay culture. As a self-nominating 'third gender' the *waria* are biologically male, but they live in particular urban villages (*Kampong*) as women. Political forces in Indonesia are seeking to ban *waria* and homosexual groups in a broad sweep of legislation designed to increase the power of Islamic moral conservatism. The patriarchy (ultra masculinity) of these conservative forces denounces the 'perversion' of gender, which is a central platform of Islamic law (*sha'riah*). Conservative Islamic groups argue that transvestites and homosexual groups breach the tradition of Islam, which is forged around family and pure gender.

Opponents of the proposed prohibition laws, however, argue that this version of tradition is itself embedded in a very modern iteration of anti-western ideology and the social and political interests of the radical Islamists themselves. Indeed, the conservatives' version of tradition critically ignores Indonesia's history of sexual tolerance and diversity, as well as the culture's own broad sexual vocabulary.

Significant transvestite communities were reported in the trading areas of Indonesia as early as the 1800s and are still evident in Jakarta, Central Java and Bali today. Seemingly unperturbed by social stigma or pejorative labelling, the *waria* continue to live on the social margins, establishing extremely powerful communities and social support networks. Various studies of *waria* communities in Indonesia present an image of very strong social networks, which includes social welfare and a socialistic micro economy constituted around sharing, mutual care, craft work and prostitution. The *waria* do not necessarily identify as female, but more as a third gender whose sexual orientation is mixed. This experience of diversity and open identity is reported by many transvestite and transgender groups across the globe, creating considerable complexity for a liberational politics which attributes specific qualities to a binary and fixed gender opposition.

This is not to say, of course, that individuals may have a strong disposition toward a particular sexuality and may seek to set their identity within a community of similar subjects. It is to suggest, rather, that these dispositions exist within a complex intersection of sexual discourses and choices, and that liberation is shaped by the capacity to choose, rather than the inevitability of a particular disposition itself. This approach broadens the reading of same-gender attraction and practices, creating more inclusive categories of 'alternative sexuality'. In particular, bisexuality represents the taxonomy of 'in-between' by which Deleuze and Guattari define the collapse of hierarchical binary structures like hetero/homo. Bisexuality, in this sense, becomes a transgressive expressivity which evades essentializing identity, providing a broader lexicon of human sexual practices, as well as a liberation from the imperatives of a fixed sexual identity (see Jagos, 1996; Halle, 2004).

More generally, these alternative expressivities that have been shaped through the emergence of queer theory have also assaulted the assumptions implicit in other binaries such as male/female. Transvestite, transgender and transsexual practices and identities necessarily compromise the fixed and biologically determinant model of gender. Thus, while second wave feminism had argued that gender was largely socially constructed, it had nevertheless fixed its liberation in a civil rights based reversal of the man/woman binary – and in doing so, essentialized and demanded the ascent of its own particular version of 'woman'. Even postmodern feminism, which seeks to valorize the expressive potential of femininity, remains set within a vision of gender that is playful and expansive, but ultimately contained within a binary formation that celebrates a particular kind of femininity. Transsexual modalities, however, hybridize biology and gender expression, creating new categories of the 'in-between' and 'outside' which usurp conventional categories.

Thus, while many transgender subjects feel impelled to 're-ascribe' the ambiguities of their biological gender, transvestites are usually comfortable with their biology but seek to express their sexuality through cross dressing and various forms of alternative gender expression. In either case, the gender with whom the subject seeks sexual engagement is extremely variable. Some cross-dressing men have sex only with men, some only with women, some with both. Cross-dressing women, while less common, have an equally variable range of sexual expressivities.

Beats, Desire, Disease and Despair

There is little doubt that consumer capitalism has appropriated these new sexual expressivities, transforming them into various modes of mainstream and popular entertainment, if not actual sexual choices. Liberation and the diversification of sexualities, that is, have become part of televisual culture – as evidenced in TV programmes like *Queer as Folk* and *The L Word*, films such as *Priscilla* and *Brokeback Mountain*, bands like *Queen* and *Anthony and the Johnsons,* and glam events like the Sydney Gay Mardi Gras. Moreover, gay characters have been featured within straight communities for largely straight audiences: programmes such as *Will and Grace, Buffy* and *Brothers and Sisters* present 'gayness' as a somewhat eccentric but vaguely pleasant interplay for the entertainment of mainstream, mass audiences.

At one level, these popular renderings of sexual alternatives represent a new and more optimistic vision of liberation and diversity. The incorporation of gay sexualities into the mainstream commodity culture is creating a new platform of normalcy as well as some genuine homoerotica for straight, bisexual and gay communities. At another level, however, this imaging of positive, young, healthy and sexually attractive gay bodies camouflages many of the continuing displeasures associated with same-gender sexual culture, experiences and practices. Of course, many of these displeasures are mere amplitudes of psycho-emotional problems associated with sexuality in the broader community. However, for some people engaged in gay sexual practices, their lives are conditioned by profound disjunctions of isolation, despair, psychological trauma and even mental illness, which bear little resemblance to the representations of mainstream or even alternative TV narratives. In this sense, the romantic ideal that is propagated by television culture and its commercial interests is fractured as individuals continue to disguise their sexuality within a community that remains disdainful of homosexuals, homosexuality and promiscuity.

Indeed, while TV programmes often glamorize gay sexualities as youthful and beautiful bodies, the actual 'gay community' is populated by people of diverse ages and degrees of physical attractiveness. The attraction pool in the gay community is far smaller than in the broader, 'hetero' community and so relationships can be fractious and unstable, with individuals periodically engaged in an intense competition for partners and sexual pleasure. The male and female gay 'scenes' are replete with transient and casual sexual activities which leave many individuals emotionally and spiritually dissatisfied, as they seek to negotiate the complex norms, expectations and practices of a community whose status remains ambiguous and vaguely clandestine, despite the honorific entertainment value that it provides for the broader culture.

The male 'beats' – toilet blocks and other places in which men have casual and anonymous sex with one another – are particularly intense locales of sexual interaction. Participants may engage in risk behaviours through non-condom concupiscence and practices that involve multiple partners and forms of physical abuse. In the lesbian community women often struggle with issues of identity, maternity and partnering. The various categories of lesbianism – butch, femme, lipstick – become indicators of a significant fracturing in the community; sex-play and partnering can often involve deception, a high level of transience and intense competition and jealousies (see Meem and Gibson, 2002). Particular categories of lesbian, such as the highly feminized 'lipstick lesbian', consciously reject the more 'masculine' styles such as the 'butch dyke'. For many 'hard core' lesbians, these femme subjects are merely visitors or players who have no real commitment to the politics of gender which seeks to oppress them: the lipstick and femme lesbians, therefore, are often seen as traitors to the lesbian cause. Even in long term partnerships, issues around sex and sexuality remain, as lesbian couples must confront issues of reproduction, and a lower rate of genital-orgasm sexual interaction than for the broader community (see Duberman, 1997). Moreover, lesbian and gay male couples appear to experience the same incidence of psychological and physical abuse that occurs in the heterosexual community (see Miller et al., 2000).

Good and Bad Sexualities

Jean Baudrillard argues that the new hyperreal mediasphere has no clearly defined moral or ideological centre; as a rampant and self-replicating stimulant, which has neither meaning, depth nor value, televisual culture is hollow at its core. The simulacra (copies of copies) which characterize televisualization are formed around the sensate and emotional engagement of audiences who are perpetually 'entranced' or 'seduced' by spectacle and their own amorphous state of arousal (Baudrillard, 1983b, 1984a). To this end, televisualization conflates libido with social knowledge, mobilizing itself through the central motif of young, beautiful (and most often female) bodies.

Of course, the motif of youthful female beauty has been central to the aesthetic and cultural iconography of many human societies, most frequently through its association with fertility, kinship and libido. In modern societies, the motif has been fortified through patriarchal and romantic ideals which have been invigorated by consumerism and commodity capitalism. Libido *as social knowledge* is critically embedded in popular narratives, commodity branding, celebrity and advertising. Thus, the young female body as the central focus of the whole culture's libido, economy and new forms of social knowledge becomes suspended within a vortex of competing and often contradictory impulses and demands – fertility and reason; arousal and restraint, family and career, beauty and denial; lust and love. Within this context, the motif and meaning of the young female body becomes subject to extraordinary cultural pressure which in turn stimulates new sexual practices and modes of representation. Within the youth cultural sub-set, for example, young women may be required to be 'chaste' and available for a serious relationship and reproduction, while being encouraged to be sexually capable and experienced. In order to promulgate an ideal of chastity, some young women experiment with their own gender or with forms of non-concupiscent sexual activities (such as oral sex) which is then culturally configured as 'not really having sex at all'. This not-quite-real sex enables young people to then create a cultural condition for the imagining of chastity which then fortifies the patriarchal ideal of marriage and reproduction.

This ideal, of course, is being seriously undermined within the evolving conditions of contemporary culture. More than half of all marriages end in divorce and increasing numbers of couples and individuals are rejecting the formal institution of marriage altogether. Fertility rates in the developed world are continuing to decline, and many women are experiencing what is being called 'social infertility' and an accelerating level of emotional dissatisfaction. Increasing numbers of women who are childless and in the last years of their fertility have claimed that their social world has simply failed to deliver an appropriate partner – a male partner with whom they could have emotional satisfaction and a family.

Marriage itself has been impugned by feminists as a patriarchal and untrustworthy institution, which oppresses women and privileges men (see Hertlein, 2006). Violence and abuse in marriage is often cited as an intrinsic deficiency of the institution. With one in nine women in the US reporting rape and other forms of coercive sex in a marriage (see Miller and Knudsen, 2006), the institution itself is being regarded increasingly as a redundant social modality that has outlived its usefulness.

This form of 'bad sexuality' challenges the general approbation of sexual diversity that is so often celebrated in postmodern academic and popular discourse. Even in a broadly permissive society, that is, the valorization of difference reaches its limits, as the culture continues to distinguish between modes of sexual practice that are sanctioned, and those that are not. The social knowledge formed in televisual texts around good and bad sexuality may be summarized in the following terms –

1   Beauty and health are central to the good/bad binary, and only occasionally are we witness to sexuality that may take place with diseased or disabled bodies. Even in more strident or 'alternative' narrative texts like *The L Word*, the characters are attractive and healthy, and relationships are forged largely around this familiar aesthetic. Lesbianism is a positive sexuality when practised by attractive, 'feminine' women.
2   Sex is rarely featured between people of vastly different cultural, class, racial or ethnic backgrounds. TV producers of programmes like *Desperate Housewives, The OC* and *Brothers and Sisters* are careful not to overstretch their audiences' expectations and imaginings of good sexuality. Where sex takes place between a black and white American, for example, it becomes a distinct feature of the narrative, and not just an incidental norm. Once it has done its work, the element quickly disappears from view. Equally, there are very few tramps or unemployed criminals presented in these programmes, and fewer still who have sex with the stars.
3   Sex is confined in age. Paedophilia and 'child abuse' have emerged as significant issues in contemporary culture. However, sexual contact between people of vastly different ages, whether as minors or adults, is treated with deep suspicion. The marriage of film-maker Woody Allen to his step-daughter has proved an uncomfortable issue – an example of a tainted and inappropriate deployment of the body.
4   Allen's romance with and marriage to his step-daughter raises further questions about the legitimacy of incestuous relationships. This taboo persists in contemporary culture, despite attempts in art-house movies like *Lone Star* to raise the issue for public consideration.

5   There is the perpetual question of polygamy. The marriage–romance ideal seems to have adapted comfortably to the notion of serial sexual partners, and can even endure a little transient multiple-partner experimentation. These experiments, however, are supposed to fail, and as we have seen in films like *Two Girls and a Guy* and TV programmes like *Desperate Housewives* or *Cheaters*, the ideal of 'the couple' ultimately imposes its normative values over other relational forms. Texts depicting positive polyamorous (multiple partner) relationships remain sparse or are fixed within a relatively conservative patriarchal paradigm (e.g., *Big Love*). And yet, even within long-term, supposedly monogamous relationships, many individuals are engaging in extra-marital sex. According to most research on long term relationships in the developed world, 60–70 per cent of men and 55–60 per cent of women have had sex with a person other than their spouse during the course of their current, long-term marriage (Hertlein, 2006).

6   Sex that involves violence, consenting sado-masochism or animals is treated with deep contempt by cultural commentary. Yet even when these elements are converted to imagination and become part of an entirely different discourse – as, for example, in Peter Shaffer's play *Equus* – the ideal is rendered silent.

7   Finally, the double code of sex/power in the workplace has produced a new anxiety, most particularly as the workplace has become a central sexual site in contemporary culture. Feminism has problematized sex between work colleagues because of the danger of differential power and exploitation. While this fear has been largely associated with women's subjugant positions in the workplace, the film *Disclosure* explores the problem for male subordinates as well.

BEAUTIFUL AND HEALTHY BODIES

Structuralist Precepts

A good deal of feminist analysis of the body has centred on questions of representation. In particular, feminists have been highly critical of advertising and other popular textualizations which constantly repeat particular images of svelte, youthful, thin, female bodies. These images are not only 'normative' or normalized as a cultural standard, they become 'mythic': an ideal toward which all women must aspire in order to complete their own identity as women. Men's institutional power enables them to construct this beauty ideal; they are the gazers and the owners of the mechanisms of gazing. In her account of this patriarchal process, Naomi Wolf (1991; see also Jeffreys, 2005) points out that the most common depiction of the body ideal has changed from a buxom size 12–14 represented in the Marilyn Monroe figure of the 1950s, to a tall, thin, size 6–8 in current imagery. Wolf argues that this shrinking of the female body ideal, at a time when men and women are actually getting larger in the developed world, represents an attempt to keep women thin, undernourished, pre-pubescent and under control.

While the broad strokes of Wolf's analysis have been severely criticized, there is little doubt that women's bodies have been iconographed as a sexual and commodificational focus for the culture at large. Feminist analysis argues that eating disorders such as bulimia and anorexia are directly related to unrealizable, media-constituted body ideals: young women deliberately starve themselves in order to suit the ideal. Paradoxically, this pandemic of body dissatisfaction is occurring as fast-food diets and declining physical activity are predisposing bodies to increased levels of obesity. Patricia Vertinsky (1998) points out that women across all age levels in the developed world are almost half as active as men, despite the clear health benefits associated with exercise.

Susan Sontag (1978) argues that the media fascination with youthful beauty carries a reciprocal social interest in the condition of ageing, constructing it as a 'problem' if not a pathology. According to Sontag, it is this horror of the ageing female body in particular which constitutes a dominant ideology in the understanding and reading of femininity. Because of the cultural intensification and prolific mediation of the young, healthy female body, female ageing is more terrible and more frightening than male ageing. Female ageing represents the fundamental loss of vitality and sexual potency, the fundamental loss of 'life'. Vertinsky goes further to argue that this horror is part of young girls' initiation into puberty; despite the great achievements of the women's movement, young girls are socialized into the culture of body-hating (Vertinsky, 1998: 87). However, according to Vertinsky and numerous other feminist commentators, even physical fitness – the leaner, fitter body – is subject to the controlling manipulations of patriarchal commodification:

> Through its immense popularity, aerobics has been linked to a changing aesthetic of the female form. … This transformed body is a fit body, and a healthy body (in stark contrast to the anorexic – a body that is fundamentally unhealthy, too far in excess of dominant standards of acceptable femininity). While this is not to deny that aerobics can serve as a vehicle of enjoyment, socioability, energy and opportunities for self-care, it embodies the complex use of power over women's bodies in a sophisticated consumer society. (Vertinsky, 1998: 89)

Whether fit, anorexic or overweight, aged or youthful, the female body is vulnerable to the controlling power of patriarchal and consumerist structures. This form of feminist analysis, however, struggles to find an escape from such powers. The beauty and health of the female body, it seems, is perpetually doomed to serve the interests of the male gaze, male sexuality and commerce.

Beauty and Labour

All cultures seem to have ordained a particular value for beauty and health, although the definition of beauty and its status against other social values are highly variable.

The prominence of beauty and health in our culture can only partly be explained by feminist structural analysis. We can identify, even within European cultural history, variations, for example, in the approbation of skin colour. Fair skin once meant wealth and leisure, significant aspects of commodifiable beauty. From the 1960s, however, skin tanning represented a healthy body which was sufficiently leisured to permit sunbathing or a beach-based lifestyle. With the public awareness of the dangers of sunburn and skin cancer, sun tans are no longer broadly acknowledged as indicators of health and well-being. Similarly, the extreme female thinness which became ascendant during the 1980s and 1990s seems to be at odds with other significant feminine idealizations – in particular the fetishization of breasts as sexual and cultural icons. That is, while the fashion industry persistently deployed the sylph-like bodies of young women, creating an imagery of perpetual pubescence or even trans-genderism, other areas of the media were increasingly exposing and deploying breasts as dominant sexual symbols. Topless bathing, increasingly explicit nudity in films, and the explosion of the breast augmentation industry – all indicated a more intense experience of feminine sexuality which in many ways transgresses the beauty myth of waif-like thinness.

Of course, this intensification of visual sexuality, especially youthful sexuality, has been accompanied by massive acceleration in beauty and youth-restoring products and services. Jean Baudrillard explains these developments in terms of the increasing visualization of contemporary culture, and the need for a generalized, commodity-driven state of arousal. The broad distribution of electronic media and mediated imagery has been accompanied historically by significant changes in the way capitalism functions. The shift from manufacturing to service economies, most particularly media-based services, has changed the way bodies are deployed in labour. Baudrillard (1981) himself acknowledges these changes, arguing that modern capitalism shifts the focus of labour from goods production to sign production. In an increasingly visual culture, it is not surprising that the exchange-value of the human body has shifted from action and thought to appearance. The value of what a subject can do (or produce) has become less important than what a subject can represent. In the symbolic exchange of beauty, therefore, the face has become centralized over the action of muscle and mind.

Complaints about the increasing superficiality of culture, the proliferation of ephemera, the increasing disconnectedness of human relationships, and so on, are directly linked to the ascendancy of this new exchange-value. The spectacle of the human form, especially the female face, provides an exchange currency. Youth equates to freshness and newness. In a culture that has so thoroughly surrendered its (modernist) imagination of deep time and chronology, where the perpetuity of newness is so highly valued, it is not surprising that youth has become such a major commercial resource. In postmodern culture, where all temporal and spatial themes are laminated into ever-self-constructing versions of the new and the present, youth is a self-feeding mechanism which must necessarily reinvent itself with each moment. Deep thought or 'knowledge' is slipping behind the visual as a commodifiable entity. And while we might speak blithely about the 'information age', it is clear that this information is not dominated by new forms of knowledge but is rather constituted out of imaged ephemera which must constantly be refreshed and reinscribed with a smiling, youthful demeanour. This constant reconstruction or re-originification of 'the new' and its promise of popular success inevitably subjugates the value of concentrated knowledge to visceral pleasure. Even the relatively new cultural facility of the Internet remained marginal until it was transformed into the World Wide Web, presenting itself and its information as narrative, image and the engagement of sensate-sexual pleasure. As a knowledge technology, the Internet was restricted to the interests of warlords and academics. Its integration with visual culture and sexual imagining brought the Net out of the unknown and into the practices of everyday users for everyday information. Once again, the human form, especially the female form, has become the dominant iconography of the Net.

Ageing and Pathology

While other cultures might respect and value the sagacity or wisdom associated with ageing, the postmodern intensification of youth and youthful appearance inevitably creates significant anxieties around ageing, disease and degeneration. Sontag and other feminists have highlighted this problematic in association with women's ageing, but the decline of bodily prowess creates significant anxieties for both genders. In fact, postmodern conceptions of cultural time as the 'ever-present' and the ever-unfolding 'new' create significant problems for cultural subjects. Subjects may wish to obey this cultural norm and be forever youthful and progressive, but the simple fact is that bodies decline and age. In broader, demographic terms, in fact, developed cultures are becoming far less youthful as a social group; the baby-boom of the post-World War Two period is well past its peak and total populations in the developed world are rapidly ageing.

At a personal level, Meyrowitz (1985) claims that this mismatch between ageing and ever-presence is associated primarily with new discursive challenges to the modernist chronologizing of the life course. Human imagining of life has changed radically, according to Meyrowitz, as children are behaving more like adults and adults more like children. There is an increasing continuity in modes of dress, cultural tastes and self-presentation as the ageing populations attempt to maintain the culture of youth against the biological necessity of decline and death.

While this characteristic is clear enough in middle and later age, it is also evident in the 'quarter-lifers' (25–35) where younger adults are experiencing an extended adolescence through the deferral of marriage and child bearing. The notional 'crisis of the quarter-lifer' refers to a social and cultural adherence to the freedoms, sexual practices and lifestyle entertainment that are common for young adults (Hassler, 2005). This temporal compression is clearly associated with postmodernization and the impact of televisual culture.

Contemporary culture's de-ritualization of life stages is part of a similar temporal realignment. Emphasis on youth and youthful perpetuity has challenged the cultural values and social rewards associated with ageing. Indeed, the presentation of idealized body types, which is so hotly condemned in much feminist analysis, operates as an obfuscation of these chronologized life phases. Youthful energy, sexual arousal and the pleasures of adventure are provided as resources for the extension of the 'mid-life'. Advertising and televisual imagery guide their adult consumers through lifestyle experiences which are only vicariously associated with chronological age; comfort and luxury are constituted as a discernment of taste, rather than a condition of bodily degeneration. Ageing, that is, becomes camouflaged through the discourses of target marketing. It is not decay, wisdom or a senior social status that draws a consumer to a product; it is bodily vitality, arousal and youthful perpetuity which enable an identity to defy its biological decline.

Featherstone and Hepworth (1991) agree that this notion of mid-life, the period between youthful adult and old age, has been reconstructed in the past few decades. However, they go on to suggest that along with the openness and increased flexibility of this reconstituted mid-life is a discourse of 'crisis' (1991: 384). In terms of televisual iconography, this crisis becomes another available resource by which subjects define themselves and adjudge their experience of relationships, health and sexuality. We have made reference to the explosion in anti-ageing products and services, relationship and psychological counselling services, and the vast array of lifestyle products designed to complete the identity that has been constituted through the mid-life. It seems, however, that mid-life becomes a point of awareness, a moment in which the perpetuity of arousal spoken about by Baudrillard may come home to roost. That is to say, the unceasing return of that arousal may lead in mid-life to an awareness of the impossibility of satisfaction. The paradoxical mingling of biology and discourse, in fact, may create the sort of fractures in subject identity which produce the sense of crisis. The mid-life crisis is the 'normal' outcome of realization: the impossibility of sexual or financial satisfaction, and the impossibility of immortality.

David Clarke (1993) suggests that the construction of marital sexual problems is linked to this normalization process. That is, the psychological, medical and pathological discourses which support the notion of 'crisis' in a relationship are built around notions of normality and abnormality. While constituting a more open approach to chronology, notions of mid-life have merely shifted 'well-being' and health problems away from ageing and toward other constituted forms of normality. Sexuality and sexual variation are barely countenanced in the construction of human sexual pathologies, Clarke argues. While some of these common sexual pathologies are identifiably physiological, many are also defined in terms of a psychological or relational 'illness'. For women, the most common problems are lack of sexual desire and failure to reach orgasm; for men the most common pathologies are erectile and ejaculant dysfunction.

For Clarke, however, it is the particular social arrangement which constitutes sexuality – marriage – which first harbours and constitutes the 'crisis'. The problematic of sex within marriage is concentrated through notions of sexual normality and the idealized marital body. The creation of relational or sexual disorders out of this normative approach, and therapies designed to cure them, deflects attention away from the relational formation itself and the broader question of sexuality. In other words, Clarke claims, the problems of the body are formed out of what is considered 'normal' in a socially and culturally sanctioned relationship. Crisis is produced because subjects' bodies are simply not able to cope with the emotional and psychological burden of these normative expectations.

The Spectacle of Muscular Bodies

While discourses on sexuality and the youthful female body have tended to dominate analyses of the body, more recent studies are considering alternative cultural presentations, including the spectacle of muscularity and 'masculinity'. Indeed, through the progress of cultural theory, a greater interest in diversity and alternative ideologies has shifted some of the interest in the body away from feminist analysis of dominant ideologies and representations. As we have noted, the prevalence of the young female body in the media, and in culture more broadly, has tended to obscure the increasing heterology of sexualities and other everyday bodily experiences. For example, recent studies on the female body have examined female muscularity as a reconfiguration of traditional female stereotypes (see Halberstam, 1998; Choi, 2000; Krane et al., 2004; Cregan, 2006). Judith Halberstam argues that women can entirely reinscribe their bodies with a muscularity that creates a form of 'female masculinity' (1998). Such analyses, either consciously or incidentally, reflect on the whole notion of body construction, body action and ascriptions of gender. The muscularity of women reflects on, for example, the constructive nature of body idealizations, including the discourses of masculinity. Leslie Heywood deconstructs masculinity through a carefully charted analysis of (female) bodybuilding in American popular culture:

> Perhaps more obviously than any other contemporary phenomenon, bodybuilding relies on a radical notion of plasticity while that plasticity paradoxically functions to bolster the most fixed, traditional masculine norms. More than any other sport, it draws attention to the fact that masculinity is a masquerade rather than an unquestionable essence. … If display places one on the side of the spectacle in the sense of film theory, and the spectacle is the position of the feminine, then bodybuilding for all its hypermasculine posturing visibly marks masculinity as both posture and literal physical construction. By definition, bodybuilding is a spectacle which performs the masculine. … Perched precariously on the balancing point between the slavish enactment of masculinity and its denaturalization and thereby deconstruction, bodybuilding is the fortification which will destroy the fortress. (1998: 65)

Bodybuilding acts in similar ways to the plasticity of cosmetic prosthetics. Strangely, the enhancement of female muscularity extends the potential of the femininity and the female form while simultaneously exposing the artificiality of the masculine. Muscles can be constructed like silicon breasts; anything is possible in the cultural construction of discourse.

While most feminists have been concerned to critique socially inscribed images of femininity, Heywood's deconstruction is designed to liberate women from the discursive and ideological limits imposed by the concept of masculinity. Heywood suggests that the extreme of bodybuilding actually constitutes a form of 'feminine spectacle' and thus self-parody. Krane et al. (2004), in their research on femininity and muscularity, found that many female athletes felt a degree of discontent over the attitudes of prospective male dating partners, who seemed to prefer the smaller bodies prescribed by conventional femininity.

Of course, this problematic of gender ascription and identity construction applies equally to males. In particular, the low-fat, highly muscled body type is critically implicated in the formation of an idealized masculinity as it is culturally imagined and experienced by men. While Heywood considers 'masculinity' to be liberatory for women, it is being seen by various commentators (see Messner and Sabo, 1990; Buchbinder, 1998; Pease, 2000; Edwards, 2006) as constraining and troubling for men. The ideal of the muscular body and the social significance attributed to size (phallic and body mass) may be constituted in similar ways as female beauty or the presentation of breasts.

As Murray Drummond (1998a, 1998b) has argued in his analysis of male body idealizations, bodies are of critical significance for the construction of male identity. While this identity has always been built around forms of bodily action, more recent displays of muscularity as spectacle in televisual culture are leading to similar pressures and dissatisfactions for men as are being experienced by women. Drummond (1998b) argues that body dissatisfaction is increasing among (especially younger) men. Susan Paxton (1998) agrees, claiming that at least 10 per cent of patients presenting with anorexia are now male and the figures for bulimia are virtually the same for men and women. Cornell (1990) claims that the desire of men to be big and muscular is not necessarily to enhance their pre-existing masculinity, but in order to match standards of social norms and to be simply acknowledged as male. This aspiration has proved particularly acute for gay men.

On a broader scale, these masculinities are implicated in thef violence of global geo-politics. As Joshua Goldstein (2001) points out, the association of masculinity with warfare is perhaps the most universal of gender-based roles across cultures. Only gestation, which is biologically prescribed, is as common in gender specialization as the link between 'maleness' and war. This inscription of masculinity with a predisposition toward violence and warfare, however, is not inevitable, and as Goldstein explains, it is the imbrication of masculinity and particular forms of political conditions which makes the connection so virulent and dangerous. For Nancy Ehrenreich (2002), the historical and cultural amplitude of masculine violence has become a central feature of American militarism and its political hegemony, most particularly in the context of the global war on terror. The reconstruction of masculinity and masculine roles in personal as well as geo-political contexts is a precondition of better human relationships, human societies and world peace.

In this way, the cultural 'deficiencies' of men and masculinity have become the central target of critique in gender, peace and human relationships studies. For many in the field, the need for reconstruction of masculinity constitutes a form of 'crisis' by which men must adjust to the increasing power of women and their own culpability in the history of violence, abuse and oppression. Even so, and as Tim Edwards (2006) notes, this notion of crisis distracts somewhat from the complex history of culture and masculinity, homogenizing men and the extraordinary diversity of the male experience into a uni-dimensional and negative disposition.

COMMODIFICATION AND SPORT

When associated with other cultural hierarchies such as race and class, the problematic of masculinity is even further intensified. Undoubtedly sport and games were once deployed in culture as forms of recreation and play. At its more functionalist levels, however, sport provided the sort of physical training necessary for labour, economy and military deployment. In more developed cultures sport was also used as a form of social differentiation, often confirming the social distance not only between performers but also between performers and spectators (see Bourdieu, 1991). The codification of sport, which took place in the late part of the nineteenth century and primarily in Britain, also provided an ideological currency for the maintenance and administration of nation, nationalism and empire. The British game of cricket provided a facility for the promotion and maintenance of imperial ideology and the hegemony of the British Empire. The potency of masculinity manifest in male sporting prowess became a useful vehicle in the public demonstration of national values and national potency. In the 1936 Berlin Olympic Games, Adolf Hitler presented the virility and machismo of the Fatherland through the performances of his German Aryan athletes. Cold War tensions between the United States and the USSR were articulated in a nuclear arms race, battles over space, and a brutish Olympic competitiveness which culminated in reciprocal boycotts of the other's hosted Games. The murder of Israeli athletes in Munich by Palestinian militia represented the brutal conjunction of politics and sport. And at the Beijing Olympics (2008) China announced itself as an advanced, global economic power through the mission of its sporting prowess.

The Televisual Sporting Body

The evolution of television, satellite and digital technology has enabled immediate, global telecast of sporting events. In fact, along with the sexuality of young women, the greatest area of image proliferation has been in men's sport. The active male body as spectacle, therefore, has become engaged in new forms of televisual economy. Scarcity and capitalist value have found a new source of commodification, new forms of labour. The transfer of amateur or recreational sport into a highly valued commodity has brought new definitions to the nature and activity of sport. Bodies, male bodies in particular, have become defined in terms of excellence in action, a capacity to function at extreme levels of performance. Thus, the muscularity associated with industrial and military labour has been transformed into a muscularity of display. The product of the display is arousal that has no palpable resolution, no product, other than visual and visceral stimulation. Men are exalted and excited by the narrative of a sporting event, but the arousal can never be completed or satisfied. Like sexual arousal, like the commodity of the youthful female face, the sports body is a form of constituted symbolic value, an ephemeron, a discourse which can never be concluded because it never actually does anything except act out a narrative which will be perpetually emerging through the carnival of play and display.

The rise of the cult of the celebrity sports star produces new modes of subjectivity or self-presentation which are available for commodity consumption and the formation of celebrity community. As with movie stars or television celebrities, the sports celebrity has become a means of marketing the sport, the constituted individual, and the promise of identity for the consumer. Audiences (see Chapter 8) or 'spectators' are now able to constitute their own communities built around teams and individual performers. Whereas once these communities may have been located in villages and urban neighbourhoods, the transferal of sport into a TV commodity facilitates much broader engagements. The Chicago Bulls may now have followers in all parts of the United States as well as in Buenos Aires, Vancouver, Berlin or Christchurch. Manchester United is no longer located in the urban centre but is a spectator commodity available for community formation and consumption all over the globe. The sports stars of athletics or tennis are no longer confined to their home nation, but are available for spectacle and consumption in transnational communities that are linked not even by language, but through the televisual image and the merchandising magic that surrounds them.

Hierarchies and Winning Ways

The televisualization and globalization of sport have created a huge economy that is sustained less by the constitution of team, but more by the symbology of success. While numerous football followers invest themselves in the iconography of 'team' or 'club', the sustaining interest in that collective is the ideology of winning. Of course, this winning, or winning potential, is the ideological basis of capitalist economics. The joys and delights of winning, or imagining victory, are the sustaining power of loyalty and identity constitution. The self-projection of success – the same self-projection that operates in the broader capitalist economy – maintains the hapless football supporter through the often excessive tribulations of loss. Were it not for the glamourous elations of (imagined) success, then the capitalist dream would undoubtedly grind to a halt. Sport has become the natural bedfellow of an ideology which obscures the inevitability of dissatisfaction through a promise of achievement and victory.

Professional football competition is, perhaps, the most spectacular example of commercial manipulation. Football is played for TV, and the controllers of the sport in most parts of the world are manipulating the game to suit advertisement intervals and the spectacle of speed and action. Amidst the imagining of team loyalty, the promise of success is nearly always invested in individuals. Individual team members or stars are heavily marketed; sponsorship and membership, along with game attendance and TV rights, are lured through the presentation and potential of the 'latest young recruit', the new coach, the return of a star. Men, in particular, pay for the drama of sport, for the visceral excitement of its unfolding and for the athleticism of its action; but above all they pay for the imagining of success, an imagining in which they can participate and with which they can identify.

Not surprisingly, the often grotesque sums of money paid to sports celebrities and the manna maniacal prospecting for new recruits and stars provide significant opportunities for social mobility. African American and other coloured men in the United States experience low levels of education and opportunities for professional careers. As Blount and Cunningham (1996) have pointed out, the subjectivity of black men in dominant white culture has been substantially constructed through physical action and physical prowess. The complex representation of black men, most particularly in sport, constitutes a certain anxiety for the dominant culture, a certain 'antagonistic co-operation' (Blount and Cunningham, 1996: xi) whereby blackness and body become a reluctantly privileged cultural category which is built around a peculiar dialogue of fear and admiration. The popularity of boxing, especially amongst men, is necessarily linked to the coliseum mentality of discharging lesser minds and greater bodies into 'mortal' combat. The success of the Sylvester Stallone *Rocky* films, meanwhile, may be partly understood as the reassertion of white supremacy, where Rocky/Stallone represents the 'great white hope' for white masculinity.

Sport, that is, has come to be associated with particular ideologies of race and gender. Boxing, as perhaps the most brutal and confrontational of all sports, is conceived fundamentally as masculine, and generally a sport of the lowest socioeconomic groups. Other Olympic sports, such as synchronized swimming, are sneered at by many men because of their putative femininity. The radical overhaul of gender ascription, however, has led to much broader transferals in bodily deployment and social conceptions. Thus, while heterosexual beauty remains highly appealing for marketing and news copy, alternative sexualities and body constructions for women and men have become increasingly evident in sports communities. Perhaps the most radical of these new bodily forms is associated with the technology of performance-enhancing drugs, especially anabolic steroids (male hormones) and growth hormones.

Sport and Bodily Enhancements

Steroids and growth hormones are used for power sports – sprinting, short distance cycling, jumping, lifting and throwing events – in order to increase muscle mass and training effects. These power events generally rely on sudden explosions of energy and muscular exertion. The Cold War tensions between the United States and the USSR and its allies (1945–89) encouraged the development of a wide range of chemical and mechanical sporting technologies. Concentrated male hormones were first used by East German female sprinters at the Helsinki Games. Along with increased muscle mass, the steroids also produce significant bodily side-effects. For women, these could include increasing male characteristics such as facial hair, deepened voice, breast shrinkage, plus labial and clitoral development with significantly increased libido. Ironically, the increased muscle size and density for men is often accompanied by testicular shrinkage as the function of the testes is supplemented by an external agent. In both genders significant health risks have been reported, including loss of bone density as well as cardiovascular, respiratory and general heart problems. Deaths have been recorded, and there is some suspicion that the premature death of Florence Griffith-Joiner, the women's 100 metres world record holder, was associated with steroid taking.

For cultural analysis these bodily modifications are indicative of the openness of the body system and its vulnerability to cultural invasion. In everyday practice the deployment of steroids has been constituted around physical display and the problematic of gender ascriptions. While sports celebrities might use the steroids to enhance the possibility of success, non-elite sportspeople are using steroids increasingly to enhance the look of their body mass. Steroid taking is popular amongst bodybuilders, including communities of gay men. It may be that the conception of beauty and sexual attractiveness which dominates heterosexual culture has its own equivalent in gay communities. The youthful, sporting, masculine body which is so ubiquitously imaged in contemporary culture may well have been adapted into areas of gay sexuality where the discourse of masculinity is intensified as a new beauty myth.

SHAPING MASCULINITIES

There is no doubt that feminism has dominated discussions of the body, most particularly the sexualized or gendered body, since the 1960s. The preoccupation with women and women's bodies has tended to frame masculinity and male bodies in terms of patriarchy and the politics of sexism. In many respects, males have been seen as the perpetrators of women's subjugation, the cause of social misery and underprivilege (see Jeffreys, 2004). Where males have accepted these critiques, they have tended to cast themselves in the shame of their masculinity, rendering themselves and their bodies invisible as they seek to support feminist politics and the redress of gender discrimination. More recently, however, cultural analysis has become more interested in the formation of gender and the issue of masculinity in its own right. Men, in particular, have become more actively engaged in the study of culture and the discursive formation of masculine identity and gender politics.

In this sense, the rise of the so-called 'men's movement' in gender-based analysis of discourse and culture can be explained in the following terms:

1 A revision of structuralist approaches to gender (and class), and a reciprocal increase in analysis based on discourse and representation. The influence of Michel Foucault, in particular, encouraged many feminists to examine the concept of gender and the relationship between men and women in more expansive ways. Such analysis acknowledges the precarious nature of a reality that is mediated by discourse and which is constituted through an enormous variety of human characteristics and traits. Feminism revised its view that all women could be homogenized and categorized as a single social class; if women's identities were to be liberated, then differences between women must be recognized and encouraged. The notion, therefore, that all men constituted a single, homogeneous social class, which was responsible for patriarchy, had to be questioned. Equally, the relationship between men and women could not always be epitomized in terms of the ideology of patriarchy, as relationships between these two broad and diverse groups were constituted through a complex imbrication of discourses and localized truths.

2 These heterologies were also filtered through Foucault's theory of power. Rather than power being fixed in structures of class or gender, Foucault conceived of it as a process, an unstable exchange of positions and discourses. In particular, Foucault's notion of the 'microphysics of power' (Foucault, 1977a) was contentious for many feminists, who returned to statistical summaries of social differentiation to justify their outrage against the structured inequality and oppression of women by men. However, as Foucault and neo-Foucauldian feminists have explained, these statistics might actually camouflage important aspects of social and cultural life, which include the social limits placed on men as much as on women. The Foucauldian approach to power, in fact, facilitates greater agency for women and for men to overcome these limits, and for the construction of new relationships and new discourses based on equality and partnership.

3 This desire to improve personal relationships through the reformulation of gender ascriptions and gender-based discourses, including the discourses of power, has been influenced by the interests and approaches of the rising generation of mothers. These new generation mothers are seeking enhanced intimacies and friendships with sons and male partners without recourse to 'hard-line' assaults on men and masculinity. These relational aspirations are occurring where the notion of gender equality is a given, rather than a radical reformulation. Women want better men, and it may be that the liberation of men is the best way of achieving that end. Moreover, the reformulation of women's subjectivities has necessarily stimulated changes for men and their relationships. The difficulties and pleasures associated with these changes have forced many men to ask

questions about their own identities and the cultural meaning of their own bodies – their role in work, military activities, sports, and so on.

4   Poststructuralism, postmodernism and discourse theory have all contributed to the broadening of the cultural politics agenda. In particular, the raising of the issue of sexuality and identity has facilitated greater interest in ethnicity, race and postcolonialism. These politics have been welded to issues of women's rights and gender; however, once problematized, the questions of gender and its relationship to other forms of cultural politics necessarily implicates the condition of men and their masculinity. Thus, the social, economic and health condition of many indigenous peoples of the world will inevitably involve gender-specific issues: the reproductivity of women, for example, and alcoholism and violence among men. This re-focusing or broadening of the cultural politics agenda demonstrates that men, as well as women, continue to suffer significant privation and oppression.

5   This has been particularly pertinent in issues of sexuality, where gay men have felt excluded from the feminist agenda. That is, while accepting the potency of feminist approaches to questions of sexuality and gender, gay men's groups have at times felt that their particular questions about masculinity, identity and sexuality have been ignored in the cultural politics of feminism.

6   The fracturing of the feminist intellectual hegemony in the 1990s has paradoxically opened a space for greater masculine self-reflection. As feminists have begun to deconstruct their feminist heritage, a number of men have found the space to consider the negative dimensions of masculinity: the problematics of their relationships with other men, including their fathers; aggression; violence; muscularity; unattainable social expectations; the denial of nurturing; and so on.

Clearly, and as Homi Bhabha (1994; also Edwards, 2006) reminds us, masculinity should not be fixed to the condition of the biologically gendered male body as opposition to the biologically gendered female body. Of course notions of femininity are often associated with female bodies, and masculinity is associated with male bodies. However, our analysis of the body has demonstrated how these cultural ascriptions may be inverted or destabilized by transgressive bodily practices and the processes of deconstruction and semiotic reconstruction. Within this general frame it is clear that the notions of masculinity and masculine identity are formed around a broad range of subject positions and discourses. Masculinity, that is, must be read as text or a set of competing discourses; inevitably these discourses engage with questions of patriarchy, privilege and power that are so often associated with the concept of male.

Anxiety and Power

A good deal of the recent discussion on masculinity has, in fact, applied a fairly familiar feminist mode of analysis, most particularly in relation to forms of social expectation and the representation of male body ideals. Just as women experience a range of psychological

Plate 9.1   *Busting Air*

Male performativity is often constituted around physical prowess and risk-taking, including the risk of bodily damage. For all its utopian idealism, surfing is dominated by a male culture and men who consistently seek the perfect wave through acculturated modes of risk-taking and interpersonal aggression. 'Busting air', a manoeuvre adopted from skateboarding, can produce horrendous injuries such as broken ankles and legs, concussion and serious spinal damage. But it is also an expression of extraordinary courage, skill and masculine grace.

and emotional dissonances through not being able to meet unrealistic body ideals, so men experience dissonance in not approximating their own muscular and powerful ideal. The privileges and power which patriarchy accords to masculinity may also function to produce men's sense of inadequacy and humiliation when they fail to fully exploit this cultural and political privilege. As David Buchbinder has put it, the key to men's social performance is the recognition of this privilege of masculinity:

The process of recognition begins with the body: for what all boys and men apparently have in common, transcending differences of race, culture and class, traversing the distinctions of occupation, and crossing the limits even of time and history, is of course the penis. (1998: 29)

As we have noted, this (minor) biological difference is constituted symbolically in discourse; the penis is not just a biological organ, it is the representative of an expansive history of power and control (phallus). As Judith Butler (1995) explains, gender itself is more than merely constructed, it is actually 'performed'; the complex meanings associated with gender are therefore rendered as operations in behaviour, choice and representation. Men perform their masculinity as the ongoing and constantly reforming process of patriarchy. The anxieties of men are embedded, therefore, in their social responsibilities as much as in their personal self-image (Pease, 2000). The system, with all its privileges and pleasures, is founded on masculinity: to fail one's own masculinity is to fail the system.

This fear of inadequacy or failure in men has often been vested in physical and sexual performance. Pathologies like impotence are the most commonly reported sexual problem for men. The ceaseless threat of attack by other males and the need to protect sexual and genetic territory create profound, if subterranean, fears for men. Comparative demographies show that at any age level men suffer much higher rates of death and bodily harm than do women. Young men are the most assaulted and murdered group in the community; they are more likely to die or be seriously injured in motor accidents than are women; they are about five times more likely to commit suicide; and they have much higher rates of disease. While the reasons for these significantly greater rates of bodily damage amongst men are varied and complex, there can be little doubt that the imperative to perform, including acts of violence and self-violence, remains remarkably resilient, even in a broader culture in which women and femininities have changed so markedly.

Masculininist analysis of this kind is designed to liberate men from the bondage of patriarchal ideologies. Many feminists and cultural commentators, however, have been hostile to the male movement, arguing that the whole notion of male 'victimism' is an offence to the project of female emancipation. George Yodice (1995) points out, for example, that a number of men may be taking up the victim position in order to rearticulate and reconstruct contemporary discourses, including liberatory discourses. Yodice points to a number of examples of males appropriating feminist discourses in order to reposition their 'hegemony'. Citing Antonio Gramsci's notion of hegemony as a form of negotiated leadership, he explains that men may simply be maintaining their domination through an interaction with feminist discourse. If males are also 'victims' of patriarchal systems, and masculinity is the outcome of that oppressive representational code, then they are justified in (re)claiming a liberated social prominence. In other words, that part of the men's movement that articulates men's cultural and social experiences in terms of an oppressive patriarchy may be surreptitiously reconstructing their dominance.

POSTHUMAN BODIES

As elaborated in our discussion of new technologies (Chapter 11), there has been a great surge in interest in the notion of posthuman bodies, most particularly those of the technology–human hybrid, the cyborg. Cultural theorists like Donna Haraway have conceived of the cyborg as a utopian ideal through which humans will evolve a more egalitarian and inclusive consciousness; the body of the cyborg will be liberated from the limiting physiognomy of race, age, gender and sexual orientation. The notion of posthumanism is also discussed by less extravagant commentators, who point to the incorporation of various technologies into human morphology as evidence of an advanced human condition. Such enhancements would include spectacles, hearing aids, wheelchairs and prosthetics (breast implants, skeletal plates, pins and joint replacements). For many theorists of the posthuman condition, digital technology, more so than mechanical and electrical analogue technologies, mimics and enhances the very essence of our humanity: our neurological (brain and nerve) system.

Perhaps the most complex of these technological supplements, one most clearly heralding changes to our humanity, is the bionic ear. The bionic ear is a replacement for the complex system of aural neuro-receptors that have been damaged or diseased. However, rather than acting as an analogue amplification of sounds, the bionic ear actually receives external stimulus (sound), which it then re-transmits to the brain. These electromagnetic stimuli must then be unscrambled and reconstituted as meaningful sounds. The sounds that a bionic ear is hearing and transmitting, in fact, are entirely different from those of a 'normal' ear; the bionic-eared human is receiving different sounds which constitute a different world experience, a different language, a different interpretational field. The bionic ear, which is a form of smart technology, may herald the sort of hybrid humanity that Haraway and others anticipate, most especially when combined with various forms of genetically engineered or cloned human organic material.

Posthuman discourse, however, also incorporates those theories which are antagonistic toward the ideology of humanism. A number of critics, especially working through radical, feminist and 'queer' liberationism, have taken a strident anti-humanist approach to the body and the ideological humanism which houses it. Judith Halberstam and Ira Livingston argue that these forms of radical posthuman bodies 'thrive in subcultures without culture' (1995: 4). What is meant here is that culture is a dominant 'imaginary' or ideology which subsumes diversity and difference. Humanism, with its ideology of inclusiveness and uniform liberationism, actually violates the forming of human meanings, closing itself and its borders around the notion of 'culture'. 'Culture' is complete and marked at the borders; 'subculture' reopens the possibilities of an ongoing exploration of subjectivity, community and meaning-making. Posthumanism allows sub-cultures to experience their difference without recourse to dominant cultural terms. In other words, the bodily forms of the sub-culture remain emancipated when they are different, uncommodified and unexploited for general perception and consumption. The posthuman body is entirely liberational as it shows the significance of the family as a patriarchal, sexual and reproductive unit. This system, which specifies 'who can fuck what and how' (Halberstan and Livingston, 1995: 11), is replaced by a heterogeneous assemblage of choosing people, a sexuality that resists gender distinctions and a reproductivity which liberates women from the onus of biological replenishment.

Michel Foucault, of course, had imagined a time when reproduction and sexuality would be entirely divorced, and the possibilities of surrogate motherhood and male pregnancy would become desirable reproductive options (Foucault, 1981: 105). This drawing from the posthuman margins might ultimately obliterate the final, biological hierarchy in gender relations. Radical posthumanism, therefore, seeks to present human bodies as the means of liberation and not its expressive limits. Masculinity and femininity would be entirely merged, reconstituting bodily variations as another opportunity in the heterology of bodily pleasures and bodily postures.

Supporters of these radical conceits are careful to insist that the liberation they envisage will always resist homogenization, that the plurality of the body is never threatened by the 'assemblage' of cultural normalism; the posthuman body cannot ossify as an essential and monadic entity. Posthumanism, that is, is conceived as an heterological phenomenon, an ephemeron which is neither atomic and infinitely unmediated, nor concrete and immovable. The heterogeneity is assured. Even so, and this remains a problem for most postmodern utopianism, the radical conceit is built around the same sort of hostilities that parade men and masculinity as the ultimate terror. Posthumanism seeks to obliterate all traces of a masculinity which is conceived as the ultimate enemy of liberation. The merging of gender is not the hybridization of particular human variations, but an assimilation of only those (feminine) characteristics which are sustaining and generative. The gender pool is thus reduced as posthumanism cannot accept those characteristics which do not fit the political formula. While claiming that posthumanism is decidedly marginal and sub-cultural, posthumanists nevertheless prescribe a social condition which excludes a variety of masculine and feminine discourses and experiences. The passion of the reform leaves little space for alternatives to the prescribed political order.

Posthumanism of this kind overlooks the generative and positive dimensions of masculinities. Indeed, the literature on bodies has tended to treat masculinity generally as negative. Indeed, maleness and male bodies are by and large ignored unless they are operating at the margins and can be easily typified as non-white, non-straight. In fact, masculinities are as broad and varied as femininities. Even the categories of distinction which currently operate are many and varied and the investment of males and females with the broad sweep of the oppositional typologies is already quite inappropriate. The literature fails to deal adequately with the complex associations which constitute differences and similarities between gender, nor does it adequately deal with the struggles which can produce joyful and generative moments. The pandemic of dissatisfaction that unquestionably plagues us can only partly be explained by the limiting effects of gendered bodily experiences. Our bodies return us pleasure and pain. Our loves and distresses, our consonances and dissonances are not to be resolved in a posthuman idealization.

10

Globalization and Global Spaces: Local Transformations

INTRODUCTION

In general, 'globalization' refers to a set of processes involving interaction between different peoples, institutions, communities and organizations across political and culturally constituted borders. Beyond this general definition, however, there is very little agreement amongst scholars about the origins, impact, value, directions and character of these processes. For many commentators, globalization processes are largely constituted around changes in the global, capitalist economy (Sklair, 2002); however, others believe that globalization is driven primarily by communications, media and cultural 'flows' (Appadurai, 1990; Fetaherstone, 1996; Tomlinson, 1999) which are themselves associated with distinct sociological, spatial and political conditions (Giddens, 1990; Castells, 1997; Held et al., 1999; Urry, 2003). While some theorists regard 'globalization' as a relatively new phenomenon, involving the formation of institutions that have transcended older political and organizational institutions like 'nation', others believe that globalization is articulated through a transformational continuum that moves toward, against and through various socially constituted formations – global, national, imperial, regional and local (Robertson, 2000; Bauman, 2004).

In this chapter we will examine these transformations in detail. As a beginning point, however, we need to identify the key variations in the ways scholars conceive of the ideological framework of globalization. These variations can be summarized as follows –

1   It is a process which is associated with the formation of a 'world system' in which economy, communications, culture and politics are integrated into a substantial transnational order. While many economists regard this system as an inevitable evolution of free market capitalism, other commentators claim that it is also being formed around global social

movements associated with 'democracy, community, gender, religion, ethnicity, age, ecology, disability, sexuality and … human rights' (Sklair, 2002: 2). This description of globalization is close to what Marshall McLuhan calls 'the global village', a site in which human diversity is being reshaped into a more or less homogeneous global order.

2   For many theorists who follow this line of argument, the homogenization of the world's diverse peoples is being largely directed through Western styles of economy and culture. As the sole superpower and dominant economic force, the United States in particular is imposing itself over the rest of the world, drawing all peoples and cultures into the web of its military, ideological and national interests. The notion of globalization, therefore is seen as a form of new imperialism ('Americanization') in which the US is the *de facto* world government.

3   It is a process by which different cultures, peoples and nations become increasingly engaged with one another, but where this contiguity provides space for enhanced, rather than diminished, localism, heterogeneity and cultural difference. While some proponents of this argument valorize resistant and 'anti-globalization' communities, others see the interaction within globalization as providing new spaces for local creativity. Thus, the cultural styles and products generated through globalization (music, TV, film, the Internet) facilitate the production of new hybrid forms and new diversity. Globalization is thus two-way, providing new cultural resources for enhanced localism and the reshaping of local identity. This 'glocalization' argument (Robertson, 2000) is generally at odds with the cultural imperialism, 'Americanization' arguments outlined above.

As we shall see in the course of this chapter, each of these arguments has a level of validity; globalization is a complex and historically dense set of processes which, like culture itself, may be simultaneously conjunctive and entirely contradictory. This chapter seeks to reconcile these different heuristic and ideological perspectives in order to more clearly define 'globalization' and the ways in which it is accelerating in the current world, cultural context. From this perspective, globalization has deep roots in history, but is assuming a more formidable demeanour through the conduit of new media and information exchange processes which are drawing complex ideologies and meanings into greater contiguity and contest.

LOCATING GLOBALIZATION

Transnational globalization begins to accelerate in the post-World War Two period, as developed nations settle into a new phase of economic interdependence and market expansion. In a broader historical reading, however, trans-cultural and trans-spatial interaction between different peoples and communities precedes the formation of 'nation', extending to the earliest periods of human migration. In fact, it appears that the major land masses of Africa, Europe, Asia and Australia were inhabited by humans at around 50–70,000 years Before Present (BP). These hunter-gatherer tribal groups, however, could not survive the new forms of territorialism and economy created by agricultural, warrior societies which first appeared around the Mediterranean and Middle East around 10,000 years BP. The pattern of military expansion and colonization, which shaped the great Classical and Eastern empires, ultimately evolved into the modern, industrial system and its immense capacity for resource expropriation, territorial control and political violence. As the large-scale social units called 'nation' evolved in Europe between 150 and 400 years ago, various forms of transnational interaction created new conditions for trade, territorialism, warfare and ultimately empire. From the eighteenth century, in particular, new discourses of 'civilization' and the validity of empire accompanied the expansion of European economic interests, constructing a complex network of administrative and ideological power grids across the globe.

As noted above, the current phase of globalization extends many of the earlier patterns of developed world imperialism. And while many people, including people in the post-colonized world, remain bitterly hostile to the history and legacy of imperialism, others regard the process as more politically neutral – a continuation of human progress and the inevitability of ever-larger social units (Hardt and Negri, 2000, also 2004). In either case, contemporary globalization integrates earlier social patterns, practices, processes and ideologies with new forms of cultural exchange. These exchanges have themselves been enhanced and facilitated by the emergence of new networked media and communications. According to Anthony Giddens, these accelerating systems of exchange and communication create the conditions for 'action at a distance' (1990: 19) or 'distant proximity' as it is called by James Rosenan (2003).

The emergence of new media and communication systems, however, does not in itself explain the increasing intensity of global cultural contiguity and exchange. The contemporary global panorama might best be understood as a series of discursive flows and assemblages formed around the imperatives of economy, media, politics and what I would call 'bionomy' (biological flows). It is the totality of these overlapping discursive forms that constitutes the best definition of globalization.

1   *Economy.* Capitalism is built around the imperative of competition, economic growth and the expansion of markets. Early capitalism was able to exploit cheap labour and resources in order to produce goods; the need continually to expand markets led capitalists to trade these goods internationally. The growth imperative led to the development of large, multinational corporations. These corporations, which are no longer bound by national borders, continue to seek the cheapest labour and the most profitable markets. While international trade has always been a significant component of capitalism, the post World War Two period has been characterized by –

   • the emergence of new media-based products and services which can be exchanged almost instantaneously

- the emergence of global financial markets which have stimulated the formation of massive, transnational corporations which are able to exert considerable economic and political pressure on sovereign governments
- the de-regulation of national economies, including strategically constructed free trade agreements
- the emergence of global free trade and market economy financial institutions, including the World Trade Organization, the World Bank, the Asian Development Bank and the United Nations Development Fund – all of which exert political and economic pressure on sovereign governments, especially in the developing world
- the intensification of the free market ideology (economic rationalism) in First World nations, creating conditions for the deconstruction of social welfare and the regulation of labour
- the decline of manufacturing and Fordist-style mass production in Western developed nations and the rise of the information economy associated with new managerial styles and 'flexible' working arrangements
- increased competition to the economic primacy of Western developed nations, especially from low labour cost countries. High levels of economic growth associated with cheap labour and efficient infrastructure strategies began in Japan, then spread outwards to Korea, Taiwan, Singapore, Central America, China and India.

2 *Media.* From the emergence of telegraphy in the nineteenth century, communication has been liberated from the constraints of space and time. Broadcast media, telecommunications, satellite technology and networked computer communication have facilitated the expansion in global cultural consciousness – the instantaneous exposure of local cultural groups to an infinite array of different cultural sites and possibilities. The flooding of global marketplaces with information and imagery has altered the cultural horizons and knowledge of all people with access to the media.

3 *Politics and ideology.* These exposures inevitably affect the formation of cultural politics, including the global distribution of ideologies. Just as print facilitated the broadening and multiplication of ideologies, electronic media have stimulated new modes of thinking and political perspectives. The constellation of these modes of political expressivity may form a 'dominant ideology' constituted around various forms of 'authority' (nationalism, 'America', capitalism, sovereign government). Equally, however, the new media facilitate the distribution of alternative and oppositional discursive modes which may themselves constitute a significant political belief system (human rights, feminism, radical Islam, gay liberation). In either case, these competing political discourses or language wars are critically engaged in the broadening of the cultural field across borders.

4   *Global institutions.* The formation of distinctly globalist ideologies such as capitalism, democracy and progress has been accompanied by attempts to form global organizations which may support or challenge these dominant beliefs and political discourses. Institutions such as the World Trade Organization, the United Nations, the World Court, the Olympic Federation and UNESCO are constructed around forms of dominant order. The International Red Cross and Care are formed as antitheses to military solutions. Greenpeace and international terrorist/freedom fighter organizations are designed to challenge global hegemony. Within this broad global framework there exist innumerable local politics which are more modest in their aspirations and designs. In many respects, these international organizations are part of an inchoate global civil order bearing the contrary impulses toward greater centralizing world government, and a more distinctly participative communal effect.

5   *Bionomy.* Human beings are among the most recently evolved organisms to inhabit the Earth's biosphere. Having distributed themselves across the globe in a relatively short period, humans have only very recently produced major disruptions to the natural ecology. In fact, the disruption and damage of the past fifty years is far more significant than for the previous two million years of human evolution and presence in the biosphere. Global economy and the proliferation of the human species are collapsing distinct natural ecosystems into a hybrid form. This hybridized, global environment is producing the greatest species extinction since the comet catastrophe which blackened the planet and obliterated 100 million years of dinosaur domination.

While a good deal of globalist discourse celebrates this new mixing of cultures and peoples, bionomic globalization is producing substantive changes to the biosphere itself. The increasing size and density of human population, along with grotesquely differentiated levels of resource consumption, represents the major feature of bionomic globalization. Human subjectivity and identity, the most personal dimensions of culture, are being radically transformed by the propinquities of other human subjectivities and bodies. Humans are on the move: at any one time there are as many as 100 million people preparing to move between national territories, at least 5–10 million of whom have no official documentation. As resources become more scarce, as wars, famines and natural disasters become more frequent, as the poorer localities of the world become more restless, and refugee camps swell, the flow of human migrations across the globe will surge to a torrent. Along with increasing business travel and tourism activities in the developed world, these vast movements of human beings will continue to alter irrevocably older biospheric forms, creating hybrid agricultural patterns, salination and expanding deserts, deforestation, polluted and touristized coastlines, and ever-broadening, continually denuded fields of urban landscape. And while the Human Security Centre report of 2005 (*War and Peace in the 21st Century*) declares that First World countries are experiencing an historically unparalleled period of security, the bionomic conditions for the vast majority of humans is precarious and wracked by disease, violence, starvation and warfare.

GLOBALIZATION, RACE AND HISTORICAL IMPERIALISM

Postcolonial Theory

The recent phase of globalization is characterized by particular forms of political and cultural realignment. The bionomic conditions outlined above are clearly the outcome of complex flows and processes associated with human mobility, interaction and the tensions generated by increasing cultural contiguity. In many respects the cultural construction of 'race' and 'ethnicity' is linked directly to these globalizing processes: within a context of extreme competition for limited economic resources, more powerful human groups seek to impose themselves, their identity and interests over other groups. During the modern period, the hierarchical divisions that had evolved around class and gender were supplemented and fortified by the social ordering of nation, empire, race and ethnicity. As part of the moral justification for their appropriation of other peoples' territories, the militarily powerful nations of the modern world categorized their conquered peoples according to variations in skin colour, skeletal structure, language and cultural practices. Race and racism was invented, therefore, as part of an imperial discourse – the cultural validation for economic exploitation.

But empire was not a pure ideology, and through the ferment of oppositional discourses and the bloody devastation of World War Two, a US-led process of de-colonization significantly changed the cultural calibre of the global order. This is not to say that the release of colonized territories was smooth or bloodless. Nationalist movements within the colonized states had been active throughout the century and the weaknesses of the colonial administration during and after the War provided significant opportunities for activism and military resistance.

Thus, whether by force or grace, the de-colonizing experience has proved complex and profoundly problematic for the peoples and cultures of the previously colonized territories. One of the most significant of these problems is the relationship between the former colonizers and their former subjects. As Homi Bhabha (1990) has pointed out, the nub of this relationship is a form of mutual dependence and antagonism, a form of identity production which never allows the formerly colonized people to be entirely free of their colonial masters and colonial past. Bhabha's point can be elaborated in three ways:

1 The actual construction of the new territory, the new nation, is produced by the colonizer's politics and cartography. The distribution of territories across the Middle East, Indochina, South-East Asia and Africa was facilitated by the interests and international relations of European nations. Cartographers simply drew lines around the map and distributed the territories according to the interests and claims of disputing colonial nations. The 'nationalism' of the colonized peoples is formed, therefore, out of the political pragmatism of the colonial administrators. The instability and ethno-sectarian

    violence being experienced in Iraq, the Balkan states and Rwanda are a direct result of this cartographic pragmatism and resonance of colonial modernization.

2   The whole notion of nation and national culture is a product of the colonizers' own cultural consciousness. Nation, that is, as a form of 'imagined community' (Anderson, 1991) is constructed out of the very fabric of European culture and has little to do with the indigenous people and culture that have been colonized. Postcolonial nationalism, therefore, was actually a transferal of the conquerors' own nationalist imaginary

3   This national consciousness, in fact, is produced locally through the formation of culture and identity. The intense interactions between colonizer and colonized produce a new subjectivity for the colonized person. He or she will think in terms of 'nation', and will locate that sensibility in cultural elements that are highlighted by colonization. For example, the nation of 'Indonesia' was constructed out of vastly differing territories, languages, cultures and ethnic groups. This blending consciousness had to reconstruct the differences in an intensely contiguous symbolic form. The Dutch colonial cartography that created the Dutch East Indies was then re-worked by Sukarno and other resistance fighters to form an assemblage of symbolic typology – the *Pancasila* which formed the basic principles of constitution and nation of Indonesia. Similarly, the Indian national flag juxtaposes the orange of Hindu, the green of Islam and the traditional wheel symbol of Buddhism. The new subjectivity of nation is supposed to harmonize these constituent and otherwise contending elements.

    One of the major resonances of the colonial period is the rise of a form of reformist cultural politics which seeks to liberate previously colonized peoples from the aftermath of ideological, cultural and economic domination. In fact, different groups who were the victims of colonization have experienced the residues of oppression in different ways. According to postcolonial reformist theory, however, all diasporic peoples have their humiliation, privation and oppression in common; this shared experience unites postcolonial people whether they are descendants of African slaves (e.g., Black Americans), minority tribal cultures (e.g., Canadian Cree) or majority agrarian cultures (e.g., Indians).

    In this sense, postcolonial theory borrows from psychoanalytic and poststructuralist theory to explain the sense of these peoples being something 'other' than what a culture deems as normal, powerful or the standard. Most particularly, postcolonized peoples of colour are defined as 'the other' or as 'different' in relation to the normative condition of 'whiteness', especially male whiteness. The challenge for postcolonial and cultural politics is to reconfigure the world in terms of a multicultural norm, where being 'different' is a condition of pride and normality, as well as a rallying point for political resistance. In particular, it is the liberation from externally imposed identities which, for postcolonial theorists, offers the greatest possibilities for the completion of de-colonization (Castells, 1997; Bauman, 2004).

Edward Said: Orientalism

Edward Said has attempted to explain the postcolonial experience in terms of discursive hegemony in the formerly colonized world. Said uses Michel Foucault's genealogical methodology (see Chapter 5) to elucidate the mechanisms by which the 'West' defines itself against the otherness of the 'East'. Said's genealogy, however, seeks a political explanation for the subjugation of the colonized world, most particularly in terms of material and discursive privation. Just as Stuart Hall's encoding/decoding theory had been deployed for the elucidation of ideology and hegemony within developed world textualities (Chapter 4), Said's genealogy seeks to elucidate the power/ knowledge discourses which inform the West's conceptions of itself in relation to the non-West. In narratizing the 'Orient', Said argues, the Western text is fundamentally telling its own story about its own superiority. Moreover, for Said, all discourses are political or ideological, and there can be no simple separation of the past from the present. The present condition draws its relevance and form from the past: 'Past and present inform each other; each implies the other, and in the totally ideal sense, ... each co-exists with the other' (Said, 1993: 2).

In *Orientalism* (1978) Said establishes the grounds for analyzing the West's discursive construction of itself in relation to the Orient. The central issue for Said relates to the means by which realities are mediated linguistically, and the ways hegemonies and dominant ideologies are imposed:

> My contention is that without examining Orientalism as a discourse one cannot possibly understand the enormously systematic discipline by which European culture was able to manage – and even produce – the Orient politically, sociologically, militarily, ideologically, scientifically, and imaginatively during the post-Enlightenment period. Moreover, so authoritative a position did Orientalism have that I believe no one writing, thinking, or acting on the Orient could do so without taking account of the limitations on thought and action imposed by Orientalism. (1978: 3)

Orientalism, in other words, is the ideologically informed system which presents the non-West as the other, the 'Orient'; in the Orientalist system it is the deficiencies of this otherness which renders it (legitimately) available for Western discipline and control.

While Said insists that the voice of Orientalism does not speak for the whole of the Orient, he makes clear that Orientalism itself represents a network 'inevitably brought to bear on (and therefore always involved in) any occasion when that peculiar entity "the Orient" is in question' (Said, 1978: 3). Said's project, therefore, is to elucidate the sources and fallibilities of Orientalism in Enlightenment scholarship. In political terms, Said seeks to deconstruct the linguistic formations themselves in order to expose their critical and ideological foundations and the ways they have continued to influence contemporary thought. Orientalism is not merely the linguistic facility deployed by colonial administration, but a product of the knowledge system of imperialism and power. Both the knowledge system and its equivalent material system functioned to control the colonized people, as well as justify this control in the minds of the imperial subjects – at home and in the colonies.

It is this theme which is more fully elaborated in Said's more recent work *Culture and Imperialism*, where Said suggests that 'the enterprise of empire depends on the idea of having an empire … and all kinds of preparations are made for it within a culture; then in turn imperialism acquires a kind of coherence, a set of experiences and a presence of ruler and ruled alike within the culture' (1993: 10). Indeed, as a Palestinian-Egyptian, born in Jerusalem and now living and working in the United States, Said is particularly sensitive to the hegemonic impositions of imperial Enlightenment discourse over the Middle East, and his own scholarship is very much influenced by what Foucault succinctly calls 'the history of the present': that is, the processes by which the world becomes modern. Most particularly, Said is concerned to demonstrate how the discursive formations of power/knowledge become identified with the material oppression of the Middle East by contemporary Western powers, especially the United States. Thus, in outlining the general scholarly project of *Orientalism*, Said insists that,

> Positively, I do believe – and in my other work have tried to show – that enough is being done today in the human sciences to provide the contemporary scholar with insights, methods, and ideas that could dispense with racial, ideological, and imperialist stereotypes of the sort provided during its historical ascendancy by Orientalism. … If the knowledge of Orientalism has any meaning, it is in being a reminder of the seductive degradation of knowledge, of any knowledge, anywhere, at any time. Now perhaps more than before. (1978: 328)

Said, while applauding what he describes as Foucault's 'imagination of power', nevertheless laments his 'profoundly pessimistic' view of modern society, a view circumscribed by 'a singular lack of interest in the force of effective resistance to it, in choosing particular sites of intensity, choices which … always exist and are often successful in impeding, if not actually stopping, the progress of tyrannical power' (1986: 151). Thus, while Said's own work on writing and discourse is clearly influenced by French poststructuralism, he finds ultimately that Foucault's microphysics does not satisfy the demands of contemporary liberation, being no more than an 'imagination' of a power that seems 'irresistible and unopposable', and which fails to condemn the banality and irresponsibility of corporate managers by its own elimination 'of classical ideas about ruling classes and dominant interests' (1986: 152).

A vocal critic of the US involvement in the Gulf War (1990–1) and US Middle East policies more generally, Said seeks a political solution to the hegemonies which continue to subjugate people of difference, people of the non-developed anglophone world. In *Culture and Imperialism*, Said insists on actual solutions to the propagation of imagined identities and cultures:

> For the purpose of this book I have maintained a focus on actual contests over land and the land's people. What I have tried to do is a kind of geographical inquiry into historical experiences, and I have kept in mind the idea that the earth is in effect one world in which empty, virtually uninhabited spaces do not exist. (1993: 6)

Most particularly, Said has been interested in the means by which the First World has been able to appropriate and administer the vast territories of the world, including Middle Asia. To this extent, he distinguishes between 'colonialism', the conquest and administration of external territories, and 'imperialism', the ongoing and cultural dimensions of identity projection and control:

> '[I]mperialism' means the practice, the theory, and the attitudes of a dominating metropolitan centre ruling a distant territory; 'colonialism', which is almost always a consequence of imperialism, is the implanting of settlements on distant territory. … In our time, colonialism has ended; imperialism, as we shall see, lingers where it has always been, in a kind of general cultural space, as well as in specific political, ideological, economic, and social practices. (1993: 8)

In this sense, imperialism works with racism to form imaginings and practices which pervade the modern and postmodern consciousness. Critics disagree about the extent of racist imagining, and while various legislative and institutional regulations have been instigated in order to ameliorate their effects, there can be little doubt that the sense of insider–outsider imagining continues to pervade culture (see also Cartells, 1997; Bauman, 2004). In his most recent book, an autobiography entitled *Out of Place* (1999), Said assaults directly the problematic of racism in contemporary American culture, most particularly as it is manifest in anti-Islamic and anti-Arabic media representation and government policy. After living and working for forty years in New York, Said expresses his own sense of alienation in a culture which constantly parades the ethos of pluralism and freedom, but which maintains deep suspicions of its own internal constituency, its own people who live precariously on the edge of different worlds and different ideologies.

Prior to his death in 2003, Said was a vehement supporter of the Palestinian cause and critic of US foreign policy in the Middle East. Moving beyond theory and textual analysis, Said was bitterly opposed to the American-led invasion of Iraq (2002), arguing that the delicacy of the tribal, cultural and ethnic constituency of Iraq would erupt into violent civil war if the political balance were disturbed by American hegemony and imperialist ambitions.

MULTICULTURALISM

Multiculturalism vs Pluralism

While Said and others regard contemporary culture as inevitably imperialist and racist, other critics draw hope from the reformulation of cultural heterogeneity. One of the effects of colonialism has been the integration of formerly colonized peoples into the ethnic mix of the First World. The once normative, in some cases exclusivist, status of homogeneous white culture within developed nations has been radically altered by migration during the past fifty years. The absorption of these various peoples into a pre-existing national–cultural formation, most especially those from non-European cultures, has required a substantial shift in ideological and discursive frames. While numerous critics, including Edward Said, have seen this integration process as largely imperfect, a series of public and government representatives have used a range of regulatory and institutional processes to promote new forms of national and cultural imagining. 'Multiculturalism', in particular, has been promoted in several countries as a means of imagining nation and national culture which is liberated from race-based identity. In fact, multiculturalism attempts to create a postmodernist ethos which forms a cultural assemblage around the notion of 'unity in diversity', a sense in which the various peoples and cultures which may constitute a national imaginary are free to experience their diversity without surrendering the validity of the whole state. This form of multicultural democracy idealizes difference by promoting a healthy interactive tolerance; the nation is no longer a contingency of racial and cultural homogeneity, but is a formation which acknowledges the great diversity in human groups and the advantages of harmonious interaction and co-operative, creative organizational processes.

Multiculturalism has been offered as a solution to the bionomic hybridities and propinquities of globalization. It is significantly different from the liberalist pluralism which had functioned as a cultural and social norm in the United States (see Modood et al., 2006). According to multicultural theory, pluralism is a form of false harmony which subsumes the diversity and dignity of migrating groups beneath the ethos of 'assimilation'. In the United States cultural difference was obliterated or significantly subjugated by an obedience to American capitalist/utilitarian principles and the grandeur of the American Dream of individual, material prosperity. American jingoism, that is, subsumed all other ideologies and discourses beneath the privilege of belonging to 'the greatest nation on Earth'.

The weaknesses of this pluralist discourse, however, are exposed in the continuation of forms of racism, Orientalism and imperialism in American culture and public policy. Multiculturalism, which liberates individuals and groups from the extremes of homogenized and collective identities, produces a more open and respectful acceptance of cultural difference, both within and necessarily outside the borders of nation. According to its proponents, multiculturalism avoids the hierarchies that are implicit in American-style pluralism and the assumptions which treat otherness as the sanctioned addendum to core cultural standards.

For Mark Poster, multiculturalism promotes an ideology of ethnic and cultural mixing both within and outside the borders of the nation-state (1995: 40–2). Poster argues that the poststructuralist/post modernist project of cultural heterogenization, the dissolution of Western *logos* and ethno-centricism, and the approbation of multiple linguistic forms are parallel with multiculturalist ambitions of dissolving geographic, cultural and ethnic borders. The new communications technologies are central for reordering and reconstituting subjectivities and cultural space. Poster recognizes that some political multiculturalists would privilege Developing World or minority group subjectivities, thus risking the return of postcolonial political essentialism; such a restoration, however, would inevitably transgress the potentialities of poststructuralist theoretics, and more particularly the opportunities presented by the new media:

> In this case, multiculturalism is a process of subject constitution, not an affirmation of an essence. As the second media age unfolds and permeates everyday practice, one political issue will be the construction of new combinations of technology with multiple genders and ethnicities. These technocultures will hopefully be no return to essence, no new foundationalism or essentialism, but a coming to terms with the process of identity constitution and doing so in ways that struggle against restrictions of systematic inequalities, hierarchies and asymmetries. (1995: 42)

The diffusion of developed national cultures into more heterogeneous forms has prompted critics like Anthony Giddens (1990, 1994) to suggest that globalized multiculturalism represents the implosion of the whole idea of Europe and the 'nation' itself. Stuart Hall (1991a, 1991b) argues similarly that the migratory movement from the ex-colonial peripheries to the old centre of Britain is deconstructing the whole systematized identity of Britain and the notion of 'being British'. The change from an older form of imperializing globalization to a reciprocal and diversifying flow of global interconnectedness is eroding the very substance of the nation-state. But it is capitalism itself, Hall argues, which is transmogrifying the experience of citizenry and national identity as it seeks new and ever-expanding resources and imaginings for its own commodification. Global commodity culture, with its emphasis on the ephemera of the 'image', seeks out new forms of representation and pleasure. It is the 'image', Hall explains, which 'crosses and re-crosses linguistic frontiers much more rapidly and more easily, and which speaks across languages in a much more immediate way … [and which] cannot be limited any longer by national boundaries' (1991a: 27).

Reviewing Multiculturalism after the London Bombings

To this extent, British policies around migration, race and racism have sought to avoid the extreme racism and racial violence which tarnish American history and its high ideals of civil rights and social pluralism. While the race riots in Brixton during the 1960s might have been prescient, the engagement of West Indian and African migrants into English, especially London, culture has largely transformed the national vision and its expressive demeanour. The reconfiguration of entire suburbs of south London, in particular, has altered the public image of the city, creating a new and vibrant cultural pageant for the consuming middle classes. This is particularly evident in the London music scene where Black music and Black musicians are a primary component of the success of European multiculturalism. The events of September 11 and the London bombings of 2005, however, have cast a shadow of doubt over these successes, re-focusing attention on religious ethnicity and public policy which, for many observers, have exposed the dangerous side-effects of multiculturalism.

In 2006 former British Home Secretary, Jack Straw, announced that he would no longer accept appointments with Muslim women who insisted on covering their faces with the traditional veil. According to Straw, the veil is a symbol of separation, a mask which obscures from public view the woman's true expression and feelings. While the proponents of multiculturalism impugned Straw's reading, many members of the British community accepted the view, believing that the ideology of diversity had taken British culture and community life beyond tolerance and into a dangerous territory of fragmentation. A similar debate had been taking place in France where Muslim girls and women had been banned from wearing the Muslim headdress or *hijab* in public schools and other secular, publicly funded institutions (Lewis, 2005: 255–59). Believing in the high value of secularism as the source and protector of freedom and diversity, the French government saw the wearing of the *hijab* (and other religious symbols) as an offence to the primacy of the state over 'the church'.

The cultural status of Muslims in the Western developed world has been foregrounded, of course, through events like September 11 and the London bombings, as well as the broader conditions of the global 'war on terror' (see Chapter 12). In many respects, however, it is also linked to the more general and abstracted misgivings about multiculturalism and postmodern culture. Diversity and difference are to be celebrated, but at what point does difference become a separation that is predisposed to hatred, social fragmentation and political violence? The ideals of a rich cultural tapestry seem somewhat limp against the powerful destructiveness of irreconcilable cultural hostility. The London bombers were second generation Muslim immigrants whose experience of cultural alienation in London provided the basis for violent radicalism and the strategies of political change through terror. While multiculturalists would claim that this violence is the direct responsibility of a government which largely ignores the plight of these young men, others argue that it is the outcome of brute and unbridgeable difference: that Islam is itself entirely incompatible with modern culture and the secular conventions of the modern state (see Ali, 2002; Bernard Lewis, 2003; Williams, 2006; Tulloch, 2006).

To this end, the London bombers were radicalized in a society that has conceived of itself as civilized and benign, a place that welcomes diversity and provides opportunities for economic and cultural progress. While the first generation migrants seem grateful for these opportunities and freedom from the insecurity associated with homeland violence or poverty, a number of second generation migrants appear dissatisfied with their status of difference, seeking a broader community experience in the global, religious ideology their parents had left behind. In either case it is clear that the fractures and suffering associated with imperialism and the cultural construction of race are far from resolved, and that a postmodern condition cannot ensure security and harmony in a complex global mediasphere.

GLOBAL IMPERIALISM – US MEDIA HEGEMONY

The arguments here are complex. Some theorists claim that multiculturalism is a formidable reconstruction of cultural pluralism; it is an ideal toward which all cultures should aspire. This multiculturalism will deconstruct national borders and release local cultures from the homogenizing effects of nationalism. The opposite argument suggests that the differences celebrated by multiculturalists are actually fallacious, and that multiculturalism is a dishonest mechanism which transforms significant Difference into palatable, consumable, First World difference. This is what Stuart Hall calls 'the international cuisine' (1991a): advanced societies welcome immigrants, largely for economic reasons, and then transform them into acceptable citizens who will readily participate in capitalist consumerism while providing a little diversity for the consuming pleasures of the hosts. In this context, diversity has distinct limits: the host society will only tolerate a particular type of difference, abjuring a broad variety of cultural practices which it finds unpalatable, offensive or criminal. Consider polygamy, arranged marriage, female circumcision, consumption of dog meat – forms of difference that are valid in other cultures but entirely unacceptable in the Anglophonic First World. In this sense, multiculturalism is pluralism by another name.

A further debate surrounds the question of the notion of cultural imperialism. This argument extends postcolonial theory, most particularly as it is expressed through writers like Edward Said (see above). Said and others claim that the commodification of culture is largely an exercise in continuing First World (especially American) cultural hegemony. Internationalization and global economy are necessarily absorbing the world into a system where dominant forces ultimately erase opposition and oppositional modes of cultural expression. While there may be some intermingling of cultures through the absorption of non-white, non-Euro/American cultural elements, the traffic has been largely one-way. That is, First World cultures import some minor cultural elements in order to transform them into new variations of familiar cultural products. By and large, however, America is a net exporter of products, images and culture, flooding the international market with its particular values, ideas, ideologies and discourses. While the English-speaking world has been the most vulnerable to American cultural exports, American popular texts are a significant presence in most locales across the globe.

Proponents of this argument tend to regard the commodification of culture as largely insidious. The absorption of international cultural elements from the peripheries into the dominant, First World culture is simply another form of cultural entropy and loss of difference. Vietnam, Korea, Jamaica, Mexico, Indonesia, Angola – all become available for the pleasures of First World consumption. In the opposite direction, the world as a market becomes more available to the cultural producers of the First World. Of course the incorporation of global cultures and peoples into the 'market' parameters of First World cultural producers parallels the broader embrace of the world into the Euro-American-dominated capitalist system. Disneyland, *Titanic, ER* and *Dancing with the Stars* are as internationally significant as Microsoft, McDonald's, Coca-Cola and Ford.

Global and Local Media

At its most pessimistic, this global domination argument points to the omnipresence of First World multinational corporations, which seem to have made their way into every part of the world, absorbing the peoples and transforming their economies, politics and ultimately their cultures. This argument points to this omnipresence as fuelling cultural imperialism, and Westernization, or, more particularly, Americanization. In Canada, for example, there are at least ten times as many American as Canadian films released in any one year; gross earnings of American films are on average ten times higher than the lower budget, limited-release Canadian films. Even the United Kingdom, which has seen something of a revival in its film industry in the last decade, struggles to dent the dominance of the American film industry. Moreover, the capacity of American economies of scale to produce large volumes of TV text at low profit margins enables the US to saturate overseas, especially English-speaking, markets with its product. It is significantly cheaper for television suppliers in Canada, Australasia or even the United Kingdom to import cheap US programming than to invest in local product. In Canada, in particular, the open-trade policy with the US has allowed a flood of American product on to the cable networks. Local television production in Australia is seriously dwarfed by the weight and volume of American and to a lesser degree British TV product, even though local TV often rates very well.

There has been little serious challenge to the dominance of American cultural products in the marketplace. While the Bombay (Mumbai) movie industry (Bollywood) generates a far greater volume of film text than the American industry, its global impact and financial power are dwarfed by the entertainment industry in the US. As numerous international surveys have demonstrated, most audiences across the English and non-English speaking world have a strong preference for US-based texts over other national product, even their own. The domination of the US has historical roots, certainly, but there is also a persistent effort on the part of these advantaged corporations to control the complete stream of production, distribution and retail.

Among many other critics, Robert McChesney argues that the impetus of global capitalism toward greater consolidation and monopoly economics has facilitated the growth of massive multinational corporations with the capacity to produce enormous volumes of scale and market domination (McChesney, 2004, McChesney et al., 2005). This competitive advantage has allowed US cultural corporations to invest heavily in high-budget productions which continually find favour with global markets. With few exceptions, the most well-attended cinema releases and frequently rented DVDs are movies with budgets of around US$100 million. While films like *The Queen* might occasionally disrupt the pattern, the Hollywood blockbusters remain the standard that other national cinema simply cannot emulate.

Americanization in these instances might seem inevitable. Fears about the dominance of American cultural exports, in fact, significantly delayed the establishment of the General Agreement on Tariffs and Trade (GATT), a largely First World initiative designed to facilitate greater free trade across the globe. The Agreement, which has now been signed and evolved into the World Trade Organization (WTO), seeks to eradicate the policies of national governments which 'protect' the local economy from external, international competition. The increased volume in trade is supposed to remove impediments to free trade, increasing the efficiency of local industry, enhancing the export orientation of local industry, and enhancing the wealth production and national economies of participants. France, in particular, saw cultural production as a special case since it directly contributed to local/national identity, aesthetics and cultural autonomy. This was not mere jingoism, but a genuine fear that American cultural products would infiltrate and alter the consciousness and dignity of French national culture.

The implications of free trade agreements and the WTO are far-reaching. The removal of protectionist policies has exposed local cultures and consumers to increasing volumes of overseas text, but more importantly it has changed the orientation of local cultural production. The United Kingdom, Canada, Australia and New Zealand, for example, have refocused local film and TV production toward a more international market. While this point is still highly debated, there is no doubt that the majority of film-makers in Australia and Canada are seeking to create films that can be understood and appreciated by American audiences. The Australian film *Babe*, for example, was created with American dictions, vocabulary and spoken accents, a not unsurprising extension of the commercial strategies of many recent Australian films. Similarly, the British film revival has been driven by a desire to exploit particular aspects of British culture which may facilitate an entrance into niche and popular American markets. Local cultural interests and needs might be served by such strategies, since the flow of American cultural product has entirely changed local cultures anyway. The question being asked is whether or not a local culture, distinct from American culture, can exist at all (McChesney et al., 2005). As we shall discuss in Chapter 12, these questions intersect dramatically with broader issues of global political hegemony and the capacity of news organizations to distinguish themselves from the dominant perspectives of American foreign policy.

INTERNATIONALISM

The alternative to the cultural imperialist argument rests on an assumption of cultural de-centring. In his seminal study of globalization and culture, Arjun Appadurai suggests that the whole notion of dominant culture is outmoded, an excessive simplification of complex processes of hybridization, appropriation and reappropriation:

> The new global economy has to be understood as a complex, overlapping, disjunctive order, which cannot any longer be understood in terms of existing center–periphery models (even those that might account for multiple centers and peripheries). Nor is it susceptible to simple models of push and pull (in terms of migration theories), or of surpluses and deficits (as in traditional models of balance of trade), or of consumers and producers (as in most neo-Marxist theories of development). (1990: 296)

Appadurai attempts to move the argument beyond the simple definitions of power and imperialism forged by Said and other postcolonialists, suggesting, in fact, that new forms of international connectedness reduce the potency and validity of theories based on ideology and differentials of power.

Ien Ang and Jon Stratton (1996) have suggested that the discipline of cultural studies needs to be more sensitive to this realignment of national relationships. Thus, the redemptive rewriting of history which is the postcolonialist project should give way to a recognition that the world has moved on. Postcolonialism, that is, falls into the category of resistance, which relies too heavily on notions of localism – including national, ethnic or regional localism – as the fount of structural opposition. For Ang and Stratton, however, Asia is no longer a fabrication of Western imagination and Western power, but is a fully functioning partner in cultural and economic interactions:

> If Asia must no longer be thought of as Other, this is not just because of the moral/ideological liability of the discourse of Orientalism, but because the region that has come to be called Asia has become an inherent part of, and force in, the contemporary global condition. (1996: 20)

At a rather more theoretical level, analysts who have been influenced by poststructuralism and psychoanalysis have suggested that postcolonialism tends to reduce complex interactions between cultures and cultural identities to a simple polemic of dominant and subordinate. Homi Bhabha (1987, 1994, 1999) argues that an extraordinary interdependence is established between self and other through discourse: this interaction necessarily destabilizes absolute differences in power, opening the individual's identity and subjectivity to the influence of otherness. Put simply, Bhabha is suggesting that, whenever two people of a different culture interact, they will necessarily be changed by the interaction since both parties are dependent on it for meaningful communication. This means, of course, that the experience of cultural interaction more broadly, including the consumption and 'use' of cultural texts, implicates change for both parties: the message sender and the message receiver.

> It is only by understanding the ambivalence and the antagonism of the 'desire of the Other'
> that we can avoid the increasingly facile adoption of the notion of homogenized 'Other', for
> a celebratory, oppositional politics of 'margins' or 'minorities'. (Bhabha, 1987: 7)

This politics of the margins, according to Bhabha, is that form of postcolonialism which centres the dominated subject as the hero of resistance. In fact, Bhabha explains, both sides of the colonialist divide must necessarily shift their worlds in order to make sense of the other, in order to make meaningful contact. To this extent, the mixing of cultures leads to a revitalization of old meanings and old values – difference is created in a new and more interdependent context.

Gayatri Spivak (1988, 1992) argues that the creation of a subaltern (subordinate) relationship with dominant cultural powers tends effectively to reinforce the hierarchical nature of that relationship. The dependency trap tends to re-create the subordinate status in the minds of non-Europeans, thus defeating the project of emancipation. In other words, the agency and liberatory potential of the postcolonized subject is diminished as the subject conceives of himself or herself as being 'trapped' as the victim of imperialist structures. An heroic resistance is imagined but can never be fulfilled because the subject continues to be a subordinate, even in his or her own imagination. This argument of course, parallels, postmodernist repudiations of Marxist typologies, which tend to locate power in immovable structures rather than in mutable relationships or interactions.

John Docker (1995; Docker and Fischer, 2000) has recognized the weaknesses of a postcolonial theoretic which attempts to fix power relationships in time and space. He points out that the whole enterprise of postcolonialism is problematic as it collapses into one category an extraordinarily diverse range of peoples, cultures and histories. Postcolonialism includes, for example, the de-colonizing experiences of the United States and Australia as much as Angola and Bangladesh – all countries which had to free themselves from European imperial control. A postcolonial analysis, therefore, is both totalizing and linear, reproducing the ideology of social and cultural 'progressivism' which draws all its subjects into a trajectory of civilization; while this trajectory for colonialism is based on notions of imperial evolution, the postcolonial project draws all diasporic people into a trajectory of collective 'liberation'. For Docker, the heroization of liberated diasporic peoples fails to appreciate the complex interactions and social fluidities which have come to produce contemporary culture. Docker is particularly critical of the essentialization of diasporic peoples, migrants and indigenous peoples as a single liberational category. Just as Marxism invests its liberational hopes in the category of the proletariat, Docker complains that new liberationists are investing a general politics in an invented category of diaspora and difference. Resistance politics, Docker concludes, 'must be understood in terms of local situations and local tactics, as well as the imperatives of global capitalism' (Docker, 1995: 71).

John Tomlinson has objected similarly to the Westernization/homogenization/cultural imperialism triad of arguments, suggesting that the global scene is far more complex than this one-way process would seem to appreciate. The whole notion that non-European cultures are so easily appropriated into the cultural empire of the West merely reinforces the status and power of the West (Tomlinson, 1999). Tomlinson suggests that the preoccupation with the presence of Western cultural elements in the non-West – fast foods, rock music, popular films – tends to distract analysis from the interests of other cultures and their peoples. The most serious deficiency of the homogenization argument, however, is its failure to appreciate the nature of culture itself and the ways in which different 'cultures' interact: 'Movement between cultural/geographical areas always involves translation, mutation, and adaptation as the "receiving culture" brings its own cultural resources to bear in dialectical fashion upon cultural imports' (Tomlinson, 1997: 169). This process has been variously described as indigenization, cultural mutation, appropriation and hybridization. Fundamentally, however, it suggests that the importation of cultural elements will always produce changes to those elements. As it falls into the mix of the importing culture, it will be adapted, used and interpreted according to the local tastes and interests. Moreover, and as we have touched upon above, this process is two-way, since the interaction with non-Western cultures will also produce effects of change and adaptation from the non-West to the West. We have seen, for example, the rapid uptake in the past two or three decades of Buddhism and other non-Christian creeds, most particularly by educated younger generations. This challenge to the orthodoxy which informs the West's basic belief system indicates that more than international cuisines are evolving through the integration of different cultural experiences within and outside the West.

More recent theories, therefore, have attempted to describe globalization in terms of global and local interactions and transformations (Castells, 1997; Crane, 2002; Rosenan, 2003; Urry, 2003; Bauman, 2004). In a sense, these ideas seek to reconcile those scholarly arguments which emphasize – either the megatrends and the formation of a 'world system' shaped by economy and macro international politics; or that culture is re-shaping the world through micro-flows of human expressivity and communication. The emphasis, therefore, is on top-down, bottom-up and multi-directional modes of complexity, flow and transformation. For George Ritzer (2004) these interactions, nevertheless, amount to a consumer and symbolic orgy which he caricatures as the 'globalization of nothing'. Seeking to establish an alternative argument to the concept of global flows, Ritzer claims that globalization is simply an expression of a chaotic impulse to express and consume – something like Baudrillard's characterization of modern culture as a vacuous and sensate hyperreality.

Hardt and Negri (2000), on the other hand, suggest that the engagement of macro and micro flows in globalization is an essential (ontological) expression of the social desire for peace through 'empire'. Looking beyond the imperialism of the European-based nation state, Hardt and Negri argue that 'empire' in their definition is an ideal, ahistorical and largely apolitical mode of human organization. In this sense, 'empire' is being shaped through broadly distributed power networks that are themselves shaped through American-style 'community' and 'new world' idealism. American empire, therefore, is not to be feared, but it is part of a much broader human enterprise which is ultimately predicated on peace, rather than violence and political domination. Cultural imperialism, and even the radical potential of multiculturalism and multi-directional, transnational flows (Nairn and James, 2005), are far less important than this megatrend toward global empire and global peace. As we shall see in the next chapter, this idealized globalization is a critical component of the 'utopianism' that prevails in digital and computer-based cultures.

Dependence, Independence, Interdependence

We might at this point summarize the basic arguments surrounding globalization theory:

1   The postcolonialist argument suggests that the new world order is built around the continued material and discursive domination of the formerly colonized peoples of the world. A system of cultural imperialism operates to maintain the privileges of Western economies and cultures.
2   Alternative arguments suggest that liberation is possible because the West and the non-West are mixing and interacting far more than ever before. Globalization is contributing to greater hybridization and localism through the force of multi-directional flows.
3   As an extension to the previous argument, some critics suggest that, in fact, 'the West' and the 'non-West' are collapsing categories. The new interdependence of cultures necessarily deconstructs these old structures.
4   As an extension to (3), it is also suggested that the whole idea of nation is imploding because of these greater, postmodern propinquities. The suggestion here is that we do not necessarily have a 'world system', but a series of interacting operational zones: economy, communications/media, migrations, and so on.
5   At the level of cultural consumption this interdependence does away with old ideas about difference based around nation or ethnicity. Difference and heterogeneity are produced through greater cultural sharing. The interaction of cultural elements produces new ideas, cultural products and cultural symbols. This is the politics of

postmodern hybridization. In this sense, the categories of West and non-West are entirely outmoded.

6 Problems around these arguments are re-emerging as the impact of global transformations is being more intensely experienced by local communities. American economic and military primacy, most particularly evident in the Middle East wars, has re-ignited anxieties about American global hegemony. Many citizens in the UK and Australia, for example, have challenged their respective government's willingness to follow American foreign policy and the invasion of Iraq. These challenges have fortified broader misgivings about the surrender of sovereignty and the domination of US culture and cultural products.

GLOBAL SPACES

Discussions on globalism tend to centre on a recurring problem of localism and local identity. Commentary during the 1990s onward has tended to recognize that globalization implicates the creation of new cultural elements, discourses and spaces, but the actual nature and definition of what constitutes 'the local' is rarely specified; rather, 'the local' is presented merely in terms of its alternative: the global. What is clearer, however, is that the parameters and substance of 'nation' are seriously challenged by the globalizing process. The 'imagined community' of the nation, which, according to Benedict Anderson (1991) was constructed in relation to the rise of print technologies, urbanization, industrialism and imperialist economies, is being dissolved through new forms of imagining. Certainly the nation continues in many of its traditional forms and discourses, but the new globalizing economic, media and bionomic conditions of contemporary culture are changing the ways we conceive of our nation and ourselves. Moreover, the physical landscape of the Earth is being radically altered as it is enveloped in the intricate webs of globalization. In the midst of significant species extinction, surviving plants and animals are being increasingly distributed beyond the borders of their old ecologies. Cities and agricultural landforms are now constituting highly assimilative and repetitive spatial patterns across the globe. The formerly distinct disciplines of urban studies, architecture and geography are converging with cultural theory in order to explain these new spatial experiences.

Postmodern Architectures

Neo-Marxist and other more strident commentaries on global space (e.g., postcolonialism, feminism) have tended to divide the world between the centre and the periphery. The centre marks the territory of the developed world, especially developed cities; the periphery or margins tend to be located in non-developed, especially agrarian, regions. These modernist forms of critique remain fixed in notions of spatial distribution, function and materialism. Postmodernism, on the other hand, appears more interested in the aesthetic and representational dimensions of space. For postmodernism the question of distribution and models of centre–periphery are no longer relevant as the world's geographies converge into a shared space of 'the imaginary'.

Charles Jencks (1995, 2005) argues that the new globalized world is propelling architecture and urban space into a new and more optimistic phase of cultural evolution. Jencks' notion of postmodernism (see Chapter 7) converges historicism and aesthetics; postmodernism is the age of humanly scaled pleasures and the liberation from modernism's stifling pessimism, orthodoxy and prescriptions of universal order. In this globalized space the imaged and constructed environment is shifted out of the suffocating uniformity of modernist functionality. Architectural space is released, that is, from the hierarchies that position and separate humans, and then attempt to overcome the separation through an artificial unity. For Jencks, modern spatial design is typified by the formalism of nineteenth-century public building with its grand entrances and oversized monuments. These self-conscious hierarchies are replaced in the post-World War Two period by grey functionalism – those rectangular concrete boxes which are self-consciously egalitarian and hideously unappealing.

Jencks celebrates a postmodern liberation from modernism's functional certitude; this new language of postmodernism, a new 'double-coding' of time and space, frees the past from itself. This emancipation facilitates the development of new forms of space which become a celebration of 'lateral' rather than 'lineal' time. Thus, the quality of pastiche (juxtaposition of diverse historical or cultural elements) that characterizes postmodern designs constitutes a new 'classicism' by which a building can again be 'beautiful' as much as functional (Jencks, 1987a, 1987b; see also Attive, 2002). This quality of pastiche is visible in a number of postmodern designs: Ralph Erskine's housing renewal project (Jencks, 1987b: 104–5); James Stirling's extension of the Tate Gallery in London (Jencks, 1987a: 288 *et passim*); and Kurokawa's Daimaru shopping complex in Melbourne, Australia (see Lewis, 1997b). This new spatial aesthetic, which celebrates time by lateral reference and propinquity, is very much in keeping with the political and ethnic diversifications now characterizing global cultural interactions (Attiva, 2002). The new space, that is, resists reduction and lineality by allowing competing voices across time, geography and culture to engage in each other's pleasures and problematics.

Kenneth Frampton's (1985) theory of critical regionalism is also designed to evade the universal grammar of modernist architecture by which cultural and representational space is characterized as (modernist) sameness and the uncritical replication of building types. For Frampton, the distinguishing characteristic of postmodern architecture is its ability to reconstruct traditional regional values and ethnic designs through new technologies. Not only can a building function as a living museum, it enhances and preserves cultural difference within the urban landscape of postmodern fusion. Thus the language of a particular region is fused with the language of postmodernism to produce unique and beautiful architectural types. Difference, geography and tradition will always be heard in this dual coding of old and new; the logocentricism, capitalist metropolitanism, functionalism and monophonic voice of modernism that had dominated the world throughout the period of Enlightenment imperialism is consequently banished, though not forgotten, since it too is a voice of history. In this way, Charles Jencks contends, the new architectural style of postmodernism produces a new ideology which can be understood as speaking to the 'elite' and the 'man in the street'; this is the necessary ideology of postmodern democracy since both 'groups, often opposed and often using different codes of perception, have to be satisfied' (Jencks, 1987b: 8). This ideology of a fused particularity is most poetically described by Frampton as an architecture of resistance by which a more complete range of symbolic senses will interact with the 'meanings' of a building:

> the intensity of light, darkness, heat and cold; the feeling of humidity; the almost palpable presence of masonry as the body senses its own confinement; the momentum of an induced gait and the relative inertia of the body as it traverses the floor; the echoing resonance of our own footfall. (1985: 28)

Jencks' periodizing of postmodernism leads him to suggest further that these architectural forms are associated with the new pastiche of the city and the postmodern globe. Nation and the separationism and alienation of modernism are being displaced by a world system in which the major cities are no longer confined to national functionalism, but are integrated into widening cultural and global relationships. Tokyo, Paris, London, Mexico City, New York, Rio de Janeiro – these are now global cities connected by significant economic, aesthetic, social and cultural matrices which enclose the whole of the world.

The Architecture of the Jumping Universe

Spatial and architectural formations are for Jencks theoretical as much as aesthetic representations. Architectural and artistic 'double-coding' is the capacity to say two potentially opposite things at once, including statements about time and space. Postmodernism is an idea which articulates the 'differences' of history or place in terms of an ever present and a unity of knowledge. This harmony in difference (difference in harmony) constitutes the major ideal for postmodern idealism, its liberatory dimensions. Thus, while the architecture and art of modernism were constructed around functionalist and mechanistic theories of the universe, postmodernism aesthetics will formulate its technologies around a purer understanding of nature and cosmic principles. The Enlightenment laid the foundations for these new understandings, but through the discoveries of the 'new physics' – post-Euclidian geometry, relativity, quantum theory, fractals and chaos theory – we now need a new way of representing the essential nature of Nature.

Thus, in a subsequent development of the original double-coding theory, Jencks suggests that the new architectural horizon should emulate the increasing complexity of the universe. Jencks' adaptation of complexity and chaos theories for cultural and aesthetic analysis claims that nature evolves through a fine balancing of order and disorder. Increasing complexity within nature leads to the potential for complete randomness and breakdown. The same is true of social and cultural history. Late modernist painting, for example, is typified by profound complexity which risks a slide into randomness and chaotic expressions of emptiness, meaninglessness and disorder. The paintings of Jackson Pollock become increasingly random; the complexity of James Joyce's *Ulysses* dissolves into the incomprehensibility of *Finnegan's Wake*. Thus, just as the universe proceeds from the simple to the complex, art and social organizations advance through increasing complexity – however, 'the reverse of complexity is not just simplicity but also entropy' (Jencks, 1995: 37): closed systems of any type must necessarily move from complexity to chaos and the expiration of energy, and ultimately death. A jumping universe, however, is an open system where development and disorder advance (and retreat) interdependently and with the ultimate, if mysterious, capacity for self-organization. The universe jumps in two ways:

1   Through evolutionary 'leaps' where there is a developmental convergence as the potential for chaos is mobilized toward greater complexity: the Big Bang, the solidification of planetary gases, the formation of air and water on Earth, the emergence of cellular life forms, the evolution of dinosaurs, the evolution of humans. According to Jencks, we are due for another spectacular jump as we produce forms of computer-based technology which will vastly outstretch the mechanistic technologies of preceding epochs; these machines will be self-replicating, self-organizing and much closer to the natural systems of organic nature. Between these leaps, of course, there have been numerous contractions where cosmic elements fall away into disorderly conditions: the cataclysm which brought the almost immediate extinction of dinosaurs is analogous to the current mass extinctions being precipitated by human activities. For Jencks, this contemporary threat to the condition of all life is directly related to the advanced state of human imagining, technologies and social life. Existence, that is, proceeds at the knife-edge of devastating chaos and generative progress.

2   The universe also jumps through the behaviour of its smallest and most fundamental particulates. According to Jencks and his theoretical mentors, the 'complexitists', the universe is structured around sub-atomic particles – quantum electrons – which display the same complex association of order and disorder that is evident throughout nature, including the 'nature' of human beings. The most basic characteristic of human knowledge is contradiction; we carry with us perpetual struggles between different attitudes, emotions and behaviours.

More generally, Jencks explains the connection between the behaviour of sub-atomic particles and human thought:

Some physicists believe, moreover, that thought is basically a wave phenomenon. This is intuitively obvious; after all, an idea weighs nothing, is contained all over the brain, is stretched out like a wave, can travel near the speed of light, and is changeable like an ocean wave. Quantum waves also have, like thoughts, paradoxical properties: unlike particles or objects, they can tunnel through walls – a miracle that happens in every television set. ... Quantum waves can add up, cancel, go through each other, and be in several places at once. (1995: 40)

Jencks goes on to explain that the modernist notion of mechanistic order, where the universe is defined and explained in terms of linear processes and laws, provides only a superficial, even partial, vision of nature. The self-organizing systems which have evolved are themselves the outcome of complex and paradoxical quantum associations:

[A] basic truth of quantum physics has been that the atom is itself an ecological entity with internal properties of organization. The electron, orbiting the nucleus as both wave and particle, jumps from quantum level to level, giving off, or taking on, energy. Its behaviour is partly self-determined and partly indeterminate. The electron cloud is said to 'choose' certain aspects of its activity just as we 'choose' whether to observe its position or momentum, particle or wave aspect. Its freedoms and our freedoms are circumscribed, but we both exhibit a degree of self-determinism and interaction. (1995: 162)

Quantum and complexity theories thus become paradigmatic for Jencks. Architecture, art and urban planning are available for complex associations of determination and self-determinism – none is complete and entirely independent of the other. Buildings, cities and social life across the globe exhibit the same contradictions and paradoxes, and it is the challenge of postmodern thinking to arrange these cultural forms in order to maximize their complexity and potential for human pleasure. In this sense, postmodernism is embedding us more deeply into the true essences, the true characteristics, of nature. Jencks summarizes as follows these principles for a new architecture which draws all of humanity into a postmodern urban web that is no longer separated from nature, but which is an intrinsic part of it:

1   Buildings should be designed and constructed in relation to nature and natural languages, including atomic and sub-atomic forms, twists, folds and waves, cyborgs, crystals and bones.
2   Buildings should represent the basic cosmological truth, including self-organization to higher (and lower) levels.
3   Building design should be constituted through organizational depth, multivalence, complexity and the edge of chaos.
4   Architecture should celebrate diversity, variety and bottom-up participatory systems which maximize difference.
5   Diversity can be supported by techniques such as collage, radical eclecticism, and superposition. This enables architecture, drawn from different historical phases and

Plate 10.1   *Gugenheim Art Museum at Bilbao*

Designed by Frank O. Gehry, the Gugenheim art museum in Bilbao represents a powerful architectural notation to the social and political transformation of Spain. Aesthetically, the building articulates the postmodern style, which defies Euclidian simplicity in favour of a more organic expression of the relationship between humans, culture and nature. Like the Opera House in Sydney, Australia, the Bilbao Gugenheim creates a broad and sweeping motif that is rich with flow and movement. This new organicism transcends the geometric rigidity of modernist architectural styles. More broadly, however, the museum has provided a new impetus for a city that was part of Spain's decaying and rusting industrial landscape. Impoverished and wracked by sectarian violence, Bilbao has now become connected by the Gugenheim to the global tourism marketplace. Budget air carriers from the UK, in particular, have ensured a massive increase in international visitors to a city which is now a major stepping-off point for many continental tours.

through different ethnicities and human interests, to co-exist in an inclusive, pluralist system of design.

6   Architecture should acknowledge the context of the contemporary culture and its agenda, including questions of ecology and political pluralism.

7   It should have a double-coding of these concerns with aesthetic and conceptual codes.
8   Architecture must look to science, especially contemporary science, for its closures of the Cosmic Code. In order to go beyond immediate concerns and fashions, architecture must look to wider fields of knowledge and understanding.

Postmodern Geographies and Thirdspace

Jencks' architectural postmodernism has been severely criticized for its celebratory and unproblematic approach to the social and political arrangement of space. His polemical utopianism has failed to impress those (especially neo-Marxist) analysts who maintain a deep suspicion of postmodern theorisations (Best and Kellner, 1997).

Howard Caygill (1990), for example, rejects all notions of a postmodern spatial democracy, arguing that this postmodernism remains critically, politically and aesthetically bound to the elitism and uneven spatial distributions of the modernism it purports to replace. Indeed, Caygill uses Theodor Adorno's model of irresolution to demonstrate the incapacity of postmodernism to resolve its contradictory parts. Adorno's work would deny the inclination of postmodern theory to resolve the Enlightenment dualities – universal/particular, past/present, rich/poor – through the processes of representation. Caygill sees the postmodern aesthetic as an unconvincing ideology which forces the alternatives into a dissonant aesthetic partnership: 'Current postmodern theory and practices succumb to the desire to reconcile the two spheres by resolving their contradictions through the erasure of differences between the profession and the public, and within the public itself' (1990: 285). Thus for Caygill and others working from the neo-Marxist critique, the aestheticization and pluralization of space remain fixed by capitalist processes which cannot diminish the pervasive unevenness of spatial and resource distribution. Globalism and the new capitalist utility would merely illuminate the shifting focus of this unevenness across the world, without clear reference to the powerful forces that control and manipulate our constructed environment.

Edward Soja (1989, 1996, 2000) attempts to overcome the divide between modernist and postmodernist conceptions of space through a reworking of Henri Lefebvre's (e.g., 1991, 1992) theories of Thirdspace, 'the trialectics of spatiality'. According to Lefebvre, the logics of modernism had always reduced space to a material and physical condition, or a representational phenomenon of the mind; Thirdspace liberates spatiality from the constraining reductivism of this dialectic. Soja identifies the defining qualities of Thirdspace as

a knowable and unknowable, real and imagined lifeworld of experiences, emotions, events and political choices that is existentially shaped by the generative and problematic interplay between centres and peripheries, the abstract and concrete, the impassioned spaces of the conceptual and the lived, marked out materially and metaphorically in spatial praxis, the transformation of (spatial) knowledge into (spatial) action in a field of unevenly developed (spatial) power. (1996: 31)

Lefebvre's notion of a ubiquitous power, like Foucault's, is appealing to Soja as it liberates the concept of power from fixed structures like class and distribution of property. Again like Foucault, Lefebvre identifies significant divisions in social power but they are elusive and mutating, occurring at the level of relationships and in discourse – at the very centre of Being. This phenomenological definition distinguishes Lefebvre from those Marxists who can only define space in terms of structure (material or ideological), and from those postmodernists who can only define space in terms of representation. Even so, Lefebvre's particular brand of nomadic and complex Marxism, while liberating his analysis from simple definitions of centre and periphery (power and powerlessness), nevertheless returns to residual forms of binary oppositionalism. Thus, while moving away from the simpler alternatives of centre–periphery in his definition of global space, Lefebvre reconstructs notions of mind–body, man–woman, West–non-West in his critique of space.

Lefebvre's analysis seeks a geography which emancipates individuals from the homogenizing, fragmenting and hierarchically organized regimes of power which are at the heart of capitalist arrangements of space. *Le droit à la ville*, the right to the city, was a concept developed by Lefebvre to announce the new aspiration of reformist politics, the right to be different. This struggle was to be experienced at all levels of the lifeworld: the body and sexuality, household designs, architecture, urban planning and monumental design, neighbourhoods, cities and the global development. These struggles for difference were conceived in contexts of centred and marginal space which was both material and metaphoric. Unlike the postmodernists who have invested much of their liberational faith in deepening individualism, Lefebvre seeks to reinvigorate collective resistance, the Thirdspace of political choice. Thus, social relations are not incidentally spatial, as many Marxists might conceive, but fundamentally spatial: there are no aspatial social processes, according to Lefebvre, no ways in which the relationships of power can be conceived without the inscription of real and imagined space.

> Thinking trialectically is a necessary part of understanding Thirdspace as a limitless composition of lifeworlds that are radically open and openly radicalizable; that are all inclusive and transdisciplinary in scope yet politically focused and susceptible to strategic choice; that are never completely knowable but whose knowledge none the less guides our search for emancipatory change and freedom from domination. (Soja, 1996: 70)

The concept of Thirdspace, then, provides a tool for the comprehension of global arrangements of space, including aspects of development, social relations within space and the construction, aesthetics and representational forms of our cities. For Soja, Thirdspace provides a valuable strategic tool for the reading of cityscapes that are now postmodern and constituted around complex simulations and media.

Thirdspace and the Olympic Games

The Olympic Games have become one of the most prominent and widely telecast of all global spectacles. Of course, the 'Games' are conducted in a physical space: arenas, swimming pools, football fields, boxing rings, and so on. However, the Olympics are also very much a part of international mediasphere and are conducted through 'language games' or the imagined spaces of discourse. Politics, economy, culture and power are all mobilized through these discourses.

The final of the men's 100 metres may be watched simultaneously by more than two billion people worldwide. A Thirdspace analysis would see the event as a form of colonization: the athletes become the representatives of the territorial and commercial interests of their home nation. The spectacle of the event, that is, engages with the historical inequities upon which capitalist competition is founded:

1 For the past sixty years or so the finalists in the 100 metres event have been the descendants of African slaves, even though they may have been representing the *nation* of Britain, Canada or the US.
2 First World nations use their successful athletes as demonstrable evidence of national virtue and virility. This success acts as a warning to those external powers. It also acts as a source of national cohesion and national consciousness.
3 Successful athletes generate income and economic activity which also benefit the home territory. Poorer nations have neither the money (public or private) nor the technology that will produce high-level athletic performances. The 100 metres final represents the unevenness of wealth distribution across the globe.
4 The glamour of the spectacle also disguises the corruption and cheating which are rampant in the Olympic movement.

A celebrational postmodernist analysis would see the representational dimensions of the Games in a rather more positive light. The community of viewers who would come to the final are deriving their own pleasures from the spectacle. Perfected human bodies, enhanced by technology and the spirit of competition, come together to form the utopia of gamesmanship. Being 'black' is no longer a point of threat, but a source of celebration. The Olympics are a space where all countries can come together to celebrate their shared humanity.

Thirdspace analysis combines these two perspectives in order to identify and critique the representational and material dimensions of space. For Thirdspace the Olympics are a set of contesting discourses which culminate in the control and distribution of space. The ideal of the Olympics and their experiential unevenness must necessarily clash. However, it is not enough to point to these clashes; genuine solutions must be found and presented. Regulations and ethics must protect against corruption. Poorer nations must have wealth distributed in their favour. African Americans must do as Tommy Smith and Don Carlos did at the Mexico Olympics (1968): they must articulate the politics of their condition and express their anger to the world.

Postmodern Playgrounds

The postmodern city has now been transformed into an integrated space of shopping, display and functional and communicative ecstasy. Edward Soja, in fact, borrows directly from Jean Baudrillard's account of the 'ecstasy of communication' (1983b, 1988, see Chapter 7) to describe contemporary Los Angeles. In a contemporary, media-centric city like Los Angeles, the old divisions of space and spatial identity are continually transformed by new simulations of space: compressions which re-create formerly separate dominions and histories into a replica, a reproduction or simulation of what might (or might not) have been. As Baudrillard has pointed out, these are forms of simulation, imitations of imitations, which have no origin and no observable context other than the here and the now:

> This ecstatic disappearance permeates everyday life, enabling the hyperreal to increasingly influence not only what we wear and what we eat and how we choose to entertain ourselves, but also where and how we choose to live, who and what we vote for, how government is run, and also how we might be agitated to take more direct political action not just against the precession of simulacra but *within* it as well. (Soja, 1996: 278)

In other words, the world of simulacra becomes unavoidable. For postmodern architects, these simulacra constitute additional resources for the design and construction of our material and iconic environment. However, the same buildings in which Charles Jencks rejoices become the source of discomfort for a critical postmodernism which seeks a deeper explanation of social and political relationships and which is distressed by the obscuration of history.

These design strategies are justifiable, according to the celebrational postmodernists, because all history is invented and all space is representational. Even so, we can see the problematic returning, even as Thirdspace, in the contemporary transformations of older industrial architecture and urban spaces that were constructed around nineteenth-century trade and manufacturing. The reinscription of such sites as museums, theme parks, recreational and cuisinal zones affirms a world of happy-endings and postmodern pleasures, but it marginalizes particular living and dead social groups. Specifically, the stories of dead workers, those who populated the former industrial spaces, are generally obliterated or obscured by the refurbishments and the sanitization of the old, industrial shells.

This postmodernization has taken place in the former industrial zones which once bordered the northern end of Melbourne, Australia's principal manufacturing city. For over a century, one particular building in the former industrial zone, the Walter Coop Shot Tower, has been the subject of enormous debates and contesting cultural discourses. During the latter part of the nineteenth century, Walter Coop constructed a lead shot factory, the most notable feature of which was the 152-foot Romanesque tower. The Shot

Plate 10.2   *Real-estate sale on Nusa Lembongan*

Plate 10.4   *The Harbourfront, Montreal*

Plate 10.3   *The Shot Tower*

Plates 10.2–10.4   The postmodernization of space. Plate 10.2 features a real-estate sale on the small Indonesian island of Nusa Lembongan. The thatched hut is situated in a fishing village which overlooks a spectacular coral reef. The pressure of global tourism is already being experienced on the island, with the international hotel corporation Hyatt establishing a major resort a few kilometres from the hut. Plate 10.3 features the postmodernization of a nineteenth-century industrial zone. The Shot Tower, which produced lead shot for artillery and kerosene lamps, has been incorporated into the Daimaru shopping complex in Melbourne, Australia. Plate 10.4 features the refurbished harbour in Montreal, Canada. Museums, restaurants and various forms of public recreational space have replaced the factories, warehouses and brothels which once dominated the harbour landscape.

Tower technology was effective but farcically primitive. Molten lead was dropped from the top of the tower; the descent cooled the material into spherical lead 'shot', which was then sorted and sold for artillery and kerosene lamps, among other uses. The enterprise continued through four generations of the Coop family until 1961, when, finally, even Australia's generous manufacturing protection policies could not save it from the challenge of more efficient and technologically advanced manufacturing techniques being used in other parts of the world. The Australian National Trust legislation became the new protector, however, and the site was saved from obliteration and redevelopment by a nostalgia which in a postcolonial nationalist discourse identified the structure with some of the great monuments of the world: the Statue of Liberty, the Eiffel Tower, Big Ben.

Even so, there seemed little interest in developing the building, and while the city continued to grow and the inner-city industrialism continued to atrophy, the old Tower's 'symbolic', rather than material, value was itself being challenged by the vigorous pragmatism of the 1980s. Discussions over the building's historic and cultural–visual value for the Melbourne streetscape began to change character. The influence of economic rationalism and globalist postmodernism began to challenge some of the established assumptions of historical–national value. While several redevelopment schemes had been mooted, they all collapsed at the door of the conserved Walter Coop complex. Finally, the giant Japanese consortium Kumagaigumi resolved the thirty years of temporal inertia by incorporating the old tower into its redevelopment plan. The acceptance of the project, which incorporated the Shot Tower into a huge shopping complex and office tower, not only marked the complete re-configuration of the northern city streetscape, it also symbolized a more general abdication in the reign of cultural modernism.

According to the conceptual designer of the Daimaru, Kisho Kurokawa, the integration of the Shot Tower into the glass cone of the Daimaru shopping complex draws together diffuse spatial and cultural elements. The people who inhabit the building are perpetually exposed to a chaotic dialogue which confronts their assumptions about space and the world at large: 'The chaotic dimensions of people distinguishes them from machines and this is what architecture for the 21st century ought to express' (Kurokawa, cited in Childs, 1991: 5). According to Kurokawa, the Daimaru design principles supersede the domination of people and their vitality which are inherent in the ordered public design of cities like The Hague, Vancouver or Washington DC. The Daimaru is a 'commercial entertainment space, so I need a surprise. It's a surprise box' (cited in Childs, 1991: 5). Like Charles Jencks and numerous other postmodern enthusiasts, Kurokawa makes grand claims about the power of his aesthetic to produce pleasures that occur at the level of the human. According to Kurokawa, his critics remain trapped in an ideological system which is always overriding the human and which inevitably produces and reproduces modes of order, dominance and displeasure.

The Daimaru building, in fact, represents another 'happy ending'. The thirty years of historical, political, commercial and cultural dissonance are finally brought together within the totemic space of postmodernism. The past can exist in a context of financial imperative. The awkward and disjunctive ghost of Australian industrialism becomes iconographed as nostalgia, a quaint and curious relic which engages the pleasures and interests of the postmodern tribe. Now the Shot Tower becomes a comedy, a linguistic interplay where the oppositions of chaos and complexity, pleasure and displeasure, old and new, are resolved in ironical dispositions. The Daimaru dwarfs the old Shot Tower, incorporating its history into video screens, walking tours and a giant waist clock which plays 'Waltzing Matilda' on the chime of every hour. The tower itself is draped in a huge red SALE sign. On the hour the shoppers stare skyward, but they are not looking at the tower; they are standing in absorbed attention at the robotic pioneers who step from the corners of the giant waist clock while it plays the 'Matilda' anthem.

The past, that is, is woven interminably into the present. But it is not a past that the ghosts of Walter Coop would recognize. Rather, it is a past that has been sanitized, standardized and re-rendered for contemporary tastes – literally and metaphorically. This new past is not merely a playground of historical references; it's a history built around untruths and the obscuration of past lives and past terrors. The ghosts cry out but the contemporary storytellers and their play are impenetrable; they continue to varnish the disease, filth and degradation of 'other' lives, condemning them to anonymity while glorifying the memories of great (men) in new modes of pleasure and info-tainment. It may be, as Alan Bryman (1995) says of Disneyland, that it is the present that is obscured by this perpetual re-rendering of the past. In fact, the present may no longer be present at all but may be rendered absent by the fabrication of an idealized history. This obscuration excludes pain and the politics of struggle, so that contemporary problems 'are not real problems at all, or ones which, with our current know-how … can easily be overcome' (Bryman, 1995: 127).

Thus, the transformation of global city spaces – ports, warehouses, working-class residences – is fashioned out of this broader transformation of global capitalism and global culture. These transformations produce particular effects, depending on the site, history and design objectives of the redevelopment. For example:

1   The redevelopment of the Thames docklands in London has replaced one hierarchical system with another. From being a site which represented the poverty of wharf labourers, imprisoned underclass felons and the imperial gateway, it has now become an exclusive residential and entertainment zone. Only the best-paid postmodern professional could contemplate the mortgage of a docklands residence.

2   EuroDisney, the expansion of Disneyland into the most chic of cities, Paris, represents the integration of Europe into the ecstasy of popular American culture. This transformation is ambiguous as it adjusts for a more distinctly European style of spectacularization and entertainment (for example, the drinking of wine, common in EuroDisney, is strictly forbidden in Disneyland). The presence of EuroDisney on the borders of Paris replaces the sense of siege which has preoccupied Paris during the period of modernity. EuroDisney now sits on the outskirts of Paris as once the German troops had done. The 'threat' posed by EuroDisney, however, is one of the complete transformation of the integrity and aloofness of Parisian culture. The changes to the Paris skyline that have also taken place over the past two decades represent, further, this conceptual re-imagining of Paris.

Plate 10.5   *The London Eye*

Urban spaces in the developed world have undergone considerable transformation over the past fifty years. As heavy industry has contracted and become more specialized, many of the old trading and port areas have been redeveloped as recreational pleasure zones. The giant ferris wheel, the London Eye, overlooks one of the world's most historically significant trading ports and the symbol of Britain's global domination in the nineteenth century. The old Victorian trading houses and the Eye exist in a peculiar historical dialogue interpolated by the Houses of Parliament, which glare back upon the bounty of their modern political vision.

3   The Tokyoization of Honolulu. One of the most significant changes to world culture and global space since the 1970s has been the success and expansion of Japanese economy and culture. As Japan has become the world's second largest economy, its rapid accumulation of capital has brought further pressure to spend and participate in global consumption, including tourist consumption. Japanese corporations and private citizens seemed suddenly to appear in world tourist and real-estate markets. Japanese investors bought prize land in the coastal and tourist zones of West coast North America, Hawaii and Australia. Even with the current ebb of the Japanese economy, the impact of

Tokyo culture and money is evident in the street signs, tourism facilities and cuisines of these coastal zones.

The notion of Thirdspace devised by Henri Lefebvre and Edward Soja would suggest that these playhouses are forms of complicated ideology. We can see how powerful groups in a society might advantage themselves and their interests by constituting the world as happy ending, as simulacra without source or conclusion. However, at the level of popular culture it is also clear that the tribe of postmodernist consumers derives genuine gratification from the spaces and the delights of design (Brown, 2004; Pinder, 2004). The homogenizing effects of repeated design and corporate hegemony are balanced, therefore, by the sorts of complicated erasures, uses and re-configurations that building-users bring to the spaces. The playground is insidious, deft and deceitful. The postmodern tribe may be blind to particular effects and determinations of power, but the principles of postmodern consumerism permit a level of freedom for the users of these playgrounds which is denied them by modernist precepts. Gastronomy, Disney pastiche, beachgoing and shopping – these are the new treasures of a postmodern, global space.

UNEVEN GLOBAL DISTRIBUTIONS

Even so, the new postmodern space is fundamentally uneven in its distribution of pleasure. Appadurai (1990) has argued that we can no longer think in terms of centre and periphery models; Lefebvre/Soja argue that centre and peripheries exist in multiple and mutating forms, some of which are characterized through the formation of space as representation and material. The concept of Thirdspace, in fact, allows us to think of space in terms of material and symbolic differentiations, while allowing for the possibility of 'meaninglessness', of space which is transformed into an absent core of simulacra. Certainly, the pleasures brought by consumerist postmodernism are not evenly distributed across the globe. The new forms of flexible accumulation of capital and the liberalization of international trade and finance are not an even bounty: wealthy countries and the majority of their citizens continue to do better, while the poorest countries continue to struggle under the burden of debt and devastating deficits in balance of trade.

As indicated in Table 10.1, the Gross National Product (GNP) of the less well developed nations of the world remained flat or fell as a percentage of the GNP of the wealthiest countries over the past 30 years. Thus, the per capita income of sub-Saharan Africa, West Asia and Latin America declined, while South Asia remained flat as a percentage of the 'core' wealthy nations. East Asian incomes, including China's from an extremely low base, rose sharply. Despite these figures, the World Bank (2001) has famously claimed that the number of humans living in 'extreme poverty' (earning less than US$1/day) had fallen in the previous decade from 1.4 billion to around 1.2 billion in the change of millennium.

Table 10.1   *GNP per capita as % of OECD-Developed World regions' GNP*

Region	1960	1980	2000
Sub-Saharan Africa	5	4	2
Latin America	20	18	12
West Africa and North Africa	9	9	7
South Asia	2	1	2
East Asia (without China or Japan)	68		13
China	1	1	3
Total Developing World	**5**	**4**	**5**
North America	124	100	191
Western Europe	111	104	98
Southern Europe	52	60	60
Australia and New Zealand	95	75	73
Japan	79	134	145
Total OECD Developed World	100	100	100

Source: Adapted from World Bank data 2004.

The main reason for this, according to the Bank, was the rise in free-market global trade and the integration of poorer countries into the global economy.

In other words, the major shift in the formation of global cultural politics and ideology had brought immense benefits to the world economy, improving the living conditions of hundreds of millions of the world's poorest people. Among many others, Robert Wade (2004) has questioned the methods employed by the World Bank to draw these conclusions. Specifically, Wade notes that the Bank changes its measurement formula for each of these figures, predisposing the 2000 poverty figures to a lower number than the earlier figures (2004: 387). In either case, even the World Bank's own figures, and the ideology of free-market 'neoliberalism' which supports them, demonstrate a clear alliance between the cultural politics of globalization and a postmodernism that subsumes the genuine suffering of individuals and communities within an aesthetic of pleasure and celebrationism. Behind the tinsel and delights of First World consumerism lies a global industrial system which condemns labourers, even in booming China, to working conditions and wages that are less than those of textile workers in England at the beginning of the industrial revolution (Kinge, 2006).

Even within developed nations the economic distance between the wealthiest and poorest people in the community is extending; social substrata are deepening as unemployment rates remain high and liberalized industrial relations laws weaken the bargaining power of ordinary wage-and salary-earners. Even in the United States, which, at the time of writing, has an extremely low unemployment rate by international standards, the image of economic success camouflages the continuation of severe poverty among many groups, including indigenous peoples, African Americans, single mothers and Hispanic immigrants. For all its enormous wealth, America has a huge proportion of underprivileged people who exist as a criminal underclass and who aren't registered in income or employment statistics. As Robert Wade points out –

> Canada excepted, all the countries of English settlement, led by the United States, have experienced big increases in income inequality over the past 20–30 years. In the United States the top 1% of families enjoyed an increase in after-tax income of about 160% over 1979–97, while families in the middle of the distribution had a 10% increase … Income distribution in the United Kingdom grew more unequal more quickly than even the United States during the 1980s, and is now the most unequal of the big European countries. (2004: 393)

With the collapse of social welfare structures and the rise of user-pay economics, the poorest members of rich, Anglophonic countries have remained just as poor as they were 30 years ago.

Globalized Finance

Since the 1970s and 1980s one of the most traded commodities around the globe has been finance, the purest form of capital. The current fashion of deregulating international currency trade has allowed individual nations to participate more fully in various forms of product exchange; however, computer linking and deregulation have also allowed currency traders to speculate on minor variations in currency value, buying and selling national currencies on minor trends to reap enormous profits. At times these minor variations are purely speculative, based on the economic performances of particular national economies, or major enterprises within those nations. The international price of agricultural or mineral products (known specifically as 'commodities') can cause major declines in the tradability and value of a nation's currency. While a decline in a major agricultural trading commodity may not upset the currency value of a large, developed economy which may have many export industries, for a Developing World economy which may export only a few agricultural products, the decline can be catastrophic. International financiers sell off that nation's currency, reducing its tradable value. The net effect of such a sell-off is to reduce that nation's capacity to buy materials from overseas (its currency is worth less) and its capacity to repay international debt (it has less income and its currency is worth less). The reduction in viability of debt repayment puts further pressure on the currency, making an already difficult economic situation much worse.

Currency trading, in fact, is one of the more insidious and mysterious global capitalist activities. An equally serious problem for Developing World economies and peoples, however, is the modernization process itself. Economies being drawn into the international capitalist network are only able to do so through a radical restructure of their own internal economic, spatial, social and cultural arrangements. While colonialism undoubtedly set the trajectory of change in motion, the globalization of economies from the 1970s has accelerated these changes, bringing an enormous burden of debt as nations struggle to participate in the global capitalist circuitry. Of course there have been some notable successes where modernization and globalization have rapidly expanded economic production in countries like Taiwan, Singapore, South Korea and the Philippines. However, as Neil Smith (1997) points out, the poorest nations of the world have merely been caught up in capitalization, most frequently as sources of cheap labour and as a vacuum receptor for the excessive accumulations of capital in the developed world. David Harvey (1989) makes this point in his discussion of postmodernity. The successes of capital accumulation in the developed world lead necessarily to the need for its redirection. Small, vulnerable economies become sites for the deposition of excess capital: tourism, development investment, loans. Of course these economic changes are accompanied by significant political and cultural incursions which in effect alter the social and cultural fabric of globalizing agricultural economies. Dislocation and social upheaval in poorer countries have been well documented, but in fact the incursions of globalized economy and internal restructure are also having devastating ecological effects. Seas, forests and formerly fertile lands are being turned to waste by the exploitative activities of multinational corporations. Great rivers are turning to sewers. As Robert Wade (2004) says, the integration of poorer nations into the global web is generally accomplished to maximize benefits for the investor without any great regard for the smaller economy.

The experience in sub-Saharan Africa is perhaps most telling. In a range of narrative films produced since 2000 – *Hotel Rwanda, The Constant Gardener, Sometimes in April, Blood Diamond,* and *The Last King of Scotland* – the terrible impact of globalization and eco-political imperialism is starkly revealed. Famine, civil war, economic exploitation, disease and the ever-present threat of a vicious warrior politics seem to mock the niceties of developed world patronage and its ideals of economic globalization. The destitution and suffering of the peoples of sub-Saharan Africa represent a blight on our own wealth and the fantasy of justice upon which our modernity is founded.

Debt

The sub-Saharan experience of the past several decades is perhaps the most spectacular example of problems of global economic integration and development. Yet, even the so-called 'tiger economies' of South-East Asia and parts of Latin America have experienced significant problems since the financial crises of the mid 1990s. These crises have been explained away by neo-classical economists of the West as part of the internal failings of a national economy which is not lean and efficient and which squanders borrowed money on non-productive activities like health and education. These neo-classical principles also underpin the policies of the international money lenders who provide funds to governments but who expect a significant profit for their financial support. As the crisis deepened, however, the major international lending organizations – the International Monetary Fund (IMF), the World Bank and the Asian Development Bank – became actively involved in the policies and spending activities of national economies like Indonesia, Thailand and Mexico. To remain solvent, that is, these independent nations were forced to surrender significant aspects of their independence and sovereignty: they had to cut back on education, health and welfare spending, open their borders to overseas investment and imports, reduce all forms of trade barriers, and allow foreigners to buy their resources, including significant natural and cultural resources. This monetary crisis, which saw the value of the Indonesian rupiah, for example, decline by 900 per cent against the US dollar, resulted in serious shortages, increased famines and destabilized the political conditions of the state (not necessarily a bad thing). It also led to the surrender of policies and legislation that had tried to protect Sumatran forests against excessive foreign exploitation and ecological devastation.

Much of the postmodern celebration of diversity is attached to the dissolution of national borders. Postmodernism, however, has not accounted fully for the dismantling of national borders where these form a protective layer against excessive exploitation and hegemonic control. In *Stop: Think* (1999) Paul Hellyer traces the rapid expansion in international indebtedness, especially by Developing World nations, arising from the 1981 global recession. According to Hellyer, the participation of Developing World and smaller economies in the trading and financial activities of large, multinational institutions like the World Bank has been bought at the cost of national sovereignty and economic independence. Developing World economies borrow money and transform their economies through developmental programmes and the sale of national assets to international interests. The sense of prosperity that may appear during periods of economic growth quickly disappears during recession. The escalation of interest rates, combined with declines in exports critically wounds the economies of dependent nations, causing savage unemployment, bankruptcies and the hollowing out of national assets and economic activity. Governments have no option but to turn further toward the international begging bowl. The entity of nation and national interests are fundamentally eroded by this uneven relationship. The protective barriers of nationhood – including education, health and welfare – are cut away by dependency. Postmodernism may bring a few tourists to the impoverished Developing World, it may bring clothing factories and plastic bags, but it seems rarely to bring security, clean water, freedom and dignity.

11

New Media Cultures

INTRODUCTION

As we have noted many times in this book, language and discourse are central to the formation of culture. Contemporary cultural theory focuses on the ways in which culture and meaning-making are constituted through the operations of language. Nineteenth-century preoccupations with knowledge and reality are replaced in cultural analysis by an interrogation of how knowledge is formed in discourse. Contemporary culture, of course, has expanded exponentially the means by which discourse is created and conveyed. Electronic and digital media have broadened human discursive processes well beyond the facilities of interpersonal (aural/oral, gesture, graphics) and print technologies. These new technologies, however, are not just the tools or machinery employed by communications media and industry; they are profoundly embedded in culture, its ideologies, discourses and meaning-making processes. In many respects a medium is distinguished by its principal technology (TV, radio, computer networked communication), and this technology is constituted in culture through its own particular sets of disputes, values and meanings.

Humans have always used technology, of course, in order to enhance 'natural' abilities in the facilitation of economy, communication, bodily performances and pleasures, relationships and social organization. Romantic philosophy, however, which evolved during the eighteenth and nineteenth centuries, conceived of technology and culture as fundamentally opposed. Reacting to the social and environmental degradation associated with modernization, Romantic philosophers and aesthetes regarded industrialization and urbanization as anathema to the richness and beauty of the human spirit (see Chapter 2). 'Culture', therefore, was defined as a sublime and spiritually exaltant release from the instrumental horrors of technological industrialism. This theme persists into the twentieth century, with particular social groups (e.g., the 1960s hippie movement) and intellectuals (Bell, 1973; Postman, 1993) questioning the social, moral and cultural value of technological progressivism and its de-humanizing effects.

In contemporary aesthetics, film-makers and artists of various kinds perpetuate the 'Frankenstein myth' created by the Romantic novelist, Mary Shelley – the idea that human interventions in nature will inevitably return to destroy their maker. From the cyborg creations of *Blade Runner* and *Gattica* to tales of global warming and climate change (*The Day after Tomorrow, Inconvenient Truth, Sunshine*), recent film-makers express their deep misgivings about technology and human manipulation of the natural environment. Once again, technology is regarded as something outside culture, where culture is the sublime of spiritual, intellectual and aesthetic transcendence.

Needless to say, however, these dystopian views of technology seem to have made little dent in the propitious and seemingly relentless force of technological progressivism. Even when it is questioned or challenged, even when it is positioned within its cultural context, technology appears to have asserted itself as a dominant idea, ideal or ideology which is associated with conceptions of individual lifestyle, social improvement, economic growth and historical progress. In the cultural analysis of technology this ideology has been characterized in its more extreme forms as a type of technological determinism: the idea that a technology exists and will necessarily produce certain historical effects. Technological determinism generally operates like this:

1   The cultural analyst looks back at history and identifies a particular new technology.
2   A causal link is established between the technology and new social trends or events. A causal link is established between the technology and the social effects. The cultural and historical trend which brought the technology into use is generally ignored.
3   The analyst claims that the technology caused or determined the effect, parenthesizing or ignoring all other associations or causations.
4   The analyst often looks forward (usually optimistically), using a 'new' technology to predict new trends.

A technological determinist perspective often surveys social and cultural history, using 'technology' as the primary definer of the particular epoch (periodization). For the study of communications technology, a determinist perspective reads the history of the world in terms of 'communications revolutions': periods that are marked and determined by the emergence of a particular communications technology. Contemporary technological periodizations, therefore, would treat history as a progress towards the current, superior technological culture. More than this, however, a technological determinist perspective also tends to be 'futurist', using the emergence of digital and computer networked communications to anticipate future social and cultural trends. For futurist technological determinists, the new computer technologies will not only transform communications, their revolutionary effects will reach across all areas of human life. Not surprisingly, this sense of an improving historical condition also affects the technological determinists' perspective of the future: undoubtedly the progress offered by these new technologies will bring us a future that is inevitably better than the past.

Marshall McLuhan's notorious 'global village' is one of the more spectacular examples of technological determinist futurism (see 1964, 1969); McLuhan predicted that the broad distribution of TV technology would compress the world into a positively homogenized global space. The current culture of networked computer technology is being represented in similar terms, with futurists anticipating such things as the end of the office, networked cities, the eradication of pollution, virtual communities and the obliteration of human conflict. Our aim in this chapter is to explore the cultural conditions that constitute these new communications technologies without recourse to a determinist perspective. While we are, of course, centralizing communications technologies, we are interested primarily in the cultural operations and meanings that flow through and around these technologies. To this extent, we are particularly interested in the ideological and discursive disputes which are associated with new communications technology.

COMMUNICATION AND TECHNOLOGY

The deployment of communications technology as a periodizing definer needs some closer attention. In particular, the problem with using technology in this way is that it may neglect or parenthesize the significant context in which the social and cultural transformations operate. That is, technologies exist because they are needed, have value or meaning for a given culture. While the culture continues to have a need for the technology, it will continue to have meaning; technological determinism tends to treat the arrival of the new technology as something 'revolutionary' and outside the interests and demands of the people who draw it from historical obscurity. Many inventions and technologies exist through historical developments, but it is only those which the culture needs or demands that become popularized and useful. Equally, the emphasis on 'the new' might also obscure the fact that particular technologies are remarkably longevitous, their use-value being obscured by the dramatic and transformative emergence of a new technology. The facility or technology of oral language, for example, has been operational for around 100,000 years; amid the excitement of the new communications technologies, this old form continues to be a major part of the human communications retinue.

To this extent, the following survey of communicative cultures needs to be understood as a series of overlapping and open assemblages, rather than as a set of closed historical categories. As Carolyn Marvin has noted in her deconstruction of the notion of communications revolutions, *When Old Technologies Were New* (1988), new technologies were nearly always constructed out of a complex set of cultural processes, including the slow and evolving confluence of social need and available apparatus. The survey that follows is meant to de-emphasize the notion of revolution by returning the communications technology to the context which produced this correlation of need and availability. At any particular historical moment there will be many cultures and many forms and levels of cultural experience; culture is never one thing, but is a series of overlapping, sometimes disjunctive, meaning formations. Our survey of communicative cultures, therefore, is merely locating culture around a particular meaning formation: communications technology. We should not, therefore, assume that this particular cultural formation represents an epitome for all the elements that constitute a particular historical epoch. We are not defining the epoch, but locating our interests in the particular cultural formation of the 'pre-eminent' communications technology, and examining how this formation relates to other cultural elements. We should also remember that a particular technology, as noted above, may continue after its predominance has subsided or been mollified by the presence of new cultural elements or technologies.

Oral Culture

Periodization analysis has tended to treat orality as a closed cultural system, beginning somewhere between 60,000 and 100,000 years ago and ending with the arrival of writing (4000 BC) or movable print (Europe, around 1451). The anthropologist Eric Michaels (1985) has demonstrated, however, that periodization overlooks the continuities of oral culture, and the ways in which new cultural technologies, forms and facilities may simply be overlaid onto pre-existing processes and experiences. In this sense, oral culture may be characterized by the pre-eminence of orality, though this fundamental language technology may have been supplemented by graphic and artistic forms, dance, music, rituals and other meaning codes like smoke signals. In any case, the beginnings of the technology of language remain elusive since spoken language leaves no residue, no artefacts for archaeological investigation. Certainly, the complex system of communication called language is associated with the migration of humans across the globe and the imperatives of new forms of economy, environmental adjustments and social organization. Oral language seems necessary for such complex social and economic activities, including the movement and settlement of people in the Americas and through South-East Asia to Australia. Recent evidence is suggesting that these migrations took place perhaps as long ago as 100,000 years before the present (BP). Clearly, these long, migratory journeys required sophisticated forms of communication and organization: the cultural need precedes the facility.

The characteristics of oral culture may be summarized as follows:

1   Oral language is fixed in time and space. Because it can't be recorded and exists only for the duration of vocal sounds, oral information is ephemeral and relies on human memory for its durability.
2   The number of people involved in any given communication process is limited by the range of the spoken voice. In direct, non-transmitted orality, the human voice becomes the range limit, and so the presence of the human body is critical to communication.

3   In oral cultures the communicator is immediately connected to the world around him/her: symbol and referent are engaged in a very close relationship. For example, the language use of the American Hopi Indians compels the speaker to consider his or her own concrete observations. For the successful transfer of information, the speaker must continually refer to the actual, physical space in which the communication is taking place. Past, present and future cannot be distinguished in abstraction as with English; the speaker must refer to a particular spatial element in order to make the information understood.

4   Information must be connected with immediacy and relies on ritualized practices of memory. Information is closely connected to 'narrative' or forms of storytelling. Social laws, therefore, are 'recorded' and communicated in repetitive practices like dance and ceremony. These practices cover birth, initiation, kinship, territory, death, hunting and gathering practices, resource distribution, fertility and sexuality.

5   Memory is imperfect and distorts information: knowledge is difficult to accumulate so only a limited corpus of knowledge can be transmitted generationally. Very often, the prized facility of memory provides a particularly high status for those with the longest memories, the elders. Elders pass their knowledge on to younger members of the tribe.

6   Rituals, totems, symbols and art are used to supplement limited knowledge, and the limits of human memory and body. The oldest human art forms consist of simple cave engravings produced by Australian Aborigines about 40,000 years ago. More recent tribal cultures produce elaborate forms of art, including cave paintings, engravings, wood carvings and stone monuments.

7   History (all-time) is revivified and restored with every utterance. History lives in the present context or lifeworld. That is, there is a sense of the perpetual in the immediacy of oral culture and oral language. Since the memory does not work like lineal time or a chronology, the past seems to be forever preserved in a present utterance. The language use of oral cultures seems to compress time into an ever-unfolding now.

8   Therefore, lived experience embodies all history, reinterpreted and refashioned to make sense of present events, social practices, relationships, and so on. For example, in Nigeria kinship obligations are rooted in a past that extends some sixty years before dropping away into mythological time. This temporal compression is produced simply out of the life-span of a living memory. The human mind flows boundlessly between present events, memory and imagination. Mythological time and present time merge through the facility of human recall.

For Australian Aborigines, knowledge of time extends only as far as the Dreaming, which is the time that surrounds the immediacy of living memory or life-span. Yet the Dreaming is also 'ever-present' in the spirit of all things: rocks, topography, the weather and animals are all imbued with the spirit of the Dreaming. Human ancestry, therefore, exists in the 'present' and present experiences of all animate and inanimate objects; while memory can only be specified through the memory of the oldest living person in the group, all-memory persists in the environment.

9   Mythology thus surrounds the immediacies of time as now. Mythology becomes the conduit to human perpetuity.

While orality has been subjugated by the ideological force of writing and print culture, it has remained a significant part of human connectedness over the past millennia. The arrival of electrical communication has not just facilitated a 'secondary orality', as McLuhan calls it; rather, orality has been a continuous presence in human communications. Postmodernism, with its emphasis on de-centralization, imagery and the compression of time, has in many respects reinvigorated this underlying orality. The communalism of decorative art, the intensification of time and immediacy as 'all-time', the experience of ephemera and the pleasures of the communicable bodily presence – all are shared by orality and postmodernism.

Writing and Print Culture

The introduction of writing in the cultures of Sumer (4000 BC), Egypt (3000 BC) and Greece (1000 BC) is undoubtedly associated with significant changes to economy, lifestyle and forms of social organization, including relationships of power. The settled communities along the Euphrates and Nile rivers employed economic and social strategies which were markedly different from those used by oral, nomadic hunter-gatherer communities. In agricultural communities territory becomes a more fixed resource, leading to changes in self-conception and notions of the cosmos. In a sense, settlement and writing are implicated in various forms of social differentiation and therefore ideology. Writing was an elite activity from its very beginnings, a tool for the control and management of resources – including property, products and human resources. Writing was also a tool for the production of political identity and the justification of privilege. It is not a question of whether the pen or the sword is mightier: it is rather a question of controlling them both.

Literacy, thus, is implicated in power and its transmutation during the period to modernity and beyond. What is interesting about the settlement process and the establishment of feudalistic social systems is that writing remained very much an exclusive practice. However, as the administration and economy of these systems became larger and more complex, the field of power began to extend and literacy served as a source and prize for those who would challenge the status quo. The administration of a complex feudal system facilitated the spread of the technology of writing, allowing alternative ideologies to challenge the dominant order. Manuscript books facilitated new forms of supplementary and sharable memory that were not confined by time and space. While the principal communicative form remained oral, the book became a new resource for exploring ideas and thoughts, some of which had been regarded as seditious. The flexibility of authorship – each scribe or copier might add or extract details of a book – permitted a certain anonymity and uncertainty. It was not until the introduction of movable typeface and large-scale printing machines that mass literacy was possible.

Again, there is the temptation to assume that the introduction of the Gutenberg printing press (first book published around 1451–3) led to specific cultural effects. This is not the case. Movable print had been used in China some time around AD 600 but was not applied in Europe until social and cultural forces had combined to construct a need. This need was associated with the development of a new and increasingly powerful group of merchants and traders, and the continuing complexity of social, economic and political administration. What is clear, however, is that mass printing facilitated the spread of literacy and with it ideology and ideas. While clearly this took some centuries to accomplish, print culture might be characterized in the following terms:

1 *Economy.* The printed, vernacular Bible was the first mass-produced capitalist product. Books, therefore, were both products and conduits of new ideas and ideologies. The vernacular Bible, in particular, was a clear challenge to the exclusivity of Latin scholarship and the power of Roman Catholicism. A vernacular Bible cracked the closed system of knowledge control which only Latin readers and writers could previously access. The printed book, therefore, becomes the ensign for a rising middle class (and bourgeois capitalism) as they access and create new forms of knowledge.

2 *Authorship.* This provides a new way of defining the individual and the ideology of individualism. The Copyright Act (England 1709) announces a significant change to the way society conceives of itself and its relationship to the individual. Previously, authorship was a highly mutable and generally collective concept: as soon as it appeared, a text could be appropriated, changed, copied and used by anyone with access to the material. The notion of authorship, however, comes to represent one of the key problematics of modern society, the division between the individual and the social whole. The public and the private, personal and governmental, individual rights and collective responsibilities are radically separated by modernism. Authorship represents the mind of the individual (intellectual property) within the context of complex interconnections in modern capitalist culture. Just as 'democracy' represents an effort to reunite politically these divisions, the notion of the author is presented as an aesthetic and intellectual resolution to social schizophrenia. The author, that is, becomes the idiosyncratic 'super-human' whose special attributes will articulate and overcome the opposite intensities of our modern individualism: freedom and alienation.

3 *Reason and individualism.* The existence of print further advances the concept of the rational self and composition of orderly text (and social order). Text objectifies the human mind, placing complex processes and ideas into an accessible, literate system. The high status of reason is clearly inscribed in the form and structure of a written text.

4 *The public–private divide.* Rational government becomes the nexus between public duties and private freedom. The written text facilitates the formation of democratic government and the integration of a new and inclusive social order. Written text facilitates the recording and rational distribution of government dicta, administration processes and laws.

5 *Durability.* This is further advanced in print. Concepts of history and time are reformulated; perpetuity becomes invested in the creative act, rationalized through

written language. The past may be reconstructed and analyzed in its own terms. The liberal humanist education is thus founded on the notion of durable and worthwhile knowledge and a chronological, systematized presentation of the past. This chronology, of course, privileges particular events, characters and systems of causality.

6   *Privilege and standardization.* The division of knowledge carries particular difficulties for modernism. Just as mythology was employed in tribal cultures in order to overcome contradictions, print culture employed education processes to inculcate particular ideologies which justified social division and privilege. Equally, the existence of mass-produced text also encourages certain standardization in language. The arrival of the first printing press in Kent led to a standardization of a previously heterogeneous English. The Kentian dialect thus became the standard written English because it was the first English to be broadly distributed in print.

7   *Dominant ideologies.* Benedict Anderson (1991) argues that the spread of mass literacy through print facilitated the development and standardization of forms of nationalism. Not only were modes of administration and the formation of an ideology of citizenship made possible by mass literacy and mass education, the emotional sensibilities of nationalism were also rendered possible through available text. Nation, thus, became the 'imagined' community of modern social agents. Their community could no longer be seen directly but had to be experienced through the imagination. Imperialism and colonialism were necessary corollaries of this imagined community. Ideologies relating to capitalist processes, social hierarchy, sexuality and sexual norms, the family and religiosity were also distributed through the mass-produced text.

8   *Alternative ideologies.* As Alvin Gouldner (1976) has pointed out, mass-produced information such as the newspaper also facilitated the spread of alternative ideologies. Undoubtedly, print facilitated specific kinds of imagination and allegiance, certain pre-eminent ideologies, but it also facilitated opposition and sedition, pleasure and aesthetic transcendence. The text, that is, becomes the source of escape and transgression, as well as obedience.

Telegraphy

Walter Benjamin's famous essay 'The work of art in the age of mechanical reproduction' (orig. 1937, 1977) refers to a significant shift in modern understanding of art and popular culture. According to Benjamin, the capacity of film art to be copied and to be watched simultaneously by innumerable audiences significantly alters the cultural status of art and its author. Benjamin's essay acknowledges that the notions of authenticity and privilege have been significantly deconstructed by the application of electricity and mechanical processes. The broadcasting of images and information could no longer be confined by the limits of space and time. In fact, the processes of mechanical and electrical reproduction had begun well before the ascent of Hollywood cinema. As James Carey has explained, 'the innovation of the telegraph can stand metaphorically for all the innovations that ushered in the modern phase of history and determined, even to this day, the major lines of development of American communications' (1989: 203). For Carey, the most 'obvious and innocent' fact about the significance of the telegraph is that it enabled for the first time the separation of communications from the spatial limits of transportation. The application of electricity to communications allowed human contact to be constituted directly and immediately beyond the constraints of time over space.

Telegraphy, in fact, heralds the beginnings of both telecommunications, including networked computer communications systems like the Internet, and the electrical broadcast media: radio, film and television. Henry Morse's codification of electrical current into a binary system of dots and dashes (1838, Morse Code) not only facilitated the reunification of the United States after the Civil War (1861–2), but also produced significant effects in networking global communications. As with newsprint, however, this networking of communications produced contradictory effects through opportunities for greater homogenization and diversification of knowledge, identity, ideology and culture. Most obviously, the telegraph further enhanced the administrative powers of the state, and the processing of national and international trade. It contributed to the creation of the first great industrial monopoly, Western Union, and facilitated the consolidation and networking of major news services. In colonial outposts, the laying of the Atlantic and Pacific cables in the latter part of the nineteenth century produced two quite distinctly homogenizing effects:

1   The relative cheapness of newsprint had facilitated the proliferation of newspapers (and ideologies) during the nineteenth century. However, for English-speaking colonies like Canada, New Zealand and Australia, the provision of local news could not fully ameliorate the tyranny of distance and the profound sense of cultural isolation. News from London or New York might take as long as nine months to be received and reprinted. The arrival of international cable news allowed immediate contact with the outside world for the first time. The growing trend toward a diversity of news styles and content in the colonies was quite suddenly shattered by the provision of news from the centres of global knowledge and culture. Local news was forced to the margins as the important information from Europe and America was centralized.

2   The great expense of telegraphed information from overseas led to the syndication of news product. The major newspapers in the English-speaking colonies pooled their resources and shared information. Smaller papers couldn't afford the cabled news. They went broke or were bought up. After the arrival of telegraphy, the number of news sources in Australia and Canada, for example, was dramatically reduced and the conditions were prepared for the development of major news conglomerates. Into the twentieth century, the larger news corporations were able to take advantage of their competitive position and form even larger and more powerful news information centres. These centres thus homogenized news stories as they contributed to the hegemony of cultural imperialism.

For non-English-speaking colonies, the arrival of telegraphy created conditions for the greater assertion of centralized, colonial control. Distance had insulated the colonies from excessive interference from the colonial centres; however, telegraphy was used to strengthen the cultural and political impact of imperialism and the construction of colonized identities and cultural landscapes. Locally stationed colonial administrators were now subject to constant surveillance and the imposition of the urban centre's interests.

James Carey (1989) has argued that telegraphy, in fact, underscores the production of particular forms of ideology and consciousness. In particular, the costing of telegraphy by the word encouraged the development of a 'parsimonious' or 'minimalist' writing style. News stories which were dispatched on the telegraph discarded all redundancies, including complex ideas, language tropes and excessively descriptive phrases. The writing style of authors like Ernest Hemingway became a paradigm for all correspondents using the telegraph lines. More than this, however, the speed and volume of telegraphic information produced new forms of social and commercial organization which stripped the language of its personality, forming processes and protocols which were essentially impersonal, commercial and rule-driven. Communications theory, law, ethics, religion, and 'common sense' produced the necessary structures for impersonal communication, leading to new forms of consciousness and the naturalization of relations through etiquette. Much the same might be said of the introduction of email, which is going through a similar transformation and production of new knowledge and etiquettes. Like emailers, telegraph users had to develop a re-conceptualized time and space, and their own sense of locally constituted identity.

As Carey points out, however, the production of a communications system through the conduit of 'electricity' seemed to bring together, for the American mind at least, the divergent poles of modernism and modernization. That is, electricity and electrical communication brought into a more contiguous relationship capitalist materialism and the 'spirit' or ethos of individualism and individual transcendence. America's parallel histories of frontier materialist secularism on the one hand, and religious emancipation on the other, seem to achieve some level of confluence in the commercial and 'ethereal' qualities of electricity. The miracle of electrical energy could be deployed for the greater commercial power of individuals and the nation; electrical communications would bring the American community together, but in a decidedly commercial context.

Broadcast Culture

This same messianic aura was deployed in the transformation of telegraphy into a point-to-point radio system, and ultimately to broadcast radio. This transformation was led initially by amateur enthusiasts, though World War I alerted governments and military officials to the importance of two-way field communications and the potential of a broadcast system. The original telegraphy legislations in Britain, Australasia, Canada and the US were extended to include the word 'voice'. With the invention of the thermonic valve, which facilitated voice amplification, broadcast radio transmission fell immediately under the control of centralized governmental powers. Raymond Williams (see 1968, 1974) has suggested a number of reasons for the developing interest in radio broadcasting:

1   Accelerating social and geographic mobility in the early years of the twentieth century led to an increased potential for alienation and isolation. Combined with the increasing insecurities associated with international relations and internal economic stress, the potential for dislocation and the fracturing of community sharpened demand for a nodal and unifying discourse. Radio's human quality (the human voice) brought an immediacy and 'personality' to the imagined community of nation.
2   The social intensification of the small family home and independent dwelling space created a new context for media reception. Urbanization and the fracturing of old communities were accompanied by the rise of the family as a social and economic unit. The family home became a source of consumption and private pleasure; radio facilitated governmental and commercial penetration into the private sphere.
3   Industrialists themselves may have understood the potential for profit. The radio, that is, constituted a commodity in itself, but more importantly offered the facility for advertising other products directly into the home. The radio, therefore, was heavily marketed as a consumer commodity.

We might also add a fourth reason to Williams' list. That is, governments themselves had identified the potential of the radio medium for gaining direct access to the minds and actions of their citizenry. While people had felt the need to be connected with each other in a mass society, governments would identify the potential of the radio for control, regimentation and propaganda. Certainly, the tight scheduling of radio programmes (including regimes of morning exercise and ablution) indicates a certain homogenizing intention in radio culture. Theodor Adorno and Max Horkheimer (1972) make the point that radio and later TV broadcasting were designed to control citizens through a certain instrumental rationality: that is, the technology and its content constituted forms of controlling ideology. Certainly, the Nazi propaganda minister, Joseph Goebbels, made sure that every citizen in Germany had access to a radio so that he or she could hear the word of the Führer directly and immediately.

The 'miracle' of radio, as it was promoted during the 1920s and 1930s, brought the sound of human voices into the everyday lives of ordinary people. Marshall McLuhan's characterization of radio as 'the tribal drum' and the 'hottest' of all media indicates the substantial appeal of a medium which amplified the human voice, bringing music, news and information directly and immediately into the private sphere of the home. The discourse of radio changed dramatically during this period, transforming the apparatus from a piece of tinkerer's technology into a fashionable and highly desirable domestic commodity. In fact, the introduction of the radio as domestic furniture marked the beginnings of commodity sexualization. Elegant and attractive young women were deployed in advertising to construct this confluence of sexual appeal and progressive media consumption. The radio became sexualized as women's bodies became the convergent public–private figures of domestic consumption. Advertising also promoted the new technology as in terms of its putative magical powers: the marriage of sound waves, sex and electricity was said to cure cancer and facilitate communication with the dead.

The arrival of TV might have spelled the death of radio, and, again, commercial, governmental and other discourses introduced the new media in revolutionary terms. McLuhan's famous 'global village' comment described a world in which TV became the information staple for all the world's citizens. Radio, however, like the technologies of orality, writing and print, maintained itself through a redefinition of role and cultural function. In particular, the application of transistor technology and the miniature battery permitted a new mobility. The radio voice changed from one of authority to one of youthful transgression. Rock and roll music and the emergence of youth culture during the 1950s and 1960s created a demand for new forms of commodification, leisure and communicative pleasure. As youth sought a space beyond the surveillance of senior generations and within the community of their peers, the transistor radio became adopted into a new cultural formation. The continuous music format, Top 40, and advertising directed specifically toward youth markets, all came to characterize new social and cultural practices. The TV displaced the radio from its central domestic location, but the radio lived on in youth parties, cars and other forms of mobile social practice. In very significant ways, the transistor radio paved the way for later mobilities, including the mobile phone, walkman and Ipod.

ELECTRONIC DEMOCRACY

Modern Technology and Politics

It is very clear that modern societies could not have evolved without some form of knowledge and memory system that enabled accurate recording and distribution of information. The organization and management of mass populations has clearly been facilitated by the development of writing and print-based technologies. Capitalism, with its large-scale and often complex transactions, could not function without an effective system of recording and regulation. Complex political systems, such as representative democracy, have been constructed around writing: electoral processes, constitutions, law, administrative government, the informed decision making of people and their rulers – are all facilities of writing.

Moreover, writing and its linear and logical patterns fortified the underpinning ideologies of modernization, most particularly as they are lionized through the concept of 'reason'. Liberal democracy, as the confluence of capitalist economics and the ideals of citizen-based political governance, is thus shaped by a fundamentally logical communicative system. According to the canon of British liberalism, John Locke's *Two Treatises of Government* (1651), the interdependence of governmental and individual reason is the basis of freedom, which in turn is the basis of effective social and political organization. To this extent, we might usefully describe the emergence of constitutional democracy in terms of its primary communicational mode: that is, as 'writing democracy' (Lewis, 2005).

Through the progress of modernism, the media, most particularly the newspaper, became what Thomas Carlyle (see 1967) called in the nineteenth century the 'fourth estate'. That is, along with government, the church and legal institutions, the news media came to represent an independent pillar in the structure of the modern democratic state. In this ideal sense, the news media supposedly informed the citizenry, providing objectively gathered and presented information necessary for debate within the public sphere. The arrival of telegraphy, as we have noted, served to reinforce the reach, speed and volumes of information for public dissemination. John Hartley (1996) argues that the self-proclaimed impartiality, rationalism and objectivity of modern news media are both exaggerated and illusory. Hartley claims, in fact, that all discourses are politically and ideologically 'positioned'. Moreover, the mass literacy so keenly sought by social and political reformers of the nineteenth century has been deployed as much for popular and sensate consumption as for the interests of political activism or rational public debate. According to Hartley, journalism, as the primary literate practice of modernity, combines intellectual and sensational experiences:

> Journalism is *the* sense-making practice of modernity (the condition) and popularizer of modernism (the ideology); it is a product and promoter of modern life. … So much a feature of modernity is journalism that it is easy to describe each in terms of the other – both journalism and modernity are products of European (and Euro-sourced) societies over the last three or four centuries; both are associated with the development of exploration, scientific thought, industrialization, political emancipation and imperial expansion. Both promote notions of freedom, progress and universal enlightenment, and are associated with the breaking down of traditional knowledges and hierarchies, and their replacement with abstract bonds of virtual communities linked by their media. (1996: 33)

For Hartley, newsmaking is embedded in all the major and minor events, institutions and personal experiences that constitute modern life – including issues of sexuality and desire.

Televisual Politics

This dimension of modernism, however, extends well beyond literate culture and newsprint. Indeed, the sensate experiences which Hartley associates with the popular news media are clearly implicated in the development of aural and televisual broadcast media. Indeed, the move from written-language information to electronic media, as Michaels explains, re-enlivens the immediacies and sensory experiences that had typified oral culture. The mediation of politics through televisual representation, in particular, inscribes democracy with a new kind of cultural presence and personality. The rigidity of institutionalized political and legal processes is compressed as human imagery. Politics becomes the 'face of politics'; official records and political forums become iconographed in the televisualized personality of the politician. Democracy thus becomes mediated not so much through delegation or representative government as in televisual campaigns, doorstop interviews, 'grabs' and news values which favour action over detail, personalities over policy, conflict over consideration.

Political theory during the twentieth century has tended to treat the emergence of electrical/broadcast technologies as essentially an extension of writing communication and its political culture. However, in 'broadcast' or 'televisual politics' the multiple and opposing claims which democratic institutions seek to accommodate, if not reconcile, in policy become highly visible. The craft of the contemporary politician is to navigate the complex of claims and discourses while maintaining a semblance of integration, consistency and honesty. Thus, language games played out in televisual politics might be better characterized as persuasion games. Politicians are trained to avoid direct answers to media questions when these might alienate particular members of the electorate. Politicians use the media, in fact, to repeat simple and generally non-specific policy positions. The media audience is available for persuasion; the televisual politician seeks to inculcate party views through various forms of personality and narrative construction. The politician uses the media to tell his or her story through various forms of narrative storytelling. To this extent, televisual politicians assume the proportion of a particular kind of media celebrity, one who operates in a highly fluid relationship with the truth.

This unhinging of the truth has become a significant feature of contemporary institutional politics. A belief that truth can be located and distributed is one of the informing principles of modern journalism and, in turn, modern democratic institutions. However, while it may be quite feasible to present a version of the truth in quite simple terms – yesterday the politician said this – it is much more difficult to locate truth in complex issues involving variant social needs. Not only do politicians tell lies quite directly, but they also hedge or obscure the truth in order to satisfy variant and opposite social interests. The availability of guns in the US, for example, may be valuable for certain interest groups, such as gun manufacturers, farmers or gangsters. But when we are told that the policy of gun availability is necessary for the protection of American 'freedom', the truth of that claim becomes far more dubious.

Marxism, poststructuralism, postmodernism and cultural studies theory have all told us that 'truth' is generally constructed out of particular social interests; the broad social acceptance of that truth is a contingency of the truth-tellers' social power.

Televisual politics in contemporary culture is clearly a game of persuasion where the various interests, including the interests of dominant groups and ideologies, are played out. As previously noted, Jean Baudrillard's book *The Gulf War did not Take Place* (1995) illustrates how contemporary broadcast media engage in the persuasion game to produce the effects of truth. Baudrillard's later account of the September 11 attacks on New York (2002, see Chapter 12) reinforces the idea that the 'spectacle' has overwhelmed the event of disaster, creating a peculiar and insidious game of violence and political celebrity (see also Kellner, 2005).

Not all commentary on electronic media is as pessimistic and deterministic as Baudrillard's account. In fact, there are some commentators who suggest that the new broadcast media provide greater access and accountability in the relationship between politicians and the electorate. The new visibility of politicians since the advent of TV has certainly intensified the relationship between public and private life. Even so, the culture of the personality politician has intensified the notion of leadership and the iconography of the individual. This personality politics and the centralization of the leader is manifest in US presidential-style campaigns and Westminster campaigns where prime minister and opposition leader have taken on presidential proportions for the media. In a sense, the election campaigns have been constructed in parallel ways to TV popularity quests; celebrity politicians are presented in carefully managed profiles as much through personality magazines as the nightly news. The development of the primaries system of selecting American presidential candidates seems to have extended the process of election campaigns, providing highly valuable copy for the sale of newspapers and advertising space on television.

This commodification of political celebrity is clearly associated with broader cultural interests in stardom and celebrity. The election of Ronald Reagan, a B-grade Hollywood actor, to the presidency in the United States and Arnold Schwarzenegger to the governorship of California symbolize the confluence, especially in America, of political power and entertainment celebrity. It is sometimes argued that the absence in American cultural and political history of an aristocratic ruling class provided an ideal context for the ascent of entertainment celebrities. This putative egalitarianism draws political power from the people, and allows personality and individualism a freer range than was possible in the aristocratic legacies of Europe. America, in this sense, may have been waiting for its Hollywood star system and a president who could fulfil both political and celebrity roles.

DIGITAL DEMOCRACY

Over the past two decades the broadcast media have begun to surrender some of their homogeneity and nodalism. Satellite TV and the introduction of cable media services are facilitating the development of new, more specialized or narrowcast forms of media dissemination. Thus, while much of this increase has merely replicated existing texts and media models, some genuine variations have occurred, especially through community broadcasting. Greater variation, more precise textual targeting and the emergence of ethnic and community broadcasting have, in fact, presented an interesting challenge for political theorists. Some would argue that these variabilities produce fracturing effects on the state and the unity promised by democratic institutions. Those commentators who maintain a faith in the efficacy of integrated social structures and the notion of delegated power and responsible government sometimes accuse media fragmentation of undermining the unifying force of the nation-state and its principles of 'shared values' and truth. This traditional, democratic model acknowledges the importance of variant voices, but insists on the pre-eminence of a shared consciousness, a national culture and a government which can resolve significant differences through the construction of consensus rule.

Other theorists have claimed that the fragmentation of the media is vastly overdue and that the new postmodern, information-based state is a more equitable and genuine political formation, one that respects and encourages the needs and interests of individuals and minority communities. The valorization of individualism and media diversity parallels broader theoretical interests in difference and otherness – the postmodern cultural politics which celebrates the margins (see Chapters 7 and 10). Networked computer communication which draws together a range of media and communicative functions has been particularly welcomed by commentators interested in cultural fragmentation and media diversity (see Pollock and Smith, 1999; Walch, 1999; Gauntlett and Horsley, 2004). A cultural politics that emphasizes the liberational dimensions of democracy has formed around interactive media systems. The flexibility of these systems can be summarized in the following terms:

1   Computer networked communication (CNC) may be broadcast, allowing users to present information across vast global territories.
2   CNC may also facilitate highly targeted information transmission. Information may be directed at individuals, communities or interest groups. As with the more broadcast functions, these narrowcasts are not contained by space and time.
3   CNC is highly interactive and, compared with other forms of broadcasting, is inexpensive and accessible.

Thus, the new medium of interactive computer communication enables users to produce, distribute and consume information and entertainment texts through the complete range of communicative casting.

Nicholas Negroponte (1995; see also Jenkins and Thorburn, 2003) claims that the new media is thoroughly transforming social, cultural and political processes. Economies in the 'information age' will be based upon the exchange of weightless information 'bits', rather than manufactured products of matter and atoms. Industrialism, with its large-scale factories and ports and its manufacturing of waste products, will be replaced by speed-of-light, non-polluting informate economies. Digitized information will thus supersede the cumbersome and wasteful forms of atomic information delivery, including the most outmoded media of all: newspapers, magazines and books. With its great advantages of flexibility, error correction and data compression, digitized information and delivery offer enormous possibilities for social and economic reformation: 'Wholly new content will emerge from being digital, as well as new players, new economic models, and a likely cottage industry of information and entertainment' (Negroponte, 1995: 18). Being digital, then, will most certainly release the everyday citizen from the clutches of large media corporations; in an age of optimism, Negroponte assures us, the negative consequences of computerization will be subsumed by its potential for liberation, social harmony and individual expression:

> The harmonizing effect of being digital is already apparent as previously partitioned disciplines and enterprises find themselves collaborating, not competing. A previously missing common language emerges, allowing people to understand across boundaries. ... But more than anything, my optimism comes from the empowering nature of being digital. The access, the mobility and the ability to effect change are what will make the future so different from the present. (1995: 230)

Negroponte's vision of a complete and sharable global language seems finally to have fulfilled Descartes's Enlightenment dream of a universal language. While Descartes imagined that language would have been mathematics, for Negroponte it is an ideal of digital information and its universal attachment to capitalist economics and liberal humanist institutions. A new democracy will be activated through 'all information for all people at all times'. Negroponte and numerous others identify the new facility as empowering, realizing the elusive democratic ideal of an informed public (cf. Barney, 2000; Slavin, 2000; Lax, 2004).

POSTMODERN COMPUTER POLITICS

Numerous writers have discussed the political potential of the new computer networked communication systems. While some, like Nicholas Negroponte and Henry Jenkins, have emphasized the capacity of the networked computer to support institutional democracy, a number of 'postmodern'-influenced writers have spoken more generally about the computer's liberational potential. This section summarizes the major features of these arguments.

Hypertext Writing

Generally speaking, 'hypertext' refers to computer-based writing, though a number of commentators restrict the term to networked communication such as email, chat-rooms, bulletin boards and Internet pages. The imperative to 'be digital' is drawing together the full range of public and academic discourses, 'forcing a radical realignment of the alphabetic and graphic components of ordinary textual communication' (Lanham, 1993: 3). Thus the hypertext (see Landow, 1992; Snyder, 1996), or 'hypermedia', in McLuhan's terms, is seen to revolutionize writing, and extend human experience and consciousness beyond the ossification of author-centred, lineal and fixed text: 'an electronic text only exists in the act of reading – in the interaction between the reader and textual structure, ... the writing space' (Boller, 1992: 20; see also Boller, 1993). The writing space, that is, becomes the field for the player of these new language games. According to hypertext enthusiasts like Ilana Snyder (1996), Richard Lanham (1993), Mark Poster (1995) and Richard Berger (2004), the qualities of this new hypertext space are intrinsically more democratic and liberational than older forms of print and script writing:

1 Hypertext is infinitely erasable and therefore it is not fixed in rigid forms and structures. For paper writing, especially formally published writing, the text remains as an archive, fixed in a stable relationship between author and reader. Hypertext is less easy to control and possess because it is necessarily ephemeral. The writer has more flexibility and creativity, as hypertext facilitates a more adventurous and less inhibiting writing space. The concept of writing errors disappears.

2 The capacity of computers to correct grammar and spelling is far more user-friendly than printed writing. Hypertext permits greater access to people with lower education and language writing skills. Writing becomes less elitist and more available to all levels of literacy. It also facilitates language use by those of non-English-speaking backgrounds, thus supporting a multiculturalism as it abrogates the privileging of native English-speakers.

3 Email writing has helped transform organizational structures, facilitating contact across hierarchical borders. Like telegraphy, email reduces the status and status etiquette of the communicators. Email is a less formal and more open writing space which also facilitates wide-reaching communication between people without the limits of bodily presence.

4 Hypertext writing is inexpensive compared with older forms of writing production. It facilitates 'desktop' publishing, which provides much wider access to creative and expressive activities. Expensive printing processes can now be by-passed and levels of specialization and training are no longer at issue.

5 The Internet provides an extremely accessible and inexpensive facility for distribution of ideas and creative activities. Whereas artists and writers would once have had to rely on expensive infrastructures and the gate-keeping processes of publishers, distributors and retailers, they can now use the Internet for global distribution and contact.

6 Hypertext also facilitates the dissolution of expressive categorizations, especially between alphabetic writing, graphics, video and animation. Especially when published on the Internet, these expressive modes can be comfortably combined. Hypertext, therefore,

doesn't privilege writing over imagery, but enables a free flow of textual experiences. Thus the Enlightenment privileging of *logos* (the word) and reason is fundamentally undermined.

7   Hypertext, therefore, restores the experiential immediacies of oral cultures. The author is no longer the privileged 'authority' of the text since the Internet dissolves many of the distinguishing and fixed characteristics of print culture. In particular, the Internet text is interactive and infinitely reproducible. Readers can take a text and make it their own. Texts are fully interactive, conducive to an unending chain of creativity. Individuals are constituted by the text in a community of knowledge and creativity without the solidifications of copyright and the authority of the author.

8   Internet writing also challenges logocentric structures or narratives which form hierarchies of reading and writing. Webpages are not written in lineal sequences but operate as mimesis, imitations of the mind. Just as the human mind links various zones of knowledge, memory and imagination, hypertext forms links between various sites or zones of knowledge. These hyperlinks are formed through association rather than lineal sequence. Readers access information as it suits their own interest, rather than through the logical and pre-arranged order imposed by the author. Linking, therefore, is a more democratic pattern, one which allows the free flow of ideas and sensibilities. Sensation, impulse, emotions and imagery are no longer subsumed beneath the authority of logic and predetermined order.

In summary, then, hypertext writing – and digital composition spaces more generally – is regarded by its enthusiasts as intrinsically liberational, most particularly as it appears to overcome many of the limitations and privileges of modernist print culture. It allows for a more flexible, de-centred and accessible creativity which dissolves privileged hierarchies of knowledge. Computer networked communication would thus be a personalized media form where information is released from the control of knowledge and 'knowers' (Numberg, 1996).

Virtual Reality and Brain Machines: Liberation of the Mind

Subjectivity and identity have become central themes in cultural studies and cultural theory, including discussions on new technology. During the late 1980s and early 1990s a good deal of discussion about the liberational effects of computers centred on the notion of virtual reality. While some commentators use this concept quite broadly to include any levels of graphic computer simulation of experiential reality, others use the concept to refer specifically to particular simulation apparatuses, including those that are worn directly over the body (Sherman and Craig, 2003). The original virtual reality suit, including helmet and gloves, completely surrounds the user in aural, visual and tactile simulations. For a number of its proponents the simulation experience represented a transcendent reality, one which could draw the user into new levels of consciousness. New Age philosophy, for example, with its emphasis on individual liberationism, ancient and Asian spiritualism, and a strange combination of alchemy and technology, has identified virtual reality as a significant pathway to expanded consciousness.

More recent experimentation with virtual reality and altered consciousness has led to the development of new kinds of machines, some of which have been adopted into electronic games and military training. While they are varied in many ways, these 'brain machines' use visual stimuli to influence receptors in the central nervous system, creating a range of mind altering and perceptual effects. The VR Lab based in Switzerland conducts extensive research on the modelling and animation of 'Three Dimensional Inhabited Virtual Worlds', extending the original concept of individual liberation toward a greater sense of real-time experiential community. In many respects this is precisely the aspiration of VR designers involved in the creation of the Second Life concept (see below), a virtual space in which networked individuals can inhabit a new form of online social experience.

The Three-D concept, in fact, liberates VR from the problems of vertigo and nausea which continue to limit the earlier helmet and glove experiences. The *Lawnmower Man* novels and films have explored the notion of expanded consciousness specifically in relation to virtual learning and virtual sexuality.

Virtual Geography/Virtual Community

The earlier studies on hypertext have evolved into much broader analyses of the Internet, 'new media', the World Wide Web and other zones of digital creativity or 'digitextuality' (Everett and Caldwell, 2003). While these studies have tended over the past few years to relinquish the title of 'postmodernism', they have nevertheless been particularly interested in the capacity of the new media to generate new digital spaces through the compression of time and space and the creation of 'virtualities', including virtual communities. Of course, print and broadcast technologies have enabled the formation of distant proximities through various forms of communicational systems, but these virtual communities (global village) have been constructed around social hierarchies and modes of social differentiation largely based around residual forms of bodily differentiation – gender, age, ethnicity, geography.

Indeed, broadcast technologies have tended to maintain dominant discourses of nation and imperial control. Edward Soja in *Postmodern Geographies* (1989) and *Postmetropolis* (2000) has noted that the reformulation of national, geographic boundaries has largely been accomplished through various forms of cultural and economic imperialism. David Harvey (1989) has made clear that multinational corporations are not so much global citizens as global raiders and rulers. The crossing of national borders by international information and entertainment corporations has not been arbitrary, but is rather a First World strategic incursion aimed at increasing market share, profit and cultural dominance.

That is, broadcast media are clearly nodalized, as they are formed around privileged economic, military and cultural zones.

Mark Poster (1995, 1997, 2006) has claimed, however, that we are moving into a more evenly distributed and less nodally controlled media epoch. In this 'second media age' the networked computer provides the ideal infrastructure for a deconstruction of centralized broadcast media. In a prescience reminiscent of Marshall McLuhan and other futurists, Poster claims that advanced technological societies are on the precipice of a cultural, social and political revolution, analogous to the emergence of an urban merchant culture in the midst of feudal society. The de-centredness of the Internet communication system necessarily produces a radical shift in the subject position of the user. A new, postmodern, informational democracy, Poster argues, is facilitated by this shifting subjectivity.

Individual users are able to connect with one another in original and necessarily de-centred forms of communication. The second media age moves the relationship between text and user into a new field of responsiveness that is no longer a predicate of differential power, wealth and infrastructure control. Thus, the 'electronic geography' of the Internet produces a belonging and an identity position which only last as long as the user's connection to the Net. The ephemeral nature of this connection and its 'geography', that is, necessarily releases the user from a fixed and stable identity or subject position. The user is now much more free as she/he moves between spaces, communities and identities. The subject no longer has to be a citizen of a nation which implicates him or her in a rigid and homogeneous value system and prescriptive social ordering. The Internet geography defines the consciousness of the linked, postmodern user in a much more flexible and open manner. As a decentralized and egalitarian space, this Internet consciousness necessarily implicates a democratic and liberational subject position. This new consciousness is particularly acute as the Internet is no space at all; rather, it is an ephemeron, an abstract and invisible 'condition' which only exists in terms of the experience and connectedness of the individual user. There can be no question of control of the space, therefore, because the electronic geography is never anything more than the creation and experience of the individual user.

According to Poster, then, this new virtual geography constitutes a zone of democracy because it implicates new forms of communicative relations which are not based upon possession and differentials of power. In his seminal book *Virtual Community* (1993), Howard Rheingold tests these theories through direct communications experience. Rheingold, an early user of networked computer communication, explains how he has formed substantial social and political relationships through the Internet. These 'virtual communities' are not constructed through spatial proximity, but are constituted through the congregation of personal interests, values and cultural predispositions. The community was formed by people who shared certain attitudes and interests, and then committed themselves to the formation of a relational space. For Rheingold, the Internet provides the ideal facility for restructuring social relationships and community, but in ways that are radically new and superior to the arbitrariness of geographic propinquity. The new community is devoid of class, gender or racial discriminations since they are essentially 'disembodied' – predicates of a shared ideal, and a desire for social improvement and social empowerment. Writing from the perspective of a Californian idealism which has also produced the hippie and counterculture movements of the 1960s, Rheingold presents this new community as a political utopia. That is, the politics of the virtual community are constituted around the sheer pleasures of connection in the free space of the Internet:

> I suspect that one of the reasons for this phenomenon is the hunger for community that grows in the breasts of people around the world as more and more informal public spaces disappear from our real lives. I also suspect that these new media attract colonies of enthusiasts because CMC [Computer Mediated Communication] enables people to do things with each other in new ways, and to do altogether new kinds of things – just as telegraphy, telephone and television did. (Rheingold, 1993: 6)

What matters to Rheingold is the community-level culture which has appropriated the Internet from the control of the US defence forces and the academy. Thus the hobbyists who connected their computers to telephone lines during the 1980s established a pattern of free engagement, where the site of the Net became available for the people to use freely and without structured impositions and regulations. Charles Ess (1994) extends this notion of a community politics to argue that the Internet now constitutes that free public sphere in which Jürgen Habermas's 'ideal speech situation' (see Chapter 7) could be realized: the Internet, that is, would become a space for democratic engagement and the production of rational and consensual communicative action. Democracy would thus return to its ideals of logical resolution, as it discarded the fixities and hegemony of institutional structure. Barney (2000) on the other hand, remains deeply suspicious of the extravagant claims of the new digital democracy.

Second Life

This notion of virtual community has been recently extended through a form of broadly participative Internet game-playing called 'Second Life'. The Internet began as a military tool designed to de-centralize and 'network' America's communications systems during the Cold War (1945–89). The US military feared that a strike from the USSR could easily cripple the country's communications system, so a network of multiple nodes was constructed around the inchoate computer-based interactive system. University academics and computer enthusiasts (geeks) quickly recognized the value of the system for experimentation and knowledge sharing. These early users of the Net, in fact, established a strong moral and ideological code, focusing on justice, community and the free flow of information, narratives and ideas.

The collapse of the Cold War and the emergence of the World Wide Web (over-coded, image-based information architecture) during the 1990s introduced a new and much wider population of users, including domestic users, students, corporate and other profit-seeking organizations and individuals. Since that time, the Internet has become a complex and expanding field of cultural participation and contestation, as various classes of user seek to dominate the space and impose their particular moral and ideological norms.

To this end, the digital utopians ('digitopians') who first entered the hypertext environment have been forced to accommodate the increasing interests of private commerce and global capitalist economics. Quite clearly, private enterprise has moved not only to colonize the Internet as a communicational space, but it has also fractured and changed the mediated utopian culture upon which it had been founded. 'Second Life', a virtual reality community space created by Phillip Rosedale, is a relatively recent permutation of this form of appropriation. However, unlike the utopia imagined by Howard Rheingold and Mark Poster, Second Life is very much embedded in the private enterprise community of which the Internet is a part as well as a key player. Extending the ideas of experimental subjectivity, Second Life invites participants to 'create' a personal avatar (animated character) who then inhabits the virtual world of avatars in an entirely created social space. Like earlier online games and modes of online communication, including dating sites, Second Life allows the participant to adopt any form of body and personality type, facilitating extreme forms of subject experimentation, idealization – and deception. More telling, however, Second Life also acts like a Monopoly game, allowing participants to purchase and develop virtual real estate, create extravagant lifestyles and material prosperity. Relationships can also be formed in Second Life, once again allowing participants to fulfil fantasy and various forms of sexual exploration without the complication of bodily effect.

The high level of participation in Second Life has enabled the creation of virtual demand and a virtual property boom. As participants vie for quality real estate, Second Life money has become transferable to 'real' money, encouraging some players to employ teams of developers and reap significant financial reward from those new players keen to have a bite of the action. Among these players are various kinds of entrepreneurs who engage in financial transactions that mirror 'real life' fiscal exchanges.

In many respects, this invasion of corporate capitalism into Second Life parallels the transformation of other online spaces which began as community share domains. Share sites like YouTube and Myspace, which have been formed around youth culture and community formation, have each been purchased by large multinational entertainment corporations (Fox and Yahoo respectively). The transgressive and democratic sites that are designed to allow individuals and communities to freely express their subjectivity, therefore, have been appropriated by the same elite powers the digitopians were seeking to subvert.

Emo on MySpace

Emo (emo-tional) music emerged out of the punk and hardcore scene in the mid 1980s in Washington DC. Particular musicians would become spontaneously emotional during performances, expressing some deeper experiences of sadness and melancholy. This musical sub-genre has spawned a broader expressive style which is being articulated through clothing, poetry, music and psycho-emotional moods. Particular teenage communities have adopted the emo style and expressive moods, fortifying a general sense of 'adolescent' alienation with a shared state of melancholy and social cynicism.

Over recent years, emo has been appropriated into the more mainstream music industry, providing yet another commodity for global media markets. And like other cultural products, emo style provides a resource for the gathering of totemic belief systems and expressive modes – both of which are necessary for the formation of community. The emo community, in particular, has expanded and reshaped itself through the communicational conduit of the Internet. MySpace, most notably, has provided an ideal vehicle for the formation of a youth community that is techno savvy, grounded in contemporary musical genres, and distinguished by its sense of emotional and psychological alienation.

And while MySpace has been broadly celebrated as an expressive cultural site, linking many people with common interests across the globe, it has also been identified as a dangerous conduit to fragmentation, despair and nihilism. The combination of emo, MySpace and adolescent psychosis has been blamed for the suicide deaths of two teenage girls in Ferntree Gully, Australia, in 2007. According to George Patton, Professor of Adolescent Health at the Royal Children's Hospital in Melbourne, the Internet has intensified suicidal moods among young people, as it provides a space for the expression and sharing of self-destructive dispositions, as well as a vocabulary of despair. The two girls had used their MySpace sites to share in emo chat and style ideas. They posted suicide notes that despaired of contemporary culture and its acquisitive demeanour: Using the MySpace site, the girls posted the following farewell poem to their friends –

Fuck this world

Everything that you stand for

Don't accept

Don't give a shit

Don't ever judge me…

Also got to love my crazy friends for being there fore me, even when I'm being really annoying, a real cunt, or a complete, stupid fuck, that u would just wanna punch out.

Thank you all so much guys. luv yas.

Virtual Reality and Cyborg Fantasy

Writers like Mark Poster argue that the Internet itself offers the greatest potential for the construction of new forms of identity and subjectivity which in themselves are politically transgressive. New identities and new subject positions, that is, are produced through the new context of Internet communication. Not only does the Internet facilitate community connection between marginalized peoples such as minority ethnic groups, gays, political lobby groups (feminists, environmentalists, etc.), it also allows for a more creative use of the space. Donna Haraway (1991, 1997) makes this point when she argues that the 'disembodiment' of Internet users liberates them from bodily, cultural ascriptions. That is, the user is free to create his or her own bodily conditions when interacting through email or chat groups; users are able to divest themselves of the norms and ideologies which are inscribed on their bodies by mainstream culture. The limits of sexuality, gender, ethnicity, age, appearance and disabilities lose their relevance for the Internet user. The egalitarian space of the Internet enables, therefore, a liberation of the body and a new regime of creative interaction that is abstract and eternally flexible. This abstract and self-ascribing body provides the foundation for the complete liberation of a subjectivity which can now invent and reinvent itself with unhindered creativity.

This new liberated subjectivity forms the basis of Donna Haraway's more radical conception of the technological body. In her 'Cyborg manifesto', published on the Internet in the late 1980s and reproduced in *Simians, Cyborgs and Women* (1991), Haraway argues the case for a utopian politics where human biology is radically enhanced by its integration with technology. This 'evolutionary' overhaul and hybridization of *Homo sapiens* would necessarily outmode hierarchical differentiations that have been historically inscribed on human biology: gender, ethnicity, health and class. While this is an 'ironic dream', Haraway's manifesto quite seriously seeks a politics in which the cyborg woman transforms social relations, 'our most important political construction'. Haraway's hybrid body, then, is transgender and ageless. As a utopian fiction, the cyborg transcends the limits of human biology and the social inscriptions of modernism:

> The cyborg is resolutely committed to partiality, irony, intimacy, and perversity. It is oppositional, utopian, and completely without innocence. No longer structured by the polarity of public and private, the cyborg defines a technological polis, based partly on a revolution of social relations in the *oikos*, the household. Nature and culture are reworked; the one can no longer be the resource for appropriation or incorporation by the other. The relationships for forming wholes from parts, including those for forming polarity and hierarchical domination, are at issue in the cyborg world. (Haraway, 1991: 151)

Félix Guattari (1992) has argued similarly that the new computerized technologies reverse modernism's tendency toward machine or industrial-controlled subjectivity. These 'pseudo-stabilities' are discarded in favour of a genuine integration of machine and subjectivity: 'The machine is placed under the control of subjectivity – not a reterritorialized human subjectivity, but a new kind of machine subjectivity' (Guattari, 1992: 29). These integrated path/voices produce a polyphony of articulations which may now link into massive data banks and forms of artificial intelligence. The new, liberated subjectivities, therefore, are immensely more powerful than the nodalized media and telecommunications systems that have produced them, because they are more than merely human, and more than merely machinery. Radical politics, therefore, are conceived in terms of an evolutionary escape from the confining borders of the human body and the social limits that have been built around them.

The cyborg manifesto

A cyborg is a cybernetic organism, a hybrid of machine and organism, a creature of social reality as well as a creature of fiction. Social reality is lived social relations, our most important political construction, a world-changing fiction. The international women's movements have constructed 'women's experience', as well as uncovered or discovered this crucial collective object. This experience is a fiction and fact of the most crucial, political kind. Liberation rests on the construction of the consciousness, the imaginative apprehension, of oppression, and so of possibility. The cyborg is a matter of fiction and lived experience that changes what counts as women's experience in the late twentieth century. This is a struggle over life and death, but the boundary between science fiction and social reality is an optical illusion.

Contemporary science fiction is full of cyborgs – creatures simultaneously animal and machine, who populate worlds ambiguously natural and crafted. Modern medicine is also full of cyborgs, of couplings between organism and machine, each conceived as coded devices, in an intimacy and with a power that was not generated in the history of sexuality. Cyborg 'sex' restores some of the lovely replicative baroque of ferns and invertebrates (such nice organic prophylactics against heterosexism). Cyborg replication is uncoupled from organic reproduction. Modern production seems like a dream of cyborg colonization work, a dream that makes the nightmare of Taylorism seem idyllic. And modern war is a cyborg orgy, coded by C3I, command-control-communication-intelligence, an $84 billion item in 1984's US defence budget. I am making an argument for the cyborg as a fiction mapping our social and bodily reality and as an imaginative resource suggesting some very fruitful couplings. Michael Foucault's biopolitics is a flaccid premonition of cyborg politics, a very open field.

By the late twentieth century, our time, a mythic time, we are all chimeras, theorized and fabricated hybrids of machine and organism; in short, we are cyborgs. The cyborg is our ontology; it gives us our politics. The cyborg is a condensed image of both imagination and material reality, the two joined centres structuring any possibility of historical transformation. In the traditions of 'Western' science and politics – the tradition of racist, male-dominant capitalism; the tradition of progress; the tradition of the appropriation of nature as resource for the productions of culture; the tradition of reproduction of the self from the reflections of the other – the relation between organism and machine has been a border war. The stakes in the border war have been the territories of production, reproduction, and imagination. This chapter is an argument for pleasure in the confusion of boundaries and for responsibility in their construction. It is also an effort to contribute to socialist–feminist culture and theory in a postmodernist, non-naturalist mode and in the utopian tradition of imagining a world without gender, which is perhaps a world without genesis, but maybe also a world without end. The cyborg incarnation is outside salvation history. Nor does it mark time on an oedipal calendar, attempting to heal the terrible cleavages of gender in an oral symbiotic utopia or post-oedipal apocalypse. As Zoe Sofoulis argues in her unpublished manuscript on Jacques Lacan, Melanie Klein, and nuclear culture, Lacklein, the most terrible and perhaps the most promising monsters in cyborg worlds are embodied in non-oedipal narratives with a different logic of repression, which we need to understand for our survival.

The cyborg is a creature in a post-gender world; it has no truck with bisexuality, pre-oedipal symbiosis, unalienated labour, or other seductions to organic wholeness through a final appropriation of all the powers of the parts into a higher unity. In a sense, the cyborg has no origin story in the Western sense – a 'final' irony since the cyborg is also the awful apocalyptic telos of the 'West's' escalating dominations of abstract individuation, an ultimate self untied at last from all dependency, a man in space. An origin story in the 'Western', humanist sense depends on the myth of original unity, fullness, bliss and terror, represented by the phallic mother from whom all humans must separate, the task of individual development and of history, the twin potent myths inscribed most powerfully for us in psychoanalysis and Marxism. Hilary Klein has argued that both Marxism and psychoanalysis, in their concepts of labour and of individuation and gender formation, depend on the plot of original unity out of which difference must be produced and enlisted in a drama of escalating domination of woman/nature. The cyborg skips the step of original unity, of identification with nature in the Western sense. This is its illegitimate promise that might lead to subversion of its teleology as star wars (from *The Cyborg Manifesto* posted on the World Wide Web by Donna Haraway)

Hackers, Crackers, Jammers and Bloggers

One of the other critical zones of contestation on the Net is formed around the issue of security and transgression. Many of the early Internet players, including the founders of the Macintosh computer organization, engaged in a recreational form of system 'hacking'. In most cases, these young computer geeks enjoyed playing cat and mouse with security coders who were employed to protect systems from outside penetration. Hackers, in this light, may be seen as playful and free spirited anti-establishment miscreants – heroes of cyberpunk – who make a nuisance of themselves as they highlight deficiencies in networked computer systems. For institutions, however, the hackers are a malicious and expensive problem, a criminal and often psychotic gang of social misfits. (The term 'cracker' or 'black hat' is sometimes applied to these more criminal or self-interested hackers, whose primary motivation is theft, fraud or malicious damage.)

Perhaps the most pernicious and damaging invasion is carried out by computer viruses. The whole notion of virus suggests an infection within the system. Thus, while hackers deliberately penetrate secured computer systems by manipulating or cracking security codes, viruses penetrate systems by attaching themselves to 'legitimate' system operations. For example, the Melissa virus (1999) distributed itself across the globe by invading normal email systems. Melissa (a set of coded instructions like all other software) specifically targeted Microsoft products, disabling communication by replicating itself over the email software fifty times whenever the receiver unwittingly opened the message attachment. What is particularly interesting about the Melissa virus (see Walch, 1999; Best and Lewis, 2000) is that it actually assaulted the system by mimicking it. That is, by accelerating the communications processes and clogging their channels, Melissa merely did what the system does normally but under the pressures of intensification. Moreover, the virus itself was initially released through the alt.sex newsgroup, as unwitting participants in global sex talk took the virus away, corrupted their systems and sent it on to their own online community. Supposedly named after a topless dancer in Florida, the Melissa virus therefore represented a consolidation of popular, computer and sexual cultures, incorporating the computer winky smile, the popular TV icon Bart Simpson, an attached list of pornographic sites, and an insatiable appetite for self-reproduction.

While viruses are often little more than a form of transgressive delinquency, 'culture jamming' is a far more strident and focused form of political computing. Culture jamming seeks to disrupt corporate or government network processes through a strategic, but generally not illegal, clogging of communication systems. One of the most common jamming tactics involves flooding the email channels of a politician or corporate office with protest messages. Interest groups and individuals simultaneously send messages into the receiver's mailbox and clog it with their particular point of view. Culture jamming approximates forms of expressive anarchy through the formation of various websites and more co-ordinated forms of global protest. In this sense, the culture jammers function more like international graffiti artists, creating spaces for parody, trickery and the reflexive practice of turning systematized facilities around on themselves in order to disrupt their instrumental operations. Like the appropriations of pop art, culture jammers use the Internet to appropriate official religious, governmental or commercial advertorial discourses. As the creator of the ABRUPT website, Daniel Moran, explains:

> There's an element of it that's purely fun and humorous. At the same time I'd like to think that in the right context, if these images that have been re-appropriated or whatever you want to call it, someone looks at them long enough to realize that something's not right. And if things like this are done enough and if people are made to see things like this a few times and they start to think, you know, maybe they've been too trusting of the imagery that they receive on a regular basis, and perhaps it will make one or two people even a little more critical of the information that they're swimming in all the time (cited in *Background Briefing*, 1999)

Moran's global culture jamming is an informational protest about information. While it uses the tools and techniques provided by informate culture, jamming seeks to disrupt the even and unremitting orthodoxies of this new form of discursive deluge. In a sense, it takes up the protest of critics like Jean Baudrillard and actively seeks to reverse the imperatives of the information society. In particular, however, the culture jammers seek to disrupt the commodification and centralization of information. Protests such as International Buy Nothing Day have been organized through a culture jamming bulletin board, one of an increasing number of bulletin board communities whose interests merge around a general contempt for cultural gluttony, commodification and the loss of discursive control.

Bulletin boards such as RtMark, CRITICAL MASS and Adbusters, for example, specifically target corporate power for its organic and flexibly invasive demeanour. Another board, ELECTRONIC CIVIL DISOBEDIENCE, functions like an electronic sit-in, crowding corporate and governmental websites and email systems with protest messages. Five electronic artists created the FLOODNET site, which constituted a means of surrounding hegemonic electronic sites in order to disrupt their operations. When FLOODNET electronically bombed the Frankfurt Stock Exchange and the Mexican president's website, the American Pentagon returned fire, attempting to hack into and close off the FLOODNET server. Further battles with the Mexican government led to what was effectively a 'browser war' where each side was attempting to close down the other's web browser. The significant thing about culture jamming is the differences in scale and resources. An electronic terrorism which is built around humour, play and mimicry, and which is constituted around little more than the publishing of political resistance movements, represents a significant challenge to the hegemony of contemporary global power. In this sense, the culture jammers are seeking to do little more than expose this hegemony and deconstruct the cultural assumptions upon which it is constructed.

Bloggers

Bulletin boards have more recently evolved into a global system of private news scripts and commentary called 'blogs' ('web logs'). In many respects, blogs have developed as an antidote to the information controls and ideologies generated by major media corporations; these private blogs offer alternative readings and appraisals of major and minor political and social affairs. While some blogs have proved extraordinarily popular with readers, assuming a high status of production and professionalism, others remain quirky and highly localized. In either case, blogs are a form of narrowcast news and social commentary, which now constitutes a major threat to professional journalism, especially in the print media. Sometimes little more than personal diaries, blogs have also become a popular way for friends to maintain contact during travel and other distance postings. In 2006 the blog search engine 'technorail' was scanning around 57 million individual blog sites in a given search operation.

Wikipedia and Google

The great advantage of blogs is also their greatest weakness: that is, they are a highly accessible and available source of information and ideas which have virtually no shared (peer-based) standards of veracity, review or proof. Thus, while the writing and information generated by professional journalists and academics are framed by particular standards of legal and institutional accountability, the amateur blog has none. While this democratization of 'knowledge' may be appealing in one sense, it may also promote the broad distribution of misinformation, ignorance, social myths, prejudice and the repetition of an infinite array of pernicious or libellous falsehoods. Students and other information-seekers, thereby, are subject to a complex of 'opinion' which may have very little genuine credibility or basis in deep knowledge.

The same issue applies for the online encyclopedia, *Wikipedia*. Designed as an entirely free contribution knowledge bank, *Wikipedia* permits any user to contribute to any topic, modify existing entries and erase information which is believed to be false. If Max Weber is correct and 'truth' is merely a generalized social consensus, then *Wikipedia* constitutes a critical cultural resource. Of course, consensus is formed around particular expert systems; and so truths are themselves subject to considerable dispute and hierarchies of interest. Dominant groups in a society have greater access to meaning-making resources, and so truths themselves are the subject of intense social competition. The 'knowledge' held in the Internet at any one time is critically confounded by this limitation: even the most popular and extraordinary search engine *Google* is subject to particular interests and ideological predispositions which perpetually colour its hierarchy of presented truths. Organizations, particularly wealthy and influential organizations, are prepared to pay *Google* to ensure that their specific website and field of knowledge-ideology are among the first listed for any given search function. The truth provided by the Internet, therefore, is as much a victim of interest and ideology as any outside its virtual borders.

CYBER-SEX AND ELECTRONIC EROS

While minority interests and large corporations fight for control of the electronic pathways, it seems that most people are using the Internet for far more personal pleasures.

Although there are a range of estimates, it seems that the greatest proportion of website visits by men are to pornography sites. And while online gambling is increasing, it is estimated that around 60 per cent of time wasting at work by men is associated with unauthorized visits to pornography sites. Along with online shopping through major sellers like Amazon and ebay, porn-based sites are also amongst the most profitable of all commercial web genres. Conventional feminist critique suggests that the populating of the Internet with male-oriented pornography represents a simple extension of existing cultural norms. Others have commented that the Internet pleasure sites represent a respite from the rational instrumentalities of work and institutional life. The Net, therefore, is 'erotic' because it is new, private, interactive and liberated from the hierarchies of broadcast media and the social conformities which constantly restrain human pleasure; the new media enhance sexuality and erotica, providing an intensely intimate space for the stimulation of desire and sexual ecstasy (see van Zoonen, 1994; Spender, 1995; Turkle, 1999; Barney, 2000; Perdue, 2002; Barry, 2003).

In this latter sense, new communications technology becomes available for the sort of transgender and trans-sexual orientation which Donna Haraway seeks in her cyborg manifesto. The new technologies facilitate a broadening of sexual identity and subjectivity. While conventional feminist theory assumes pornography, for example, is constructed around broad ascriptions of gender (males gazing on women), more recent discussions have opened the possibility of mixed gazing and the auto-erotic pleasure of display. According to Laurence O'Toole (1998), pornography appeals to a wide variety of users, not simply heterosexual men: gay men, heterosexual, bisexual and lesbian women, fetishists, sex therapists, the disabled, the elderly, and so on. New communications technologies like the Internet provide the ideal facility for these interactions and for the ferment of new ideas on sexuality. O'Toole's commentary seems prescient as the zones of sexual interaction, dating and pornography have continued to expand in the decade or so since he pronounced:

> The feelings and ideas behind such developments continue to thrive on web sites and newsgroups. People are speaking about porn as they've never done before. … Likes and dislikes, cravings and disgruntlements. The posters and operators of the alt.sex groups treat porn as a legitimate product, not something to be ashamed about, but something to be critically evaluated. It would be nice to think that the views of the users could influence the style of the commercial, hard-core product. A new connectivity could find porn becoming more responsive to what users favour. (O'Toole, 1998: 285)

In this sense, cyberspace becomes a non-regulated arena for the exploration of fantasies and the forbidden, for both the consumption and production of sexual imagery. The facility of low-cost media production in the new technologies has permitted, in fact, the broader creation and dissemination of non-commercial imagery, a good deal of which is posted by couples and individuals. Chat groups, dating sites and amateur sex sites represent a volunteering of sexual imagery and a forum for sexual play and identity bending. These non-commercial home pages are used by women to present themselves in various modes of sexual display, effectively challenging the ideal typologies or stereotyped bodies which are created and controlled by professional site producers. Thus, while some feminists might criticize the sexualization of women when it is controlled by patriarchal systems, the amateur or 'home girl' nude sites allow women of all body types to publicly display their bodies in ways which provide personal as well as shared pleasures (see Kerby, 1997). This form of self-presentation and identity manipulation problematizes structuralist precepts on power and power relations, most especially in terms of definitions of victim and oppression. The use of the Net for the personal pleasures of display enables a liberational agency which places the gazed-upon body in an uncertain relationship with the gazer.

Online Dating/Email Romance

A number of theorists of postmodernism have suggested that the intense sexualization of culture is associated with the proliferation of mediated sexual imagery. Jean Baudrillard (1988), for example, believes that this proliferation has degraded erotica, producing a condition of perpetual arousal that has no source and no focus. Kroker and Kroker have suggested that the current digital age is 'typified by a relentless effort on the part of the virtual class to force a wholesale abandonment of the body, to dump sensuous experience into the trashbin, substituting instead a disembodied world of empty data flows' (1997: 3; see also Kroker, 2004). Thus, while some critics welcome the virtualization of the body as a means to sexual and identity liberation, others believe it to be an exercise in superficiality which debases sexuality and limits liberation. During the 2000s, critics have also become concerned that the Internet poses a threat for the sexual exploitation of children, who have unparalleled access to pornography and chat sites that render them vulnerable to sexual predators (Jenkins, 2001). In any case, there has certainly been a proliferation of explicit sexual imagery and sexual discourse in contemporary European and Anglophone culture during the past two to three decades, and the Internet has provided another facility for those discourses.

Even so, sexualization has not dissolved nor excluded the discourses of romantic love. Amidst the frenzy and furtive exigency of popular music, videos, films and TV programmes, romance and the possibilities of substantial, intimate connections remain substantially present – almost as though it were the final, imaginary vestige in the tidal wave of sexual exploration, expression and experience. Indeed, with divorce rates running at over 50 per cent and increasing numbers of people choosing serial monogamy, same-sex relationships and sole-occupancy lifestyles, romantic intimacy appears a strangely atavistic yet potent part of contemporary cultural imagining.

Online dating sites, chat-room and email romances are clearly connected with broader cultural norms, values and practices, though they have also evolved a number of quite specific qualities. In particular, the anonymity and 'disembodiment' of the communicating individuals seem to facilitate a freer engagement with fantasy and dalliance. The exploration of one's own and the other person's mind, experiences and emotions is liberated from the drive to meet, or even be truthful. This anonymity allows for a freer flourishing of an idealized experience. Like fiction, though with the hauntingly exciting possibility of meeting and consummating the dalliance, email romance draws together fantasy and self-projection; the romancers can choose at any point to withdraw, create or re-create the romance (and their own character) in any way they choose.

A number of online romance analysts, in fact, regard this anonymity as the fundamental precipitant of the virtual dating and romance, permitting a kind of flirtatiousness that face-to-face and even phone communication couldn't allow. Thus, professional and work-related email communications become a space for romantic and sexual dalliances. The instrumentalities and rationalism of work, as illustrated in the film *You've Got Mail* (1999), are challenged, as they are eroticized, by the reconnection of people through the corporation's email system. As we have discussed, modernization has always implicated the threat of alienation and the dissolution of community. One function of interpersonal communications systems (telegraphy, telephony and now computer mediated systems) has been to ameliorate the negative effects of separation and 'social massification'. While it presents itself as a rationalizing mode of information transfer, corporate email systems provide a de Certeauian space (see Chapter 8) for the conduct of love and romance; work becomes a site for bodily pleasure as well as rationalized obedience.

In fact, there are those theorists who argue that the Internet itself brings particular qualities to human interaction. Lewis Perdue (2002) argues that the whole character of the Internet (specifically the World Wide Web) has been formed predominantly around human sexuality, and the tension between rationality and clandestine desire. Adams and Motta suggest that 'the Internet is a medium which often encourages users to open up and become more personally involved than they might in a real-life setting. Sharing of intimate thoughts and feelings is commonplace. Individuals lower defences quickly because they feel safe and less vulnerable in cyberspace' (1996: 105). The qualities of newness, anonymity, privacy and intimacy, however, become the life-line of the romance; they precipitate, sustain and then depend upon it. Reports on the outcomes of email romances are varied. Sometimes they are consummated online with specific sexual engagements, actions and emotions being posted in real time. Sometimes the consummation exhausts the relationship; sometimes it leads to the imperatives of actual meeting. Sometimes the romance disappears along with the imagined personae of the romancers. The anonymity, of course, permits chicanery and false identities, with many reports of men taking the identity of women and vice-versa. Some of the romances on same-sex date-lines have provided a forum for the fantasies of 'heterosexuals'. In fact, most online romances fizzle without a trace. When 'couples' actually do meet, it seems that the fantasies and intimacy that have sustained the romance are immediately surrendered; most romances end quickly. But not all, and there are many reports of correspondents meeting online and converting their dalliance into a real-flesh encounter that proves durable and satisfying for both parties.

Clearly, the Internet and the new media more generally are predisposed to the conditions of sexual simulacra. The increasing popularity of dating sites for all modes of sexuality and sexual identity indicates a genuine social need for interactive spaces and the free expression of desire. As sexual durability, marriage and monogamy fracture, individuals of all ages are increasingly compelled to locate and populate new venues in which they may find pleasure and happiness. New forms of courting and courting venues are being created through the Internet, as innumerable individuals post their profile and trawl the library of potential sexual partners and lovers, listing from hope to disappointment in a world that has become increasingly connected, but crushingly lonely.

12

Global Terror and the New Language Wars

INTRODUCTION

From the mid 1980s until around 2001 cultural studies was besieged by a fatuous and largely unproductive bickering between those scholars who had become interested in the notion of transgressive textual pleasure, and those who were focused on 'materialism and the heuristic potential of cultural policy studies' (see Lewis, 2002a: 419–34). For many British and Australian cultural policy scholars, in particular, the 'postmodern turn' represented a betrayal of the political project which had been initiated by Raymond Williams and the original Birmingham scholars (see Chapter 3). Thus, neo-Marxist and materialist cultural studies researchers such as Tony Bennett (1985, 1986, 1997, 1999) invoked Michel Foucault's essays on 'governmentality' (1988, 1991) in order to propitiate a 'new' form of cultural analysis, one which was driven by a more politically precise utilitarian engagement in key cultural debates. Thus, as many English literature, art and media schools were seeking to reconstruct themselves in terms of a postmodern textual and cultural aesthetic, the governmentality scholars had assumed a more pragmatic posture – announcing their relevance to industry, educational training and civic debate. In denouncing the fatuousness of the postmodern turn, these scholars impugned the wretched self-indulgence of textual analysis and its flagging methodologies of 'deconstruction', identity politics and ideological subversion.

In the previous edition of this book, I had thought it necessary to challenge this rather unproductive debate. My view then and now is that cultural studies offers an extraordinary range of theoretical and analytical options. I could see no great value in the oppositional framework that had evolved since the 1980s nor the compulsion to choose between textual aesthetics and a highly focused policy analysis: these strategies of cultural investigation are both legitimate and entirely complementary. Cultural studies, thus, is a rich epistemology which presents itself as a genuinely trans-disciplinary and trans-cultural alternative to historically ossified modes of study that remain fixed in traditional disciplines. The great strength of cultural studies, most particularly as it problematises processes and ordering of meaning-making, resides in its engagement in the critical dialogue between aesthetics and social power. And while the self-ascribed 'policy' specialists like Tony Bennett (1997), Jim McGuigan (1996) and Douglas Kellner (1995, 2005) have sought to divest cultural and media analysis of the 'contaminant effects' of poststructuralism and postmodernism, there is little evidence that their work deviates significantly from the original analytical paradigms established by Raymond Williams, Richard Hoggart and Stuart Hall. The erasure of French language theory achieves very little, other than a conceptual slimming which limits the force of cultural enquiry itself. The application of Foucault's governmentality thesis is barely satisfactory, as it leaves underdeveloped the theoretical difficulties which Foucault himself was not able to resolve (Lewis, 2002a: 426–7).

My view remains, therefore, that cultural studies offers an original mode of thinking which focuses on the political *and* aesthetic density of social meaning-making. This precept is starkly evident in the September 11 attacks on New York and Washington in 2001. The attacks were not simply a physical event – an act of war – that had devastating material and corporeal consequences. Rather, the meaning and significance of the attacks reside in the complex intersections of culture and history, most particularly as they are articulated in conditions of power, policy and mediated expressivity. To this end, 'terrorism', as a formulated discourse of power, has become a central trope in the global mediasphere – that socially constituted and mediated public space in which governments, media and 'the people' engage with one another through a dynamic of ongoing language war. As we noted in Chapter 1, however, this is not a coherent, static or homogeneous realm, but rather represents a complex of disjunction and meaning assemblages where power and people interact through a perpetual stream of encounters and semiotic dispute. This chapter examines the ways in which these language wars have been forming around the cultural conditions of a post-9/11 mediasphere.

THE MEANING OF TERRORISM AND ACTS OF TERROR

The Concept of Terrorism

While they are somewhat exceptional in terms of the general history of politically generated violence, events like 9/11 create a spectacle of horror which inscribes itself into the cultural imaginary of the international mediapolis. The mediated vision of a chaotic and terrible death, of burning and shattered bodies, and of the destruction of our towering symbols of progress and social order have become amplified into a new consciousness, a new fear, that is both pessimistic and strangely ennobled by the momentum of an heroic defence. 'Terrorism' becomes the rubric for an insidious and darkly imagined power – the risk conditions of an annihilation which randomly assaults the majesty of our history, institutions, community and being. The global order represented by New York, Bali, Madrid and London is cast into shadow. And out of these shadows, vaguely imagined forces condemn us, attacking the foundations of our civilization and the values which separate good from evil, the innocent from the guilty, the knowing from the damned. In many respects, terrorism, as it is infused through the spectacle of media discourses, becomes the antithesis of our modern project, creating a new threat, a new disorder, that challenges the 'essence' of our constituted global political–social harmony.

Some commentators suggest that this level of community fear is somewhat disproportionate to the actual risk posed by global terrorism (see Wilkinson, 1997; Human Security Centre, 2005). This view, however, tends to parenthesize the symbolic amplitude of terrorism and the ways in which the media and public discourse shape a cultural imaginary that re-presents the world of phenomena as social knowledge. The danger and likelihood of physical attack are shaped through a cultural imaginary that draws upon the deep expressivities of history and a pre-existing social knowledge which operates through institutional discourses and the broader resources of culture. In telling their stories, governments, the media and publics engage in the limitless dynamics of language and meaning which reconstitute or re-present experience in terms not only of what is known, but what can be known. As noted throughout this book, the media is thoroughly implicated in the formation of social knowledge, most particularly through the broadcasting of televisual information. We can only know the events of 9/11, Bali and London – we can only share in the agony and grief of the victims – through a vicarious system of experiential representation. Our understanding and experience of terrorism must be forged, therefore, through an understanding of the media, and the ways in which our culture creates its meanings through the discourses of political violence.

To this end, it is important to distinguish between a given social action, and the discourses and cultural knowledge that give it meaning. A definition or history of 'terrorism' needs to separate the application of the term and the political violence it describes. Thus, the *concept* of terrorism first appears during the French Revolution and the notional Reign of Terror that occurred in 1793. The term *terrorisme* described the violence and brutality inflicted by a new ruling group as it attempted to impose itself over the country, most especially those who were deemed to be enemies of the new citizen government. From its beginnings, then, the notion of terrorism was associated with dissidents and militia, though initially it was regarded as a legitimate weapon of the state. In this sense, the new rulers in France invoked a 'reign of terror' in order to fortify their own power and legitimacy while terrorizing their opponents into submission.

As the French Revolution descended into chaos, however, British liberals like Matthew Arnold became increasingly convinced that revolution was dangerous, and thus the Reign of Terror became equated with political infamy and injustice. In English, therefore, *terrorisme* was almost immediately associated with sedition and a political violence that sought to overthrow social progress and legitimate parliamentary reform. When novelist Joseph Conrad uses the term in *The Secret Agent* (orig. 1907) to describe the 'madness' of anarchy and political violence, his comments become prescient for the anxieties of all democratic states in the twentieth century: 'The venomous spluttering of the old terrorist without teeth was heard'.

David Rapoport (2001) claims that until the end of World War One, 'terrorism' was often treated as a noble compendium to democratic and anti-colonial freedom movements, particularly in relation to Imperial Russia and the Ottoman Empire. However, groups like the anti-imperial *Narodnaya Volya* (People's Will) lost their gloss as they became identified with the Russian Revolution and the ascent of an authoritarian communist regime, which ultimately evolved into the anti-democratic nemesis of western culture and values. The popularization of the concept of terrorism as a negative description, however, was marshalled through two key movements: the Provisional Irish Republican Army (IRA), and the Palestine Liberation Organization (PLO). Both groups were largely anti-colonial and both sought the overthrow of governments which, in their view, were imposed by external powers that were themselves opposed to the liberation and rights of the respective groups they represented. In both cases, the forces that opposed them – the British government, and Israeli (with US) government respectively – identified the political militia as 'terrorists' .

Mediating Terrorism

Quite clearly, however, there remain significant differences over the definition of the concept of terrorism and the type of political violence it describes. George W. Bush's own invocation of legislative authority which declared a 'war on terror' referenced a specific definition which distinguishes the legitimacy of 'war' against the illegitimacy of 'terrorism'. To this end, US law defines terrorism as 'premeditated, politically motivated violence against noncombatant targets by sub-national groups or clandestine agents' (22, USCA, 2656 [d]). This definition privileges 'the state', which is legitimized by the citizenry and rule of law, and which is protected by military and paramilitary agents who conduct 'policing' and 'war' so as to maintain social order. The US Department of Defense expands the definition slightly, suggesting that this 'calculated use of violence or threat of violence against individuals or property' is an act of terrorism when it is designed 'to inculcate fear, intended to coerce or intimidate government or societies in the pursuit of goals that are political, ideological or religious' (DoD, 1986: 15).

Combined, these definitions specifically exempt the state as a potential perpetrator of terrorist action. Moreover, they suggest that the motivation for terrorism cannot be random or criminal in the sense that the violence is not specifically or exclusively designed to obtain property or engender some intrinsic pleasure. Rather, the terrorist action is politically motivated, though politics in this sense might include ideological or religious motivation. Not surprisingly, a number of commentators have questioned this dichotomy of legitimacy, noting in particular that rulers throughout history have perpetrated incredible atrocities and threats against conquered peoples, and indeed their own citizens. Annamarie Olivero, for example, suggests that definitions, like those offered by the US government, marshal the concept of 'terrorism' for the specific ideological interests of the state. In these terms, terrorism:

> … contains its own rhetoric, which has been transformed throughout history by different states. By claiming to be defining a type of violence, i.e., one that threatened the site of legitimate violence (the state), it is clear that this term is reserved for the art of statecraft. (1998: 142)

In other words, the accusation of terrorism becomes a tool in the management and durability of state-based hegemony.

It is clearly for this reason that organizations like the Irish Republican Army (IRA) referred to themselves as an 'army' which is fighting a 'civil war' against an imperial force; for the British authorities, however, the IRA's attacks on noncombatants and their sub-national status condemns them as 'terrorists'. Critics such as Robert Fisk, Edward Herman and Noam Chomsky (see *Znet*.com) argue that the whole notion of a 'war on terror' serves merely to legitimate the military and discursive hegemony of the US over its opponents and their political claims. The dichotomy between a legitimate, state-sponsored 'war', and an illegitimate act of 'terror' is blurred, these critics argue, when the state acts brutally or unjustly or when rebels act with just cause. Noam Chomsky claims, moreover, that America's own official strategy of 'low intensity warfare', which is explained in various military manuals and in the 'US Code' (2001: 57), in many ways parallels the strategies of sub-national militant groups. The low intensity strategy of the US military code includes, for example, the 'coercion of civilians' which may result in death and the destruction of social and material infrastructure such as transportation lines, communications, hospitals and so on. As Chomsky points out, this is precisely the strategy adopted by those who destroyed the World Trade Center.

Equally, the targeting of citizens and infrastructure by clandestine paramilitary organizations like the Central Intelligence Agency (CIA) would fit within many definitional boundaries of terrorism. Direct CIA assaults on state agencies, and involvement in the political processes of Nicaragua, the Sudan and various parts of the Middle East, are not entirely dissimilar to the activities of national and international terrorist organizations that have been sponsored by specific states such as Libya, Taliban Afghanistan, Iran and Saudi Arabia. In his seminal work on the formation and operations of modern terrorism, Walter Laqueur argues that terrorism can, in fact, be perpetrated by the state and state agencies. Laqueur distinguishes between top-down and bottom-up terrorism, both of which are characterized by a long and widely dispersed history of systematic political brutality. Thus, while '[n]o definition of terrorism can possibly cover all the varieties of terrorism that have appeared throughout history' (1987: 11, see also 2003), the strategies and tactics of terror are common to all modes of politically motivated violence. To this end, terrorism –

> ... aims to induce a state of fear in the victim that is ruthless, and does not conform to humanitarian rules ... [P]ublicity is an essential factor in the terrorist strategy. (1987: 143)

Laqueur and other more recent analysts of terrorism argue that the notion of 'victim' or 'target' needs to be widely interpreted. While the terrorist act will produce 'corporeal' victims of the specific act of assault, the violence of terrorism has its percussive effects on those who witness the event. The publicity to which Laqueur refers is the central strategy of a violence which is specifically rhetorical (Tuman, 2003). Nareen Chitty (2003) argues that terrorism is effectively 'anti-democratic' since it adopts strategies that lie beyond the borders of humanitarian values. Subjects seek to influence opinion through a form of violent 'theater' –

> Terrorist acts are often deliberately spectacular, designed to rattle and influence a wide audience, beyond the victims of the violence itself. The point is to use the psychological impact of the violence or of the threat of violence to effect political change. As the terrorism expert Brian Jenkins bluntly put it in 1974, 'Terrorism is theater'. (Chitty, 2003: x)

Alex Schmid (1983) suggested some time ago that terrorism is essentially a communicational act by which 'the immediate human victims of violence are chosen randomly (targets of opportunity) or selectively (symbolic or representative targets) from a target population, and serve as message generators' (1983: 70). These messages may seek to elicit a range of responses in the broader audience, including fear, increased awareness or sympathy about an issue, or even change in government policy. Whether this use of the media by terrorists to publicize their interests and create fear is 'anti-democratic' is a question we will return to later. What is clear, however, is that the strategy of engaging distant publics through the spectacle of violence is effective inasmuch as global media networks seem thoroughly absorbed by the current phase of political violence. At the simplest level, the September 11 attacks on America generated a dramatic increase in media coverage of Islamicism and issues pertaining to the Middle East. Brigitte Nacos (2002) demonstrates that the issues raised by Osama bin Laden's 9/11 video – the Palestine–Israeli issue in particular – achieved significant penetration in media and public discussion. Sandra Silberstein (2002), Joseph Tuman (2003), Pippa Norris et al. (2003), and Stephen Hess and Marvin Kalb (2003) have all shown that the terrorist attacks on New York and Washington have significantly raised the profile of, and interest in, al-Qa'ida and America's role in the Middle East.

Nacos (2002) argues specifically that communications is the central element of terrorism and anti-terrorism (see Lewis, 2005). Indeed, it might be suggested further that the relationship between terrorism and the media has become more or less symbiotic over the past decades. Following Sissela Bok's (1999) examination of media violence as crime-based entertainment, Nacos claims that terrorist organizations have employed critical marketing strategies designed to meet the demands of media networks' interests, style and scheduling. Citing 9/11 as the most dramatic and sophisticated example of this strategy, Nacos argues that al-Qa'ida timed the attacks in order to achieve maximum television coverage, most particularly through presentations on the evening news bulletins. A violence-obsessed media could do little else but be entranced by the narrative and horror of the attacks, repeating over and again the spectacle of falling bodies and the inferno of the collapsing towers.

In this way, the victims of the attacks on New York and Washington were only conduits to a broader audience. The 'terrorists' are neither arbitrary nor motivated by petty material gain; rather, they seek to communicate specific messages through the mass mediation of brutal and frightening details (Nacos, 2002: 10). Thus, the mass media is absolutely implicated in the political activities of the terrorist organization:

> The starting point is the notion of mass mediated terrorism and its definition as political violence against noncombatant/innocents that is committed with the intention to publicize the deed, to gain publicity and thereby public and government attention. (Nacos, 2002: 17)

This emphasis on the media acknowledges the substantive link between the material and discursive dimensions of political violence in the exercise of power. It is reasonable to suggest, in fact, that terrorism is critically bound to the contemporary world's compulsive communicationalism, a drive to 'expressivity' which constitutes the very fabric of the culture (Deleuze and Guattari, 1987). In this sense, the terrorists' use of the media might be understood as a response to their enemies' communicational power – most particularly the capacity of hegemonic social groups, like governments, the military and multinational corporations, to generate and broadly disseminate their own interests, perspectives and ideologies. Paradoxically, though, it might also represent the integration of the dissident groups into the world of symbolic warfare and symbolic exchange: that is, the world in which language and persuasion are principal tools in creating, ordering and contesting community and culture.

The Attributes of Terrorism as Political Violence

In this context, we can see how several thousand deaths in the twin towers attacks came to 'change the world', while several hundred thousand civilian deaths associated with the invasion and occupation of Iraq (see Roberts et al., 2004) have been rendered virtually invisible by the Coalition governments and the mainstream global media. In given circumstances, therefore, the state, including the democratic state, may be prone to the deployment of 'terrorist' tactics – including the infusion of a communicational violence which is designed to publicize its interests, as well as intimidate, coerce and persuade its audiences. Within a global mediasphere, therefore, the label of 'terrorism' is a critical part of the discourse of political violence (language wars) which centres on the control and management of people, economy, resources and modes of governance. Each side in the current context of political violence, therefore, is engaging in a form of modern (or postmodern) persuasion game, using the media to demonize their opponents as 'terrorists'. In this context, it is more productive to consider various acts of politically motivated violence in terms of specific attributes we might call 'terrorism'. These attributes can be summarized as follows –

1   Terrorism exists in a contingent relationship with global media networks. As has been argued, modern terrorism is fundamentally communicational; it could not exist without the network of communicational channels that convey its impact and message to broad audiences across the globe. As a cultural form, terrorism is a violence that has its semiotic roots in the culture of the modern media. This contingency of violence, however, becomes a facility or strategy which is available to governments, as well as sub-national and transnational militant groups. The strategy of silence or censorship, in this sense, constitutes a form of representation, a media strategy that is designed to shape meanings and social knowledge. Thus, the strategy of imposed silence (censorship) is as much a manifestation of the contingent relationship between violence, power and mediation, as is the release of specific messages (public relations). As we have seen in Russia and the United States, governments may typically invoke the rubric of security in order to justify the management and control of information surrounding terrorism and terrorist events.

   While a number of commentators have acknowledged the importance of the media for modern terrorism, these studies tend to treat the process as one of simple message delivery. When we remind ourselves that the media is formed through a set of relationships – producer, text, audience– within a cultural and governmental context, it becomes obvious that the predisposition toward violence is reflexive and somewhat paradoxical. Violence generally, and political violence in particular, are major revenue generators for the media industries: violence, through its various permutations, is part of the fiscal and semiotic foundations of the modern media. Media audiences, who are also the polis, the community and the public, seem also to be implicated in this reflexive contingency of violence.

2   Terrorism is a category of political violence which is intended to influence foreign, occupying and domestic–home governments, as well as communities. Terrorism uses its immediate victims and material targets for semiotic and symbolic purposes. Attacks may be designed to create fear or a sense of threat. As in Beslan and occupied Iraq, hostages may be used as bargaining tools with foreign governments. Successful attacks may be used to promote causes and attract new recruits. It is certainly true that the 9/11 attacks were critical to the survival of al-Qa'ida.

3   To this extent, terrorism is both material and highly abstract. Its meanings are shaped by culture's immanent complexities and tensions – its language wars. The current wave

of terrorism and political violence is bound, therefore, by ethnic, religious, discursive and political differences which are being shaped by a resurgence of an historical east–west divide (see Chapter 10). This cultural politics of difference manifests itself in terms of equally problematic disputes over territory and economic resources, especially oil. However, these resource wars are themselves the predicate of a globalizing culture which implicates differentials of power and the uneven distribution of discursive resources. The east–west divide is the abstract manifestation of cultural disputes which use violence to maintain or subvert this global hierarchical order.

In fact, the whole notion of a 'war on terror' signifies the level of abstraction that is driving the highest level of policy-making and legislative–military authority in the developed world. The enemy of this new 'war' is a concept, a metaphor, that fills the heart and mind with dread – not merely because it is insidious but because it can never be seen other than through the lens of a highly politicized cultural imaginary. Culture, therefore, is an absolutely critical feature of terrorism.

4   Terrorism tends also to focus its violence against non-military or civilian targets and infrastructure. Attacks like 9/11, Bali, Madrid and London are clear examples of this strategy. The carpet bombing of Afghanistan and Iraq by American-led forces is less clear – even though innumerable civilians have been killed and maimed in the attacks. Whether this sort of 'collateral damage' can be seen as a form of terrorism pivots upon the issues of intentionality, military strategy and morality. US military strategists claim that these bombings were focused on military or 'strategic' targets and civilian death and injury are largely unintentional (collateral). The smart- bomb technology, proven to be a fraud in the first Gulf War, has nevertheless been designed to minimize civilian casualties.

Certainly for many Iraqi citizens, the invasion and occupation of their countries by American-led forces constitutes a form of political violence which is both brutal and oppressive. The US forces deliberately destroyed water, electricity and sewerage infrastructure in Baghdad, for example, leading to the suspension of hospital facilities, and the spread of water based diseases. Along with the continuing violence, the destruction of infrastructure is creating considerable risk of disease and death for many non-military Iraqis.

The use by US forces of scatter and percussion bombs, which are designed to inflict maximum damage and death to personnel, if nothing else, seems an astonishingly careless approach to the lives of noncombatants and non-military infrastructure; the UK and Australian forces refused to support this weaponry precisely for this reason. For the US authorities, however, it is the issue of 'targeting' which exempts them from the accusation of terrorism. For our purposes, however, this question of incidental or intended target seems less important than the corporeal and symbolic effects of the military strategy. Certainly, there are many commentators who believe that the aggressive military response to Islamic insurgency by America and its allies, particularly Israel, is actually contributing to the forward spiral of global violence, oppression and human rights abuse – especially in the Middle East. For this reason, I would argue that this ambiguous category of government and military assault on civilians should be seen as a distinct category of terrorist violence.

AMERICA AND THE WAR ON TERROR

Hell's Gate: In the Void of Ground Zero

As we noted in Chapter 1, the 9/11 attacks on the United States created a massive rupture in the physical and cultural landscape of America and the symbolic capital of the global economy. The destruction of the twin towers, in particular, was a powerful rendering of the Islamic militant mission, striking at the very heart of America's global domination and sense of historical destiny (Lewis, 2005). Indeed, the very notion of 'America' was suddenly profoundly assaulted, creating a yowling semiotic void where the assumed meanings of the trope were shattered and scattered in a devastating moment of cultural irruption.

Not surprisingly, many commentators, including the US President at the time, invoked the deeper contingencies of American culture and history in order to explain the catastrophe. Calling up the Biblical imagery of Hellfire and damnation, these commentaries regarded the perpetrators of the attacks as emissaries of Satan – 'terrorists' who had dared to challenge the purity of God's chosen, the pinnacle of civility, morality and ideological history. This was not a political or military battle, but a deadly and cosmological engagement with the Devil.

To this end, the President, George W. Bush, spoke on behalf of the citizenry as well as the complex of religious and cultural historicism, when he sought to restore the meaning of America. In what he initially called 'Operation Infinite Justice', Bush announced a scale of retribution that would resonate throughout history and perhaps beyond. The convolution of a direct assault on ordinary people and America's unique status in the world constituted for Bush the ultimate offence, an offence against the pinnacle of civilized being, morality and social progress. On the day of the attacks Bush's public statements repeated a common theme of shock, belligerence and indignation. Bush's address to the nation, in many ways, became the foundation for much of the rhetoric of the war on terror –

> Good evening. Today, our fellow citizens, our way of life, our very freedom came under attack in a series of deliberate and deadly terrorist acts. The victims were in airplanes, or in their offices: secretaries, businessmen and women, military and federal workers, moms and dads, friends and neighbors. Thousands of lives were suddenly ended by evil, despicable acts of terror … A great people has been moved to defend a great nation. Terrorist attacks can shake the foundations of our biggest buildings, but they cannot touch the foundations of America. These acts shattered steel, but they cannot dent the steel of American resolve. America was targeted for attack because we're the brightest beacon for freedom and opportunity. And no-one will keep that light from shining. Today our nation saw evil, the very worst of human nature … This is a day when all Americans from every walk of life unite in our resolve … None of us will ever forget this day. Yet, we go forward to defend freedom and all that is good and just in the world. (*The White House*, 2001)

While regarded by many commentators, especially in the Internet blog community, as incompetently 'belated' (Wood and Thompson, 2003), Bush nevertheless was drawn to fill the semiotic void of 9/11 with an epiphanal polemic. An 'infinite' justice, of course, is one that marshals the divine powers against evil. Bush calls on a divine retribution in his hastily coined, but extraordinarily effective, 'war against terror'. The ritual of prayer and the interlacing of blessings on the nation, its people and its ideology punctuate the speeches on September 11. Bush attributes to the events a cosmological meaning, one which elevates the victims as heroes and condemns the perpetrators as evil, inhuman and perverted by a hatred which would 're-make the world ... imposing its radical beliefs on people everywhere'.

As we have noted, however, the battleground for the military, cultural and cosmological war is formed largely through the communicational spaces of the media. Bush and many others who rallied America invoked their sense of history, justice and destiny through American popular culture – films, television and commemorations (Lewis, 2002c). Novelist and 9/11 eyewitness , John Updike, viewed the whole event as a mysterious but compelling conflation of phenomenal and televisual realties: the destruction of the World Trade Center twin towers had the false intimacy of television, on a day of perfect reception ... [T]here persisted the notion, as on television, this was not quite real' (2001: 28). This 'not quite real', of course, is the essence of a hyperreal and televisual culture which forms its social knowledge around a complex aesthetic of image and meaning dynamics. The *Towering Inferno,* the Christ-like victim–hero, the national anthem – motifs drawn directly from a catastrophe movie that has already been seen, already been digested in the rich iconography of the trope 'America'.

In his book, *Ground Zero* (2002), Paul Virilio suggests that these language wars are fundamentally implicated in the cultural formation of the televisual technologies themselves. This is not merely a matter of message conveyance, but of the cultural complicity of the apparatuses of war and the apparatuses of mediation. As noted above, the meaning of terrorism is clearly bound to the global media and its context of cultural politics. Virilio elaborates on this point, claiming that the 'telescopic' or 'ocular' technologies of mediation and war now function within a single techno-sphere, a sphere that is shaped around the cultural effects of speed and progress –

> [W]hat is troubling about the covert state of transnational terrorism ... is its growing subordination to a techno-scientific progress which is, itself, unauthored and dependent on the development of its own audio visual media and platforms ... The scientific imagination ultimately suffers the same fate as 'e-tainment'; it comes to resemble ... that of the Islamic suicide-attackers no doubt dying happy at becoming actors in a global super-production in which reality would tip over once and for all into electronic nothingness. (2002: 68)

In contrast to George Bush's cosmological effect, Virilio raises the prospect that 9/11 may mean very little or nothing at all – a prospect which no doubt prompted many commentators and public officials to enter the fray and seek to fill the semiotic void created by the collapse of the twin towers. Most particularly, Americans rushed to fill the void with a form of zealot patriotism which would not, under any circumstances, tolerate criticism or vacuous nihilism. The nothingness to which Virilio refers, however, sits within the vector of televisual culture and a politics which evinces itself through the semiosis of a nascent broadcast democracy and its mediasphere.

It is not, however, that an attack on US interests was exceptional in itself. Since the 1980s US citizens and soldiers had been targeted by militants, both domestically and internationally; the Trade Center itself had been bombed in 1993, killing six people and injuring around a thousand more. Against this context, moreover, various other forms of political violence over recent years have produced many more casualties than September 11 – in Rwanda, for example, around 800,000 people were killed in a campaign of 'ethnic cleansing', while in Serbia, Kosovo, Sierra Leone and most recently the Sudan and Darfour tens of thousands of people were slaughtered in ethno-territorial warfare. The distinguishing feature of the 9/11 attacks, in fact, centres on the sudden exposure of America's vulnerability, not merely as a material and social space, but as a semiotic system.

Following the September 11 attacks on New York, Jean Baudrillard expanded on this point, suggesting that American domination of the mediated global 'system' was of itself the essence or 'spirit' of terrorism. This global domination manifests itself through the hyperreal of media communications, but is also critically linked to American military and economic primacy – which is the essence of globalization. This is not merely to say, as Noam Chomsky (2001, 2003a) and others might, that American foreign policy contributed to the attacks on New York; it is rather to suggest that the actual existence of a single, and unitary global superpower constitutes its own predicate of violent reprisal. Michel Foucault (1977a, 1981) has said something similar, of course, in arguing that power generates its own inevitable resistance. For Baudrillard, however, it is the sheer singularity and mass of this power which cannot of itself be directly and genuinely opposed, altered or exchanged. The terrorism which assaults the megapower of US global domination is merely reactive, an inevitable response to singularity itself –

> To a system whose very excess of power poses an insoluble challenge, the terrorists respond with a definitive act which is also not susceptible of exchange. Terrorism is the act which restores an irreducible singularity to the heart of a system of generalized exchange. All the singularities (species, individuals and cultures) that have paid with their deaths for the installation of a global circulation governed by a single power are taking their revenge today through this terroristic situational transfer. (Baudrillard, 2002: 9)

In this sense it is 'terror against terror' though without the density of ideas or ideology. In a 'not quite real' (or hyperreal) cultural condition, therefore, the triumph of globalization leads inevitably to a battle against itself. This Fourth World War, as Baudrillard defines the current agonisms, is not a battle of ideologies or a clash of civilizations as Samuel Huntington claims (1993, 1996), but rather it is the world or globe battling against the inevitable flows of globalization. In other words, it is a world system in which power is both feeding on itself and attacking itself – 'if Islam dominated the world, terrorism would rise against Islam' (Baudrillard, 2002a:12). In line with Baudrillard's wider thinking, this duality is reflected in the symbology of the 'Twin' Towers themselves – the mirror of good and evil which inevitably advance together in a tandem of often indistinguishable and irrevocable opposition.

The void created by 9/11, thereby, has been flooded with secular, political and theological discourses which have all been constructed around a cultural and ideological re-rendering of 'America'. The flush and force of American nationalism which followed the 9/11 attacks has itself formed a policy platform for the war on terror , the continued expansion of US-dominated global capitalism and the transmission of political ideologies – democracy, freedom and 'the west'. Within this discursive forcefield, the meaning of 'America' and 'Muslim' form a global battleground for despair, death and an unrelenting war *of* terror. As the occupation of Iraq, Afghanistan and Palestine continues, these meanings will be scattered like toxic manna across the Middle East: the carnival of global information–entertainment will ensure that the mediasphere is rich with dramatic accounts of a civilizational and cosmological divide, distinguishing western integrity from Islamic infamy.

War and Democracy in the Global Mediasphere

According to Susan Carruthers (2000), the successful waging of war by a modern, democratic state is contingent upon a broad tripartite consensus between the government, the public and the media. Thus, the 'war on terror' has been propagated around an alignment of 'values' which seek to inscribe the mission of 'infinite justice' with a shared and defining set of cultural values. The three governments of the Anglophonic Coalition of the Willing (US, UK, Australia) have thus bound themselves into a mission that was not simply retribution for 9/11, the erasure of Taliban-based terrorism in Afghanistan, or the threat of Weapons of Mass Destruction (WMDs) in Iraq; rather, they amplified the mission as a restoration of the supreme condition of their cultural status, privilege and meaning. The 'liberation' of Iraq from ignorance and oppression became the flowering of democracy and a truly civilized, modern state.

As Slajov Zizek (2004) reminds us, however, this 'war on terror' and the WMD fantasy in particular was constituted around the 'twisted logic of dreams'. The world publics became mesmerized by the narrative of the war, watching the British and American soldiers, clad in chemical protection masks and suits, marching into the desert, into the cradle of time. Like the not-quite-real of the twin towers collapse, the masked soldiers appeared in the desert with the Messianic force of a Hollywood blockbuster, a science fiction fantasy in which the other-worldliness of Iraq succumbed to the purity and normalcy of the American narrative ideal. Thus, the extemporized hero comes forth to save the world from evil – the mask, a technological panoply which, like the mask of the Lone Ranger, compounds the wearer as pure identity, pure hero.

And while the Coalition cameras followed the masked crusaders into battle, home audiences watched in deep consternation for the madman's WMDs and the hellfire of his final stand. When the whole thing fizzed, of course there was a collective sigh of relief. The Coalition troops removed their masks and protective clothing, marching almost unhindered into the Iraqi capital, Baghdad. Yet even as the dust of the conquest was barely settling, the voices of cynicism began to emerge; the fabled Weapons of Mass Destruction remained invisible. While UK Prime Minister, Tony Blair, held out hope that these weapons – and the reasons for war – actually existed, commentators around the world were pointing the finger at government leaders and intelligence agencies which had clearly duped the global polity. Opponents of the invasion queried the value of 100,000 Iraqi deaths and the ensuing political instability in the Middle East. A dark shadow was being cast across the meaning of America and the lives of those people who had been sacrificed for the campaign of violence. These shadows seemed all the more tragically rendered as many critics pointed out that the United States possesses undoubtedly the most deadly WMD arsenal ever known to humankind. In particular, the percussive and scatter bombs which other Coalition partners had refused to use because of their imprecise and indiscriminate effects, had caused terrible harm to civilians and urban infrastructure in Iraq. Damage to water supplies and electricity, in particular, continues to wreak havoc on city populations and civilian health. A further dimension to this tragic irony, according to peace activists, relates to America's own forms of ethnic cleansing. Paralleling Saddam's treatment of the minority Kurds, America's treatment of its own indigenous, black and Hispanic populations has been constructed around a history of exclusion, criminalization and incarceration. Activists ask profound questions about the moral authority of a nation whose history is so steeped in blood and institutionalized persecution.

Thus, the image of the American Coalition as 'heroes' and 'liberators' has been questioned. Without the shield of the WMDs' rhetoric, the march into Iraq has been more broadly vaunted as an emancipation from the tyranny of Saddam Hussein. No doubt that many Iraqis are happy to be rid of Saddam and his brutal military dictatorship, but they are asking very strong questions about the validity of the American invasion and its 'collateral' damage. According to Rampton and Stauber (2003), the image that was beamed around the world of Iraqis tearing down the statue of the hated tyrant may well have been a public relations stunt. Reuters, the BBC and the *Boston Globe* all reported that the crowd in Firdos Square that day was very small, and that American tanks had entirely ringed the area, admitting only a few Iraqis into the event. Long shots of the square were largely edited out of the final reports, as they showed only a few Iraqis joining the celebrations which the American troops had themselves orchestrated (2003: 3). While Rampton and Stauber refer to these propaganda events as a 'clash of symbolizations', they are attached to a far more substantial cultural politics involving the critical discourse of freedom and liberation. As we noted above, this discourse is powerfully rendered by the Bush administration for the fight against terror and the 9/11 retribution.

In this light, the 'liberation' of Iraq reaches to the more substantive dimensions of the ideology and meaning of America. Thus, while Iraq's cultural heritage and museums were being pillaged in the early stages of the Coalition occupation, the toppling of the Saddam statue announced the dawn of a 'new history'. According to the invaders, this new history would transform Iraq's social and political infrastructure into a modern, democratic state. As the WMD rhetoric faded, in fact, the discourse of democracy and transformation became the primary focus of the US propaganda machinery. The discourse of 'freedom' remained redolent within the war on terror, but its powerful and evocative abstraction – its theological and relentlessly Romantic intensity – was substantially fortified through its adhesion to the more pragmatic and politically precise discourse of 'democracy'. As the 'graven image' of Saddam Hussein came down, it was draped in an American flag, announcing not only the arrival of the conquering nation, but its raft of ideals, values and ideologies.

MEDIA AND POLITICAL VIOLENCE IN IRAQ

Did the Gulf War Take Place?

Following the first Iraq War (1990–1), Jean Baudrillard (1995) outraged many commentators with his claim that 'the Gulf War did not take place'. In essence, Baudrillard was making the simple point that the first invasion had been successfully camouflaged from public view by the US government's deft erasure of death and violence. The televisualization of the war, according to Baudrillard, created a 'war without bodies', which could not be called a war at all –

> Electronic war no longer has any political objective strictly speaking: it functions as a preventative electroshock against any future conflict. Just as in modern communication there is no longer any interlocutor, so in this electronic war there is no longer any enemy, there is only a refractory element which must be neutralized and consensualized. This is what the Americans seek to do, these missionary people bearing electroshocks which will shepherd everybody towards democracy. (1995: 84)

At the time of the second invasion (2003–) the US administration and its Coalition supporters extended these strategies, creating a vision of the invasion that was clinical, clean and consigned by destiny. Not atypically, the government sought to control the representational breadth of discourses through various means of information management. In many respects, the powerful discourses of nation, culture and unity, most particularly as they were fortified by the post-9/11 rhetoric on freedom and democracy, seemed to quell even the possibility of alternative perspectives. The vitriolic criticism of Susan Sontag and others who raised questions about American foreign policy in the aftermath of 9/11 (see Chapter 1) provides a clear prescience for a good deal of the social and media management that was to follow: a criticism of any aspect of US policy or government action was considered 'treasonable', an attack on all of America, its values and way of life. Thus, radio and television outlets refused to broadcast alternative perspectives on the Iraq invasion. Protest voices of musicians like Michael Franti and the Dixie Chicks were censored by various broadcasters in the United States. The Dixie Chicks, in fact, dramatically retreated from their musical dispute with the US government after receiving death threats which accused them of anti-Americanism. While many of these protest voices have found their way onto the Internet, there is no doubt that the patriotic fervour of the United States made it difficult for alternative perspectives to be produced and disseminated.

Rampton and Stauber (2003) have described the range of communications strategies which were designed to ensure the primacy of the government perspective. Within a globalizing market-based corporate economy, it is not surprising that the United States has adopted, among the more familiar military-based PR strategies, a form of national branding that has been designed to promote the virtues and values of the USA – especially the ideal of liberal democracy. In other words, and as Rampton and Stauber go on to argue, the new ideology of a corporatized and privatized democracy becomes both the tool and the object of the US communications strategy on the Middle East. In the aftermath of 9/11, preparing the way for direct military actions in Afghanistan, the US launched two advertising campaigns: the first featured the President's wife speaking in reassuring and maternal tones as she sought to lift the spirits of the American people and soothe their anxieties; the second was designed to remind Americans that they are part of a tolerant and virtuous society which is blameless but which must act to defend its greatness and high ideals. This second advertising campaign promoted US democratic pluralism – the idea that America is a tolerant and welcoming place which admits people from diverse backgrounds, ethnicities and nations into its national–cultural embrace. At around the same time, the US government established a number of instant communication offices in Washington, London and Islamabad (Pakistan). These PR offices facilitated regular contact between senior US officials and the Arabic media. The *Wall Street Journal* reported, in fact, that the US had exerted considerable pressure on Arabic TV and print news editors to release stories which were favourable or at least clarified the US perspective on events in the Middle East and South Asian regions.

This move toward a branding model is perhaps best illustrated by the appointment of advertising executive Charlotte Beers into the position of State Department Undersecretary for Public Diplomacy. In seeking to influence the opinions of Muslims and Muslim governments, Beers considered the possibility of using American celebrities, including sports stars, to generate a positive and more emotional impression of America and American culture. According to Beers, public diplomacy is 'a vital new arm in what will combat terrorism over time. All of a sudden we are in the position of redefining who America is, not only for ourselves under this kind of attack, but also for the outside world' (cited in Rampton & Stauber, 2003: 12). Beers and others who have been attracted from the private sector into the realm of 'public duty' are developing new strategies for neutralizing the antipathy of domestic and global citizens of the mediasphere. The branding of America might be the pre-emptive discursive strike against those over whom George Bush puzzles, those who 'hate us'.

While the deployment of propaganda processes is nothing new, the corporatization and branding model is clearly a part of a new incarnation of 'democracy' and the new public sphere we are calling the 'mediasphere'. The Rendon Group, a major PR consulting firm employed by various administrations, now specializes in the corporate imaging of politicians and the support of US military campaigns. Having worked with the CIA to create anti-Saddam Hussein materials after the first Gulf War, Rendon has consulted for the US military in Argentina, Colombia, Haiti, Kosovo, Panama and Zimbabwe. Readers and viewers in various countries of the globe have been exposed to the perspective created by the Rendon Group and the US military. In fact, it was the Rendon Group that developed and financed the formation in 1992 of the Iraqi National Congress (INC), an assembly of key opponents of the Saddam regime. Under the leadership of Ahmed Chalabi and funded by covert CIA money (Jennings, 1998, cited in Rampton & Stauber, 2003: 43), the INC was able to forge strong links with the Project for the New American Century, a neo-conservative think-tank chaired by William Kristol, a strong proponent of US military assertiveness in the Middle East (see Chapter 2). At the time of the war preparations in 2002, the White House began working with a new group, the Committee for the Liberation of Iraq, which was also closely linked with the New American Century people.

This stage-managing of the political transformation of Iraq is dramatically illustrated by the construction of specific stage sets. The first is the well-publicized stage set of US military command constructed in the small Middle East country of Qa'tar. According to the *Army Times,* the military media centre, designed by Hollywood art director, George Allison, is a high-tech stage set covering around 17,000 square feet. The set, while giving the impression of proximity, was constituted for journalists working at distance from the actual hostilities. Like the stage-managing of the liberation of Private Jessica Lynch and the $45m military commission to the Institute for Creative Technologies, the Qa'tar media centre was charged with the task of creating an effective impression of the emancipation of Iraq. The second major media set was established on the US aircraft carrier, the *Abraham Lincoln.* On May 1 2003 Bush was flown out to the carrier where, dressed in a naval flight suit, the President declared victory over Iraq. The image of Bush's declaration was played live on the media networks and replayed during the evening bulletins. The image of Bush in his flight suit, indicating a noble connection with the Iraq victory, became a centrepiece of the 2004 presidential election campaign. As a major public relations exercise, however, the bulletins omitted to tell their audiences that the *Abraham Lincoln* was actually situated only 39 miles off the San Diego coast and that Bush's pilot suit actually linked him to a barely reputable stint in the National Guard where he appears to have spent at least twelve months absent without leave (AWOL).

This confluence of corporatized communications with the polemics of political positioning is clearly located within a hyperreal mediasphere which blurs the distinction between private and public interests. Through an electronic polis, public information penetrates the private domain within a broad field of competing signifiers, images, texts and media. Subjects receive the information within the private domestic setting, engage with it and create perspectives in terms of their own cultural resources. Thus, while Jurgen Habermas has called for a revitalization of the public sphere through an invigorated participative democracy and 'communicative action', this sphere is already being generated through the interaction of the hyperreal with the private–domestic.

Bedding Down

In many respects, the strategy of 'embedding' allied journalists during the US-led invasion of Iraq represented an attempt by the US military to exploit this confluence of the public and private spheres by bringing the 'war' into the lived experiences of the domestic audience. As is typically the case, public support for the military campaign in Iraq increased once the troops were committed (Gallup, 2003). However, in order to galvanize and maintain public consent, the US communications machinery sought to strengthen the sense of 'being with the troops'. While this strategy had been developed during the Vietnam–America War (Carruthers, 2000), it turned against the US authorities as scenes of violence and bloody warfare nightly invaded the domiciles of American citizens. Sympathy and support for the home troops was compromised by significant political questions which arose out of the vision of a close combat depicting Americans killing and being killed. The information managers realized that there needed to be a balance between propinquity, empathy and dramatic effect. The deaths of civilians and American troops were especially alienating and disturbing for home audiences; the propinquity needed, therefore, to maximize the sense of American courage and the justness of the war, and minimize the negative aspects of military engagement.

The practice of embedding journalists into the invading military forces represented a key strategy for managing sympathy and identification by home audiences with their troops without the exposure of excessive violence and loss of life. Embedding may be defined as a highly managed inclusion of accredited journalists in direct military action.

Journalists are embedded as they are housed within specific military units under the direct control of military authority. The Pentagon guidelines on embedding include –

- no information on ongoing engagements will be released unless authorized by an on-scene commander, and information about previous engagement will be released only if discussed in general terms
- reports giving information on 'friendly force' troop movements and deployment are prohibited
- information on future operations is strictly prohibited
- journalists will be assigned to a specific unit
- no private transport
- no personal firearms
- all interviews with military personnel are to be 'on the record'.

As we noted above, this careful management of death has been a critical strategy for governments and their military since the first Gulf War. However, while the first Gulf War was largely deployed through aerial bombing, it was not particularly difficult to camouflage the significant numbers of Iraqi deaths (40–200,000) and virtually erase the American and allied casualties (around 200). The invasion of 2003, which involved ground assaults, created far greater challenges for the Coalition authorities, most especially as journalists would have greater access to Iraqi civilian deaths (around 100,000), as well as American and British casualties. As in the first Gulf War, the US communications authorities devised a system of accreditation by which registered journalists would have access to information, protection and military personnel (as 'talent'), as well as a contiguous and intimate view of the invasion. Consequently, the vision and reporting was generated exclusively from the perspective of the American and Coalition troops. Using sophisticated digital imaging and satellite technology, reporters were able to present to the home audience a strong sense of immediacy, action and rapid success, the precondition of domestic public consent. Journalists would lose their accreditation if any of their stories 'compromised' American strategic interests.

The embedded and closely managed information releases were also designed to counter alternative news stories being generated by independent first world journalists and Arab-based networks, including al-Jazeera and al-Arabia. What was particularly troubling for the US communications authorities was the reporting and distribution of stories, especially through the Internet, of the slaughter of noncombatants, including women and children. The view from 'behind enemy lines' was to be minimized, if not censored altogether, since it represented the enemy as people and compromised the image of a highly sophisticated, targeted and liberational military conquest. Robert Fisk, one of the non-embedded journalists working from behind enemy lines, argues that American troops deliberately targeted independent journalists in order to eliminate these alternative perspectives. Fisk points specifically to the American attack on Reuters and al-Jazeera journalists, who were reporting from the Palestine Hotel, as evidence of information control in the Iraq invasion. The killing of these and numerous other journalists during the invasion indicates an insidious distrust by the Americans of a media they cannot directly control. Fisk asks – 'Is there an element of the American military which has come to hate the press and wants to take out journalists based in Baghdad ... working "behind enemy lines"?' (2003: 3).

Fisk's interrogation of the notion of 'enemy lines' points to a far broader problematization of geography in the war and its mediation. Clearly, the territory of Iraq is re-imagined through the reporting, as mainstream media networks recapture the territory for the informational and cultural gratification of the invaders' home culture. This is not reporting at a 'distance', as Phillip Taylor (1992) discusses in the context of the 1991 Gulf War, and as Paul Virilio historicizes it in his book, *The Vision Machine* (1994). Rather, it is an attempt by the private and military media networks to speak directly and 'immediately' to domestic audiences, giving them a sense of the presence and value of the US democratic mission. The war is conjured through the broadcast media as a presence, a reality and a lived community experience which compounds distance as simultaneously distant *and* contiguous. As we noted above, the media perpetuates itself and its vision in terms of a deficit of meaning. Each image, segment or instalment seems to confirm the story, and what is absent – death, bodies, scorched earth, contention, Weapons of Mass Destruction, Saddam himself. But this absence is irradiated through an insistent presence which generates its belief and verisimilitude through the gathering momentum of an emotional and dramatic narrative. This momentum is personified in the voice and body of the journalist who shouts from the back of an invading transport vehicle, assuring us that all is going according to plan and that the spearhead of this dawning democracy is not the abstract words of politicians and leaders at home, but the brave young men who represent all that is virtuous, healthy and good in the culture. These young men (and women), who may be as familiar and everyday as the boy-next-door, are prepared to risk all for the justness of the cause. By drawing the journalist and the soldier together and bringing them into the domestic living space of the home citizen, distance and absence are folded into a moment of identification and forceful propinquity. The message is the medium; the soldier is the citizen; the citizen is the medium.

Information Machines: The Fox Paradigm

Of course, what appears to be present, is also absent. What is absent from the story of the invasion of Iraq is what is intrinsic to the information and imagery itself: that is, the actuality of the lived experience. The identification and the propinquity are always and inevitably ephemeral. Whatever the conjuration of the image-voice and the story, the imagining of the lived experience is always and inevitably a representation and a meaning deficit. This is not merely the financial deficit that impels the production of the story, but the deep demands of a meaning-rabid media which must create a story out of the bare bones of its own semiotic resources, its own 'lived experience'. In this way, the media feeds on its own proliferating and compulsive imagining, creating the story, as it creates itself, through an association or consonance of already existing supplements – images, ideas and texts which have already told the story of America's heroic democracy over and over again. These supplements, through fictional narratives, news bulletins or propaganda, create the preconditions for audience (public) belief or consensus which might constitute a self-actualizing semiotics that is grounded in what we conveniently epitomize as 'American culture'. This is not in an exact science of information control or simply the propagation of ideology, as many opponents of the war, following Althusser's paradigm, frequently proclaim. It is rather a complex interaction of signs and meanings over which governments and their information systems seek to impose an order that will somehow delimit the inevitability of semiotic stupefaction. The ideology or information structure that governments would impose, that is, inevitably encounter the whirring disorder of culture and a slippage that releases audiences' own expressive capacity.

Quite clearly, the US information authorities have entirely surrendered the notion of objectivity, replacing it with notions of 'values' and self-interest. The version of democracy to which they work is 'positioned', established through the perspective of what the Project for the New American Century might call 'the national interest': what's good for America is good for the world. It is precisely this alignment of political interest and communications strategy which is central to a broadcast democracy. Not surprisingly, the editors who manage information at home through the various national and global news networks are also critically positioned. As has been widely discussed, the editing process, particularly as it seeks to converge the interests of the private and public sphere of Coalition viewers, contributes significantly to the construction of meanings and the ways in which the representations are formed. Not surprisingly, the most watched TV coverage of the war in the US was the one with the fewest depictions of death, maiming and the complex politics of violence. The Fox network presented a war which closely aligned itself to the principles of nationalism, the invasion policy and a powerful, global democratic ideal, one which resolved conflict through the heroics of American enterprise and morality.

To this extent, the narrative of a pleasing but powerful nation is transposed from fictional to news texts by the Fox Network paradigm. And while there have been moves to interrogate the ethics and efficacy of its news model (see Greenwald, 2004), the Fox audience remains loyal to the illusion or ideals of a perfect state. The typical Fox war report is generated through three scales of interaction, each of which is designed to engage the audience through a narrative of information and entertainment. First, the embedded journalist tells his or her story, exclusively presented from the perspective of the invading American forces. The journalist often reports through real time, constructing a narrative of implacable American heroism and the force of liberation. These narratives interconnect with the cultural experience of the world as picture. Texts feed into one another and the embedded journalist, in a flak jacket and helmet, advances the story of American military might and right. The dichotomous national motif of victim–hero is the perpetually unfolding foreground of reports which are inevitably shot from the perspective of the American troops: the camera sees the world of hostility and violence literally over the shoulder of the obviously endangered American soldier.

At the second level, studio anchors – often a male and female – 'domesticate' the stories for homeland consumption. The anchors represent a critical framing for the extremes of adventure, bringing it into the realm of the familiar body; the host becomes an anchorage for fixing our understanding of the terrors of war and the excess of political violence. Now the story is oscillating from public experience into the familiar and private sphere, restoring the ideal of pleasure against the abominable and abnormal. The horrors of war and the distance of the military campaign becomes 'speakable' through what might be called the Ma and Pa Kettle effect – the translation of the unimaginable into the comforting values of home, parentalism and domestic familiarity. A third framing is also frequently offered. This framing brings the 'expert systems' of advanced societies into domestic living rooms. In the case of the Fox network, and its imitators across the world, these experts are drawn from the political or academic dominions of conservative thinkers. They provide a context and interpretation of events based on historical, cultural, strategic or political 'expertise'. While these experts will provide a bridge from the external to the internal modes of information and knowledge, they also confirm the ideological and cultural superiority of the invaders over the invaded. They are, in effect, a source of enlightenment and modernizing supremacy.

Cultural Democracy: Abu Ghraib and Beyond

It is now very clear that the moral authority by which Coalition forces justified the war on terror and invasion of Iraq has been severely compromised. As the tide of public opinion in the Coalition countries turned more severely against the bloody and chaotic occupation of Iraq, the absurdity of the Coalition's ethical and ideological vindications has become starkly evident. This absurdity is not simply evinced in the widely predicted outbreak of sectarian violence and collapse of the Iraqi economy (see Said, 2002), it is also manifest in the degradation of democratic and cultural values which were supposedly the liberators' bequest to the Middle East. The contamination of these ideals and normative values is symbolized most evidently in the calamity of Abu Ghraib prison.

Used as one of Saddam's torture camps, the prison at Abu Ghraib was re-furbished and re-commissioned by the US authorities after the fall of Baghdad. The cells were cleaned and re-bricked, floors were tiled, and toilets, showers and a medical centre were installed in the new military prison. By September of 2003 there were several thousand Iraqis being 'detained' in the prison. These prisoners, however, were not primarily military personnel, but civilians who had been arrested during random military sweeps at checkpoints on the major highways. While some reports suggest that the inmates included around 107 'children' (UNICEF, *Sunday Herald,* Scotland), it is certainly clear that teenagers of unspecified ages were detained at Abu Ghraib, along with women and men. All of these prisoners fell into one of the following three categories – common criminals, security detainees suspected of committing crimes against the Coalition, and a small number of 'high-value' insurgency leaders. The prison came under the broad command of army reserve Brigadier General Janis Karpinski. Karpinski, while having experience with intelligence and operations with the US Special Forces, had no prison experience. In Iraq she was placed in charge of the 800th Military Police Brigade, which included three large prisons and eight battalions in which there were 3,400 reservists, most of whom had no experience in penal operations or administration.

While Karpinski reported to the St Petersburg *Times* that her prison system was working exceptionally well, others within the system were feeling outraged by the extreme and routine abuses to which they were daily witness (see Lewis, J. and Lewis, B, 2006). One military police specialist, Joseph Darby, had been handed a CD from a fellow MP, Charles Graner; the CD contained images of naked prisoners in various submissive and sexual poses. Darby reported the incident to his superiors and an investigation was undertaken by Major General Antonio Taguba. According to Taguba's eventual report (February 26, 2004), the abuses at Abu Ghraib, first detailed by the International Red Cross, took place between October and December of 2003. As Seymour Hersh outlined in *The New Yorker,* Taguba's report, which was not available for public dissemination, identified 'sadistic, blatant, and wanton criminal abuses' at Abu Ghraib –

> Breaking chemical lights and pouring the phosphoric liquid on detainees; pouring cold water on naked detainees; beating detainees with a broom handle and a chair; threatening male detainees with rape; allowing a military guard to stitch the wound of a detainee who was injured after being slammed against the wall in his cell; sodomizing a detainee with a chemical light and perhaps a broom stick; and using military working dogs to frighten and intimidate detainees with threats of attack; and in one instance actually biting a detainee. (cited in Hersh, 2004: 1)

As well as the evidence provided by detainees, Taguba referred to photographs and videos which were taken by the prison guards themselves, but which were not included in the report because of their 'extreme sensitivity'. A number of these videos and photographs were later to be shown by the US TV program *60 Minutes II* in stark revelations about the Abu Ghraib abuses.

As local Iraqis were quick to note, the bearers of law and justice were themselves guilty of exploitation, brutality and tyranny. The grand projects of democracy and rule of law seemed duplicitous to a people whose safety and security was becoming increasingly imperilled by the US-led 'liberators'. In fact, the public exposure of these tyrannies was

Plate 12.1 *Abu Ghraib*

The abuse at Abu Ghraib included a violence and sexual humiliation which compromised the Coalition forces' moral credibility.

an unintended effect of 'mediaization', and was only partially related to the exercise of the conquerors' ethical and legal responsibilities. The guards' videos and photographs, which represented their activities at Abu Ghraib prison, constituted the critical evidence for Taguba and ultimately the global publics. It is the guards' own 'productive' participation in media culture which leads them to judgement – that is, to the trials that are an intrinsic part of audience discernment within a 'broadcast democracy'. The texts produced by the guards become the conduit which engages citizens in the matrix of representations, ideas, images and persuasive perspectives that constitute the political mediasphere (see Lewis, J. and Lewis, B., 2006).

While these recordings are ultimately absorbed into the official discourses of democracy and law via the mainstream media, they are nevertheless generated through the democratic field of personal and community-based political expression. No matter how heinous this expression may appear, it is at least legitimate inasmuch as it is 'of the people', an iteration of personal and corporeal politics. In fact, the events at Abu Ghraib may have entirely escaped notice by the global media networks and US authorities had they not been represented for the visual and visceral pleasure of the guards themselves. A number of scholars and media commentators have questioned why the mainstream media took so long to absorb and develop the story. While the media made some attempt to explore the detention system, there seemed little interest or willingness to pursue the story – at least until the publication of the Abu Ghraib photographs. As Sherry Ricchiardi laments –

> During a town-hall style meeting with Pentagon workers on May 11[2004], the defense secretary smugly noted that it was 'the military, not the media' that discovered and reported the prisoner abuse at Abu Ghraib. (2004: 1)

Despite reports from the International Red Cross and a number of minor or incidental media references, the Abu Ghraib abuses seemed to pass unnoticed until the airing of the photographs on *60 Minutes II* (April 28, 2004) and two days later Seymour Hersh's article in *The New Yorker*. Ricchiardi expresses her own confusion about the tardiness of media interest in the abuses which only became a major international story three and a half months after the completion of Taguba's report. Ricchiardi cites several reasons for the torpid work of the US media –

> Media critics and newsroom professionals cite a wide array of factors: the Bush admin-istration's penchant for secrecy and controlling the news agenda; extremely dangerous conditions that limited reporting by Western reporters in much of Iraq; the challenge of covering the multifaceted situation in the embattled country with a finite amount of reporting firepower. Some see a media still intimidated by the post 9/11 orgy of patriotism. Yet there's little doubt that missed cues and ignored signals were part of the mix. (Ricchiardi, 2004: 3)

It is clearly the first of these reasons that most irritates Ricchiardi and other members of the more critical or 'liberal' media. The Bush administration's close management of information is seen as the nemesis of quality journalism and the primary challenge for on-the-ground reporters. However, what breaks this cell of silence on Abu Ghraib is less the work of professional journalists, and more the work of amateurs – the Abu Ghraib wardens themselves. Their own very direct participation in the mediasphere – the recording, publication and distribution of their narrative – is what actually exposes them to military authority and the broader conditions of the democratic legislative process. As the guards record their narrative – a fantasy of sexual, military and national power – they are engaging in a pleasure game which, to their own minds, accords with the essentially vile imperatives of their duty. In terms of their own legal defence and the sexual politics of their bodies, the guards seek to explain their actions through an upward delegation of responsibility – to their senior officers, the US authorities and their culture generally. According to their defence lawyers, the guards were acting in accordance with what they perceived to be their 'duty' or more broadly their cultural expectations.

Guantanamo Bay

The military prison at Guantanamo Bay represents one of the lowest points in American and western democratic history. Constructed in territory expropriated from the sovereign state for Cuba, Guantanamo has become infamous as the storage place for prisoners of America's war on terror. Labelling these detainees as 'alleged terrorists', the US military and government have denied this enemy the rights afforded other war prisoners under the International Court and Geneva Convention. More significantly, as accused terrorists, the detainees have become subject to a judicial system which bears little resemblance to the legal processes and rights afforded America's own citizens. Under special legislation, the accused criminals have been denied the rights of *habeas copus* (detention of 'bodies') which ensures that individuals cannot be denied liberty without due legal process and trial. Moreover, the military commission, which has been established by this special legislation, can admit 'evidence' which would not be permitted in the normal American judicial framework. 'Hearsay' (second hand re-telling), for example, is excluded as evidence in a conventional trial system as it can never be corroborated; such hearsay evidence, however, is permitted in the military commission.

Accusations of torture and intimidation have also been levelled against the interrogators, casting serious doubt on any evidence (or 'intelligence') which may have been derived through the Guantanamo system. The justification for this transgression, of course, is scripted into the propaganda processes which have denied this enemy, the terrorists, their humanity, as much as their rights as citizens or even enemy combatants. These detainees are tainted by association with the hell-hounds and monsters who perpetrated the 9/11 attacks; as preternatural creatures contaminated by cosmological evil, they cannot be regarded as having 'rights' in the same manner as 'normal' human beings.

Of course, the public execution of Americans and other Coalition citizens in occupied Iraq were the moral and ideological equivalent of Guantanamo. These appalling acts of barbarity that were broadcast through al-Jazeera, al-Arabia and the Internet were a form of trial by ordeal (Lewis, 2005, Lewis, J. and Lewis, B., 2006) which, like the medieval atrocities, evince the same level of spectacle and horror that is inscribed in the essential communicational purpose of terrorism itself. While it may be a matter of degree, Guantanamo and Abu Ghraib parallel the impious and medieval character of the public execution as it is performed for global audiences. The Guantanamo system is a vicious parody of rule of law and the deep dignity that is inscribed in the American Bill of Rights and justice system. In many respects the Guantanamo system represents that unrestrained 'other' of the democratic ideal, a chaotic and impetuous political violence which rule of law was designed to subdue, if not dissolve altogether. The violent spectacle that is evinced in Guantanamo is a lurking and dangerous narrative which is perpetuated in the cultural politics of power and the fantasy of America, globalization and modernity.

FREEDOM OF EXPRESSION AND THE IMAGINING OF DOMESTIC SECURITY

Domestic Anti-terrorism and Surveillance Laws

September 11 exposed gaps in the social ocular system as it then existed. The failure of intelligence agencies to identify the risk and predict a cataclysm of this kind sent the authorities scuttling into various legislative paroxysms and public commissions. The pre-emptive strikes on Afghanistan and Iraq were the most spectacular responses to the 9/11 attacks and America's newly exposed vulnerability, but the US also led the democratic world into new modes of social surveillance and governmental management. If a handful of individuals could effectively hold the nation to ransom, then clearly some radical measures for controlling individual actions and thoughts needed to be devised. The Patriot legislations in the US, while aiming to enhance domestic security and limit terrorist penetration, seriously impacted on the rights and privacy of individual citizens. Along with some astonishingly Draconian measures affecting prisoners of war and any person suspected of a terrorist crime, these new surveillance measures constitute a significant challenge to the ideals of the legal protection of individual rights and access to law. In this context, the meaning of September 11 is forcefully linked to questions of civil and human rights, and the problematic confluence of individual and collective interests.

David Lyon (2003) has addressed the issue of surveillance and 9/11 very directly. Lyon argues that the development of transnational media networks has provided the technological facility necessary for an increasingly globalized surveillance system. At its seemingly more innocuous, we might identify these systems with various kinds of synoptic and panoptic visions. A synoptic vision is typified by the satellite and cable television networks and the creation of a 'celebrity' system by which the many watch the few. The great danger of synoptica, of course, is that the information that is delivered to citizens, and upon which democracy is founded, may be compromised or positioned by those groups who have greatest control over the media systems.

The panopticon, vision of the many by the few, is perhaps even more threatening for civil rights and the freedoms terrorists are supposedly assaulting. Borrowing from Foucault, Lyon describes the evolution of modern surveillance in terms of increasing state management and modes of 'governmentality' (Foucault, 1991). The state, Lyon argues, has generated and adapted a range of technologies and strategies of observation and checking to ensure that populations are acting, behaving and thinking in ways which maintain state legitimacy, authority and management principles. Beyond specific governments, the state seeks to negotiate individual freedoms against other individual and collective freedoms for the perpetuity of an orderly social and political system. Surveillance provides the ideal mechanism for the identification of crime and other 'excesses' of human action which may threaten this order.

Such measures, of course, may seem necessary where individualism is supported by a capitalist economic system which rewards adventurism, personal risk and self-interest, and which advantages specific individuals and groups over others. These differentials in rewards, pleasures and quality of life create a range of complex psychological and social problems which may manifest themselves in actions that threaten the security of individuals, privileged groups, the system and the social aggregate. An excess of individualism disrupts the orderliness of structured hierarchy; but an excess of collective-authoritarian order threatens the potentiality of individual effort, creativity and the 'liberalism' of democratic processes. Democracy collapses where the individual is not able to express that individuality. In order to prevent the unravelling of this nexus of opposite effects (individual collective balance), states in the modern developed world have adapted surveillance as a principal mechanism for the control and coercion of its citizens. This has become particularly pertinent as modern societies have evolved through the processes of globalization, corporatization and marketization. These processes have created complex associative cellular social structures which frequently elude classification or delineations based around nation or other discursive borders. The citizen, that is, has become increasingly complex as she/he is formed through interactions with new modes of social agency and action, and new modes of information and media networks. With an increasingly cosmopolitan lifestyle, these interactions create the potential for cultural contiguities which usurp older meanings as they generate new conceptions, lifestyles and modes of social knowledge which inevitably threaten with fragmentation the perpetuity and security of the state (Jameson, 1991).

The state and its representative governments respond to this threat by a greater assertion of unity and control. The move to greater surveillance and restraint, therefore, is not merely a response to 'terrorism' and political violence. Yet terrorism has certainly become the discursive referent which justifies many of the recent legislative measures that extend social policing, creating conditions for greater controls on individual freedom and greater intrusion into the private lives of the citizenry. At its most basic level, this intrusion creates and determines an individual and a group's 'identity', creating new modes of prescription and obedience, new modes of inclusion and exclusion. Individuals are increasingly being required to identify themselves through various forms of documentation, including fingerprinting, identity cards and passports. A reasserted and aggressive form of border control has denied millions of refugees the rights of 'identification', including the sense of 'home'. Across the developed world, police and intelligence agencies have been granted increased powers of detention, phone tapping, and access to private email and web transactions. Digital communications, in fact, have created an ever-expanding resource for observation and information collection; private interests, beliefs and political actions are exposed to the panoptic view of suspicious intelligence services.

> One important aspect of this is that the flows of personal and group data percolate through systems that once were much less porous, much more discrete and watertight. ... The use of searchable databases makes it possible to use commercial records previously unavailable to police and intelligence services and thus draws on all manner of apparently 'innocent' traces. (Lyon, 2003: 32)

Information derived from drivers' licences, commercial transactions, banking, marketing, mobile phone billing, education records, email, television subscriptions and so on are all part of the individual citizen's 'observable' profile.

After 9/11, these sorts of data files were used to track the perpetrators. But they have also been used as the focus for extensions to security laws that were already causing concerns for civil libertarians and human rights activists. George Bush's rhetoric following the attacks, as we noted above, invoked a resurgent unity for the American people (and its friends); in practice this unity has enabled the imposition of radical new restrictions on civil and human rights. In Australia, the UK and the United States, the key (Anglophonic) partners in the 'Coalition of the Willing', a range of legislative measures designed to enhance the powers of security agencies, were met with considerable opposition from civil rights advocates. Feeding on the profound anxieties of the public, the government and security officials in these countries devised a raft of legislative and managerial strategies which would enable greater synoptic vision of potential attackers, but which encroached considerably on the privacy and legal rights of ordinary citizens

The authors of America's first Patriot legislation, for example, seem to have circumvented any wide-spread public objection through the adhesion of a nationalist discourse and by the very speed of the bill's enactment. Again, rushing to fill the discursive void created by 9/11, the US administration wrote the 342 page legislation, passed it with a 98–1 Senate majority, and signed it within seven weeks of the September 11 attacks. The acronym – 'Uniting and Strengthening America by *Providing Appropriate Tools Required to Intercept and Obstruct Terrorism*'– was also adopted into a Patriot 2 legislation 'The Domestic Securities Enhancement Act' (2003) which extended the power to observe citizens and access data, as well as increase the range and reach of crimes that could be nominated and punishable as 'terrorism'. According to organizations such as the American Civil Liberties Union and the Village Voice, the new provisions would render organizations such as Greenpeace and Operation Rescue vulnerable to the 'terrorist' tag and hence penalties which would include the death sentence. Moreover, the death penalty itself would be extended to include 15 new offences.

Security legislation in the UK and Australia, though somewhat less enthusiastic about the death penalty, has been similarly encouraged by the need for greater powers of surveillance and for restricting the legal rights of suspected terrorists. While there is an increasing level of public debate and disquiet over the more recent legislative programmes around terrorism and security in the first world, many third world and non-democratic nations seem rather unrestrained in their use of terrorism issues as a justification for enhancing government control over their people. The 2004 Amnesty International, *Human Rights Report,* while criticizing the US security measures, was even more concerned about a number of third world regimes which used the rubric of terrorism to suppress legitimate protest and crack down on political or religious dissidents. Using the banner of 'controlling terrorism', these regimes are incarcerating and torturing minorities in places like Chechnya, the Democratic Republic of the Congo, Sudan, Nepal and Colombia. Muslim dissidents in China and Egypt have been labelled as Islamists and terrorists, and have had their civil rights seriously impinged by hostile governments (Amnesty, 2004).

For Amnesty and other human and civil rights organizations, the 'freedom' that the US and other first world nations are trying to protect is in fact compromised by the restrictions they are placing on individuals' privacy and access to law. The discourse of 'freedom' is challenged within the language wars we have been describing, and while it is certainly the case that the criminal perpetrators of September 11 should be brought to justice, using all appropriate strategies and technologies, it is also true that these measures must never be allowed to compromise the basis for that justice. Essentially, the contest of values which informs the discourse of freedom is embedded critically in our cultures and the meaning systems that support it. Indeed, the freedoms that are structured into the hierarchy of order we have outlined are inevitably linked to their opposite effect. As governments seek to protect freedom, they restrict it; as these restrictions take effect, individuals and groups will seek out and exploit new expressive spaces in order to subvert restraint and enhance expressivity. We can take some solace in the inability of these restrictive structures to override the capacity of individuals, groups and communities to forestall the pervasive power of surveillance and governmentality, both through effort and through the underlying gaps of language and its supporting media systems.

These gaps are to some extent evident in the systemic deficiencies identified by the US Congressional Report on September 11 (2004). The failure of intelligence agencies to anticipate 9/11, and the failure of policing and military authorities to prevent it, are not merely symptoms of technological or strategic failure; nor indeed do they represent an intrinsic human fallibility. Rather, they represent the underlying gaps in text which will always and inevitably expose themselves through the dynamic of culture and the imperfections of systems, organization and communication. The Commission Report itself concedes as much, noting that 'nearly everyone' expects the terrorists to come again, even though 'the United States and its allies have killed or captured a majority of al Qaeda's leadership; toppled the Taliban, and severely damaged the organization' (US Government, 2004: 16). But the reason they will come again is not because of the material power of al-Qa'ida or other terrorist organizations so much as their discursive or 'ideological' force –

> The problem is al Qaeda represents an ideological movement, not a finite group of people. It initiates and inspires, even if it no longer directs. In this way it has transformed itself into a decentralized force. Bin Laden may be limited in his ability to organize major attacks from his hideout. Yet killing or capturing him, while very important, would not end terror. His message of inspiration to a new generation of terrorists would continue. (2004: 16)

Al-Qa'ida and related attacks on human targets are an absolutely abhorrent expression of global cultural formation. But the grim effects of political violence in terrorism, counter-terrorism and war are not resolvable through further acts of brutality. The cultural spaces that are created in globalization emit both the possibilities of intelligence failure and intelligent solutions.

Narratizing the Horror

Perhaps the most frequently repeated mythologies of nation are constituted around the motif of hero–victim. National narratives often represent the story of nation through a particular person or people who must assert themselves over injustice or adversity. In retelling the 9/11 story, two major film studios selected the same elements of the event, intensifying both the tragic circumstances of the attack as well as their heroic transcendence. Both *Flight 93* (Peter Markle, 2006) and *United 93* (Paul Greengrass, 2006) tell almost identical stories of the passengers' courageous counter attack on the Islamic militants who had hijacked the aeroplane as part of the 9/11 suicide fleet. The films are politically uncomplicated, providing a dramatic and chilling account of the mission and the desperate tragedy of the passengers. With no other major studio releases on the 9/11 events, the narratives are particularly significant in terms of their rendering of American culture and its vocalization against the rupture and void created by 9/11. In a sense, the films represent a critical phrasing of the event, as it becomes the significant memory or articulated presence of the event, creating a resonance that, once again, seeks to reconfirm the mythology upon which American nationalism and national self-interests are grounded.

As 9/11 evolved into a 'war on terror', the borders between fiction, fact and persuasion have become increasingly blurred, most particularly as the major media networks and movie production houses announced themselves as enthusiastic supporters of the White House administration and the Iraq invasion. While the news media and Internet are deluged with onsite reporting and analysis, fictional versions of the Iraq invasion have also proliferated. Emerging out of the powerful lineage of military cinema, a range of film projects have been developed, including *No True Glory (The Battle for Fallujah), The Tiger and the Snow* (comedy), *Gunner Palace* (documentary), and the somewhat bizarre Jerry Buckheimer project on the 'liberation' of Private Jessica Lynch (*Saving Private Lynch*). What is evident through all these projects, however, is the absence of critical distance and artistic scepticism which might challenge the political and military hegemonies which authorized the Iraq invasion and occupation. The TV series *Over There*, written and directed by Steven Bochco, evinces a new mood of artistic patriotism which seeks to redeem American military heroics from the savage nihilism of Vietnam. Bochco's production, like his earlier series, *NYPD Blue,* focuses on the gritty and hard-edged experiences of the 'ordinary American'. In *Over There* Bochco specifically celebrates the US soldier in Iraq who is burdened by duty and the arduous demands of 'a tough job'. Like an embedded journalist, Bochco directs his camera through the vision of the US soldier, whose personal story must necessarily ascend, without challenging, the abstruse and abstract politics of US foreign policy. The business of the soldier is to endure hardship and prevail irrespective of, or in some ways despite, the great power and great civilization under which s/he labours.

We now know, of course, that these fictional perspectives are generated not only out of respect for national ideology; they are also an historical and highly strategic effect of government intervention. Casting off the failings of the Vietnam information experience, the US government and its military have embarked on very direct policies of media management. While the management of the news media has been discussed at length in the course of this book, it is also clear that the military is directly participating in the formation of fictional representations. Not only does the military encourage troops to produce their own video and photographic records of actual combat, rendering them available for 'newsreel' texts distributed through American cinemas, they are also contributing directly to those films and TV programmes which subscribe to the ideals and policies of the Department of Defense. Writing in the *Washington Post*, David Robb (2002) has pointed out that the Department's media liaison division assesses film and TV scripts in order to judge their ideological status. Those texts which submit to the persuasive interests of the Department, films like Tony Scott's *Top Gun,* are supported with equipment, aircraft, ships, personnel and artillery fire – those extremely expensive contextual elements which render the film 'believable'. Under these circumstances, scripts are assessed and often heavily edited to ensure that the military, military personnel, the government and nation are presented in the best possible light. Those films which may be critical of war, the military or the US, films such as *Thin Red Line, Apocalypse Now!* or *The Windtalkers,* are denied the largesse of the Department of Defense.

At one level, this may seem fair enough. The military is not in the business of exposing itself to public or artistic critique. But in the context of 'democracy' and the Iraq invasion and occupation, culture is once again being marshalled in order to support a propagated east–west divide. Bochco's *Over There* is exceptional inasmuch as it enters the mediasphere while the war it represents is still being waged. The violent politics in which the state is engaged are drawn into the artifice of representationalism, contributing further to a broadcast democratic sphere in which the absent and the present clash in a confused predicate of semiotic disorder. The real, that is, encounters its fictional other in a greeting place of domestic doubt which, while reiterating the force of the east–west divide, moves us further away from the ideals and moral dignity of democracy. The intersection of propaganda, news reporting and fictional representation becomes the kaleidoscope of distrust through which the electronic polis views its values, its media and its political leaders.

Muslims, Martyrs and Murderers: London Bombings

The attacks of 9/11 and the subsequent wars (9/11 wars) have escalated pre-existing, historical tensions that are associated with various forms of Middle East sectarianism, religious animosity and European colonialism (Ali, 2002; Lewis, 2005). Significantly, the violence of the 9/11 wars has also stimulated communal tensions within the west itself. Islamic militant attacks in Bali, Madrid and London have been largely perpetrated by local or 'home-grown' Islamic militants, who have been provoked by the wars and a deep sense of economic and cultural alienation. Even in Bali, Indonesian militants have spoken very directly of their profound hostility toward tourism and western appropriation of the island (Lewis, J. and Lewis, B., 2007).

The London bombings (7/7, 2005) were also linked by the perpetrators to a strong sense of social alienation, most particularly as it is represented in British participation in the Iraq invasion and occupation. More generally, however, these 'home grown' terrorists have been associated with a complex blending of global conditions and international violence, as well as an increasing level of cultural isolation. Of course, Britain's experience of terrorism has been conditioned through Irish–Catholic nationalism and the radical militantism of the Provisional Irish Republican Army (IRA). As with ETA in Spain, the relative calming of Irish nationalism has coincided with the rise of Islamic extremism, a form of sectarianism which (also like the Irish experience) is directly linked to the social and economic resonance of Britain's colonial history.

Bassam Tibi (2001) has argued that Islamic discord in the UK and other parts of the developed world is a direct outcome of the complicated blending of traditional values and modernity. The politicisation of Islam is not an intrinsic or inevitable disposition of Islamic faith; it is rather associated with the jarring effects of modernization, both within Islamic territories and the developed nations to which Muslims migrate. Islamic political radicalism and militancy, as Tariq Ali (2002) also notes, are simply the manifestation of a modern condition associated with change, material aspiration and cultural disjunction. Euro–Islam, in this sense, is undergoing the same struggles as any other transitional culture, but these changes are critically compounded by the emergence of second generation alienation. Within the 1.6 million Muslim community in the UK, there is a broad range of issues associated with transition, not the least of which is the relevance of a democratic system which, unlike the material prosperity offered by the new homeland, has little direct relevance to Islamic tradition itself .

Williams (2006) points out that the first generation of Islamic migrants in the UK, mostly from Pakistan and North Africa, were largely content in their adopted country as it provided direct relief from the penury, health risk and other dangers associated with life in the developing world. The perpetrators of the London bombings, however, experienced a much greater level of discontent and alienation. Their urban lifestyles and experience of ethnicism and racism has stimulated their interest in alternative ideologies and a mode of cultural politics which fortifies their sense of Islamic identity. The 'global community' of Islam fostered a sense of belonging which promised security and sanctuary from the genuine hardships of 'Britishness' and an urban lifestyle that was fostered around hyper-individualism and hyper-materialism.

For many non-Muslims, these attacks represent a clear breach of faith, not only for the migrants whom they had welcomed into their country, but to the principles of multiculturalism (see Chapter 10). In either case, the cultural fault-lines that are appearing in the developed world cannot be assuaged by rhetoric or an idealism which bears little relevance to alienated groups. As the most rapidly expanding religion in the world, the Muslim faith is attracting people who feel genuinely and deeply dissatisfied with the momentum and demeanour of a capitalist–western mode of global culture. The invasion and extremely problematic occupation of Iraq has flushed out much of the weakness of western – especially Anglophonic – hegemony. For many Muslims living in Muslim and non-Muslim majority nations, the Iraq war is a rubric for an excessive and arrogant consumerism which will stop at nothing to feed its unseemly and often voracious desire for self-interest and pleasure. The young people who continue to martyr themselves in the name of Allah are expressing a psychological and emotional disturbance that is rooted in a far deeper cultural psychosis. In the madness of the global mediasphere, this psychosis becomes grotesque as culture loses its capacity for compassion and understanding.

Glossary of Key Terms

Agency (individual agency): Studies of society and culture often debate the degree to which individuals have control of their own destiny. This capacity for self-determination is called 'agency'. It is contrasted to the power of society to control the actions, attitudes and free thinking of individuals.

Bricolage: The rearrangement of cultural elements and styles in order to produce new meanings and styles. For example, the reassignment of denim cloth, originally used in the US prison system, into a teenage fashion style; the reworking of African rhythms, Caribbean music, rhyming couplet poetry and talking blues to form rap music (rhythm and poetry).

Capitalism: The economic system based on trade and private ownership that begins in Europe in the Middle Ages and flourishes during the modern period (from the seventeenth century).

Class (social class): Capitalism inevitably produces differentials in power and financial success. Karl Marx argued that there are two principal classes of people in a modern, industrial society: the bourgeoisie (middle class who own capital and property); and the proletariat (who have nothing to sell except their labour). While Marx was describing the developed societies of the nineteenth century, recent commentators argue that class is more diffuse and complex. Even so, in most modern societies there exists a very small group of people who are extremely wealthy, and a much larger group who are quite poor. Between these extremes is a broad social group often called the middle class.

Codes: A code is a meaning system which may be based on language, images, colour, sounds, music, etc. Coded meanings may be clear, broadly shared and understood, and literal (e.g. an English language statement such as 'I am hungry', or the red light in a traffic signal). A code may also be subtle, restricted and abstruse (e.g. the metaphoric coding in Jim Jarmusch's film *Dead Man*).

Commodification: The idea that capitalism is taking over all aspects of social life, converting everything into a form of commercial product or commodity. Thus, we can talk about the commodification of love, women or 'the body' inasmuch as advertising and other commercial codes present human experience as a sellable commodity.

Cultural imperialism: Powerful social groups have historically invaded and occupied the territory of other social groups. In the modern period this form of territorial expansion by one nation over another has been called 'colonialism' and 'imperialism' (the creation of empires). Colonial administration was supported by a symbolic conquest through which the invaders imposed their culture over the invaded group. While the direct colonization of other national territories is no longer regarded as politically legitimate (with some exceptions), the symbolic 'control' of other national groups' cultural consumption practices is regarded as a legitimate part of capitalism and cultural trade. The concept of cultural imperialism suggests that powerful nations like the US are able to dominate global cultural markets with their information, news, media, fashion and styles. Through these products, cultural imperialists are able to influence disproportionately the ideas, ideology, belief systems and overall culture of other nations.

Cultural materialism: A theory of culture that draws on Marxism and anthropology to explain social inequality. In particular, cultural materialism suggests that the uneven distribution of cultural materials (products and artefacts) in a society is directly linked to differences in social power and access to the resources of meaning-making. Cultural materialists seek to understand the mechanisms used by powerful groups in a society (e.g. media owners and governments) to exploit and control more vulnerable groups. This theory is often associated with Raymond Williams and his followers.

Culture: An assemblage of meanings which are generated and consumed by a given social group.

Deconstruction: An analytical strategy pioneered by French philosopher Jacques Derrida which focuses on the historical and cultural assumptions that inform a belief system and its discourses (language). For Derrida and his disciples, the core of every belief system is ultimately constructed around these assumptions. In Western civilization such assumptions are formed in a language that is fundamentally *binary* in structure(e.g. present/absent, truth/untruth, culture/nature). Deconstruction exposes and deconstructs these binaries and their correlative assumptions in order to present a new mode of thinking which liberates a broader spectrum of social 'difference'.

Diaspora: Originally referring to the dispersal of Jews across Europe, diaspora now refers to any human group that has no clearly defined homeland. Many of today's refugees, for example, may be seen as part of a new global diaspora.

Digitopia: A utopia formed around digital technology. Digitopians are those individuals and communities who believe that digital, computer based technologies will provide the answer to the world's political and social problems.

Discourse (discursive): This term was popularized by Michel Foucault, who used it to describe the interdependence of meaning systems (such as language), social power and knowledge. Foucault argues that meaning systems or 'discourse' shape knowledge and vice-versa. Both knowledge and the meaning system are formed through relationships of power. Therefore, the term discourse is usually deployed in order to indicate that meanings are always shaped in relation to what Foucault calls power/knowledge.

Emancipatory Politics (liberational politics): Since its inception, cultural studies has been interested in issues of power, hierarchy and social inequality. In its recent incarnations, some areas of cultural studies have been focusing on individual subject's potential for personal emancipation through new expressive modes of pleasure, creativity and self-actualization. This approach to emancipation believes that freedom is only possible through the liberation of subjects from all fixed structural forms. Thus, a 'collective' freedom is only possible through the liberation of each individual, rather than by replacing one oppressive system with another (as in the communist revolutions of the twentieth century).

Epistemology: The study of knowledge – what it is and how we acquire it. This was a central focus of philosophy in the eighteenth and nineteenth centuries. From this period, however, epistemology has been supplemented by an interest in the way knowledge is shaped by language.

Essentialism (see ontology below)

Globalization: Process of increasing contact between people from different nations and cultural backgrounds. It is usually identified as a modern process which has been accelerating over the past fifty years as a result of increased volumes of trade and new forms of global communication.

Governmentality: A concept established by Michel Foucault and used by a number of more recent cultural analysts. Governmentality describes the broadly distributed strategies and techniques that modern societies employ to manage complex relationships and material conditions. While recent analysts often use the term in relation to government and policy processes, Foucault refers to a much broader expanse of bureaucratic processes, material management and hierarchical systems in a society.

Hegemony: This term was popularized by Antonio Gramsci. It refers to the forms of 'leadership' which are infused in significant social institutions – political, economic, educational and religious. As it has been more broadly applied in cultural studies, hegemony refers to an authority which is expressed through institutionally sanctioned meaning systems. This authority is not entirely closed, and people have the opportunity to influence their leaders and their authority in a modern society. Thus, meanings may be generated by powerful groups (governments and mass media corporations), but individuals are able to rework or 'negotiate' how these meanings are to be deployed in terms of their own personal life circumstances.

Hybridization (hybridity): Globalization has brought different peoples and cultural elements into greater interaction and contiguity. Some theorists argue that this process is leading to greater global homogeneity, particularly as it is dominated by cultural superpowers like the United States. However, others believe that this contiguity transforms older cultural elements, creating new and hybrid forms of culture. At the 'local' level individuals and communities absorb and transform dominant cultural modes (music, film, clothing styles, food chains), adapting them to their own customs and practices: the mix of the internal and external creates a 'hybrid' cultural form (e.g. Bollywood, Asian Rap, vegetarian McDonalds).

Hyperreality: A concept popularized by Umberto Eco and Jean Baudrillard, 'hyperreality' suggests that contemporary culture is shaped around a new form of mediated reality. That is, contemporary culture is so dense with media texts and competing meanings that reality itself has been utterly transformed. For Baudrillard, in particular, a hyperreality is characterized by meaninglessness, or at least an agitated and dynamic process whereby everything is merely an imitation (**simulacrum**) of everything else.

Identity: The way an individual sees him- or her-self, and projects that self into the world. This concept marks a key debate in contemporary cultural studies. An individual's 'identity' is shaped by biological, social and personal factors. Some theorists believe that identity is rooted in deep history, culture and ethnicity; others believe that identity is almost entirely constructed in culture and discourse. The first of these positions is **essentialist** in that 'identity' is seen as something fixed and largely immutable. The second suggests that individuals have a degree of choice about who they are and which cultural elements they wish to mobilize in order to express their identity. In effect, our individual identity is both conditioned by external forces, and by our own choices and sense of expressive agency. Identity has become a critical part of contemporary cultural politics – for example, in the notional 'war on terror' a great deal of popular, governmental and academic debate surrounds the condition of 'being Muslim' and the ways in which identity is being mobilized in cultural agonisms.

Ideology: This is an extremely complex term which is frequently debated in cultural studies. At the simplest level it is a system of beliefs and attitudes which are formed politically by a given social group. Adapting the ideas of Karl Marx, however, Louis Althusser argues that ideology is really the mechanism by which powerful elites impose their own interests and beliefs over the masses in a given society. It is the difference between the things people believe about themselves and the real conditions of their lives. These powerful groups infuse their self-interest over the masses through the manipulation of a symbolic order. Media texts, government discourses, laws, education, information – all contribute to the formation of a dominant ideology.

Intertextuality: According to Jacques Derrida, all texts are necessarily related to all other texts through the process of meaning deferral. This simply means that the words that comprise a text are dependent upon prior (and future) meanings that are contained in other words. In order to understand the meaning of a statement like 'the dog is black', a reader will be tracking back to prior readings of each of these words and their formulation in grammar. If the reader goes to the dictionary, s/he will find a whole new set of words whose meanings must also be tracked to other texts and meanings. Thus, all meanings are subject to a process of 'supplementarity', where any given word supplements the meaning of any other.

Marxism (neo-Marxism): This is a set of ideas derived from the nineteenth century German philosopher and social theorist Karl Marx. Marxist theory focuses on the means of production, historical materialism, political economy and various forms of social inequality. Marxian studies focus on the man himself, as opposed to his theories.

Mediasphere: The notion of a 'public sphere' refers to citizenship (belonging to a nation state) and participation in democratic institutional processes. In its original form, the public sphere was seen as the physical and cultural spaces in which citizens engage in political discussion, information sharing, decision making and electoral processes. It is not about private profit or pleasure, but public duty and democratic participation. With the emergence of mass media, the public sphere has been transformed through a new merging of private and public cultural spaces. Political participation is now formed in relation to mediated texts, entertainments and information. The mediasphere represents the convergence of the public sphere with new forms of mass mediation.

Myth: According to Claude Lévi-Strauss, myths are stories and legends developed by cultures in order to resolve underlying community tensions. While Lévi-Strauss focuses on traditional and tribal societies, the same process of myth-making (as meaning-making) is evident in modern societies. Roland Barthes argues that myths are 'naturalised' (formed as a natural or inevitable truth) by a modern society in order to make sense of things and provide an historical density to their meaning-making. At this level, myths are not necessarily 'untruths' or fallacious narratives; they are an essential part of a social group's identity and sense of belonging.

Ontology (essentialism): This is a philosophical idea about the true and essential nature of things. Often the concept is applied to explain the essence of human nature, human spirit, the cosmos, nature, identity or history. Cultural studies is often seen as 'anti-essentialist' as it treats culture as constructed meanings, rather than as some mysterious or nefarious essence.

Patriarchy: Feminists argue that social history is marked by a significant gender hierarchy by which males have dominated females. This patriarchal system is shaped by material divisions, law and cultural meanings which insist that women are inferior to men; the world has been shaped by this fundamental belief system and the interests and ideology of males.

Performativity: The focus on social performance (action) which has been determined by culturally embedded discourses and laws. For example, men will perform as men because they are obeying specific social rules and expectations that are continually confirmed through repetition in movies, sports programmes, television and social interactions, etc.

Phallocentrism: A phallus is a symbolic penis. It represents the belief system that surrounds patriarchy and male political and cultural power. Phallocentricism refers to the subconscious male ego.

Political economy: This concept is drawn from Karl Marx and usually refers to a critical framework for studying society. This framework focuses on the interdependence of politics and economics as the core of social relationships and inequality.

Polysemy: This concept was developed through **semiotics** (see below). It is the idea that a sign (unit of meaning) may carry many potential meanings. However, the selection of a dominant meaning is generally shaped by dominant social groups. For example, the word 'democracy' is politically charged and subject to considerable debate between national, ethnic and religious groups across the globe. This potential for multiple meanings is nevertheless subject to the dominant interests of, for example, the United States government and its cultural power.

Position (to): A number of cultural studies scholars argue that a text and its ideology 'position' readers and their meaning-making. Thus, some feminists might argue that fashion magazines position teenage female readers, creating the urge to imitate thin, heavily made up, high consuming models. The text positions or situates the reader in terms of specific identities and ideologies (capitalism, patriarchy) and behaviours (consuming, wearing make-up, dieting).

Postcolonialism: An analytical framework designed to explain the cultural and political experiences of peoples in formerly colonized territories. Such analyses usually point to the evolution of complex power relationships in countries that were once directly administered by colonialists such as Britain, the US, France, Spain and Germany. They will study, for example, the contemporary experiences of indigenous people in countries like Australia and Canada. The ethnic, racial and political disharmonies associated with colonization, foreign settlement and de-colonization in Africa, India and the Middle East are also common sites for postcolonial analysis.

Post-Fordism: Henry Ford perfected the system of mass, assembly-line, industrial production (Ford motor cars). Many historians believe that we have entered a new economic phase in which mass production has been replaced by flexible, low scale and creative industry (typified by tourism, hospitality, media and information industries). It is argued that this post-industrial society is characterized by flat management styles and a flexible, highly trained workforce. The major OECD countries are seen as post-Fordist, while emerging economies like China remain in a typically Fordist phase.

Postmodernism (Postmodernity): Usually refers to a set of texts and ideas that are characterized by multiplicity of meanings and forms that are self-challenging and self-reflexive. In particular, postmodernism challenges the notion of an integrated, modernist, unified and absolute truth. To this end, we might think of 'postmodern' films like David Lynch's *Mulholland Drive,* literature such as Joseph Heller's *Catch-22,* paintings like Andy Warhol's *Green Coca Cola Bottles,* and architecture such as the Sydney Opera House. Postmodernity describes the historical phase in which postmodern ideas and texts are pre-eminent. A number of scholars argue that we have entered such a phase, claiming that time and space have been compressed and there is no overriding truth or reality in a globalized cultural context.

Poststructuralism: A philosophical idea which focuses on the way language shapes knowledge and power. It is 'post' structuralism because it challenges the idea that language, society and history are constructed around durable, fixed and powerful 'structures'. Poststructuralism claims that meanings are dynamic, elusive and often unstable. Power is treated as a contingency of relationships, rather than as something that is historically fixed, as Marx claims.

Reflexive (reflexivity): This concept is associated with postmodernism. It refers generally to a social or aesthetic perspective which reflects upon and challenges itself. Thus, in a multiple irony, reflexive text such as *Mulholland Drive,* the storytelling reflects on the processes of storytelling, narrative and creating film.

Representation: The re-presentation of experience or phenomena in discourse and text. In cultural studies 'representation' is not merely the reproduction or mirror reflection of reality in text; rather, the process of representation is ultimately one of engagement between the self and all other cultural elements. Reality (or more precisely meaning) is created through representation. This is why many cultural studies scholars treat everything as a potential text, including lived experience, bodies and nature as well as recognizable media texts in film, literature and television.

Semiotics (semiology): The study of 'signs' as meaning systems. Semiology has a more scientific demeanour and is centred in French scholarship.

Signification (signifiers, signifieds): Signification is the process of making meaning through sign systems. Signs are formed in any meaning system such as language, colour schemes like traffic lights and so on. A sign is divided into the signifier (the material sign such as a word or traffic light), and signifieds (the mental concept or potential meaning to the signifier). Thus, in a sign such as red light on a traffic signal, the signifier is the bulb and colour red, while the signified is linked to the meaning of stop.

Simulacra: Literally refers to simulations or imitations. Jean Baudrillard uses the concept to explain his **hyperreality** in which everything is an imitation of everything else; thus, there is no distinct or valid meaning within a hyperreal cultural context.

Society (social formation): Society is the assemblage of people into a mass organizational unit, most often constituted in modern history around the nation-state. A 'social formation' is also an assemblage of people with a distinct organizational and/or ideological purpose (not necessarily the nation-state). Thus, the workers in a multi-national corporation, global Islam, or an intra-state ethnic community may be seen as a specific social formation.

Structuralism: This concept most often refers to the idea that invisible social structures provide the essential framework of a society. Such structures are carried through history by durable institutions and their belief systems, ideology and fixed meanings. Karl Marx, most famously, refers to social class as the primary and defining social structure of modern society. Many other social theorists have also seen society as being based upon social structures (such as patriarchy) and related institutions (such as the family). A number of language theorists (e.g. C.S. Peirce and Ferdinand de Saussure) believe that society is largely determined by the structures and recurring patterns that are inherent in all language.

Subculture: For theorists who believed that culture was a relatively fixed system of meanings attached to a relatively fixed and stable social group, 'subculture' denotes a social sub-section which deviates from the majority or dominant group and its 'norms' (sense of normality and values). Subcultures are usually seen as a distinctive and separate group with their own norms, beliefs, rules, clothing styles and cultural practices. Thus, analysts might append the notion of subculture to drug-user groups, motor cycle gangs, criminals and so on. Scholars who believe that the concept of 'culture' implicates difference and multi-forming constituencies are less inclined to use the concept of subculture because it suggests that there is a fixed main culture and deviant appendices.

Subject (subjectivity): An individual member of a social group is called a 'subject'. Subjects pertain to a culturally formed 'identity' or 'subjectivity' (sense of self) over which they have a degree of control or choice. Subjectivity is thus formed in discourse and culture. It is the new focus of an emancipatory politics which encourages choice and the liberation of subjectivity from socially determined rules and prescribed beliefs and practices.

Televisualization (televisual culture): As meaning production, dissemination and consumption are the central processes of culture, different cultures may thus be characterized in terms of their dominant communications technologies. The notion of a televisual culture refers to the pre-eminence of image-based mass mediation. Televisualization clearly affects the consciousness of individuals and hence their shared meaning-making and sense of reality.

Text: In cultural studies 'text' refers to any organized set of discourses (and meanings). A text may be related to particular media forms or publications as in film, television and literature. However, we might also refer to 'the body' as a text which has meanings inscribed on it and which may be 'read' or interpreted. Thus, a body can be decorated and clothed according to a given meaning system (punk, businessman, prostitute, etc); it may also be read according to biologically determined tags such as age, 'colour', gender, etc. Landscapes, social practices and built environments may also be read and interpreted as texts.

References

Abbas, A. and Erni, J. (2005) *Internationalizing Cultural Studies: An Anthology,* Blackwell, Malden, MA.

Adams, M. and Motta, S. (1996) *Online Friendship, Chat Room Romance and Cybersex,* Health Communications Inc., Deerfield Beach, FL.

Adorno, T. (1994) 'On popular music' in J. Storey, ed., *Cultural Theory and Popular Culture: A Reader,* Harvester Wheatsheaf, Hemel Hempstead.

Afary, J., Anderson, K., Foucault, M. (2005) *Foucault and the Iranian Revolution: Gender and the Seductions of Islamicism,* University of Chicago Press, Chicago.

Alexander, J., ed. (1988) *Durkheimian Sociology: Cultural Studies,* Cambridge University Press, Cambridge.

Ali, T. (2002) *The Clash of Fundamentalisms: Crusades, Jihads and Modernity,* Verso, London.

Althusser, L. (1969) *For Marx,* Allen Lane, London.

Althusser, L. (1971a) 'Ideology and ideological state apparatuses' in L. Althusser, *Lenin and Philosophy and Other Essays,* New Left Books, London.

Althusser, L. (1971b) 'Letter on art' in L. Althusser, *Lenin and Philosophy,* trans. B. Brewster, New Left Books, London.

Anderson, B. (1991) *Imagined Communities: Reflections on the Origin and Spread of Nationalism,* rev. edn, Verso, London.

Ang, I. (1985) *Watching Dallas: Soap Opera and the Melodramatic Imagination,* Methuen, London.

Ang, I. (1996) *Living Room Wars: Rethinking Media Audiences for a Postmodern World,* Routledge, London.

Ang, I. and Stratton, J. (1996) 'Asianing Australia: notes toward a critical transnationalism in cultural studies', *Cultural Studies,* 10 (1).

Appadurai, A. (1990) 'Disjuncture and difference in the global cultural economy' in M. Featherstone, ed., *Global Culture: Nationalism, Globalization and Modernity,* Sage, London.

Appadurai, A. (1996) *Modernity at Large: The Cultural Dimensions of Globalization,* University of Minnesota Press, Minneapolis.

Appadurai, A. (2006) 'Disjuncture and Difference in the Global Cultural Economy' in M. Durham and D. Kellner, eds, *Media and Cultural Studies: Keywords,* Blackwell Publishing, London.

Arac, J., ed. (1988) *After Foucault: Humanistic Knowledge, Postmodern Challenges,* Rutgers University Press, New Brunswick, NJ.

Arnold, M. (1949) *Culture and Anarchy*, Everyman's Library, London.

Attive, Z., ed. (2002) *The New Generation of International Architecture*, Skira, Milan.

Bacchi, C. (1996) *The Politics of Affirmative Action: Women, Equality and the Politics of Category*, Sage, London.

Background Briefing (1999) 'Culture jamming: how to make trouble and influence people', ABC National Radio, 18 October.

Bakhtin, M. (1984) *Problems of Dostoevsky's Poetics*, trans. C. Emerson, Manchester University Press, Manchester.

Barney, D. (2000) *Prometheus Wired: The Hope for Democracy in the Age of Network Technology*, University of Chicago Press, Chicago.

Barry, K. (2003) *Citizen Sex: The Girl Next Door on the Adult Internet*, Trafford Publishing, Victoria, BC.

Barthes, R. (1967) *Elements of Semiology*, trans. A. Lavers and C. Smith, Jonathan Cape, London.

Barthes, R. (1973) *Mythologies*, trans. A. Lavers, Paladin, St Albans.

Barthes, R. (1975) *The Pleasure of the Text*, trans. R. Miller, Hill and Wang, New York.

Barthes, R. (1977) *Image–Music–Text*, trans. S. Heath, Fontana, London.

Barthes, B. (1990) *The Fashion System*, trans. M. Ward and R. Howard, University of California Press, Berkeley.

Baudrillard, J. (1975) *The Mirror of Production*, trans. M. Poster, Telos Press, St Louis.

Baudrillard, J. (1981) *For a Critique of the Political Economy of the Sign*, trans. C. Levin, Telos Press, St Louis.

Baudrillard, J. (1983a) *In the Shadow of the Silent Majorities*, trans. P. Foss, S. Johnson and P. Pallon, Semiotext(e), New York.

Baudrillard, J. (1983b) 'The ecstasy of communication' in H. Foster, ed., *The Anti-Aesthetic: Essays on Postmodern Culture*, Bay Press, Seattle.

Baudrillard, J. (1984a) *Simulations*, trans. P. Foss, Semiotext(e), New York.

Baudrillard, J. (1984b) 'The procession of simulacra' in H. Wallis, ed., *Art After Modernism: Rethinking Representation*, Museum of Modern Art, New York.

Baudrillard, J. (1987) *Forget Foucault*, Semiotext(e), New York.

Baudrillard, J. (1988) *The Ecstasy of Communication*, trans. B. Schutze and C. Schutze, Semiotext(e), New York.

Baudrillard, J. (1990) *Seduction*, trans. B. Singer, Culturetext, New York.

Baudrillard, J. (1993) *Symbolic Exchange and Death*, trans. I. Hamilton, Sage, London.

Baudrillard, J. (1994) *The Illusion of the End*, trans. C. Turner, Polity, Cambridge.

Baudrillard, J. (1995) *The Gulf War Did Not Take Place*, trans. P. Paron, Power Publications, New South Wales.

Baudrillard, J. (1996) *The System of Objects*, trans. J. Benedict, Verso, London.

Baudrillard, J. (1998) *The Consumer Society: Myths and Structures*, trans. C. Turner, Sage, London.

Baudrillard, J. (2002) *The Spirit of Terrorism and Requiem for the Twin Towers*, trans. C. Turner, Verso, London.

Bauman, Z. (2004) *Identity*, Polity, Oxford.

Becker, H. and McCall, M. (1990) *Symbolic Interaction and Cultural Studies*, University of Chicago Press, Chicago.

Bell, D. (1973) *The Coming of Post-Industrial Society*, Basic Books, New York.

Bell, D. (1976) *The Cultural Contradictions of Capitalism*, Basic Books, New York.

Benjamin, W. (1977) 'The work of art in the age of mechanical reproduction' in *Illuminations*, trans. M. Zohn, Fontana, London.

Bennett, T. (1985) 'The politics of the popular' in V. Beechey and J. Donald, eds, *Subjectivity and Social Relations*, Open University Press, Milton Keynes.

Bennett, T. (1986) 'Hegemony, ideology, pleasure: Blackpool' in T. Bennett, C. Mercer and J. Woollacott, eds, *Popular Culture and Social Relations*, Open University Press, Milton Keynes.

Bennett, T. (1997) 'Towards a pragmatics of cultural studies' in J. McGuigan, ed., *Cultural Methodologies*, Sage, London.

Bennett, T. (1999) 'Putting policy into cultural studies' in S. During, ed., *The Cultural Studies Reader*, 2nd edn, Routledge, London.

Bennett, T., Mercer, C. and Woollacott, J., eds (1986) *Popular Culture and Social Relations*, Open University Press, Milton Keynes.

Bennett, T., Frith, S., Grossberg, L., Shepherd, J. and Turner, G., eds (1993) *Rock and Popular Music: Politics, Policies, Institutions*, Routledge, London.

Berger, P. (1967) *The Sacred Canopy*, Doubleday, Garden City, NY.

Berger, P. and Luckmann, T. (1966) *The Social Construction of Reality*, Doubleday, Garden City, NY.

Berger, R. (2004) 'Digital media futures' in D. Gauntlett and R. Horsley, eds, *Web.Studies*.

Best, K. and Lewis, J. (2000) 'Hacking the democratic mainframe: (Dis)Organising transgressive computing', *Media International Australia*, 95, May.

Best, S. and Kellner, D. (1997) *The Postmodern Turn*, Guilford Press, New York.

Bhabha, H. (1987) 'Interrogating identity' in H. Bhabha, ed., *Identity: The Real Me*, ICA, London.

Bhabha, H. (1990) *Nation and Narration*, Routledge, London.

Bhabha, H. (1994) *The Location of Culture*, Routledge, London.

Bhabha, H. (1999) 'Liberalism's sacred cow' in S. Okin and J. Cohen, eds, *Is Multiculturalism Bad for Women?*, Princeton University Press, Princeton.

Bleitch, D. (1978) *Subjective Criticism*, Johns Hopkins University Press, Baltimore.

Blount, M. and Cunningham, G. (1996) *Representing Black Men*, Routledge, New York.

Blumer, H. (1933) *The Movies and Conduct*, Macmillan, New York.

Bok, S. (1999) *Mayhem: Violence as Public Entertainment*, Perseus, New York.

Boller, D. (1992) 'Literature in the electronic writing space' in M. Tuman, ed., *Literacy Online*, University of Pittsburgh Press, Pittsburgh.

Boller, D. (1993) 'The information superhighway: roadmap for renewed public purpose', *Tikkum,* 8 (4).

Bourdieu, P. (1977) *Outline of a Theory of Practice,* trans. R. Nice, Cambridge University Press, Cambridge.

Bourdieu, P. (1984) *Distinction: A Social Critique of the Judgement of Taste,* Routledge, London.

Bourdieu, P. (1990) *Language and Symbolic Power,* Polity, Cambridge.

Bourdieu, P. (1991) 'Sport and social class' in C. Mukerji and M. Schudson, eds, *Rethinking Popular Culture,* University of California Press, Berkeley.

Bradbury, M. and McFarlane, J., eds (1978) *Modernism,* Penguin, Harmondsworth.

Brown, G. (2004) 'Sites of public (home) sex and the carnivalesque spaces of reclaim the streets' in L. Lees, ed., *The Emancipatory City?,* Sage, London; Thousand Oaks, CA.

Bryman, A. (1995) *Disney and His Worlds,* Routledge, London.

Buchbinder, D. (1998) *Performance Anxieties: Reproducing Masculinity,* Allen & Unwin, Sydney.

Burchell, G., Gordon, C. and Miller, P., eds (1991) *The Foucault Effect: Studies in Governmentality,* University of Chicago Press, Chicago.

Burroughs, W. (1966) *Exterminator,* Viking, New York.

Butler, J. (1995) 'Melancholy gender/refused identification' in M. Berger, B. Wallis and S. Watson, eds, *Constructing Masculinity,* Routledge, London.

Carey, J. (1989) *Communication as Culture,* Unwin Hyman, Boston.

Carlyle, T. (1967) *Essays: English and Other Critical Essays,* Everyman's Library, London.

Castells, M. (1997) *The Power of Identity,* Blackwell, London.

Caygill, H. (1990) 'Architectural postmodernism: the retreat of an avant-garde?' in R. Boyne and A. Rattasnsi, eds, *Postmodernism and Society,* St Martin's Press, New York.

Chambers, I. (1988) *Popular Culture: The Metropolitan Experience,* Routledge, London.

Childs, K. (1991) 'Daimaru man defends his vision of the future', *The Age,* 28 October.

Chitty, N. (2003) 'Introduction: subjects of terrorism and media' in N. Chitty, R. Rush, and M. Semeti, *Studies in Terrorism: Media Scholarship and the Enigma of Terror,* Southbound, Penang.

Choi, P. (2000) *Femininity and the Physically Active Woman,* Routledge, London.

Chomsky, N. (2001) *September 11,* Unwin, Crows Nest.

Chomsky, N. (2003a) *Middle East Illusions,* Rowman and Littlefield, London.

Chomsky, N. (2003b) *Hegemony or Survival,* Metropolitan Books, New York.

Cixous, H. and Clément, C. (1986) *The Newly Born Woman,* trans. B. Wing, University of Minnesota Press, Minneapolis.

Clarke, D. (1993) '"With my body, I thee worship": the social construction of marital sexual problems' in S. Scott and D. Morgan, eds, *Body Matters: Essays on the Sociology of the Body,* Falmer Press London.

Collins, J. (1989) *Uncommon Cultures: Popular Culture and Post-modernism,* Routledge, New York.

Connor, S. (1989) *Postmodernist Culture: An Introduction to Theories of the Contemporary*, Blackwell, New York.

Cornell, D., ed. (2000) *Feminism and Pornography*, Oxford University Press, New York.

Cornell, R.W. (1990) 'An iron man: the body and some contradictions of hegemonic masculinity' in M. Messner and Donald Sabo, eds, *Sport, Men and the Gender Order*, Human Kinetics Books, Champaign.

Cowie, E. (1984) 'Fantasia', *m/f*, 9.

Crane, D. (2002) 'Culture and globalization: theoretical models and emerging trends' in D. Crane, N. Kawashima, and K. Kawasaki, eds, *Global Culture: Media, Arts, Policy and Globalization*, Routledge, New York.

Cregan, K. (2006) *The Sociology of the Body: Mapping the Abstraction of Embodiment*, Sage, London.

Darwin, C. (1859) *On the Origin of Species by Means of Natural Selection, or the Preservation of Favoured Races in the Struggle for Life*, John Murray, London.

Davies, J. (1999) *Diana: Constructing the People's Princess*, Macmillan, Melbourne.

Davies, P. (1983) *God and the New Physics*, Penguin, Harmondsworth.

Davies, P. (1987) *The Cosmic Blueprint*, Heinemann, London.

de Beauvoir, S. (1972) *The Second Sex*, trans. H.M. Parshley, Penguin, Harmondsworth.

de Certeau, M. (1984) *The Practice of Everyday Life*, trans. S. Rendall, University of California Press, Berkeley.

de Certeau, M. (1988) *The Writing of History*, trans. T. Conley, Columbia University Press, New York.

de Lauretis, T. (1987) *Technologies of Gender: Essays on Theory, Film and Fiction*, Macmillan, London.

de Saussure, F. (1974) *Course in General Linguistics*, Fontana, London.

Deleuze, G. (1977) 'Discussion with Michel Foucault' in M. Foucault, *Language, Counter-Memory and Practice: Selected Essays and Interviews*, trans. D.F. Bouchard and S. Simon, Blackwell, Oxford.

Deleuze, G. and Guattari, F. (1983) *Anti-Oedipus: Capitalism and Schizophrenia*, trans. R. Hurley, M. Seem and H. Lane, University of Minnesota Press, Minneapolis.

Deleuze, G. and Guattari, F. (1987) *A Thousand Plateaus: Capitalism and Schizophrenia*, trans. B. Massumi, University of Minnesota Press, Minneapolis.

Denzin, N. (1992) *Symbolic Interactionism and Cultural Studies: The Politics of Interpretation*, Blackwell, Cambridge, MA.

Derrida, J. (1970) 'Discussion' in *The Structuralist Controversy: The Languages of Criticism and the Sciences of Man*, R. Macksey and E. Donato, eds, Johns Hopkins University Press, Baltimore.

Derrida, J. (1974) *Of Grammatology*, trans. G.C. Spivak, Johns Hopkins University Press, Baltimore.

Derrida, J. (1979) *Writing and Difference*, trans. A. Bass, Routledge and Kegan Paul, London.

Derrida, J. (1981) *Dissemination*, trans. B. Johnson, University of Chicago Press, Chicago.

Descombes, V. (1980) *Modern French Philosophy*, Cambridge University Press, Cambridge.

Desmond, C., ed. (1997) *Meanings in Motion: The Cultural Studies of Dance*, Duke University Press, Durham, NC.

Dews, P. (1984) *Logics of Disintegration: Post-structuralist Thought and the Claims of Critical Theory*, Verso, London.

Docker, J. (1994) *Postmodernism and Popular Culture: A Cultural History*, Cambridge University Press, Cambridge.

Docker, J. (1995) 'Rethinking postcolonialism and multiculturalism in the *fin de siècle*', *Cultural Studies*, 9 (3).

Docker, J. and Fischer, G. (2000) *Race, Colour and Identity in Australia and New Zealand*, UNSW Press, Sydney.

Douglas, M. (1978) *Implicit Meanings: Essays in Anthropology*, Routledge and Kegan Paul, London.

Drew, A. (1998) 'Elizabeth Tudor and Diana Spencer: Charming an image; Recovering a life' in A. Hall, ed., *Delights, Desires and Dilemmas: Essays on Women and the Media*, Praeger, Westport, CT.

Driscoll, C. (1995) 'Who needs a boyfriend? The homocentric virgin in adolescent women's magazines' in P. van Toorn and D. English, eds, *Speaking Positions: Aboriginality, Gender and Ethnicity in Australian Cultural Studies*, Victoria University of Technology, Melbourne.

Drummond, M. (1998a) 'When size matters: confusions and concerns over the ideal male body', *Body Image Research Forum* (Conference proceedings), Body Image and Health Inc., Melbourne.

Drummond, M. (1998b) 'Bodies: an emerging issue for boys and young men', *Everybody*, 2, August.

Duberman, M., ed. (1997) *A Queer World*, New York University Press, New York.

Durkheim, É. (1960) 'Preface to *L'Année sociologique 2*' in K. Wolff, ed., *Émile Durkheim et al. on Sociology and Philosophy*, Free Press, New York.

Durkheim, É. (1977) *The Evolution of Educational Thought*, Routledge and Kegan Paul, London.

Duvall, J. and Dworkin, J., eds (2001) *Productive Postmodernism: Consuming Histories and Cultural Studies*, Suny Press, New York.

Dyer, R. (1985) *Heavenly Bodies: Filmstars and Society*, Macmillan, Basingstoke.

Eagleton, T. (1978) *Criticism and Ideology*, Verso, London.

Eco, U. (1984) 'Postmodernism, irony and the enjoyable' in *Postscript to The Name of the Rose*, trans. W. Weapon, Harcourt Brace Jovanovich, New York.

Eden, D. (2006) *The Thrill of the Chaste: Finding Fulfilment while Keeping Your Clothes on*, Nelson, New York.

Edwards, T. (2006) *Cultures of Masculinity*, Routledge, London.

Ehrenreich, N. (2002) 'Masculinity and American militarism', *Tikkim*, 17 (6).

Elliott, G. (1994) *Louis Althusser: A Critical Reader*, Blackwell, Oxford.

Engels, F. (1994) 'Letter to Joseph Bloch' in J. Storey, ed., *Cultural Theory and Popular Culture: A Reader*, Harvester Wheatsheaf, Hemel Hempstead.

Ess, C. (1994) 'The political computer: hypertext, democracy and Habermas' in G. Landow, ed., *Hyper/Text/Theory*, Johns Hopkins University Press, Baltimore.

Everett, A. and Caldwell, J., eds (2003) *New Media: Theories and Practices of Digitextuality*, Routledge, New York.

Featherstone, M. (1990) *Consumer Culture and Postmodernism*, Sage, London.

Featherstone, M. (1996) 'Globalism, localism and cultural identity' in R. Wilson and W. Dissanayake, eds, *Global Local: Cultural Production and the Transnational Imaginary*, Duke University Press, London.

Featherstone, M. and Hepworth, M. (1991) 'The mask of ageing and the postmodern life course' in M. Featherstone, M. Hepworth and B. Turner, eds, *The Body: Social Process and Cultural Theory*, Sage, London.

Featherstone, M., Hepworth, M. and Turner, B., eds (1991) *The Body: Social Process and Cultural Theory*, Sage, London.

Fischilin, D., ed. (1994) *Negation, Critical Theory, and Postmodern Textuality*, Kluwer Academic, New York.

Fish, S. (2002) 'Don't blame relativism', *The Responsive Community*, The Communications Network Symposium, Published papers, University of Illinois, Chicago.

Fisk, R. (2003) 'Does the US military want to kill journalists?' *The Independent*, April 8.

Fiske, J. (1987) *Television Culture*, Methuen, London.

Fiske, J. (1989a) *Reading the Popular*, Unwin Hyman, Boston.

Fiske, J. (1989b) *Understanding Popular Culture*, Unwin Hyman, Boston.

Fiske, J., Hodge, B. and Turner, G. (1987) *Myths of Oz: Reading Australian Popular Culture*, Allen & Unwin, Sydney.

Forman, M. (2000) '"Represent": race, space and place in rap music', *Popular Music*, 19 (1).

Foucault, M. (1972) *The Archaeology of Knowledge and the Discourse on Language*, trans. A.M. Sheridan, Pantheon, New York.

Foucault, M. (1974) *The Order of Things: An Archaeology of the Human Sciences*, Tavistock, London.

Foucault, M. (1977) *Discipline and Punish: The Birth of the Prison*, trans. A.M. Sheridan, Penguin, New York.

Foucault, M. (1980) *Power/Knowledge: Selected Interviews and Other Writings*, Pantheon, New York.

Foucault, M. (1981) *The History of Sexuality, Volume One: An Introduction*, trans. R. Hurley, Penguin, New York.

Foucault, M. (1984) 'What is Enlightenment?' trans. C. Porter in P. Rabinow, ed., *The Foucault Reader*, Penguin, London.

Foucault, M. (1988) 'Technologies of the self' in L. Martin, H. Gutman and P. Hutton, eds, *Technologies of the Self*, University of Massachusetts Press, Amherst.

Foucault, M. (1991) 'Governmentality' in G. Burchell, C. Gordon and P. Miller, eds, *The Foucault Effect: Studies in Governmentality*, University of Chicago Press, Chicago.

Frampton, K. (1985) 'Towards a critical regionalism' in H. Foster, ed., *Postmodern Culture*, Pluto Press, London.

Frith, S. (1996) *Performing Rites: On the Value of Popular Music*, Harvard University Press, Cambridge, MA.

Frith, S. and Horn, D. (1987) *Art into Pop*, Methuen, London.

Frow, J. (1991) 'Michel de Certeau: the practice of representation', *Cultural Studies*, 5 (1).

Fukayama, F. (1992) *The End of History and the Last Man*, Free Press, Toronto.

Gans, H. (1973) *Popular Culture and High Culture*, Basic Books, New York.

Gauch, S. (2006) *Liberating Shahrazad: Feminism and Postcolonialism*, University of Minnesota Press, Minneapolis.

Gauntlett, D. and Horsley, R., eds (2004) *Web.Studies*, 2nd edn, Arnold, London.

Geertz, C. (1973) *The Interpretation of Cultures*, Basic Books, New York.

Geertz, C. (1976) 'Art as a cultural system', *MLN*, 91.

Geertz, C. (1988) *Works and Lives: Anthropologist as Author*, Stanford University Press, Stanford.

Geertz, C. (1991) 'Deep play: notes on the Balinese cockfight' in C. Mukerji and M. Schudson, eds, *Rethinking Popular Culture: Contemporary Perspectives in Cultural Studies*, University of California Press, Berkeley.

Giddens, A. (1990) *The Consequences of Modernity*, Polity, Cambridge.

Giddens, A. (1994) *Beyond Left and Right: The Future of Radical Politics*, Polity, Cambridge.

Gilbert, S. and Gubar, S. (1988) *No Man's Land: The Place of the Woman Writer in the Twentieth Century, Volume 1*, Yale University Press, New Haven.

Giles, J. and Middleton, T. (1999) *Studying Culture: A Practical Introduction*, Blackwell, Oxford.

Gilroy, P. (1998) *The Black Atlantic*, Verso, London.

Goffman, E. (1959) *The Presentation of Self in Everyday Life*, Doubleday, New York.

Goldstein, J. (2001) *War and Gender: How Gender Shapes the War System and Vice Versa*, Cambridge University Press, Cambridge.

Gouldner, A. (1976) *The Dialectic of Ideology and Technology*, Macmillan, London.

Gramsci, A. (1971) *Selections from the Prison Notebooks*, trans. Q. Hoare and G. Nowell-Smith, Lawrence and Wishart, London.

Greenwald, R. (2004) *Outfoxed: Rupert Murdoch's War on Journalism*, DVD.

Grossberg, L. (1997) *Bringing it All Back Home: Essays on Cultural Studies*, Duke University Press, Durham and London.

Grossberg, L., Fry, T. and Curthoys, A. (1988) *It's a Sin: Essays on Postmodernism, Politics and Culture*, Power Publications, Sydney.

Guattari, F. (1992) 'Regimes, pathways, subjects', trans. B. Masumi in J. Crary and S. Kwinter, eds, *Incorporations*, Zone Books, New York.

Gunew, S. (1993) 'Multicultural multiplicities: US, Canada, Australia', *Meanjin*, 32 (3).

Habermas, J. (1975) 'Towards a reconstruction of historical materialism', *Theory and Society*, 1 (3).

Habermas, J. (1981) 'Modernity versus postmodernity', *New German Critique*, 22, Winter.

Habermas, J. (1983) 'Modernity – an incomplete project' in H. Foster, ed., *The Anti-aesthetic: Essays on Postmodern Culture*, Bay Press, Seattle.

Habermas, J. (1984a) *The Theory of Communicative Action, Volume One*, trans. T. McCarthy, Beacon, Boston.

Habermas, J. (1984b) 'The French path to postmodernity: Bataille between eroticism and general economics', *New German Critique*, 33.

Habermas, J. (1987a) *The Theory of Communicative Action, Volume Two*, trans. T. McCarthy, Beacon, Boston.

Habermas, J. (1987b) *The Philosophical Discourse of Modernity*, trans. F. Lawrence, MIT Press, Cambridge, Mass.

Habermas, J. (1989) *The Structural Transformation of the Public Sphere: An Inquiry into a Category of Bourgeois Society*, MIT Press, Cambridge, MA.

Halberstam, J. (1998) *Female Masculinity*, Duke University Press, Durham, NC.

Halberstam, J. and Livingston, I. (1995) *Posthuman Bodies*, Indiana University Press, Bloomington.

Hall, S. (1980) 'Encoding/decoding' in S. Hall, D. Hobson, A. Lowe and P. Willis, eds, *Culture, Media, Language*, Hutchinson, London.

Hall, S. (1982) 'The rediscovery of ideology: the return of the repressed in media studies' in M. Gurevitch, T. Bennett, J. Curran and J. Woollocat, eds, *Culture, Society and the Media*, Methuen, London.

Hall, S. (1988) 'Recent developments in theories of language and ideology: a critical note' in S. Hall, D. Hobson, A. Lowe and P. Willis, eds, *Culture, Media, Language*, Hutchinson, London.

Hall, S. (1991a) 'The local and the global: globalization and ethnicity' in A. King, ed., *Culture, Globalization and the World-System*, State University of New York at Binghampton, Binghampton.

Hall, S. (1991b) 'Old and new identities, old and new ethnicities' in A. King, ed., *Culture, Globalization and the World-System*, State University of New York at Binghampton, Binghampton.

Hall, S. (1996) 'Cultural studies and its theoretical legacies' in D. Morley and K.H. Chen, eds, *Stuart Hall: Critical Dialogues in Cultural Studies*, Routledge, London.

Hall, S., Critcher, C., Jefferson, T., Clarke, J. and Roberts, B. (1978) *Policing the Crisis: Mugging, the State and Law and Order*, Macmillan, London.

Hall, S., Held, D. and McGraw, T. (1992) *Modernity and its Futures*, Open University Press, Milton Keynes.

Halle, R. (2004) *Queer Social Philosophy: Readings from Kant to Adorno*, University of Illinois Press, Illinois.

Haraway, D. (1991) *Simians, Cyborgs and Women: The Reinvention of Nature*, Free Association Books, London.

Haraway, D. (1997) *Modest_Witness@Second_Millennium.FemaleMan_Meets_Onco-Mouse: Feminism and Technoscience*, Routledge, New York.

Hardt, M. and Negri, A. (2000) *Empire*, Harvard University Press, Cambridge, MA.

Hardt, M. and Negri, A. (2004) *Multitudes*, Penguin, New York.

Hartley, J. (1992) *Tele-ology: Studies in Television*, Routledge, London.

Hartley, J. (1996) *Popular Reality: Journalism, Modernity, Popular Culture*, Arnold, London.

Harvey, D. (1989) *The Condition of Postmodernity: An Enquiry into the Origin of Cultural Change*, Blackwell, Oxford.

Hassan, I. (1982) *The Dismemberment of Orpheus: Towards a Postmodern Literature*, Oxford University Press, New York.

Hassan, I. (1985) 'The culture of post modernism', *Theory, Culture and Society*, 2 (3).

Hassan, I. (1987) *The Postmodern Turn: Essays in Postmodern Theory and Culture*, Ohio State University Press, Columbus.

Hassler, C. (2005) *20 Something, 20 Everything*, New World Library, New York.

Hebdige, D. (1979) *Sub-culture: The Meaning of Style*, Methuen, London.

Hebdige, D. (1988) *Hiding in the Light: On Images and Things*, Comedia, London.

Heidegger, M. (1952) *Being and Time*, trans. J. Macquarie and E. Robinson, Harper, New York.

Heidegger, M. (1977) 'The age of the world picture' in *The Question Concerning Technology and Other Essays*, trans. William Lovitt, Garland Publishing, New York.

Hekman, S., ed. (1996) *Feminist Interpretations of Michel Foucault*, Pennsylvania University Press, University Park.

Held, D. (1987) *Prospects for Democracy*, Polity, Cambridge.

Held, D. (1992) 'Democracy: from a city state to a cosmopolitan order?' in D. Held, ed., *Prospects for Democracy, Political Studies Special Issue*, 40.

Held, D., McGrew, A., Goldblatt, D. and Perraton, J. (1999) *Global Transformations: Politics, Economics and Culture*, Polity, Cambridge.

Hellyer, P. (1999) *Stop: Think*, Chimo Media, Toronto.

Hersh, S. (2004) 'Torture at Abu Ghraib', *The New Yorker Fact*, May 10, <www.newyorker.com/fact>.

Hertlein, K. (2006) 'Internet infidelity: a review of the literature', *Journal of Family Studies*, 14 (4).

Hess, S. and Kalb, N., eds (2003) *The Media and the War on Terrorism*, Brookings Institution Press, New York.

Heywood, L. (1998) *Bodymakers: A Cultural Anatomy of Women's Body Building*, Rutgers University Press, New Brunswick, NJ.

Heywood, L. and Drake, J., eds (1997) *Third Wave Agenda: Being Feminist, Doing Feminism*, University of Minnesota Press, Minneapolis.

Hoggart, R. (1958) *The Uses of Literacy*, Penguin, London.

Horkheimer, M. and Adorno, T. (1972) 'The culture industry: Enlightenment as mass deception' in *Dialectic of Enlightenment*, Seabury Press, New York.

Hoy, D.C., ed. (1986) *Foucault: A Critical Reader*, Blackwell, Oxford.

Hoy, D.C. (1988) 'Foucault: modern or post- modern?' in J. Arac, ed., *After Foucault: Postmodern Challenges*, Rutgers University Press, New Brunswick, NJ.

Huffer, L. (2001) 'There is no Gomorrah: narrative ethics in feminist and queer theory', *Differences: Feminist Cultural Studies*, 12 (3).

Hume, M. (1998) *Televictims: Emotional Correctness in the Media AD (After Diana)*, Informinc, London.

Hutcheon, L. (1988) *A Politics of Postmodernism: History, Theory, Fiction*, Routledge, New York.

Hutcheon, L. (1995) *Metafiction*, Longman, New York.

Huyessen, A. (1986) *After the Great Divide: Modernism, Mass Culture, Postmodernism*, Indiana University Press, Minneapolis.

Iser, W. (1978) *The Act of Reading: A Theory of Aesthetic Response*, Johns Hopkins University Press, Baltimore.

Jacka, E. (1994) 'Researching audiences: a dialogue between cultural studies and social science', *Media International Australia*, 73, August.

Jackson, S. (1996) 'Ignorance is bliss: when you are *Just Seventeen*', *Trouble and Strife*, 33.

Jaffe, A. (2005) *Modernism and the Culture of Celebrity*, Cambridge University Press, London.

Jameson, F. (1981) *The Political Unconscious: Narrative as a Socially Symbolic Act*, Methuen, London.

Jameson, F. (1983) 'Postmodernism and consumer society' in H. Foster, ed., *The Anti-aesthetic: Essays on Postmodern Culture*, Bay Press, Seattle.

Jameson, F. (1984) 'Postmodernism, or, the cultural logic of late capitalism', *New Left Review*, 46.

Jameson, F. (1991) *Postmodernism, or, the Cultural Logic of Late Capitalism*, Verso, London.

Jameson, F. (1998) *The Cultural Turn*, Verso, London.

Jarrett, L. (1997) *Stripping in Time: A History of Erotic Dancing*, HarperCollins, London.

Jeffreys, S. (2004) *Unpacking Queer Politics: A Lesbian Feminist Perspective*, Polity Press, Cambridge.

Jeffreys, S. (2005) *Beauty and Misogyny: Harmful Cultural Practices in the West*, Routledge, London.

Jencks, C. (1986) *What is Postmodernism?* Academy Editions, London.

Jencks, C. (1987a) *Post-Modernism: The New Classicism in Art and Architecture*, Academy Editions, London.

Jencks, C. (1987b) *The Language of Post-Modern Architecture*, Academy Editions, London.

Jencks, C. (1995) *The Architecture of the Jumping Universe*, Academy Editions, London.

Jencks, C. (2005) *The Iconic Building*, Frances Lincoln, London.

Jenkins, H. (1992) *Textual Poachers: Television Fans and Participatory Culture*, Routledge, New York.

Jenkins, H. and Thorburn, D., eds (2003) *Democracy and New Media*, MIT Press, Cambridge, MA.

Jenkins, H., McPherson, T. and Shatruc, J. (2003) *The Hop and Pop: The Politics and Pleasure of Popular Culture*, Duke University Press, Durham, NC.

Jenkins, P. (2001) *Beyond tolerance: Child Pornography and the Internet*, NYI Press, New York.

Johnson, R. (1979) 'Elements of a theory of a theory of working class culture' in J. Clarke, ed., *Working Class Culture's Studies in History and Theory*, Hutchinson, London.

Katz, E. (1959) 'Mass communication research and the study of popular culture', *Studies in Public Communication*, 2.

Kellner, D. (1989) *Jean Baudrillard: From Marx-ism to Postmodernism and Beyond*, Polity, Cambridge.

Kellner, D. (1995) *Media Culture: Cultural Studies, Media and Politics between the Modern and the Postmodern*, Routledge, London.

Kellner, D. (2005) *Media Spectacle and the Crisis of Democracy*, Paradigm Publishing, New York.

Kerby, M. (1997) 'Babes on the web: sex, identity and the home page', *Media International Australia*, 84 May.

Kinge, J. (2006) *China Shakes the World: The Rise of a Hungry Nation*, Weidenfeld and Nicholson, London.

Krane, P., Choi, P., Baird, S., Aimar, C. and Kauer, K. (2004) 'Living the paradox: female athletes negotiate femininity and muscularity', *Sex Roles: A Journal of Research*, 50 (5/6).

Kristeva, J. (1980) *Desire in Language: A Semiotic Approach to Literature and Art*, trans. T. Gora, Columbia University Press, New York.

Kroker, A. (2004) *The Will to Technology and the Culture of Nihilism: Heidegger, Nietzsche and Marx*, University of Toronto Press, Toronto.

Kroker, A. and Kroker, M. (1997) 'Code warriors' in *C. Theory* <http://www.ctheory.com/a36-code_warriors.html>, 19 September.

Kuhn, T. (1970) *The Structure of Scientific Revolutions*, Chicago University Press, Chicago.

Lacan, J. (1977) *Ecrits: A Selection*, Tavistock, London.

Laclau, E. (1996) *Emancipation(s)*, Verso, London.

Laclau, E. and Mouffe, C. (1985) *Hegemony and Socialist Strategy: Towards a Radical Democratic Politics*, Verso, London.

Laing, S. (1986) *Representations of Working-class Life*, Macmillan, London.

Landow, G. (1992) *Hypertext: The Convergence of Contemporary Critical Theory and Technology*, Johns Hopkins University Press, Baltimore.

Langley, E. (1997) *The Lusty Lady*, Scalo Zurich, New York.

Lanham, R. (1993) *The Electronic Word: Democracy, Technology and the Arts*, University of Chicago Press, Chicago.

Laqueur, W. (1987) *The Age of Terrorism,* George Weidenfeld and Nicolson, London.

Laqueur, W. (2003) *No End to War: Terrorism in the Twenty First Century,* Continuum, New York.

Lax, S. (2004) 'The internet and democracy' in H. Jenkins and D. Thorburn, eds, *Web.Studies.*

Lefebvre, H. (1991) *The Production of Space,* trans. D. Nicholson-Smith, Blackwell, Oxford.

Lefebvre, H. (1992) *Critique of Everyday Life,* trans. J. Moore, Verso, London.

Leonard, M. (1997) '"Rebel girl you are the queen of my world": feminism, subculture and grrrl power' in S. Whitely, ed., *Sexing the Groove: Popular Music and Gender,* Routledge, London.

Lewis, Bernard (2003) *The Crisis of Islam: Holy War and Unholy Terror,* The Modern Library, New York.

Lewis, J. (1997a) 'The inhuman state: nature, media, government', *Media International Australia,* 83, February.

Lewis, J. (1997b) 'Shot in the dark: Australia's industrial culture', *Cultural Studies,* 11 (3).

Lewis, J. (1998) 'Between the lines: surf texts, prosthetics and everyday theory', *Social Semiotics,* 8 (1).

Lewis, J. (2002a) 'From Culturalism to Transculturalism', *Iowa Journal of Cultural Studies,* 1 (1).

Lewis, J. (2002b) *Cultural Studies: The Basics,* 1st edn, Sage, London.

Lewis, J. (2002c) 'Propagating terror: 9/11 and the mediation of war', *Media International Australia,* August, 104.

Lewis, J. (2005) *Language Wars: The Role of Media and Culture in Global Terror and Political Violence,* Pluto Press, London.

Lewis, J. and Lewis, B. (2006) 'Trial by ordeal: *Abu Ghraib* and the global mediasphere', *Topia: The Canadian Journal of Cultural Studies,* Spring, 15.

Lewis, J. and Lewis, B. (2007) 'Transforming the *Bhuta Kala:* the Bali bombings and Indonesian civil society' in D. Staines, ed., *Interrogating the War on Terror,* Cambridge Scholars Press, Cambridge.

Lewis, Justin, and Miller, T. (2002) *Critical Cultural Policy Studies: A Reader,* Blackwell, Malden, MA.

Lull, J. (1980) 'The social uses of television', *Human Communication Research,* 6 (3).

Lyon, D. (2003) *Surveillance after September 11,* Polity, London.

Lyotard, J. (1984a) *The Postmodern Condition: A Report on Knowledge,* trans. G. Bennington and B. Massumi, University of Minnesota Press, Minneapolis.

Lyotard, J (1984b) 'Answering the question: what is postmodernity?' in *The Postmodern Condition: A Report on Knowledge,* trans. G. Bennington and B. Massumi, University of Minnesota, Minneapolis.

Lyotard, J. (1991) *The Inhuman: Reflections on Time,* trans. G. Bennington and R. Bowlby, Polity, Cambridge.

MacCabe, C. (1974) 'Realism and the cinema: notes on some Brechtian theses', *Screen*, 15 (2).

McChesney, R. (2004) *The Problem of the Media: US Communications Policy in the 21st Century*, Monthly Review Press, New York.

McChesney, R., Newman, R. and Scott, B. (2005) *The Future of the Media: Resistance and Reform in the 21st Century*, Seven Stones Press, New York.

McClintock, A., Mufti, A. and Shohat, E., eds (1997) *Dangerous Liaisons: Gender, Nation and Postcolonial Perspectives*, University of Minnesota Press, Minneapolis.

MacDonald, N. (2001) *The Graffiti Subculture: Masculinity, Youth, and Identity*, Palgrave, New York.

McElroy, W. (2003) 'Iraq War may kill feminism as we know it', Online essay, July 23, <http//www.wendymcelroy.com>.

McGuigan, J. (1992) *Cultural Populism*, Routledge, London.

McGuigan, J. (1996) *Culture and the Public Sphere*, Routledge, London.

McGuigan, J., ed. (1997) *Cultural Methodologies*, Sage, London.

McHale, B. (1987) *Postmodernist Fiction*, Methuen, London.

Macherey, P. (1978) *A Theory of Literary Production*, trans. G. Wall, Routledge and Kegan Paul, London.

McLuhan, M. (1964) *Understanding Media*, Routledge and Kegan Paul, London.

McLuhan, M. (1969) *Counterblast*, Rapp and Whiting, London.

McNair, B. (2002) *Striptease Culture: Sex, Media and Democratization of Desire*, Routledge, London.

McRobbie, A. (1982) '*Jackie*: an ideology of adolescent femininity' in B. Waites, T. Bennet and G. Martin, eds, *Popular Culture: Past and Present*, Croom Helm. London.

McRobbie, A. (1989) *Zoot Suits and Second-hand Dresses*, Macmillan, London.

McRobbie, A. (1991) *Feminism and Youth Culture: from* Jackie *to* Just Seventeen, Macmillan, London.

McRobbie, A. (1994) *Postmodernism and Popular Culture*, Routledge, London.

McRobbie, A. (1997) '*More*: new sexualities in girl's and women's magazines' in A. McRobbie, ed., *Back to Reality: Social Experience and Cultural Studies*, University of Manchester Press, Manchester.

McRobbie, A. and Garber, J. (1991) 'Girls and subcultures' in A. McRobbie, *Feminism and Youth Culture*, Macmillan, London.

McRobbie, A., Cohen, P. and Nana, M. (1989) *Gender and Generation*, Macmillan, London.

Mailer, N. (2003) *Why Are We at War?* Random House, New York.

Marcuse, H. (1964) *One Dimensional Man: Studies in the Ideology of Advanced Industrial Society*, Beacon Press, Boston.

Marshall, P.D. (1997) *Celebrity and Power*: *Fame in Contemporary Culture*, University of Minnesota Press, Minneapolis.

Marvin, C. (1988) *When Old Technologies were New*, Oxford University Press, New York.

Marx, K. (1963) *Early Writings*, trans. T.B. Bottomore, McGraw-Hill, New York.

Marx, K. (1970) *Critique of Hegel's 'Philosophy of Right'*, trans. A.J. and J. O'Malley, Cambridge University Press, London.

Marx, K. (1976) *A Contribution to a Critique of the Political Economy*, Foreign Language Press, Peking.

Marx, K. and Engels, F. (1970) *The German Ideology*, Lawrence and Wishart, London.

Matthews, J., ed. (1997) *Sex in Public*, Allen & Unwin, Sydney.

Meem, D. and Gibson, M., eds (2002) *Femme/Butch: New Considerations in the Way We Want to Go*, Haworth Press, New York.

Messner, M. and Sabo, D. (1990) *Sport, Men and the Gender Order: Critical Feminist Perspectives*, Human Kinetics Books, Champaign, IL.

Meyrowitz, J. (1985) *No Sense of Place: The Impact of Electronic Media on Social Behaviour*, Oxford University Press, New York.

Meyerowitz, J. (2002) *How Sex Changed: A History of Transexuality in the United States*, Harvard University Press, Cambridge, MA.

Michaels, E. (1985) 'Constraints on knowledge in the economy of oral information', *Current Anthropology*, 26 (4).

Mill, J.S. and Taylor Mill, H. (1970) *Essays on Sex Equality*, University of Chicago Press, Chicago.

Miller, A., Bobner, R. and Zereski, J. (2000) 'Sexual identity development: A base for same-sex couple partner abuse', *Contemporary Family Therapy*, 22 (2).

Miller, J. and Knudsen, D. (2006) *Family Abuse and Violence: A Social Problems Perspective*, Altamira Press, Lanham, MD.

Millett, K. (1971) *Sexual Politics*, Rupert Hart-Davis, London.

Milner, A. (2002) *Re-imagining Cultural Studies*, Sage, London.

Mitchell, J. (1984) *Women: The Longest Revolution. Essays in Feminism, Literature and Psychoanalysis*, Virago, London.

Modood, T., Triandofylidou, A. and Barrero, T. (2006) *Multiculturalism, Muslims and Citizenship: A European Approach*, Routledge, London.

Moe, K. ed. (2003) *Women Family, and Work: Writings on the Economics of Gender*, Blackwell, New York.

Moi, T. (1991) *What is a Woman? and Other Essays*, Oxford University Press, Oxford.

Moores, S. (1993) *Interpreting Audiences: The Ethnography of Media Consumption*, Sage, London.

Morley, D. (1980a) *The Nationwide Audience*, British Film Institute, London.

Morley, D. (1980b) 'Texts, readers, subjects' in S. Hall, D. Hobson, A. Lowe and P. Willis, eds, *Culture, Media, Language*, Hutchinson, London.

Morley, D. (1986) *Family Television: Cultural Power and Domestic Leisure*, Comedia, London.

Morley, D. and Silverstone, R. (1990) 'Domestic communication – technologies and meanings', *Media, Culture and Society*, 12 (1).

Morris, M. (1993) 'Panorama: The live, the dead, the living' in G. Turner, ed., *Nation, Culture, Text: Australian Cultural and Media Studies*, Routledge, London.

Morris, M. (1998) *Too Soon, Too Late: History in Popular Culture*, Indiana University Press, Bloomington.

Muggleton, D. (2002) *Inside Subculture: The Postmodern Meaning of Style*, Berg Publishing, Oxford.

Mulvey, L. (1975) 'Visual pleasure and narrative cinema', *Screen*, 16 (3), Autumn.

Nacos, B. (2002) *Mass Mediated Terrorism: The Central Role of the Media in Terrorism and Counter Terrorism*, Rowman and Littlefield, London.

Nairn, T. and James, P. (2005) *Global Matrix: Nationalism, Globalism and State Terrorism*, Pluto Press, London.

Neale, R.S. (1987) 'E.P. Thompson: a history of culture and culturalist history' in D.A. Broos, ed., *Creating Culture*, Allen & Unwin, London.

Negroponte, N. (1995) *Being Digital*, Hodder and Stoughton, Rydalmere, New South Wales.

Nietzsche, F. (1956) *The Birth of Tragedy and the Genealogy of Morals*, trans. F. Golffing, Doubleday, Garden City, New York.

Norris, C. (1987) *Derrida*, Fontana, London.

Norris, C. (1990) 'Lost in the funhouse: Baudrillard and the politics of postmodernism' in R. Boyne and A. Rattansi, eds, *Postmodernism and Society*, St Martin's Press, New York.

Norris, P., Kern, N. and Just, M., eds (2003) *Framing Terrorism: The News Media, the Government and the Public*, Routledge, New York.

Numberg, G. (1996) 'Farewell to the information age' in G. Numberg, ed., *The Future of the Book*, University of California Press, Berkeley.

Olivero, A. (1998) *The State of Terror*, State University of New York Press, Albany.

Osterweil, A. (2004) Andy Warhol's *Blow Job*: toward the recognition of an avant-garde pornography' in L. Williams, ed., *Porn Studies*, Duke University Press, Durham, NC.

O'Toole, L. (1998) *Pornocopia: Porn, Sex, Technology and Desire*, Serpent's Tail, London.

Parsons, T. (1961) 'An outline of the social system' in T. Parsons, E. Shils, K. Naegele and J. Pitts, eds, *Theories of Society, Volume 1*, Free Press, Glencoe, IL.

Parsons, T. (1967) *Essays in Sociological Theory*, Free Press, New York.

Paxton, S. (1998) 'Do men get eating disorders?', *Everybody*, 2, August.

Pease, B. (2000) *Recreating Men: Postmodern Masculinity Politics*, Sage, London.

Perdue, L. (2002) *Eroticabiz: How Sex Shaped the Internet*, Universe, Lincoln, NE.

Pinder, D. (2004) 'Inventing new games: unitary urbanism and the politics of space' in L. Lees, ed., *The Emancipatory City?*, Sage, London; Thousand Oaks, CA.

Poster, M. (1989) *Critical Theory and Poststructuralism*, Cornell University Press, New York.

Poster, M. (1995) *The Second Media Age*, Polity, Cambridge.

Poster, M. (1997) 'Cyberdemocracy: internet and the public sphere' in D. Porter, ed., *Internet Cultures*, Routledge, New York.

Poster, M. (2006) *Information Please: Culture and Politics in the Age of Digital Machines*, Duke University Press, Durham, NC.

Postman, N. (1993) *Technopoly: The Surrender of Culture to Technology*, Vintage Books, New York.

Prendergast, C. and Knottnerus, J. (1990) 'The astructural bias and presuppositional form of symbolic interactionism: a noninteractionist evaluation of the new studies in social organization' in L. Reynolds, ed., *Interactionism: Exposition and Critique*, General Hall, New York.

Queeley, A. (2003) 'Hip hop and the aesthetics of criminalization', *Souls* 5 (1).

Rabinow, P., ed. (1991) *The Foucault Reader*, Penguin, London.

Radway, J. (1987) *Reading the Romance: Women, Patriarchy and Popular Literature*, Verso, London.

Rampton, S. and Stauber, J. (2003) *Weapons of Mass Deception: The Uses of Propaganda in Bush's War on Iraq*, Hodder, Sydney.

Rapoport, D. (2001) 'The fourth wave: September 11 in the history of terrorism' *Current History*, December.

Redhead, S., Wynne, D. and O'Connor, J., eds (1997) *The Clubcultures Reader: Readings in Popular Cultural Studies*, Blackwell, Oxford.

Reynolds, L., ed. (1990) *Interactionism: Exposition and Critique*, General Hall, New York.

Rheingold, H. (1993) *The Virtual Community: Homesteading on the Electronic Frontier*, Addison Wesley, Reading, MA.

Ricchiardi, S. (2004) 'Missed Signals', *American Journalism Review*, August/September.

Richards, J., Wilson, S. and Woodhead, L., eds (1999) *Diana: The Making of a Media Saint*, I.B. Tauris, London.

Robb, D. (2002) 'To the shores of Hollywood: Marine Corps fights to polish image in "Wiindtalkers"', *Washington Post*, June 15.

Robertson, R. (2000) *Globalization: Social Theory and Global Culture*, Sage, London.

Rojek, C. (2003) *Stuart Hall*, Polity Press, Cambridge.

Rose, G. (1988) 'Architecture to philosophy – the postmodern complicity', *Theory, Culture and Society*, 5 (2–3), June.

Roseman, J. (2003) *Distant Proximities: Dynamics Beyond Globalization*, Princeton University Press, Princeton.

Ross, A. (1991) *Strange Weather: Culture, Science and Technology in the Age of Limits*, Verso, London.

Said, E.W. (1978) *Orientalism*, Pantheon Books, New York.

Said, E.W. (1986) 'Foucault and the imagination of power' in D.C. Hoy, ed., *Foucault: A Critical Reader*, Blackwell, Oxford.

Said, E.W. (1993) *Culture and Imperialism*, Chatto and Windus, London.

Said, E. (1999) *Out of Place: A Memoir*, Knopf, New York.

Sawicki, J. (1991) *Disciplining Foucault: Feminism, Power and the Body*, Routledge, London.

Schatz, T. (1981) *Hollywood Genres: Formulas, Filmmaking and the Studio System*, Temple University Press, Philadelphia.

Schmid, A. P. (1983) *Political Terrorism: A Research Guide to Concepts, Theories, Data Bases and Literature*, Transaction Press, New Brunswick, NJ.

Scott, L. (2005) *Fresh Lipstick: Redressing Fashion and Feminism*, Palgrave Macmillan, New York.

Seidman, S., ed. (1996) *Queer Theory/Sociology*, Blackwell, Oxford.

Shaw, S. (2002) 'Shifting conversations on girls' and women's self-injury: an analysis of the cultural literature in historical context', *Feminism and Psychology*, 12 (2).

Sherman, W. and Craig, A. (2003) *Understanding Virtual Reality: Interface, Application and Design*, Morgan Kaufmann, New York.

Shilling, C. (1993) *The Body and Social Theory*, Sage, London.

Shilling, C. (2005) *The Body in Culture, Technology and Society*, Sage, London.

Silberstein S. (2002) *War of Words: Language, Politics and 9/11*, Routledge, London.

Silverstone, R. (1990) 'Television and everyday life: toward an anthropology of the television audience' in M. Ferguson, ed., *Public Communication: The New Imperatives*, Sage, London.

Skelton, T. and Valentine, G., eds (1998) *Cool Places: Geographies of Youth Culture*, Routledge, London.

Sklair, L. (2002) *Globalization: Capitalism and its Alternatives*, Oxford University Press, Oxford.

Slavin, J. (2000) *The Internet and Society*, Polity, Cambridge.

Smith, J. (2004) 'The Gnostic Baudrillard: a philosophy of terrorism seeking pure appearance', *International Journal of Baudrillard Studies*, July, 1(2).

Smith, N. (1997) 'The Satanic geographies of globalization: uneven development in the 1990s', *Public Culture*, 10 (1), Fall.

Snyder, I. (1996) *Hypertext: The Electronic Labyrinth*, Melbourne University Press, Melbourne.

Soja, E. (1989) *Postmodern Geographies: The Reassertion of Space in Critical Social Theory*, Verso, London.

Soja, E. (1996) *ThirdSpace: Journeys to Los Angeles and other Real-and-Imagined Places*, Blackwell, Cambridge.

Soja, E. (2000) *Postmetropolis: Critical Studies of Cities and Regions*, Blackwell, Oxford.

Sontag, S. (1966) *Against Interpretation*, Deli, New York.

Sontag, S. (1978) 'The double standard of ageing' in V. Carver and P. Liddiard, eds, *An Ageing Population*, Hodder and Stoughton, London.

Sontag, S. (2001) 'On the cowardice of the 9/11 attackers', *The New Yorker*, September 21.

Spender, D. (1995) *Nattering on the Net: Women, Power and Cyberspace*, Spinifex, Melbourne.

Spivak, G.C. (1987) *In Other Worlds*, Methuen, London.

Spivak, G.C. (1988) 'Can the subaltern speak?' in G. Nelson and L. Grossberg, eds, *Marxism and the Interpretation of Culture*, Macmillan, London.

Spivak, G.C. (1992) 'Teaching for the times', *MMLA Journal for the Mid-West Modern Language Association*, 25 (1), Spring.

Stuart, E. (1984) *All Consuming Images: The Politics of Style in Contemporary Culture*, MIT Press, Cambridge, MA.

Taylor, J. (2000) *Diana, Self-interest and British National Identity*, Praeger, Westport, CT.

Taylor, P. M. (1992) *War and the Media: Propaganda and Persuasion in the Gulf War*, Manchester University Press, Manchester.

Thade, D. (1991) 'Text and the new hermeneutics' in D. Wood, ed., *On Paul Ricoeur: Narrative and Interpretation*, Routledge, London.

Thomas, H. (2003) *The Body, Dance and Cultural Theory*, Palgrave, London.

Thompson, E.P. (1976) 'Interview', *Radical History Review*, 3.

Thompson, E.P. (1980) *The Making of the English Working Class*, Penguin, Harmondsworth.

Tibi, B. (2001) *Islam: Between Culture and Politics*, Palgrave, New York.

Tomlinson, J. (1997) 'Cultural globalisation: placing and displacing the west' in H. Mackay and T. O'Sullivan, eds, *The Media Reader: Continuity and Transformation*, Sage, London.

Tomlinson, J. (1999) *Globalization and Culture*, Polity, Cambridge.

Tompkins, J., ed. (1980) *Reader Response Criticism: From Formalism to Poststructuralism*, Johns Hopkins University Press, Baltimore.

Tulloch, J. (2006) *One Day in July: Experiencing 7-7*, Brown, London.

Tuman, J. (2003) *Communicating Terror: The Rhetorical Dimensions of Terrorism*, Sage, Thousand Oaks, CA.

Turkle, S. (1999) 'Identity in the age of the Internet' in H. Mackay and T. O'Sullivan, eds, *The Media Reader: Continuity and Transformation*, Sage, London.

Turner, B. (1996) *The Body and Society: Explorations in Social Theory*, 2nd edn, Sage, London.

Turner, G. (1996) *British Cultural Studies: An Introduction*, 2nd edn, Routledge, London.

Turner, G. (2004) *Understanding Celebrity*, Sage, London.

Turnock, R. (2000) *Interpreting Diana: Television Audiences and the Death of a Princess*, British Film Institute, London.

UNICEF (2007) 'Women and children: the double dividend of gender equality', *The State of the World's Children Annual Report*.<www.unicef.org/sowc07>. November 2007.

United States Department of Defense (1986) DOD directive, 2000.12, 'Protection of DOD resources against terrorist acts', June 16.

United States Government (2004) *The 9/11 Commission Report*.

Updike, J. (2001) Untitled contribution to *The New Yorker*, 24 September, p. 28.

Urry, J. (2003) *Global Complexity*, Polity, Cambridge.

van Zoonen, L. (1994) *Feminist Media Studies*, Sage, London.

Vertinsky, P. (1998) 'Run, Jane, run: central issues in the current debate about enhancing women's health through exercise', *Women and Health*, 27 (4).

Virilio, P. (1994) *The Vision Machine*, British Film Institute, London.

Virilio, P. (2002) *Ground Zero*, trans. C. Turner, Verso, New York.

Wade, R. (2004) 'Is globalization reducing poverty and inequality?' *Journal of Health Services*, 34 (3).

Walch, J. (1999) *In the Net: An Internet Guide for Activists*, Zed Books, London.

Walter, N. (1999) *The New Feminism*, Virago, London.

Weber, M. (1930) *The Protestant Ethic and the Spirit of Capitalism*, trans. T. Parsons, Unwin, London.

Weber, M. (1946) *From Max Weber: Essays in Sociology*, Oxford University Press, New York.

Weber, M. (1949) *The Methodology of the Social Sciences*, Free Press, New York.

White, M. and Schwoch, J. (2006) *Questions of Method in Cultural Studies*, Blackwell, Malden, MA.

Williams, E. (2006) *The Puzzle of 7/7: An In-depth Analysis of the London Bombings and Government Sponsored Terrorism*, Lulu Press, London.

Williams, L. (1989) *Hard Core: Power, Pleasure and the Frenzy of the Visible*, University of California Press, Berkeley.

Williams, L. (1992) 'When the woman looks' in G. Mast, M. Cohen and L. Braudy, eds, *Film Theory and Criticism*, Oxford University Press, New York.

Williams, L. (2004) 'Porn studies: proliferating pornographies on/scene' in L. Williams, ed., *Porn Studies*, Duke University Press, Durham, NC.

Williams, R. (1958) *Culture and Society*, Chatto and Windus, London.

Williams, R. (1965) *The Long Revolution*, Penguin, London.

Williams, R. (1968) *Communications*, Penguin, Hammondsworth.

Williams, R. (1974) *Television, Technology and Cultural Form*, Fontana, London.

Williams, R. (1976) *Keywords*, Fontana, London.

Williams, R. (1981) *Culture*, Fontana, London.

Williamson, J. (1978) *Decoding Advertising*, Marion Boyars, London.

Wilson, T. (1993) *Watching Television: Hermeneutics, Reception and Popular Culture*, Polity, Cambridge.

Wilson, T. (1995) 'Horizons of meaning: the breadth of television narrowcasting', *Media International Australia*, 75, February.

Wilson, T. (2004) *The Playful Audiences: From Talk Show Viewers to Internet Users*, Hampton Press, New Jersey.

Winship, J. (1987) *Inside Women's Magazines*, Pandora, London.

Wittgenstein, L. (1922) *Tractatus Logico-Philosophicus*, trans. C.K. Ogden, Routledge and Kegan Paul, London.

Wolf, N. (1991) *The Beauty Myth: How Images of Beauty are used against Women*, Vintage, London.

Wolff, J. (1990) 'Feminism and modernism' in A. Milner and C. Worth, eds, *Discourse and Difference*, Monash University Press, Clayton.

Wood, A. and Thompson, P. (2003) 'An interesting day: President Bush's movements and actions on 9/11', The Center for Co-operative Research, <www.cooperativeresearch. org/timeline/main/essayaninterestiongday.html>.

Woolf, V. (1978) *A Room of One's Own*, Hogarth Press, London.

Woolf, V. (1979) 'Dorothy Richardson' in M. Barrett, ed., *Virginia Woolf: Women and Writing*, The Women's Press, London.

World Bank (2001) *World Development Indicators 2001*, World Bank, New York.

Wright, W. (1975) *Sixguns and Society: A Structural Study of the Western*, University of California Press, Berkeley.

Yodice, G. (1995) 'What's a straight white man to do?' in M. Berger, B. Wallis and S. Watson, eds, *Constructing Masculinity*, Routledge, New York.

Zizek, S. (2004) *Iraq: The Borrowed Kettle*, Verso, London.

Index